PENGUIN REFERENCE BOOKS

A DICTIONARY OF ART AND ARTISTS

Peter and Linda Murray were both trained as painters but turned to the history of art and went to the Courtauld Institute as students immediately after the war. They were married in 1947, in the middle of their Final examinations. They published their first joint work, a translation of Heinrich Wölfflin's *Classic Art*, in 1952. Since then they have collaborated on several translations as well as a book on the art of the Renaissance, but this was their first book. Each wrote a complete entry which the other then picked holes in and rewrote; as a result they are now unable to tell who wrote which entries and must take joint responsibility for everything.

Both prefer teaching to anything else: Linda Murray is an Extra-Mural Lecturer for the University of London and Peter Murray is Professor of the History of Art at Birkbeck College in the University of London.

Peter and Linda Murray

A DICTIONARY OF ART
AND ARTISTS

PENGUIN BOOKS

Penguin Books Ltd, Harmondsworth, Middlesex, England
Penguin Books Inc., 7110 Ambassador Road, Baltimore, Maryland 21207, U.S.A.
Penguin Books Australia Ltd, Ringwood, Victoria, Australia
Penguin Books Canada Ltd, 41 Steelcase Road West, Markham, Ontario, Canada
Penguin Books (N.Z.) Ltd, 182–190 Wairau Road, Auckland 10, New Zealand

—

First published 1959
Reprinted with revisions 1960
Reprinted 1962, 1963, 1964, 1965, 1966, 1967
Revised edition first published by Thames & Hudson 1965
Further revised edition published in Penguin Reference Books 1968
Reprinted 1969, 1971 (twice)
Third edition 1972
Reprinted 1973, 1975 (twice)

—

Copyright © Peter and Linda Murray, 1959, 1960, 1965, 1968, 1972

—

Made and printed in Great Britain
by Hazell Watson & Viney Ltd
Aylesbury, Bucks
Set in Monotype Times

FOR OUR PARENTS

ABBREVIATIONS USED IN THE DICTIONARY

Acad.	Academy, Academia	Md	Maryland
Accad.	Accademia	Mass.	Massachusetts
Akad.	Akademie	Met. Mus.	Metropolitan Museum
ARA	Associate of the Royal Academy	Mich.	Michigan
b.	born	Middx	Middlesex
B.C.	Before Christ	MS, MSS	Manuscript, manuscripts
Berks.	Berkshire	Mus.	Museum, Musée
Bib.	Bibliothèque	N.	North
BM	British Museum	Nat. Marit. Mus.	National Maritime Museum
Bucks.	Buckinghamshire	Naz.	Nazionale
c.	circa, about	NEAC	New English Art Club
Cal.	California	NG	National Gallery
Cath.	Cathedral	NG of S	National Gallery of Scotland
cf.	confer, compare	NJ	New Jersey
Ch. Ch.	Christ Church	NPG	National Portrait Gallery
Col.	Colorado	nr	near
Coll.	Collection, College	NSW	New South Wales
Conn.	Connecticut	NY	New York
d.	died	NZ	New Zealand
DCL	Doctor of Civil Law	OED	Oxford English Dictionary
ed.	edition	OM	Order of Merit
e.g.	exempli gratia	Pa	Pennsylvania
Fdn	Foundation	Pal.	Palais, Palace, Palazzo
ff.	following	PRA	President of the Royal Academy
Fitzwm	Fitzwilliam	PRB	Pre-Raphaelite Brotherhood
Fla	Florida	RA	Royal Academy, Royal Academician
Fr.	French	RAMC	Royal Army Medical Corps
Gall.	Gallery, Galleria	RI	Rhode Island
Ger.	German	Rijksmus.	Rijksmuseum
Gk	Greek	RSA	Royal Scottish Academy
Hist.	Historical		
Hosp.	Hospital		
i.e.	id est		
Inst.	Institute		
Ital.	Italian		
K-H	Kunsthistorisches		
Lat.	Latin		
M of MA	Museum of Modern Art		

S.	Saint, San, South	Sto	Santo
SC	South Carolina	Univ.	University
S.M.	Santa Maria	US	United States
SNPG	Scottish National Portrait Gallery	USSR	Union of Soviet Socialist Republics
Soc.	Society		
Span.	Spanish	V & A	Victoria and Albert Museum
SS.	Saints, Santissimo (a)		
St	Saint	Va	Virginia
Sta	Santa		
Staffs.	Staffordshire	Wilts.	Wiltshire

LIST OF GENERAL ARTICLES

Counterproof
Craquelure
Cross-hatching
Cubism

Dada
Dance of Death
Danube School
Deësis
Del., Delin.
Desco da Parto
Design
Diptych
Disegno
Distemper
Divisionism, *see* Optical Mixtures
Doelenstuk, Schutterstuk
Dotted Print
Drill, *see* Stone Carving
Drypoint, *see* Engraving
Dugento

Eclectic, *see* Carracci
Encaustic Wax
Engraving
Etching, *see* Engraving
Euston Road
Exc., Excudit
Expressionism

F., Fec., Fecit
Facture, Fattura
Fauve
Fine Manner
Fixative
Fontainebleau, Schools of
Foreshortening
Found Object
Fraglia
Fresco
Frottage
Futurism

Garzone
Genre
Gesso
Giotteschi, Giottesques
Glazing
Glyptic, *see* Sculpture
Golden Section
Gothic
Gouache

Graffito, *see* Sgraffito
Graphic Arts
Graver, *see* Burin
Grisaille
Grotesque
Ground
Guild

Handling
Hatching
History Painting
Hortus Conclusus
Hot Colour, Tone
Hours of Turin
Hudson River School

Icon
Ideal Art
Illusionism
Imago Pietatis
Impasto
Impressionism
Imprimitura
Inc.
Intaglio
International Gothic
Intimisme
Intonaco, *see* Fresco
Inv., Invenit
Italianizers

Journeyman
Jugendstil, *see* Art Nouveau

Keeping, *see* Values
Key
Kit Kat
Kortegaardjes

Laocoön
Lay Figure
Liber Studiorum, *see* Liber
  Veritatis
Liber Veritatis
Limning
Linear Composition
Linocut, *see* Engraving
Lithography, *see* Engraving
Local Colour
London Group
Lukasbrüder, *see* Nazarener

Macchiaioli

8

Madonnieri
Maestà
Mahlstick
'Mai'
Malerisch
Mandorla
Manière Criblée, *see* Dotted
   Print
Manner
Mannerism
Maquette
Masses
Matière
Mattoir, *see* Engraving
Medici e Speziali
Medium
Merz, *see* Schwitters
Mezzo-rilievo, *see* Relief
Mezzotint, *see* Engraving
Miniature
Misericordia, Madonna della
Mixed Method
Mobile
Modelling
Modello, Modelletto
Monochrome
Monotype
Montage
Monumental
Morbidezza
Mosaic
Mural, *see* Wall-Painting

Nabis, Les
Nature Morte, *see* Still-Life
Nazarener
NEAC
Neoclassicism
Neo-Impressionism
Neue Sachlichkeit
New English Art Club, *see*
   NEAC
Niello
Nocturne
Norwich School
Novecento

Objet Trouvé, *see* Found Object
Œuvre
Offset, *see* Counterproof
Oil Painting

Optical Mixtures
Orphic Cubism, Orphisme
Ottocento

P., Pinx., Pinxit
Painterly, *see* Malerisch
Painting Techniques, *see* Encaustic
   Wax, Fresco, Gouache, Oil
   Painting, Pastel, Size Colour,
   Tempera, Watercolour
Pala
Paliotto
Papier Collé
Paris, the School of
Pastel
Pastiche, Pasticcio
Patina
Pedigree, *see* Provenance
Peinture à l'Essence, *see* Degas
Pencil
Pentimento
Perspective
Picture Plane
Picturesque
Pietà
Plaster Casting
Plasticity
Plein Air
Pochade
Pointillism, *see* Optical
   Mixtures
Pointing Machine
Polychromatic Sculpture
Polyptych
Post-Impressionism
Poussinisme, *see* Rubénisme
PRB, Pre-Raphaelite
   Brotherhood
Predella
Primary Colours
Priming
Primitive
Profil Perdu
Proof
Proportion
Provenance
Punch, *see* Stone Carving
Putto

Quadraturista
Quadro Riportato

9

Quattrocento

Rayonism
Realism
Recession
Refusés, *see* Salon
Relief
Remarque Proofs
Renaissance
Replica
Repoussoir
Reredos
Retroussage
Rilievo, *see* Relief
Rococo
Romanists
Romantic, *see* Classic
Royal Academy, *see* Academy
Rubénisme

Sachlichkeit, Die Neue, *see* Neue
   Sachlichkeit
Sacra Conversazione
Salon
Sanguine
School
Schutterstuk, *see* Doelenstuk
Scorzo, Iscorzo
Sculp.
Sculpture
Scumbling
Section d'Or, *see* Golden Section
Seicento
Sepia
Serigraphy
Settecento
Sezession
Sfumato
Sgraffito
Shop Work, *see* Workshop
   Production
Significant Form
Silk-screen, *see* Serigraphy
Silver Point
Sinopia
Size Colour
Sketch
Social Realism
Soft Ground Etching, *see*
   Engraving
Soft Style

Sopra Porte
Sotto in Sù
Spolvero
Squared
Stabile
Staffage
Stained Glass
Stanze
State
Steel Engraving, Steel-faced
Stiacciato, *see* Relief
Stijl, De
Still-Life
Stippled Drawing
Stone Carving
Stopping Out, *see* Engraving
Study
Stump
Style Criticism
Super-Realism, *see* Surrealism
Suprematism
Surrealism
Synthetism

Tachisme
Tactile Values
Taille-Douce, *see* Engraving
Tectonic, *see* Architectonic
Tempera
Tenebrism
Terracotta, *see* Plaster
Terribilità
Tesserae
Tondo
Tone Values, *see* Values
Torso
Totentanz, *see* Dance of Death
Trecento
Triptych
Trompe-l'œil, *see* Illusionism

Underpainting

Values
Vanishing Point, *see* Perspective
Vanitas, *see* Still-Life
Variant
Veduta
Vehicle
Vesperbild, *see* Pietà
Vingt, Les
Vorticism

PREFACE TO THE FIRST EDITION

The purpose of this Dictionary is to act as a companion to the inquiring gallery visitor, and, we hope, to serve as a useful quick reference book. We have restricted the scope to the arts of painting, sculpture, and engraving in Western Europe and North America, and to a period beginning about the year 1300 and continuing up to the present day. One good reason for this restriction is that we are almost totally ignorant of the arts of other periods and places; since writing this book we have come to realize that we have a restricted knowledge of the field we have undertaken to cover. Like the companion *Dictionary of Music* in this series we have to combine articles on technical terms and processes with biographies of as many artists as possible, and we decided to try to cover all the technical terms, processes, and artistic movements as fully as we could, even at the expense of biographies. There have been many thousands of painters and sculptors in the last six centuries and most of them are in that monument of scholarship Thieme and Becker's *Allgemeines Künstlerlexikon* in forty-odd large volumes.

There is one exception to our desire to give a definition for all technical terms, and that is when it is already adequately defined – even in the technical sense – in a normal English Dictionary (we have used the *Concise Oxford*): examples of this are 'Vignette', 'Diorama', or 'Retable'. Where a definition seemed to us not to cover a common usage in the arts we have given it here.

In the biographical articles our aim has been threefold. We have tried, first, to give the dates of birth and death, or known activity, and such other dates as seemed important for an understanding of an artist's career. Next, we have tried to give the reader some idea of what his works look like, usually by relating them to other and perhaps better-known artists by means of frequent cross-references. Thirdly, we have given, in most cases, a list of museums which have pictures or sculpture by him. These lists are not intended to be exhaustive or critical. We have obviously tended to include museums in Great Britain or the United States and to omit those in Russia or, say, Bulgaria. For equally obvious reasons we have not mentioned pictures in private collections unless they are crucial to the artist's development, but this is very rare indeed. As far as we know, the pictures stated to be in a given museum are in that museum, but this is less simple than it sounds, for many museums are still recovering from the War and no modern catalogue is available, while others – such as the National and Tate Galleries in London – seem to play a constant game of musical chairs with their possessions.

Cross-references. Capital letters are used to indicate cross-references, and we have made this systematic so that, by following up the cross-references, the reader can not only expand the information in the original entry but should also gain a better idea of X's relationship to his contemporaries. In any given entry several other names will occur in normal type: these may or may not have separate entries of their own, but we do not think that following them up will, in this case, add anything to the reader's knowledge of X.

Spelling. The spelling of names may present some difficulties, especially as de This or van That will be found under T, the prefixes being disregarded, while the Italian Giovanni di Paolo will be found under G and not P. In many cases we have given cross-references, but the best rule will be to look under everything possible before deciding that whoever it is has been left out.

Dates. Dates are given with as much precision as we can manage, and the distinction between 1520/25 and 1520–25 should be noted. The first means 'at some point in the period, but the exact point is unknown', the second, 'beginning in 1520 and ending in 1525'. Authorities, of course, are not cited: we hope our fellow-professionals will find some amusement in spotting them, and to those who spot themselves we offer our grateful thanks.

London, September 1957

PREFACE TO THE SECOND PENGUIN EDITION

Since this Dictionary was published in 1959 it has been reprinted with a number of minor revisions, but in 1965 an edition was published by Thames & Hudson in London, and in America, which contained a revision of the original text and a considerable number of new articles. This edition was very fully illustrated and also contained two bibliographies. In this new Penguin edition the text is substantially the same as that of the illustrated edition with a small number of revisions and new entries. The principal difference between this and the original Penguin edition lies therefore in the larger number of biographies contained in this new edition, since the principal general articles are virtually unchanged and only a comparatively small number of new biographies of earlier artists will be found in this edition. We are inclined to feel that many 19th- and 20th-century artists are included in this edition because of their topical interest rather than their merits, but it is certainly true that there is a lively interest in their work and we have therefore provided an outline of their careers. From a historical point of view the book is now out of balance, but it may well be that this is justifiable on other grounds.

January 1968

A

ABBATE, Niccolò dell' (c. 1512–71), was a Modenese painter whose style was founded on Mantegna's illusionism and especially on Correggio's softness. He painted frescoes in Modena (1546) and Bologna (1547: now in the University), and was in France by 1552, helping PRIMATICCIO with the decoration of the Royal château at Fontainebleau. Most of his work there has disappeared. He spent the rest of his life in France, where, with Primaticcio, he represents the end of the First School of FONTAINEBLEAU. He introduced the Mannerist landscape into France: there is a fine example in the NG, London, and other works are in Florence (Uffizi), Modena, Oxford (Ch. Ch.), Paris (Louvre), Rome (Borghese), Vienna, and elsewhere.

ABBOTT, Lemuel Francis (c. 1760–1803), was an English portrait painter, famous for his *Nelson*, of which many replicas and variants exist. These and other portraits are in London (NPG, Nat. Marit. Mus., Tate).

ABSORBENT GROUND. A chalk ground, on canvas or panel, prepared without oil so that it will absorb the oil from the paint, leaving it matt and very quick-drying.

ABSTRACT ART depends upon the assumption that specifically aesthetic values reside in forms and colours and are entirely independent of the subject of the painting or sculpture. This view is of great antiquity and has resulted in much art of a semi-magical character as well as pure decoration. It also prevails in Moslem countries, where representation of the human figure is prohibited. The 'liberating' influence of the camera allowed the painter to neglect his social duty as a recorder of things and events, and, at the same time, late in the 19th century, Impressionism came to be regarded as a dead-end of naturalism, thus leading to an increased emphasis on formal values and ultimately to CUBISM, CONSTRUCTIVISM, TACHISME, and the rest.

The philosophical justification of abstract art may be found in Plato: 'I do not now intend by beauty of shapes what most people would expect, such as that of living creatures or pictures, but . . . straight lines and curves and the surfaces or solid forms produced out of these by lathes and rulers and squares. . . . These things are not beautiful relatively, like other things, but always and naturally and absolutely' (*Philebus*).

ABSTRACT EXPRESSIONISM. A combination of ABSTRACT ART and EXPRESSIONISM which amounts to little more than automatic painting – i.e. allowing the subconscious to express itself (a SURREALIST idea) by the creation of involuntary shapes and dribbles of paint. Abstract Impressionism – which appears to be another name for the same thing – is supposed to derive from the intricate mesh of paint which forms the surface of MONET'S last pictures, as, half-blind, he struggled to find pictorial equivalents for his optical sensations. Abstract Impressionism has been defined (by E. De Kooning, 1956) thus: 'Retaining the quiet uniform pattern of strokes that spread over the canvas without climax or emphasis, these followers keep the Impressionist manner of looking at a scene but leave out the scene'. *See also* ACTION PAINTING, TACHISME.

ACADEMY. The name, derived from Plato's Academy, was used in Italy in the 15th century by groups of humanists meeting together for discussion. The first academies of art are connected with LEONARDO da Vinci in his Milanese period and BERTOLDO in Florence. Little is known of the aims and activities of the 'Academia Leonardi Vinci', as it was called, but Bertoldo was in charge of the statues and sculpture-school in the Medici Garden, fostered by Lorenzo de' Medici, 'Il Magnifico' (*d.* 1492), and had the distinction of helping the young Michelangelo. During the 16th century these groups acquired more formal aims and character, and the term was, by extension, applied to groups of artists meeting privately for study. Baccio BANDINELLI founded one in 1531, in the quarters granted him in the Vatican, and another in Florence *c.* 1550. The first Academy of Fine Arts, properly speaking, was founded in 1563 in Florence by VASARI, with at its head the Grand Duke Cosimo and the absent and eighty-eight-year-old MICHELANGELO, who, by his personal prestige, had done more than anyone to raise the fine arts from the level of the mechanical to the equal of the liberal arts. Vasari's Accademia di DISEGNO was intended to be a teaching as well as an honorific body, for the main purpose of an academy was always to raise the social status of the artist; but though almost every artist of repute in Italy became a member, its teaching programme was soon abandoned. The Accademia di S. Luca, founded in Rome in 1593, with Federico ZUCCARO as its president, also had a similarly ambitious programme which came to nothing. Other such bodies were founded in Italy – notably in Bologna in 1598, where it became intimately associated with the CARRACCI – and the custom of artists meeting under the patronage of an enlightened nobleman or connoisseur, to draw from the nude, thus forming private teaching academies, was widespread by the middle of the 17th century.

The French Academy, charged with the study and preservation of the language, was founded by Richelieu in 1634: the Academy of Painting and Sculpture, first founded in 1648, was closely modelled on the Italian ones, but did not reach its all-powerful position until 1661, when it came under the control of Colbert, who saw in it a golden opportunity to make the arts play a part in the aggrandizement of the monarchy. By 1664 he had obtained a new constitution for it, which made it primarily a teaching body, responsible for the training of artists who could then carry out the artistic programmes which he planned. He also founded the French Academy in Rome in 1666, as a school to which the most successful students could be sent for further training, and intended to make POUSSIN its head, but the latter's death prevented this. The French Academy reached perhaps its greatest power under LEBRUN, who became Director in 1683. This dual character of learned body, with a strict hierarchy of members graded according to the form of art they practised (history painters at the top, portraitists next, and so on down to landscape and genre) and with the privilege of public exhibition exclusively reserved to it, combined with a state school, became the pattern for most of the Academies founded during the 17th and 18th centuries. The majority were not, however, successful until after the middle of the 18th century, when academies of all kinds were an established part of the pattern of intellectual life.

The Royal Academy in London, founded in 1768 with provision for forty Academicians and (in 1769) twenty Associates, later increased to thirty, was one of these late-comers. But it is an exception to the generality in that it was the outcome of private enterprise among artists, and though it enjoyed Royal patronage from the start (in fact, it owed its initial success to the keen interest of George III), has never had any state control, subsidies, or monopoly of exhibitions. The efforts of its first President, REYNOLDS, established it as a school, and his personal prestige and intellectual attainments were reflected in the social status which membership conferred, while the open character of its yearly exhibitions ensured a flow of new talent. The first American Academy, founded in Philadelphia in 1805, grew out of a private institution, and the National Academy of Design was founded in 1826, under MORSE.

It was mainly during the reign of late 19th-century conservatism that Academies became the centre of opposition to all new ideas in art, with results that have brought nothing but discredit on themselves, so that the term 'academic' has become the synonym of dullness, conventionalism, and prejudice. This cleavage between official bodies and the mass of artists outside the academic fold has bedevilled the relations between artists and public, fostered unfortunate extremes of taste, and rendered the fair appreciation of academic art difficult and the criticism of art particularly unfruitful. There are, however, signs that it is now realized, inside and outside the Academies, that this cleavage is to the detriment of all.

ACADEMY FIGURE. A painting or drawing, generally about half life-size, of a nude figure executed solely for purposes of instruction or practice and not as a work of art.

ACRYLIC paint – properly acrylic vinyl polymer emulsion paint – is an entirely new synthetic paint which allows a combination of the traditional oil and watercolour techniques. It is a plastic emulsion which is soluble in water, so that very thin, transparent, washes can be applied, as in classical watercolour. At the same time, it is possible to apply a very thick impasto, as in ALLA PRIMA oil-painting, and there is also a special polymer medium which has a function similar to that of oil in oil-painting. The synthetic substances are said to be permanent and to adhere to almost any surface, but it is perhaps early to judge this.

ACTION PAINTING. Splashing and dribbling paint on canvas. The basic assumption is that the Unconscious will take over and produce a work of art. The technique is claimed to go back to Leonardo, who suggested using stains on walls as a starting point for designing (cf. BLOT): the essential difference is that Leonardo used the method solely as a means of stimulating the creative imagination and not as an end in itself. Action Painting should not be confused with the intellectual type of Abstract art in which some thought is necessary, but its advocates claim that the beauty of the 'calligraphy' – i.e. the movements of the artist's wrist – constitutes its justification, as well as distinguishing it from TACHISME. *See* POLLOCK *and* TOBEY.

ADAM, Lambert-Sigisbert (1700–59), a French sculptor, went to Rome in 1723 and there won the competition for the Trevi Fountain (1731), which he did not execute. He returned to Paris in 1733 and was received into the Academy on his *Neptune calming the Waves* (1737: Louvre), which is derived directly from Bernini, while his *Neptune* at Versailles is also markedly Baroque; yet he also published a collection of Greek and Roman sculpture ('Recueil des sculptures antiques . . .', Paris, 1754).

AERTSEN, Pieter (1508/9–75), was a painter, born in Amsterdam, who continued the tradition of peasant genre established by BRUEGEL, and was unaffected by the ROMANISTS. He settled in Antwerp *c.*1535, where he married and entered the Guild, but he returned to Amsterdam in 1556, possibly on account of religion. Many of his pictures were destroyed in the religious troubles of 1566, but there are many survivors, mostly with kitchen or genre scenes in the foreground and a religious scene (such as Christ in the House of Martha and Mary) in the background. His still-life painting was important in the development of the genre in the Netherlands and even in Italy: it has been argued that he influenced both Caravaggio and VELAZQUEZ, though it is difficult to see how they could have known his work, and BASSANO is a more likely source, at least for Caravaggio. His surviving religious pictures, while less influential, show the straightforward, realistic tradition of Netherlandish art. His wife's nephew, Joachim BUECKELAER, was his pupil. There are works by him in Amsterdam (Mus. and Mus. Mayer van den Bergh), Berlin, Birmingham, Brussels, Copenhagen, Cracow, Genoa, Leningrad, Pisa, Rotterdam, Rouen, Stockholm, Uppsala (University) and Vienna.

AFRO (*b.*1912) is an Italian abstract painter whose real name is Afro Basaldella. He lives in Rome, but his style derives from Picasso and Braque; he has worked a good deal in the US. There are murals by him in the Banco Nazionale del Lavoro, Rome. There is a painting in Berlin and a drawing in London (Tate).

AGOSTINO di Duccio (1418–81), sculptor, was born in Florence. He became a mercenary soldier in 1433, and did not return to Florence until after 1442, by which date he had executed the altar in Modena Cathedral, accepted as his earliest independent work. Its figures in deep relief against a plain background suggest that he was probably a pupil of Jacopo della QUERCIA, who worked at S. Petronio, Bologna, from 1425 to 1438. By 1446 he had again left Florence, accused, with his brother, of theft from a church. From about 1450 until 1457 he worked on his masterpiece – the tombs and the extensive series of low reliefs forming the sculptural decoration of the interior of the Tempio Malatestiano in Rimini, reconstructed by Sigismondo Malatesta who employed Alberti as architect and PIERO della Francesca as painter. Agostino worked on the façade of the Oratory of S. Bernardino, Perugia, until 1462, and in 1463 returned to Florence, where he entered the Guild, and began work on a block of marble which later was used by Michelangelo for his *David*. In 1473 he went back to Perugia, remaining there until his death.

Agostino's marble reliefs are usually of an even flatness, and his flat, decorative, and intensely linear style has none of the illusionistic effects used by DONATELLO or the ROSSELLINO brothers. There are further examples in Florence (Bargello), London (V & A), Paris (Louvre), and Washington (NG).

AIKMAN, William (1682–1731), was a Scottish portrait painter, pupil of MEDINA, who succeeded to his business in Edinburgh, but after KNELLER'S death in 1723 migrated to London, where he had many literary friends, including Swift and Pope. Allan Ramsay, the poet and father of the painter, was portrayed by him; the picture is inscribed: 'Here painted on this canvas clout By Aikman's hand is Ramsay's snout'. He is chiefly remarkable as having studied in Rome (1707–10) before this became common; after this he went on to Constantinople and Syria. There are self-portraits in Edinburgh (NG of S) and Florence (Uffizi).

ALBANI, Francesco (1578–1660), a Bolognese painter contemporary with Guido RENI whose fellow-pupil he was, first under CALVAERT and then at the CARRACCI Academy. There are many works by him in Rome, Bologna, Paris, and in most of the older galleries.

ALBERTINELLI, Mariotto (1474–1515), was a Florentine painter who collaborated with Fra BARTOLOMMEO from before 1500, and was taken into partnership in 1508 in the S. Marco workshop. After three years he abandoned painting for inn-keeping, which he said was less exacting and less open to criticism, declaring, so the tale goes, that he was 'sick of this everlasting talk of perspective'. His best work is the *Visitation* (1503) in the Uffizi, Florence, but there is a charming example in London (Courtauld Inst.).

ALGARDI, Alessandro (1595 or perhaps 1598–1654), was a Bolognese sculptor who worked in Rome and represented the classicism of the Bolognese Academy in opposition to BERNINI. He was a pupil of Lodovico CARRACCI and worked in the Carracci Academy in Bologna before going to Rome *c*.1625, where he became a friend of DOMENICHINO, also a Bolognese Carracci pupil. His early works – the tomb of Cardinal Millini (*d*.1629) in Sta Maria del Popolo, and the Frangipane portrait busts in S. Marcello – show his marked dependence on antique portrait types. His *S. Philip Neri* (Sta Maria in Vallicella), an imaginary portrait of the saint (canonized 1622), is another example of his skill in portraying people he never set eyes on; but his *Cardinal L. Zacchia* (1626/37: Berlin) shows what he could do when working from life. A terracotta bust of Cardinal P. E. Zacchia (*d*.1605) dates from very late in Algardi's career (? 1654): it is now in London (V & A), and the marble made from it is in a private coll. in Florence. This, however, is probably by an assistant since Algardi grew so fat in his last years that he was apparently unable to carve. The bust of Bracciolini, also in London (V & A), once attributed to him and now attributed to Finelli, is one of several which have been given to Bernini as well as to Algardi. On the whole, Algardi's are graver in deportment and have greater inward characterization than Bernini's highly extrovert portraits. There can be no doubt, however, that Algardi borrowed from Bernini, whose portrait statue of Urban VIII underlies Algardi's *Innocent X*, begun in 1645 for the Conservatori Palace in Rome as a companion to Bernini's *Urban*; while the tomb of Leo XI (St Peter's 1634–52) is a chastened and plain white marble version of Bernini's polychrome tomb of Urban VIII. Algardi's leadership of the classical opposition to Bernini was recognized in 1640 by his election as Principe of the Academy of S. Luke, but his real success came under Innocent X (1644–55), when Bernini was in disgrace. His only important relief also dates from this period: the *Attila* in St Peter's of 1646–53, which is a piece of technical virtuosity, but is less a relief than a Carracci altarpiece in marble. There are other works elsewhere in Rome and in S. Paolo, Bologna, Cleveland Ohio, Minneapolis, New York (Met. Mus.), Paris (Louvre), and Ravenna.

ALLAN, David (1744–96), sometimes called the 'Scottish Hogarth', was, more accurately, a painter of genre and portraits anticipating WILKIE. He lived in Rome 1764–*c*.1777 and won a medal for a history picture in 1773. There are works in Edinburgh and Glasgow.

ALLA PRIMA (Ital. at first) describes the technique, general since the

19th century but considered freakish and slapdash before then, of completing the picture surface in one session in full colour and with such opacity that neither previous drawing nor underpainting – if these exist – modifies the final effect. *Au premier coup* is the French term.

ALLSTON, Washington (1779–1843), was the first important American landscape painter. He was trained in London (1801–3) and travelled in Europe before returning to America. He made a second visit to Europe in 1811 and was elected ARA in 1818, the year in which he returned to America. His early works were Italianate landscapes in the Claude manner, but his intensely Romantic outlook caused him to admire FUSELI and TURNER, and ultimately to imitate the hyper-romanticism of MARTIN. Most of his works are in America, but his portrait of his lifelong friend, S. T. Coleridge, is in London (NPG) and Birmingham has an extravagant landscape attributed to him. *See* HUDSON RIVER SCHOOL.

ALTDORFER, Albrecht (*c.* 1480–1538), a Bavarian painter, worked in Regensburg (Ratisbon), becoming City architect and a councillor. In 1511 certainly, and probably earlier, he travelled along the Danube and visited the Austrian Alps where the scenery moved him to become the first landscape painter in the modern sense. His earliest dated paintings (1507: Berlin and Bremen) show the influence of CRANACH and DÜRER, but the landscape is already very important, and by 1510 the figure is quite unimportant – only the rustle of the trees beside the mountain lake matters. The figures in his pictures are the complement of his romantic use of landscape (*S. George in the Forest*, Munich), and their gestures and facial expressions, as well as their colour, show his use of subjective distortion for dramatic and emotional ends. He also made many drawings and etchings of pure landscape, the importance of which makes him the head of the DANUBE School. His major works are the *S. Florian Altar* (1518: mostly still in S. Florian's Monastery, near Linz) and *Alexander's Victory* (1529: Munich): other works are in Regensburg and in Basle, Cleveland Ohio, Cologne, Florence (Uffizi), London (NG), Luton Hoo, Beds. (Wernher Coll.), Nuremberg, and Vienna.

ALTICHIERO was a Veronese painter of the late 14th century, whose style was formed on Giotto's frescoes in Padua. With his helper Avanzo he painted frescoes in Padua (Il Santo and, after 1377, Oratorio di S. Giorgio), and, at the end of the century, he founded the school of Verona with his frescoes in Sant' Anastasia.

ALTO-RILIEVO *see* RELIEF.

'ALUNNO DI DOMENICO', i.e. 'Pupil of Domenico' (GHIRLANDAIO). A name invented by Berenson for the Florentine painter to whom he ascribed most of the designs for Florentine woodcut book-illustrations of the late 15th century. This wholesale attribution has not won general acceptance, but the actual pupil and assistant of Ghirlandaio postulated by Berenson has been identified as Bartolommeo di Giovanni, who was commissioned to paint the predella of Ghirlandaio's *Adoration* in the Foundling Hospital, Florence, in 1488.

AMANNATI is the more correct form of AMMANATI.

AMBERGER, Christoph (*c.*1500–61/2), was an Augsburg portrait painter whose works resemble those of Holbein, but with a strong Venetian influence, perhaps due to Paris BORDONE, who may have visited Augsburg in 1540. There is a signed altarpiece, of 1560, in S. Anna, Augsburg, but the only signed portrait by him seems to be the *Emperor Charles V* (Berlin). There are works in Augsburg, Birmingham (Barber Inst.), Glasgow, Munich, Philadelphia (Johnson), Toledo Ohio, Vienna, and York.

'AMICO DI SANDRO' (Friend of Sandro, i.e. Botticelli) was the name given by Berenson to the artist he invented as the painter of several pictures which seemed between the styles of BOTTICELLI and Filippino LIPPI; e.g. two Filippinos in the NG, London, and a Botticelli in the V & A, London. His creator later repudiated him and the pictures have been redistributed, although an attempt has been made to resuscitate him.

AMIGONI (Amiconi), Jacopo (1682?–1752), was a Venetian history and portrait painter who worked all over Europe in a more or less international style, the Venetian Rococo, with elements compounded from Sebastiano RICCI and French Rococo, and, later, TIEPOLO. He worked for some years for the Elector of Bavaria and then came to London in 1730, where he painted several decorative cycles and portraits; though these, according to VERTUE, were 'not his inclination – nor Talent'. In 1739 he returned to Venice with a small fortune, and it was he who persuaded Canaletto to visit London (1746). In 1747 he went to Madrid as Court painter: Vertue records that news of his death there reached London just as his finest works – in St James's Square – were destroyed. The altarpiece of Emmanuel College, Cambridge, is his: other works are in Darmstadt, London (Tate), Madrid, Schleissheim, Sheffield, Venice, and York.

AMMANATI, Bartolommeo (1511–92), was a Florentine sculptor influenced by Michelangelo and Sansovino. His best-known work is the *Neptune* fountain (1563–75) in the Piazza della Signoria at Florence, of which a contemporary said: 'Ammanato, Ammanato, che bel marmo hai rovinato!' (what fine marble you have ruined!). In his old age, affected by Counter-Reformation austerity, he is said to have destroyed some of his secular works. He also wrote an important letter (published in 1582) setting out his ideas on decency and on the sculptor's responsibility for his work, which is a document of Mannerist art-theory after the Council of Trent. His chief claim to fame rests on his work as an architect. In 1550 he married Laura Battiferri, who was well-known as a poet.

AMORINO (Ital. little love). A small Cupid or PUTTO.

ANAMORPHOSIS. Prominent in the foreground of HOLBEIN's *Ambassadors* (1533: London, NG) is an extremely elongated and distorted representation of a skull which can only be recognized by viewing it through a special lens or at an extreme angle. Such a representation – not unlike the reflection in a distorting mirror – is called an Anamorphosis. They are rare as serious works of art, and no convincing explanation for the skull has so far been proposed, but there is a similar, contemporary, *Edward VI* (1546: London, NPG).

ANCONA (Ital.). A large altarpiece composed of several compartments made in one piece with the frame. *See* POLYPTYCH.

ANDREA del Castagno *see* CASTAGNO.

ANDREA del Sarto (1486–1530) was, with Fra BARTOLOMMEO, the most important painter working in Florence at the time when Raphael and Michelangelo were active in Rome. He was the best painter (as opposed to draughtsman) in 16th-century Florence and had more feeling for tone and colour than any of his contemporaries south of Venice. He was the first Florentine to depart from the coloured drawing approach in favour of composition by patches of coloured light and shade, although his actual draughtsmanship is derived from Michelangelo. He also borrowed from the newly arrived engravings of Dürer. As a fresco painter he made his name with a series of grisailles in the Church of the Scalzi (1511–26) and the *Miracles of S. Filippo Benizzi* (1509–10) in SS. Annunziata. These were followed by his most famous frescoes, epitomizing the High Renaissance style in Florence, the *Birth of the Virgin* (1514) and the *Madonna del Sacco* (1525), both also in the Annunziata. Andrea went to France in 1518/19 at the invitation of Francis I and was well received there, but he broke his contract in order to return to his wife, who, in the opinion of contemporaries, ruined him. Browning's poem is probably the best explanation of his failure to live up to his early promise, but his works are of great importance in the evolution of Florentine painting, especially the *Holy Families*, often in half-length. The *Madonna delle Arpie* (1517) in the Uffizi, Florence, is a purely classical work comparable with Raphael's Madonnas: it is also a starting-point for MANNERISM, since his pupils included PONTORMO, ROSSO, and VASARI. Outside Florence there are works by him in the Royal Collection and in Berlin, Dresden, London (NG and Wallace Coll.), Madrid, New York (Met. Mus.), Paris (Louvre: including some painted in France), Philadelphia, Vienna, and elsewhere.

ANGELICO, Fra (c. 1387 or perhaps c. 1400–55). Fra Giovanni da Fiesole, known as the Blessed Angelico, was a Dominican friar who was a friend of S. Antoninus and knew Popes Eugenius IV and

Nicholas V. As a member of the Order of Preachers he used his art for
didactic rather than mystic purposes and the style he evolved was cor-
respondingly simple and direct; conservative, and yet based on the
largeness of form of Giotto and Masaccio, so that the general development of his style begins with a Gothic quality akin to LORENZO
Monaco and runs counter to the trend of Florentine painting in the
1440s as shown e.g. by Fra Filippo LIPPI. He entered the convent at
Fiesole and shared in its vicissitudes at Cortona and Foligno, but he
does not seem to have painted much before 1428, although he seems
to have been both a layman and a painter in 1417. The new theory
that he was born c. 1400 goes a long way towards explaining this. The
first certainly datable work by him is the *Linaiuoli Madonna* (Florence,
S. Marco), commissioned in 1433. The convent of S. Marco was
taken over by his Order in 1436 and he decorated it with a series of
about fifty frescoes, most of them in the cells of the friars and intended
as aids to contemplation. At the same time (c. 1440) he painted the
altarpieces for S. Marco and two other convents: these show the
Madonna surrounded by Saints and are important in the development of the type of altarpiece known as the SACRA CONVERSAZ-
IONE. He was called to Rome, probably by Eugenius IV, to decorate
a chapel in the Vatican (c. 1446–9), which still exists. In 1447 he also
painted two frescoes in Orvieto Cathedral as part of a *Last Judgement*,
a scheme which was later finished by SIGNORELLI. He was elected
Prior of Fiesole in 1449 and probably returned to Rome after his
three year term expired to paint the Chapel of the Sacrament in the
Vatican, now destroyed. He died in Rome in 1455. The biggest collection of his works is in the Museo di S. Marco, Florence, his own convent. Others are in Cortona, Fiesole, Florence (Uffizi), Perugia, and
the Vatican, as well as Berlin, Cambridge Mass., London (NG),
Madrid, Paris (Louvre), Munich, and elsewhere. His most important
pupil was Benozzo GOZZOLI.

ANONIMO (Ital. anonymous). Often applied to any unknown Italian
painter, but specifically it refers either to the Anonimo Morelliano
(i.e. Marcanton Michiel), a writer on the art of Venice and N. Italy in
the first half of the 16th century, or to the Anonimo Magliabechiano
(or Gaddiano), a Florentine writer of the same period.

ANTELAMI, Benedetto, was the chief Italian sculptor before the
PISANI. In 1178 he signed and dated a relief of the *Deposition* in
Parma Cathedral; the Baptistry at Parma, begun in 1196, and some of
the sculpture at Borgo San Donnino (now called Fidenza) are attributed to him.

ANTI-CERNE (Fr. *cerne*, outline). A contour managed by leaving a
white line of bare canvas between two or more areas of colour. It is,
in fact, the opposite of a black outline, and is a favourite device of
FAUVE painters.

ANTONELLO da Messina (*c.*1430–79) was the only major S. Italian painter of the 15th century and the only Italian decisively influenced by the minute oil-technique associated with the EYCKS. He may have been a pupil of the half-legendary Colantonio in Naples (where he could have seen Flemish paintings) and there is no reason to suppose he actually visited Flanders. His mature style combines Flemish detail and technique with Italian breadth of form. In 1475/6 he was in Venice, where he painted the S. Cassiano altarpiece (now known only from copies and fragments in Vienna): this was contemporary with the altarpiece of PIERO della Francesca (Milan, Brera) and the one (now destroyed) by Giovanni BELLINI for SS. Giovanni e Paolo. One of these three was the first great SACRA CONVERSAZIONE to treat the picture space as a continuation of the real space – like a chapel opening out of the church – so that the spectator is drawn into the scene in active participation. Antonello's virtuoso technique also influenced the Venetians, especially Giovanni Bellini's portraits, which show traces of the Flemish type of design favoured by Antonello. Apart from the Vienna fragments there are works in London (NG) (*Salvator Mundi* 1465, the first dated work, and others); Paris (Louvre) and Antwerp which both have works dated 1475, presumably painted in Venice; Berlin, Bucharest, Messina, Munich, New York, Philadelphia, Rome (Borghese), Washington, and elsewhere.

ANTWERP MANNERISTS. A term used to describe a group of Antwerp painters, mostly unidentified, working in the early 16th century (*c.*1510–30), and who, strictly speaking, have nothing to do with MANNERISM. Their style is characterized by its use of affected poses and florid ornament, some of which is Italianate in type. ISENBRANDT is related to this group. *See also* ITALIANIZERS, ROMANISTS.

APPEL, Karel (*b.*1921), is a Dutch painter, born in Amsterdam, who works in Paris. He exhibited with the group known as Cobra (i.e. Copenhagen, Brussels, Amsterdam) from 1949. In 1951 he painted a mural for the Stedelijk Museum, Amsterdam, and he has also produced some book-illustrations, but most of his works are in immensely thick layers of frenziedly moulded oil paint, Abstract Expressionist in type and similar to the work of the American KOONING. There are examples in Antwerp, Auckland NZ, Brussels, Buffalo, Copenhagen, The Hague, Liège, London (Tate), Manchester (Whitworth), New York (Guggenheim), Ottawa, Pittsburgh (Carnegie), Sheffield, and Utrecht.

APT, Ulrich the Elder (*d.*1532), was active in Augsburg in 1481. He painted many portraits, mostly in the style of Hans Holbein I, and several have been confused with HOLBEIN the Younger's. There are pictures by him in Augsburg, Florence (Uffizi), Munich, Vienna; and there are two replicas of a *Man and his Wife*, 1512, in the Royal Coll. and New York (Met. Mus.).

Aquatint *see* Engraving.

Arabesque. A flowing linear decoration. *See* Grotesque.

Archipenko, Alexander (1887–1964), was a Russian-American abstract sculptor. He went to Paris in 1908 and was much influenced by Cubism. There are works by him in New York (M of MA), Detroit, and London (Tate).

Architectonic in the sense in which it is used in art criticism means 'having the massive stability and calm grandeur of noble architecture'. A handy synonym for Monumental.

Arcimboldi, Giuseppe (1527–93). A Milanese painter of fantastic heads composed of fragments of landscape, vegetables, flowers, etc., much overrated in his own day (and now) and claimed as an ancestor by the Surrealists. He worked in a normal style for Milan Cathedral (1549–58) and designed tapestries for Como (1558). Court painter at Prague (1562–87), his bizarreries appealed to the Hapsburgs, especially Rudolf II, who made him a Count Palatine. Vienna has several pictures painted for Rudolf II; other works are in Brescia, Cremona, Graz, Hartford Conn. (Wadsworth Atheneum), and Innsbruck.

Aretino *see* Spinello.

Armature. A metal skeleton, usually of flexible lead piping, used to support clay or wax in the making of a piece of sculpture.

Armitage, Kenneth (*b.*1916), is a British sculptor who now works almost exclusively in modelled plaster, subsequently cast in bronze. His figures are exceedingly thin and sail-like, with much attention given to the effect of movement. In 1956 he won a competition for a war memorial at Krefeld, and in 1958 he was the British representative at the Biennale in Venice. There are works by him in Antwerp (Middelheim Park), Brussels, Buffalo, Leeds, London (Tate, V & A), New York (Brooklyn and M of MA), Paris, Rome, and elsewhere.

Armory Show. Held in 1913 in a regimental armoury in New York this exhibition was the principal means of introducing 'modern' – i.e. Post-Impressionist – art to the United States.

Arnolfo di Cambio (*d.*probably 1302). Italian architect and sculptor, designer of Florence Cathedral (1300). A pupil of Nicola Pisano, Arnolfo worked on his master's Shrine of S. Dominic, Bologna (1264–7), and Pulpit at Siena (1265–8), before going to Rome in 1277 where he made a portrait of Charles of Anjou (Rome, Conservatori Gall.), which is one of the first modern portrait statues. His tomb of Cardinal de Braye (*d.*1282) in S. Domenico at Orvieto, now much altered, set the type of wall-tomb for more than a century, with its arrangement of the dead man lying on a bier below the Madonna and Child in glory, set in a vertical architectural frame. He also made a tomb and a bust of Boniface VIII, as part of the Pope's campaign of artistic propaganda, and built ciboria in S. Paolo fuori (1285) and

Sta Cecilia (1293), both in Rome. The famous bronze statue of S. Peter in S. Peter's is attributed to him. The remains of his sculptural decoration for Florence Cathedral are in the Cathedral Museum, and other works are in the Bargello, Florence; Boston, and the V & A, London.

ARP, Jean (Hans) (1887–1966), was born in Alsace and studied in Paris, but also knew Ernst, Klee, and Kandinsky, and exhibited in the second Blaue Reiter exhibition. In Zürich in 1916 he was one of the co-founders of DADA, and later, after settling in France, he became a Surrealist, which may explain the evident sexual symbolism of his forms. There are works by him in Leeds, London (Tate), and New York (M of MA). His autobiography was published in 1948.

ARPINO, Giuseppe Cesari, called Cavaliere d'Arpino (1568–1640), was 'the last melancholy champion' of conservative and anaemic MANNERISM in opposition to CARAVAGGIO's naturalist revolution (he employed Caravaggio and outlived him by 30 years), and was patronized by the Vatican and the Roman Princes. He designed the mosaics of the dome of S. Peter's, painted the frescoes of S. Martino, Naples (1589–91), and painted huge and dull histories in the Conservatori Palace, Rome, the earliest of 1591 and the last of 1636. Most old galleries have examples, including London (Wellington Mus.), Oxford (Ch. Ch.), the Vatican, and Vienna.

ARRICCIATO (ARRICCIO) *see* FRESCO.

ARS MORIENDI (Lat. The Art of Dying). One of the most famous BLOCK-BOOKS, printed in Germany *c.*1466. It is a devotional work, like the *Biblia Pauperum*, and is based either on a Netherlandish block-book of *c.*1450 (in London, BM) or on a set of engravings (Oxford) by the anonymous Master E.S.

ART BRUT *see* DUBUFFET.

ART NOUVEAU was a 'new art' which spread across Europe and America in the 1890s. It was mainly a style of architecture and interior decoration (Horta, van de Velde) and flourished in Belgium and Britain especially, using flat patterns of writhing vegetable forms based on a naturalistic conception of plants rather than a formalized type of decoration. Cast-iron lilies and copper tendrils are still with us, as is furniture with heart-shaped holes in it. ENSOR was associated with the creators of the movement in Belgium, but he is much less typical than MORRIS, whose Arts and Crafts movement may be the progenitor of *Art nouveau*, or, better still, BEARDSLEY, whose drawings appeared in the first issue of 'The Studio' (1893), a periodical which helped to spread the style. In Germany the movement was called *Jugendstil*, after a magazine 'Jugend' (Youth), which was first published in 1896.

ASCRIPTION *see* ATTRIBUTION.

ASHCAN SCHOOL. A group of 19th/20th-century American 'realist' painters and illustrators – the best-known was BELLOWS, although he was not one of the original eight – whose interest in the sordid side of city life (especially in New York) justifies the nickname.

ASSELYN, Jan (1610–52). A Dutch Italianate painter, probably a pupil of E. van de VELDE, but who formed his style on the imitation of the Arcadian landscapes of CLAUDE. His best-known work is a political allegory of Dutch independence, *The Angry Swan*, in Amsterdam (Rijksmus.), but *Beggars at a Monastery* (1647) in Dresden is more typical.

ATELIER (Fr. studio). The *atelier libre* is a common feature of the Continental art world. It is a studio, open freely but not free, which provides a nude model in fixed sessions, but no tuition or control. The most famous was opened *c.*1825–30 in Paris by a model called Suisse, and was used by Delacroix, Courbet, Manet, Monet, Pissarro, Cézanne, and other Impressionists. The Atelier Julian, opened in Paris in 1860, was not an *atelier libre* since it provided a teacher, though it was more liberal than the official École des Beaux-Arts for which it often served as forcing-ground or alternative. Most of the NABIS worked at the Julian, as did Matisse, Derain, and Léger. Sometimes these *ateliers libres* are called *Académies*.

ATTRIBUTION. When a picture is signed or recorded in a document there can be little doubt that it is by the painter to whom it is attributed: 'attribution', however, usually means assigning a picture to its painter on the grounds of its likeness to works known to be his. This, which involves STYLE CRITICISM, can range from moral certainty to mere guess-work, depending on such factors as the number of certain works known to the person making the attribution, as well as the degree of his intimacy with them. For this reason, a conscientious cataloguer gives at least the main reasons for his decisions, and it is desirable to use phrases like 'Attributed to . . .', 'Ascribed to . . .', 'Circle of . . .', or 'Studio of . . .' with some precision. In normal English usage there is no distinction between Attributed and Ascribed, but it may be suggested that a useful terminology would be to keep 'Ascribed to . . .' to imply a slightly greater degree of dubiety than 'Attributed to . . .'. The distinction between 'Studio of . . .' and 'Follower of . . .', maintained in the catalogues of the National Gallery, is similar – Follower not implying any direct contact with the artist. A Follower may well be considerably later, whereas an Imitator is self-explanatory.

AU PREMIER COUP (Fr. at the first shot) *see* ALLA PRIMA.

AUTOGRAPH. A painting or other work of art is said to be autograph when it is thought to be entirely from the hand of the artist to whom it is attributed. In the case of frescoes or other very large undertakings it can hardly be expected that the artist should execute every part with his own hand, but the expression 'Studio of . . .' in connexion with smaller works indicates a desire not to suggest that the work is a copy. In some cases, especially that of RUBENS, one often finds that the original sketch is autograph and the execution of the finished, large, canvas was entrusted to assistants.

AUTOMATISM. Doodling. Shut your eyes and draw – the subconscious will do the rest; hence it was a favourite SURREALIST technique.

AVANZO, Jacopo. A 14th-century Paduan painter who was the pupil and apparently inseparable partner of ALTICHIERO.

AVED, Jacques (1702–66). A French portrait painter trained in Amsterdam, who became a friend and collaborator of CHARDIN, whose splendid portrait of Aved is now in the Louvre, Paris. There are portraits by Aved in the Louvre, Versailles, and other French museums, as well as Amsterdam (Rijksmus.), Cleveland Ohio, and The Hague.

AVERCAMP, Hendrik (1585–1634). A landscape painter born in Amsterdam but influenced by BRUEGEL the Elder and CONINXLOO and making the transition to the realistic Dutch landscape of the 17th century. He specialized in ice scenes and there are works in Amsterdam (Rijksmus.), Edinburgh (NG of S), London (NG), Rotterdam, St Louis, Toledo Ohio, and Vienna. Barent Avercamp (1612–79) was his nephew, pupil, and imitator.

B

BABUREN, Dirck van (c.1590–1624), was one of the three principal painters of the UTRECHT SCHOOL. He was in Rome 1617–20/2 and there painted the *Deposition* (S. Pietro in Montorio) which is derived from Caravaggio's (now in the Vatican). His career was very short and only a handful of pictures survive, others being in Utrecht, Boston, Oslo, and York.

BACICCIA, Giovanni Battista Gaulli called (1639–1709), was a Genoese whose style was formed by the study of Rubens and van Dyck. He soon made a name as a portrait painter but went to Rome very young and made a greater reputation as one of the most daring of all the Baroque decorators. He was friendly with BERNINI and studied the Correggio frescoes in Parma: his most celebrated work, the ceiling of the Gesù in Rome (1668–85), is a staggering piece of illusionism, with the painted figures merging into stucco figures which break out of the apparent frame into the plane of the spectator. It goes beyond even the ceiling of the Barberini Palace, by PIETRO da Cortona, and has in addition a Rubensian warmth of colour. Many other Roman churches were decorated by him and his portraits are also to be found in Roman galleries. Some of his later portraits have a quieter, almost Marattesque, character.

BACKER, Jacob Adriaensz. (1608–51), was a pupil of Rembrandt about 1632 and painted portraits in Amsterdam. Occasionally he crossed the influence of Rembrandt with that of Hals, particularly in his use of light colour. Amsterdam and The Hague have good examples.

BACKHUYSEN, Ludolf (1631–1708), was a Dutch marine painter, a pupil of A. van EVERDINGEN. He is well represented in the NG, London, and his *Boats in a Storm* (London, Dulwich) may well have been one of the sea-pieces that influenced Turner.

BACON, Francis (b.1909), is a self-taught painter who destroys a large part of his output, so much so that virtually nothing of his early work has survived. Through his highly personal subject-matter, which concentrates chiefly on dogs, carcasses, and evocations of men, including elderly tycoons, and Velazquez's *Innocent X*, caged in plate glass and screaming in a silent world of horror, dissolution and fear, he expresses with energy and singleness of aim all the gradations of emotion from pity and disgust to horror, traumatic revulsion and the unbalance of panic. His work, which can be interpreted as an attempt to evoke an essentially partial, since incomplete, catharsis in the spectator, raises in its most acute form the problem of the relationship between art and pleasure. There are pictures by him in

Aberdeen, Batley, Belfast, Birmingham, Buffalo NY, Chicago, Detroit, London (Tate), New York (M of M A), Ottawa, and Yale.

BACON, John (1740–99), began by modelling china figures. He also worked in Coade's artificial stone, and for Wedgwood and the Derby porcelain factory. He became an RA in 1770. He was a fashionable sculptor who executed many tombs, including the huge Chatham monument in Westminster Abbey (1779) and the one to Dr Johnson in St Paul's Cathedral (1796). He was considered the best sculptor of his day for tombs, as BANKS was for history pieces and NOLLEKENS for busts, and prided himself on his Christian sentiment: he was 'pious and zealously attached to Methodism . . . yet knowing in the ways of the world . . . and eager among stockbrokers'. His son John (1777–1859) was his pupil and finished his equestrian *William III* in St James's Square, London, and also executed a large number of tombs.

BALDINUCCI, Filippo (c. 1624–96), succeeded VASARI as historiographer of Florentine Art, his 'Notizie de' Professori . . .' appearing in many volumes, 1681–1728. He made greater use of documents than his predecessor, and the vast collection of drawings in the Uffizi is due to his appreciation of their importance in the study of paintings.

BALDOVINETTI, Alesso (c. 1545–99), was a Florentine painter and worker in mosaic and stained glass who was influenced by DOMENICO Veneziano. His experiments with the technique of fresco painting were unfortunate, witness the frescoes in SS. Annunziata (1460/2) and S. Miniato (1466), in Florence. He painted three panels in the series on the doors of the Silver Cupboard of SS. Annunziata (now in the Museo di S. Marco, Florence) which had been begun by Fra Angelico. There are other works by him in Florence as well as in London, Paris, and elsewhere.

BALDUNG, Hans (1484/5–1545), called Grien, was a Strasbourg painter and designer of woodcuts and stained glass. His woodcuts in particular show the influence of DÜRER, in whose shop he may have worked before 1505. His principal picture is the altarpiece in Freiburg Cathedral (1512–16), but his favourite theme was the female nude, often in horrible allegories such as the *Death and the Woman* (1517: Basle). Outside Germany and Austria there are pictures in the Royal Collection and in The Hague, Liverpool, and London (NG).

BALLA, Giacomo (1871–1958), signed the FUTURIST Manifesto of 1910 and painted Futurist pictures for a while, including the only amusing one produced by that dreary movement – the *Dog on a Leash*. He later returned to more traditional forms of expression. Examples of his Futurist phase are in London (Tate), and New York (M of MA).

BAMBINO (Ital. baby). Usually specifically the Christ child.

BAMBOCCIATA (Ital.). The name given to low-life and peasant subjects, generally small, with small figures, of the type painted by several Dutch and Flemish artists in Italy in the 17th century. These were popular even in Italy, although frowned on by the theorists of the Grand Style, as well as in the North. The name perhaps derives from BAMBOCCIO, although it also means 'jest, triviality'.

BAMBOCCIO (Ital. fat and lively baby). Name given as BENTNAME to Pieter van Laer (1592 or 1595–1642), a Dutch painter who lived in Rome 1627–39, where he was a friend of Poussin, Claude, and Sandrart. His pictures of peasants, soldiers, brigands, and similar subjects became popular in Italy and were much imitated by other Northern artists. He returned to his native Haarlem in 1639 and died there. There are pictures by him in the Royal Collection and in Amsterdam, Budapest, Cambridge (Fitzwm), Dresden, Florence (Uffizi), Munich, New York (Met. Mus.), Oxford (Ch. Ch.), Paris (Louvre), Rome (Gall. Naz.), and elsewhere.

BANDINELLI, Baccio (1493–1560), was a Florentine sculptor, gold-smith, and painter whose constant efforts to outdo Michelangelo generally rebounded on his own head. He was the rival of Cellini, who hated him both on his own account and on behalf of Michelangelo, but he enjoyed the favour of the Medici and through them he got the commission for his *Hercules and Cacus* (1534: Florence, Piazza della Signoria), made in direct emulation of Michelangelo's *David*. It was not much liked and Cellini and Bandinelli had a highly public quarrel over it. His best works are the reliefs in the choir of Florence Cathedral, but his greatest importance lies in the part he played in the development of ACADEMIES. There are examples in London (V & A), and Paris (Louvre).

BANKS, Thomas (1735–1805), was one of the first British sculptors to be influenced by Neoclassic ideals. He went to Rome in 1772 on a scholarship from the R A and remained there seven years: while there he carved the *Thetis* (London, V & A). He spent 1781–2 in St Peters-burg but in 1786 was elected R A and worked for the rest of his life on busts and monuments, the most famous of which was the dead child, *Penelope Boothby* (Ashbourne, Derbyshire), which moved Queen Charlotte to tears. There are works in London (NPG, Soane Mus., Westminster Abbey, and St Paul's), and elsewhere.

BAPTISTE *see* MONNOYER.

BARBARI, Jacopo de' (*d.c.*1515/16), is said to have been a Venetian painter, but from 1500 he worked in Germany and the Netherlands; about 1501 he wrote a curious letter to the Elector of Saxony called *De la eccelentia de la pictura*. He influenced DÜRER and was also influenced by him; certainly his engravings fit into the development of German graphic art. There is a portrait of Pacioli, the mathema-tician and pupil of Piero della Francesca, with another man, signed and dated 1495 (Naples), but this is sometimes held to be the work

of a different painter: on the other hand he certainly painted the first
STILL-LIFE, the *Dead Bird*, of 1504, at Munich. The reason for the
doubt over the attribution of the *Pacioli* is that it is signed 'Jaco. Bar.
vigennis P. 1495' – i.e. the painter was in his twenties and thus born
*c.*1475, which accords ill with an application for a pension (1511/12)
which describes him as 'old and weak'. Both documents may well be
correct. Berlin, Dresden, Paris, Philadelphia (Johnson), Verona, and
Weimar also have works of his.

BARBIZON SCHOOL. A mid-19th-century group of landscape painters,
centred on the village of Barbizon in the Forest of Fontainebleau. Its
chief members were MILLET, Théodore ROUSSEAU, and DIAZ,
their aims being an exact and unprettified rendering of peasant life
and scenery, painted on the spot. This last makes them the precursors
of IMPRESSIONISM, although the major influences upon them were
COROT, MICHEL, Dutch 17th-century landscape painters such as
Hobbema and Ruisdael, and, to a lesser degree, CONSTABLE and
BONINGTON. There are good collections of their work in Boston
and London (V & A), as well as the Louvre and other French
museums.

BARISANUS of Trani was a bronze founder and sculptor working in
South Italy in the last quarter of the 12th century. There are three
large pairs of bronze doors by him at the Cathedrals of Trani, Ravello,
and Monreale. Those at Trani have a self-portrait and a signature and
are thought to date from *c.*1175. The doors at Ravello are dated 1179
but are not signed. Those at Monreale are signed and are thought to
be contemporary with the other set of doors made for the same
cathedral by the Pisan BONANUS in 1185. The difference in style is
considerable and emphasizes the much greater dependence of
Barisanus upon Byzantine models – in some cases he even retains
Greek inscriptions – as well as his far greater interest in decorative
forms. Many of Barisanus's figures are repeated, even on the same
door, and were thus cast from a single mould. His doors are made of
plates of bronze nailed on to an oak framework, since the technique
of bronze casting in the 12th century was still comparatively rudimentary.

BARLACH, Ernst (1870–1938), was a German EXPRESSIONIST
sculptor and illustrator of great tragic power. His pessimistic art was
condemned by the Nazis and many of his works destroyed: survivors
are now in many German museums and there is a small Barlach
Museum near Lüneburg. His best works are perhaps the woodcarv-
ings of single figures of peasants, beggars, and similar subjects, many
of them inspired by a visit to Russia (cf. KOLLWITZ). His wood-
carving technique was closely based on German Late Gothic
work.

BARNA was a Sienese painter, active *c.*1350/6, who was the greatest of

Simone MARTINI's followers. In the Collegiata at S. Gimignano he painted the *Life of Christ* and he is said to have died as a result of a fall from the scaffolding, leaving the frescoes unfinished. The *Christ carrying the Cross* (New York, Frick Coll.) is attributed to him.

BARNABA da Modena (active 1362–83) was a N. Italian painter who combined an almost purely Byzantine tradition with some Giottesque elements. There are dated works in Berlin (1369), Turin (1370: Sabauda Gall.), London (1374) and elsewhere.

BAROCCI, Federico (c.1535–1612), was, after Raphael, the most important painter of Urbino. His soft, colouristic, and emotional art is a perfect expression of one aspect of the Counter-Reformation, and it is not surprising that S. Philip Neri regarded him highly. He was also a sensitive portrait painter. He was in Rome in the mid-1550s, when Michelangelo is said to have encouraged him, and he returned in 1560, making his name with the decorations in the Casino of Pius IV (1561–3: Vatican). Most of the rest of his life was spent in Urbino, where he worked for only two hours a day, crippled by ill-health (yet he lived to extreme old age). He became a Tertiary of the Order of S. Francis in 1566 and his greatest patron was the austere and pious Duke of Urbino, although he is better known for his connexion with S. Philip. Many drawings made as studies for his carefully-prepared paintings survive – e.g. the finished MODELLO in Oxford (Ashmolean) for the *Madonna of the Rosary* (c.1589–93: Senigallia, Bishop's Pal.), for which at least 27 other drawings and studies are known. Apart from the numerous works in Urbino, there are others in Brussels, Copenhagen, Florence (Uffizi, including the big *Madonna del Popolo*, 1575–9), London (NG), Madrid, Milan (Brera), Munich, Paris (Louvre), Perugia Cath. (1567, a *Descent from the Cross*, showing the influence of PONTORMO and CORREGGIO), Rome (Borghese and churches), the Vatican, Vienna, and Weimar.

BARONZIO, Giovanni, was a Riminese painter, working in 1345 and earlier, who was much influenced by CAVALLINI and GIOTTO. He was dead by 1362. He is the best evidence for Giotto's activity in Rimini, recorded in old sources. There are two dated pictures (1345) in Urbino and Mercatello, near Urbino (but the attribution of this is open to doubt), and frescoes in Ravenna and Tolentino. Others are in Rimini, Birmingham (Barber Inst.), Baltimore, Berlin, Munich, New York (Met. Mus.), Paris (Jacquemart-André), Rome, Venice, and elsewhere.

BAROQUE. This is the style that succeeded MANNERISM and lasted, though with profound modifications, until well into the 18th century. The style is seen at its purest in the so-called 'High Baroque', which is virtually confined to Italy (to Rome even) and to the period covered by the years c.1630–80, that is, roughly the maturity of its greatest exponent, BERNINI. The High Baroque, at its best and fullest, is a union of the arts of architecture, painting, and sculpture, acting in concert on the emotions of the spectator; inviting him, for example, to participate in the agonies and ecstasies of the Saints. Its blend of illusionism, light and colour, and movement is calculated to overwhelm the spectator by a direct emotional appeal. Owing to its essential links with Counter-Reformation Catholicism, pagan antiquity, and the Mediterranean generally, many Northerners are – or were until recently – queasy about it. At the beginning of the 17th century there was an upsurge of spiritual confidence and a new direction in religious art which combined with a new approach to classical art to create a new style. The confused and flaccid forms of late Mannerism gave place to the simple subject matter, the unidealized naturalism, the uncomplicated iconography, and strong chiaroscuro of CARAVAGGIO; the clarity of composition, the revival of the balance and harmony of Raphael and the tenderness of handling of Correggio, the nobility of form, the directness of meaning and imagery of Annibale CARRACCI, DOMENICHINO, Guido RENI, and GUERCINO. Of the painters of the High Baroque, LANFRANCO, PIETRO da Cortona, BACICCIA, and, at the end of the century, Padre POZZO specialized in the florid and exuberant illusionism which is one of the characteristics of the style, while Bernini pushed to their furthest limits the use of painterly effects in sculpture, the dissolved contour, the rendering of movement by means of flickering light, the expression of the most profound and passionately felt religious emotion. Some Roman artists, such as SACCHI, MARATTA, and ALGARDI, were always more restrained: POUSSIN, who lived and worked in Rome for most of his life, developed the classical and intellectual aspects of the Baroque style almost to the exclusion of its emotional side. Outside Italy, astute politicians like Colbert, Louis XIV's great Minister, were quick to see that the religious style could easily be made to subserve autocratic regimes, by the glorification of the monarch, but in this process a good deal of pompous inflation was superimposed on the original religious fervour; and the French exponents of the Baroque, in LEBRUN and his team, replaced its emotional qualities with a conscious and frigid use of the antique. Even RUBENS, the greatest Northern Baroque artist, sometimes allowed himself to be used in this way. The style lasted longest in Catholic Germany and Austria, and had the least influence in Protestant countries – Britain, Scandinavia and Holland, although there are aspects of Rembrandt which place him among the greatest artists of the Baroque, and there is certainly such a thing as English Baroque. In the North it is still possible to use the term as one of simple abuse (i.e. non-Gothic, unRuskinian), but this is now confined to the very old or the very unsophisticated. A more dangerous misuse is as a synonym for 'Seventeenth Century'. Late Baroque merges almost imperceptibly into the ROCOCO and the Age of Reason finally rejected both and produced NEOCLASSICISM.

BARRY, James (1741–1806), was an Irish painter who was brought to London by Edmund Burke in 1764. He was encouraged by Reynolds to persist in grand manner historical painting, and Burke paid his expenses to Italy, 1766–71, where he studied Raphael and Michelangelo with more enthusiasm than discretion. He was made an RA in 1773, and from 1777 to 1783 worked on a huge decoration in the Great Room of the Society of Arts of six pictures (two are 42 feet long) representing *The Progress of Human Culture*. When they were exhibited in 1783 Dr Johnson said of them: 'Whatever the hand may have done, the mind has done its part. There is a grasp of mind there which you find nowhere else.' He became Professor of Painting at the RA in 1782, but in 1799 was expelled for his bitter attacks on his fellow-members and on the memory of Reynolds. BLAKE's projected poem 'Barry' exists only as a fragment, which is a diatribe against Reynolds. He died in great poverty and squalor. There are works in Dublin (NG), Cork, London (Tate), and Manchester. He represents, with FUSELI and HAYDON, another instance of the failure of the English patron to appreciate history painting on a gigantic scale and on heroic themes, based on a studious adaptation of the Italian Grand Style. His portraits are very fine, but he could only rarely be persuaded to demean himself to paint one.

BARTOLO di Fredi was a Sienese who died in 1410 but who worked in the style of the LORENZETTI and of BARNA.

BARTOLOMMEO di Giovanni *see* 'ALUNNO DI DOMENICO'.

BARTOLOMMEO della Porta, Fra (*c.* 1474 – probably 1517), was born in Florence and apprenticed to Cosimo ROSSELLI in 1484. He was in the convent of S. Marco in 1498 when it was stormed and its Prior, Savonarola, dragged to prison, and he is said to have vowed then to become a monk, which he did in 1500. His earliest remaining work (a *Last Judgement*, 1499, Mus. di S. Marco) is now in very bad condition but enough remains to show its profound influence on the young RAPHAEL. In 1504 he became head of the monastery workshop, a position once held by Fra Angelico. He visited Venice in 1508 and after his return took Mariotto ALBERTINELLI into partnership, and he was in Rome in 1514 or 1515, both these visits being important for the development of his ideals of simplicity and balance in composition, decorum of presentation, the use of telling gestures and rapt expressions, the exclusion of picturesque detail, and the adoption of sober and rather generalized settings. He introduced figures in strong *contrapposto* for its own sake, and was among the first to replace contemporary costume with nondescript drapery in his religious figures, using this to stress the gulf between the divine and the earthly.

All these ideas mark the change from the style of the 15th century to that of the 16th century, and he was one of its most important initiators, his influence being spread by his huge output of drawings. After his death the S. Marco workshop petered out. There are works in Berlin, Besançon (Cath.), Cambridge Mass. (Fogg Mus.), Florence (Accad., Pitti, Uffizi, Mus. di S. Marco), London (NG), Lucca (Mus. and Cath.), Paris (Louvre), Philadelphia (Johnson Coll.), Rome (Gall. Naz.), Stuttgart, the Vatican, Vienna, and Washington (NG).

BARYE, Antoine-Louis (1796–1875), the son of a Paris goldsmith, served in the Napoleonic Armies 1812–14 and began to study sculpture only in 1816. He worked for a goldsmith from 1823 to 1831 in the Jardin des Plantes, making models of the animals, and from then on devoted himself almost exclusively to animal sculpture. In 1848 he went bankrupt but was appointed Keeper of Casts at the Louvre (1848–50) and was later teacher of zoological drawing at the Musée d'Histoire Naturelle, Paris. His first major work of a non-animal subject was the *Napoleon dominating History and the Arts* (1855–7), a pediment on the Pavillon de l'Horloge of the Louvre, and in 1860 he made the equestrian *Napoleon* for Ajaccio, Napoleon's birthplace. He was one of the major Romantic artists of the 19th century and his choice of violent subjects – tigers, jaguars, and other carnivores, often shown devouring other animals and even human beings – gives him a certain affinity with DELACROIX, although Barye was never able to invest the human figure with Romantic overtones. One or two small statues of women are almost Greek in feeling. There is a large collection of his works in the Louvre and over 100 in Washington (Corcoran).

BASAITI, Marco (c. 1470–1530), was a Venetian painter much influenced by Giovanni BELLINI (c. 1500–10) and then by GIORGIONE. There is a signed *Madonna* in London (NG) which shows him using Bellini's types.

Pseudo-Basaiti is probably only a name for one aspect of Bellini.

BAS-RELIEF *see* RELIEF.

BASSANO. This was the name of a family of Venetian painters of which there were four main members. Francesco da Ponte the Elder (c. 1475 –1539) worked in Bassano and was a modest provincial follower of the Bellini. His son Jacopo (c. 1510/18–92) was the most considerable artist of the family. He was a pupil in Venice of BONIFAZIO de' Pitati, and was independent by the early 1530s. Although he worked almost entirely in Bassano he was by no means a provincial painter, and his works show successive waves of influence, proving him to have been in constant and sensitive touch with Venice. His was a highly personal style, robust and energetic, with stocky figures in strong chiaroscuro and heavy impasto, and he pioneered the large, rustic genre scene depicting the seasons, or the trades, with many figures and animals, often set in a mountainous and stormy landscape, and favoured religious subjects that allowed him to introduce peasants and animals (in which he was one of the first to be interested) and heaped-up still-lifes of fruit, game, vegetables, and utensils (cf. AERTSEN, BUECKELAER). Jacopo had three painter sons. Francesco the Younger (1549–92) ran the Venetian branch of the workshop. His paintings are often based on his father's drawings and closely, but more weakly, follow his style.. He committed suicide a few months after his father's death. Leandro (1557–1622) worked in the Venetian studio under Francesco, and after the latter's death took over the workshop. He was the chief portrait painter of the family, and his portraits are closely allied to those of TINTORETTO. Gerolamo (1566–1621) entered the workshop under Leandro.

There are works by the family in the museums and churches of Bassano and Venice, and in the Royal Collection, Bergamo, Berlin, Budapest, Cambridge (Fitzwm), Cambridge Mass. (Fogg Mus.), Chicago, Cleveland Ohio, Copenhagen, Detroit, Dresden, Edinburgh (NG), Florence (Uffizi, Pitti), Greenville S. Carolina, Grenoble, London (NG, V & A), Madrid (Acad., Prado), Manchester, Mantua, Milan (Brera, Ambrosiana, Castello), Munich, Naples, New York (Met. Mus., Frick), Paris (Louvre), Philadelphia (Johnson), Prague, Rome (Gall. Naz., Borghese, Capitoline), Rouen, Stockholm, Toronto, Turin, Vienna, and elsewhere.

BASTIEN-LEPAGE, Jules (1848–84), exhibited at the Salon from 1870 until the end of his short life. Most of his exhibits were portraits, but he is now remembered for his rustic genre scenes – his masterpiece, *The Haymakers* of 1877 is in the Louvre – and there was much discussion of his truthfulness to the Lorraine countryside. By comparison with MILLET he seems sentimental, which may explain the popularity of his pictures in Scotland (Aberdeen, Edinburgh and Glasgow), and he may have influenced the Glasgow School. His *Joan of Arc* is in New York (Met. Mus.), and there are works in Lille, Melbourne, Moscow and Verdun.

BATONI (Battoni), Pompeo (1708–87), was the principal rival of MENGS in Rome, but, although he was an enthusiast for Raphael and the Antique, he was less whole-heartedly Neoclassic. The minute delicacy of his handling won him many foreign patrons and the greater part of his output must consist of portraits of Princes and Grand Tourists painted while they were in Rome. He painted three Popes and most Princes of Europe, but the idea of a portrait of an educated man, standing against a background of classical antiquity (e.g. the Colosseum), seems to be Batoni's speciality and was well suited to the travelling Englishman. Many of these still exist in private collections, and there is even one of *General Gordon* (1766: Fyvie Castle, Aberdeenshire) which shows the sitter in full Highland dress with a claymore, set against the Colosseum. Reynolds was more influenced by these than he would admit, and, in the 14th Discourse, he goes out of his way to praise Gainsborough at the expense of Mengs and Batoni. From 1735 Batoni had a great many commissions for altarpieces and also for historical and mythological pictures: in 1760–1 he painted an altarpiece for St Peter's but this was not very successful and is now in S. M. degli Angeli, Rome. There are works in Roman churches and galleries and in Berlin, Birmingham, Cardiff, Dresden, Dublin (NG), Edinburgh (NPG), Florence (Uffizi and Pitti), Frankfurt (Städel), Greenville S. Carolina, Leeds, London (NG, V & A, NPG), Madrid (Acad. and Prado), Milan (Brera), Minneapolis, Munich, Oxford, Paris (Louvre), and Vienna.

BAUHAUS, The. This was the most famous school of architecture, design and craftsmanship of modern times and has had an inestimable influence on art school training all over the world. It was founded in 1919 at Weimar, in Germany, by W. Gropius, the architect. It moved to Dessau in 1925 and then to Berlin, where, in 1933, it was closed by the Nazis. Its great importance lay in the fact that its teachers included FEININGER, KLEE, and KANDINSKY, and it attempted to face the problem of machine production, which MORRIS had evaded. The influence of DOESBURG, DE STIJL, and SCHLEMMER may be seen in this. The New Bauhaus was at Chicago, opened by MOHOLY-NAGY in 1937.

BAUMEISTER, Willi (1889–1955), was a German abstract painter who began as a Constructivist. He was in Paris in 1912 and 1914 and was influenced at first by Lautrec, Gauguin, and Cézanne, but was later decisively influenced by the mechanical forms of LÉGER. He was dismissed from his teaching post for 'degeneracy' in 1933, but, unlike most others, he remained in Germany and was, in due course, reinstated. From c.1936 his works were entirely abstract: examples are in Cologne and Frankfurt (Städel).

BAYEU, Francisco (1734–95), was a Spanish painter who worked under MENGS on the decoration of the Royal Palace, but is better known as GOYA's master 1766–c.71 and brother-in-law. There is a portrait of him by Goya in the Prado, Madrid, which also has some of his own works. His brother Ramón (1746–93) was also a painter and worked with Goya.

BAZAINE, Jean (b.1904), denies that he is an abstract painter, but since 1945 he has produced non-figurative pictures as well as stained glass and mosaics (churches at Assy (1950), Audincourt (1951), and for the UNESCO building in Paris). In 1948 he published Notes sur la peinture d'aujourd'hui, which went into a second edition in 1953. In 1953–4 he was in Spain. There is a painting by him in Paris (Mus. d'Art Moderne), and glass in St Séverin.

BAZILLE, Frédéric (1841–71), was a pupil of the academician Gleyre at the same time as Renoir, and through him came into close contact with most of the IMPRESSIONISTS and with Manet. His chief aim was the study of figures painted out-of-doors, so as to relate the tones of the flesh with those of the landscape. He was killed in the Franco-Prussian War when still on the threshold of his career. Most of his pictures are in Paris (Mus. de l'Impressionnisme) and his native Montpellier.

BEARDSLEY, Aubrey (1872–98), was an illustrator whose highly wrought, stylized black and white drawings exude a typically *fin-de-siècle* atmosphere and express perfectly the ART NOUVEAU of which they were an ingredient. He is best known for his work on the 'Yellow Book' in 1894, and for illustrations to Wilde's 'Salome', and to the 'Rape of the Lock'. There are drawings by him in London (V&A, Tate).

BECCAFUMI, Domenico (1484/6–1551), was, with PARMIGIANINO, the most interesting of the non-Florentine Mannerist painters, and the last of the great Sienese. A member of the High Renaissance generation, his years in Rome (1510–12) saw the painting of Raphael's Stanze and Michelangelo's Sistine Ceiling, both of which influenced him. In such works as the *S. Catherine receiving the Stigmata* (*c.* 1514: Siena, Accad.) he appears also to have been affected by Fra BARTOLOMMEO, whose work was known in Siena. From soon after his return to Siena in 1513, his highly personal style displays characteristics usually associated with the Mannerism of the following decade; his use of strong effects of perspective and *contrapposto*, his intensity of emotion, and his use of subtle, shot colour, as well as of lurid effects, are stylistic features of central Italian painting of the 1530s and 1540s, which he probably knew of as a result of the dispersal of Roman artists after the Sack in 1527. Most of his best works are in Siena, but there are others in Baltimore, Berlin, Birmingham (Barber Inst.), Cambridge (Fitzwm), Detroit, Dresden, Dublin, Florence (Uffizi, Pitti, and Horne Mus.), Leicester, London (NG, V & A), Munich, Naples, Pisa (Cath.), Rome (Gall. Naz., Borghese, S. M. Maggiore), Sarasota Fla, Washington (NG), York, and elsewhere.

BECKER, Paula Modersohn *see* MODERSOHN.

BECKMANN, Max (1884–1950), was one of the leading German EXPRESSIONIST painters. He met MUNCH in 1906, exhibited with DIX and GROSZ and other NEUE SACHLICHKEIT painters and taught in Frankfurt until 1933, when he was dismissed as 'decadent'. On the opening day of the Degenerate Art exhibition sponsored by the Nazis in 1937 he emigrated to Holland, going to America in 1947, where he died. His nine Triptychs, painted from 1932 onwards, show that the main influences on him were Bosch and the German primitives, apart from his contemporaries. He is represented in American museums (e.g. Harvard Univ.), and now in Germany as well.

BEECHEY, Sir William (1753–1839), was a portrait painter of far less skill than Sir Thomas Lawrence, but he may have had a more truthful eye and he was certainly more sober in approach. He was elected ARA in 1793 and made Portrait Painter to the Queen; in 1798 he exhibited the huge *George III and the Prince of Wales reviewing Troops* (Royal Coll.) for which he was knighted and elected RA. He was a very careful craftsman and most anxious to ensure the durability of his pictures, examples of which are in London (Tate, NPG, Dulwich, Soane, Courtauld Inst.), Ottawa, and many American museums.

'BEFORE ALL LETTERS' *see* PROOF.

BEGGARSTAFF Brothers *see* NICHOLSON, William.

BELLECHOSE, Henri, *see* MALOUEL.

BELLINI. There were three painters in this Venetian family: Jacopo, and his sons Gentile and Giovanni.

Jacopo (*c.* 1400–70/1) was a pupil of GENTILE da Fabriano, with whom he was in Florence where, in 1423, he was involved in a prosecution as a result of an affray with a youth who threw stones into the workshop yard. Only four certain pictures are known, all rather stiff and hieratic in pose and treatment. In 1441 he defeated PISANELLO in a competition portrait of Lionello d'Este of Ferrara, but this portrait cannot be identified with certainty. His major surviving works are his two sketchbooks (British Museum and Louvre) which were the source of many of the ideas and designs used by his sons and by Mantegna. Four signed works are in Lovere (near Bergamo), Milan (Brera), Venice (Accad.), and Verona; other, attributed, pictures are in Florence (Uffizi), Milan (Poldi-Pezzoli), Padua, Verona, and elsewhere.

Gentile (*c.* 1429/30–1507) probably worked in the family shop until his father died (an altarpiece said to have been signed by all three and dated 1460 is recorded), but he had achieved sufficient fame to be ennobled by the Emperor in 1469, though nothing is known of the work that procured him his honours. In 1479–81 he was in Constantinople, painting portraits for Sultan Mahomet II. He worked on the cycle of history pictures in the Doge's Palace in 1474 and again on his return from Turkey, but all were burnt in 1577. His series depicting the processions and ceremonies of two major charitable foundations in Venice became the popular type for this kind of picture, full of portraits and views of the city. His large *S. Mark preaching at Alexandria* (Milan, Brera) was unfinished at his death, and he bequeathed one of his father's sketchbooks to his brother on condition that he finished it. He also bequeathed to two of his pupils his sketchbook of Roman drawings (now lost), which may be evidence for his having visited Rome. There are works in Berlin, Boston (Gardner), Budapest, Chicago, Istanbul (University Library), London (NG), Milan (Brera), New York (Frick Coll.), San Francisco, Venice (Accad., Correr, S. Marco Mus.), and elsewhere.

Giovanni (c. 1430–1516) is usually accepted as the younger son, but his birth date is pure conjecture. There is some evidence that he was independent by 1459, but he can be presumed to have been connected with the family workshop until Jacopo's death. His early work derives much from his father, but, like Gentile, he was strongly influenced by MANTEGNA, who married their sister Nicolosia in 1454. The chronology of his works is difficult because he became the main teacher of his generation, the main source of new ideas and forms, with a large workshop of pupils and assistants, so that 'OP. IOH. BELL.' is not only a signature, but a trade-mark, the sign of the workshop rather than the artist. His pupils included Giorgione, Titian, Palma Vecchio, and Sebastiano del Piombo, and he influenced directly or indirectly all the painters of his own and the next generation, even when they were the pupils of his brother or the Vivarini; Cima, Catena, Basaiti, Montagna, and Carpaccio are examples of this. Dürer wrote home from Venice in 1506 that he was 'very old, but still the best in painting'. He became the greatest of the Venetian *Madonnieri*, or Madonna painters, evolving a succession of designs and types of unparalleled imaginativeness and versatility for official commissions, such as the votive offerings of the Doges, large altarpieces, and small devotional works. He was influenced by ANTONELLO, and from the latter's S. Cassiano altarpiece and one of his own, painted for SS. Giovanni e Paolo (and burnt in 1867), stem the great SACRE CONVERSAZIONI painted for S. Giobbe (c. 1483/5; now in the Accad.) and S. Zaccaria (1505; in the church) and the later developments of the form, notably those by Giorgione and Titian. His compositions of the Pietà, particularly those with the dead Christ supported in the tomb either by angels or by the Virgin and S. John, derive ultimately from Donatello and Jacopo Bellini, and were intended more as private devotional works than for churches. He frequently included landscapes as a background, and in the *Agony in the Garden*, painted in emulation of Mantegna's similar work (both in London, NG), he combines observation of nature with rare poetic feeling, but naturalistic details are never allowed to overwhelm the figures. In 1479, when Gentile went to Turkey, he took over the work in the Doge's Palace and eventually became chief painter to the State, a position he held until his death, despite Titian's attempts to displace him. The loss of these history paintings (together with those by Pisanello and Gentile da Fabriano) in the fire of 1577 means that the early style of Venetian history painting can only be surmised. His official work included painting portraits of the Doges – the *Doge Loredano* (c. 1501; London NG) is the finest of these – and his portraits, many of which adapt the Flemish type of the three-quarter view against a landscape background, are simple, sensitive, and compelling. His last works break new ground. His *S. Jerome* (1513; Venice, S. Giovanni Crisostomo), with its spatial device of the saint seated in a landscape and seen through the arch before which the other life-size figures stand, is an entirely new invention. He had painted Christian and classical allegories before, but never a mythology on such a scale as the *Feast of the Gods*, painted in 1514 for the Duke of Ferrara (now in Washington), which depicts a rustic Olympian picnic in a mildly erotic pastoral vein. Titian later repainted the landscape background to make it suit his own mythologies painted for the same room. The *Lady at her toilet* (1515; Vienna), a semi-mythological subject which possibly started as a portrait, combines the composition used for late Madonna pictures with genre detail and a nude figure. These three works show the old Bellini coming to terms with the new century. Technically, he learned from Antonello; stylistically, he digested Mantegna, yet survived as an independent personality; iconographically, he was the most inventive painter Northern Italy produced. There are works in the Royal Collection, Baltimore (Walters), Bergamo, Berlin, Boston (Gardner), Bristol, Cambridge Mass. (Fogg), Detroit, Dresden, Florence (Uffizi), Glasgow, Houston Texas, Kansas City, London (NG, Courtauld Inst.), Milan (Brera, Poldi-Pezzoli), Naples, New Orleans, New York (Brooklyn, Frick Coll., Met. Mus., Morgan Library), Ottawa, Oxford (Ashmolean), Padua, Paris (Louvre, Jacquemart-André), Pesaro, Philadelphia (Johnson), Rimini, Rome (Borghese, Capitoline Mus.), San Diego Cal., San Marino Cal. (Huntington), Stuttgart, Toledo Ohio, the Vatican, Venice (Accad., Correr, Cà d'Oro, Doge's Palace, Querini-Stampalia, and churches), Verona, Vienna, Washington (NG), and elsewhere.

BELLOTTO, Bernardo (1721(1720 Venetian style)–80), was the nephew and pupil of CANALETTO, and is sometimes confusingly so called: he himself started the habit, doubtless because it paid. They appear to have separated by 1746, perhaps after a quarrel, for Canaletto came to London and Bellotto began travels in N. Italy before leaving for Dresden, in 1747. Before then he had visited Rome (probably in 1742) and Florence, Lucca, Lombardy (1744), and Turin (1745). He became Painter to Frederick Augustus II in 1748 and painted many views of Dresden, Pirna, and Königstein for him. He also visited Vienna and Munich before going to Poland in 1767. Although nominally on his way to Russia, he settled in Warsaw and worked for King Stanislas Poniatowski until his death. His *vedute* of Warsaw are of great topographical exactness (and were used in the reconstruction of the city after the Second World War), and in general his style is very similar to that of his uncle; his colour is colder and he has a feeling for landscape and a certain humour in his figure groups lacking in Canaletto's work. Almost all his best works are in Dresden and Warsaw but there are examples in Boston, Cambridge (Fitzwm), Dublin, Glasgow, London (NG), New York (Met. Mus.), Vienna, and elsewhere.

BELLOWS, George (1882–1925), was an American illustrator and painter of city life, who was influenced by the ASHCAN School and was one of the organizers of the ARMORY show. He also painted a number of fine portraits in a bold style – e.g. *Mrs T., No.* 2 (Minneapolis).

BENEDETTO da Maiano (1442–97) was a Florentine sculptor of the post-Donatello generation. His major work is the pulpit in Sta Croce, Florence (*c.*1475), three sketches for which are in London (V & A). He also made several fine portrait busts, examples being those in Florence (Bargello), London (V & A), Paris (Louvre), and Washington (NG).

BENTNAME (Dutch), the nickname given to Dutch and Flemish members of the *Schildersbent*, or group of painters in Rome. They were also called *Bentvueghels* (birds of a flock) because they formed a group in 1623, partly in solidarity against the Italians and against the law, but ostensibly to defy the dues levied by the Roman Academy of S. Luke. The founders included BABUREN and BOR, but most of the members painted BAMBOCCIATE (Bamboccio was the Bentname of Pieter van Laer). As more Northerners flocked to Rome the Bentvueghels got more rowdy and held huge drinking parties ending in Sta Costanza, where scores of their names are still scratched on the walls. Their riotousness and mock baptisms caused the Pope to suppress them in 1720.

BERCHEM, Nicolaes (Claesz.) (1620–83), was born in Haarlem and studied under an assortment of masters, but his style was really formed in Italy, where he went with J. B. WEENIX 1642–5. He painted a few religious (e.g. *The Angel appearing to the shepherds*, 1656: Bristol) and allegorical subjects and some portraits, as well as some realistic Dutch landscapes (e.g. *Winter Scene, Haarlem* of 1647: Amsterdam, Rijksmus.); but most of his works are Italianate landscapes, seen through a golden haze and peopled with travellers and their mules or Arcadian shepherds and their flocks. The ruins and taverns blend to a nicety the classic past and the spirit of BAMBOCCIO, and it is not surprising that he and his rival, BOTH, were the principals among the popular ITALIANIZERS, the landscape painters influenced by Claude and, above all, by a nostalgic longing for the South. He may have returned to Italy 1653/6. Not only did he paint many pictures of his own but he also added the figures for others, including Hobbema and Ruisdael: he also made a number of etchings. There are representative works in London (NG, Wallace Coll., Dulwich).

BERCKHEYDE, Gerrit (1638–98), was a Haarlem painter of town views. He was the pupil of Hals and of his own brother Job (1630–93) and was influenced by his Haarlem contemporary, the great architectural painter SAENREDAM. After 1660 he went to Germany and painted views of Cologne, Heidelberg, and Bonn; on his return he painted

Amsterdam and The Hague, but in many cases he rearranged the buildings to improve the composition – i.e. he painted VEDUTE long before the Italians.

BERGOGNONE *see* BORGOGNONE.

BERLINGHIERO was active in Lucca from *c.* 1215 and died in 1242 or earlier. His signed crucifix in Lucca is of the more old-fashioned CHRISTUS TRIUMPHANS type which was to be superseded by those of GIUNTA Pisano. Berlinghiero's three sons were all painters and one, Bonaventura, painted the *S. Francis* (1235: Pescia) which is one of the earliest altarpieces dedicated to the saint. The Berlinghiero family exerted considerable influence on Florentine painting before CIMABUE.

BERMEJO, Bartolomé (active 1474–95 or later), was a Spanish painter who was much influenced by the Flemings and was one of the first to practise oil painting in Spain. In 1474 he painted the *S. Dominic of Silos* (Madrid, Prado), which is very close to Jan van EYCK. From 1475 his contracts stipulate the use of oil, but the *Pietà* of 1490 in Barcelona Cathedral is less Eyckian and reflects a certain influence from later Flemish, and possibly even from French painting. There are other works by him in Berlin, Boston (Gardner Mus.), and Luton Hoo (Wernher Coll.).

BERNARD, Émile (1868–1941), was the friend of van Gogh, GAUGUIN and Cézanne. He experimented with Signac's POINTILLISM, *c.* 1886, but subsequently quarrelled with Signac and destroyed all the works of this type. He then went to Brittany, where he met Gauguin in 1886, and he evolved a style known as *Cloisonnisme* from its resemblance to *cloisonné* enamels; this was a method of painting strong, flat, forms in strong, flat colours with blue or black contours separating the colour-patches. It was to lead eventually to a quarrel with Gauguin, who got all the credit. Bernard subsequently travelled in Egypt, Spain, and Italy (1893–1900); his later works are reactionary in style and often vitiated by a sentimental religiosity. Paris (Mus. d'Art Moderne) has a good early picture.

BERNINI, Gianlorenzo (1598–1680), was born in Naples, the son of Pietro Bernini, a Tuscan sculptor in the late Mannerist style, who moved to Rome *c.* 1605 to work for Pope Paul V. The young Bernini early attracted the patronage of the Pope's nephew, Cardinal Scipione Borghese. His first known work, the *Goat Amalthea* (*c.* 1615: Rome, Borghese), for long passed as an antique, and the *Aeneas and Anchises* (1618–19: Borghese) shows him working, perhaps with his father's help, within the Mannerist tradition; the group has no fixed viewpoint and the spectator is encouraged to walk round it, thus obtaining a varying silhouette which, coupled with the slipping movement and the strongly emphasized details of muscles, veins, and joints, creates an impression of uncertainty and strain. The *Neptune and*

Triton (1620: London, V & A) shows this uncertainty resolved into energy and movement, though still within the tradition of the multiple viewpoint, but in the group of works executed for the Cardinal (*Rape of Proserpina* 1621–2; *David* 1623; *Apollo and Daphne* 1622–4: all Borghese) Bernini adopts a single frontal viewpoint and the indecisions are resolved into a clearcut expression of supreme energy, coupled with a psychological insight and a delicacy of finish that established him as the greatest sculptor since Michelangelo.

The roots of his style are not only in Michelangelo and the Antique, but also in contemporary painting, for his attitude to the Antique is conditioned by his admiration for Annibale Carracci, his naturalism is stimulated by Caravaggio, and his gestures and facial expressions are influenced by Guido Reni. He rejected Michelangelo's concept of the figure adhering closely to the block, just as he rejected the Mannerist multiple silhouette, and evolved the new concept of the figure with a single action and viewpoint freed from the limitations of the block and infringing the limits of its own space by breaking into that of the spectator, who is thus drawn into the action. This new concept lay at the root of the BAROQUE, of which Bernini was the virtual creator and greatest exponent. His search for a means of expressing different realms of the divine, the mystical, and the earthly led him to imaginative mixtures of white and coloured marbles, bronze, stucco, stone, painting, and even coloured light through stained glass, and the combination of these varying materials has often been condemned, by uncomprehending critics, as tasteless overdecoration. The finest examples of this use of mixed materials are in the Cornaro Chapel (1645–52: Rome, S. Maria della Vittoria) with the *Ecstasy of S. Theresa*, and the tombs of Urban VIII and Alexander VII in S. Peter's, the latter a dramatic conception, in white and coloured marbles, with a bronze figure of Death writing the Pope's name in his book. His busts prove his insight into character, and his religious statues and groups show his passionate concern with the expression of states of mind and soul, while his feeling for the unity of sculpture and its setting led him to become the architect who has most fully expressed the upsurge of religious confidence and militant faith that characterize the Counter-Reformation. He was a man of difficult and stormy character – his son, Domenico, described him as '*terribile nell'ira*' – but of deep piety who regularly practised the Jesuit Spiritual Exercises.

Papal patronage provided him with enormous architectural commissions (in and around St Peter's and the Vatican, tombs, fountains, churches) which demanded the participation of numerous assistants, and of these MOCHI, BOLGI, and Raggi were the best of his frequent helpers, while DUQUESNOY was a friendly, and ALGARDI a bitter, rival. Louis XIV invited him to Paris to redesign the Louvre in 1665;

nothing came of the visit but the magnificent bust of the King (Versailles), and a later equestrian statue of Louis (1669–77) was, when it arrived in Versailles in 1685, so disliked by him that GIRARDON was employed to convert it into a garden ornament. This only too truly fulfils Bernini's prediction that after his death his reputation would suffer a decline. It is impossible to see his work properly outside Rome, and on no city has one man left a stronger imprint of his vision and personality. There are also works in Birmingham, Bologna (Mus. Civico), Bordeaux (S. Bruno), Cambridge Mass. (Fogg), Copenhagen, Detroit, Florence (Bargello, Contini Coll.), London (V & A), Modena, New York (Met. Mus.), Paris (Louvre, Jacquemart-André), Washington (NG). Several paintings have been attributed to him, the two most important being a *Self-portrait* in Florence (Uffizi) and *Two Saints* (London, NG).

BERRETTINI *see* PIETRO da Cortona.

BERRUGUETE, Alonso (c. 1489?–1561), was the son of Pedro Berruguete and became the major Spanish sculptor of the 16th century. He was trained in Italy and brought back Italian Mannerist ideas both in sculpture and in painting. He went to Florence about 1504 where he saw and copied Michelangelo's lost *Battle* cartoon (he is even mentioned in Michelangelo's letters). He may have been in Rome before returning to Florence for about five years before his final return to Spain in 1517. He was, therefore, acquainted with the early work of PONTORMO and ROSSO at the very beginning of the Mannerist style. His own work as a painter is close to Rosso and he probably finished the *Coronation of the Virgin* (Paris, Louvre) which was left incomplete by Filippino LIPPI.

He was active in Spain principally as a sculptor on such works as the altar of the Irish College in Salamanca (1529–32) and especially the choir stalls in Toledo Cathedral (on the Epistle side) executed 1539–43. These works, like his paintings, show a combination of the influences of LEONARDO da Vinci, ANDREA del Sarto and RAPHAEL. He had an extremely successful career, being made Painter to the King on his return from Italy and ennobled in 1559. Other pictures attributed to him are in Arezzo, Budapest, Florence (Uffizi), Munich and Rome (Borghese).

BERRUGUETE, Pedro (c. 1450–1503/4), was Court Painter to Ferdinand and Isabella. He was a Castillian who worked at Avila and in Toledo Cathedral from 1483. At some date before this he may have been in Italy since it is often held that he painted some of the pictures in the Palace at Urbino which are usually given to the Fleming JOOS van Gent. This problem is much confused by a document, purporting to be of 1477, which says that 'Pietro Spagnuolo' – Peter the Spaniard – was working in Urbino. Unfortunately nobody has set eyes on the document since 1822. On the other hand, a 16th-century

Spanish writer says that the *Famous Men* at Urbino were by an unspecified Spanish painter. Some further evidence in favour of the attribution may be found in works by Berruguete at Avila and in his native village, Paredes de Nava, and also in the fact that his son Alonso studied in Italy. Other works by Pedro are in Madrid (Prado) and Paris (Louvre), these latter being part of the disputed series from the Palace at Urbino.

BERTOLDO di Giovanni (*d.* 1491) was the pupil and assistant of Donatello and the master of Michelangelo, since he was employed by Lorenzo de' Medici as Keeper of his Sculpture Garden, which was one of the earliest of all ACADEMIES. This was in the 1480s and Bertoldo was said to be 'old', but he is first recorded (as Donatello's assistant) in 1460, so the date of his birth may be later than *c.*1420, which is the current guess. There are works by him in Florence (Bargello), Modena, and Paris (Louvre).

BERTRAM of Minden, Master. A German painter working in Hamburg from 1367 to *c.*1415. The most important work attributed to him is the *Grabow Altar* (*c.*1379/83: Hamburg, Kunsthalle). Others are in Hanover, Paris (Mus. des Arts Décoratifs), and London (V & A). He was a precursor of the realistic Flemish approach of the 15th century but also of the SOFT STYLE, and may have had some contact with THEODORIC of Prague and with France.

BEUCKELAER *see* BUECKELAER.

BEWICK, Thomas (1753–1828), was the father of modern woodengraving. His numerous book-illustrations, beautifully observed from nature, are expressed in terms of white-line engraving, which he revived. There are drawings by him in London (BM and Courtauld Inst.) and Newcastle (his home town).

BIBIENA. A family of Bolognese stage-designers and architects active from the 1670s to the 1780s in most European countries. They were the most famous exponents of the elaborate perspectives and settings provided for theatrical productions and state occasions. The Opera House at Bayreuth was their work and about 200 engravings also exist.

BIEDERMEIERSTIL is the name given to the style, roughly corresponding to Early Victorian, of furniture and decoration in Germany in the period 1815–48. It is an unaristocratic style, clear and simple, and is sometimes extended to cover painting and sculpture of the same period (cf. SPITZWEG). The name derives from two fictitious characters, Biedermann and Bummelmeier, who were supposed to represent genuine German Philistines.

BILL, Max (*b.*1908), is a Swiss abstract sculptor who is also active as a painter, architect, and writer. He was trained in Zürich and at the BAUHAUS in Dessau (1927–9). In 1951 he went to Ulm to teach for six years, exerting considerable influence on young German artists.

His writings include essays on the mathematical elements in modern art and on Kandinsky.

BINGHAM, George Caleb (1811–79), was an American painter of the great settlements in the Far West in the 19th century. Bingham was the most important of the so-called Frontier painters, but he had no real training, apart from a few months in Philadelphia in 1837–8. He worked for a time in Washington, but returned to Missouri *c.* 1844 and painted scenes from everyday life which were widely engraved. In 1856 he went to Düsseldorf and was much influenced by the sentimental German art of the period, but in 1859 he returned to America and wasted most of the rest of his life in politics.

BIOMORPHIC ART is a form of Abstract Art which purports to take its abstract forms from living organisms rather than from the geometrical basis of such abstract movements as CONSTRUCTIVISM.

BIRD, Francis (1667–1731), was born in London, but studied in Flanders and Rome, and after his return about 1689 under Grinling Gibbons and Cibber. He executed most of the statuary on the outside of St Paul's Cathedral from before 1706 to 1721 (including the *Conversion of St Paul* in the pediment, for which he was paid £620 in 1706), and made the *Queen Anne* of which a poor replica now stands before the Cathedral. He also made many tombs in Westminster Abbey.

BISTRE (Fr.). A brown pigment, made from charred wood, used as ink, or chalk, or – principally in the 17th century – as a wash. Rembrandt's drawings are mostly in bistre.

BITUMEN. A rich brown pigment made from asphaltum. Its use, though pleasant, is very dangerous, since it never dries completely. It was popular during the 18th and 19th centuries and has been the cause of severe damage in many paintings of those periods.

BLAKE, William (1757–1827), earned a meagre living by working for publishers as an engraver, usually of other men's designs, but between his bread-and-butter work he produced his own poems in books which he made and published himself, engraving the text and surrounding it with an illustration which he coloured by hand. In this manner he issued the 'Songs of Innocence' (1789) and 'Songs of Experience' (1794), and his various 'Prophetic Books' (1783–1804). His greatest works are his twenty-one large watercolours illustrating the Book of Job, produced from 1820 and engraved in 1826, 102 illustrations to Dante, of which seven were published in 1827, and his colour-printed drawings, which include the *Nebuchadnezzar*, the *Hecate*, and the *Elijah in the Chariot of Fire*. These were made by printing off a design prepared in distemper on millboard, and then finishing each individually. Most of his designs were carried out in normal watercolour technique, but his so-called 'frescoes' are in a highly unorthodox form of tempera which has deteriorated badly.

His early work is within the current Neoclassical style, but as his verse and philosophy acquired a more visionary quality, so he turned to forms and ideas evolved from medieval and Mannerist examples, abandoned logical arrangement in space, and developed a purely subjective use of colour, light, and form to give substance to his visions. Whatever his sources, he always transmuted everything by the power of his imagination; this is his salient quality and marks the sharpest reaction against the Age of Reason and the dawn of Romanticism.

In 1800 he moved to Felpham, near Bognor, where he lived uneasily for three years in the circle of the poet Hayley, which included FLAXMAN and Romney. His difficulties with the engraver Cromek, over his illustrations to Blair's 'Grave' (1808) and his picture and engraving of the *Canterbury Pilgrims* (1810), are reflected in one of his typically pungent epigrams: 'A petty sneaking knave I knew – Ah! Mr Cromek, how d'ye do?'. His detestation of Reynolds's theory was expressed in his annotation to the 'Discourses': 'This Man was Hired to Depress Art'. He was also of the opinion that all the parts of Reynolds's 'Discourses' with which he found himself agreeing were due to BARRY or FUSELI. In his last years he was helped by LINNELL, and his circle of friends included Varley, Richmond, CALVERT, PALMER, and Fuseli, who admitted that he found Blake 'damned good to steal from'. The Tate Gallery, London, has a fine collection of his work, and there are also examples in Aberdeen, Boston (Mus.), Cambridge (Fitzwm), Cambridge Mass. (Fogg), London (BM, V & A), Manchester (City Art Gall. and Whitworth), Melbourne, New York (Met. Mus., Morgan Library, Brooklyn), San Marino Cal. (Huntington), and elsewhere.

BLANCHARD, Jacques (1600–38), was born in Paris, but was in Rome 1624–5 and in 1626 moved to Venice, where he saw the work of LISS. He then went to Turin, where he worked for the Dukes of Savoy, before returning to France in 1628. The principal influence on him was Veronese, whose blond and silvery colour and limpid light he used most effectively in his small religious and mythological subjects. The several versions of *Charity*, depicted as a young woman with two or three children, are excellent examples of his tenderness of colour handling, and of a softness of sentiment more reminiscent of the 18th than the 17th century. He was also a sensitive portrait painter. There are examples in London (Courtauld Inst.), New York (Met. Mus.), Paris (Louvre and Notre Dame), Toledo Ohio, Venice (Accad.), and in French provincial museums.

BLAUE REITER, Der (The Blue Rider), was the name given to a group of Munich artists in 1911 by the two most important members, KANDINSKY and MARC. They invented this name, according to Kandinsky, because they both liked blue, Marc liked horses and

Kandinsky liked riders. The group was later joined by KLEE and, with Die BRÜCKE, was the most important manifestation of modern art in Germany before 1914. There is a large collection in Munich.

BLAUEN VIER, Die (The Blue Four), *see* JAWLENSKY.

BLECHEN, Karl (1798–1840), was a German Romantic painter influenced by FRIEDRICH, whom he probably met in Berlin in 1823. Blechen worked for the Berlin Theatre and went to Italy in 1828–9. On his return he became Professor of landscape painting at the Berlin Academy (1831). He visited Paris in 1835. His later works are more realist and show him moving away from his early romanticism. Most of his pictures are in Berlin, but there are others in Hanover, Karlsruhe, and Vienna.

BLOCK-BOOK. An early form of illustrated book, of a popular devotional character, in which the text and illustrations were cut together, from the same block. Oddly enough, the earliest block-books seem to date from *c.*1460, after the invention of movable type, and are contemporary with books printed from movable type and illustrated with separately cut blocks. Nevertheless, recent research seems to show that *Apocalypse I* (Manchester, Rylands Library) dates from 1451/2, i.e. somewhat earlier than Gutenberg. The influence of Roger van der WEYDEN and MEMLINC, seems to confirm dates in the 1460s. Some early examples are the Biblia Pauperum 1465, the Song of Songs, 1466, and the ARS MORIENDI, 1466.

BLOEMAERT, Abraham (1564–1651), was an Utrecht Mannerist. He was in Paris 1580–3 and returned to Utrecht to paint elaborate history and genre subjects, bright in colour and with an exaggerated figure style reminiscent of WTEWAEL. He is important in the formation of the UTRECHT School because he was the master of so many other painters, including Both, J. G. Cuyp, Gerard HONTHORST, TERBRUGGHEN, Weenix, and others. He himself came strongly under the influence of Caravaggio in the early 1620s, just when his pupil Honthorst returned from Italy with the new ideas. His son Hendrick (*c.*1601–72) was also a painter and his pupil. There are works by Abraham in the Royal Collection and in Amsterdam, Barnard Castle (Bowes Mus.), Berlin, Brunswick, Brussels, Cape Town, Copenhagen, Dublin, Frankfurt, Grenoble, Haarlem, The Hague, Hamburg, Leamington Spa, Leyden, London (V & A (Ham House)), Ottawa, Paris (Louvre), Stockholm, Toledo Ohio, Utrecht, and Vienna (K-H Mus.).

BLOT DRAWING was the name given by Alexander COZENS to the practice of evolving a composition from the forms suggested by allowing a few blobs of ink or colour to fall at random on a sheet of paper, if necessary folding the paper to create further blots. The method seems to have been known to Leonardo, who advocated the study of stains on a wall or the shapes in the fire as a stimulus to the creative imagination. Cozens's advocacy of the method as a means of teaching his numerous pupils led to his being dubbed 'Blotmaster to the Town': at the end of his life he published his system as 'A New Method of assisting the Invention in Drawing Original Compositions of Landscape' (c.1785).

BLUE FOUR, The, see JAWLENSKY.

BOCCIONI, Umberto (1882–1916), was one of the original FUTURISTS, signing the Manifesto of 1910 and issuing the Manifesto of Futurist Sculpture in 1912. He also wrote a book about it (1914). He volunteered for the War in 1915 and died as a result of an accident after being wounded. He had been the most active of the Futurists and the group never recovered from his death. His work realized, in attempting to render movement, two of the clauses of the Manifesto: 'Universal dynamism must be rendered in painting as a dynamic sensation . . . . Motion and light destroy the materiality of bodies'.

BÖCKLIN, Arnold (1827–1901), was, with HODLER, the major Swiss painter of the 19th century, and he exerted a tremendous influence on the German-speaking countries through the expression of a heightened Romanticism and poeticism. He was trained in Germany, Flanders, and Paris, and spent seven years in Rome (1850–7), where he began to evolve a kind of heroic landscape. He was in Munich 1871–4, where he met THOMA, but, like many other German artists of the period (e.g. FEUERBACH), he spent much of the rest of his life in Italy, where he died. His most famous work was, and is, the *Island of the Dead*, which exists in several versions from 1880 onwards: it has a curious haunted quality which can be felt even in the elementary German grammars, where many people first saw it in reproduction. The same quality can be found in his *Pan* and some other landscapes. Most of his works are in Basle (the Museum also has a frescoed staircase), Munich, and other German museums. New York (Met. Mus.) has a good version of the *Island of the Dead*.

BODEGÓN (Span. tavern). Kitchen scenes in which the interest in still-life predominates. Typical examples are Velazquez's pair in Edinburgh and London.

BODY COLOUR is watercolour mixed with white to make it opaque: it is therefore identical with GOUACHE. Body colour is often used in drawings done on tinted paper, or on watercolours, to heighten the effect of highlights or give accent to strong passages of local colour.

BOL, Ferdinand (1616–80), was a pupil of Rembrandt before 1640, and for many years imitated his master so closely that many of his works have passed as Rembrandt's (e.g. *Lady*; London, Kenwood). By about 1660, when Rembrandtesque portraits were less in demand, Bol adapted his style to a more French manner, lighter and more courtly. He painted several big group portraits, such as the *Governors of the Leper Hospital* (1649: Amsterdam, Rijksmus.).

BOLDINI, Giovanni (1845–1931), was a fashionable portrait painter, the Italian equivalent of SARGENT, whom he knew. He was born in Ferrara, but in 1867 went to Paris and was swept off his feet by MANET, whose dazzling skill he imitated, but without Manet's impeccable taste. He visited London before settling in Paris c.1872, where he spent the rest of his life. Whistler and the Impressionists also influenced him, but he is best remembered as a virtuoso who recorded the Paris of La Belle Époque. There is a Boldini Museum in his native town, and other works are in Paris as well as Florence, London, and New York (Brooklyn Mus.: *Whistler*).

BOLGI, Andrea (1605–56), an Italian sculptor, was a pupil of BERNINI. His best-known work is the *S. Helena*, one of four huge statues in the crossing of S. Peter's in Rome. The others are by Bernini, MOCHI, and DUQUESNOY. A bust of Laura Frangipane is signed and dated 1637 (Rome, S. Francesco a Ripa).

BOLOGNA, Giovanni (da), (Giambologna, Jean de Boulogne) (1529–1608), the most famous sculptor in Florence after the death of Michelangelo, was born in Douai and trained in Flanders before arriving in Italy c.1555. After a period in Rome he settled in Florence, where he competed with AMMANATI and CELLINI for the commission for the Fountain in the Piazza della Signoria. Ammanati won, but Giambologna assisted him and later made his own *Neptune Fountain* in Bologna (1563–7). His *Rape of the Sabines* (1579–83: Loggia de' Lanzi, Florence) shows the fully developed Mannerist principle of sculpture to be seen from all points of view equally by walking round it instead of regarding it from one main viewpoint. All his marbles are in Florence except the *Samson slaying the Philistine* (London, V & A, begun c.1565). The best-known of his bronzes are the *Mercury* (Florence, Bargello, 1564; Vienna, and other versions) and the equestrian statues of the Grand Dukes Cosimo I (1594: Florence, Piazza della Signoria) and Ferdinando (Piazza dell' Annunziata). Small bronze replicas of his works were produced in his shop in huge quantities. There are four wax models (London, V & A, and Brisbane) for the bronze reliefs in Genoa University Chapel (c.1580).

BOLTRAFFIO, Giovanni Antonio (1467–1516), was one of LEONARDO's Milanese followers. Most of his works are in Milan, but others are in Berlin, Budapest, Cambridge Mass. (Fogg), Florence (Uffizi), London (NG), New York (Met. Mus.), Paris (Louvre, Jacquemart-André), and Philadelphia (Johnson). An interesting portrait by him is at Chatsworth, Derbyshire.

BOLUS GROUND. The canvas or panel is prepared with a dark brown or reddish earth (bole). The colour of the ground eventually shows through and affects the painting.

BONANUS made the bronze doors of Pisa Cathedral in 1179, but they were destroyed in 1595. The side door (Porta di S. Ranieri) is attributed to him as it is identical in style with the bronze doors of Monreale Cathedral, signed by him and dated 1185 (modern style). The other bronze doors at Monreale are by BARISANUS.

BONE, Sir Muirhead (1876–1953), was an architectural draughtsman and etcher, whose *Demolition of S. James's Hall* (1905) was the first major work in a field he made his own. There are many drawings and etchings by him of the First World War in the Imperial War Museum, London, while the Second World War produced the huge *Ruins of London from S. Bride's*.

BONHEUR, Rosa (1822–99), was, with LANDSEER, the most famous animal painter of the 19th century, but her works are free from anthropomorphic sentimentality. The huge *Horse Fair*, exhibited at the Salon of 1853, established her reputation. She made studies at the Marché aux Chevaux in Paris dressed as a man and received formal police *permission de travestissement*. The original, offered to her native Bordeaux and refused, was bought by an English dealer and is now in New York (Met. Mus.). In order to facilitate the engraving (by Landseer's brother Thomas) she had a reduced version (still over 8 feet wide) made by her friend, Natalie Micas, which she then finished herself: it is now in the National Gall., London. She enjoyed great popularity in Britain and was fascinated by the Highlands of Scotland, which she visited in the 50s. In 1894 she became the first woman Officer of the Legion of Honour. There are no works by her in the Louvre, but there is a Musée Bonheur at Fontainebleau, good examples in the Wallace Collection, London, and a *Self-portrait* in the collection in Florence, Uffizi.

BONIFAZIO de' Pitati (Bonifazio Veronese) (1487–1553) was born in Verona but trained under PALMA Vecchio and ran a large workshop in Venice. His style was much influenced by Giorgione and Titian, and to some extent his name is used to cover works which the owner dare not quite attribute to either of them.

BONINGTON, Richard Parkes (1801/2–28), was an English landscape painter who went to France as a boy and was trained there. He was a friend of DELACROIX as well as a pupil of GROS and began exhibiting in 1822. He returned to England in 1825 and 1827 and went to Italy in 1826. His historical pictures are much influenced by the Venetians, but Delacroix's remark that Bonington was carried away by his own skill is truer of them than of his landscapes. There are works by him in his native Nottingham, Paris (Louvre), and London (Tate, Wallace Coll., V & A, BM, and Courtauld Institute).

BONNARD, Pierre (1867–1947), became a painter after selling a poster to a champagne maker in 1889. In 1890 he shared a studio with VUILLARD and DENIS, which was a meeting-place for the Nabis, with whom he was associated until the group broke up in 1899. Until then his work was strongly influenced by Japanese prints, and based on flat decoration and asymmetrical composition. It was subdued, even dark, in colour. After 1900, his palette became richer, he used heavier impasto and more strongly modelled forms, and his – and Vuillard's – more Impressionist technique and choice of subjects became known as *Intimisme*. His subjects varied little: quiet interiors, many with a woman bathing, dressing or sleeping, family scenes round a table, sunlit landscapes, all increasing as the years passed in dazzling intensity of light and colour, which made his work so influential on later painters. He also produced many lithographs, both black-and-white and coloured. Most museums of modern art have a picture by him.

BONNAT, Léon (1833–1922), was born in Bayonne and brought up in Spain, receiving his first training in Madrid. Early impressions of RIBERA and Caravaggio were succeeded by the influence of the Bolognese School during a stay in Italy (1858–60). There is a certain similarity to COUTURE in some of his sketches, but he does not seem to have shared MANET's Spanish interests. In the latter part of his career he became an enormously successful portrait painter (many Presidents of the Third Republic, Victor Hugo, and many American millionaires). He also painted murals in the Hôtel de Ville, Palais de Justice, the Panthéon and many Paris churches, but his best memorial is the Musée Bonnat at Bayonne, which contains his own splendid collection of drawings. There are many works in the Louvre and others in Boston, Lille, New York (Met. Mus.), Poitiers and in French public buildings and museums.

BOR, Paulus (c. 1600–69), was born in Amersfoort, Holland, and went to Rome in the 1620s, where he was one of the founders of the BENT. He returned to Amersfoort about 1628 and painted at first in a manner deriving from the young Rembrandt, but the influence of Caravaggio – whose works he must have seen in Rome – seems to have grown on him and he became a member of the UTRECHT School. There are works in Amersfoort, Amsterdam (Rijksmus.), Liverpool, and Utrecht.

BORCH, Gerard ter, *see* TER BORCH.

BORDONE, Paris (1500–71), was a Trevisan painter who spent most of his life in Venice, but probably visited France (in 1538?) and Augsburg; a portrait in the Louvre is signed and dated 1540 and inscribed 'Augusta', so he was probably in Augsburg in that year, and the Venetian influence on AMBERGER may well come from this visit. Vasari says that he was apprenticed to Titian but set himself to imitate GIORGIONE. There are works by him in the Royal Collection and in Augsburg, Baltimore, Bergamo, Boston (Mus. and Gardner Mus.), Cologne, Dublin, Edinburgh, Florence (Uffizi, Pitti),

Genoa, Glasgow, London (NG), Milan (Brera), Munich, Paris, Philadelphia (Johnson), Rome (Borghese), Toronto, Treviso, the Vatican, Venice, Vienna and Washington.

BORGOGNONE, Ambrogio (*c.* 1450/60–1523), was a Milanese painter, influenced by FOPPA and not by Leonardo, whose best works are in the Certosa at Pavia, including some *trompe-l'œil* frescoes of monks looking through windows. Other works are in Bergamo, Birmingham, London (NG), and Milan (Brera).

BOSCH, Hieronymus (*c.* 1450–1516), perhaps the greatest master of fantasy who ever lived, is first recorded in 's Hertogenbosch in 1480/1. He may have been born there and his name probably derives from it; certainly he spent his life there and died there. His obsessive and haunted world is that of Gothic twilight and is the best surviving expression of some aspects of the waning of the Middle Ages, but it is now largely incomprehensible. The Surrealists have claimed him as a sort of Freudian *avant la lettre*, but it is certain that his pictures had a very definite significance and were not free expressions of the unconscious mind. For example, the *Hay Wain* (Madrid, Prado) once belonged to Philip II of Spain and is obviously an allegory on the general theme 'All flesh is grass'; just as the *Ship of Fools* (Paris, Louvre) is a well-known late medieval allegory. About 1600 a Spanish writer apparently thought it necessary to defend Bosch's memory against imputations of heresy, which would seem to show that by then the real meaning of the pictures had largely been lost. In recent years there has been an elaborate attempt to 'explain' many of the pictures – in particular the *Earthly Paradise* (Madrid, Prado) – as altarpieces painted for a heretical cult which was addicted to orgiastic rites. Not only is there no evidence for this but it also fails to explain why so many of Bosch's pictures belonged to people of unimpeachable orthodoxy, such as Philip II. The problem of Bosch's patrons resembles that of BRUEGEL'S, and there is much in common between the two although Bosch's fantasy is always far more inventive and seems to have deeper levels of symbolism, even in what appear to be purely erotic scenes. It is also worth noting that, according to a mid-16th-century Spanish writer, there were already forgeries in circulation apparently signed by Bosch: he cites the *Seven Deadly Sins* (Madrid, Prado) as an example, but it is now universally accepted as authentic. The chronology of Bosch's pictures is not clear, but it may be safe to assume that the *Crucifixion* (Brussels) is his earliest known work, on the grounds that the style is closer to that of BOUTS or Roger van der WEYDEN – the dominant styles in the Netherlands *c.* 1480 – than at any other time in Bosch's career. His master is unknown, and the origins of his style are very obscure but are probably to be sought in popular woodcuts and devotional prints. Other early works are probably the *Christ mocked* (London, NG), the *Cure for*

Madness (Madrid, Prado), and the *Seven Deadly Sins*: the later works seem to be those with greater numbers of small-scale figures, painted in pale, bright, transparent colours on a very white ground. There are examples in Antwerp, Berlin, Boston (Mus.), Chicago, Cologne (Wallraf-Richartz Mus.), Denver Col., the Escorial, Frankfurt (Städel), Ghent, Lisbon, Munich, New York (Met. Mus.), Philadelphia (Johnson), Princeton NJ, Rotterdam (Boymans Mus.), San Diego Cal., Valenciennes, Venice (Doge's Pal.), Vienna (Akad. and K-H), and elsewhere.

BOTH, Andries (*c.*1608–41/9) and Jan (*c.*1618–52), were Utrecht painters who were supposed to have worked together, Andries painting the figures and Jan the landscapes, until one day Andries fell into a canal in Venice on his way home from a SCHILDERSBENT party. Andries was probably in Rome *c.*1636–41 and Jan *c.*1638–41; Jan returned to Utrecht after his brother's death. Such a picture as the *Boors carousing* (Utrecht), signed and dated 1634, shows Andries as a painter of BAMBOCCIATE in a style closer to Brouwer than to his brother's idyllic landscapes. Jan was profoundly influenced by the works of CLAUDE in the period 1638–41. He became one of the leading ITALIANIZERS, and, like his chief rival, BERCHEM, painted Claudian landscapes with a golden light falling on the picturesque peasantry. The treatment of light in Cuyp's work owes much to him. Both brothers were pupils of the Utrecht Mannerist BLOEMAERT, and in their several ways they show the new directions taken by Dutch painting in the 17th century. Jan is represented in most older galleries, and there are typical works in London (NG, Wallace Coll., Dulwich), Detroit, Indianapolis, Toledo Ohio, and Worcester Mass.

BOTTEGA (Ital. shop). The workshop or studio of an artist; specifically, that part in which pupils and assistants worked on productions commissioned from, and usually signed by, the master.

BOTTICELLI, Sandro (*c.*1445–1510), was the most individual, if not the most influential, painter in Florence at the end of the 15th century. He was probably a pupil of Fra Filippo Lippi but was influenced by the POLLAIUOLI for a short time around 1470, when he painted a *Fortitude* to go with a set of six other *Virtues* by Piero Pollaiuolo (all now in the Uffizi). The chronology of his work is difficult to establish since it ranges between the vigorous realism of the 1470 *Fortitude* and the languorous and anti-naturalistic ecstasy of his last dated (and only signed) work, the *Mystic Nativity* (1500: London, NG). It seems certain that the Victorian interpretation of his style as progressively more naturalistic (and more Pre-Raphaelite) is topsy-turvy: we know that he was neurotic, much troubled by the religious crisis of the late Quattrocento and yet ambiguous in his attitude to Savonarola, and that he was at any rate accused of pederasty (this charge seems to have been made as freely in 15th-century Florence as that of Communism in modern America, and on about the same evidence). His extreme dependence on outline as a means of emotional expression is a summary of Florentine tendencies in the 15th century, but his style seems nevertheless to have been deliberately archaic; just as his most celebrated mythological pictures – the *Primavera* and the *Birth of Venus* (both in the Uffizi) – have very involved allegorical and Christianizing meanings. These were probably painted for a member of the Medici family, then ruling Florence, but we know almost nothing about the commissioning or his relationship with the Medici and their humanist circle. In 1481/2 Botticelli was in Rome, painting frescoes in the Sistine Chapel along with Ghirlandaio, Rosselli, Signorelli, and Perugino, but these do not seem to have been particularly successful. During the last twenty years of the 15th century he ran a large shop for the production of *Madonnas* of a gently devout kind well suited to the piety of the age: these made him prosperous and many of them are repetitions by different hands from a cartoon by him. They were also extensively forged in the 19th century, but these are now beginning to look strangely Victorian.

By about 1500 his style was so obviously opposed to the new ideas of Leonardo da Vinci and Michelangelo that he suffered a decline in popularity and the last ten years of his life are mysterious. It is probable that the clumsy and almost hysterical style of pictures like the *Pietàs* in Munich and Milan (Poldi-Pezzoli) or the S. Zenobius series in London (NG), Dresden, and New York (Met. Mus.) is that of his last period, i.e. after the 1500 *Mystic Nativity*, rather than works of his youth. Probably in the 1490s he made a series of splendid outline drawings illustrating Dante (Berlin and the Vatican), which show his sensitive feeling for contour at its most subtle. There are pictures by him in Bergamo, Berlin, Boston (Mus. and Gardner Mus.), Cambridge Mass. (Fogg Mus.), Chicago, Detroit, Dresden, Edinburgh (NG), Florence (Accad., Uffizi, Pitti, and Ognissanti and other churches), Frankfurt, Glasgow, London (NG, V & A, Courtauld Inst.), Milan (Ambrosiana, Poldi-Pezzoli), Munich, New York (Met. Mus.), Ottawa, Paris (Louvre, Jacquemart-André), Philadelphia, Rome (Borghese), the Vatican, Washington (NG), and elsewhere. Filippino LIPPI was his pupil. *See also* AMICO di Sandro.

BOTTICINI, Francesco (*c.*1446–97), was a Florentine painter who imitated many others, including Botticelli. The most interesting picture ascribed to him is the *Assumption* (*c.*1474/6: London, NG) which is the only Quattrocento picture known to have been painted to illustrate a heresy: Matteo Palmieri, the donor, held that human souls are the angels who remained neutral when Lucifer rebelled.

BOUCHARDE *see* STONE CARVING.

BOUCHARDON, Edme (1698–1762), was a French sculptor who worked under G. Coustou I and then went to Rome (1723) where he remained for nine years and enjoyed considerable fame. He worked at Versailles, but is best remembered for his Fontaine de Grenelle, Paris (1739–45); his *Cupid* (1750: Louvre); and his *Equestrian Louis XV*, designed as the centrepiece of the Place de la Concorde, Paris, but destroyed in the Revolution: it had *Virtues* by PIGALLE which evoked the epigram:

> Oh! la belle statue! Oh! le beau piédestal!
> Les vertus sont à pied et le vice à cheval!

BOUCHER, François (1703–70), was the most typical ROCOCO decorator and the friend and protégé of Mme de Pompadour. One of his best portraits is of her (1758: London, V & A – others are in the Wallace Coll. and Edinburgh NG). He began as an engraver of Watteau, won the Prix de Rome of the Academy in 1723, but did not go to Italy until 1727: there he admired little but Tiepolo, the greatest decorator of the age. He returned to France in 1731, became an Academician in 1734, and Director in 1765. He made many tapestry designs and painted charmingly indelicate mythological scenes, ultimately inspired by Veronese, Rubens, and Watteau. Reynolds, who visited his studio, was scandalized by his working without a model: 'he said, when he was young, studying his art, he found it necessary to use models; but he had left them off for many years.' The best collection of his works is in the Wallace Coll., London, but there are others in London (NG, Kenwood), New York, Paris, Waddesdon, Bucks. (National Trust), and Washington.

BOUDIN, Eugène (1824–98), was a direct precursor of Impressionism. He was born at Honfleur, son of a pilot, and he painted seascapes and harbour scenes with luminous skies taking up most of the picture space. These skies are the link between his friend Corot and his younger friends the Impressionists, especially MONET. He exhibited at the First Impressionist Exhibition, 1874.

BOUGUEREAU, Adolphe William (1825–1905), won the Prix de Rome in 1850 and spent 4 years in Italy. He painted 'Renaissance-type' nudes, rather cloying religious subjects, and portraits of photographic verisimilitude: this probably explains why Renoir, on being fitted with a new pair of glasses to correct his myopia, threw them on the floor, crying: 'Bon Dieu, je vois comme Bouguereau!' There are works in the Louvre, Bordeaux, Dijon, La Rochelle and in many US museums, especially Williamstown, Mass.

BOURDELLE, Émile Antoine (1861–1929), was a pupil of RODIN, but soon reacted against his loose and impressionistic modelling and began to study Greek and Gothic sculpture for its more stylized forms. He did the sculpture and decorative paintings in the Théâtre des Champs-Élysées, Paris, but his major work is the *Virgin of Alsace*, an enormous statue on a mountain in the Vosges, the sketch for which is in Edinburgh. There is a Musée Bourdelle in Paris.

BOURDON, Sébastien (1616–71), was born in Montpellier, and spent his early years in Paris and Bordeaux. In 1634 he went to Rome; there he imitated current styles – the landscapes of CLAUDE, the genre subjects of CASTIGLIONE, and BAMBOCCIATE, the speciality of Dutch and Flemish painters in Italy. In 1637 he returned to Paris, visiting Venice on the way, and continued along the same lines, before turning to large religious and classical subjects in a more Baroque manner, with a Venetian richness of handling, though the influence of POUSSIN eventually subdued their exuberance. In 1652 he went to Sweden as Court portraitist to Queen Christina, and after her abdication and his return to Paris in 1654 he continued to paint portraits with great success. The years 1659–63 were spent in Montpellier, but he was finally compelled to leave through the jealousy of local artists, and he passed his remaining years in Paris. His late works show the strong influence of Poussin, with tenderness, charm, and cool colour.

There are works in Amsterdam (Rijksmus.), Cambridge (Fitzwm), Greenville SC (Bob Jones Univ.), The Hague, Hartford Conn. (Wadsworth), London (NG, Dulwich), Madrid (Prado), Montpellier, Montreal, Munich, Paris (Louvre), Providence RI, Sarasota Fla (Ringling), Stockholm, and elsewhere.

BOUTS, Dieric (c. 1415–75), was a Netherlandish painter, born in Haarlem but active in Louvain (where he died) in 1457, and probably before 1448. His figures are stiff and unemotional, but his treatment of light and landscape is of great beauty and delicacy, especially in colour. With Roger van der WEYDEN, who influenced him strongly, he was a powerful influence on German 15th-century painting. His only certain works are the *Mystic Meals* (1464–8: S. Pierre, Louvain) and the large pair of *Justice Scenes* (Brussels), one of which was unfinished at his death and may have been completed by Hugo van der GOES. Bouts had a great influence – like his fellow-Dutchmen OUWATER and the MASTER OF THE VIRGO INTER VIRGINES – on the beginnings of woodcut book-illustration. He was also a fine portrait painter, as is shown by the *Man* (1462: London, NG). Other works are in Lille, Madrid, New York, Philadelphia, and elsewhere.

His two sons, Dieric II (c. 1448–90/1) and Aelbrecht (d. 1549), were also painters: of Dieric nothing certain is known; Aelbrecht's chief work is an *Assumption* in Brussels.

BOZZETTO (Ital. sketch), or MAQUETTE. Usually applied to models for sculpture, but can so be used for painted sketches, more usually called MODELLI.

BRANCUSI, Constantin (1876–1957), was a Rumanian sculptor whose most successful works are often simple, highly-polished shapes. He settled in Paris in 1904 and was influenced by RODIN, but by 1907 was more concerned with abstract shape: he was the friend of MODIGLIANI and induced him to turn to sculpture. He exhibited at the ARMORY Show (1913) in New York, and was involved in a notorious case in 1926–8, when the US Customs refused to admit a work of his as sculpture, claiming that it was turned metal and thus dutiable. In 1937 he began a column some 90 feet high at Targu Jiu, in Rumania. There are works in London (Tate), and the Museums of Modern Art in New York and Paris, but the biggest collection is in Philadelphia. He bequeathed many works to France, on condition that his studio be kept intact.

BRANGWYN, Sir Frank (1867–1956), was a Welsh painter of huge mural decorations, usually with many figures executed in a brilliantly colourful handling. He became an RA in 1919, and was knighted in 1941. There are examples of his decorations in the Skinners' Hall, the Royal Exchange, and Lloyd's Register, all in London; the Court House, Cleveland Ohio; Missouri State Capitol, and the Rockefeller Centre in New York (where it replaced one by RIVERA). After many troubles his projected decorations for the House of Lords were erected in the Guildhall, Swansea. Most English provincial museums have an example of his paintings or his large and important etchings, and there are many scattered throughout the world. Bruges (his birth-place) and Orange in Southern France have museums devoted to his works.

BRAQUE, Georges (1882–1963), learned to paint as an apprentice in a decorator's business, hence his superb technique. He was at the École des Beaux-Arts in Le Havre and, later, in Paris, but preferred to work on his own. He was friendly with Dufy and Friesz (both were from Le Havre) and by 1906 was in the FAUVE circle, but by 1909 he knew PICASSO well, and with him had started to work out the basis of a new approach to painting which developed into CUBISM. By the outbreak of war in 1914 this close collaboration was at an end: when Braque resumed painting in 1917 he tried to pick up Synthetic Cubism where he had left off, but by 1920–1 a less arbitrary spatial composition and not so much a return to reality as an acknowledge-ment of its existence, led to the ample, vigorous, splendid still-life and figure compositions, with a perfection of balance and harmony between the colour and the design, which he continued to develop for the rest of his life.

He also executed a certain amount of sculpture, incised plaster plaques, and plaster reliefs. There is a small body of graphic work – between forty and fifty lithographs, some woodcuts for book illustra-tion, and some etchings for which the drawings were originally pro-duced in 1931 as illustrations for Hesiod's Theogony. There are works in Basle, Buffalo, Copenhagen, Detroit, Frankfurt (Städel),

Glasgow, Le Havre, London (Tate), New York (M of MA, Guggenheim Fdn), Ottawa, Oxford, Paris (Mus. d'Art Moderne, Petit Pal.), Philadelphia, San Francisco, Toledo Ohio, Washington (Phillips), and elsewhere, including many French museums.

BRAY, Jan de (c. 1626/7–1697), was the son and pupil of Salomon. He worked in Haarlem and was much influenced by HELST, as well as by HALS. His best works are portraits and portrait groups such as the *Regents of the Children's Hospital* (1663: Haarlem), which clearly shows the influence of similar group portraits by REMBRANDT (e.g. the *Staal Meesters* of 1662), and Hals, but is much less free in handling. He also painted some more consciously poetical works such as *Antony and Cleopatra* of 1669 (replicas in the Royal Collection and at Nuremberg). These works show him, like LIEVENS and MAES, aping the grand manner of contemporary French historical painting. Other works are in Amsterdam (Rijksmus.), Edinburgh (NG), London (NG), and Worcester Mass.

BRAY, Salomon de (1597–1664), was an Amsterdam painter, poet, and architect who settled in Haarlem c. 1625. He was the pupil of GOLTZIUS, whose manner he occasionally imitated, but his portraits, like those of his son Jan, are often close to HALS. There are works by him in Bristol, Dresden, The Hague (1651: *Decorations for the House in the Wood*), and London (V & A).

BREU, Jörg (c. 1475–1537), was a painter and designer of woodcuts who worked in Austria 1496–1502, but settled in Augsburg in 1502 and came under the influence of HOLBEIN the Elder and BURGKMAIR. There are works by him in Augsburg, Basle, Berlin, Herzogenburg, London (Courtauld Inst.), Melk, Munich, San Diego Cal., and Vienna.

BREUGHEL *see* BRUEGEL.

BRIL (Brill), Mattheus (1550–83) and Paul (1554–1626), were brothers, born in Antwerp, but who both worked in Rome and painted landscapes which form the link between the panoramic views of Patenier or Bruegel and the ideal landscape evolved by Poussin and Claude. Mattheus was in Rome by about 1570 and painted several large frescoes, including the *Seasons* in the Vatican, but he died young and much of his work was completed by Paul, who also succeeded him in the Papal favour. Paul seems to have followed his brother to Italy c. 1574, and was certainly in Rome in 1582. He also painted frescoes, including the landscapes in the Casino Rospigliosi, Rome, accompanying Guido RENI's *Aurora*; but he is best known for his small easel pictures on copper, many of which are much influenced by ELSHEIMER. Among his pupils was Agostino Tassi, later to become Claude's master. His influence was also spread by his engravings. Among his pictures (some signed with a pair of spectacles – *Brille*) are examples in Amsterdam, Antwerp, Basle, Berlin, Brussels, Dresden, Dunedin NZ, Edinburgh, Florence (Uffizi, Pitti), Glasgow, Leeds, London (NG, Wellington Mus.), Milan, Munich, Paris (Louvre), Rome (Gall. Naz. and Borghese), Stockholm, the Vatican, and Vienna.

BROAD MANNER *see* FINE MANNER.

BROEDERLAM, Melchior (active 1381 – *d.*1409 or later), was a painter in Ypres who became Painter to Philip the Bold, Duke of Burgundy, in 1385 and was in Paris 1390/3. In 1392 he was commissioned to paint two wings for an altar, which he completed in 1399 (Dijon, Musée): this is probably the earliest example of INTERNATIONAL GOTHIC.

BRONZE was used as a material for sculpture in ancient Greece and Rome as well as in Africa and China, but the art seems to have become almost lost in the Middle Ages, when bronze effigies were made by hammering thin plates of bronze on to a wooden core. The *S. Peter* attributed to Arnolfo di Cambio is one of the earliest modern cast bronzes on a big scale, but by the early 15th century the craft was well established in the hands of masters like Ghiberti. Modern bronzes are made either in sand moulds or by the *cire perdue* method, both these techniques being very ancient. Sand casting is done by simply making a mould of special sand from the original PLASTER model, inserting a core, and pouring in the molten bronze. *Cire perdue* (Fr. lost wax) is economical of bronze because it consists of a model which is a few millimetres smaller in all directions than the enclosing mould, the space between being filled with wax and vent pipes inserted at top and bottom. The outer side of the wax is exactly what the desired bronze should look like; and molten bronze is poured through the top vent, taking the place of the wax which has previously been melted out. The amount of wax run out serves as a guide to the quantity of bronze needed. Any number of such casts can be taken. In Renaissance times it was usual to work on the casts with files and chasers, polishing and engraving the surface, but it is now the fashion to prefer a rough surface, showing the thumb-marks of the original clay model. Patina is the lovely greenish tint and matt surface which age and chemical reaction have imparted to Greek bronzes, but which is now artificially imitated by chemical means. A peculiarly vivid green bronze is characteristic of Epstein's work.

BRONZINO, Agnolo (1503–72), was a Florentine painter who was the pupil of PONTORMO and was also influenced by Michelangelo. He was Court painter to Cosimo I de' Medici, the first Grand Duke of Tuscany, and one of the most important Mannerist portrait painters, concentrating on expressing an inhuman elegance and restraint in his sitters, totally unlike the nervous sensibility of Pontormo. From Michelangelo he learned little but tricks of foreshortening. His few religious works are highly wrought and devoid of any kind of feeling, while his *Venus, Cupid, Time and Folly* (London, NG) has a kind of icy obscenity. Most of his works are in Florence; others are in Antwerp (Mayer van den Bergh), Berlin, Boston (Gardner), Budapest, Chicago, Cincinnati, Detroit, London, Madrid, Milan, New York (Met. Mus. and Frick Coll.), Ottawa, Oxford, Paris, Pisa (S. Stefano), Rome (Barberini, Borghese), Toledo Ohio, Vienna, Washington (NG), and Worcester Mass.

BROUWER (Brauwer), Adriaen (1605/6–38), was the link between Flemish and Dutch genre painting. He was born in Flanders but spent some time in Holland and may have been a pupil of Frans Hals. His pictures, apart from a few landscapes, represent sordid tavern scenes, usually with boors carousing. He himself lived like that and has been compared to Villon in consequence. His earliest works may start from the village scenes of BRUEGEL, and he may have known one of Bruegel's sons before going to Amsterdam in 1625 and on to Haarlem where he met Hals. In 1631/2 he was in the Guild in Antwerp and came under the influence of Rubens, who in turn admired him. His political activities led to imprisonment in 1633: the prison baker was Joos van Craesbeck, who became his pupil and imitator. His best works are comparable with those of STEEN and David TENIERS II (both of whom were influenced by him) and have a delicacy of colour combined with a breadth of handling that compensate for his subjects, in which his most fervent admirers see an almost Rembrandtesque pathos. The best collection of his works is in Munich: others are in Amsterdam, Antwerp, Berlin, Brussels, Dresden, Frankfurt (Städel), Haarlem, The Hague, Leipzig, London (NG, V & A, and Wellington Mus., Wallace Coll., and Dulwich), Madrid (Prado), New York (Met. Mus.), Paris (Louvre, Petit Pal.), Philadelphia (Johnson), Rotterdam, Vienna (Akad.), and York.

BROWN, Ford Madox (1821–93), was born in Calais and studied in Belgium, Paris, and Rome (where he met and was influenced by OVERBECK) before returning to England in 1845. In 1848 ROSSETTI asked him for lessons and in this way Brown was brought into contact with the PRB. He never actually became a member but his work was profoundly influenced by them for many years, as may be seen in his best-known works *The Last of England* (1855: Birmingham) and *Work* (1852–65: Manchester). He carried out decorations for the Town Hall at Manchester, and there are other pictures in the Tate Gallery, London.

BRÜCKE, Die (The Bridge), was the name taken by a group founded in 1905 in Dresden by E. L. KIRCHNER, K. SCHMIDT-ROTTLUFF, Erich HECKEL, and F. Bleyl. There was no particular programme, but the name was chosen to indicate their desire to link like-minded artists. The group-style, however, was that of EXPRESSIONISM and was manifested in forms very close to those of FAUVISM, since they admired the works of Gauguin, van Gogh, and Munch. The group broke up in 1913, but it had exerted considerable influence on public taste, and it was particularly important in the revival of woodcut and other graphic arts. *See also* BLAUE REITER, Der.

BRUEGEL, Jan I (1568–1625), called 'Velvet Bruegel', was the younger son of Pieter I and brother of Pieter II. He was a successful painter of still-life and landscape in a highly detailed style which elicited much admiration from contemporaries. His chief claim to fame is the fact that Rubens collaborated with him. There are pictures in London (NG), Oxford, and many other museums. His son Jan II (1601–78) was also a painter.

BRUEGEL (Brueghel, Breughel), Pieter I (*c.*1525/30–69), sometimes also called 'Peasant Bruegel', was the most important satirist in the Netherlands after BOSCH and one of the greatest landscape painters. The date of his birth is unknown but may be guessed at from the fact that he became Master in the Antwerp Guild in 1551: immediately after this he went to France and Italy (*c.*1552), travelling as far south as Sicily. He was in Rome in 1553 and returned over the Alps, probably in 1554. The Alps, and to a lesser extent the scenery of Italy, made a tremendous impact on him, as may be seen from the drawings he made on the journey and also from the whole development of his landscape style. The art of Italy seems to have made almost no impression on him. On his return he began to make drawings for engravers, very much in the manner of Bosch and dealing with the same subjects. His earliest painting to be dated is of 1553 and in the last ten or twelve years of his life he produced the genre scenes and the religious subjects set in vast landscapes which are his finest works. The old nickname 'Peasant Bruegel' is misleading if it is held to mean that he was himself a peasant: on the contrary he was highly cultivated and is known to have enjoyed the friendship of humanists and the patronage of the Emperor's representative, Cardinal Granvella. Later, many of his pictures belonged to Rudolf II. His attitude, and that of his patrons, is hard to define since it is not merely condescending but seems to show a real interest in village customs coupled with a satirical approach to drunkenness, gluttony, and other sins of the flesh. Some pictures – for example the *Massacre of the Innocents* – have been held to be veiled allusions to the Spanish Fury and the subjection of the Netherlands in general, and it has also been held that Bruegel's move from Antwerp to Brussels *c.*1563 was due to his membership of a heretical sect and fear of persecution; yet he was certainly patronized by Cardinal Granvella and Brussels was the centre of orthodoxy and of government. The great series of the *Months* consists of five pictures (now in Vienna, Prague, and New York), all but one dated 1565. They have no moral message comparable with his earlier works, such as the *Fall of the Rebel Angels* or the *Dulle Griet*, but they are among the great landscape paintings of the age, influenced by PATENIER and even Titian but surpassing both in their feeling for nature and the unity of man and his surroundings. The best collection of his works is in Vienna (K-H Mus.) but there are others in the Royal Collection and in Antwerp (Musée Mayer van den Bergh), Berlin, Boston (Mus.), Brussels, Budapest, Darmstadt, Detroit, London (NG), Madrid (Prado), Munich, Naples, Paris (Louvre), Philadelphia, Rome (Doria), Rotterdam, Upton House (National Trust) Banbury, and Washington (NG).

BRUEGEL, Pieter II (c. 1564–1638), called 'Hell Bruegel', was the son of Pieter I and frequently copied his father's works. He was the master of Snyders and presumably of his own son, Pieter III.

BRUSHWORK. With the development of the technique of oil-painting it soon became clear that the use of stiff bristle brushes charged with oil paint and applied to a grainy surface such as canvas could give a special texture and quality of handling which is aesthetically pleasing in itself, independently of its function in representing form. A painter's brushwork is as personal as his handwriting (and is occasionally so referred to) and it is even harder to imitate. The encrustations of Rembrandt, the frenzied drama of the actual strokes of van Gogh's brush, the thin film of Gainsborough, the gem-like luminosity of Vermeer's small dabs of paint; all these are possible in one and the same medium, so that brushwork is one of the painter's most powerful tools in the creation of his own world. In some cases it becomes the end rather than the means, as in certain forms of Abstract Expressionism, where the word can perhaps hardly be legitimately applied to paint trickled, rather than brushed, on to the ground.

BRUYN, Barthel (1492/3–1555), was a Cologne painter, chiefly of portraits. His religious works are much influenced by Netherlandish painters of the late 15th century and his portraits, which are grimly realistic representations of unaristocratic sitters, are very close to those of JOOS van Cleve. In 1515–16 he is documented as a painter of altarpieces, and the Xanten altar was commissioned in 1529. His career, 1515–55, invites parallels with HOLBEIN and LUCAS van Leyden, although a beautiful *Nativity* of 1516 (Frankfurt) is closer to GEERTGEN. There are works in Cologne (Mus. and churches), churches in Essen and Xanten, and in Antwerp, Basle, Berlin, Brussels, Copenhagen, Dresden, Frankfurt (Städel), Göteborg, Gotha, The Hague, Hanover, Leipzig, London (NG, Courtauld Inst.), Munich, Oberlin Ohio, Ottawa, Paris (Louvre), Prague, Siena, Toronto, Vienna, York, and several other German museums.

BRZESKA *see* GAUDIER.

BUECKELAER (Beuckelaer), Joachim (c. 1530/35–1573/4), was the nephew by marriage and pupil of AERTSEN, and painted very similar still-life pictures with ostensibly religious subjects. He often worked as a journeyman for other artists, but became a master in the Antwerp Guild in 1560. His first dated work is of 1561. There are pictures by him in Amsterdam (Rijksmus.), Antwerp (Mus. and Mayer van den Bergh), Brussels, Florence (Uffizi), Genoa, Hull, Paris (Louvre), Stockholm, Vienna, and York (The Treasurer's House).

BUFFET, Bernard (b.1928), is a French painter of extreme precocity who made his name as early as 1948. He is the principal figurative painter in Paris and was much influenced in the 1940s by the movement known as *Misérabilisme*; sad greys, thin spiky forms, and an obtrusively angular signature characterize his style. In later years he has painted views of London, Paris, and New York, as well as series of Toreadors and S. Joan of Arc. There are works in Cincinnati, New York (Brooklyn), and Toronto, as well as London (Tate) and Paris (Mus. d'Art Moderne).

BUON, Bartolommeo (c.1374–1464/7), was the leading Venetian sculptor of the first half of the 15th century. His work is strongly influenced by South German sculpture and most of it is in Venice (e.g. Porta della Carta, Doge's Palace) but there is a *Madonna della Misericordia* (1441–5) by him in London (V & A).

BURGKMAIR, Hans (1473–1531), was an Augsburg painter who was not influenced by Dürer but, like him, formed his style by contact with Venetian art. He soon outdistanced the elder Holbein and also had a good connexion with publishers, designing woodcuts. He was patronized by the Emperor Maximilian. There are works in Augsburg, Cologne, Munich, Nuremberg, Vienna, and elsewhere.

BURIN or Graver. The principal tool used in ENGRAVING on wood or metal to plough the lines out of the surface of the plate or block.

BURNE-JONES, Sir Edward (1833–98), was one of the painters in the circle round William MORRIS and ROSSETTI, by whom he was greatly influenced. He travelled in Italy in 1859, and was in Milan and Venice in 1862 with Ruskin, for whom he copied works by Tintoretto. He produced many tapestry and stained-glass designs for William Morris's firm, and these and his paintings evoke a dreamy, romantic, literary never-never land of Botticelli and Mantegna, executed in a flat technique and a colour aptly described by the phrase 'greenery-yallery, Grosvenor Gallery'. He was made a baronet in 1894.

The largest collection of his works is in Birmingham City Art Gallery (his native town), and there are many in the Tate, London; Cardiff, and in provincial museums in England.

BURR *see* ENGRAVING 2(b).

BURRI, Alberto (b.1915), an Italian abstract painter, began by practising medicine, but started painting in a prisoner-of-war camp in Texas in 1944. He settled in Rome in 1945 and exhibited in New York in 1954. He was awarded a prize at the 1960 Biennale. His works are not so much paintings as compositions in patched sacking with an occasional blob of colour. There are examples in London (Tate) and New York (Guggenheim).

BUSHNELL, John (d.1701), fled from England owing to matrimonial difficulties and went to Rome. He worked in Italy, France, and Flanders before settling in Venice, where he made the huge Alvise Mocenigo monument in S. Lazzaro dei Mendicanti. He returned to England after 22 years, but his impossible pride and conceit suggest that he was mentally unbalanced. He executed a number of tombs, including two in Westminster Abbey and a bust of Mrs Pepys (St Olave's) in the City of London, but his work is very uneven in quality. A terracotta bust of Charles II at Cambridge (Fitzwm) is attributed to him.

BUTLER, Reg (b.1913), one of the leading British sculptors, was originally an architect and has also worked as a blacksmith: most of his work is in metal, either forged or cast. He won the 1953 competition for a monument to The Unknown Political Prisoner, and he produced another version in 1957. His first one-man show was in 1949 and the works of this period were all Constructivist, but in the later 1950s he returned to figurative work and his most recent works are superbly sensual figures of girls. He has also written a book on the processes of artistic creation. There are works by him in Cologne, London (Tate), New York (M of MA), and Ottawa.

BYLERT (Bijlert), Jan van (1603–71), was an UTRECHT painter who was the pupil of BLOEMAERT and then went to France and Italy, returning to Utrecht by 1625. His work between 1620 and 1630 is based directly on Caravaggio's in subject and handling; after c. 1630 he used much lighter and brighter colours and chose subjects which have a certain pastoral prettiness, as well as painting some portraits. There are works in Amsterdam (Rijksmus.), Belfast, Berlin, Brunswick, Budapest, Cassel, London (NG), Lyons, Rotterdam, Utrecht (Mus. and elsewhere).

C

CABINET PICTURE. A small easel picture, usually not more than about 3 or 4 feet across, and often much less. The minor Dutch masters were the principal painters of this type of furniture picture at its best.

CALDER, Alexander (*b.* 1898), is an American sculptor, abstract painter and illustrator of children's books. He was originally an engineer and his main inventions – STABILES (so named by ARP) and MOBILES (so named by DUCHAMP), both dating from *c.* 1931 – can be regarded as a marriage between engineering and sculpture. His paintings are influenced by MIRÒ. Most of his works are in America, but there is a Mobile (of 1959) in Leeds, and others in London (Tate).

CALLIGRAPHIC is an adjective applied to an artist's handling. In drawing it means 'freely and rhythmically treated, with pen squiggles like handwriting': in painting it means 'free and loose BRUSHWORK'.

CALLOT, Jacques (1592/3–1635), was one of the greatest of etchers and produced some 1,500 plates. He was born in Lorraine, at Nancy, and went to Rome at some time between 1608 and 1611, when he went to Florence. There he made many etchings of fairs and festivals as well as of courtiers, beggars, and hunchbacks, many of them based on *Commedia dell'arte* types. In 1621 he returned to Nancy, where his work took a more serious turn, culminating in his masterpiece the *Grandes Misères de la Guerre* (1633), which was at least partly inspired by Richelieu's invasion of Lorraine. It is the most terrifying record of the savageries of the Thirty Years War, comparable with Goya's later *Desastres*.

CALRAET, Abraham van (1642–1722), was a Dordrecht painter who may have been a pupil of CUYP. The similarity between some of Calraet's small pictures and those by Cuyp has led to a great deal of misattribution, some of it deliberate. The initials A C apply equally to both artists, but the still-life pictures so signed are certainly Calraet's and many of the stable scenes probably are his. There are three pictures signed A C in the National Gallery, London, all of which were previously attributed to Cuyp.

CALVAERT, Dionisio (Denis) (*c.* 1545–1619), was an Antwerp painter who went to Italy *c.* 1562. He eventually set up an Academy in Bologna and became the first master of Reni, Albani, and Domenichino; his Academy seems to have inspired the CARRACCI one. There are works by him in Bologna and other Italian museums and in Hull, Vienna, and Worcester Mass.

CALVERT, Edward (1799–1883), joined the Navy as a young man and first exhibited at the RA in 1825. He met PALMER there in 1826, who described him as 'a prosperous, stalwart country gentleman ...

redolent of the sea, and in white trousers': between 1827 and 1831 he was deeply influenced by BLAKE and Palmer, but he lost his innocent eye and spent the rest of his long life absorbed in anti-Christian mythological musings. There are works by him in the Tate Gallery, London.

CAMAÏEU (Fr.). For paintings *en camaïeu see* GRISAILLE, and for engravings *see* CHIAROSCURO.

CAMBIO, Arnolfo di, *see* ARNOLFO.

CAMDEN TOWN GROUP. A small secession from the NEAC which later developed into the LONDON GROUP. GILMAN and GORE were the major figures in it, but SICKERT was the principal inspiration. The group is usually said to have introduced Post-Impressionism into English art.

CAMERA OBSCURA, LUCIDA. A mechanical means of securing accuracy in drawing, particularly of topographical detail. The *camera obscura* was invented in the 16th century and consists of an arrangement of lenses and mirrors in a darkened tent or box. The view seen by the lens is reflected through the mirrors on to a sheet of paper, so that all the draughtsman has to do is to trace round the edges. CANALETTO is known to have used the machine in making studies for his *Vedute,* and its use was undoubtedly widespread; CARLEVARIS also used it. Drawings made in this way are sometimes identifiable by distortions at the edges due to primitive lenses. A *camera lucida* is a more sophisticated optical instrument, incorporating a prism.

CAMPENDONK, Heinrich (1889–1957), was the youngest member of the BLAUE REITER, which MARC and KANDINSKY invited him to join in 1911. He emigrated to Holland in 1933 and taught at Amsterdam. Most of his works are woodcuts, but his paintings are rich in colour with small, puppet-like figures reminiscent of Chagall and the Russians.

CAMPIN, Robert (1378/9–1444), is known to have been a painter active in Tournai from 1406. No pictures are certainly known to be his, but he had two pupils, Jacques DARET and (probably) Roger van der WEYDEN: he may therefore have been identical with the MASTER OF FLÉMALLE.

CANALETTO, (Giovanni) Antonio (1697–1768), Venetian *vedutista,* went to Rome *c.*1719 (and probably again *c.*1740) and was influenced in some not clearly definable way by PANINI. He had already worked as a scene-painter with his father and was back in Venice by 1720, where he is recorded in the Guild 1720–67. His earliest datable works are four views of Venice painted in 1725–6 for Stefano Conti of Lucca (now in a private collection in Montreal): these show the strong contrasts of light and shade which made him famous at the expense of CARLEVARIS (who may have been his master, although this is not likely). It is clear that these *vedute* were extremely unusual in that they were painted on the spot instead of from drawings, although he later abandoned this practice and returned to the traditional method of working from drawings, some of which were made with the help of the CAMERA OBSCURA; occasionally he even worked from etchings by Carlevaris. By 1726 he was already working for the English market and by about 1730 he had come to an agreement with Joseph Smith, later British Consul in Venice, who had the pick of his output, arranged other sales, and probably forwarded his visit to England, which, with short intervals in Venice, lasted from 1746 until *c.*1756. During this time he painted several English views and Capricci, although on his arrival he had some difficulty in establishing himself, as Vertue observed that 'on the whole of him something is obscure or strange. he dos not produce work so well done as those of Venice or other parts of Italy ... especially his figures in his works done here, are apparently much inferior to those done abroad. which are surprizeingly well done and with great freedom and variety – his water and his skys at no time excellent or with natural freedom. and what he has done here his prospects of Trees woods or handling or pencilling of that part not various nor so skillfull as might be expected ... which has much strengthend a conjecture that he is not the veritable Cannalleti of Venice.' This was perhaps partly due to BELLOTTO's use of his uncle's name. During and after his English period Canaletto's style, as Vertue observed, became much harder and tighter, losing all the breadth and freedom of his earliest works. These later works were much imitated by English painters such as SCOTT and Marlow (who also seems to have forged Bellottos).

The Royal Collection has the largest and best collection of Canaletto's works, with more than 50 paintings and over 140 drawings from the Smith Collection. Most other galleries have an example. About 1741/4 he issued his etched *Vedute* ... with a dedication to Smith.

CANO, Alonso (1601–67), was one of the leading painters and sculptors of Seville. He was the son of a sculptor who specialized in the construction of elaborate altars and he himself continued the business, but became a master painter in 1626. His early works were influenced by ZURBARÁN, but his style later became softer in handling. In 1636 he was imprisoned for debt; in the following year he was in trouble for duelling, and in 1638 he left Seville for the Court where he may have been invited by VELAZQUEZ, who had been his fellow apprentice under PACHECO. In 1644 his young wife was found stabbed to death; he was arrested but subsequently freed. He returned to Madrid in 1645, but obtained the salary of a Prebendary at Granada Cathedral, although he does not seem to have been very satisfactory to his ecclesiastical superiors. He designed the façade of Granada Cathedral *c.*1664. A contemporary records his systematic use of prints, even the crudest street ballads, as a means of stimulating his imagination. Most of his sculpture is in Granada, but there are paintings and some carved wooden figures in Berlin, Budapest, Dresden, Kansas City, London (Wallace Coll.), Los Angeles, Madrid (Prado and Acad.), Munich, New York (Hispanic Soc.), Paris (Louvre), Seville, Stockholm, Worcester Mass., and York.

CANOVA, Antonio (1757–1822), was brought up as a mason and already had his own studio, in Venice, by 1774: he became the most famous NEOCLASSIC sculptor, whose international reputation surpassed even those of FLAXMAN, THORWALDSEN, and GIBSON. His early work is still very much in the 18th-century tradition and reminiscent of French portrait sculpture in its liveliness, but by 1779 he had been converted to Neoclassic theory and this was confirmed by his visit to Rome and Naples in 1780 and his residence in Rome from 1781. He is said to have been influenced by Gavin HAMILTON. In 1782 he received his first major commission, the Monument to Pope Clement XIV (1782–7: Rome, SS. Apostoli), followed by that to Clement XIII (1787–92: St Peter's). The French invasion caused him to go to Vienna in 1797, and there he got the commission for the Monument to Maria Christina (in the Augustinerkirche). In 1802, pressed by the Vatican, he accepted Napoleon's invitation to Paris; although he did not approve of the French lootings of Italian works of art he became an admirer of Napoleon and made a bust of him from life. This was followed by many others and in the years 1806–8 he began several, including an equestrian bronze for Naples and two gigantic standing figures of the Emperor, stark naked. One of these, in bronze, is in Milan (Brera): another, in marble, was captured by Wellington and is now in the Wellington Mus., London. In 1807 he also began (but abandoned) a Nelson Monument. His best-known work is the portrait of Napoleon's sister, *Pauline Bonaparte Borghese as Venus* (1808: Rome, Borghese Gall.), one of several statues of members of Napoleon's family. In 1815, after the fall of Napoleon, Canova was sent by the Pope to Paris to try to secure the return of the works looted by the French. He succeeded in large measure, with English help, and he visited London on his way back, where he studied the Elgin Marbles (bought, after much controversy, for the British Museum in 1816). For his part in securing the return of the Italian treasures the Pope made him Marchese d'Ischia. In 1817 he transformed his equestrian *Napoleon*, destined for Naples, into *Charles III Bourbon* and in the same year he adapted his colossal *Religion* into a smaller figure for a Brownlow Monument in Belton, Lincs, where it is said to represent *Protestant Faith*. Two years later, at the expense of George III, he made the Monument to the Stuarts now in St Peter's, and in 1820 he made a *Washington* for N. Carolina (now destroyed). He seems to have been an extremely kind and generous man, spending his large fortune freely in helping young students and sending patrons to struggling sculptors. There is a large collection of casts of his works in his native village, Possagno near Treviso: other works are in Bassano, Bergamo, Berlin, Florence (Pitti and Sta Croce), Forlì, Genoa (Pal. Bianco), Liverpool (a *Self-portrait*), London (V & A), Milan (Ambrosiana), Munich, Naples (Mus. Nazionale and Filangeri), Ottawa, Padua, Paris (Louvre), Parma, Rome (Mus. Capitolino and Napoleonico, S. Antonio dei Portoghesi, SS. Luca e Martina, S. Marco), Treviso, Turin, the Vatican, Venice (Accad., Mus. Correr, Mus. dell'Arsenale, Querini-Stampalia, Seminario Arcivescovile), and Vienna (K-H Mus.).

CAPPELLE, Jan van de (*c.*1624/5–79), was an Amsterdam painter of calm seas with fleecy white clouds. He also painted a few winter landscapes. His style was based on that of Simon de VLIEGER, by whom he owned 9 paintings and 1300 drawings: Cappelle seems to have been wealthy, since his collection also included 500 Rembrandt drawings and portraits of him were painted by Rembrandt, Hals, and Eeckhout. Examples of his work are in many Dutch museums and in Antwerp, Berlin, Birmingham (Barber Inst.), Brussels, Chicago, Detroit, Dublin, Glasgow, London (NG and Kenwood), Munich, New York (Met. Mus., Frick Coll.), Ottawa, Toledo Ohio, Vienna, Washington (NG), and elsewhere.

CAPRICCIO (Ital. caprice). Any fantasy; but usually applied to quasi-topographical subjects and VEDUTE, e.g. Marlow's *St Paul's, London, with the Grand Canal, Venice* (London, Tate Gallery). *Los Caprichos* is the title of a set of highly phantasmagoric etchings by Goya.

CARACCIOLO, Giovanni Battista called 'Battistello' (*d.*1637), was one of the first Neapolitan painters to be influenced by CARAVAGGIO, whose works he may have seen in Rome before Caravaggio went to Naples in 1606–7. He thus exerted a decisive influence on Neapolitan painting of the 17th century. There is a fine work attributed to him in St Mary's Church, Newmarket.

CARAVAGGIO, Michelangelo Merisi da (1573–1610), so called from his birthplace near Milan. In 1584 he was apprenticed for four years to Simone Peterzano, a Bergamasque who claimed to have been a pupil of Titian. After his apprenticeship ended he went to Rome, but his early years are so obscure that it is uncertain when he arrived there, and when he worked for the Cavaliere d'ARPINO. His earliest works were still-life subjects and small dramatized self-portraits of a distinctly Northern and vaguely Venetian character, with strong chiaroscuro and detailed execution. From the 1590s he worked for Cardinal del Monte, who commissioned several genre subjects, and through him he obtained in 1597 the commission to decorate a chapel in S. Luigi dei Francesi, the French church in Rome, with 3 scenes from the life of S. Matthew. This – his first public work – was finished only after many difficulties, including the rejection of the original altarpiece of *S. Matthew and the Angel* on the grounds of indecorum, and radical repaintings of the *Calling* and the *Martyrdom* of the Saint on the side walls, probably due to difficulties with the scale of the figures occasioned by unfamiliarity with working on such large canvases and on related works on opposing walls. The present altarpiece was substituted for the original one, and with the extensive repaintings the work may have lasted until 1603, although the chapel was opened in 1601.

During these years he also painted the *Martyrdom of S. Peter* and the *Conversion of S. Paul* for Sta Maria del Popolo (1600–1), and these too were rejected by the clergy and replaced by more acceptable renderings. These are smaller than the works in S. Luigi, with fewer figures much larger in scale, but with an even more dramatic chiaroscuro. Three further large altarpieces were bitterly criticized: the *Madonna di Loreto*, the *Virgin and Child with S. Anne,* and the *Death of the Virgin*. Basically, the objections were on the grounds of indecorum – the sweaty headcloth and dirty feet of the pilgrims in the *Madonna di Loreto*, the naked Child and peasant air of the Virgin and S. Anne, the coarse peasant types used for the Apostles, and the bloated figure of the dead Virgin, reputed to have been painted from a drowned strumpet fished out of the Tiber. These accusations, and opposition to his works among the Academic later Mannerists such as ZUCCARO, were founded on his vivid realism, his use of contemporary costumes and settings, his rejection of idealization, the immediacy and simplicity of his approach, and the novelty of his use of strong chiaroscuro with a wealth of detail which, though appearing to conform to the new ideas favoured by Counter-Reformation artistic theory, were radically opposed to the forms and ideas expressed by the CARRACCI. But all his rejected works found ready buyers among Cardinals and noblemen against whom no accusations of insincerity and sensationalism can be made. His reputation as a stormy petrel was probably added to by the libel action brought against him in 1603 by Baglione (later his biographer) because of scurrilous verses circulated by Caravaggio, and by the numerous fracas with the police due to his violent temper. His career in Rome was brought to an inglorious end in 1606 by just such an outburst, for during a game of tennis he quarrelled with his opponent and stabbed him. He fled to Naples where he painted several works before going on to Malta in 1607. Here he was well received by the Grand Master of the Order of S. John, of whom he painted a full-length portrait (now in the Louvre), was made a Knight and commissioned to paint two works still in Malta. After assaulting a Justiciary, he was imprisoned but escaped and fled to Sicily in 1608. He was expelled from the Order, and pursued by its agents from Syracuse to Messina, then to Palermo, and finally back to Naples in 1609, where at a low tavern, haunt of German mercenaries and cut-throats, he was seriously wounded in a brawl and his death was generally reported. Meanwhile, in Rome, efforts were being made to obtain a pardon, but not daring to return to Rome until he was sure of it, he left Naples by sea for Porto d'Ercole, a Spanish enclave on the Tuscan coast. Here he was imprisoned by mistake and was released in time to see the felucca sail, as he thought, with all his goods. His rage brought on an attack of fever, and a few days later he died in a tavern. After his death, the Spanish Viceroy sent to Port' Ercole for his effects which were awaiting him in the customs house.

His last works in Malta and Sicily are very dark and somewhat damaged, but their direct iconography, their inspired simplicity and poignancy embody a new intensity of dramatic feeling. His technical methods were revolutionary and brought him into endless controversy: he is recorded as painting directly on to the canvas from a model, instead of working from sketches and squared-up preparatory drawings. Apart from Naples his methods and ideas had little lasting effect in Italy, where his principal followers were Orazio GENTILESCHI and his daughter Artemisia, MANFREDI, Borgianni, Serodine, and a number of lesser men who imitated his manner without catching more than his realism and light effects. He had some influence on Guido RENI and GUERCINO, and a decisive one on the UTRECHT School and in Naples. The realism of RIBERA and Maino links him with the early work of VELAZQUEZ and MURILLO, and in France LA TOUR and the LE NAIN brothers show the spread of his ideas. RUBENS also was a profound admirer of Caravaggio, and much of REMBRANDT'S work stems from him.

There are works in Berlin, the Escorial, Florence (Uffizi, Pitti), Hartford Conn., Kansas City, Leningrad, London (NG), Madrid (Prado), Messina, Milan (Ambrosiana, Brera), Naples (S. Domenico Maggiore, Misericordia), New York (Met. Mus.), Palermo (S. Lorenzo), Paris (Louvre), Rome (Gall. Naz., Borghese, Capitoline, Corsini, Doria Galls. and churches), Rouen, Valletta Malta, the Vatican, and Vienna.

CARLEVARIS, Luca (1665–1731), was the precursor of CANALETTO as the painter of Venice, and his *Vedute*, 103 etchings, were published in 1703. A sketch-book with preparatory drawings for these is in the British Museum; a volume of 53 oil sketches is in the V & A Museum, and there are paintings in the Royal Collection, Detroit, Dresden, Venice, and elsewhere. The large picture of *Lord Manchester's Embassy to Venice in 1707* (Birmingham) was probably the cause of his patronage by the English.

CARO, Anthony (b.1924), English sculptor, was an assistant of Henry MOORE'S 1951–3. From 1959 he began making large non-figurative works, abstract assemblages of metal forms in painted steel or aluminium.

CARON, Antoine (c.1520–c.1599), is first recorded in the 1540s at FONTAINEBLEAU, where he worked under PRIMATICCIO and was much influenced by Niccolo dell' ABBATE. In 1559 he became Court painter to Catherine de' Medici. He was an exponent of the most exaggerated and sophisticated Mannerist Court art, executing works based on court ballets and festivities, which he was employed to design. His use of strange colour-schemes, especially yellows, orange and pinks, and lurid skies, and his fantastic architecture peopled by wildly gesticulating figures of extraordinarily elongated proportions blend peculiarly with some of his depictions of battles and mass-acres suggested by the Wars of Religion. There are works in Beauvais, Blois, and Paris (Louvre), and drawings in Edinburgh and Florence.

CARPACCIO, Vittore (c.1460/5–1523/6), was probably a pupil, and certainly a follower, of Gentile BELLINI. He was also influenced by Giovanni Bellini, whose assistant he was in 1507, and perhaps also by Giorgione. His best work is the cycle of large pictures of the Legend of S. Ursula, in Venice (Accad.), the earliest of which is dated 1490. In 1511 he offered to sell a View of Jerusalem, from which it has been in-ferred that he had been there. His Knight in a Landscape (Lugano, Thyssen Coll.) is obscurely dated 1510?/26?, and may be the earliest full-length portrait, preceding CRANACH and MORETTO: if so, it clearly derives from pictures of Saints, such as the S. Liberale in Giorgione's Castelfranco Madonna. Other works by Carpaccio are in Berlin, London (NG), Milan (Brera), New York (Met. Mus.), Paris (Louvre, Jacquemart-André), Philadelphia (Johnson), Rome (Bor-ghese), and Washington.

CARPEAUX, Jean Baptiste (1827–75), was the principal French sculptor of his day and is, in some ways, parallel to Delacroix. He was a pupil of RUDE, whose influence he combined with the Romanticism of BARYE; he was also a precursor of Rodin and Rosso in the impor-tance he attached to chiaroscuro in sculpture. He went to Italy in 1854 and made his name with a dramatic statue of Ugolino, before return-ing to Paris in 1862. His most famous works were a pediment for the Pavillon de Flore of the Louvre (begun 1863) and The Dance, begun in 1865 for the new Opera House in Paris. This caused a great sensa-tion and was attacked on grounds of morality. It was even suggested that the group should be removed, but the outbreak of the Franco-Prussian War in 1870 prevented any action, although the original is now in the Louvre and has been replaced by a copy on the Opéra. He worked in England in 1871, to avoid the Commune. His last years were clouded by persecution mania and he died, at 48, of cancer. He worked as a painter as well as a sculptor and his native Valenciennes has a museum of his works: others are in Paris (Louvre and Petit Pal.), and in Birmingham, Copenhagen, London (Tate), New York, Providence RI, and Washington.

CARRÀ, Carlo (1881–1966), was one of the original FUTURISTS, but his study of Giotto (1915) convinced him that the Italian tradition was not yet exhausted. In 1917, while serving in the army, he met CHIRICO in Ferrara and they evolved PITTURA METAFISICA. He was associated with MORANDI in a quest for a heightened realism, thus departing entirely from his original Futurism.

CARRACCI. There were three Carracci, all Bolognese: Ludovico, and his cousins Agostino and Annibale, who were brothers.

Ludovico (1555–1619) probably entered the Bologna Guild in 1578. With his cousins, he founded a teaching Academy in Bologna in 1585/6, which became the most celebrated of its kind and was responsible for the training of most major Bolognese painters of the next generation, including Domenichino, Reni, and Guercino. He ran the Academy alone after his cousins left Bologna, but after this there was a notable falling off in his work, and he dwindled into a painter of large, rather sentimental, and didactic Counter-Reformation altarpieces, with none of the originality that his cousins, particularly Annibale, had stimulated in him.

Agostino (1557–1602) was principally an engraver who executed many plates after works by High Renaissance, and particularly Venetian, artists. He visited Venice and North Italy in 1580–1 and was in Parma with Annibale c.1585. His wide knowledge of North Italian painting reinforced the trend away from the dying forms of Roman Mannerism towards a fresh evaluation of the part to be played by the High Renaissance and classical tradition in the creation of the new and revitalized painting which culminated in the Baroque. He was in Rome in 1597–9, working with Annibale on the Farnese Gallery, but by 1600 had moved to Parma and was working there for the Farnese family when he died. His major altarpiece, the *Last Communion of S. Jerome* (Bologna), greatly influenced Domenichino.

Annibale (1560–1609) was a pupil of Ludovico, and was by far the greatest artist of the three. He may have travelled in Tuscany c.1583–4, was in Parma with Agostino and almost certainly visited Venice c.1585/6. He participated with Ludovico and Agostino in the Academy, and they all shared in the decoration of the Fava (1584) and Magnani (1588–91) palaces in Bologna. In 1595 he went to Rome to work for Cardinal Farnese on the decoration of the Farnese palace, and for this he first executed the 'Camerino', with an elaborate ceiling with subjects from classical mythology in fresco surrounding an oil-painting of *Hercules at the Crossroads* (now in Naples). The Gallery, which he next undertook, is a room some 66 feet long by 22 feet wide, and he designed for the barrel vault of the ceiling an elaborate illusionistic arrangement of mythological pictures supported by herms against an open colonnade, with, seated above the cornice, nude male figures reminiscent of those in Michelangelo's Sistine ceiling. The Farnese Gallery ranks with Raphael's decorations in the Stanze and the Farnesina and Michelangelo's Sistine ceiling as one of the great schemes of decoration. In its illusionism and imaginative scope it has a lightness of touch, a sense of humour, and a freshness of vision and fancy transcending his other works, where the conscious recreation of the grander aspects of the style of High Renaissance painters, particularly Raphael, Correggio, Andrea del Sarto, and the Venetians, is more readily perceptible. He was helped in the Gallery by Agostino until 1599, and by Domenichino (particularly in the landscapes) and Albani. It was finished by 1604, and in 1605 Annibale was first attacked by the illness which virtually prevented him from working and which eventually killed him.

There are works by one or more of the Carracci in the Royal Collection, Amsterdam (Rijksmus.), Berlin, Birmingham (City Mus.), Bologna (Mus., and churches), Boston (Mus.), Brussels, Dresden, Florence (Uffizi), London (NG, V & A), Milan (Brera), Modena, Munich, Naples, Oxford (Christ Church), Paris (Louvre), Parma, Rome (Borghese, Capitoline; Colonna, Doria and Spada Colls.), Sheffield, the Vatican, Venice (Accad.), Vienna, and elsewhere.

Antonio (c. 1583–1618), an illegitimate son of Agostino, and Francesco, an illegitimate brother of Agostino and Annibale, were also painters and worked as assistants.

The term Eclectic, now discredited, was formerly applied to the Carracci as an imputation that their use of the High Renaissance and classical tradition involved a deliberate policy of selection and combination of the forms and concepts, often mutually incompatible, characterizing the style of their predecessors. There is no evidence of any such specific programme underlying either the teaching in their Academy or their own works, which illustrate the truism that all art is nourished by tradition.

CARRIERA, Rosalba (1675–1757), was a Venetian woman pastellist who had a great vogue in Venice, Paris (1720–1), Vienna, and among English tourists. A famous example, *Horace Walpole in Fancy Dress*, does not represent him, as there are pastels at Houghton Hall (private coll.) of Horace and his two brothers, with inscriptions by himself, and the faces differ. She painted numerous portraits in pastel, but she also had great success with her nearly pornographic girls, which are considerably earlier examples of the genre than those of GREUZE. There are 157 of her pastels in Dresden.

CARRIÈRE, Eugène (1849–1906), was taken prisoner in 1870 and thus had the opportunity to see, in Dresden, some pictures by Rubens which influenced his style at the beginning of his career: the 'mistiness' which is so characteristic of his works (giving many of them the appearance of a smudgy sepia-print) dates from his later years. His famous portraits of Daudet and his daughter, of Verlaine (both 1891), and of Edmond de Goncourt on his death-bed (1896), are all in the Louvre, along with many others. Another *Verlaine* is in Boston and there are works in Avignon and Toulon.

CARSTENS, Asmus (Erasmus) Jakob (1754–98), was Danish-born, but was the most *ernst* of the German Neoclassic artists; his difficult temperament prevented him from obtaining due recognition. He made his first Italian journey in 1783, but money soon gave out and he had to return. He was helped to settle in Berlin in 1787 and became Professor at the Academy (1790), but in 1792 he was able to return to Rome, where he died. He made almost no paintings and his work consists of large cartoons in black and white chalk, very much influenced by Michelangelo, so that the combination of Neoclassical rectitude with Mannerist form is curiously reminiscent of BLAKE. There are examples in Berlin and Copenhagen and, especially, Weimar. His works became better known through the publication of engravings, 1864–84.

CARTELLINO (Ital. a little paper). A small scroll or piece of paper painted on a picture to appear like a real scroll affixed to the background or the small foreground parapet which is often supplied to limit the front of the foreground plane and provide something for the *cartellino* to be stuck to. The commonest use for a *cartellino* is to take the painter's signature, as in the works of Giovanni Bellini and Antonello da Messina, but it sometimes carries a religious invocation or the motto of the sitter in a portrait.

CARTOON. Nowadays this normally means a drawing with a humorous or satirical intention, but the original meaning (from Ital. *cartone*, a big sheet of paper) is quite different. A cartoon in this sense is a full-size drawing for a painting, usually worked out in complete detail, ready for transfer to the wall, canvas, or panel. The cartoon was rubbed on the back with chalk and the main lines were then gone over with a stylus thus transferring them to the canvas or panel; sometimes the main lines had their contours pricked through and fine charcoal dust was then 'pounced' through or a SPOLVERO was used to preserve the cartoon itself. The procedure for FRESCO was more complex but essentially the same. Several cartoons still survive and it is possible to tell which were used for transfer, from the presence of prickings or the indentation of the lines. The most famous of all, by Raphael, were for tapestries and therefore were not transferred in this way.

CASSATT, Mary (1844–1926), was born in Pittsburg, the daughter of a banker who offered little encouragement to her desire to be a painter.

In 1868, after travelling widely in Europe, she settled in Paris to study under Chaplin, a typical Academic painter, but was far more interested in Courbet, Manet, and the Impressionists. In 1877 she met Degas, who invited her to exhibit with the Impressionists, which she did in 1879, 1880, 1881, and 1886. She bought Impressionist paintings for herself and her family, tried to get other Americans to do so, and helped their dealer Durand-Ruel in some of his more difficult moments. She was partly blind by 1912, and totally so at her death. In 1914 she was awarded the Gold Medal of Honour of the Pennsylvania Academy, where she had studied 1861-6. She is well represented in American museums. She also made several fine coloured etchings, intended to make original works available at reasonable prices. These are mostly of domestic scenes and show a combination of Japanese colour printing techniques with the vision of Degas and Renoir. They are a unique and significant (though still undervalued) contribution to Impressionism and probably influenced BONNARD and VUILLARD.

CASSONE is an Italian word for a special kind of coffer used as a marriage-chest and containing the bride's household linen. They were often very richly decorated, with carved and gilt mouldings and painted panels at the front and sides and sometimes also inside and outside the lid. The great age of *cassoni* was from the 14th to the 16th century, and the subjects were usually mythological, of the *Rape of Helen* type, or from classical antiquity. The exact significance of some of the paintings inside the lids is still not clear and may have been quasi-magical. Many panels from the fronts of *cassoni* are now framed and hung as Old Masters, although most of the original painters were not regarded as more than craftsmen by their contemporaries: Uccello is an exception. A panel from a *cassone* is nearly always recognizable on account of its shape – some four to six feet wide by about a foot or eighteen inches in height.

CASTAGNO, Andrea del (perhaps 1421-57), was one of the most influential Florentine painters of the generation after Masaccio. The date of his birth is now thought to be as late as 1421/3, although it was formerly put at 1412 or even in the 14th century. He seems to have been precocious: traditionally he painted some effigies of rebels hanged by the heels, *c.*1440, from which he derived the nickname Andreino degli Impiccati (of the hanged men). He was certainly in Venice in 1442, when he signed and dated some frescoes in S. Zaccaria; but these do not give an unequivocal picture of his style in his youth, since they were painted in collaboration with the unknown Francesco da Faenza. He was back in Florence in 1444, designing a stained glass window for the Cathedral (still there), and soon after this he must have painted his frescoes of *Passion Scenes* and the *Last Supper* (Florence, S. Apollonia, now the Castagno Mus.). These were his first famous works and show the influence of Masaccio's scientific realism. In 1449–50 he painted an *Assumption* for S. Miniato fra le Torri (now in Berlin), which is far closer to the International Gothic style; and, for the last seven years of his short career, Castagno broke with the style of Masaccio (whom he could not have known) in favour of one based on the emotional and linear style of DONATELLO (who was alive and very famous): in fact Castagno translated Donatello's sculpture into terms of painting and thus influenced all 15th-century Florentine painters. The major examples of this Donatellesque style are the *Famous Men and Women,* painted for a villa at Legnaia, near Florence (now in the Castagno Museum). His last dated work was the equestrian fresco portrait of *Niccolò da Tolentino* in the Cathedral, a pendant to Uccello's *Hawkwood*. This is of 1456 and shows a more dynamic style than Uccello's, based partly on Donatello's *Gatta-melata*. In recent years a number of Andrea's *sinopie* have been recovered, justifying the praise lavished on him by contemporaries as a draughtsman. There are other works by him in Florence (SS. Annunziata) and in Edinburgh (NG), London (NG), New York (Met. Mus. and Frick Coll.), Venice (S. Marco), and Washington (NG).

CASTIGLIONE, Giovanni Benedetto (*c.* 1600 ?–65 ?), was a Genoese and a pupil of van DYCK, in whose studio in Genoa he worked from 1621. He was – for an Italian – much influenced by foreigners, for his style was formed by Flemish painters and Rembrandt's etchings, and later he was much influenced by POUSSIN and Rubens. Like Bassano, he was a great animal painter. He was in Rome by 1634, when he was in the Academy of S. Luke, and he remained until 1650 at least: it was at this time that he was influenced by Poussin. About 1648/50 he began to work for the Mantuan Court, which perhaps explains the influence of Rubens. His latest works have a deep mystical fervour, but he is principally remembered as the inventor of a kind of drawing in thin washes of oil-paint, and, more important, of the MONOTYPE. Excellent examples of both are in the Royal Collection (Windsor) and other works are in Bergamo, Birmingham, Dresden, Dublin, Genoa, Hartford Conn., Munich, Madrid, Montpellier, Ottawa, Paris (Louvre), Rome (Doria), Rouen, and Turin.

CASTING *see* PLASTER and BRONZE.

CATENA, Vincenzo (*c.* 1480–1531), was a Venetian painter who began as an imitator of Giovanni BELLINI and CIMA, but who entered into some kind of partnership with GIORGIONE in 1506 (according to an inscription on the back of Giorgione's *Laura* in Vienna); nevertheless, the influence of Giorgione did not make itself felt until after 1510 when Giorgione died. In the last twenty years of Catena's life he was also influenced by Palma Vecchio, Titian, and others. There are works by him in Berlin, Boston (Gardner), Budapest, Dresden, Edinburgh (NG), Frankfurt (Städel), Glasgow, Liverpool, London

(NG), Madrid (Prado), Milan (Brera), New York (Met. Mus.), Ottawa, Paris (Louvre), Venice (Accad., Correr, Querini, S.M. Mater Domini), Vienna (K-H Mus.), Washington (NG), and elsewhere.

CAVALLINI, Pietro (active 1273–1308), was the great representative of the Roman School slightly before GIOTTO. He painted fresco cycles and designed mosaics in a purely classical style which forms the link between the painting of antiquity and the revived forms introduced principally by Giotto. The mosaics in Sta Maria in Trastevere in Rome are recorded as having been signed and dated 1291 (but the evidence is very unsatisfactory); the fragmentary *Last Judgement* fresco in Sta Cecilia, also in Rome, is probably of 1293. He was in Naples in 1308 and the frescoes in S.M. Donna Regina are probably his.

CAVALLINO, Bernardo (1616–56), was a short-lived Neapolitan painter of small-scale figures set in a murky background. He was the major Neapolitan painter of the 1640s and early 50s until his death in the great plague of 1656. His few signed works include those in Molfetta (Apulia), Moscow, Rome, Stockholm, and the *S. Cecilia* of 1645, acquired by Hitler in 1941 and now the property of the Italian Government: the sketch for it is in Naples along with other works. Barnard Castle (Bowes Mus.), Birmingham (Barber Inst.), Boston, Cleveland Ohio, Detroit, Hartford Conn. (Wadsworth Atheneum), London (NG), Melbourne, Munich, New York (Met. Mus.), Sarasota Fla, Verona, Vienna (K-H Mus.), Washington (NG), and York also have examples.

CAVO-RILIEVO *see* RELIEF.

CELLINI, Benvenuto (1500–71), Florentine sculptor, goldsmith, and amorist, is best known for his *Autobiography* (1558–62: several English editions exist). This is one of the great autobiographies and gives us a glimpse of the processes of artistic creation as well as an insight into the troubled Italy of the years following the Sack of Rome in 1527; Cellini's love-life also features in considerable detail, not all of it quite credible. In 1519 he refused an invitation to go to England with TORRIGIANO, on the grounds that he could not do anything with the man who had broken the divine Michelangelo's nose. Instead he went to Rome, and, according to his own account, played a heroic part in the defence of the city during the siege. He also claims to have killed Charles de Bourbon, one of the Imperial commanders in the siege. As an artist Cellini was first influenced by the pupils of Raphael but later came very much under the shadow of Michelangelo, and his *Perseus* (1545–54: Florence, Loggia dei Lanzi) stood fittingly near Michelangelo's *David* and Donatello's *Judith*, its other main prototype. In 1537 and again in 1540–5 Cellini went to France to work for Francis I, for whom he made a salt-cellar (1540–3: now in Vienna) and the *Nymph of Fontainebleau* (1543–4: Paris, Louvre), whose sophisticated elegance and elongatedly Mannerist forms sum up the whole of the Second School of FONTAINEBLEAU. Imprisoned in 1556, apparently for immorality, in 1558 Cellini took the first steps towards becoming a priest but in 1560 he obtained his release from his vows. He also designed coins and medals and there are other works by him in Boston (Gardner Mus.), the Escorial, Florence (Bargello), and Oxford.

CENNINI, Cennino, wrote, *c.* 1390 or a little later, the earliest Italian treatise on painting, 'Il Libro dell'Arte', which is the source of most of our knowledge of early TEMPERA technique. He says in it that he was a pupil of Agnolo GADDI – and could therefore trace his artistic descent back to Giotto – but no works of his are known.

CERANO *see* CRESPI, G.B.

CÉSAR (*b.* 1921) was born César Baldacchini in Marseilles, but has lived in Paris since 1943. He is a sculptor who works with characteristic 20th-century materials – mostly crushed motor-cars and similar industrial debris. He has three workshops, one in a foundry, so that material is handy, and he can then weld the crushed scrap into assemblages that often take their titles from the location of the workshop, e.g. *Man of Saint-Denis* (London, Tate).

CÉZANNE, Paul (1839–1906), was probably the greatest painter of the last 100 years. He was born in Aix-en-Provence, the son of a wealthy banker and tradesman, and was educated at the Collège Bourbon where he became friendly with Zola. The friendship, which meant a great deal to Cézanne, lasted until the publication of Zola's 'L'Œuvre' in 1886: the character of Claude Lantier seemed a travesty of Cézanne, and not only to Cézanne. In 1861, after abandoning the study of law, Cézanne went to Paris, where he met PISSARRO and from 1862 he devoted himself to painting, living in Paris until 1870. The Franco-Prussian War drove him to L'Estaque and in 1872 he joined Pissarro at Pontoise. In the 1860s his ardent Southern temperament expressed itself in a series of more or less erotic and melodramatic pictures – in particular the *Rape* of 1867 – which were not unnaturally received with no enthusiasm. While closely associated with Pissarro Cézanne began to paint landscapes in an Impressionist technique and he exhibited at the first IMPRESSIONIST Exhibition of 1874. One of his pictures was among those which incurred the greatest public displeasure. This was the most extraordinary of all his erotic fantasies, the *Modern Olympia*, so called as a rather dubious compliment to MANET: it represents a fat squatting female being disrobed by a negress while a man (probably Cézanne himself) watches with interest. In the midst of the chaste Impressionist landscapes the effect must have been startling, particularly as these pictures are painted with great violence and the colour is often piled on with a palette-knife. During the 1870s Cézanne digested the theories of colour and light which the Impressionists were then developing: in the 3rd Impressionist Exhibition (1877) he showed 16 pictures and one critic praised them highly. Gradually he calmed down the exuberant Romanticism of his temperament and abandoned a Delacroix-like technique, to which he was not really suited. His great achievements lay in the direction of an ever more subtle analysis of colour and tone, totally different from the Impressionists' analysis in that they sought to capture the surface, the impression, and therefore painted quickly. Cézanne's analysis was infinitely prolonged and laborious because he sought to use colour as a means of modelling and as the ultimate expression of the underlying forms of visible objects. In this he was, of course, following classical prototypes and some of his recorded sayings are of great importance. He said that he 'wanted to do Poussin again, from Nature' and that he wanted 'to make of Impressionism something solid and durable, like the art of the Museums'. This was clearly because Impressionism was lacking in formal qualities, but 'when colour has its greatest richness then form has its plenitude': in particular, the basic ideas of CUBISM have been claimed to be implicit in his teaching that the painter ought to look for the cone, the sphere, and the cylinder in Nature. Cézanne himself was no theorist and constant insults from public and critics made him very chary of exposing himself. When his father died in 1886 he found himself rich and able to live in seclusion in Provence, mainly at the Jas de Bouffan, near Aix, a house his father had bought and which once contained some very early Cézanne decorations. In 1890 he was invited to exhibit in Brussels by Les XX, in 1895 he had his first big show, and from about 1900 his genius was fairly widely recognized. In the last years of his life he returned to some of his favourite early themes – in particular, the big compositions of *Bathers*, with nude figures in a landscape setting. His great contribution was to show that colour and tone values must be considered as one thing and not two; in doing this he made Impressionism into something solid, like Poussin. Because his analysis was pursued with agonizing care many of his pictures were never finished – he is said to have abandoned a portrait of Vollard the dealer, after more than a hundred sittings, with the remark that he was not displeased with the shirt-front! Naturally, still-life and landscape offered the greatest freedom in this respect and most of his flowerpieces were probably painted from artificial flowers; his few portraits were of himself or of people whose sittings could be protracted almost indefinitely.

There are pictures by him in Amsterdam (Stedelijk Mus.), Basle, Berlin, Berne, Boston, Budapest, Cardiff, Chicago, Cleveland Ohio, Columbus Ohio, Edinburgh, Essen (Folkwang Mus.), Glasgow, The Hague (Gemeente Mus.), Hamburg, Helsinki, Leningrad, London (NG, Tate, and Courtauld Institute), Los Angeles, Mannheim,

Merion Pa (Barnes Foundation), Minneapolis, Munich, New York (Met. Mus., Brooklyn Mus., and Guggenheim), Northampton Mass. (Smith College), Oslo, Ottawa, Paris (Louvre), Philadelphia, Prague, Providence RI, St Louis, São Paulo, Stockholm, Washington (NG and Phillips), and Zurich.

CHADWICK, Lynn (b. 1914), is a British abstract sculptor who works in welded iron and steel, copper, bronze, metal compositions, plaster, and glass. Like his contemporary BUTLER he was trained as an architect. After war service he turned to sculpture and produced mobiles under the influence of CALDER (he made three big mobiles for the 1951 Festival of Britain), but has now evolved 'balanced Sculptures' which do not attempt to exploit the quality of movement. He was awarded a prize at the 1956 Venice Biennale and is now represented in museums in Adelaide, Brighton, Bristol, Brussels, Buffalo, Chicago, London (Tate and V & A), Manchester (Whitworth), Montreal, New York (M of MA), Ottawa, Paris (Mus. d'Art Moderne), Pittsburgh, Rome, Rotterdam, and Turin.

CHAGALL, Marc (b.1887). Born in Vitebsk, Chagall was trained in St Petersburg and came under the influence of Bakst and the Ballet. He was in Paris 1910–14 and was influenced by Cubism; in 1917 he was made Commissar of Fine Arts in the Vitebsk area and founded an Academy. After disagreements with MALEVICH he resigned and worked for theatres in Moscow, returning to Paris in 1923. By now his highly imaginative style was fully formed, and he was painting more or less recognizable objects in unusual juxtapositions and floating rather insecurely in space, his colour was very rich and most of his subjects were poetic evocations of Russian village life, but he came increasingly to paint religious pictures. His fantasies have greatly influenced the SURREALISTS. In 1941 the Museum of Modern Art, New York, invited him to America, where he remained until 1946. In 1961 he completed a series of stained glass windows of the Twelve Tribes of Israel for a synagogue near Jerusalem, followed by mosaics and tapestry for the Knesset in 1966. He also did decorations for the Metropolitan Opera, New York, in 1966, following the success of his ceiling for the Paris Opéra, completed in 1964, and a memorial window in Tudeley, Kent (1967). There is a Chagall Mus, at Cimiez, Nice.

CHAMPAIGNE, Philippe de (1602–74), was born in Brussels and received his first training there as a landscape painter. He went to Paris in 1621, and worked with POUSSIN on the decoration of the gallery in the Luxembourg Palace which was to house Rubens's series of the Life of Marie de' Medici. In 1628 he became Painter to the Queen Mother, Marie de' Medici, and also worked for Louis XIII and Richelieu, painting for the Cardinal the dome of the Sorbonne church, the full-length portrait, and the triple portrait similar to Van Dyck's one of Charles I, made for the same purpose – to be sent to Bernini as a model for a portrait bust. About 1643 he began to work for the Jansenists of Port Royal. This austere Catholic sect deeply influenced him and accentuated his tendency, observable as early as the middle 1630s, towards a form of classicism parallel to that then being developed independently in Rome by Poussin. His early portraits show his links with Rubens and van Dyck, but there is no strong Baroque feeling in his later works – no ecstasies, radiances, visions. All is kept clear and lucid, to appeal to reason rather than to the emotions, with severe composition, frequently of the frieze type used by Poussin, cool strong colour, and an unexaggerated though strict naturalism. His portraits of lawyers, merchants, and the group portraits of the sheriffs of Paris, show his human and sensitive grasp of character, and are as grave and sober as his sitters. His finest portraits are those in the votive picture made on the recovery of his daughter, a nun at Port Royal, who was stricken with paralysis and cured in 1661 by the prayers of the community. There are works in the Royal Collection and in Alençon, Amsterdam, Barnard Castle (Bowes Mus.), Berlin, Boston, Brussels, Detroit, Florence (Pitti, Uffizi), The Hague, Hull, Le Mans, London (NG, Wallace Coll.), Lyons, New York (Met. Mus.), Paris (Louvre), Rome (Gall. Naz.), Rouen, São Paulo, Toledo Ohio, Toulouse, Versailles, Vienna, and Washington.

CHANTREY, Sir Francis (1781–1841), was a celebrated sculptor of portrait statues and busts, whose large fortune was bequeathed to the RA for purchase of 'works of Fine Art of the highest merit ... executed in Great Britain'. The choice of many works has been criticized. There are works by Chantrey in the Royal Collection, in Edinburgh (NPG), London (NPG, V & A, Soane Mus., RA, Westminster Abbey, St Paul's), Oxford (a large collection of casts), and elsewhere.

CHAPUS see MASTER OF THE AIX ANNUNCIATION.

CHARCOAL is made from twigs of willow or vine which have been charred away from the air. Each twig will then make a blackish mark that is easily rubbed off if necessary. Charcoal is sometimes used for drawing on paper, but its principal use is for making the preliminary drawings on walls or canvases as the first stage in a painting.

CHARDIN, Jean Baptiste Siméon (1699–1779), the finest 18th-century French painter of still life and genre, became a member of the Academy in 1728 and was its treasurer and hung its exhibitions for over 20 years. His early works are not so much inspired by similar Dutch paintings as extensions of the Netherlandish cabinet pictures so popular in France in the 18th century: they take up the modest size and restricted range of subjects, adapting them to French tastes and feeling. His still-lifes, composed of the simplest elements – kitchen utensils, vegetables, game, baskets of fruit, fish, and similar materials – are exceptional in their impasted technique and solid colour, with tremendous depth of tone achieved by extreme delicacy of touch and the subtle use of dragged and scumbled colour. They have a straightforward honesty of vision and truth of representation untainted by mere verisimilitude. His genre scenes are small in format, with small figures in homely interiors, redolent of the simple domesticity of every-day bourgeois life, unsentimentalized and unidealized, but not rendered picturesque by any concessions to low life, or titillating by excursions into modish society. In the 1775 Salon he exhibited two self-portraits and one portrait of his wife in pastel (all now in the Louvre) which are masterpieces of acute analysis and breadth of vision and technique, far excelling LATOUR's more fashionable pastel portraits. Fragonard was his pupil for a short time.

There are works in Amiens, Angers, Berlin, Boston, Cambridge Mass. (Fogg Mus.), Chicago, Detroit, Dublin, Edinburgh, Glasgow (Hunterian Mus. and Burrell Coll.), The Hague, Hartford Conn., Indianapolis, Kansas City, Leningrad, London, Merion Pa (Barnes Foundation), Minneapolis, New York (Frick Coll. and Met. Mus.), Oberlin, Ottawa, Paris (Louvre and Jacquemart-André), Potsdam, Princeton, Rotterdam, St Louis, Springfield Mass., Stockholm, Vaduz (Liechtenstein Coll.), and Washington (NG and Phillips Gall.).

CHARONTON see QUARTON.

CHASSÉRIAU, Théodore (1819–56), was a pupil of Ingres who was deeply influenced by Delacroix – the only artist of his time to make this difficult synthesis with any success. He used subject matter from the repertory of both: Biblical and Shakespearean illustration, scenes from North African life, reconstructions of classical life, religious and allegorical decorations, and portraits, often – like Ingres' – in lead pencil. He is well represented in the Louvre in Paris, and in French provincial museums.

CHAVANNES, Puvis de, see PUVIS.

CHIAROSCURO (Ital. light-dark). As generally used, chiaroscuro (or the French *clair-obscur*) means the balance of light and shadow in a a picture, and the skill shown by the painter in the management of shadows. The word tends to be used mainly of painters like Rembrandt or Caravaggio whose works are predominantly dark in tone. A *chiaroscuro woodcut* is a woodcut, linocut, or other similar engraving which is printed from several blocks, in exactly the same way as a colour print, in imitation of a drawing in several shades of monochrome wash, each shade being cut on a separate block. Intermediate tones may be obtained by careful overprinting of two or more blocks. The first artist to specialize in this technique was Ugo da Carpi (*c*.1480–*c*.1525), and many designs for such woodcuts go back to PARMIGIANINO.

CHIRICO, Giorgio de' (*b*.1888), an Italian painter who founded the quasi-Surrealist PITTURA METAFISICA movement with CARRÀ at

Ferrara in 1917. In the 1930s he abandoned his 'modern' ideals and returned to a form of imitation of the Old Masters. There are works by him (mostly unregenerate) in Rome (Gall. d'Arte Mod.) and in Chicago, Detroit, London (Tate), New York (M of MA), and elsewhere.

CHRISTUS PATIENS AND CHRISTUS TRIUMPHANS are the names given to the two main types of the very large painted crucifixes which normally stood on the rood screens of medieval churches. Very few still exist in their original positions, most of the surviving examples having been cut down in size and transferred to side chapels or sacristies. The Christus Patiens (Suffering Christ) represents Christ as dead on the Cross whereas the Triumphans type represents Him with open eyes and outstretched arms standing on, rather than hanging from, the Cross. The dramatic emphasis of the Patiens type is certainly to be connected with the influence of S. Francis. An early example is provided by the work of GIUNTA Pisano.

CHRISTUS (Cristus), Petrus (d.1472/3), was the major Bruges master after the death of Jan van EYCK (1441). Christus settled there in 1444, but he is nevertheless sometimes said to have been Jan's pupil: two pictures – a *S. Jerome* (1442: Detroit) and a *Madonna* (probably finished 1443: New York, Frick Coll.) – have been claimed as works by Jan finished by Christus. His own dated works range from 1446 to 1452 (or 1457), the latter being a *Madonna* in Frankfurt (Städel) which has some of the characteristics of a *Sacra Conversazione* in the Italian manner. This is signed, but the date is not clear: there is also a portrait in Los Angeles which is very similar in style to ANTONELLO da Messina, but it is not signed and may not be his. These two pictures are often read with a Milanese document of 1457 referring to 'Piero di Burges' to endow Christus with an Italian period and an influence on Antonello. In fact, Christus's style is a simplification of Jan van Eyck's with very smooth, rounded forms; but he also painted two versions of the *Lamentation* (Brussels and New York, Met. Mus.) which both derive more or less from Roger van der Weyden's Escorial *Deposition*. The New York picture is simpler and the two are put at opposite ends of Christus's career; whether early or late depending on individual choice of the moment of maximum Eyckian influence. There are other pictures by him in Berlin, Copenhagen, Dessau, Kansas City, London (NG), Madrid (Prado), and Washington (NG).

CIBBER, Caius Gabriel (1630–1700), sculptor to William III, carved the bas-relief at the base of the Monument, London, in 1673–5 while imprisoned for debt. He worked at Hampton Court (1692–4) and at St Paul's Cathedral (1698–1700), but his best-known works are *Melancholy* and *Raving Madness* (inspired by Michelangelo's Medici tombs) formerly over the gate of Bedlam and now in the Guildhall Museum, London.

CIMA da Conegliano, Giovanni Battista (1459/60–1517/18), was a Venetian painter much influenced by Giovanni BELLINI and also by Antonello. There are pictures by him in Amsterdam, Baltimore (Walters), Berlin, Birmingham, Bologna, Boston (Mus. and Gardner), Cambridge (Fitzwm), Conegliano near Treviso (Cath. and S. Fiore), Detroit, Dresden, Edinburgh (NG), Florence (Uffizi), Frankfurt (Städel), London (NG, Wallace Coll., Courtauld Inst.), Milan (Brera, Poldi-Pezzoli, Ambrosiana), New York (Met. Mus.), Paris (Louvre), Parma, Philadelphia (Johnson), Vicenza, Washington (NG), York, besides a large number in Venice.

CIMABUE (c. 1240–1302?) is generally put at the beginning of modern art, as the teacher of GIOTTO (which he may, in fact, have been). The basis of his fame is due to the choice of his name by Dante as an example of the transitory nature of earthly glory: 'Cimabue thought that he held the field in painting, but now Giotto is acclaimed and his fame obscured' (Purg. XI, 94–6). The early commentators drove home the moral by insisting that Giotto was Cimabue's pupil and he is consequently credited with the introduction of a more naturalistic style into the Byzantine formulae current in Tuscan Dugento painting. In fact, he is known to have been in Rome in 1272 and may well have been influenced by the classical current which is represented by CAVALLINI; but the sole securely documented work by Cimabue is a *S. John*, part of a large mosaic in the apse of Pisa Cathedral, on which he was working in 1302. This affords only the most tenuous grounds for stylistic generalizations, but there are several works attributed to him on what seem good traditions. These include the very damaged frescoes in the choir of the Upper Church at Assisi and the repainted *Madonna of S. Francis* in the Lower Church as well as the very large and impressive *Sta Trinita Madonna* (Florence, Uffizi) which can reasonably be compared with the *Ognissanti Madonna* by Giotto or the *Rucellai Madonna* attributed to DUCCIO (both in Florence: the latter was formerly attributed to Cimabue). Other works attributed to him are in Arezzo (S. Domenico), Bologna (S. M. dei Servi), Florence (Baptistry, Sta Croce – a Crucifix very badly damaged in the floods of 1966 – S. M. Novella), Paris (Louvre), and Washington (NG).

CINQUECENTO (Ital. five hundred). The 16th century, i.e. the fifteen hundreds.

CIONE, Nardo and Jacopo di, *see* ORCAGNA.

CIRE PERDUE *see* BRONZE.

CLASSIC, CLASSICAL, ROMANTIC. In addition to the meanings given in any standard English Dictionary there are some extra ones in common use in writing on art. *Classic* is usually used to mean an established excellence and *classicism* a form of art derived (or thought to be derived) from the study of Antique exemplars, which are by definition *classic*: this became a fixed dogma in the mid-18th century, though prevalent enough from the 16th century or even earlier. The 18th-century form is better referred to as NEOCLASSICISM, and, with its passion for rules and Academies, it soon led to a marked reaction. It is a curiosity of history that the French Revolution fostered both ideals simultaneously, but the Romantic movement, with its unbridled expression of the passions, its love of the exotic, and its occasional absurdities, reached its apogee about 1830 in France, Britain, and Germany. In France the situation was clarified by the presence of INGRES and DELACROIX as the living embodiments of the two approaches to life and art, and indeed the dichotomy is still apparent in CUBISM and SURREALISM, the antithesis between form and content (or subject). The culmination of 19th-century art can be seen to some extent in CÉZANNE, who began as a positively orgiastic Delacroix follower and ended as one of the great classic French artists, like Poussin.

CLAUDE Gellée (Claude Lorraine) (1600–82) was born near Nancy, and, according to Sandrart, was first trained as a pastry-cook. By *c.*1613 he was in Italy, working as *garzone* for the Cavaliere d'ARPINO and the landscape painter Agostino Tassi. From 1618 until 1620 he was probably in Naples, then he settled in Rome as Tassi's pupil and assistant. In 1625 he returned to Nancy, but by 1627 was back in Rome; there is no certain work before 1630, but by the end of the 1630s he had a big reputation as a landscape painter and his popularity has remained undimmed ever since. The 195 drawings in the LIBER VERITATIS (now in London, BM), begun *c.*1635, were his own record of his paintings, made to guard against copies and forgeries.

The obvious comparison is with POUSSIN, but while the latter derived his heroic landscapes from Titian and Annibale Carracci, Claude's sources lie chiefly in the romanticized poetic landscapes of the later Mannerists such as Tassi, and the northerners, ELSHEIMER and the BRILLS. Like them, Claude used the later Mannerist traditions of the division of the picture into areas of dark greenish-brown foreground, light green middle distance, and blue far distance, with the composition set out in COULISSES to create a sense of infinite distance, and tree forms treated as feathery fronds in silhouette. He also developed Elsheimer's landscape of mood created by poetic lighting effects, though not so much with strong chiaroscuro as by looking into the sun in a blaze of golden light. His composition remains virtually constant: a large mass of trees on one side counterbalanced by a smaller mass on the other, a middle distance with some small feature such as a bridge or a farm, and a far distance of mountains, rivers, or the Campagna in the most delicately atmospheric handling. In his seascapes and port scenes, the additive detail of shipping, masonry, rigging, merchandise lying on quays, does not really alter this arrangement of the parts, and allows him to concentrate on the magical effects of sunlight shimmering on water. He also uses small figures (possibly sometimes by other artists) not for themselves but as a part of Nature, the drama of their action absorbed into immensities of light and space. His working drawings, loose and free in their handling, exemplify his way of looking at landscape by gradations of tone rather than colouristically, and his poetic rather than formal vision. SANDRART describes Claude's working methods and claims (perhaps wrongly) to have persuaded him to make paintings in the open air, as well as drawings. He also claims to have gone on sketching parties with Claude, Poussin and BAMBOCCIO. Most older galleries have examples.

CLAW CHISEL *see* STONE CARVING.

CLEVE, JOOS VAN, *see* JOOS.

CLODION, Claude Michel, called Clodion (1738–1814), was a French sculptor who won the Rome Prize in 1759 and went there in 1762. In 1767 he left the French Academy in Rome but stayed on in the city working for Catherine II of Russia and other patrons until he was sharply reminded that he had been sent to Rome at the King's expense for the glory of France. He went home in 1771, but did not become an associate of the Academy until 1793; never became a full Academician; and never received official commissions, other than the *Montesquieu* for the King (1779–83; the marble now in the Institut, Paris). His works were almost entirely small figures of nymphs, satyresses, and similar subjects treated in a frankly sensual way and he was nearly ruined by the Revolution and Republican Virtue. He rallied, however, and adopted the Greek taste so successfully that he was able to get work on the Colonne de la Grande Armée (1806–10) and the Arc de Triomphe du Carrousel (1806–9). There are works by him in the Louvre, Paris; London, Wallace Collection and V & A; Versailles and other French museums.

CLOISONNISME *see* BERNARD.

CLOUET, François (*d*. 1572), was the son of Jean Clouet, whom he succeeded as Court Painter in 1541. He was sometimes called Janet. His earliest signed painting is the *Pierre Quthe* (1562: Paris, Louvre), which seems to indicate that he had been to Italy as it closely resembles the work of BRONZINO and other Florentines. He specialized in portrait drawings, most of which are now in Chantilly (Musée Condé): there are paintings in the Royal Collection and in Edinburgh (NG), Florence (Uffizi and Pitti), London (Wallace Coll.), New York (Met. Mus.), Rouen, Versailles, Vienna, and Worcester Mass.

CLOUET, Jean II ('Janet') (*d*. 1540/1), was probably the son of the Flemish painter Jean Clouet, painter to the Duke of Burgundy. Jean II is first recorded in a poem of 1509 – where he is referred to along with Leonardo and others. He later became Court Painter in France, his son François succeeding him in 1541. He made a number of portrait drawings (mostly in the Musée Condé, Chantilly) which are comparable to those of Holbein as records of a Court though quite different in style. Paintings ascribed to him are in the Royal Collection and at Antwerp, Edinburgh (NG), New York (Met. Mus.), and elsewhere.

COBRA *see* APPEL.

COELLO, Claudio (1642–93), was of Portuguese descent but became the last great painter of the School of Madrid. The principal influences on his work seem to have been RUBENS, van DYCK, and TITIAN – that is, he used his opportunities to study in the Spanish Royal Collection, but he also visited Italy at some time 1656/64 and was influenced by contemporaries such as DOLCI. He became Painter to the King in 1683, and was promoted Pintor de Cámara in 1686. His pictures tend to be overcrowded and rather complicated, and are reminiscent of Neapolitan Rococo. His masterpiece is *Charles II adoring the Blessed Sacrament* (1685–90: Sacristy of the Escorial), the space of the actual sacristy being continued in the picture, which contains the portraits of many courtiers and priests. There are other works by him in Frankfurt, London (Wellington Mus.), Madrid (Prado, Acad., and churches), and Munich.

COELLO, Sánchez, *see* SÁNCHEZ.

COLD COLOUR, TONE: COOL COLOUR, TONE. Those colours and tones which are blue, blue-green or blue-violet in general effect. The opposite of HOT or WARM.

COLE, Thomas (1801–48), was the principal painter of the HUDSON RIVER School of American landscape painting. He was born in England and worked as an engraver before emigrating to the US in 1818. In 1819 he went to the W. Indies and was deeply impressed by the beauties of the scenery. His efforts as a landscape painter met with little success until he settled in New York in 1825, when he began to be recognized, and in 1826 he was one of the founders of the National Academy of Design. He returned to England in 1829 and went to Italy in 1832, living in a studio that traditionally had been Claude's: Cole admired Claude (and therefore Turner) more than any other painter, but his works are far more dramatically Romantic than theirs. He returned to America in 1832, but made another trip to Europe in 1841. He is represented in Cleveland, Hartford Conn., Minneapolis, New York (Met. Mus.), Toledo Ohio (an extraordinary fantasy, *The Architect's Dream*, 1840), and other US museums.

COLLAGE (from Fr. *coller* to stick). A picture built up wholly or partly from pieces of paper, cloth, or other material stuck on to the canvas or other ground. The device was much used by the early Cubists, who would stick pieces of newspaper on to pictures painted in an otherwise normal way, and by the Dadaists. In his last years Matisse used pieces of coloured paper as a complete substitute for painting. *See also* FROTTAGE.

COMPLEMENTARY COLOUR. Each primary colour – red, blue, yellow – has a complementary formed by a mixture of the other two, and it is part of Impressionist theory that every primary has its complementary colour in the shadow cast by it. Thus, a yellow object will have violet in the shadows.

COMPOSITION. The art of combining the elements of a picture or other work of art into a satisfactory visual whole: in art the whole is very much more than the sum of the parts. A picture is well composed if its constituents – whether figures or apples or just shapes – form a harmony which pleases the eye when regarded as two-dimensional shapes on a flat ground. This is the sole aim of most abstract painting but in more traditional forms the task is made much more difficult by the need to project the forms in an ordered sequence into an imaginary depth or picture space without losing their effectiveness as a pattern. The word is often also used loosely to mean a work of art, a group, etc.

CONCA, Sebastiano (1680–1764), was a belated Baroque decorator. He was born near Naples and trained under SOLIMENA before moving to Rome in 1706. He was much employed in churches and also had a great reputation as a teacher. In 1751 he was commissioned to decorate the church of Sta Chiara in Naples (totally destroyed 1939/45) and he spent the rest of his life there. There are works by him in Augsburg, Dresden, London (NG), Parma, Rome (Accad., Borghese, Gall. Naz., and churches), Sarasota Fla, and elsewhere.

CONCRETE ART. A term used occasionally as a synonym for Abstract Art (e.g. by van DOESBURG).

CONEGLIANO *see* CIMA.

CONINXLOO, Gillis van (1544–1607), was an important link in the chain of landscape painters between Bruegel and the early 17th-century Dutch realist painters such as E. van de Velde, van Goyen, or S. van Ruysdael. Coninxloo travelled in France and Germany as well as his native Flanders before settling in Amsterdam, where he died. His type of landscape has much realist detail, especially in the trees and foliage, but is combined with fantasy of shape and of viewpoint, as well as adhering closely to the 'three tone' scheme – warm brownish foreground, green middle distance, and blue distance. There are works in Brussels, Dresden, Graz, Rouen, and Vienna.

CONSTABLE, John (1776–1837), was, with TURNER, the major English landscape painter of the 19th century. He first exhibited in 1802, but achieved only limited recognition, becoming an ARA in 1819 and an RA in 1829. His comment on the Suffolk countryside,

'These scenes made me a painter', takes little account of his skill in composition and his brilliant use of chiaroscuro as a unifying factor. In 1806 he travelled in the Lake District, but he was happiest with the vivid, dewy greens of water-meadows and mills, under fresh, windy skies, his deep knowledge of which he owed to the sky studies made under the influence of Luke Howard's 'The Climate of London' (1818–20). In 1824 his *Hay Wain* (shown at the Academy in 1821: now London, NG) and a *View on the Stour* were awarded a Gold Medal at the Paris Salon, and the great success of these and other works imported into France had an appreciable effect on the development of the BARBIZON School, and on the painting of the Romantic Movement – Delacroix, for instance, was enormously impressed by them.

He left few successors. His art lay in the representation of nature modified by the tradition inherited from the Dutch landscape painters of the 17th century, and he was the last great painter in this tradition. After him, Turner's 'airy visions, painted with tinted steam' – the phrase is Constable's – and the meticulous descriptive attitude of the Pre-Raphaelites exploited different, and contradictory, aspects of nature.

A large collection of his work was bequeathed to the Victoria & Albert Museum, London, by his daughter. There are also examples in Boston (Mus.), Cambridge Mass. (Fogg), Chicago, Cincinnati, Detroit, Dublin (NG), Dunedin NZ, Edinburgh (NG), Hartford Conn., Leeds, Le Mans, London (NG, BM, RA Diploma Gall., Tate, Guildhall, Courtauld Institute), Manchester, Montreal, New York (Met. Mus., Frick), Ottawa, Oxford (Ashmolean), Philadelphia (Mus.), San Marino Cal., Toledo Ohio, Toronto, Washington (NG, Corcoran, Phillips), Worcester Mass., and Yale University.

CONSTRUCTIVISM was principally a Russian movement which grew out of COLLAGE. Vladimir TATLIN in Moscow developed this into hanging and relief constructions, abstract in conception, and made of a variety of materials, including wire, glass, and sheet metal. He later turned to architectural and engineering schemes such as the projected monument to the Third International – a leaning spiral about 1,300 feet high with counter-rotating central sections. PEVSNER and his brother GABO evolved from Cubism, but only after returning to Moscow in 1917 did they become abstract Constructivists, publishing in 1920 – the year of the big Constructivist exhibition – their 'Realistic Manifesto', in which they restated the ideas of Archipenko and Boccioni that only movement in space and not volume was important in art.

By 1921 the movement was dead in Russia for political reasons and its practitioners turned to furniture design, the stage, typography – in fact, anything but painting and sculpture. Pevsner went to Paris in 1923, and Gabo worked in Germany until 1932. Constructivist ideas have had considerable influence on architecture and decoration, and their manifestations include abstract sculpture employing non-traditional materials such as perspex, or industrial methods such as welding.

CONTÉ. A proprietary name for synthetic black, red, or brown chalk.

CONTINUOUS REPRESENTATION. In many medieval – and some Mannerist – pictures there are representations of several successive incidents in the story, shown as taking place in different parts of the same picture. For example, a picture of the martyrdom of a saint may show all his miracles dotted about in the background. This is conveniently known as Continuous Representation.

CONTOUR (Ital. *contorno*). The outline which, in drawing or painting, forms the boundary of one shape, defining it in relation to another, so that the outline of a head against a wall is at once the pattern made by the head at that particular position against the wall, and also the shape as it were cut out of the wall by the impingement of the head. Contour means slightly more than outline, because an attentive study of any good drawing – and more especially one by INGRES – will reveal that the modulation of the contour traced by the point of the pencil can express the fullness and recession of forms and even the variety of texture and surface between bony structure and fatter tissue; whereas outline is no more than a boundary of forms or silhouette.

CONTRAPPOSTO. An Italian word used to mean a pose in which one part of the body is twisted in the opposite direction from that of the other – usually with the hips and legs in one way and the chest and shoulders twisted on the opposite axis. Michelangelo's fantastic virtuosity in this led to a sort of mania in the 16th century to see who could invent the most elaborate and improbable *contrapposto* for a figure supposedly performing some simple action.

CONVERSATION PIECE. A special kind of genre picture consisting of two or more small portraits of people represented in appropriate surroundings, usually domestic. It is an informal group portrait and usually represents members of the same family. HOGARTH, DEVIS, and ZOFFANY are among the best-known exponents of the genre.

COOPER, Samuel (1609–72), was an English miniaturist who enjoyed a European reputation: Aubrey called him 'the prince of limners' and his prices were not far short of LELY's. Unlike Hilliard, he regarded the miniature as a painting, not a drawing or piece of goldsmith's work, and he modelled his heads in light and shade. Walpole said: 'If a glass could expand Cooper's pictures to the size of Vandyck's they would appear to have been painted for that proportion. If his portrait of Cromwell could be so enlarged, I do not know but Vandyck would appear less great by the comparison . . .'. The

Cromwell is the best known image of the Protector (Coll. of the Duke of Buccleuch, replica in the Royal Coll.). Evelyn's Diary (10 January 1662) records 'Being call'd into his Majesties Closet, when Mr Cooper (the rare limner) was crayoning of his face and head, to make the stamps by, for the new *mill'd* mony, now contriving, I had the honour to hold the Candle whilst it was doing; choosing to do this at night & by candle light, for the better finding out the shadows ...'. A few days earlier, Pepys had been disappointed in his hopes of meeting Cooper; later, however (30 March 1668), he visited his house and saw his work 'which is all in little, but so excellent as, though I must confess I do think the colouring of the flesh to be a little forced, yet the painting is so extraordinary, as I do never expect to see the like again. ... Being infinitely satisfied with this sight, and resolving that my wife shall be drawn by him ...'. In fact, this miniature of Mrs Pepys cost him £30, and another £8. 3. 4. for its crystal and gold case, a large sum of money. Samuel's elder brother, Alexander (*d*.1660), was also a miniaturist who worked in Holland, Sweden, and Denmark. Both were the pupils of their uncle John HOSKINS, who probably anticipated them in treating a miniature like an oil painting. Both Coopers are represented in the Royal Coll. and London (V & A).

COPLEY, John Singleton (1738–1815), was a Boston painter, almost self-taught, who evolved a distinguished and direct portrait style for his New England clientèle. In 1774 he left America for good, visited Italy and much of Europe before settling in London, where competition with Reynolds and West profoundly altered his style, although his children retain an engaging vivacity. His *Brook Watson and the Shark* (1778: Christ's Hospital and Boston), *Death of Chatham* (1780: London, Tate) and *Death of Major Pierson* (1783: Tate) are notable for being among the first large pictures of modern history and grand scale genre subjects, of a type common in France during the Napoleonic period and the Romantic movement. There are examples in the Royal Collection, Cambridge Mass. (Fogg, Harvard), Cleveland Ohio, Dundee, New York (Met. Mus., Brooklyn), N. Carolina, Philadelphia (Hist. Soc.), Providence R I, Washington (N G, Corcoran), and Yale. The American museums contain most of his early portraits, of which there are many in Boston (Mus., and public buildings).

CORINTH, Lovis (1858–1925), was, like LIEBERMANN, one of the leading German Impressionists. He worked in Paris 1884–7 and painted in an Impressionist style until 1911, when he had a stroke. He was crippled by this, but forced his hand to work and from then on painted in a more violent and pessimistic way: some of his later works are crude and harshly Expressionist. There is a museum at Tapiau, in East Prussia (his birthplace), and he is well represented in German museums: other works are in Basle, Belgrade, London (Tate), New York (M of MA), Pittsburg, Vienna, and Zurich.

CORNEILLE de Lyon (active 1533/4–74) was a painter of small-scale portraits who was born in The Hague but worked in Lyons and was Painter to Henri II and Charles IX of France. There is no certain work by him, but a group of small portraits, similar to the work of François CLOUET but faintly Northern in style, is associated with him. They usually show half-length figures in black against a green or blue background: examples are in Boston, Cleveland Ohio, London (NG and Wallace Coll.), and New York (Met. Mus.).

CORNELIUS, Peter von (1783–1867), went to Rome in 1811 and there worked with OVERBECK and the NAZARENER until 1819. He then returned to Munich and became head of the so-called Munich School which sought to revive monumental fresco painting. Most of his works are in Munich, but he was also important as a teacher and administrator.

COROT, Jean Baptiste Camille (1796–1875), was born in Paris. His early training, from 1822 onwards, was with the classicizing landscape painters Michallon and Bertin, and in 1825 he went to Italy, via Switzerland, for two years. He spent most of his time in and around Rome, where he developed, through painting actually on the site, his sensitive treatment of light, form, and distance in terms of tonal values rather than by colour and drawing. In this he resembled MICHEL (whom he knew), but never to the point of abandoning, for works to be exhibited, the traditional classical or religious subject; this he used as a disguise for his unconventional vision, although these carefully composed landscapes have little of the spontaneity of his sketches from nature. He travelled widely in France in 1827–34, and returned to Italy for several months in 1834 and 1843, his journeys being recorded in his drawings or his *pochades*, which are small and very freely handled, and remarkable for the justness of their tonal values and the freshness of their colour.

By the early 1850s the tide of official and public favour had turned, possibly because by then he had developed for his Salon exhibits a fuzzy, woolly, poeticizing manner entirely different from the directness and keenness of observation found in his sketches. This muzzy treatment of the landscape and trees in soft, grey-green tones became immensely popular, and has assured to Corot the most notoriously prolific of all posthumous productions. His very late portraits and figure studies are entirely free from the blurred and formless approach of his public manner, and show that in his seventies he was able to absorb the ideas of younger men, such as Courbet and Manet. His personal prestige with the younger generation was very great, and he did all in his admittedly limited power to soften the rigours of the Salon jury towards the works of unacademic artists. He was a man of great simplicity and generosity and extremely charitable, as witness his support of Daumier in his blindness, Millet's widow, and his benefactions during the Franco-Prussian War. There are examples of his art – autograph or attributed – in almost every museum of any size all over the world; the works of Caruelle d'Aligny and Édouard Bertin, who were his companions in Rome in 1825-7 on many of his painting expeditions, are all too frequently confused with his.

CORREGGIO, Antonio (1494, or 1489–1534), worked mostly in Parma, in a style that looks forward to the Baroque and even, in its softness, to the French 18th century. His earliest works show the combined influences, oddly disparate, of MANTEGNA, whose pupil he traditionally was, and LEONARDO (who influenced all early 16th-century painters in North Italy). From Leonardo he developed a very soft painterly style, extolled by 18th-century critics as MORBIDEZZA, or the 'Correggiosity of Correggio'. This softness, which in works like the SS. *Placid and Flavia* (Parma) is allied to a virtually Baroque movement and emotion, is characteristic of all his oil-paintings and achieves, in his mythologies, a tender and voluptuous quality. His frescoes show so much of the influence of Michelangelo and Raphael as to make a visit to Rome before 1520 fairly certain. He is first documented as a painter in 1514, and his first set of frescoes was painted about 1518: these are the decorations in the Camera di S. Paolo, Parma, which derive partly from the SOTTO IN SÙ perspective of Mantegna's Mantuan frescoes and from his *Madonna della Vittoria*, and partly from Leonardo. Other frescoes in Parma are the cupolas of S. Giovanni Evangelista (1520-3) and the Cathedral (documented from 1522, but probably executed 1526-30). Both these have extremely illusionistic effects as seen from below, and anticipate the ceilings and domes of the 17th century, particularly those of LANFRANCO. The Cathedral dome, representing the *Assumption*, is composed of ascending concentric circles of flying figures and is said to have been described unkindly (but not altogether unreasonably) by one of the canons as 'a hash of frogs' legs'.

Apart from Parma there are no other frescoes by Correggio, but oil-paintings are in the Royal Collection and Berlin, Budapest, Chicago, Detroit, Dresden, Florence (Uffizi), Frankfurt (Städel), London (NG, Wellington Mus.), Madrid (Prado, Acad.), Milan (Brera, Mus. Civico), Modena, Munich, Naples, New York (Met. Mus.), Paris (Louvre), Philadelphia (Johnson Coll.), Pavia, Rome (Borghese), Vienna, and Washington.

CORTONA, Pietro da, *see* PIETRO.

COSMATI. A name given to the marble and mosaic workers in Rome from the 12th to the 14th centuries, many of whom were of the same family. They made many pavements, pulpits, tombs, and other ecclesiastical furnishings in marble with inlays of coloured stones and glass, mosaic and gilding. Towards the end of the period they also produced sculpture. 'Cosmati work' is thus a generic term for work in coloured stone.

COSSA, Francesco del (1435/6–probably 77), worked in Ferrara from 1456 as a follower, to some extent, of Cosmè TURA; but his style was probably first formed in Florence and his *Crucifixion* (Washington, NG) although probably a late work shows clear traces of the style of Castagno. Like all the other Ferrarese of the 15th century he was basically influenced by MANTEGNA and also by Piero della Francesca, whose lost frescoes in Ferrara may well have influenced Cossa's best-known works, the frescoes of the *Months* in the Palazzo di Schifanoia at Ferrara. These were completed in 1470 and Cossa – who did not paint all of the cycle – was so ill-satisfied with his pay that he left the city and spent the rest of his life in Bologna. The Schifanoia frescoes are charming and mildly lascivious, but they can hardly rank with the Camera degli Sposi at Mantua, in which Mantegna also depicted the daily life of a Court, nor (presumably) would they have compared with the lost Pieros. Parts of the Schifanoia frescoes are lost, parts are by pupils, and one Month, *September*, is possibly the earliest work of Ercole ROBERTI. There are works by Cossa in Berlin (Schloss Mus.), Bologna (Pinacoteca and churches), Dresden, Forlì, London (NG), Milan (Brera), Paris (Jacquemart-André), and Washington (NG).

COSTA, Lorenzo (c.1460–1535), was trained in Ferrara and brought up on the style of TURA, COSSA, and ROBERTI. He moved to Bologna by 1483 and worked there for the Bentivoglio Court, becoming the partner of Francesco FRANCIA and tempering the ferocity of his Ferrarese style with Francia's Umbrian softness. In 1506 he was appointed Court Painter at Mantua in succession to Mantegna and painted two *Allegories* for Isabella d'Este (now in the Louvre, Paris); later in life, however, ill-health led to his eclipse by GIULIO Romano. There are works by him in the Royal Collection and in Amsterdam, Berlin, Bologna (Pinacoteca, S. Giacomo Maggiore, and other churches), Boston, Dresden, Dublin, Florence (Uffizi), London (NG), Lyons, Mantua (S. Andrea), Milan (Brera), New York (Met. Mus.), Paris (Louvre, Jacquemart-André), Toledo Ohio, Vaduz (Liechtenstein), and Washington (NG).

COSTRUZIONE LEGITTIMA. An early PERSPECTIVE system described in the Treatise on Painting written in 1435 by the architect, humanist, and aesthetic theorist Leon Baptista Alberti (c.1404–72). It is based on geometrically constructed picture space, in which the height of the figures to be represented in the finished picture is taken as the norm by which the base-line of the picture and also the height of the horizon are to be fixed and proportioned. A point approximately in the centre of the horizon then becomes the central Vanishing Point, on which all lines that recede into the picture are made to converge:

lines which are parallel to the Picture Plane can have no point on which to converge and an element of distortion is thus introduced, since a house in the picture will seem to have one side subject to the effects of perspective while the other side remains unaffected, as a quadrilateral parallel to the picture plane. Examples of this construction can be found in e.g. the works of UCCELLO.

COSWAY, Richard (1742–1821), was a fashionable miniaturist of great charm and ability. He became an RA in 1771, was a collector of Old Master drawings, dealt in pictures as a side-line, was a famous fop and a friend of the Prince of Wales (later George IV). In 1781 he married Maria Hadfield, who had been born and brought up in Florence, and was also a miniaturist, though not in her husband's rare class. They entertained lavishly, and perhaps imprudently in view of the odd rumours which circulated about their house. After her husband's death Maria Cosway returned to Italy, where she ran a girls' school at Lodi until her death in 1838.

COTES, Francis (1726–70), first made his mark in 1748 as a pastellist. He was a pupil of KNAPTON, but used brighter colour than his master, and shows the influence of Rosalba Carriera and Liotard. During the 1760s he worked more in oils, and adopted Reynolds's portrait style, in contrast to the more conservative patterns of Knapton. He was Reynolds's most serious competitor before Gainsborough arrived in London, but his portraits have neither Reynolds's inventiveness nor Gainsborough's charm, though at his best – in e.g. his portrait of Sandby (London, Tate) – he is fine indeed. He occupied the house and studio in Cavendish Square later used by Romney. There are examples in the Royal Coll., Cardiff, Edinburgh (NPG), Leicester, London (Tate), Oxford (Ch. Ch.), and elsewhere.

COTMAN, John Sell (1782–1842), was a painter in watercolour and oil, whose austere sense of design produced some of the finest English landscape paintings of the early 19th century. He was born in Norwich but worked in London, partly with Dr MONRO, and exhibited at the RA 1800–6. He then returned to Norwich, where he first exhibited in 1807, becoming the leading member of the NORWICH SCHOOL. While living in East Anglia he visited Normandy in 1817–18 and 1820, making drawings for Dawson Turner's 'Architectural Antiquities of Normandy' (1820–2), and in 1834 he returned to London. From 1831 he used watercolour mixed with rice-paste, producing an impasted and richly wrought surface which (to modern taste) is rather vulgar and totally different from his earlier work, which depends solely on simple flat washes of colour and clearly defined, almost geometric planes. There are works by him in Norwich, London (BM, NG, Tate, V & A), and in Birmingham, Hull, Leeds, and Port Sunlight (Lady Lever Gall.). His sons Miles Edmund (1810–58) and John Joseph (1814–78) were also painters, and are well represented in Norwich.

COULISSE (Fr.). The side-pieces at either side of the stage, so arranged as to give room for exits and entrances. The idea has been taken over to describe the type of composition in which the effect of recession into space is obtained by leading the eye back into depth by the overlaps, usually alternately left and right, of hills, bushes, winding rivers, and similar devices.

COUNTERPROOF. A mirror-image reproduction made by damping an original drawing or engraving, laying a damp sheet of clean paper on it, and then running both through a press. It is sometimes done by the artist himself in order to bring a fresh eye to his work by seeing it in reverse, but it is also the commonest and simplest method of faking 'original' drawings. Such fakes are easily detected because reversal turns right hands into left, makes the normal diagonal direction of shading appear left-handed and so on. An offset is the same as a counterproof, but has a wider meaning, e.g. in printing.

COURBET, Gustave (1819–77), was born at Ornans, near the Swiss border of France. After he went to Paris in 1840 he taught himself partly by copying in the Louvre, partly by working in the Atelier Suisse. He evolved a vigorous naturalism, tinged with Venetian and Caravaggesque influence, which he used in scenes from everyday life, portraits, nudes, still-life, flowers, seascapes, and landscapes; these last are often of the mountain scenery near Ornans and sometimes include nudes, hunting scenes, or deer amid snow, and his scenes from daily life extend from the depiction of abject poverty in the *Stonebreakers* (1849: formerly Dresden, destroyed in 1945), to the representation of a peasant funeral in the *Burial at Ornans* (1850: Louvre) which contains over forty lifesize figures, and to a quasi-philosophical manifesto in the huge *Painter in his studio* (1855: Louvre). He was rabidly anti-clerical – his *Return from the Conference*, depicting drunken priests, was rejected both by the official Salon and the Salon des Refusés in 1863, and was finally bought by a strict Catholic who destroyed it – and he further injured himself by meddling in politics and involving himself in the aftermath of the 1848 revolution and the Commune in 1871. The first added to his reputation of being a dangerous firebrand, as violent as his painting; the second caused him to be imprisoned and heavily fined for his part in the destruction of the column commemorating Napoleon in the Place Vendôme and eventually brought about his flight to Switzerland, where he died.

Courbet was strongly anti-intellectual, despite his friendship with Baudelaire and with the socialist writer and theorist Proudhon. He rejected all idealization in art, rebelled against both classicism and romanticism for their literary and exotic subjects, proclaimed that only realism was truly democratic, and that the noblest subject for the artist was the worker and the peasant. He also rejected selection and composition in landscapes, though his own prove this to have been more theory than practice. He exhibited regularly at the Salon, which awarded him a gold medal in 1849, but his works generally incurred bitter criticism. In 1855 and 1867, on the occasion of International Exhibitions in Paris, he held large private exhibitions of his works in an attempt to offset official neglect. Both attracted more unfavourable than helpful notice, but they established the precedent of privately organized exhibitions, also followed by Manet and the Impressionists. His flight from France in 1873 prevented him from knowing much of the Impressionists, though he knew Monet personally; he was particularly valuable to them as an example of fairly successful intransigence towards academism. Courbet was a convivial Bohemian, of inordinate vanity, and with an unendearingly caustic tongue. His technique was imperfect; reworkings and bitumen have played havoc with many works, and his brushwork and use of the trowel-shaped palette knife are often as insensitive as his colour, though in his best works this can be extraordinarily rich, his chiaroscuro deeply satisfying and his vivid, unconventional approach dramatically exciting. Many of his nudes range from the mildly to the highly erotic. In his last years, he employed unworthy assistants in what was virtually a production-line system of painting Swiss landscapes, though at this time he was crippled by the payment of the indemnity exacted by the French State for the Vendôme Column. His ideas and works were more favourably received in Belgium, Holland, and Germany than in France; although he had a certain influence on Whistler, this was indignantly repudiated by the American. There are works in Baltimore, Basle, Berne, Birmingham (Mus.), Boston (Mus., Gardner), Bristol, Budapest, Cambridge (Fitzwm), Cambridge Mass. (Fogg), Chicago, Cincinnati, Cologne (Mus.), Columbus Ohio, Detroit, Dublin (NG), Glasgow (Mus., Burrell Coll.), Hartford Conn., Kansas City, Leeds, Liverpool, London (NG, Tate, V & A), Manchester, Mannheim, Minneapolis, Montpellier, Montreal, New York (Met. Mus., Brooklyn), Northampton Mass. (Smith College), Ornans, Ottawa, Paris (Louvre, Petit Pal.), Philadelphia (Mus., Acad.), Portland Oregon, Providence RI, Rochester NY, St Louis, Toledo Ohio, Toronto, Washington (NG, Corcoran, Phillips), Yale University, and many French provincial museums.

COUSTOU, Guillaume I (1677–1746), was one of a family of French sculptors. He was a pupil of his uncle COYSEVOX and went to Rome. He became Director of the Academy and worked for the Crown from 1707; his masterpieces, the *Chevaux de Marly*, were made for the Royal park at Marly 1740/5 and are based on antique prototypes. They are now at the entrance to the Champs-Élysées in Paris. His son,

Guillaume II (1716–77), became an Academician in 1742 and produced much sculpture for churches and public buildings. There is a bust by him in London (V & A) and his *Vulcan*, made for the Academy, is in Paris (Louvre). Liverpool has a fine bust by him of his brother Nicolas (1658–1733), who was also a sculptor.

COUTURE, Thomas (1815–79), was a French history and portrait painter whose best-known work is the *Romans of the Decadence* (1847: Louvre), which united the soft colour of the 18th century to the contemporary classic strictness, but is in fact a 19th-century orgy picture of a recognizable type. He was a pupil of GROS and was a good portrait painter, with a bold attack, and is now remembered as an outstanding teacher, whose pupils included FEUERBACH as well as MANET. His *Etex* (Birmingham) shows his influence: much of the so-called Spanish influence on Manet's early work is in fact derived from Couture's freedom of handling and sharp tonal contrasts. Outside France there are pictures in Boston, Bristol, Budapest, Cambridge (Fitzwilliam Mus.), Cambridge Mass. (Fogg Mus., a sketch for the *Decadence*), Cleveland, Edinburgh, Glasgow, London (Wallace Coll., including the first idea of the *Decadence*, dated 1843), Philadelphia, Providence RI, and Toledo Ohio.

COX, David (1783–1859), was a watercolour painter who studied for a while under Varley (1804) and first exhibited at the RA in 1805. He lived by teaching and published several books, of which the best-known is the 'Treatise on Landscape Painting and Effect in Watercolours', 1813–14 (reprinted 1922). His favourite painting ground was North Wales, but he visited Holland and Belgium in 1826 and France in 1829 and 1832. His effects are extremely broad, with a vigour of handling that sometimes appears forced, as if for exhibition. In 1836 he discovered accidentally a kind of cheap wrapping paper made in Dundee, which exactly suited his style, since the rough, slightly tinted paper absorbed the washes quickly. A similar kind of paper is now marketed as 'Cox Paper'. In 1840 he took lessons in oil-painting from MÜLLER, but his watercolours have always been more prized. The best collection of his work is in his native Birmingham, but other works are in Cardiff, London (BM, Tate, V & A, and Courtauld Institute), Manchester (City Gall. and Whitworth), and other provincial museums. His son David (1809–85) was also a painter.

COYPEL, a dynasty of French painters active in the 17th and 18th centuries. The founder was Noël (1628–1707) whose career began in 1646 and who painted in a style derived from POUSSIN. He decorated the Invalides in Paris (*c.* 1700–7), worked for the Gobelins tapestry factory from 1674 and had a distinguished career in the Academy. He became a Member in 1663, Professor 1664, and Director in 1695. The influence of LEBRUN got him the appointment as Director of the French Academy in Rome 1672-4. Some of his writings were published posthumously. There are pictures by him in Paris (Louvre), Madrid, and many French provincial museums.

His son Antoine (1661-1722) was the most famous of the family. He began his training in Rome in 1672 with his father and was made a member of the Academy in Paris in 1681, becoming Director in 1714, and Rector in 1716. In 1717 he was ennobled. His works are evidence of the triumph of RUBÉNISME by the 1690s, but the vast ceiling of the Chapel at Versailles (1708) is much more reminiscent of Roman High Baroque illusionism as practised by BACICCIA at the Gesù. There are works by him in Berlin, Florence, Madrid, Paris (Louvre), and many French provincial museums.

Antoine's half-brother Noël Nicolas (1690-1734) was also a painter and pastellist, and became a Member of the Academy in 1720. Antoine's son Charles Antoine (1694-1752) also had a distinguished academic career, becoming First Painter to the King in 1743 and Director of the Academy in 1747. He was widely read and himself wrote forty pieces for the stage; Voltaire remarked that there was no other example in his day, 'De rimeur peignant de sa force, Ni de peintre rimant comme lui.' His huge output included book-illustrations and tapestry designs as well as religious pictures, portraits and writings on art. He was the originator of the idea of the École des Élèves protégés which was a special school for promising Academy students who received a state pension and an education fitting them for further training at the French Academy in Rome and subsequent membership of the Academy itself. The programme of the school consisted of professional studies in painting and sculpture and courses in ancient and modern literature and history, mythology, and all the learning thought proper to the painter of history in the 18th century. There are works by him in Paris (Louvre, Jacquemart-André and Gobelins Mus.) and in other French museums, and in Berlin, Cleveland Ohio, Hartford Conn., Minneapolis, New York (Met. Mus.), Philadelphia, and Sarasota Fla.

COYSEVOX, Antoine (1640-1720), was the chief sculptor to Louis XIV of France and worked much at Versailles, in a vigorous Baroque style derived ultimately from Bernini. This may also be seen in his portraits, such as the *Charles Lebrun* (London, Wallace Coll., the original terracotta) or the *Matthew Prior* (Westminster Abbey). He is well represented in the Louvre, Paris and in Versailles. COUSTOU was his nephew and pupil.

COZENS, Alexander (c.1717-86), was born in Russia (though the picturesque story that Peter the Great was his father is not now credited). He was in Rome in 1746 and appears to have gone to the Continent again in 1764, but most of his time was spent as a drawing master. He is best known for his system of 'BLOT drawings' – in

1781 Beckford described him as 'almost as full of systems as the Universe' – which developed an idea adumbrated by Leonardo da Vinci. A blot or dots made haphazard on the drawing paper would suggest a landscape or other composition, which could then be worked out in full. This system was set out in his 'New Method of assisting the Invention in the Composition of Landscape' (1785/6). He also wrote several other books. There are drawings and blottings by him in London (BM, V & A, Tate Gall., and Courtauld Institute), and in Bedford, Birmingham and Manchester (Whitworth).

COZENS, John Robert (1752–97), was the son of Alexander Cozens and was, according to Constable, the 'greatest genius that ever touched landscape' . . . 'Cozens is all poetry'. His entire work consists of landscape painting in watercolours and only one oil-painting, of 1791, is known (in a private collection). He went to Switzerland and Italy with the famous connoisseur Payne Knight in 1776–9 and was in Rome in 1778–9, when his style seems to have been modified by contact with Swiss watercolourists, notably Ducros, who was said to be an innovator in technique. He returned to Switzerland and Italy, going as far south as Naples, in 1782–3, this time in the train of William Beckford, the eccentric author of 'Vathek'. On these journeys Cozens discovered the grandeur of the Swiss Alps as well as the better-known classical beauties of the Italian landscape; his gentle and poetic landscapes are muted in colour and soft in lighting, being predominantly blue-green or blue-grey in tonality. Some time in 1793 his mind gave way, and early in 1794 he was under the care of Dr MONRO, who regarded him as incurable. He died in 1797 without recovering. He exercised an enormous influence on the next generation since both Turner and Girtin worked for Dr Monro and copied drawings by Cozens. There are watercolours by him in the Royal Collection and in Aberdeen, Birmingham, Cambridge (Fitzwm), Leeds, London (BM, V & A, Tate, Soane Mus.), Manchester (Whitworth), Oxford (Ashmolean), and elsewhere.

CRANACH, Lucas I (1472–1553), painter, etcher, and designer of woodcuts, was in Vienna in 1503 and had probably been there since 1500. In 1505 he went to Wittenberg to become Court Painter to the Electors of Saxony and there he met Luther, became his friend and designed propaganda woodcuts for him. His earliest works are religious subjects in which the landscape plays a great part; they are therefore linked with the ideas of the DANUBE School. In Wittenberg his style changed considerably, partly on account of the large shop he set up. He seems to have invented the full-length portrait as an independent work of art, for the splendid pair of *Henry the Pious of Saxony* and his *Duchess* (1514: both in Dresden and probably originally on one panel) certainly ante-date the Italian examples by MORETTO and others, and probably ante-date other German examples; only

CARPACCIO's *Knight* has a claim to be earlier. All his life Cranach continued to paint splendid portraits, including a large number of versions of *Luther*, but at the same time he developed a new kind of highly erotic female nude, usually full-length, painted with a glossy enamel-like finish and purporting to represent Lucretia, Venus, or some other character. From about 1505–9 he made a number of woodcuts, much influenced by Dürer, and from about 1520 he designed many more, often rather crudely executed, to illustrate the Bible or the writings of the Reformers. Most of his pictures are signed with a winged snake and the monogram LC, but it is very difficult to distinguish his own works from those produced in his shop or by his sons Hans (*d*. 1537) and Lucas II (1515–86). There are pictures in the Royal Collection and in Augsburg, Basle, Berlin, Boston, Breslau (Mus. and Cath.), Bristol, Brunswick, Brussels, Budapest, Cincinnati, Cologne (Wallraf-Richartz), Darmstadt, Detroit, Dresden, Florence (Uffizi), Frankfurt (Städel), Glasgow (Burrell), Kansas City, Leipzig, Leningrad, Lisbon, Liverpool, London (NG, Courtauld Inst.), Milwaukee, Munich, New York (Met. Mus.), Nuremberg, Oslo, Ottawa, Paris (Louvre), Philadelphia, Sarasota Fla, Stockholm, Vaduz (Liechtenstein), Vienna (K-H Mus., Akad., and Albertina), Weimar, Yale, and many other museums.

CRAQUELURE. The network of fine cracks which covers the surface of any old painting, caused by shrinkages and the movement of the ground and the paint film and varnish. There are characteristic crack-formations for each type of ground and paint film and they also vary with age and with the skill of the original painter. *Craquelure* remains one of the principal means of proving forgery, even though really high-class forgers use elaborate electrical and chemical means of counterfeiting the effects of time.

CREDI, Lorenzo di (*c*. 1458–1537), was a Florentine painter who was the fellow-pupil of LEONARDO under VERROCCHIO, whose principal assistant on the painting side of the business he seems to have become. He was in Verrocchio's shop in 1480/1 and was still there in 1488, when Verrocchio died. His style is technically admirable but is otherwise an insensitive and highly-coloured version of Leonardo's earlier works. There are several works by him in Florence and others in Berlin, Boston (Gardner), Cambridge Mass. (Fogg), Cleveland, Dresden, Liverpool, London (NG), Naples, New York (Met. Mus.), Oxford (Ashmolean), Paris (Louvre), Philadelphia (Johnson), Princeton NJ, San Marino Cal., the Vatican, Yale, York, and elsewhere.

CRESPI, Daniele (*c*. 1598–1630), was probably related to G.B. Crespi and was much influenced by him. His career was cut short by the plague of 1630, but like Cerano he expressed Counter-Reformation piety, and his best-known work is the *S. Charles Borromeo's Lenten Meal* (*c*. 1628) in S. Maria della Passione, Milan, which has many other paintings by him. His *S. Bruno* cycle in the Certosa at Gareg-nano, Milan, of 1629, shows the influence of Rubens and van Dyck and was followed by a similar, less good, cycle in the Certosa at Pavia. There are works in Milanese museums and churches and also in Berlin, Budapest, Florence (Uffizi), Madrid (Prado), Munich, Piacenza (S. M. di Campagna), Vienna (K-H Mus.), and Wellesley College, Mass.

CRESPI, Giovanni Battista 'Il Cerano' (*c*.1575–1632), was the major Lombard Mannerist of the early 17th century. He was born at Cerano, near Novara, and visited Rome and Venice; as a result, the main influence on his early style, Gaudenzio FERRARI, was overlaid by the influences of BAROCCI, Tintoretto and Veronese. He settled in Milan *c*.1598 and worked for Cardinal Federigo Borromeo, con-tributing to the scenes from the life of S. Charles Borromeo, painted for Milan Cathedral between 1602 and S. Charles's canonization in 1610. In 1620 he was appointed first Director of the painting section of the Cardinal's newly-founded Accademia Ambrosiana, and in 1629 he became head of the sculpture workshop of the Cathedral (his designs for sculpture are in the Cath. Mus.). His paintings reflect the piety of the age of S. Charles (*d*.1584) and are Mannerist principally on account of their emotional quality and their pale, clear tonality with a favourite lemon, grey, and pink colour scheme. With MORAZ-ZONE and G. C. PROCACCINI he was the leading Milanese painter of the early 17th century and a curious *Martyrdom* (Milan, Brera), painted before 1625, shows all three collaborating in 'the three-handed picture'. There are works in many Milanese churches and in the Ambrosiana, Brera and Castello Museums and also in Bristol, Detroit, Florence (Uffizi), Pavia (Certosa), Princeton NJ, Turin, Varese (S. Vittore), and Vienna.

CRESPI, Giuseppe Maria (1665–1747), was a Bolognese painter, trained in the academic tradition, which he came to loathe. In his youth, Bologna was still the Mecca of foreigners studying in Italy, but he predicted its end as a School and lived long enough to see it replaced by Rome. He developed a vivid genre style: dark shadows and very strong lights – time has accentuated the contrasts – and a passion for effects of light, which often involved a surrender to anecdote and gives the details of his settings an almost Dutch character, although they are, in fact, derived from the Caravaggesque tradition. He influenced PIAZZETTA, who used his low tones, rich greys, and his light effects. He died blind. There are works in Birmingham, Bologna, Boston (Mus.), Cambridge Mass. (Fogg), Dresden (the *Sacraments*, his best-known works), Florence (Uffizi, Pitti), Munich, Paris (Louvre), St Louis, the Vatican, Vienna, Washington (NG), and else-where.

CRISTUS, Petrus, *see* CHRISTUS.

CRITZ *see* GHEERAERTS.

CRIVELLI, Carlo (*d*.1495/1500), was a Venetian painter, probably trained in the VIVARINI workshop, imprisoned in Venice for adultery in 1457. Some Paduan training is also likely, since his strongest stylistic affinities are with SQUARCIONEsque painters such as Schiavone, and his hard, wiry style is powerfully influenced by MANTEGNA. In 1465 he was recorded in Zara (now Zadar), Dalmatia, and must soon after have moved to the Marches of Italy, where he is documented from 1468, mostly in Ascoli Piceno. Though he always signed himself as a Venetian, he never returned to Venice. In 1490 he was knighted – a rare distinction for an artist. All his pictures are of religious subjects, and old-fashioned in type since he did not use the SACRA CONVERSAZIONE form until it had been current in the rest of Italy for some 30 years; he also used, until the 1480s, the old-fashioned device of raised plaster details, such as crowns and saints' attributes, giving a three-dimensional quality to his linear and highly stylized forms in which there is a strong element of Late Gothic fantasy. His iconography is very elaborate, and the gourds and fruits in garlands, and other complicated details, all further the inner significance of his hieratic images. Vittorio Crivelli, possibly a younger brother, worked in a similar style, but was less accomplished. Many of Carlo's works are still in the churches for which they were painted, but 12 pictures are now in London (NG), and the Brera in Milan also has important examples.

CROME, John (1768–1821), was, with COTMAN, the major artist of the NORWICH School. He began life as an errand boy but apprenticed himself to a sign painter and is said to have taught himself by being allowed to copy Gainsborough and Hobbema in the collection of Thomas Harvey of Catton, who was his patron from 1790. Certainly the Dutch 17th century is the principal influence on his style, together with that of Wilson. His observation of Norfolk scenery has the same freshness as Hobbema and Ruisdael, while Cuyp and Wilson influenced his sense of design and of light. He founded the Norwich Society of Artists in 1803 and exhibited regularly there. In 1814, along with many other British artists, he went to Paris to see the pictures looted by Napoleon, and on the way he visited Belgium. He was a notable etcher and is well represented in the BM. There are paintings by him in Norwich and in Boston, Edinburgh, London (NG, Tate, Kenwood, Courtauld Institute), New York (Met. Mus.), Ottawa, and elsewhere. He is often called 'Old Crome' to distinguish him from his son John Bernay Crome (1793–1842), who imitated him. The *Water Frolic* (London, Kenwood) is probably a joint work: others by the son are in Norwich.

CROSS-HATCHING *see* HATCHING.

CUBISM is the parent of all abstract art forms. It grew out of the efforts of PICASSO and BRAQUE to replace the purely visual effects of Impressionist preoccupation with the surface of objects with a more intellectual conception of form and colour. Their starting point was Cézanne, who had striven to the same ends, but Cubism carried much further the ideas of the unity of the two-dimensional picture surface, and the analysis of forms and their inter-relation, since they deliberately gave up the representation of things as they appear in order to give an account of the whole structure of any given object and its position in space. This meant, in practice, combining several views of the object all more or less superimposed, expressing the idea of the object rather than any one view of it. The first exhibition of such pictures was in 1907 in Paris. The name Cubism was derisive, for it excited as much opposition as Impressionism itself, or the then recent FAUVISM: it was much influenced by Negro art, by Picasso's interest in Iberian sculpture, and by reaction from the pattern-making of Fauvism. Gris, Léger, Delaunay, and Derain were among the early adherents and the new aesthetic was soon preached by two practising Cubist painters, Gleizes and Metzinger, whose book, 'Du Cubisme', was published in 1912 and later translated into English, while the poet Apollinaire followed in 1913 with 'Les Peintres Cubistes'. The first phase, under the influence of Cézanne, lasted from 1906 to 1909; the second, sometimes called High or Analytical Cubism, lasted from 1909 to 1912 and excluded interest in colour or handling while concentrating on the breaking down of forms; finally, Late or Synthetic Cubism (1912–14) allowed a re-emergence of tactile qualities, colour, and handling. ORPHIC CUBISM is a derivative.

CURRIER, Nathaniel, published in 1840, three days after the disaster, a highly-coloured print of the burning of the steam-boat Lexington in Long Island Sound. The edition went like wildfire, and established him as the most important publisher of 'Colored engravings to the People'. James Ives joined the firm in 1852, and it became Currier and Ives in 1857. The prints were lithographs, hand-coloured on a mass-production system of one girl to each colour, and for some 50-odd years they published about three new prints each week on every aspect of American life – views, portraits of notabilities, Wild West, Indian, sporting and pioneering scenes, fires and other disasters, the Civil War, temperance and political tracts – which reached into the farthest confines of the land, and also had a considerable sale abroad.

CUYP, Aelbert (1620–91), was a Dordrecht painter, principally of landscape and animals, but also of sea-pieces, portraits, and still-life, such versatility being rare in the Dutch School. He was the son and pupil of Jacob Gerritsz. Cuyp (1594–after 1651), a painter of portraits and landscapes. In his earlier works Aelbert was influenced by van GOYEN and S. van RUYSDAEL and painted landscape with the same fidelity to nature; later, however, he became more and more interested in the play of light, and especially of those effects of golden glow which the Italianate Dutch landscape painters had learned from Claude. In his later works Cuyp resembles Jan BOTH in his light effects and his use of semi-Italian scenery and *staffage*. His light is, however, always poetic in feeling and exerted an incalculable influence on the development of English painting, since nearly all his best works are still in Britain; in the Royal Collection, in Glasgow (a rare religious work), London (NG, Wallace Coll., Dulwich, Kenwood), Oxford, and in other galleries and many private collections. Others are in Amsterdam (Rijksmus.), Antwerp, Berlin, Brussels, Cape Town, Dordrecht, Dublin, Frankfurt (Städel), The Hague, Munich, New York (Met. Mus.), Paris (Louvre), Philadelphia, Rotterdam, Toledo Ohio, Toronto, Vienna (K-H Mus.), Waddesdon, Bucks. (National Trust), and Washington (NG). Many pictures signed A C are by his imitator Abraham CALRAET.

Benjamin Gerritsz. Cuyp (1612–52) was Aelbert's father's half-brother and painted genre scenes in the manner of OSTADE, with some influence from the early Rembrandt.

D

DADA (Fr. hobby-horse) was a nihilistic precursor of SURREALISM, invented in Zürich during World War I, a product of hysteria and shock lasting from about 1915 to 1922. It was deliberately anti-art and anti-sense, intended to outrage and scandalize, and its most characteristic production was the reproduction of the *Mona Lisa* decorated with a moustache and the obscene caption LHOOQ (read: *elle a chaud au cul*) 'by' DUCHAMP. Other manifestations included ARP'S COLLAGES of coloured paper cut out at random and shuffled, ready-made objects such as the bottle drier and the bicycle wheel 'signed' by Duchamp, Picabia's drawings of bits of machinery with incongruous titles, incoherent poetry, a lecture given by 38 lecturers in unison, and an exhibition in Cologne in 1920, held in an annexe to a café lavatory, at which a chopper was provided for spectators to smash the exhibits – which they did.

DADDI, Bernardo (c.1290–1349/51), was a pupil of Giotto but was influenced by the Lorenzetti: that is to say, he attempted to fuse the plastic qualities of Giotto with some aspects of Sienese art and in this he represents the trend of the generation after Giotto, both in Florence and Siena. His triptych of 1328 in Florence, Uffizi, is a typical work; other works are in Florence and in the Royal Coll. and Baltimore, Berlin, Boston (Mus. and Gardner), Cambridge Mass. (Fogg), Edinburgh, London (Wallace Coll., Courtauld Inst.), New York (Met. Mus., Historical Soc.), Paris (Louvre, Mus. des Arts Décoratifs), Philadelphia (Johnson), the Vatican, Washington (NG), and York.

DAHL, Michael (1656/9–1743), was a Swedish painter who was KNELLER's only serious rival. He probably came to London about 1682, made a Grand Tour in 1685, travelling through Paris, staying long in Rome, and visiting Venice and Naples before returning via Frankfurt to London, where he decided to settle in 1689. He had a long and successful career. His style is softer than Kneller's, warmer and less forced. There are works in London (NPG, Nat. Marit. Mus., Dulwich), English provincial museums, and Stockholm.

DALI, Salvador (b.1904), was originally a Cubist but became one of the leading Surrealists until he abandoned its implied Marxism and returned to the Catholic Church. New Brunswick, New York, and other US museums have pictures. There are examples in Glasgow and London (Tate).

DANCE OF DEATH (Ger. *Totentanz*). A typically macabre late medieval subject, in which Popes, Emperors, Lords, and so on down to Artisans are shown as being whirled off in a dance with skeleton Popes,

Emperors, and so on, and not enjoying the experience. The most celebrated of these cycles (which were sometimes frescoed in cemeteries) is the woodcut series by HOLBEIN the younger.

DANTI, Vincenzo (1530–76), was a Perugian sculptor much influenced by Michelangelo. His first work was the bronze *Julius III* (1555: Perugia) but he later worked mainly in Florence, where he is best known for his completion of SANSOVINO's *Baptism of Christ*, on the Baptistry, and for his own bronze group of the *Decollation of S. John Baptist*, also on the Baptistry. There are other works in Florence, in the Bargello and elsewhere.

DANUBE SCHOOL (Ger. *Donauschule, Donaustil*). This is really only a name for the pre-eminence of the Danube region in the formation of modern landscape painting: the romantic effects and the emotional sympathy between landscape and human action found in ALTDORFER's pictures are the principal examples but other major painters of the 'School' are the young CRANACH and Wolf HUBER.

DARET, Jacques (*d.* after 1468), was a painter in Tournai who, in 1427, became the apprentice of CAMPIN. He painted an altarpiece for S. Vaast, Arras, 1433–5 (now in Berlin, Lugano (Thyssen Coll.), and Paris (Petit Pal.)), which is documented as his, and which shows very strongly the influence of the MASTER of FLÉMALLE: hence the identification of Flémalle with Campin receives strong support. Some light is also cast on the origins of Roger van der WEYDEN.

DAUBIGNY, Charles François (1817–78), was a French landscape painter much influenced by the BARBIZON School, who worked mostly near Paris but who went to Italy in 1836 and also visited England, Spain, and Holland. He was a friend of Corot and was admired by Monet; he thus forms a link between the Impressionists and their predecessors of the Barbizon School. There are pictures by him in Aberdeen, Boston, Budapest, Edinburgh (NG), Glasgow, London (NG, Tate), Montreal, New York (Met. Mus.) and Washington, as well as many French museums.

DAUMIER, Honoré (1808–79), worked as a cartoonist on 'La Caricature', founded in 1830, and was imprisoned in 1832 for representing King Louis Philippe as Gargantua. After the suppression of 'La Caricature' in 1835, he joined 'Charivari', and made, for this and other similar journals, some 4,000-odd lithographs, mostly of the aptest and bitterest political and social satire. His watercolours and wash drawings of scenes in the Courts of Justice, and every-day life, are untouched by any romantic feeling for picturesque poverty and his large oil-paintings, many on the theme of Don Quixote, are loosely handled, with calligraphic brushwork and intense light and shadow. He became blind in his old age, and was rescued from desperate poverty by Corot. He also made some sculptures.

There are works in Baltimore (Mus., Walters), Boston (Mus.), Cambridge Mass. (Fogg), Cardiff, Glasgow, London (NG, BM, V & A, Tate, Courtauld Inst.), Montreal, New York (Met. Mus., Brooklyn), Ottawa, Paris (Louvre, Petit Pal.), Philadelphia (Mus.), Washington (NG, Corcoran, Phillips), and elsewhere.

DAVID, Gerard (d. 1523), was born in Oudewater in Holland but was in Bruges by 1484. He was the last master of the Bruges School, painting gently pious pictures in a 15th-century style which was superseded in his own lifetime by the new, Italianate, Antwerp style, just as the commercial prosperity of Bruges faded before the rise of Antwerp. David seems to have gone to Antwerp and joined the Guild there in 1515, but he was certainly back in Bruges by 1521 and he died there. His only documented picture is a *Sacra Conversazione* (1509: Rouen), but two *Justice Scenes* of 1498 are certainly his (Bruges). Many pictures are ascribed to him, in Amsterdam (Rijksmus.), Antwerp, Berlin, Brussels, Chicago, Cleveland, Denver, Detroit, Dublin, Edinburgh, the Escorial, Florence (Uffizi), Frankfurt (Städel), Granada, Greenville SC, London (NG), Madrid (Prado), Munich, New York (Met. Mus., Frick Coll.), Paris (Louvre), Philadelphia (Johnson), St Louis, Stockholm, Toledo Ohio, Vienna, Washington (NG), Worcester Mass., and elsewhere.

DAVID, Jacques Louis (1748–1825), was distantly related to Boucher, who recommended his being placed under VIEN in 1765. He won the Prix de Rome in 1774, and went there with Vien in 1775, remaining until 1781. He abruptly forsook Boucher's Rococo in favour of the new NEOCLASSICISM and at the same time adopted the strong chiaroscuro of the Caravaggesques. In 1782 he became an Academician and in 1784 he returned to Rome to paint the *Oath of the Horatii* (1785: Paris, Louvre), which was acclaimed in Rome and again in Paris at the Salon of 1785. It was perhaps the most important French Neoclassic picture, simple, severe, and uncompromising in its subordination of colour to drawing; it was also highly topical in its Republican implications. It was followed by other large pictures extolling classical and republican virtues. During the Revolution David became a Deputy and voted for the death of Louis XVI. He became dictator of the arts, designed huge propaganda processions – such as the Feast of Reason – abolished the Academy, and helped found the Institut which replaced it; he also painted memorial portraits of the martyrs of the Revolution, Lepelletier de Saint Fargeau and Marat. After the fall of Robespierre he was imprisoned, and his release was due to the intercession of his pupils and his wife, who had divorced him because of his Revolutionary activities but who now remarried him and lived happily with him for another 31 years. The *Sabine Women* was begun in 1798, partly in recognition of her devotion, partly as a manifesto of his passion for the Antique. In the same year he met Napoleon and became an ardent Bonapartist. Napoleon fully appreciated the uses of a great painter as a propagandist, and as part of the Napoleon Saga David painted *Napoleon crossing the Alps* and worked 1805–7 on the huge *Coronation*, containing over a hundred portraits, and followed this with *The Emperor distributing the Eagles*. After Waterloo he fled to Switzerland and eventually retired to Brussels, where he died.

Several contradictory strains combine in David's art – from the stern Neoclassicism of his youth he moved, in the Napoleonic pictures, towards a Venetian use of colour and light, and yet contemporary and later pictures of classical subjects show a concentration on drawing and a rigid antiquarianism at variance with all that Venetian influence implies. His portraits are always supremely well designed and full of realism, yet his later classical subjects betray a progressive sweetening of style, perhaps due to the stultifying influence of his self-imposed exile, cut off from the stimulating conflict of ideas resulting from the rise of Romanticism. He was a great teacher, whose many pupils included GÉRARD, GIRODET, GROS, and INGRES. Most of his large pictures are in Paris (Louvre, Petit Pal., Jacquemart-André, and École des Beaux-Arts); others in Aix-en-Provence, Algiers, Angers, Avignon, Berlin (Charlottenburg), Besançon, Boulogne, Buffalo NY, Cambridge Mass. (Fogg Mus.), Cherbourg, Chicago, Cincinnati, Cleveland Ohio, Detroit, Hartford Conn., Kansas City, Le Mans, Lille, Lyons, Montauban, Montpellier, New York (Met. Mus. and Rockefeller Inst. for Medical Research), Northampton Mass. (Smith Coll.), Rome (Mus. Napoleonico), Rouen, Springfield Mass., Toledo Ohio (a version of *The Horatii*, perhaps by Girodet), Troyes, Versailles, Vienna (Belvedere), and Washington (NG).

DAVIS, Stuart (1894–1964), was an American painter who exhibited in the ARMORY SHOW. He was influenced by Cubism, but later moved from flat, low-toned townscapes (many of Paris) to simple, loud-coloured patterns in which letters and words are major elements. Paintings of commercial artifacts and packages – *Lucky Strike*, 1921; *Odol*, 1924 – are more than prototypes for POP ART: they are Pop *avant la lettre*.

DEAD COLOUR *see* LAY-IN.

DEËSIS (Gk). A group of Christ enthroned in Majesty, with the Virgin and S. John on either side. The idea is Byzantine, but the best-known representation is in the Eycks' Ghent Altar. It is often used as the central group in a Last Judgement.

DEGAS, Edgar (1834–1917), was born in Paris of a wealthy family. He studied at the École des Beaux-Arts under a pupil of Ingres, whom he knew and deeply admired. His early works – family portraits and some history pictures – suggest that he was to develop into an academic painter in the Ingres tradition. By the late 1860s, however, he had begun to develop a deceptively casual composition, probably influenced by Manet and possibly also by Whistler. He knew Manet well, as he did Bazille, Berthe Morisot, and Tissot, and was a frequent member of the circle which gathered round Manet, where he also met Fantin-Latour, Renoir, Constantin Guys, Cézanne, Monet, Sisley, and Pissarro. During the Franco-Prussian war he remained in Paris and in 1872–3 he visited relations in New Orleans. Here he painted only a few works, but these – and those executed after his return to Paris – show him using unusual viewpoints and purely contemporary subject matter. He ceased exhibiting at the Salon in 1870, and in 1874 he took part in the first Impressionist Exhibition, as he did in six of the subsequent seven. His works could only be seen in public at these group exhibitions (always received with hostility and ridicule) and at the dealer, Durand-Ruel, whose patient and persevering faith in IMPRESSIONISM nearly ruined him. Unlike Monet, and some others in the group, Degas had a private income which made him independent of sales of his work, and he was less than understanding over their defections from the group exhibitions (which he largely organized) in order to send works to the Salon in an endeavour to attract purchasers.

His first pictures of dancers were painted about 1873, and from then on ballet girls, working girls, models dressing and bathing, and cabaret artists became his principal subject matter. He recorded the manners and movements of a society which he observed almost as if it were another world, and these figures were treated as the material of his investigations into light, colour, and form as much as the pastel or paint he used. Technically, he was one of the greatest experimenters and innovators. His sound knowledge of the traditional technique of oil-painting enabled him to make endless trials of various media and mixtures such as oil-paint thinned with turpentine after the oil has been partly extracted with blotting-paper (*peinture à l'essence*), pastel used in superimposed layers, or with watercolour or spirit-thinned oil-paint, or thinned with water, gouache, egg tempera, etching, drypoint, monotype, lithography, aquatint, and drawing in every material. In later life, he used pastel more than any other medium, and as his eyesight weakened his handling became broader and freer.

There are also 74 pieces of sculpture – late works – including ballet dancers and figures in movement, originally executed in wax, but now generally cast in bronze. The most unusual is the large figure of the little ballet girl wearing a real net *tutu* (London, Tate).

There are works in Baltimore (Walters), Berlin, Birmingham, Boston (Mus., Gardner), Cambridge Mass. (Fogg), Chicago, Cleveland Ohio, Columbus Ohio, Copenhagen, Detroit, Dumbarton

Oaks, Edinburgh, Frankfurt (Städel), Glasgow (Burrell Coll.), Hartford Conn., Liverpool, London (NG, Tate, V & A, Courtauld Inst.), Los Angeles, Lyons, Minneapolis, Moscow, New York (Met. Mus., M of M A, Brooklyn, Frick Coll)., Ottawa, Paris (Louvre, Mus. de l'Impressionnisme, Mus. Gustave Moreau), Pau, Philadelphia (Mus.), Rochester N Y, São Paulo, St Louis, Stockholm, Toledo Ohio, Toronto, Vienna, Washington, and elsewhere. London (Tate) and New York (Met. Mus.) have good collections of the sculptures.

DEL., DELIN. (Lat. *delineavit*, he drew it) after a name on an engraving or drawing is an assertion of authorship.

DELACROIX, Eugène (1798–1863), was the major painter of the Romantic Movement in France. He was a pupil of Baron Guérin (teacher also of GÉRICAULT) whose lack of artistic authority made his studio tolerant of new ideas. Delacroix was the ardent admirer rather than an intimate friend of Géricault, but in the grim year which preceded his death was a frequent visitor to his studio. To Géricault's influence is probably due Delacroix's interest in English art and in animal painting, and his revolt from the classicizing forms and classical literary subject which still dominated French painting in the early 19th century. He admired GROS, studied Rubens and Veronese, and was a friend of Bonington and an admirer of Constable. He was in England in 1825 and was much impressed by the charm of English colour and freshness of handling, particularly in landscape, and the predominance of medieval and anecdotal subject pictures.

His first Salon exhibit (*Dante and Virgil crossing the Styx*, 1822: Paris, Louvre) was well received, but subsequent ones (*The Massacre at Chios*, 1824; *Sardanapalus*, 1829: both Louvre) were bitterly attacked for his use of brilliant colour, contemporary and exotic literary subjects, and free handling, in which was seen the influence of Géricault and English art and a rejection of traditional French classicism. In 1832 he visited North Africa and this opened to him a whole new field of subjects: scenes from Arab and Jewish life, animal subjects, innumerable combinations of illustrations to Byron and allusions to the Greek wars against the Turks abound in his gigantic *œuvre* after this, and share the honours with Scott and Shakespeare as constant sources of inspiration. From the mid-1830s he was in official favour, receiving commissions for large-scale decorations in which INGRES, his greatest rival and inveterate opponent, was unsuccessful. His principal decorations were the *Justice of Trajan* for Rouen Town Hall (1840: now in Rouen Mus.), the ceiling of the Salon d'Apollon in the Louvre (1849), and works in the Libraries of the Chamber of Deputies and the Senate (1838–47), S. Sulpice (1857–60), and the Hôtel de Ville (destroyed in 1870). But the works he is happiest with are small, freely handled, colourful subjects – battles, hunts, animals in combat, and portraits of intimate friends such as Chopin (1838: Louvre). His Diary, kept from 1822 to 1824 and again from 1847 to 1863, is a precious source for his life and work and as a commentary on the social, intellectual, and artistic world of Paris. Delacroix only occasionally had pupils, and never taught in the sense that Ingres did, though he had assistants for his large decorations. He left no artistic succession, for the essence of Romanticism is its personal quality. His contribution to the struggle of the non-conforming artist against entrenched classicism is reflected in his long wait for election to the Institute (1857), the frequent battles over the admission of his works to the Salon and the veneration in which he was held by younger artists.

There are works in Baltimore (Mus., Walters), Bordeaux, Boston (Mus., Gardner), Bristol, Budapest, Buffalo, Cambridge Mass. (Fogg), Chantilly, Chicago, Cincinnati, Cleveland Ohio, Dublin, Edinburgh (NG), Glasgow, Hartford Conn. (Wadsworth), Lille, London (NG, Wallace Coll.), Los Angeles, Metz, Minneapolis, Montpellier, Montreal, New York (Met. Mus., Brooklyn), Northampton Mass. (Smith), North Carolina (Univ.), Paris (Carnavalet), Philadelphia, Princeton Univ., Reims, São Paulo, St Louis, Toledo Ohio, Toronto, Toulouse, Versailles, Victoria NSW, Washington (NG, Corcoran, Phillips), and elsewhere.

DELAUNAY, Robert (1885–1941), was the inventor of ORPHIC CUBISM. He was mainly concerned with the emotional effects of pure colour, which may have grown out of his early preoccupation with Impressionism. In 1911 he exhibited with the Independents in the Cubist Room and was also invited by KANDINSKY to exhibit with the BLAUE REITER group. Delaunay began to paint a series of the city of Paris and the Eiffel Tower in 1910–12 and he returned to these themes in 1924, after a seven-year stay (1914–21) in Spain and Portugal. In 1937 he was commissioned to paint vast murals – one was 9,000 square feet – for the Universal Exhibition in Paris. There are works by him in Amsterdam (Stedelijkmus.), London (Tate), Minneapolis, New York (Guggenheim), and Paris (Mus. d'Art Moderne). Delaunay's wife Sonia Terk (b.1885) was a Russian who went to Paris in 1905, where she was influenced by Gauguin. She married Delaunay in 1910. In 1937 she also painted a huge mural for the Paris Exhibition.

DELVAUX, Laurent (1698–1778), was a Flemish sculptor who came to London in 1717 to work with SCHEEMAKERS. In 1728 they went to Italy together, but soon afterwards Delvaux returned to Brussels where in 1733 he received a Court appointment. In Brussels he made a large number of statues for churches, several important pulpits, and a number of tombs; he worked on two tombs in Westminster Abbey with Scheemakers, and there are works (including terracotta models) by him in the V & A and the R A in London, and in Brussels (Mus. d'Art Moderne).

DELVAUX, Paul (*b.* 1897), is a Belgian painter, trained in Brussels, who was first influenced by the Expressionism of PERMEKE and SMET, but, under the influence of MAGRITTE and CHIRICO turned to Surrealism in the 30s. In 1939 he visited Italy and was deeply impressed by Roman architecture, so that a typical Delvaux consists of a meticulously detailed representation of a full-breasted Rubensian nude contemplating a Roman temple in the company of a man in a bowler hat. He is well represented in Brussels and there is a *Venus Asleep* in London (Tate).

DENIS, Maurice (1870–1943), was a co-founder and principal theorist of the NABIS. In Paris in 1888 he met BONNARD, VUILLARD, and SÉRUSIER, who knew Gauguin. Denis's early style, in reaction against Impressionism, was strongly decorative and much influenced by PUVIS de Chavannes, as well as Gauguin: in 1900 he painted his celebrated group portrait, *Homage to Cézanne* (Paris, Mus. d'Art Moderne). He made several trips to Italy and particularly studied the decorative style of Giotto, Fra Angelico, and Piero della Francesca; in 1903 he accompanied Sérusier to Beuron, the German Benedictine monastery which was a centre of religious art, and from 1910 he painted many religious works, including the decoration of S. Paul, Geneva (1914). In 1919 he founded the Ateliers d'art sacré. His interest in subject-matter seems to run counter to his famous dictum that a picture is essentially a flat surface covered with colours assembled in a certain order, but the contradiction is more apparent than real. Denis was a prolific writer on art, his best-known works being *Théories* and *Nouvelles Théories*. There are paintings by him in Paris (Mus. des Arts Décoratifs, and d'Art Moderne).

DERAIN, André (1880–1954), was one of the original FAUVES. He was much influenced by Vlaminck, Matisse, and Cézanne and, before 1914, painted in very bright colours and a pointillist handling: after 1919 he became more traditionalist and used principally browns and olive green. There are works in Paris (Mus. d'Art Moderne), and in Chicago, Cleveland, Detroit, Glasgow, Leeds, Liverpool, London (Tate), Manchester (Rutherston), New York (M of MA), Oxford, Washington (NG), and elsewhere.

DESCO DA PARTO (Ital. birth plate). In medieval Italy there was a charming custom of visiting a woman who had just given birth to a child and carrying her sweets or small gifts on a special small tray: these *deschi da parto* were frequently painted with appropriate subjects, e.g. a visit to a lady in childbed by ladies carrying *deschi*, as in the famous *desco* in Berlin, attributed to Masaccio.

DESIDERIO da Settignano (1428/30–64) was probably the most promising sculptor of the followers of Donatello. He adopted the technique of very low relief (*rilievo schiacciato*) which had been invented by Donatello, but Desiderio used it for purposes of extreme delicacy of effect quite different from the heroic style of Donatello. Desiderio's sensitive treatment of women and children is best seen in his busts: examples are in Berlin, Florence (Bargello), London (V & A), Paris (Louvre), Philadelphia, Toledo Ohio, Washington (NG). His major monumental work is the tomb of Carlo Marsuppini (*d.*1453) in Sta Croce, Florence, which derives from Donatello and the ROSSELLINI.

DESIGN. Roughly the same, in normal usage, as COMPOSITION. It may mean a part of a composition considered in isolation, as 'The design of the lower left-hand group of Mr Blank's composition . . .'. The arts of design are the visual arts. For the distinction between Design and Disegno *see* DISEGNO.

DE SMET *see* SMET.

DESPIAU, Charles (1874–1946), was a French sculptor who was influenced by RODIN from 1903 and worked for him 1907–14. Despiau's *Paulette* of 1907 (Paris, Mus. d'Art Moderne), his earliest major work, attracted Rodin's attention, but later Despiau rejected the softness and vagueness of Rodin's forms and, like MAILLOL, returned to the simplicity and formal severity of antique sculpture, particularly of the archaic period. His only large-scale work was the war memorial for his native Mont-de-Marsan (Landes), of 1920–2, but he was a sensitive and famous portraitist. There are works by him in Buffalo, Detroit, London (Tate), New York (M of MA), Philadelphia, and Rotterdam, and several in the Musée d'Art Moderne, Paris.

DESPORTES, Alexandre François (1661–1743), was a French painter trained in the Flemish tradition by a pupil of Snyders. He was in Poland, painting royal portraits, in 1695–6, and on his return to France became the official painter of hunting scenes to Louis XIV and Louis XV, painting also dogs, the animals in the royal menagerie, and profuse still-life subjects. He worked on decorations for the royal palaces, and like OUDRY made cartoons for the Gobelins. His small landscape studies made for the backgrounds of his hunting scenes are early examples of direct painting from nature. His rich still-life and animal pictures helped to turn French taste from an exclusive concentration on Italian art to a greater interest in Flemish painting. There are examples in Compiègne, London (Wallace Coll.), Munich, Paris (Louvre), and elsewhere.

DE STIJL *see* STIJL.

DEVIS, Arthur (1711–87), was a successful painter of small portraits and conversation pieces of great charm, cool delicate colour, and high finish. His solidly middle-class patrons are usually portrayed in their gardens or parks, or in sparse interiors detailed with as much care as the personages, who are assembled rather than grouped before the painter. His brother Anthony (1729–1816) was a minor landscape painter, and his son Arthur William (1763–1822) was also a painter and draughtsman in the service of the East India Company.

There are works in Hull, Liverpool, London (Tate, V & A), Manchester, Preston (his native town), Yale, and elsewhere.

DE WINT, Peter (1784–1849), was born at Stone, Staffs., of Dutch-American descent. He was trained in London and, through Dr MONRO, was influenced by Girtin. He was also helped by Varley. Apart from a visit to France in 1828 and to North Wales in 1829 he painted only the English landscape, and especially the flat country round Lincoln which lends itself to his favourite format, very wide in comparison to its height. In breadth of handling he sometimes approaches Cox, but his washes are simpler and more liquid, and the whole atmosphere calmer. There are examples in Cambridge (Fitzwm), Edinburgh, Leeds, Lincoln, London (BM, Tate, V & A), Manchester, and elsewhere.

DIAZ de la Peña, Narcisse Virgile (1807/8–76), was a French landscape painter of the BARBIZON School, but his earlier works were Romantic compositions in the manner of Delacroix. There are pictures by him in Boston, Glasgow, London (NG, Tate), New York (Met. Mus.), and French museums.

DIDEROT, Denis (1713–84), was the most important 18th-century French writer on art and a precursor of the modern critic. He wrote informative and penetrating accounts of the SALONS in 1759–71, 1775, and 1781, which circulated in Grimm's privately subscribed *Correspondance Littéraire*. His plays, the earliest examples of the *comédie larmoyante*, by their emphasis on tableaux and on incident rather than character, explain his admiration for GREUZE'S development of narrative bourgeois genre.

DIPTYCH. A picture consisting of two parts, usually hinged together like the pages of a book: a POLYPTYCH in two parts. A *Consular Diptych* is a pair of ivory reliefs commemorating a Consulship. There are several extant examples of Flemish 15th-century diptychs which consist of a portrait of the owner, represented in prayer, gazing at the Madonna and Child on the other panel: these were intended as objects of private devotion and as memorials.

DISEGNO. An Italian word, capable of a variety of meanings, the simplest of which is Drawing, and the next simplest DESIGN. The *arti del disegno* are the visual arts in general, not just drawing alone, and the 16th-century usage became more and more complicated as the MANNERISTS evolved theories about design which perhaps found their climax in the anagram *Disegno, segno di Dio* – i.e. Design is the sign-manual of God. This may be an over-statement. In this involved theory the idea of *disegno interno* plays an important part;

the artist is thought of as having a Platonic Idea of an object in his mind, implanted by God, so that the perfect idea of a human figure which exists in the painter's mind is what he has to realize, not contenting himself with the mere copying of any figure which he happens to have in front of his eyes. This theory, explicit in Mannerists like Federico ZUCCARO, is implicit in all theories of IDEAL ART and is at the back of most anti-naturalistic modern movements. In its purest 16th-century form it has much in common with the Counter-Reformation, a fact which might well surprise some of its more recent exponents.

DISTEMPER. A painting technique in which the powdered colours are mixed with size. As anyone who has ever done home decorating will know, it is easy and cheap but very impermanent; for this reason alone it should not be confused with TEMPERA.

DIVISIONISM see OPTICAL MIXTURES.

DIX, Otto (b.1891), learned to paint in Dresden. His experiences in 1914–18 and in the Inflation after the War led him to paint with a pitiless realism, even in his portraits, though never in quite so caricatural a manner as Georg GROSZ. He was naturally attracted to the NEUE SACHLICHKEIT group and in 1933 his big triptych 'disappeared' from Dresden Gallery and Dix himself was later arrested by the Gestapo. Since 1946 he has painted mainly religious subjects, and in his later works the influence of early German masters such as Altdorfer and Baldung has been evident.

DOBSON, William (1610–46), was born in London. He was described by his contemporary Aubrey as the 'most excellent painter England hath yet bred', and as such he succeeded to the office of van Dyck as Court Painter and to some of the position of van Dyck, whose assistant he may have been. Nevertheless, his impasted and robust style is more Italianate than van Dyck's and may have been partly formed by a study of the superb Venetian pictures in the collection of Charles I. He appears first in 1642, at Oxford where the Civil War had driven Charles I and his Court; between then and his early death he painted many of the Royalists and also the Royal children, but never the King himself. There are works in the Royal Collection, Birmingham, Dunedin NZ, Edinburgh (NPG), Hull, Liverpool, London (Tate, NPG, Nat. Marit. Mus., Courtauld Inst.), and elsewhere.

DOELENSTUK, Schutterstuk. Dutch words meaning group portraits of the Civic Guards formed in Dutch towns during the Wars of Independence. HALS and REMBRANDT painted the most celebrated examples, but most of the late 16th- and early 17th-century portrait painters received commissions.

DOESBURG, Theo van (1883–1931), was born in Utrecht and began his career as a painter (there are pictures by him in Amsterdam and The Hague), but in 1917, with MONDRIAN, he founded the magazine

De Stijl and most of the rest of his life was spent as a publicist. He had some influence on BAUHAUS ideas.

DOLCI, Carlo (1616–86), was the leading painter in Florence in the mid-17th century, and an exponent of the restrained style of Late Baroque comparable with SACCHI'S Roman works. Dolci was extremely precocious and one of his finest pictures is the portrait, painted when he was 16, of Fra Ainolfo dei Bardi (1632: Florence, Pitti). Nevertheless, he became very neurotic and felt himself to be professionally inadequate. Most of his later works are small devotional pictures, often painted on copper in an extremely finicky and detailed style: when GIORDANO was in Florence in 1682 he said jokingly that his own virtuoso style had brought him a fortune of 150,000 scudi, but if Dolci spent so much time in finishing his works he would starve, an idea which preyed upon Dolci's mind. One of his best works is *The Martyrdom of S. Andrew* of 1646 (Florence, Pitti) for which there is a sketch of 1643 in Birmingham.

DOMENICHINO (1581–1641), one of the chief pupils of the CARRACCI, was an assistant to Ludovico in Bologna before he joined Annibale in Rome in 1602 to work in the Farnese Palace. He exemplified the Carracci doctrines of a return to the antique and Raphael and was also, with Annibale Carracci and the Northerners Elsheimer and the Brills, one of the pioneers of landscape painting.

In 1621 he returned to Rome from Bologna – where he had been since 1619 – to work as papal architect for the newly elected Pope Gregory XV, but his main work of this period was the decoration of the choir and pendentives of S. Andrea della Valle (1624–8), the dome being by LANFRANCO. The bitter enmity between them was exacerbated by Domenichino's neurotic temperament and his jealousy at having to share the commission. In 1631 he went to Naples to decorate the chapel of S. Gennaro in the Cathedral, a commission that had been hawked around due to the difficulty of getting any major Roman artist to brave the hostility of the Neapolitan artists, before whom the Cavaliere d'Arpino prudently retired, and Guido Reni fled after the murder of one of his assistants. Domenichino's acceptance of this ungrateful task was prompted by the increasing unpopularity of his style in Rome, where the day was being carried by the more exuberant Baroque of Lanfranco and Pietro da Cortona. Domenichino also had trouble with the Neapolitan faction and worked reluctantly and not very successfully, with several flights, and again in bitter competition with Lanfranco, until his death there. Outside Rome and Naples (where there are too many to list) examples may be found in the Royal Collection, and in Berlin, Béziers, Bologna, Bristol, Cambridge (Fitzwm), Chatsworth, Edinburgh (NG), Florence (Pitti, Uffizi), Genoa (Pal. Rosso), Glasgow (University), Grottaferrata, Hartford Conn., Indiana, Leeds, Leningrad, London (NG),

Madrid (Prado), Milan (Brera), Montpellier, Munich, Newcastle (King's College), Oxford (Christ Church), Paris (Louvre), Vicenza, and York.

DOMENICO Veneziano (d.1461) was probably a Florentine painter, although his name may be held to imply that he came from Venice. The date of his birth is unknown, but he is first recorded in 1438, in Perugia, when he wrote to the Medici in Florence asking for a job. He may have been successful in this, for he was working in Sant' Egidio (SM Nuova) in Florence 1439–45, on frescoes which are now lost. One of his assistants was PIERO della Francesca, and Domenico's greatest influence on the future was probably exerted through Piero rather than in Florence proper. His main concern was with the mutation of colour by light, a subject that hardly interested the Florentines, obsessed as they were by drawing. In recent years there have been attempts to represent Domenico as the most important influence after Masaccio, but there are only two signed pictures by him and barely half-a-dozen plausibly attributed. What is probably his earliest surviving work is the *Carnesecchi Madonna* and two *Saints* from the same street tabernacle (London, NG): these fresco fragments are in bad condition, but the *Madonna* is signed. The other signed picture is his masterpiece, the *S. Lucy Altarpiece*, painted for a church in Florence and now dispersed. The main panel is in Florence (Uffizi) and represents the Madonna and Saints in one of the earliest SACRE CONVERSAZIONI; the *predelle* are now in Berlin, Cambridge (Fitzwm), and Washington (NG).

It has been suggested that, before this, he painted the lower half of Angelico's *Coronation of the Virgin* (Paris, Louvre) and after the *S. Lucy Altar* he was sufficiently influenced by Castagno to paint the fresco of *SS. John and Francis* (Florence, Sta Croce): there is no compulsion to believe either of these theories. One of the few things known with certainty about him is that he died in 1461, and therefore could not have been murdered by Castagno (d.1457). Nevertheless, this story was current in the late 15th century. Other works attributed to him are in Berlin, Boston (Gardner Mus.), New York (Met. Mus.), and Washington (NG).

DONATELLO (c.1386–1466) was not only the greatest Florentine sculptor before Michelangelo; he was the most influential individual artist of the 15th century. Much of the later 15th-century painting in Florence stems from him, as does the whole Paduan School, while, through MANTEGNA and the BELLINI, his influence was felt even in Venice. Practically every later sculptor, including Michelangelo, was deeply indebted to him; while the heroic types he invented have coloured our whole conception of 15th-century Florence. He was apprenticed to GHIBERTI and worked on the First Doors in 1403 but had left by 1406, when he was working with NANNI di Banco on the Cathedral: he continued to work for the Cathedral on and off for the next 30 years. In 1408/9 he carved his marble *David* (reworked 1416: Florence, Bargello): this shows him as still very influenced by Gothic formal ideas, but his own heroic style is first seen in the *S. Mark* (1411–12: Florence, Orsanmichele) and the *S. John Evangelist* (1413–15: Cathedral) which made his reputation. In both these he created a new kind of humanity, slightly larger than life and exemplifying those qualities of will that were so highly prized in the Early Renaissance. In 1415 he began his series of statues for the Campanile and from 1416 to *c.*1420 he worked on his *S. George* for Orsanmichele (now in the Bargello). The Saint is a portrayal of the Christian hero, but perhaps even more significant was the relief below (still on Orsanmichele) of *S. George killing the Dragon*. This is the earliest datable example (*c.*1417) of the new science of perspective being used to create a definite, measurable space for the figures to inhabit: it was probably contemporary with the theoretical studies of Brunelleschi, Donatello's friend, but precedes the work of MASACCIO by many years. About 1425 Donatello entered into partnership with the sculptor and architect MICHELOZZO, with whom he produced a series of works, including the Tomb of the Antipope John XXIII (Florence, Baptistry) and the Tomb of Cardinal Brancacci (S. Angelo a Nilo, Naples), both of which were being worked on in 1427, in which year he also finished the *Salome* for the Baptistry Font, Siena. The Tomb of John XXIII established a type of wall-tomb, with the dead man lying on a bier, which derived from earlier examples (e.g. by ARNOLFO di Cambio) but which was decisive for the later Florentine examples (e.g. those by the ROSSELLINI or DESIDERIO). Both the marble relief from the Brancacci Tomb and the bronze one of *Salome* show Donatello exploiting the dramatic possibilities of a combination of very low relief (*rilievo schiacciato*) with the new perspective effects, and these mark his full maturity as a tragic artist. (The *Ascension* in London (V & A) is another example of about the same date.) In 1431–3 he was in Rome, probably with Brunelleschi, and there he seems to have produced little, presumably as he was absorbed in studying the classical remains. Certainly his later work is saturated in the spirit of antiquity, which he understood more fully than any other 15th-century artist, with the possible exception of Mantegna. It was probably after his return to Florence that he made the very classic bronze *David* (Bargello), one of the earliest of Renaissance independent nudes. He was also commissioned to carve the *Cantoria* ('Singing Gallery') for the Cathedral (1433–9: Cath. Mus.) to match the one already begun by Luca della ROBBIA. During these years he also made the Pulpit for Prato Cathedral and carried out the elaborate decorations for the Old Sacristy in S. Lorenzo, Florence, including the bronze doors, which, much less ambitious than Ghiberti's, far surpass his in the interpretation of human character. From 1443 to 1453 Donatello was in Padua, where he made the High Altar of the Santo (now altered) and the equestrian monument to Gattamelata, the first reworking in modern times of the ancient Roman type and clearly owing much to the most famous antique example, the *Marcus Aurelius* in Rome. His works in Padua were the models for all North Italy.

On his return to Florence Donatello explored new possibilities of romantic distortion and religious emotion in his carved wood *Magdalen* (c.1455: Baptistry), which shows the dramatic impact of extreme ugliness. This statue was of great importance in the development of Florentine painting, for it has the qualities of expressive contour and tense drama that painters like Castagno or, later, Botticelli sought. At his death he left two unfinished pulpits in S. Lorenzo which show the extreme distortion he was prepared to practise in his old age. They were completed by his pupil BERTOLDO. Apart from those mentioned there are works by or attributed to Donatello in Berlin, Boston, Faenza, Florence (Sta Croce Mus. and Piazza della Signoria), Lille, Pisa, Rome (St Peter's, Aracoeli), Siena (Cath.), Venice (S.M. de' Frari), and Washington (NG).

DONGEN, Kees van (1877–1968), was a Dutch painter who lived in Paris from 1897. From 1905 he was influenced by the FAUVES (especially MATISSE and DUFY), and from their formal simplifications he evolved a style which, coupled with the experience of making satirical drawings for newspapers, allowed him to become a successful painter of 'cruel' portraits of the rich and fashionable. There are examples in Chicago, New York, and Paris (Mus. d'Art Moderne).

DONNER, Georg Raphael (1693–1741), was the leading Austrian Baroque sculptor and a pupil of PERMOSER. He probably went to Italy before 1715, although the evidence for such a journey is purely stylistic. The influence of Michelangelo is very marked in his works, as well as that of contemporaries. He worked in Salzburg 1725–8, in Pressburg (now called Bratislava or Pozsony) 1728–38, and then in Vienna. Most of his best works are in lead (e.g. the *S. Martin* of 1735 in Pressburg Cath.), but the lead figures for the Fountain in the Mehlmarkt, Vienna (now in the Barockmus.), of 1737–9, had to be replaced by bronze copies. This was his masterpiece, and in the opinion of some critics it shows him moving away from Baroque exuberance.

DORÉ, Gustave (1832–83), was the most productive and celebrated designer of wood-engraved book-illustrations of the 19th century. He began by supplying lithographs for a weekly paper in Paris, but soon turned to making drawings which could be engraved on wood by teams of skilled craftsmen: in this way he soon achieved international fame (there was even a special Doré Gallery in London). His books included Rabelais, Balzac, Dante's *Inferno* and 'the Doré Bible', and his engravings of the squalor of London life still provide material for social historians. He produced a few paintings and some sculpture in his later years: Grenoble has the *Lac en Écosse sous l'Orage*, and there is a huge landscape in Boston. He is well represented in Britain and America and there are works in Paris (Mus. d'Art Moderne), in Bayonne, Montpellier, Reims, Rouen, Troyes, Versailles and other French museums.

DOSSI, Dosso (*c.*1479/90–1542), was the last of the Ferrarese painters, much influenced by Giorgione and Titian and also by Raphael. He is first recorded in Mantua in 1512, but had presumably already been in Venice. His most famous work, the *Circe* (Rome, Borghese), shows the unearthly light which plays about his fantastic landscapes inhabited by gorgeously dressed actors. There are works in the Royal Collection and in Baltimore, Detroit, Dresden, Ferrara, Florence (Uffizi, Pitti), Glasgow, London (NG), Modena, Naples, New York (Met. Mus.), Parma, Philadelphia (Johnson), Rome (Borghese, Capitoline), Trent, Vienna (K-H Mus.), Washington (NG), Worcester Mass., and elsewhere.

His brother, Battista Dosso (*d.*1548), was his helper, but pictures in Modena and Dresden may be by Battista alone.

DOTTED PRINT. Among the earliest forms of ENGRAVING were prints made from metal plates treated as relief blocks, the white lines being cut out of the metal. The surface was extensively ornamented with dots made by using punches to produce a decorative effect, often regardless of the design as a whole.

DOU, Gerard (1613–75), a portrait and genre painter of Leyden, was a pupil of the young REMBRANDT 1628–31, although it is difficult to see any trace of Rembrandt's handling (or intellectual powers) in the elaborately wrought small scenes of everyday life that brought Dou great prosperity and are now in every major gallery. Nevertheless, the *Parable of the Treasure* (Budapest) and the *Tobit* (London NG) are reasonably attributed to Rembrandt and Dou jointly. The extreme minuteness of his handling may be connected with his horror of dust – he would sit immobile in his studio, waiting for it to settle, before beginning work. SANDRART visited his studio with BAMBOCCIO and admired the finish of a broomstick, but Dou claimed it still needed three days' work. METSU was his pupil.

DOWNMAN, John (*c.*1750–1824), travelled in Italy with Wright of Derby in 1773–5, and made a number of landscape drawings, but on his return to London he turned to small portraits (often on copper), being particularly successful with pencil and charcoal drawings delicately tinted with watercolour. He became an ARA in 1795. There are examples in London (Tate and Wallace Coll.).

DRILL *see* STONE CARVING.

DROUAIS, François Hubert (1727–75), was a French portrait painter who studied under his father, BOUCHER, and others. His father painted actresses and so did he: his *Mme Favart* (1757: New York, Met. Mus.) is a good example. He became a serious rival to NATTIER and worked for Mme du Barry and the Royal family, being particularly successful with children. There are works in Paris (Louvre), London (NG), and New York (Met. Mus. and Frick Coll.).

DRYPOINT *see* ENGRAVING.

DUBUFFET, Jean (*b.*1901), is inspired by *graffiti* on walls ('the art of the ordinary man') and produces works, called *pâtes*, which are not painted but made of junk – tar, sand, glass and so on – which has been scratched, coloured, and manipulated into shapes resembling human beings – e.g. aggressively female women. He prefers amateur spontaneity to professional skill, and has a large collection of what he calls *art brut* (raw art), much of it produced by psychotics. He has travelled a good deal and worked for a while in America, producing *Bowery Bums*. There are examples in Amsterdam, Belfast, Edinburgh (M of MA), London (Tate), and New York (M of MA) as well as in France.

DUCCIO di Buoninsegna (*c.*1255/60–in or before 1318, probably 1315/18) was the first great Sienese painter, and he stands in relation to the Sienese School as GIOTTO does to the Florentine; yet without the powerful naturalism which makes the art of Giotto so revolutionary, for Duccio rather sums up the grave and austere beauty of centuries of Byzantine tradition and infuses it with a breath of the new humanity which was spreading from the new Orders of S. Francis and S. Dominic. He is first recorded in 1278 and 1279, working for the Comune, and then in 1280 he was heavily fined for an unspecified offence, probably a political one. It was the first of many fines to be inflicted on him, but the others were all very much smaller. In 1285 a large *Madonna* was ordered from him for the Florentine church of Sta Maria Novella: this was very probably the *Rucellai Madonna* (now temporarily in the Uffizi, Florence), but the picture is sometimes called a work of the Master of the Rucellai Madonna, and Vasari, in one of his patriotic moods, ascribed it to the Florentine Cimabue. The picture was probably painted in Siena, where Duccio is recorded at intervals (1285–99), when he was again fined for refusing to swear fealty to the *Capitano del Popolo*, a civil official. In 1302 he was fined again – probably one of several for debts incurred – and was also commissioned to paint a *Maestà* for Siena Town Hall, but the picture is now lost. He was also fined again, this time for refusing military service, and yet again for some activity apparently connected with sorcery. This last accusation cannot have been very serious since in 1308 Duccio achieved the consummation of his career with the contract for the huge *Maestà* for the High Altar of the Cathedral. The work was finished in 1311 and carried in solemn procession from the workshop to the Cathedral. Most of the *Maestà* is now in the Cathedral Museum at Siena, a few small pieces are missing, and the other panels (all small ones from the *predelle*) are in London (NG), New York (Frick Coll. and a private (Rockefeller) coll.), and Washington (NG). Wellesley College, Mass., has an *Angel* which may have come from the *Maestà*. In its original form the *Maestà* proper – that is, the Enthroned Madonna and Child surrounded by Saints and Angels – occupied the whole of the main panel facing the congregation. Above and below were scenes from the Life of Christ and the Virgin, with small figures of Saints. Most of these smaller scenes would have been visible only to the officiating priest. The whole of the back of the main panel was taken up by 26 scenes from the Passion, while above and below, as on the front, were smaller panels with scenes from the Life of Christ. The whole of this narrative cycle, being in the Sanctuary, was normally easily visible only to the clergy, and it is perhaps for this reason that the narrative is more important, as a kind of commentary on the Scriptures; while the front is principally an image for the contemplation of the devout. From the artistic point of view both sides show Duccio as a profound innovator, for the front has figures with greater weight and solidity, and more characterization, than had been seen previously in Siena; while the back shows him as a master of narrative, equal to Giotto in his power of story-telling though less fresh in iconographical invention, for Duccio was content to use the old Byzantine models for most (though not all) of his scenes from the New Testament. The superb craftsmanship, the use of gold as a decoration and a compositional feature at the same time, the rich and subtle colour which is made into an aesthetic feature in its own right rather than treated (as in Giotto's works) as explaining the forms, and above all the use of varied and elegant outlines as a surface pattern as well as a description of form; all these features characterize the Sienese School for nearly two centuries. In the next generation artists as profoundly different as Simone MARTINI and the LORENZETTI started from aspects of Duccio's work, although the influence which Giovanni PISANO'S sculpture had had on Duccio himself was also a potent factor in the development of the Lorenzetti.

Other works ascribed to Duccio are in the Royal Collection and in Badia a Isola near Siena (a *Madonna* often ascribed to the Badia a Isola Master rather than to Duccio himself), Berne, Boston, Budapest, Cambridge Mass. (Fogg), London (NG), New York (Met. Mus., Frick Coll.), Perugia, Philadelphia (Johnson), Siena (Pinacoteca, Opera del Duomo, and Cathedral itself (stained glass, although this is also ascribed to Cimabue)), and Utrecht (Archiepiscopal Mus.).

DUCHAMP, Marcel (1887–1968), brother of R. DUCHAMP-VILLON and J. VILLON, was one of the original Dadaists even though he had gone to New York in 1915, before the invention of DADA. In the ARMORY SHOW he exhibited his *Nude descending a Staircase* (two versions, 1911 and 1912, both in Philadelphia). This was a relatively straightforward Cubo-Futurist work, but it was soon to be succeeded by ready-mades (i.e. anything that comes to hand). The first ready-made, a bottle rack, was exhibited in 1914 and was followed by a urinal, entitled *Fountain* and 'signed' R. Mutt, 1917. His version of the *Mona Lisa* was made in 1919, but his major work is *The Large Glass*, or *The Bride stripped bare by her Bachelors, Even* (1915–23: Philadelphia). This is not a painting, but a transparent construction made of wire and painted foil sandwiched between carefully dirtied plate glass. The original version (1915, unfinished) was broken by accident in 1926 and was repaired by Duchamp himself, retaining the cracks so that the work could be considered finished 'by chance'. He published a complete documentation of all this, but the last 40 years of his life were largely devoted to chess.

DUCHAMP-VILLON, Raymond (1876–1918), was the brother of Marcel DUCHAMP and Jacques VILLON. From 1898 his sculpture was under the influence of RODIN, but he later came to sympathize with Cubist ideals, and, from 1912 to 1914, there is a series of *Horses* which have something of the quality of a Cubist manifesto, combined with BOCCIONI's interest in movement. He was gassed in 1916 and died in 1918. Paris (Mus. d'Art Moderne) has one of the *Horse* series (1914). There is another example in London (Tate).

DUFY, Raoul (1877–1953), worked in a sub-Impressionist manner until 1905, when the impact of the FAUVE movement (particularly of Matisse's *Luxe, Calme et Volupté*) impelled him to adopt simplified form and bright colour. He designed textiles and ceramics and developed a gay, light-hearted, decorative style, eminently suited to his range of subjects – esplanades, racecourses, regattas, etc. – and used odd tricks of technique, such as white patches ('neutrals') for shadows, and a rapid, modish, calligraphic draughtsmanship. There are examples in London (Tate and Courtauld Inst.), New York (M of MA), Paris (Mus. d'Art Moderne), and large collections at Le Havre and Nice.

DUGENTO (*Duecento*: Ital. two hundred). The 13th century, i.e. the twelve hundreds.

DUGHET, Gaspard, *see* POUSSIN.

DUJARDIN, Karel (1622–78), was born in Amsterdam. He was a pupil of BERCHEM, and twice went to Italy. He painted chiefly Italianate landscapes with figures, occasional religious subjects, and an exceptionally fine group portrait of the *Regents of the Women's*

Prison in Amsterdam (1669: Rijksmus.). He died in Venice. There are examples in the Royal Collection, Berlin, Brussels, Dresden, Edinburgh (NG), The Hague, Hartford Conn., Leningrad, London (NG, Dulwich, Wallace Coll.), Munich, Paris (Louvre), Vienna, Yale, York, and elsewhere.

DUNLAP, William (1766–1839), was an American painter of portraits – e.g. the picture of himself, on his return from London in 1788, showing his *Hamlet* to his parents (New York, Hist. Soc.). He was also a playwright and kept 30 volumes of Diary (1786–1834) of which 11 survive and have been published; above all, he wrote 'A History of the Rise and Progress of the Arts of Design in the United States', 1834, which is the best source-book on early American painting.

DUQUESNOY, François (1594–1643), known as *Il Fiammingo*, was a sculptor, born in Brussels, who worked in Rome from 1618 to 1643. He died on his way to Paris to become Court Sculptor. He was the most famous non-Italian sculptor of his day, and, like ALGARDI, he represented a more classical tendency than the full Baroque of BERNINI, by whom he was nevertheless influenced, especially in portraiture. Poussin, the most classical artist of the age, was his close friend. His major works are the *S. Andrew* (1628–40: St Peter's; *see* BOLGI) and the *S. Susanna* (1629–33: Sta Maria di Loreto, Rome). Numerous smaller works spread his fame outside Italy: there are examples in Berlin, London (V & A), Paris, and elsewhere. His *putti* were especially praised by contemporaries: good examples are those in Sta Maria dell'Anima, Rome.

DURAND, Asher B. (1796–1886), began as an engraver whose reputation was established in 1820 with the engraving, after TRUMBULL'S painting, of the *Declaration of Independence*. As early as 1830 he projected a serial publication of engravings devoted to the American landscape but it was not successful and had to be suspended after the first number. By this time he had turned to painting portraits and landscapes, and he eventually became one of the leading landscape painters of the HUDSON RIVER School. In 1840 he made a trip to Europe and copied the old masters, and in 1846 he was elected President of the National Academy of Design, one of the first landscape painters in any country to receive such recognition. Unlike his friend COLE, he worked out-of-doors and the artless realism of his landscapes is their principal attraction, but he began by working in a tradition close to that of the Dutch 17th-century painters (e.g. Hobbema). There are pictures by him in many American museums, but there do not seem to be any outside the United States.

DÜRER, Albrecht (1471–1528), was the son of a goldsmith who settled in Nuremberg in 1455, and in 1467 married his master's daughter. The young Albrecht was first apprenticed to his father, and was then bound for three years to the painter Michael WOLGEMUT, whose large workshop also produced woodcut book-illustrations for the printer Anton Koberger, Dürer's godfather. He travelled for eighteen months, from Easter 1490, afterwards visiting Colmar (intending to work under Martin Schongauer), Basle, and Strasbourg, and in May 1494 he returned to Nuremberg and married. In the autumn of 1494 he went to Venice (his great friend, the humanist Wilibald Pirckheimer, was then a student at Padua) and returned home by spring 1495. Late in 1505 he again went to Venice, travelling via Augsburg, and stayed until February 1507. During this visit he met Giovanni Bellini, whom he greatly admired, and painted several works including the *Madonna of the Rose Garlands* (Prague; now very damaged) for the German merchants in Venice, and the *Christ among the Doctors*, which shows some knowledge of Leonardo. On his return he intensified the learned side of his art and personality; he studied mathematics, geometry, Latin and humanist literature, and sought the company of scholars rather than that of his fellow artisans. This departure in mode of life and thought was directly traceable to the influence of Leonardo and Mantegna and the example of Bellini, and though it was common enough in Italy, it was unprecedented in Germany. In 1512, he became Court Painter to the Emperor Maximilian, and in July 1520 he journeyed to the Netherlands to obtain from his successor, Charles V, the ratification of his post and pension. He saw the coronation of the new Emperor at Aix-la-Chapelle and was confirmed in his office, visited Antwerp, Brussels, Malines, Cologne, Middelburg, Bruges, and Ghent, and was honoured and feted all along the route. He returned home in July 1521, and despite ill-health resulting from fever, probably contracted in the swamps of Zeeland, where he had ventured in the hope of seeing a dead whale, he worked unremittingly until his death.

Dürer's enormous *œuvre* consists of woodcuts and engravings, paintings, preparatory and independent drawings, and he also wrote treatises on measurement (1525), fortification (1527), proportion and artistic theory (1528), besides his detailed diary of his Netherlands journey. He was the main channel through which Italian Renaissance forms and ideas were introduced into the North, and he combined these with the individualism general in German art and inherited from the Gothic tradition. His greatest influence was through his graphic work. He is one of the supreme masters of woodcut and copper engraving, and these easily transportable models carried his technique, subjects, designs, and style all over Europe, and even had a considerable influence in Italy. He extended the range of woodcut and engraving by perfecting the technique of both, and raised the standard of graphic art by the training he gave to the workmen who executed his designs.

His main works in woodcut were series such as the *Apocalypse* (1498), the *Great Passion* (1498–1510), and the *Little Passion* (1509–11), the *Life of the Virgin* (1501–11), and single prints such as the *Men's Bathhouse* (1497), and in engraving the *Engraved Passion* (1507–12) and the many single plates such as the *Sea Monster* and the *Prodigal Son* (1497), the *S. Eustace* (c.1501), the *Great Fortune* (1501/2), the *Adam and Eve* (1504), the *Knight, Death and the Devil* (1513), *S. Jerome* and the *Melencolia* (1514). The *Apocalypse* was the first book to be entirely the work of an artist; Dürer here was his own artist, printer, and publisher. All his works combine vivid imagery, technical refinement, expressiveness, and masterly draughtsmanship with deeply thought out, and often involved, iconography which must be read, layer upon layer, before the meaning of the design becomes clear, although its visual impact is immediate. He shared in the Emperor Maximilian's commissions for the huge woodcut *Triumphs*, and executed some blocks for them, but they added little to his fame.

Compared with his graphic work, his paintings are few in number; they are more traditional in type and usually less packed with significance. One of his greatest contributions is his watercolour and gouache landscapes, some made during his Italian journeys, for they are among the most evocative expressions of mood and atmosphere in landscape painting. In October 1526, he presented to his native city, as a memorial of himself, the *Apostles* (Munich), probably designed as a part of a *Sacra Conversazione* which was not executed because of the Reformation. In form, the Saints owe much to Bellini's Saints in the Frari Altarpiece (Venice), and their significance is bound up with the spiritual conflicts of the Reformation, which affected him deeply. Melancthon was a close friend, and he knew and admired both Luther and Erasmus. Despite his large workshop he left no succession; his art was too universal and yet too personal to breed imitators.

There are works in Augsburg, Berlin, Boston (Gardner), Budapest, Cassel, Cologne (Wallraf-Richartz), Dresden, Florence (Uffizi), Frankfurt (Mus. and Städel), Lisbon, London (NG), Madrid (Prado), Munich, New York (Met. Mus.), Nuremberg, Ober St Veit (near Vienna), Paris (Louvre, Bib. Nat.), Toledo Ohio, Vienna, Weimar, and elsewhere.

DYCE, William (1806–64), painter, scientist, and administrator, was born in Aberdeen and studied in London and Rome. He was much influenced by the NAZARENER and introduced their ideas to England with a *Madonna* in 1828: he thus transmitted the new German ideas to the Pre-Raphaelite Brotherhood (founded in 1848). There are works in the Royal Collection and in Aberdeen, Edinburgh (NG), Liverpool, and London (Tate).

DYCK, Sir Anthony van (1599–1641), was born in Antwerp. He became RUBENS's chief assistant while still in his teens, his forte being for subjects requiring pathos rather than movement. He visited England in 1620 (James I desired to employ him as Court Painter), but after four months returned to Flanders and in 1621 he went to Italy where, except for a visit to Flanders in 1622 when his father died, he remained for four years. He was in Rome, Florence, Venice, Palermo, and particularly in Genoa, where he laid the foundation of his great career as a portrait painter, and evolved the repertory of patterns of which he made such constant use during his years in England. He was not at his best in Rome, which was then full of brilliant artists – Domenichino, Guercino, Bernini, Pietro da Cortona – and the Baroque that Rubens saw coming to birth was fully developed.

Between his return to Flanders in 1625/6, when he tried to obtain the patronage of the Regent Isabella, and worked for the House of Orange, and his departure for England, he produced most of his finest portraits for, less forceful as a personality than Rubens, he was more sensitive to his sitter's individuality, which he expressed with an unfailing sense of style that reflects something of his own introspective melancholy. In religious works, he leaned heavily on Rubens, and on Titian and Correggio, though he digested these influences less successfully than Rubens did. Technically, his paint is thinner than Rubens's, drier, more dragged, and with greyer underpainting, less limpid and free in handling. His years in England – from 1632 until his death – were outwardly successful, with immense prestige at the Court of Charles I, a knighthood, and an enormous practice as a portrait painter, for he supplanted MYTENS and overshadowed JOHNSON. But his efforts to re-establish himself on the Continent in 1640, first to succeed Rubens (cf. JORDAENS), and then to obtain the commission for the decoration of the gallery in the Louvre which, when he arrived in Paris, had already been given to Poussin, suggest that he realized how precarious Charles I's position had become, and how limiting was the patronage of the English Court. But by now he was very ill, and he returned to England to die.

His nine years in England were prolific, but involved the constant repetition of his Genoese types, with varying success according to whether he himself or a studio hand executed the work. None of his helpers was of any significance, and he lacked Rubens's ability to control a large workshop. Among the most famous of his English portraits are the equestrian ones of Charles I, the triple portrait of the King sent to Bernini to serve as a model for a bust, the groups of the Royal children, and the great family group at Wilton. These show him creating a model that lasted until the end of the great tradition of English portrait painting, through DOBSON, Lely, Reynolds, and Gainsborough to Lawrence.

Most of the older galleries have one or more examples, Antwerp, Brussels, London (NG, Wallace Coll.), and the Royal Collection being exceptionally rich. The following American and Canadian museums also have examples: Baltimore, Boston (Mus., Gardner), Chicago, Cincinnati, Cleveland Ohio, Columbus Ohio, Denver, Detroit, Hartford Conn. (Wadsworth), Kansas City, Los Angeles (Mus., Univ. of S. Cal.), New York (Met. Mus., Frick), Ottawa, Raleigh N. Carolina, St Louis, San Diego, Toledo Ohio, Toronto, Washington (NG, Corcoran, Nat. Coll.), Yale, and others.

E

EAKINS, Thomas (1844–1916), was an American painter, principally of portraits. He went from Philadelphia to Paris in 1866, where he came under the influence of MANET's realism. After a visit to Spain in 1870 he returned to Philadelphia and became a successful teacher whose quest for realism led him to attend medical classes to improve his knowledge of anatomy and led indirectly to his *Gross Clinic* (1875), with its representation of a surgeon operating, which caused an uproar, as did his *Agnew Clinic*. These Rembrandtesque subjects were treated in the 'Spanish' style of Manet, which also caused uproar rather earlier in Paris. His works are well represented in US museums.

EARL, Ralph (1751–1801), was an American portrait painter who is first recorded in 1775, making sketches for engravings of the Revolution. He worked in England 1778–85, exhibiting at the RA 1783–5 and probably coming into contact with the Loyalist WEST. In 1785 he returned to New England and painted portraits there until his death: he was twice married and deserted both wives, and from 1799 his work deteriorated under the influence of the alcoholism which killed him. His *Roger Sherman* (*c*.1775/7: Yale Univ. Gall.) has a gaunt Yankee quality which seems preferable to the pastiche of fashionable English painting apparent in his later works. Many American museums have a picture by him: the only one outside the US appears to be the *Admiral Kempenfelt* (1783) in the NPG, London.

ECLECTIC *see* CARRACCI.

EECKHOUT, Gerbrand van den (1621–74), was an Amsterdam painter who was the pupil, friend, and close imitator of Rembrandt. About 1655 he painted a number of scenes in the totally different manner of TER BORCH.

ELIAS, Nicolaes, called Pickenoy (1590/1–1654/6), was an Amsterdam portrait painter of the generation before Rembrandt. His *Company of Captain Jan van Vlooswijck* (Amsterdam, Rijksmus.) was painted in 1642, the year of Rembrandt's *Night Watch*.

ELSHEIMER, Adam (1578–1610), was a German landscape painter whose most important work was done in Italy. He was in Venice *c*.1598 and in Rome by 1600, where he spent the rest of his life. His landscapes are among the first ideal ones, in which the figures have a considerable but not overwhelming part to play, and in which the effects of light are studied with great care. He probably learned the effectiveness of a variety of points of light from Tintoretto and Caravaggio and many of his small landscapes have several sources of light – e.g. a warm sunset with the cold light of the moon in another part of the picture, together with the light of a torch elsewhere. His works are small, always on copper, and executed with great precision: they had great influence on his friend Rubens and on younger men such as Rembrandt and Claude. The works of Paul BRIL are very similar.

Rubens, in a letter of 14 January 1611, refers to Elsheimer's death as causing him great grief and goes on: 'I pray that God has forgiven Signor Adam his sin of sloth by which he has deprived the world of most beautiful things, caused himself much misery and finally, I believe, reduced himself to despair; whereas with his own hands he could have built up a great fortune and made himself respected by all the world.' He then goes on to offer to sell any of Elsheimer's pictures on behalf of the widow – an Englishwoman he married in 1606 – for considerable sums of money: 'and if the painting should not be sold immediately, we shall in the meantime find a way to advance her a good sum of money on it without prejudice to the sale.' SANDRART, however, says that Elsheimer was afflicted by melancholia and could not work, so that he was exploited by his own pupil Goudt, who eventually had him imprisoned for debt. There are pictures by him in Cassel, Cambridge (Fitzwm), Dresden, Edinburgh, Florence (Uffizi), Frankfurt (Städel), The Hague, London (NG, Wellington Mus.), Munich, Paris (Louvre), Venice (Accad.), Vienna (K-H Mus.), Yale, and elsewhere.

ENCAUSTIC WAX was a painting technique apparently practised in antiquity with success but since fallen into disuse. The principle seems to have been to work on a wall with colours mixed with wax, which, when heated with irons or similar means, were driven into the wall itself. Pliny gives an account, and this probably inspired LEONARDO's disastrous attempt at reviving the technique in 1503–5 as well as the late 19th-century attempts.

ENGRAVING. A generic title often used to cover all the methods of multiplying prints, although strictly the word should apply only to the second of the processes described below. The first distinction to be drawn is between Reproductive and Original Engravings, a reproductive engraving being a means of divulgating an idea expressed in a painting, drawing, statue, or other medium, invented by an artist other than the engraver. An original engraving is an independent work of art invented by the engraver himself.

The three main types of engraving may be classified as (1) Relief or cameo, (2) Intaglio, and (3) Surface or planar. Each of these types corresponds to one or more of the main techniques, and each type has a special method of printing. (1) Relief. The main techniques are Woodcut and Wood-engraving, Linocut and its simpler forms, such as Potato cuts. A plain block of wood, if covered with printing ink and pressed on a sheet of paper, would print as a black rectangle: but if channels were cut into the surface with a gouge these would not catch the ink, and, therefore, would print as white patches. The principle of a woodcut is therefore to leave the black lines or patches as untouched wood and to cut away the parts intended to print as white. A single black line has to have the wood on each side of it cut away, and this is done with special knives and gouges. Woodcuts are done on blocks of soft wood, cut plank-fashion, and will give hundreds, or even thousands, of impressions before wearing out. Lino is often used nowadays, as it is easier to work, but its life is shorter. Colour prints are produced by cutting a special block for each colour as well as a key-block, usually printed black, which carries the linear structure (*see* CHIAROSCURO *woodcut*), and these have to be printed 'in register', so that the forms do not overlap. The earliest woodcuts date from the end of the 14th century, but wood-engraving hardly occurs before the mid-18th century, and found one of its greatest exponents in Thomas BEWICK, who revived white-line engraving. Wood-engraving is very similar to engraving on copper, using the same kind of tool, called a graver or burin. The main difference between wood-engraving and woodcut is in the block itself, which is of boxwood, cut across the grain, for wood-engraving. On this smooth, grainless surface the sharply pointed graving tools can plough very fine furrows each of which will print as a fine white line. Obviously, it is far easier to think in terms of white lines on a predominantly black ground, and the great modern revival (since about 1920) of wood-engraving has been of the white-line or Xylographic type, which offers a means of stylized design.

2) Intaglio. The intaglio techniques are all forms of engraving on metal, usually copper, and they are distinguished from the other techniques by the method of printing. When the plate has been engraved by one or more of the processes to be described – and several processes are often used in combination – the plate is dabbed all over with a thin kind of printing ink, which is then rubbed off again with muslin or the palm of the hand, leaving the ink in the engraved furrows. A piece of paper is then damped and laid on the plate and both are rolled through a heavy press not unlike a mangle. The damp paper is forced into the engraved lines and so picks up the ink in them: when dry the engraved lines stand up in relief. This explains the great difference between a copper-engraving, or any other intaglio print, and a wood-engraving which has been cut in a very similar way – the ink lies on the surface of a wood-engraved block instead of being forced into the lines cut (*intagliate*) into the metal plate. A wood-engraving cannot be printed in the intaglio manner as it would break under the great pressure. The main intaglio processes are: (*a*) Line (or copper) engraving, (*b*) Dry-point, (*c*) Etching, including Soft-ground etching,

(*d*) Stipple and crayon engraving, (*e*) Mezzotint, and (*f*) Aquatint and the related processes.

a) *Line-engraving*. The sharp graver is pushed into the copper, exactly like a plough'into the earth, throwing up small shavings and leaving a line which has a V-section. This is the earliest of the intaglio techniques, as the earliest dated print is of 1446, but it is also the one demanding the greatest discipline and precision of hand since the sharp tool has to be pushed ahead of the hand – and polished copper is very slippery. DÜRER is incomparably the greatest artist in this medium, which was later used mainly for reproducing pictures and other works of art.

b) *Dry-point*. This is the simplest technique, since it consists of drawing on the metal plate with a 'pencil' made of hard steel. The great quality of dry-point lies in the burr, which is the shaving of metal turned up at the side of the furrow. When burr occurs in line-engraving it is scraped off, but it is left in a dry-point because it catches the ink and prints with a richness which adds to the directness of the artist's work. Unfortunately, it is soon crushed by the pressure of printing, so that less than fifty good impressions can be taken. Dry-point is often used to reinforce etching or even engraving; Rembrandt, in particular, often combined it with etching.

c) *Etching*. Here the plate is covered with a resinous ground, impervious to acid, and then the etcher draws on the ground with a needle, exposing the copper wherever he wants a line to print. The plate is put in an acid bath, which eats away the exposed parts, but subtlety is given by taking the plate out of the acid as soon as the faintest lines are bitten. These faint lines are then 'stopped-out' with varnish and the plate re-bitten until the medium-dark lines are stopped-out in their turn, and so on. The first dated etching is of 1513, but the great period came with the 17th century, culminating in Rembrandt, and the process has been popular ever since. *Soft-ground Etching* looks like a pencil or chalk drawing, because the ground is mixed with tallow, and has a sheet of thin paper laid on it, on to which the etcher draws directly with a pencil; part of the ground sticks to the paper giving a grainy effect when the plate is bitten. A *Photographic Etching* is made by drawing with a stylus on a grounded glass plate which is then treated like a photographic negative and printed on photographic paper. More than 60 such 'etchings' were made by Corot from *c*.1853, but the technique never became popular.

d) *Stipple, crayon engraving*, and *colour printing* were popular 18th-century techniques. Stipple and crayon engraving were used particularly for the reproduction of portrait drawings, giving an effect remarkably similar to that of a chalk drawing. It is obtained by a combination of etching and engraving techniques, stippling dots over a grounded plate with the point of an etching needle or, more usually, by the use of special tools; a *Roulette* is a spur-like wheel which gives an effect similar to the grainy quality of chalk, and it can be combined with a *Mattoir*, which is an instrument like a tiny club with sharp points projecting from the head. These points produce a grained effect on the bare copper which prints as black, chalk-like dots. Occasionally the effect of two-colour chalks is obtained by printing from two plates, usually black and red.

Colour engravings of the 18th century fall into two main categories, English and French. The finest English colour prints are usually based on the aquatint process (see (*f*) below) and are made by a single printing from a plate coloured in the appropriate areas. Some English colour prints are, in fact, monochrome aquatints hand-coloured in watercolour, and both GIRTIN and TURNER earned a living colouring engravings at the beginning of their careers.

The French technique, sometimes called *manière de lavis*, is an imitation of a wash drawing or a watercolour obtained by the use of a great number of *roulettes*, *mattoirs* and gravers. The use of these tools gave the tones, but the actual colours were printed from four separate plates – yellow, red, blue, and black, printed in that order, the black being the most important since it defined the contours. The most difficult part of this technique is to ensure that one plate is printed exactly on top of another – 'in register'.

e) *Mezzotint*. This was the great reproductive process of the 18th century (though invented in the 17th century), especially famous and successful in England, where the portraits of Reynolds and Gainsborough were normally reproduced by it. The plate is first covered with a mesh of small burred dots, made by a toothed chisel-like 'rocker'. In this state the plate would print as a solid, rich black. The half-tones and lights are obtained by scraping off the burr with a scraper, or polishing the plate smooth again with a burnisher so that the ink may be wiped off the highest lights. The technique is rarely practised now, as photographic methods have superseded it for reproduction.

f) *Aquatint*. Like mezzotint, aquatint is a tone process rather than a line method, but it is admirably adapted to the rendering of transparent effects, such as watercolour gives. It is basically a form of etching, using a porous ground which the acid can penetrate to form a network of fine lines. Any pure whites are stopped out in the usual way before the biting begins, then the palest tints are bitten and stopped out, and so on as in etching. Variations of texture can be obtained by pressing a piece of sand-paper on the grounded plate, mixing sugar with the ground, or attacking the plate with sulphur ('sulphur-tint'). Paul SANDBY was the first imaginative artist to use the process, followed by the greatest of all aquatinters, GOYA, but it has been revived by John Piper, and Picasso used the sugar process for his illustrations to Buffon.

3) Surface Printing. The one major process which involves no cutting into the block or plate, and therefore no 'engraving' in the proper sense, is Lithography, usually executed on a thick slab of stone, although zinc is now more common as it is both lighter and less fragile. The whole technique, invented in 1798 by Alois Senefelder, is based on the fact that water runs off a greasy surface. The design is drawn or painted on the stone with a greasy chalk and then the stone is wetted. When the greasy ink is rolled on the stone it will not take on the wet parts but it sticks on the parts which are already greasy, off which the water ran. The new process was taken up by several 19th-century artists, including Delacroix, Goya, Géricault, Daumier, Manet, and others, and it is still a popular medium. It is used very widely for posters and other forms of commercial art. Its great advantage is that there is almost no limit to the number of prints it is possible to take. *See also* SERIGRAPHY.

ENSOR, James (1860–1949), was a Belgian painter whose father was English. Apart from his training in Brussels Ensor spent his life in Ostend. He had a peculiarly macabre outlook, taking the subjects of Callot, Bosch or Bruegel and treating them in the technique of Manet, Courbet, and Rubens. He frequently used masks and skeletons for Expressionist purposes before EXPRESSIONISM was invented. In 1884 he exhibited with Les XX, who, in 1889, rejected his *Entry of Christ into Brussels in 1889* (1888: Knocke-le-Zoute, Casino) and voted for his expulsion. His best work was done by 1900: in 1929 he was made a Baron. There are pictures in Antwerp, Brussels, Detroit, London (Tate), New York (M of MA), and Paris (Mus. d'Art Moderne).

EPSTEIN, Sir Jacob (1880–1959), was born in New York and went to Paris in 1902; from 1905 he lived in England. In 1907 he was commissioned to carve 18 statues for the British Medical Association building. They were erected in 1908 and caused great scandal: after that, it became customary for any new imaginative work of his to be greeted with uproar – e.g. the *Rima* in Hyde Park (1925) or the carvings on the London Transport Building in Westminster (1928–9). His portraits in bronze have an over-lifesize quality, partly due to the rugosity of the handling, reminiscent of Rodin, and are generally admired: the last example was the official commission of *Smuts* outside the Houses of Parliament. Other works are in Aberdeen, Auckland NZ, Birmingham, Edinburgh, Hull, Llandaff Cathedral, London (Westminster Abbey, St Paul's, Tate, Imperial War Mus., and in Cavendish Square), Manchester, New York (M of MA), Oxford (New College), Paris (Cemetery of Père Lachaise, Tomb of Oscar Wilde), and elsewhere.

ERCOLE de' Roberti *see* ROBERTI.

ERHART (Erhaert), Gregor (*d.*probably 1540), was a German sculptor, born in Ulm, who worked in Augsburg from 1494 until his death. There are no documented works by him, although he is known to have made a stone crucifix in 1498, and in 1509 he was working on an equestrian monument for the Emperor Maximilian. Nothing is known of his later work, but he seems to have been an important sculptor of the transitional period, whose work was influenced first by MULTSCHER, the leading Ulm artist, while his later works come close to those of RIEMENSCHNEIDER. The most important attributions to Erhart are the altarpiece at Blaubeuren (1493-4), and *Madonnas* in Berlin (1502-4) and Frauenstein, Austria (*c.*1515). Other works attributed to him are in Cleveland Ohio, Detroit, London (V & A), and Paris (Louvre).

ERNST, Max (*b.*1891), introduced the Dadaist movement into Cologne in 1919. He also made *collages* and *frottages* and from 1924 was a Surrealist. He has published *collage* novels. There are examples in Edinburgh, Hartford Conn., Manchester, and New York (M of MA).

ESQUISSE is French for sketch.

ETCHING *see* ENGRAVING.

ETTY, William (1787-1849), was one of the very few English artists to paint the nude almost exclusively. This he did in a manner derived from Titian and Rubens, and therefore glowing and sensual, but subject to the requirements of IDEAL ART. Many of his pictures consist of extremely faithful studies from the nude, done in the Academy Life School which he frequented all his life, presented as mythological characters. He made several journeys to the Continent and met Delacroix in 1825, so he must have been aware of the French Romantic movement. The best collection of his work is in his native York, but there are other pictures in Boston, Leeds, London (Tate), Manchester, New York (Met. Mus.), Oxford, Port Sunlight (Lever Gall.), Preston, and elsewhere.

EUSTON ROAD was the name given to an English group, founded in the late 1930s, which takes its name from the Euston Road in London. They sought to return to a more realistic conception of painting, neither abstract nor Surrealist. The principal members were Coldstream, Gowing, Rogers, and PASMORE (who has since become an abstract painter).

EVERDINGEN, Allart van (1621-75), was a Dutch landscape painter who visited Scandinavia (1640-4) and returned to Holland with a new type of romantic mountain landscape, with pine forests and waterfalls, which was strange and successful. His type of scenery influenced some of the later works of J. van RUISDAEL. There are pictures by him in many Dutch and German galleries, the NG and Wallace Coll., London, and elsewhere. He also produced over one hundred landscape etchings. His elder brother, Caesar Boetius (1617–78), was a figure painter in Alkmaar and Haarlem who was much influenced by Caravaggio and therefore represents a sort of offshoot of the UTRECHT School. There are pictures by him in Alkmaar, Amsterdam, Dresden, The Hague, Rouen, and Stockholm.

EWORTH, Hans, who signed his pictures HE, was an Antwerp painter, probably identical with Jan Euworts, recorded in the Antwerp Guild in 1540. Eworth worked in London from1549 (or 1545) to 1574. His first work with both HE and a date is the *Turk on Horseback* of 1549, but he painted chiefly portraits, sometimes allegorical, such as the *Sir John Luttrell* of 1550, or straightforwardly Holbeinesque, such as the *Mary Tudor* (1559: London, Soc. of Antiquaries). His style is sensitive and nervous, employing a great deal of delicately rendered detail, ultimately dependent on HOLBEIN – who preceded him as Henry VIII's Court painter – yet without his robustness. The *Queen Elizabeth confounding Juno, Minverva and Venus* (1569: Royal Coll.) is an example of the unsubtle flattery expressed in highly sophisticated and involved Mannerist imagery which was typical of Elizabeth's Court, especially in literature. The style of this picture, however, and also the form of the monogram differ from those of the portraits, and it has been suggested that it is the work of a different painter: on the other hand, a picture of 1570 (Copenhagen), of a similar subject, may be held to bridge the gap. The *Lord Darnley and his Brother* (1563: also Royal Coll.) is a straightforward portrait, but equally introspective and elegant, with the pale complexions typical of Eworth's figures. There are several of the HE pictures still in private collections and others attributed to him in the Royal Collection and in Antwerp, Cambridge (Fitzwm), London (NPG, Tate and Wallace Coll.) Ottawa, Oxford (Ashmolean), and Wellington NZ.

EXC., EXCUDIT (Lat. he executed it) on an engraving usually refers to the publisher, who was often identical with the engraver.

EXPRESSIONISM. The search for expressiveness of style by means of exaggerations and distortions of line and colour; a deliberate abandon of the naturalism implicit in Impressionism in favour of a simplified style which should carry far greater emotional impact. In this general sense of emotional force Expressionism is a feature of non-Mediterranean art in general, GRÜNEWALD being the standard example. In the more limited context of modern art, the Expressionist movement may be said to spring from van GOGH's use of drastically simplified outline and very strong colour. In France this has clear affinities with FAUVISM, but the principal exponents, apart from Toulouse-Lautrec, were mostly German (or at least 'Nordic', like the Norwegian MUNCH, whose hysterical art is one of the foundations of the movement). The tendency to a sentimental hysteria and the clear derivation from Negro art are two of the factors which explain Hitler's denunciation of 'Degenerate Art' and the esteem it now enjoys. The BRÜCKE and the BLAUE REITER are two of the principal sub-groups, while some of the major individual artists are BECKMANN, ENSOR, NOLDE, KOKOSCHKA, ROUAULT, and SOUTINE. The nature of their subject-matter and the emphasis placed on outline are two reasons for the important part played by Expressionist graphic art.

EYCK, van. On the frame of the polyptych of the *Adoration of the Lamb* in S. Bavon, Ghent, is a Latin quatrain which may be roughly translated as 'The painter Hubert van Eyck, than whom none was greater, began it; Jan, second in art, having completed it at the charge of Jodocus Vyd, invites you by this verse on the 6th May to contemplate what has been done'. The last line is a chronostich containing the date 1432. On the problems raised by the meaning of this verse, more ink has been spilt than on any other subject in the history of art. The only facts assumed to relate to Hubert are these four: in 1424/5 a Master Luberecht was paid by the Ghent Magistrates for two designs for an altarpiece, and in 1425/6 a Master Ubrechts was visited by the Magistrates in his workshop; in 1426, a 'Master Hubrechte the painter' had in his workshop a statue and other works connected with an altarpiece, and later in that year the heirs of Lubrecht van Heyke (not specified as a painter) paid inheritance tax on his property. Except for two copies said to have been made of the epitaph on his tomb before its destruction in 1578, and according to which he died on 18 September 1426, that is all that is known of Hubert.

Jan van Eyck is well documented. From 1422 to 1424 he was working for Count John of Holland at The Hague, and around, or before, this date was perhaps connected with the Turin HOURS. In 1425 he was appointed Court Painter and 'varlet de chambre' to Philip the Good, Duke of Burgundy, and from then until late in 1429 he lived in Lille. He removed to Bruges probably in 1430, bought a house there in 1431 or 1432, and lived there until he died. Between 1426 and 1436 he made several secret journeys on the Duke's business, two of which – concerned with marriage negotiations – took him to Spain in 1427 and to Portugal in 1428. Many records testify to his presence and activity in Bruges (payments of salary, a visit in 1432 to his workshop by the town councillors, and one by the Duke himself in 1433) until the final record of his burial in July 1441. In addition to the documented facts, there are a number of signed and dated pictures: the *Portrait of a man*, inscribed 'Tymotheos Leal Souvenir 1432', the *Man in a red turban*, 1433, bearing the painter's challenging motto 'Als ich kan' (As I can) on the frame, and the *Arnolfini marriage group*, 1434, with the declaration of his own participation as a witness – 'Johannes de Eyck fuit hic' (. . . was here) – all in London, NG; the *Madonna and Child* in Melbourne, 1433 (but although the inscription is authentic, many scholars reject the attribution); the *Madonna of Canon van der Paele*, 1436, in Bruges; the *S. Barbara*, an elaborate drawing on a gesso ground, 1437, and the *Madonna*, in Dresden, which cleaning has revealed to be dated 1437; the *Madonna of the Fountain*, 1439, in Antwerp; the *Portrait of his wife*, 1439, in Bruges. In all these works the stupendous Eyckian technique is a major factor. For long the brothers were credited with the invention of oil painting, and though this is no longer a tenable idea, it is clear that Jan perfected an oil medium and varnish which has enabled his brilliant colour to survive almost unchanged, and which was fluid enough to allow him to achieve the subtlest effects of light and the most detailed rendering of objects. It is through his astounding analysis of surfaces that he reached the larger understanding of form and space; from his capacity to observe the minute he achieves a complete expression of the whole, and his technique is the perfect servant of his realistic, unidealizing, and unemotional attitude.

The Ghent Altar is a very large and complex polyptych. It consists of two superimposed rows of paintings: the upper row has, inside in the centre, *Christ as King* flanked by the *Virgin* and *S. John the Baptist*, and on the insides of the wings *Musician* and *Singing Angels*, and *Adam* and *Eve*; the lower row has, in the centre, the *Adoration of the Lamb*, and on the insides of the wings are continuations of the processions of the faithful coming to adore the Lamb, in the form of four groups of *Judges*, *Knights*, *Hermits*, and *Pilgrims* (the panel of *Judges* is a modern copy of the original, stolen in 1934). On the outside of the wings, in the upper row, is an *Annunciation*, and in the lower row portraits of the *Donor and his wife*, flanked by their patron Saints, *John the Baptist* and *John the Evangelist*. This huge and heterogeneous work is rendered more difficult to interpret by the extensive restorations and repaintings disclosed by recent scientific investigation. The quatrain would make it – with the *Leal Souvenir* portrait – the earliest of Jan's dated works, but it is impossible to decide how much or what parts are due to an earlier hand (that is, to Hubert). The theory has been advanced that the quatrain is a later forgery and Hubert a legendary figure to whom no works or participation in the Ghent Altar can be allowed. This is certainly going too far, for the verse appears to be genuine, and there exist certain works (the *Three Maries at the Sepulchre*, Rotterdam, and the so-called Friedsam *Annunciation*, New York, Met. Mus.) which are related to works by Jan, but not to the point of being attributable to him, and which possess characteristics from which his style could well have developed.

Other works attributed to Jan with reasonable certainty include the *Virgin in a Church*, Berlin; *Annunciation*, Washington, NG; *Madonna and Donor*, Warwick Castle; *Madonna with Chancellor Rolin*, Paris, Louvre; *Madonna and Child*, Frankfurt, Städel; and the so-called

'*Cardinal Albergati*', Vienna, the preparatory drawing for which, in Dresden, is the only surviving silverpoint unanimously attributed to Jan.

Jan's ability and inventiveness make him easily the major artist of the Early Netherlandish School, and his position is challenged only by the MASTER of FLÉMALLE. In Jan, the opulent, politically opportunist, and aristocratic Burgundian Court found its most complete artistic expression. The Ghent Altar was extremely influential throughout the 15th century and the technique evolved by Jan became the accepted Flemish one. His formal influence, however, in the succeeding years was less than that of Roger van der WEYDEN, due to the greater appeal of Roger's warmer and more emotional approach. Jan's chief follower was Petrus CHRISTUS, who is believed to have completed the *Madonna and Child with Saints* (New York, Frick Coll.) commissioned in 1441 a few months before Jan died, and who probably took over his workshop and something of his position as the principal Bruges painter of his day.

Margaret van Eyck, said to have been a sister of Jan and a miniaturist, is pure fiction.

Besides the works already mentioned there are others in Berlin, New York (Met. Mus.), Philadelphia (Johnson), Turin, and Vienna.

F

F., FEC., FECIT (Lat. he made it) frequently follows a name on paintings, engravings, etc. as an assertion of authorship.

F.F. is an abbreviation of Fieri Fecit (Lat. he caused to be made) and should not be confused with a signature: *Johannes Smith F.F.* means that John Smith paid for the picture, not that he painted it.

FABRIANO *see* GENTILE da Fabriano.

FABRITIUS, Barent (1624–73), was the younger brother of Carel. Like his brother, he was probably a pupil of Rembrandt *c.*1640, but unlike Carel he remained a Rembrandt imitator all his life. He painted portraits and Biblical and mythological subjects, good examples of which can be found in Amsterdam. The Hague, Hartford Conn., and London.

FABRITIUS, Carel (1622–54), was the finest of Rembrandt's pupils, whose brilliant promise was cut short by the great Delft explosion of 12 October 1654, which killed him as he was working on a portrait. He was in contact with Rembrandt about 1641–3 and was himself probably the master of VERMEER: the extraordinary gap between Rembrandt and Vermeer being bridged by Fabritius's reversal of Rembrandt's practice, in that he painted dark objects against a light background (e.g. the *Self-portrait*, Rotterdam). Several Rembrandtesque portraits have recently been attributed to him, but the few known works – only five are dated, and less than ten are signed – do not seem to confirm these attributions, and there is still considerable confusion with his brother's work. The *Goldfinch* (1654: The Hague) is almost unique in Dutch art, but it has much more in common with Vermeer than with Rembrandt. There are pictures in Amsterdam (Rijksmus.: one apparently dated 1640, but probably either 1648 or 1649), Groningen, The Hague, Innsbruck, London (NG: dated 1652 and 1654), Paris (Louvre), Rotterdam, Schwerin (dated 1654), and Warsaw.

FACTURE, FATTURA are the French and Italian equivalents for HANDLING.

FALCONET, Étienne-Maurice (1716–91), worked under J. B. LEMOYNE and was accepted into the Academy in 1744. In 1757 he was appointed Director of Sculpture at the Sèvres Porcelain Manufactory, where he remained until 1766, supervising the production of many pieces from his own models. He also worked for Mme de Pompadour. Through Diderot the Empress Catherine II invited him to Russia in 1766 to make a bronze equestrian monument to Peter the Great at St Petersburg: this is his masterpiece and a great feat of technique as the horse rears up on its huge plinth of rough granite with both forelegs unsupported. He left Russia in 1779, before the statue was unveiled, returning to France in 1781. A stroke in 1783 forced him to stop working. He also wrote on sculpture and was notorious for his opinion that the warmth and softness of the human body were better rendered by his own contemporaries than by the Ancients ('Réflexions sur la sculpture', 1761); most of his own works are of Venus, nymphs, and similar subjects tending to warmth and softness. His more formal *Milo of Croton* (1754: made for the Academy) is in the Louvre, and the *maquette* for the *Peter the Great* is in the Hermitage, Leningrad: the Wallace Coll. and V & A, London, and the Frick Coll., New York, have more characteristic works.

FANTIN-LATOUR, Henri (1836–1904), was a French painter of romantic figure subjects, portrait groups, and still-life. He exhibited at the Salon regularly from 1861, but found himself in the SALON des Refusés in 1863, and, for all that he seems a straightforward Salon painter, he was friendly with most of the advanced artists of the day, including Manet and Whistler, and also admired the Pre-Raphaelites. He painted several portrait groups, the best-known being the *Hommage à Manet* (*L'Atelier aux Batignolles*) (1870: Louvre, Paris), but his Romantic imagination and, later, a passion for Wagner, led him to paint some extraordinary figure subjects. In England he has always been popular for his still-life and flower paintings, executed in a meticulous 'Dutch' manner totally unlike his sub-Delacroix fantasies. There are pictures in Birmingham, Boston, Cambridge (Fitzwm), Cleveland, Dublin, Glasgow (Burrell Coll. and University), Kansas City, London (NG, Tate, V & A), Manchester, Ottawa, Oxford, Port Sunlight (Lever Gall.), Toledo, St Louis, Washington (NG and Phillips), and elsewhere.

FARINGTON, Joseph (1747–1821), was a topographical draughtsman of no great ability who became an RA in 1785 and whose talent for intrigue gave him an enormous influence in that institution. He kept a very full Diary which is one of the principal sources for the history of English art (and the RA) in the last years of the 18th and the early 19th century: extracts from it have been published and a complete edition is in preparation. The original text is mostly at Windsor Castle, but some parts have been dispersed. Farington's drawings are in London (BM, V & A) and elsewhere.

FAT. Pigment is said to be fat when it is mixed with oil to make an oleaginous paste, giving a rich IMPASTO. Lean paint has been thinned with turpentine or other spirit, which helps to make it dry quicker. A studio maxim used to be: 'Start lean and finish fat'.

FATTORI, Giovanni (1825–1908), was one of the leading members of the MACCHIAIOLI. He was trained in Florence and then fought in the War of Independence 1848–9: in 1861 he won a prize with his *Battle of Magenta* (1861–2: Florence, Gall. d'Arte Moderna). This was followed by other military subjects as well as landscapes and scenes of peasant life. He visited Paris in 1875, the year after the Impressionist Exhibition, but was little influenced by them. There are works by him in Florence, Leghorn, Milan and Rome, as well as about 200 etchings (a technique unusual in 19th-century Italy).

FAUVE. At the Paris Salon d'Automne of 1905, the works of a number of painters were hung together in one room: these were MATISSE, MARQUET, DERAIN, VLAMINCK, ROUAULT, Manguin, Camoin, Jean Puy, and Othon Friesz. Their works, full of distortions and flat patterns and painted in violent colour, created a furore, and a critic dubbed them collectively '*Les Fauves*' (the wild beasts). They were not, until then – or even afterwards – a particularly coherent group. Matisse came to be regarded as their leader, possibly because he was not unwilling, but the parts of the group had various origins. Matisse, Marquet, Rouault, and Camoin had all been pupils of Gustave MOREAU at the École des Beaux-Arts; Matisse and Marquet had often worked together; Rouault pursued a solitary course and found himself among the Fauves rather than sought their company; Derain and Vlaminck worked together, strongly influenced by EXPRESSIONISM; the others adhered temporarily, mostly out of rebellion against the academic system and because their brightly coloured works could be hung in no other company. In 1906 DUFY, and in 1907 BRAQUE and METZINGER, exhibited with them, but by 1908 the Fauves had fallen apart as a group and a number of its members had seceded to CUBISM.

FEININGER, Lyonel (1871–1956), was born and died in New York, but was really a German Cubist. He went to Germany in 1887 and finally returned to America only in 1937: he was trained in Germany and went to Paris in 1892–3. From 1911 he was interested in Cubism, and DELAUNAY was the main influence on his painting. In 1912 he met the members of the BRÜCKE group and in the following year exhibited with the BLAUE REITER. He was particularly close to KLEE and KANDINSKY, but after his return to the US his works became more abstract. Many German and American museums have examples.

FERGUSON, William Gouw (1632–95), was a Scottish painter of still-life so much in the Dutch manner that he is often confused with painters like Jan WEENIX. He worked in Holland and England. There are four pictures by him in Edinburgh and others in Aberdeen, Barnsley, Berlin, London (Tate, V & A at Ham House), Manchester, and elsewhere.

FERNELEY, John (1782–1860), was an English sporting painter whose works were made widely popular in reproduction. He worked in Ireland 1809–10. His *Bay Horse* (1826: London, Tate) is typical.

FERRARI, Gaudenzio (1471/81–1546), was a Lombard painter who combined the influence of Leonardo with that of both Perugino and

Correggio and sometimes added a strong dash of German art. His earliest works (1507) were for Varallo, near the Swiss border, and his principal fresco cycles are in Lombardy; in the Sacro Monte, Varallo (begun 1517), in S. Cristoforo, Vercelli (1529–32), and in Saronno (1534–6). The Sacro Monte frescoes, which contain an element of overcrowding derived from German examples, are further complicated by the addition of terra-cotta figures in the round, also by Gaudenzio, to add to the illusion. From 1539 he worked in Milan. There are pictures by him in Amsterdam, Bergamo, Berlin, London (NG), Milan (Brera, Poldi-Pezzoli, Castello, and churches), Paris (Louvre), Sarasota Fla, Turin, and elsewhere.

FERRI, Ciro (1628/34–89), was the closest follower of PIETRO da CORTONA, some of whose frescoes he completed in the Pitti Palace, Florence, and elsewhere. He worked mainly in Rome, Florence, and Bergamo and he also made many designs for engravers.

FETI (Fetti), Domenico (c. 1588/9–1623), was born in Rome and began as a follower of Caravaggio's followers and an admirer of ELSHEI- MER. He was taken to Mantua in or before 1613 by Cardinal Ferdi- nando Gonzaga (who became Duke of Mantua) and worked there as Court Painter until he went to Venice in 1621. In 1622 he settled there and is recorded as gravely ill early in 1623. In Mantua he saw the Rubens portraits and was also influenced by Venetian painting, and these influences, together with his early admiration for Elsheimer, led him to produce smallish genre pictures, usually representing one of the Parables, which are very broadly treated and rich in colour. He paint- ed some frescoes in Mantua, but they are less successful. There are examples in the Royal Coll. (a series at Hampton Court) and in Baltimore, Birmingham (Barber Inst.), Dresden, Florence (Uffizi, Pitti), Frankfurt (Städel), Kansas City, Manchester, Mantua (Palazzo and Cath.), Munich, New York (Met. Mus.), Paris (Louvre), Prague, Venice (Accad.), Vienna, Washington (NG), and York.

FEUERBACH, Anselm (1829–80), was, like BÖCKLIN, a German Ro- mantic painter who came under the spell of Italy and Italian art (in his case, Raphael). He was trained in Germany and Antwerp before going to Paris and working in COUTURE's studio (1852–3); he was also simultaneously influenced by Delacroix and Courbet. In 1855 he went to Italy and spent most of the rest of his life there except for three unsuccessful years (1873–6) teaching in Vienna. He painted some fine portraits, 16th-century Italian in feeling, especially those of Nanna, whose features obsessed him from 1860 to 1865. Karlsruhe has a whole room of his works and most German galleries possess examples.

FIAMMINGO see DUQUESNOY.

FINE MANNER. Early Florentine engravings, of the mid and later 15th century, are divided into two classes – the Broad and Fine

Manners. The Fine Manner is so called because it uses fine lines, often cross-hatched, to give a general effect not unlike a wash drawing. The Broad Manner uses bolder lines, parallel but further apart, often with small hooks at the end, the general effect being similar to a bold pen drawing. MANTEGNA, although not a Florentine, was influenced by the Broad Manner.

FINSON (Finsonius), Ludovicus (before 1580–1617), was a rather mysterious Caravaggesque who was born in Bruges, died in Amsterdam, formed his style in Naples and seems to have worked principally in Aix-en-Provence. He was there in 1610, but his *Annunciation*, still there, is signed and inscribed '1612 in Naples', and another version is in Naples Mus. His style was closely modelled on Caravaggio's Neapolitan followers (cf. the UTRECHT School) and he actually owned a part-share of Caravaggio's *Madonna of the Rosary*. There are two pictures of 1613 in Marseilles, and the *Martyrdom of S. Stephen* (1614) is in Arles Cathedral; most of his works are in S. France, especially Aix, but there are attributed pictures in Chicago, London (Wellington Mus.), and Oxford.

FIXATIVE. A kind of thin varnish sprayed on to drawings and pastels to prevent their being rubbed.

FLAXMAN, John (1755–1826), was an English NEOCLASSIC sculptor with an enormous European reputation in his own day. He first exhibited in 1767 and became friendly with ROMNEY early in his career. He went to the RA Schools in 1770 and met BLAKE at about this time: much of his sympathy for Gothic art is probably due to this friendship. In 1775 he began to work for Wedgwood, who was then popularizing Neoclassical designs in his new 'Etruscan' ware. With Wedgwood's help he went to Italy in 1787, where he remained until 1794, looking at a great variety of works of all periods. A sketchbook in the V & A, London, shows the catholicity of his tastes, for it includes drawings after Bernini although he loathed everything he stood for. His dislike of the Baroque was probably partly religious in origin, reflecting his Low Church sympathies; and it is interesting that BACON was a Methodist and BANKS an atheist, and all employed only generalized Christian symbolism – non-Catholic – in their funerary sculpture, although Flaxman prided himself on Christianizing monumental sculpture. After he returned from Italy Flaxman devoted himself almost exclusively to monuments, two of his most famous having been begun in Rome. These are the *Mansfield*, erected in Westminster Abbey in 1795, and the *Collins* of the same year in Chichester Cathedral. While still in Rome he had also begun the book-illustrations which brought him the greatest fame on the Continent and influenced later generations – INGRES and the NAZARENER among them. These are pure outline drawings of strictly Neoclassical simplicity, which give the impression of being sketches for relief sculpture: they include long series of plates for the Odyssey and the Iliad, Aeschylus, Hesiod, Dante, as well as Milton and Bunyan drawings. He became an RA in 1800 and was made Professor of Sculpture in 1810, his lectures being published posthumously in 1829. Among his few statues in the round which are not monuments are the *Fury of Athamas* (1791-2: Nat. Trust, Ickworth House) and *S. Michael overcoming Satan* (1821) and the *Pastoral Apollo* (1824: both Nat. Trust, Petworth). University College, London, has a large collection of his drawings and models, and the Soane Mus., London, also has models. Other works are scattered as far as Madras and Quebec and include works in Bath, many in Chichester Cath., Copenhagen, Edinburgh (NPG), Glasgow, Gloucester, London (NPG, V & A, RA, Westminster Abbey, and St Paul's), and many English churches and cathedrals.

FLINCK, Govaert (1615–60), was a pupil of REMBRANDT, and imitated him until the mid 1650s, though always with a greater striving for elegance, which brought him a successful practice as a portrait painter. He had ambitions, however, as a historical painter, and was commissioned by the City Council of Amsterdam to decorate the interior of the new Town Hall with large historical works, but he died before executing the work, which was then divided among different artists – including Rembrandt. There are works in Amsterdam (Rijksmus.), Antwerp, Berlin, Boston (Mus.), Brunswick, Cape Town, Dresden, Dublin, London (NG, Wallace Coll.), Leningrad, Munich, New York (Met. Mus.), Paris (Louvre), Rotterdam, Vienna, and elsewhere.

FLORIS, Frans (Frans de Vriendt) (c.1517–70), was a Flemish painter who went to Italy, where he studied Michelangelo, Raphael, and the Antique. He entered the Antwerp guild in 1540, and was prominent among the Antwerp ITALIANIZERS. There are works in Amsterdam (Rijksmus.), Antwerp, Berlin, Brussels, Dresden, Florence (Uffizi), The Hague, Madrid, Prague Castle, Vienna, and elsewhere. His two sons, Jan Battista and Frans, were also painters; the second worked in Rome.

FONTAINEBLEAU, First and Second Schools of. The First School of Fontainebleau is the name given to the combination of Mannerist painting and stucco decoration introduced by the Italians ROSSO, PRIMATICCIO, and Niccolò dell'ABBATE into the Royal Palaces of France, particularly that of Fontainebleau, under the patronage of François I. The style begins in 1530, with Rosso's arrival in France, and continues to c.1560 under Niccolò dell'Abbate. The extreme elegance of Parmigianino's art is characteristic of this First School. The Second School of Fontainebleau represents an attempt at a similar decorative tradition in the second half of the 16th century, mostly under Henri IV. The palaces decorated by him have suffered greatly, but the Salle Ovale at Fontainebleau is an example of the revival. The names usually associated with the Second School are not illustrious: Ambroise Dubois (1542/3–1614), Toussaint Dubreuil (1561–1602), and Martin Fréminet (1567–1602).

FOPPA, Vincenzo (1427/30–1515/16), was the leading painter of the Milanese School before it was transformed by the influence of Leonardo da Vinci. He was born near Brescia and may have been a pupil of the Paduan SQUARCIONE, who was Mantegna's master: in any case his first dated work, the *Crucifixion* (1456: Bergamo), shows the influence of Jacopo Bellini, and Foppa's later works amply prove that he knew the work of Jacopo's son Giovanni and son-in-law Mantegna. From 1456 to 1490 he worked in Pavia and was employed a good deal by the Dukes of Milan. There are works by him in Milan (Brera, Castello, Poldi-Pezzoli, S. Eustorgio) and in Baltimore (Walters), Bergamo, Berlin, Brescia (Accad. and Carmine), London (NG and Wallace Coll., all that is left of the frescoes in the Medici Bank), Milan, New York (Met. Mus.), Pavia, Philadelphia (Johnson), Washington (NG), and Worcester Mass.

FORAIN, Jean Louis (1852–1931), was a draughtsman and illustrator working for satirical papers in Paris from 1876 onwards. He was greatly influenced by Rembrandt and Goya, by DAUMIER, who preceded him in his chosen field, and by Manet. He was a friend and follower of Degas, and exhibited four times with the Impressionists between 1879 and 1886. Until *c.* 1909 his subjects were chiefly scenes from Parisian life, with occasional cartoons on political scandals, e.g. the Panama Canal; after 1909 he turned to the depiction of social misery and the callousness and inhumanity of the processes of justice. He also illustrated the New Testament. Most of his drawings are in limpid watercolour washes of sepia on a loose and evocative outline, full of movement and luminosity, highly reminiscent of Daumier. There are works in Boston (Mus.), Chicago, Dresden, London (Courtauld Inst., Tate), Paris (Louvre), Washington and elsewhere.

FORESHORTENING is perspective applied to a single object. An arm pointing directly at the spectator so that little more than the hand can be seen is said to be strongly foreshortened. Extreme foreshortening can have emotional overtones, as is best demonstrated by Mantegna's *Dead Christ* (Milan, Brera). The work of Uccello is sufficient proof that a mastery of foreshortening is not necessarily accompanied by the ability to construct coherent perspective systems.

FOUND OBJECT (*Objet trouvé*). In SURREALIST theory an object of any kind, such as a shell found on a walk, can be a work of art; and such 'Found Objects' have been exhibited. If a little judicious touching-up has been indulged in, the object is known technically as a 'Found Object Composed'.

FOUQUET, Jehan (*c.* 1420–in or before 81), was the major French painter of the 15th century. He went to Italy and was in Rome at some time between 1443 and Feb. 1447, since he is said to have painted a portrait of Eugenius IV and two attendants: this, however, depends on the identification of Jehan the Frenchman with *Giachetto francoso*, which is not self-evident. He may have gone to Rome with a French embassy in 1446, or he may have gone to get a dispensation to enter the priesthood, since there is a letter of 1449 from Nicholas V to 'Johanni Fouquet Juniori clerico . . .'. By 1448 he was back in his native Tours, where he soon began to work for Charles VIII. He was appointed Painter to the King in 1475. He is known to have designed sculpture and to have worked for the Order of S. Michel, but the only documented works extant are the miniatures in a copy of 'Les Antiquités Judaïques' (Paris, Bibliothèque Nationale). On grounds of style several other MSS. and some easel pictures are attributed to him: they include works in Paris (Louvre (portraits of *Charles VII* and *Jouvenel des Ursins*) and Bib. Nat.), Antwerp and Berlin (the two halves of the Melun diptych: *Étienne Chevalier* and *Madonna*), Chantilly (Musée Condé), London (BM), Munich (Staatsbibliothek), and Nouans Indre-et-Loire, Parish Church (*Deposition*).

A very fine portrait of a young man, dated 1456, in the Liechtenstein Coll., Vaduz, used to be attributed to Fouquet but is now generally given to the Master of 1456, and another portrait, *Man with a Glass of Wine*, in the Louvre, has also been attributed to him.

FRAGLIA. The Venetian painters' GUILD.

FRAGONARD, Jean Honoré (1732–1806), was the typical painter of gallant and sentimental subjects in the reign of Louis XV during the ascendancy of Mme du Barry, and during the reign of Louis XVI. He was a pupil of Chardin for a few months in 1750 and then went to BOUCHER until 1752, when he won the Rome Prize: he did not go directly to Rome, however, but worked under Carle van Loo 1753–6. From 1756 until 1761 he worked at the French Academy in Rome, where he studied the living TIEPOLO more than any of the Old Masters. He also went, with Hubert ROBERT, to the South under the patronage of the Abbé de Saint-Non, who later wrote a book about the trip. In 1761 Fragonard returned to Paris and made his name in 1765 with his *High Priest Coresus sacrificing himself to save Callirhoe* (Paris, Louvre), a piece in the very Grand Manner. He soon abandoned History (having been elected *Agréé* of the Academy) and turned to more congenial subjects, such as *The Swing* (c.1766: London, Wallace Coll.). This was originally commissioned from a serious history painter by the Baron de St Julien: 'I desire', he said, 'that you should paint Madame [pointing to his mistress] on a swing which is being set in motion by a Bishop. You must place me where I can have a good view of the legs of this pretty little thing . . .'. The serious history-painter could think of nothing else to say except to recommend M. Fragonard as a more suitable executant. He continued in this light-hearted and sometimes frankly erotic vein with great success, being commissioned by Mme du Barry to paint a series of the *Progress of Love* for her new house; unaccountably, however, she rejected them and Fragonard took them back to his native Grasse when he fled there during the Terror. They are now in New York (Frick Coll.). In 1773 he went to Italy again, returning via Austria and Germany. The Revolution put an end to his patrons and to the demand for his kind of art, which was entirely superseded by the high-mindedness of DAVID and Republican Virtue. In desperate poverty, he returned to Paris from Grasse, and it was David who got him a job in the Museums Service. He died in Paris, almost totally forgotten. There are works by him in Besançon, Paris (Louvre and Banque de France), and other French museums: outside France the best collection is in London (Wallace Coll.), and there are others in Boston, Cincinnati, Cleveland, Detroit, St Louis, New York (Met. Mus.), Toledo Ohio, Washington (NG), and else- where. Splendid examples of his *portraits de fantasie*, based on Rembrandt and Tiepolo, are in Barcelona and Liverpool.

FRANCESCO di Giorgio (1439–1501/2) was a Sienese who worked principally as an architect and designer of fortifications, and was perhaps the inventor of the land-mine. He also executed sculptures, and a few paintings in a tender and linear style reminiscent of Botticelli, including a documented altarpiece of 1475 (Siena). There are examples in Amiens, London (NG), New York (Met. Mus.), and Siena.

FRANCIA, Francesco (*c.* 1450–1517/18), was a Bolognese goldsmith who is first recorded as a painter in 1486. It used to be thought that a *Madonna* (London, NG) of 1492 was his earliest known dated work; this is now regarded as a forgery, and the earliest picture would now seem to be the large *Felicini Madonna* (signed and dated 1494: Bologna, Pinacoteca), which shows a blend of the style of PERUGINO with that of COSTA and the Ferrarese – COSSA and ROBERTI – and almost no personal character. Until 1506, when Costa went as Court Painter to Mantua, they worked in partnership, but after that date he was more and more influenced by Raphael and the soft style of Perugino and the Umbrians. Raphael's *S. Cecilia* is supposed to have caused him to die of depression at his own inferiority. There are works by him in the Royal Coll. and in Berlin, Bologna (Pinacoteca, Mus. Civico, and several churches), Boston (Gardner), Budapest, Chantilly, Dresden, Dublin, Ferrara (Cath.), Florence (Uffizi), Glasgow, London (NG), Milan (Brera, Poldi-Pezzoli), Munich, New York (Met. Mus.), Paris (Louvre), Philadelphia (Mus. and Johnson), Rome (Gall. Naz., Capitoline, Borghese), San Marino Cal. (Hunting- ton), Turin, Vienna (K-H Mus., Akad.), Washington (NG), Worcester Mass., Yale, and elsewhere.

FRANCIABIGIO (*c.*1482/3–1525) was a Florentine painter who was the assistant of ANDREA del Sarto and a pupil of ALBERTINELLI. Franciabigio's best works are his rather introspective portraits, and he is a characteristic representative of the generation between Andrea del Sarto and Fra BARTOLOMMEO, as may be seen in his frescoes in the Chiostro dello Scalzo, Florence, of about 1518. There are works by him in Florence (Uffizi, Pitti, and churches) and in the Royal Collection, Barnard Castle (Bowes Mus.), Berlin, Brussels, Detroit, London (NG), Munich, New York (Met. Mus.), Oxford, Paris (Louvre), Rome (Borghese and Gall. Naz.), and Vienna.

FRANCIS, Sam (*b.*1923), is a Californian Tachiste painter. He served in the US Air Force 1943–5, and, after a long spell in hospital, became an abstract painter in 1947. In 1950 he went to Paris, joining the circle of American painters around RIOPELLE. He has painted murals for the Kunsthalle, Basle (1956–8) and, on a visit to Japan in 1957, for a School of Flower Arrangement there. His technique of dribbling paint differs from the more 'calligraphic' style used by many Americans. There are paintings by him in London (Tate) and New York (M of MA).

FRANCKE, Master (active *c.*1405–after 24), was the most important Hamburg painter after Master BERTRAM, but was (like KONRAD von Soest) an exponent of the SOFT STYLE. He was probably in France about 1405, since his style owes much to French illuminated MSS. His major work was the *S. Thomas à Becket Altar*, painted for the merchants trading with England, of which only fragments are known (begun 1424: Hamburg). Other works are in Hamburg, Helsinki, and Leipzig.

FRESCO (Ital. fresh). Wall-painting in a medium like watercolour on plaster. *Fresco secco*, painted on dry plaster, gives an effect not unlike an ordinary distempered wall and suffers from the same defect of the paint scaling off, but true fresco, or *buon fresco*, practised in Italy from the 13th century and perfected in the 16th century, is one of the most permanent forms of wall decoration known. The wall is first rough-plastered and then a coat, known as the *arricciato* (or *arriccio*) is applied. On this the CARTOON is traced, so that the whole composition is transferred to the wall, and then an area sufficient for one day's work is covered with the final layer of plaster, called the *intonaco*. The cartoon is redrawn over this, joining up with the parts still uncovered, and the damp plaster is then painted with pigments mixed with plain water or lime-water, allowance being made for the fact that the colours dry much lighter. Because the plaster is still damp a chemical reaction takes place and the colours become integrated with the wall itself, so that scaling cannot occur. The use of a detailed, full-size cartoon means that several assistants can work simultaneously on different parts of the wall, provided that all work is done from the top downwards so that the splashes fall on the unpainted parts. At the end of the day all the unpainted *intonaco* is cut away, to be re-laid next day, so that the working surface is always damp: careful examination of a fresco reveals the joins in the plaster and from these the number of days taken to paint the whole can be estimated approximately. *Fresco secco* may legitimately be employed to retouch or to add accents, but during the 16th century it was almost obligatory to work entirely in *buon fresco*, and some of the finest examples of the technique are Raphael's decorations in the Stanze of the Vatican. Climatic conditions outside Central Italy are not always favourable and the attempts to revive the technique for the decoration of the House of Lords, early in the 19th century, were not successful, although RIVERA practised a form of fresco in Mexico in the present century.

FRIEDRICH, Caspar David (1774–1840), was the most purely Romantic of German landscape painters, and in his vision of the great forests one of the purest of European Romantics. He was trained in Copenhagen and never went to Italy – he said that he was afraid he would never want to return if he ever saw Rome. He was particularly interested in the expression of effects of light and of the seasons, but his feeling for the haunted silence of the woods has no parallel outside Altdorfer. In 1808 he exhibited the *Cross in the Mountains* (Dresden), which was painted as an altarpiece for a private chapel, although it has no specifically religious subject-matter. It started a debate over the suitability of landscape for religious purposes: in fact, all Friedrich's pictures of this kind are landscapes with religious implications, and not 'religious' subjects at all. He spent most of his life in Dresden, which has the best collection of his works.

FRITH, William Powell (1819–1909), was the son of an innkeeper in Harrogate, who virtually forced him to become an artist. He started as an itinerant portrait painter, and after 1840 specialized in costume history and genre subjects, becoming one of the most successful painters of contemporary life. *Ramsgate Sands* (1853: Royal Coll.), *Derby Day* (1858: London, Tate), *The Railway Station* (1862: Royal Holloway College, near Windsor) depict with minute detail an enormous variety of anecdotal incidents, which made his works so popular that barriers had to be erected at the Royal Academy to protect them from the crush of admirers. He travelled a good deal in Holland, and visited Italy; he published three volumes of memoirs, recounting in the most matter-of-fact way the sources of his subjects, and the details of his phenomenal success.

FROMENT, Nicolas (active 1450–90), worked in the South of France and was painter to René of Anjou. There are two documented works by him: the curious *Mary in the Burning Bush* (1476: Aix-en-Provence, Cath.) and the *Raising of Lazarus* (1461: Florence, Uffizi). A diptych of René and his wife, attributed to Froment, is in Paris (Louvre).

FROTTAGE (from Fr. *frotter*, to rub). Most people know the parlour game which consists of putting a piece of thin paper over a penny and rubbing a soft pencil over it, causing an image of the monarch's head to appear on the paper. This simple device, dignified by the name of *frottage*, has frequently been used to obtain effects of texture in abstract or semi-abstract painting. It is normally done by making a *frottage* on a piece of paper and then applying one or more of these to a canvas as COLLAGES. Max ERNST frequently used the method, employing the floorboards and other wooden surfaces.

FRUEAUF, Rueland I and II, were Austrian painters from Passau. Rueland I (*c.*1440/5–1507) worked in Passau and Salzburg from 1470 in a style derived from Flemish painters such as Jan van Eyck and the Master of Flémalle. There are four *Passion Scenes* of 1490–1 by him in Vienna (K-H Mus.).

His son Rueland II (*c.*1470/5–1545 or later) was a citizen of Passau before 1497, a Councillor in 1533, and was still active as a painter in 1545. He painted a series of scenes from the life of S. Leopold, some of which are signed R F and dated 1507, for Klosterneuberg, near Vienna, as well as a *S. Anne with the Virgin and Child* (1508: Vienna K-H Mus.). Other works by father or son are in Boston, Budapest, Cambridge Mass. (Fogg), Detroit, Munich, Prague, and Venice (Correr).

FULLER, Isaac (*d.*1672), was probably trained in France and was working in Oxford in 1644, at the same time as DOBSON. He seems to have been a very Bohemian character, and his few surviving works are all painted with a fierce bravura and an impasto distantly reminiscent of Rembrandt. His altarpiece in All Souls College, Oxford, is now lost but was described by Evelyn as 'too full of nakeds for a chapell' (*Diary*, 1664). He died in London. There are works in London (Tate, NPG, and Dulwich) and Oxford (*Self-portrait*, 1670, in the Bodleian Library and a version in Queen's College).

FUSELI, Henry (1741–1825), was Swiss by birth, his name, Füssli, being modified to suit the Italian tongue. His father, a painter, forced him to become a clergyman, and he was ordained in 1761, but his exposure of a dishonest magistrate ended his career as a parson. In 1763 he began studying art in Berlin and later came to England to work as a hack translator of French, German (WINCKELMANN, as early as 1765), and Italian books, and occasional illustrator. He was encouraged by Reynolds to become a painter, and in 1770 went to Rome for eight years, where he taught himself, mainly by copying Michelangelo in the Sistine Chapel. On his return to England he began exhibiting works of imaginative power, executed in a deficient technique, his first success being *The Nightmare* (1782), a picture redolent of Romantic horror. He then worked for Boydell's Shakespeare Gallery, became an ARA in 1788 and an RA in 1790, and began a series of huge paintings illustrating Milton (46 in all) to which public and patrons remained indifferent. He was made Professor of Painting at the Academy in 1799 and Keeper in 1804, and he held the double office until his death. Among his pupils were Etty, HAYDON, Mulready, Leslie, Constable, Landseer, and the artistic memoirs of the period are full of anecdotes of his eccentricities and sarcasms. Fuseli's art, with its extravagance of movement and gesture, its distortions and stylizations of form (particularly in his often erotic drawings of women), its exploitation of the murky layers of horror and fear in the imagination, is the antithesis of Reynolds's classicism and Gainsborough's charm, but is a less dedicated form of the visionary quality which inspired BLAKE, whom he first met *c.* 1787. He also knew DAVID (in Rome 1775/8) and GÉRARD. In 1831 a *Life* was published with an edition of his writings.

There are works in Auckland NZ, Birmingham, Cambridge (Fitzwm), Frankfurt (Goethe Mus.), London (Tate, Courtauld Inst.), Weimar, Zürich, and elsewhere.

FUTURISM. This word, sometimes used to mean any art more recent than 1900, has in fact a precise meaning. It was the only important modern movement before the New York School to be largely independent of Paris (for which reason it is not popular in France), and it can be dated from 20 February 1909 to its virtual demise in the First War (*c.* 1915). It was actually born in Paris, in an article in 'Le Figaro' by MARINETTI, poet, dramatist, mountebank, and future friend of Mussolini, in which he announced '... a new beauty ... a roaring motorcar, which runs like a machine-gun, is more beautiful than the *Winged Victory of Samothrace*. ... We wish to glorify war ...'. This general Manifesto was followed by a 'Manifesto of Futurist Painting' (1910) and a 'Technical Manifesto' (also 1910), which is the key to the aesthetics of Futurism. They wished to represent machines or figures actually in motion – 'We proclaim ... that universal dynamism must be rendered as dynamic sensation; that movement and light destroy the substance of objects'. The 'Manifesto of Futurist Painting' was signed by BOCCIONI, CARRÀ, Russolo, BALLA, and SEVERINI; Boccioni also issued a Manifesto of his own, on sculpture, in 1912. In that year the Futurist Exhibition was held in Paris and caused great scandal; from Paris it went on to London and Berlin and eventually all over Europe, causing riots and general excitement. Nevertheless, Futurism as an aesthetic force died early in the First World War and all the major Futurists who survived have since returned to a more traditional method of expressing their ideas.

G

GABO, Naum (*b*.1890), was born in Russia and is the younger brother of PEVSNER. He abandoned a medical career and began to study in Munich under the great German art historian Wölfflin. In 1910 he met KANDINSKY and in 1913/14, while visiting his brother, then a Cubist painter in Paris, he met other artists and, on returning to Russia in 1917, he found himself involved in art and politics. He and his brother opposed TATLIN and in 1920 issued their 'Realistic Manifesto', beginning: 'We deny volume as an expression of space . . .'. Inevitably, he had to leave Russia and he spent the years 1922–32 in Berlin, leaving at the time of the Nazi rise to power. He spent many years in England, broadcasting for the BBC during the war, and in 1946 he settled in America. There are works by him in London (Tate) and New York (M of MA).

GADDI, Taddeo (*d*.1366), was one of the most faithful of the followers of GIOTTO, for whom he is supposed to have worked for 24 years – thus transmitting, through his son Agnolo, the Giotto tradition to the very end of the Trecento, and even, through Agnolo's pupil Cennini, into the Quattrocento. Since Giotto died in 1337 Taddeo must have been apprenticed to him not later than 1313, but by 1332 he took an important independent commission to paint the fresco cycle of the *Life of the Virgin* in the Baroncelli Chapel in Sta Croce, Florence, where Giotto himself painted four chapels. These frescoes were completed in 1338 and form his most important work; they show a strong dependence on Giotto and also a certain desire to break away, which is confirmed by the signed and dated triptych (1334: Berlin) which shows an affinity with the art of Bernardo DADDI. Several other dated works are known, and in 1347 his name heads the list of famous painters who might be employed to paint a polyptych for S. Giovanni Fuorcivitas, Pistoia. He was given the commission, and the altarpiece (dated 1353) is still in the church. He also painted a series of scenes from the Life of Christ and of S. Francis on the panels of a Sacristy cupboard door (now in Florence, Accad., Berlin, and Munich): these are often adapted from Giotto's frescoes in Sta Croce and Assisi. Other works are in Berne, Bristol, Esztergom, Florence (Uffizi, Accad., Horne Mus., Bargello, and churches), New York (Met. Mus.), Pisa (S. Francesco), Yale University, and elsewhere.

His son, Agnolo (*d*.1396), was working in the Vatican as an assistant to his brother Giovanni in 1369 and seems to have had a very prosperous career, founding the fortunes of the Gaddi family. He painted a series of frescoes in Sta Croce, so that his style is easily comparable with that of both Giotto and his own father: the most important of his frescoes is the cycle of the *True Cross* in the choir (perhaps of the early 1380s). There are documented frescoes in Prato Cathedral (1392–5) and panels in S. Miniato al Monte, Florence (1393–6). Other works are in Florence and in Berlin, London (NG), Montreal, Munich, Paris (Louvre), Perugia (Cath.), Washington (NG), Yale, and elsewhere.

GAINSBOROUGH, Thomas (1727–88), was born in Sudbury, Suffolk, but went to London in 1740, where he worked for the next few years under GRAVELOT and probably met HAYMAN, then working on his Vauxhall decorations. The connexion with Hayman is not very clear, but it is certain that many of the small portrait-groups, with the figures set in a realistic landscape, which Gainsborough painted at the beginning of his career are markedly dependent on Hayman. One of the principal influences on him at this stage, however, was Dutch 17th-century landscape painting. In London he seems to have copied and restored such pictures for the dealers, and it is certain that he thought of himself as a landscape painter in this style. His earliest landscapes, painted in Suffolk, are very close to the example of Wynants, Ruisdael, and Hobbema as may be seen from the most famous of them, the *Cornard Wood* (finished 1748: London, NG), of which Gainsborough himself wrote: '. . . as an early instance how strong my inclination stood for Landskip, this picture was actually painted at Sudbury in the year 1748; it was begun *before I left school*; – and was the means of my Father's sending me to London . . .'. All his life he was to regard landscape as his real bent, but he painted portraits for a living and set up in Sudbury *c*.1748. He moved to Ipswich *c*.1750 and remained there until he moved to Bath at the end of 1759. In Suffolk he continued to paint landscapes as well as the little portrait groups, like conversation pieces in a park, which distantly echo Watteau – perhaps through the French influence of Gravelot as well as from Hayman. A pair of early landscapes at Woburn Abbey (1755) are also French in style. His move to Bath, then a highly fashionable town, was probably in order to find more sitters. This he did, and he remained the most sought-after painter there until his final removal to London in 1774. His Bath period is characterized by a loss of the ingenuous quality of his early work, which gives way to a sense of fashionable elegance, now often displayed in full-length portraits, life-size, set against an imaginary landscape background. The influence of van Dyck, whom he now had opportunities to study, is very apparent in such pictures as the *Blue Boy* (San Marino, Calif.) and some others in which he actually dresses the sitter in van Dyck costume. He continued to paint landscapes but they are now more Arcadian in quality, obviously composed rather than observed, although the finest of them, such as the *Harvest Wagon* (Birmingham, Barber Inst.), have a new richness of colour. He began to exhibit in London (at the Society of Artists) in 1761 and was sufficiently well-known there to be among the original members of the Royal Academy when it was founded by George III in 1768. He was later elected to the Council of the Academy, but his relations with it were always uncertain: in 1773 he quarrelled with the hanging of his pictures and did not exhibit again until 1777; after another dispute in 1784 he ceased to exhibit there. His move to London in 1774 was in order to match himself against Reynolds, and most people relished the rivalry. Their styles are utterly different and Gainsborough, who was fortunate in seizing a likeness much better than Reynolds could, is often empty and mechanical in his later portraits; yet he has always, as Reynolds has not, a superb handling of paint. The rivalry was rendered all the more piquant by the fact that Reynolds was knighted and the head of the King's own Academy – yet all the Royal Family preferred Gainsborough to paint them, although RAMSAY was Painter to the King until his death in 1784, when Reynolds succeeded to the title but not the favour. From about 1780 Gainsborough painted several 'Fancy Pictures', more or less in imitation of Murillo, of a poetic quality which was an extension of his interest in landscape. His later landscapes are much influenced by Rubens and were composed of 'broken stones, dried weeds and pieces of looking-glass ... magnified and improved into rocks, trees and water'. The *Watering Place* (RA 1777: Tate) was described by Horace Walpole: 'the landscape in the style of Rubens is the most beautiful which has ever been painted in England and equal to the great masters'.

Contrary to normal 18th-century practice Gainsborough painted all his pictures himself and never employed a drapery man. His technique was, he realized, an essential part of the effect he sought and he made it a beauty in its own right: it is best described in the noble tribute paid by his rival Reynolds in an obituary 'Discourse' (the 14th) at the RA in which he says, 'all those odd scratches and marks which, on a close examination, are so observable ... and which even to experienced painters appear rather the effect of accident than design; this chaos, this uncouth and shapeless appearance, by a kind of magic, at a certain distance assumes form ...'. He seems to have used very long brushes and to have diluted the paint with turpentine to the consistency of watercolour. As a result, his works have lasted much better than those of almost any other 18th-century British painter. His wife's nephew Gainsborough Dupont (*c.* 1755–97) was his pupil and imitator. There are pictures by Gainsborough in almost every major museum.

GALGARIO, Fra, *see* GHISLANDI.

GARZONE is an Italian word for a boy apprentice, less skilled than an assistant or JOURNEYMAN. When a part of a picture is apparently ill-executed it is usual to blame the *garzone*.

GASPAR. The usual English 18th-century form of Gaspar(d)
POUSSIN.

GAUDIER-BRZESKA, Henri (1891–1915), was a French sculptor
who lived in London (Brzeska was the name of a Polish woman he
lived with). He was associated with the Vorticist movement, but he
joined the French Army in 1914 and was killed before he had time
to develop as a sculptor: he is perhaps at his best in the calligraphic
drawings made in the Zoo, where the taut pen line perfectly expresses
the grace of a puma or a jaguar. He is well represented in the Tate
Gallery, London, and also in Chicago, Liverpool, Manchester, New
York (M of MA), Southampton, and elsewhere.

GAUGUIN, Paul (1848–1903), was born in Paris. Part of his childhood
was spent in Peru, whence his mother's family came, and from 1865–
71 he was at sea. He became a stockbroker in 1871, and a Sunday-
painter who collected the works of the Impressionists and joined in
their exhibitions (1881–6). He gave up his job in 1883, and after many
vicissitudes separated from his family and went to live in Brittany at
Pont-Aven and Le Pouldu, where he worked from 1886–90, except
for visits to Paris, a trip to Panama and Martinique in 1887 and a
disastrous stay of two months with van Gogh in Arles in 1888. In
1891 he went to Tahiti, returned to Paris in 1893 for lack of money,
but went back to the South Sea Islands in 1895. His health was
failing and he had been seriously hurt in a brawl with sailors in
Brittany in 1894. His remaining years were spent in poverty, illness,
and continual strife with the colonial authorities through his cham-
pioning of native causes. He died at Atuana in the Marquesas.

His early works may be ranged with those of the Impressionists,
particularly with Pissarro and Cézanne, but after 1886 when his
works hung in the eighth and last Impressionist Exhibition with those
of Seurat he endeavoured to introduce more colour and this tendency
became more marked after his voyage to Martinique. In 1888 at
Pont-Aven he met Émile BERNARD, the influence of whose knowledge of medieval art joined with Gauguin's interest in primitive
sculpture, Japanese, Romanesque, and Far and Near Eastern art,
to encourage him to abandon Impressionism and all attempts at the
representation of nature in favour of SYNTHETISM. His rejection of
Western civilization led to his departure for Tahiti, and to his efforts
to express through an art free from the conventions of the naturalistic
tradition the simplicity of life among primitive and unspoiled peoples.
His influence has been enormous, since he is one of the main sources
from which non-naturalistic 20th-century art has emanated.

There are works, including sculpture, in Baltimore, Basle, Birmingham (Barber Inst.), Boston (Mus.), Brussels, Budapest, Buffalo,
Chicago, Cleveland Ohio, Edinburgh (NG), Essen, Glasgow, Grenoble, Hartford Conn., Indianapolis, Kansas City, London (Tate,

Courtauld Inst.), Los Angeles, Manchester (City Mus.), Minneapolis, Moscow, Newcastle, New York (Met. Mus., M of MA), Oslo, Ottawa, Paris (Louvre, Petit Pal.), Prague, Reims, Stockholm, Toledo Ohio, Washington (NG, Phillips), and elsewhere.

His son, Émile (b.1899), now living in America, is also a painter and sculptor.

GAULLI *see* BACICCIA.

GEDDES, Andrew (1783–1844), studied from 1807 onwards in the RA Schools, where he met Wilkie, whose lifelong friend he became. He painted portraits in Edinburgh from 1810 to 1814, when he removed to London although he frequently visited Edinburgh. In 1828 he travelled in France, Germany, and Italy, and was elected an ARA in 1832. He died soon after a visit to Holland. His portraits, direct and in a solid technique with a skilful use of grey, have much charm; his subject paintings tend to be sentimental and vaguely Nazarene in type. He is well represented in Edinburgh (NG).

GEERTGEN tot Sint Jans (i.e. 'little Gerard of the Brethren of S. John') was a Dutch painter active in the late 15th century. He was born at Leyden and is said to have died at about 28, perhaps c.1485/ 95. He was a pupil of Albert van OUWATER and the only works which can reasonably be connected with his name are two very large panels in Vienna (K-H Mus.), originally back and front of a single panel from an altarpiece in the Monastery of S. John at Haarlem, for which Geertgen worked. They represent the *Lamentation over the Dead Christ* and *Julian the Apostate burning the bones of S. John Baptist, with members of the Order saving some relics.* The curious egg-shaped heads make it easy to group some other works around these two, but a picture of the Cathedral at Haarlem (in the Cathedral) which is traditionally his shows no characteristics in common. The principal pictures attributed are in Amsterdam (Rijksmus.), Berlin, Cleveland Ohio, Leipzig, Leningrad, London (NG), Milan (Ambrosiana), Paris (Louvre), Prague, and Utrecht.

GELDER, Aert de (1645–1727), was a pupil of Rembrandt in the 1660s and continued his late style well into the 18th century, giving it a Rococo flavour by lightening Rembrandt's palette and using pinks and violets. He painted principally Biblical subjects and portraits, and his Old Testament scenes are often markedly Rembrandtesque in their strong, warm colour as well as in their use of Oriental types and costume. There is a series of New Testament scenes, of c.1715, in the galleries of Aschaffenburg and Munich and other pictures in Amsterdam, Berlin, Birmingham (Barber Inst.), Boston, Brighton, Chicago, Dordrecht, Dresden, Frankfurt, The Hague, London (Dulwich), Melbourne, Paris (Louvre), Providence RI, Rotterdam, Vaduz (Liechtenstein Coll.), and Vienna.

GENRE (Fr. kind, variety). A type of picture, usually small in size, depicting not so much a subject as everyday life and surroundings, though the opportunity for narrative content leads easily into subdivisions such as moralities and the conversation piece, which is a form of genre portrait. The important thing is that it should not represent idealized life. Small touches of genre – interest in setting, in objects – can be found in 14th- and 15th-century Italian painting and in early Flemish painting, but not so strongly developed as to affect its status as religious art. Although genre appears in Italy in e.g. CARPACCIO and, later, in CARAVAGGIO, CRESPI, and Piazzetta, it plays a minor role until the 18th century when Pietro LONGHI devoted his whole life to it. It is in the North that it first gains a strong hold and appears as a distinct form, as in the engravings of the MASTER OF THE HOUSEBOOK and in the *Bankers* of Massys and Reymerswaele. In 17th-century Holland the absence of patronage for religious and decorative painting stimulated the development of genre, and OSTADE, STEEN, METSU, TER BORCH, VERMEER, and de HOOCH produced little else, each specializing in subvarieties such as peasant and tavern scenes, musical or genteel drinking parties, with displays of glittering satin, or simple interiors with dazzling effects of light. In the 18th century, in France CHARDIN imbued his humble subjects with supreme dignity and beauty; in England the main forms were the moralities of HOGARTH, the 'fancy pictures' of GAINSBOROUGH, and the rustic scenes of MORLAND. In the 19th century the genre subject became the commonplace anecdotal painting of the Victorian narrative painters like Mulready, and the PRE-RAPHAELITES, with their mixture of costume-history and religious subjects and scenes from contemporary life, blurred further the line dividing genre from History Painting. MANET used the form occasionally and so did the IMPRESSIONISTS, RENOIR and DEGAS, and it survives into our own times with Sickert and the Camden Town Group, the Euston Road painters, and even the new Realists, for much the same reasons as caused its enormous development in Holland.

GENTILE da Fabriano (*c.* 1370–1427) is first recorded in 1408, when he was in Venice. In 1409 he was working on historical frescoes in the Doge's Palace which were later finished by PISANELLO but were subsequently destroyed. From 1422 to 1425 he was in Florence where he completed, in May 1423, the resplendent altarpiece of the *Adoration of the Magi*, now in the Uffizi. This was one of the masterpieces of the INTERNATIONAL GOTHIC style and exerted enormous influence on Florentine art; it was followed by the *Quaratesi Altarpiece*, completed in May 1425, of which the *Madonna* is now in the Royal Coll. and the remainder divided between the Uffizi, the Vatican, and Washington. In 1425 he left Florence and worked in Siena and Orvieto, and by 1427 he was working on frescoes in the

Lateran Basilica in Rome, which have also been destroyed. His art is the charming, elegant, and courtly art of the International Gothic style; he shows little or no interest in the intellectual problems of space and volume which exercised MASACCIO, who was working in Florence at precisely the same time (cf. the *Madonna* in the Royal Coll. with Masaccio's Pisa Polyptych *Madonna*, in the NG, London).

There are other pictures by him in Berlin, Harvard Univ. Gall., Milan (Brera and Poldi-Pezzoli), New York (Met. Mus. and Frick Coll.), Orvieto, Paris (Louvre: part of the Uffizi *Adoration*), Perugia, Pisa, Washington (NG), and Yale Univ. Gall.

GENTILESCHI, Orazio (1563–1639), was a follower of CARAVAGGIO who worked in Paris *c.*1623/4 and arrived in London as Court Painter to Charles I in 1626. He remained in England until his death and was – with HONTHORST – one of the first practitioners of Caravaggism in England. The ceiling painted by him for Inigo Jones's Queen's House at Greenwich is now in Marlborough House, London. There are works by him in the Royal Coll. and in Berlin, Birmingham, Fabriano (Cath. and churches), Florence (Pitti), Madrid, Milan, Paris (Louvre), Prague, Rome (Corsini and churches), Turin (Mus. Civico and Sabauda), Vienna (K-H Mus.), and Washington (NG).

His daughter Artemisia (*c.*1597–1651/3) worked in a similar style, mainly in Naples. She joined her father in London in 1638–9. Detroit is one of the few museums to possess works by both.

GÉRARD, Baron François (1770–1837), was born in Rome. While he was a pupil of DAVID – from 1786 onwards – he worked for engravers to earn a livelihood and during the Revolution, to evade military service, he obtained through David's influence a position as judge on the Revolutionary tribunal, but contrived to be continuously ill so as to avoid its dreadful duties. His reputation as a portrait painter was made in 1795, and during the first Empire he rivalled David in court favour. It was Gérard who suggested to David that in his huge *Coronation of Napoleon* the Emperor should crown Josephine rather than himself. Later, there was bitter animosity between them, and also between him and GROS, whom he defeated both in the speed with which he turned his political coat and in his efforts to secure the Court appointment to the restored Bourbons. He was ennobled by Louis XVIII, and kept a large studio of assistants to help with his glossy, showy, superficial portraits that compete with Lawrence for facility and charm, but lack the vision and solidity which make David's portraits outstanding. There are works in Paris (Louvre, Carnavalet), Versailles, London (Wellington Mus.), Barnard Castle (Bowes Mus.), and elsewhere.

GERHAERT, Nicolaus (von Leyden or Leyen) (active 1462–73/8), was the last great German Gothic sculptor in the realist tradition – at least, if he was not Dutch, as the 'Leyden' often added to his name would imply. He is first recorded in Trier in 1462, when he signed and dated the Tomb of Archbishop von Sierck (Diocesan Mus.), but he was in Strasbourg from 1463 until 1467 (a tomb in Strasbourg Cath. is signed and dated 1464). In 1467 he carved the Baden-Baden Crucifix and went to Vienna to work on a Tomb for Friedrich III (Vienna, S. Stephan). He seems to have died in Vienna between 1473 and 1478. Other works by him are in Chicago, Downside Abbey Somerset, Frankfurt, New York (Met. Mus.), Passau Cath., and Ranshofen. A fine *Madonna* formerly in Berlin was destroyed 1939/45.

GÉRICAULT, Théodore (1791–1824), was born in Rouen of well-to-do parents. In 1808 he became the pupil of Carle VERNET, but left him after two years ('One of my horses would have devoured six of his', he said) for Guérin, in whose studio DELACROIX was also a pupil. He was strongly influenced by GROS, particularly in his painting of horses, and his choice of contemporary subjects. His technical innovations, too, are noteworthy: he abandoned the use of detailed preparatory drawings and squared-up studies, painting directly on to the final canvas from models posed according to a painted sketch. From being an ardent Bonapartist he eventually sided with the liberal opponents of the Restored Monarchy, an alignment reflected in many of his drawings (scenes from the Greek Wars of Independence, anti-slavery subjects, the ending of the Inquisition) and particularly in his most celebrated work, the *Raft of the 'Medusa'*, a shipwreck which was a political scandal of the day (1819: Louvre). In 1816 he visited Italy for a year, and in 1820–22 he was in England, where his *Raft* was shown in a travelling exhibition. During this long stay, he made many lithographs of horses and scenes of the poverty in the London streets, as well as small paintings of horses and racing subjects. His influence on the development of the Romantic movement exceeded what might have been expected from his total of no more than three exhibited works, a few portraits and horse pictures, and his lithographs and drawings. But his art, as much as that of Gros and Rubens, was one of the starting points for the young Delacroix, who admired him deeply.

In 1822–3, he painted a series of ten movingly realistic portraits of inmates of the Paris asylum of the Salpêtrière, of which only five survive (Ghent, Louvre, Lyons, Springfield Mass., Winterthur). They were inspired by his friend, the alienist Georget, a follower of Pinel in the humane treatment of the insane, but the idea behind them – that certain types of physiognomy accompany certains kinds of insanity – has now been abandoned. There are works in Alençon, Baltimore (Walters) Bayonne, Buffalo, Cambridge Mass. (Fogg), Chicago, Detroit, Geneva, Glasgow, Hartford Conn., London (NG), Montpellier, Munich (Bavarian State Mus.), Northampton Mass.

(Smith College), Paris (Louvre), Providence R I, Rouen, and elsewhere.

GESSO is the name given to the ground used in TEMPERA painting and in certain types of oil painting. It is a dense and brilliantly white ground with a rather high degree of absorbency (in Italy it was usually gypsum, but in N. Europe usually chalk). In Italian practice it was usual to prepare a panel with several coats of *Gesso Grosso*, which is simply gesso mixed with size, like white distemper. This is highly absorbent. The panel was then given ten or more coats of *Gesso Sottile*. This is plaster of Paris slaked in water for a month or more, so that all the setting power goes out of it. It is then made into a silky smooth mixture with size and painted on over the *gesso grosso*. The result is a smooth, brilliant white surface with a pleasant 'feel' and low absorbency.

GHEERAERTS. The Gheeraerts, the de Critzes, and Isaac OLIVER were all Huguenot refugees in England who intermarried and were probably members of one workshop, to which most English portraits of the later Elizabethan period tend to be attributed. John de Critz (*c.*1554–1642) was well established in England by 1598 and was Sergeant Painter to the Crown from 1605 until his death, at a very great age, in 1642. His sister, Susanna, married in 1571 Marcus Gheeraerts the Elder, a decorative painter from Bruges who fled from the Alvan persecution in 1568 and was in England 1568–77: he died before 1604. He made a signed engraving of the *Garter Procession* in 1576 and may have painted the *Queen Elizabeth* (Coll. the Duke of Portland), which is signed M G F (but this may also be his son's signature). Marcus Gheeraerts the Younger was a child of an earlier marriage (*c.*1561–1636) and married, in 1590, Magdalen de Critz, his stepmother's younger sister. No works can be attributed to John de Critz, and there is not much evidence for Marcus Gheeraerts I as a portrait painter. Marcus the Younger is documented as a portrait painter and as working for the Crown: the *Duke of Württemberg* (Royal Coll.) is of *c.*1608 and is signed 'Gerardi Brugiense'. There are other works, notably in Oxford (Bodleian), in the Duke of Bedford's Coll., and at Penshurst, which are certainly by him. The portraits (there was no other possible subject) which usually sail under the Gheeraerts colours are full or half length, life-sized effigies of noblemen and women in full dress with heavy curtains, a table, or chair or a Turkey carpet as accessories. They have a formal, heraldic air and, when clean, are bright in colour. The portraits of Queen Elizabeth in English country houses are always lumped together under the name Gheeraerts (when not called 'ZUCCARO').

Emmanuel de Critz (*d.*1665) was a younger son of John. He is usually credited with the fine de Critz and Tradescant family portraits (one is dated 1645) in the Ashmolean Mus., Oxford, but no convincing reason can be adduced in support.

GHENT ALTAR *see* EYCK.

GHIBERTI, Lorenzo (1378–1455), was the Florentine sculptor who made two of the three bronze doors of the Baptistry in Florence. He was younger than Brunelleschi but older than DONATELLO or Masaccio, and in spite of his collection of antique sculpture and his desire to be regarded as a humanist he was not really like the Masaccio-Brunelleschi-Donatello triumvirate and had only a superficial feeling for classical art, at least in the earlier stages of his career, although it deepened in his later years. In 1401 a Competition was announced for a bronze door for the Baptistry, to match the one by Andrea PISANO, but to consist of Old Testament scenes. The competition was won by Ghiberti in 1402, against Brunelleschi (who subsequently devoted himself to architecture), Jacopo della QUERCIA, and four others: according to his own account 'The palm of victory was conceded to me by all the experts and by all my fellow-competitors. By universal consent and without a single exception the glory was conceded to me. . .'. Up to this time Ghiberti had been active as a goldsmith and painter but the rest of his life was principally devoted to his first Doors (1403–24) and to the second pair commissioned immediately afterwards (1425–52). The reliefs, of the *Sacrifice of Isaac*, submitted by Ghiberti and by Brunelleschi survive (Florence, Bargello), but all the others are lost. When the commission was given to Ghiberti in 1403 (and renewed in 1407) the subjects were changed from Old to New Testament but the doors remained very close to the type established by Andrea Pisano, with high reliefs enclosed in Gothic frames, the figures being gilt and set against a neutral ground. Ghiberti established a large workshop to carry out this great undertaking, and this shop was the principal training-ground for the next generation of artists – including Donatello as well as painters like MASOLINO and UCCELLO.

In spite of a restrictive clause in his contract Ghiberti made several other works during the period 1403–24. Two large statues – the *S. John Baptist* (1414) and the *S. Matthew* (1419–22, but dated 1420) – made for the church of Orsanmichele, show the movement of his style away from Gothic linear rhythms towards a graver and more antique treatment. Between 1417 and 1427 he made two reliefs for the Font of the Baptistry in Siena, where the pictorial treatment of the relief foreshadows his own second Doors but is probably derived from Donatello's contribution to the Font. Finally, in 1418 Ghiberti was paid for a model of the dome of Florence Cathedral, thus proving that he was also involved in the greatest architectural enterprise of the day: his share in the dome as built by Brunelleschi is still controversial.

After a trip to Venice in 1424 Ghiberti returned to Florence and was commissioned in 1425 to make the remaining (third) pair of doors.

Such had been the success of his first pair that he was left to exercise his own judgement. He altered the whole layout and reduced the number of Old Testament scenes to 10 (against 28 New Testament scenes on the earlier doors), allowing each rectangular field to appear like a picture in a frame, with the plane of the background representing the sky or the ground, and not simply a neutral foil as in the earlier door. The perspective is carefully calculated and depends on the recent researches of Brunelleschi and Donatello: Ghiberti himself described the doors thus 'There were ten scenes, each framed so that the eye measures them from a distance and they appear in relief. The relief is very low and the figures are so disposed on the planes that those which are nearest are seen to be larger than those further off, just as happens in reality. The whole work is based on these principles.' These doors were very richly gilded, thus adding to the painterly effect, but the gold was completely obscured by time and dirt until the doors were taken down during the Second World War and cleaned. (Some panels suffered in the flood of 1966.) This pair is often called the Door of Paradise – the *Porta del Paradiso* – because Michelangelo is said to have called them worthy to be the Gates of Paradise.

During this period 1425–52 Ghiberti also made the bronze shrine of the Three Martyrs (1428: Florence, Bargello) and the bronze Reliquary of S. Zenobius (1432–42: Florence, Cath.) as well as another statue, the *S. Stephen*, for Orsanmichele (1428). There are other works by him in Florence (Sta Croce, S. Egidio, and Sta Maria Novella) and he also designed a number of stained glass windows for the Cathedral.

In the last years of his life Ghiberti wrote his 'Commentarii' – already quoted from – the Second of which is the principal source of our knowledge of Trecento art in Florence and Siena and also includes Ghiberti's Autobiography, the earliest to survive by an artist. His interest in the art of the Trecento links him firmly with his Gothic predecessors: his consciousness of his own individuality in his Autobiography shows him to have been also a man of the Renaissance and perhaps the vital link between the two worlds.

GHIRLANDAIO, Domenico (1449–94), was the best fresco executant of his generation in Florence, whose main claim to fame is that he had Michelangelo as an apprentice. With his brother Davide (1452–1525) and other relatives he ran an extensive and well-organized studio, but he himself preferred fresco to tempera, and he never attempted oil painting. He worked in the Sistine Chapel in the Vatican (1481–2), along with Botticelli and others, and his contribution is notable for the fact that it is nearest in spirit to Masaccio – i.e. it was old-fashioned in the 1480s – and that the nominal subject, the Calling of the First Apostles, is half-swamped in the rows of lifelike portraits of prominent Florentines living in Rome. His essentially prosaic mind and the naturalistic detail in all his works made him very popular in his own day and in the late 19th century, but it is significant that he received only one commission (now lost) from the Medici family and none from any cultivated patron. His frescoes are, of course, of great historical interest. Most of them are in Florence: the *S. Jerome* (1480: Ognissanti) shows strong Flemish influence in the treatment of detail, and the two major cycles are those in the Sassetti Chapel, Sta Trinita (completed 1485), and in the choir of Sta Maria Novella (completed 1490). Outside Florence, there are works of his in Berlin, Cambridge (Fitzwm), Cambridge Mass. (Fogg), Detroit, London (NG), Munich, New York (Met. Mus.), Paris (Louvre), Philadelphia (Johnson), Washington, and elsewhere.

His son Ridolfo (1483–1561) was much influenced by his friend Raphael and was a portrait painter of distinction. He is well represented in Florence, and there are portraits by him in Chicago, London (NG), Philadelphia (Johnson), Washington (NG), Worcester Mass., and Yale.

GHISLANDI, Vittore, called Fra Galgario (1655–1743), was an Italian portrait painter, active mainly in Bergamo, who was trained in Venice and whose portraits reflect the best qualities of Late Baroque Venetian painting in their solid handling and strong but subdued colour. His sitters are usually simple people and he represents them in informal poses, often with a strength of light and shade indicating a knowledge of Rembrandt. He has lately been connected with the Realist tendency in Lombard painting of the early 18th century, but the closest parallels among his contemporaries seem to be Hogarth's portraits, although his best-known work, the *Boy Painter*, in some ways anticipates GREUZE. His works are best represented in Bergamo, but there are others in Hartford Conn., Milan, Minneapolis, and Venice.

GIACOMETTI, Alberto (1901–66), was a Swiss sculptor, painter and poet. He was trained in Italy 1920–22 and then spent three years in Paris under BOURDELLE, but he was also much influenced by BRANCUSI and became a Surrealist in the 1930s. The sculpture of this period has been called 'still-life sculpture' or 'magic objects', and the most famous is *The Palace at 4 a.m.* (1932–3: New York, M of MA). Later he returned to more realistic single figures, extremely emaciated in form, usually built up by working directly in plaster of Paris on a wire foundation. A characteristic example is the *Man Pointing* (1947: London, Tate).

GIAMBOLOGNA *see* BOLOGNA.

GIAMBONO, Michele, was a Venetian painter and mosaic worker. He is recorded in 1420 as a married man and is last recorded in 1462. He came of a family of painters but his Venetian workshop tradition was profoundly influenced by the International Gothic style imported into Venice by GENTILE da Fabriano and PISANELLO in their major works in the Doge's Palace (destroyed in the 16th century, and known to us mainly from reflections in the style of artists like Giambono). He worked on the mosaics in the Mascoli Chapel in S. Mark's from 1444 and his *Coronation of the Virgin*, ordered in 1447, is probably the painting now in Venice (Accad.) which was copied from an earlier picture of the same subject. There are other works by him in Rome (Gall. Naz.) and Venice.

GIAQUINTO, Corrado (1703–65), was a Neapolitan painter who was a pupil of SOLIMENA until 1723, when he went to Rome and began to work under CONCA who had also been a Solimena pupil. Giaquinto worked with Conca in Rome and Turin and was elected to the Academy of S. Luke in Rome in 1740 and became President in 1750. In 1752 he was invited to Madrid to succeed AMIGONI as Court Painter. He arrived in 1753 and became Director of the Academy, but in 1761 Charles III summoned MENGS to Madrid, and Giaquinto, whose Neapolitan Rococo style was the antithesis of Mengs' Neoclassicism, at once returned to Italy. One of his most important works is the vast *Birth of the Virgin* in Pisa Cathedral (1751/2) for which several sketches exist, one in Oxford (Ch. Ch.). There are pictures in Madrid and a sketch in London (NG) for a proposed ceiling in the Royal Palace at Madrid.

GIBBONS, Grinling (1648–1721), was born in Rotterdam of English parents but came to England by 1672. He was one of the most skilful woodcarvers who ever lived, as witness such virtuoso performances as the wooden cravat in the V & A Museum, London. With the help of Evelyn the diarist he was introduced to Charles II and became Master Carver in Wood to the Crown: as a sculptor proper his finest work is certainly the *James II* outside the National Gallery, but, as with all his work other than wood-carving, it is probable that most of it is by others. He worked with Arnold QUELLIN on the chapel at Whitehall Palace (1685–6) and it is likely that Quellin actually modelled the *James II*, although Gibbons was paid for it.

GIBSON, John (1790–1866), was apprenticed to a mason in Liverpool in 1804 but contrived to get to Rome in 1817 and spent the rest of his life there ('I thank God for every morning that opens my eyes in Rome'). He worked under CANOVA and THORWALDSEN and enjoyed a reputation little below theirs, revisiting England only in 1844 and 1850, on both occasions to work for the Queen. His principal innovation was to re-introduce the tinting of marble, which, although certainly practised by the Greeks, seemed to a contemporary 'a dangerous departure from true art'. Many stories are told of his simplicity: a woman pupil said of him that 'he is a god in his studio, but God help him out of it', and to a puzzled railway porter he is said to have replied 'No, I am not a foreigner, I am a sculptor'. Nevertheless, he left a large fortune and his bequest to the Royal Academy (to which he was elected in 1838) paid for most of the building of the Diploma Gallery, which contains work by him: there are others in the Royal Collection and in Cardiff, Durham (Cath.), Liverpool (which has his rediscovered Tinted Venus), and London (NG, NPG, Tate, V & A, Wellington Mus., and Westminster Abbey).

GILL, Eric (1882–1940), English engraver, letter-cutter, sculptor, typographer, and writer. The *Stations of the Cross* (Westminster Cath.) and *Prospero and Ariel* (Broadcasting House) are his best-known carvings: others are in the Tate Gallery. He will probably best be remembered as the designer of the lettering known as Gill Sans-serif, and for many other fine alphabets.

GILMAN, Harold (1876–1919), was trained at the Slade School, met GORE, and joined SICKERT's circle, against which he subsequently reacted violently, coming under the influence of van Gogh. He was a member of the CAMDEN TOWN GROUP and became the first President of the LONDON GROUP on its foundation in 1913. He is represented in Cardiff, Liverpool, London (Tate), and Ottawa.

GILPIN, Sawrey (1733–1807), was an English animal painter of Romantic ambitions. He was the younger brother of the Rev. William Gilpin, the celebrated writer on the PICTURESQUE. Sawrey studied in London from 1749 under SCOTT: his work is less sensitive than that of STUBBS and is somewhat marred by anthropomorphism. This may be seen in his *Election of Darius* (York) – according to legend the election was influenced by the neighing of Darius's horse – but most of his works are straightforward sporting pictures. He exhibited at the RA from 1786, and was elected RA in 1797.

GIORDANO, Luca (1632–1705), was a Neapolitan painter known as 'Luca fa presto' (*Luke, paint quickly*) from the alleged habit of his father in urging ever greater speed and facility. Certainly he was able to paint in an amazing variety of styles, which has earned him praise and disdain in about equal measure. He was probably a pupil of RIBERA in Naples but went on to Rome, where he was influenced by the lighter style of PIETRO da Cortona, and to Florence and Venice, where the influence of Venetian art was instrumental in getting away from the darkness of Ribera's style. In Florence he painted a chapel, and, in 1682–3, the huge ceiling of the Ballroom of the Pal. Medici-Riccardi. His great renown led Charles II to summon him in 1692 to Spain, where his ceilings in the Escorial are probably his masterpieces. He returned to Naples in 1702 and spent his last years there. He was the most important Neapolitan painter of the second half of the 17th century, and his lighter and more colouristic style marks a great change from the Neapolitan painting of the first half of the century. His output was huge and most older galleries have examples of his easel-paintings.

GIORGIONE (*c.*1476/8–1510) was a Venetian painter, a pupil of Giovanni BELLINI, who was ranked by Vasari with Leonardo da Vinci as one of the founders of modern painting. He was the first exponent in Venice of the small picture in oils, intended for private collectors rather than for churches, and frequently mysterious and evocative in subject. Many of his contemporaries were unable to interpret the subject of such a picture as the *Tempest* (Venice, Accad.), of which we can say only that it appears to be the first 'landscape of mood', expressing the heat and tension of an approaching thunderstorm. His career is almost entirely mysterious. In 1506 he shared a studio with, of all people, CATENA; in 1507/8 he was working in the Doge's Palace, but these works are lost; in 1508 he was painting frescoes on the outside of the Fondaco dei Tedeschi, the headquarters of the German merchants in Venice, and TITIAN was also working there in a subordinate capacity. Only faded fragments of these frescoes now exist, but the link with Titian is important, for it seems to prove that it was Giorgione, and not Titian, who was the great innovator. This would be less controversial if we had more knowledge of Giorgione's style, but no extant pictures can be regarded as completely documented and there are only about half a dozen which are generally agreed to be attributable to him on adequate evidence. The problem is much complicated by the fact that he died, of the plague, in 1510 and several pictures seem to have been completed by Titian and SEBASTIANO del Piombo, both of whom were, at that date, profoundly influenced by him; nevertheless, optimistic attributions to him continue to be made. The *Castelfranco Madonna* (Castelfranco Veneto – his birthplace – S. Liberale) is derived from the large altarpieces of Giovanni Bellini, and is therefore probably an early work: it is universally accepted as Giorgione's. Other works, in Dresden, Leningrad, Venice, and Vienna (K-H Mus.), including the *Laura* in Vienna which is dated 1506, are almost beyond controversy, but the debate continues over works in the Royal Collection and in Berlin, Boston (Gardner), Budapest, Florence (Uffizi and Pitti), Glasgow, London (NG, Courtauld Inst.), Madrid, Oxford, Paris (Louvre), San Diego Cal., and Washington as well as other less likely candidates. The portrait in San Diego has a 16th-century inscription attributing it to 'Zorzon' (the Venetian form of his name) and a date which has been read as 1508 and 1510, but may be neither. The *Adoration* in Washington is very controversial but may be an early work.

GIOTTESCHI, Giottesques. The name given to a number of 14th-century painters working in the shadow of GIOTTO. Many of them are anonymous, others are known by names like the MASTER OF S.

CECILIA, while others again are distinct personalities such as DADDI, GIOTTINO, Taddeo GADDI, or MASO di Banco.

GIOTTINO, active in the mid-14th century, probably painted the *S. Remigio Deposition* in Florence (Uffizi) which was regarded as a work of MASO by Vasari and earlier writers. The distinction of hand is evident, but it is by no means certain that Giottino was identical with a Giotto di Maestro Stefano who was painting in the Vatican in 1369, who in turn cannot be reconciled with Vasari's Maso/Giottino figure. No other work can reasonably be attributed to the painter of the Uffizi *Deposition*, unless one accepts the attribution of it to ORCAGNA's brother Nardo di Cione.

GIOTTO (1266/7 or, less probably, 1276–1337) was a Florentine, who, with CIMABUE, is generally regarded as the founder of modern painting, since he broke away from the stereotyped forms of Italo-Byzantine art and tried to give his figures the maximum solidity and naturalism. He gave passion and imagination to his scenes, just as Giovanni PISANO had done slightly earlier in sculpture. His dramatic power can be felt in his frescoes of scenes from the lives of SS. Joachim and Anne and the Virgin, and of the Life and Passion of Christ, in the Arena Chapel, Padua. These were completed by 1313, perhaps *c*.1306. Before then Giotto had probably designed the fresco cycle of the Legend of S. Francis in the Upper Church at Assisi, although his authorship is denied by many critics on stylistic grounds. These frescoes are imbued with the humanity which S. Francis himself had brought into the religious life of the 13th century, and which was so potent an influence on the arts.

Probably just after 1300 Giotto designed the *Navicella*, a huge mosaic of the Ship of the Church, in St Peter's, but this has been so reworked that his hand is no longer discernible in it. Much later, perhaps in the 1320s, he decorated four chapels in Sta Croce, Florence, of which two chapels (Bardi and Peruzzi: *Life of S. Francis* and *Lives of SS. John Baptist and Evangelist*), and an *Assumption* (doubtfully attributed) from a third chapel, survive. A slight influence from Gothic sculpture is perceptible in them. Giotto also worked in Naples (1329–33), but all his work there is lost. There are several panel pictures – some of them signed – attributed to him: in Bologna, Florence (Sta Croce), London (NG), Munich, Paris (Louvre), Raleigh N.C., Upton Park (National Trust) near Banbury, Washington, and elsewhere, but all of these are held to be works of his school or shop, and even the signed ones are, as it were, trade-marked rather than signed in the modern sense. This is true even of the *Stefaneschi Altar* in the Vatican, which is mentioned as his in a document of 1342; on the other hand, the *Ognissanti Madonna* (Florence, Uffizi) is universally accepted as his although it is neither signed nor documented. Other works with a good claim to be considered as his include the

Dormition of the Virgin (Berlin) and a Crucifix in Sta Maria Novella, Florence.

On account of his great fame – he and Cimabue are both mentioned by Dante – Giotto was appointed supervisor of Florence Cathedral in 1334, and he began work on the Campanile ('Giotto's Tower'), but his design was altered later. Nearly all Florentine and many Sienese painters of the mid-14th century were influenced by him (the Giotteschi), but his influence waned in the later 14th century, to be revived in MASACCIO and even in Michelangelo.

GIOVANNI d'Alemagna *see* VIVARINI.

GIOVANNI da Bologna *see* BOLOGNA.

GIOVANNI di Paolo (1403–82/3) was, with SASSETTA, the leading Sienese painter of the 15th century. There are documented works from 1426 down to about 1475 and it is likely that he ceased painting towards the end of his long life. His style is a rather more archaic and tortured version of Sassetta's, with a certain influence from GENTILE da Fabriano (who was in Siena 1424/6): his later works seem to show that he had visited Florence. Nevertheless, like Sassetta, he seems always to be looking back over his shoulder to the masters of the Trecento. There are works in Altenburg, Baltimore (Walters), Berlin, Boston (Mus. and Gardner), Cambridge (Fitzwm), Cambridge Mass. (Fogg), Chicago, Cologne (Wallraf-Richartz, Rheinisches Mus.), Florence (Uffizi, Bargello), London (NG), Minneapolis, Modena, Münster, New York (Met. Mus. and Frick Coll.), Oxford (Ashmolean and Christ Church), Paris (Louvre), Philadelphia (Johnson), Siena (Pinacoteca, Cath. Mus., and churches), Utrecht, the Vatican, Vienna (Akad.), Washington (NG), and Yale University.

GIRARDON, François (1628–1715), was the most classical of the sculptors working at Versailles for Louis XIV. His *Apollo and the Nymphs*, commissioned in 1666 for the Grotto of Thetis and now much altered by the regrouping of the figures, is severely classical in style and based on the Apollo Belvedere and on Poussin, whose type of composition it translated into sculpture. His *Rape of Proserpine*, in the gardens, though full of movement, consciously avoids both the Mannerism of Giovanni da Bologna's group, and the Baroque movement in depth of Bernini's group of the same subject.

GIRODET de Roucy-Trioson, Anne-Louis (1767–1824). He became a pupil of DAVID in 1785 and won the Prix de Rome in 1789. He was in the Academy in Rome when in 1793 David's order to replace the Royal arms by the Republican ones touched off the riot in which the mob wrecked the Academy and murdered the French agent. Girodet escaped to Naples, but there found his republicanism dangerous and after a gruelling flight across Italy arrived, very ill, in Genoa where he was succoured by GROS. His *Endymion*, sent from Rome in 1793, reflects not only his romantic temperament but also the drift from

David's classicism towards more poetic and romantic themes. David disapproved of him, and of GÉRARD, declaring that they had debased the art by their pandering to poetry and portraiture: indeed, his notorious *Danäe* of 1799 (now in Minneapolis) was a portrait of a well-known *demi-mondaine*, with her current protector represented as a peacock. In 1812 Girodet inherited a large fortune and abandoned painting to compose unreadable poems on aesthetics, writing in a house shuttered against daylight. There are works in Leipzig, Montpellier, Malmaison, Orléans, Paris (Louvre), Smith College Mass. (1804: *Mme Trioson*), Versailles, and elsewhere.

GIRTIN, Thomas (1775–1802), was the friend and contemporary of TURNER, but all his important work was done in watercolour and in his short life he revolutionized landscape painting in that medium. With Turner he worked for Dr MONRO and also copied Canaletto drawings, from which he learned much about topographical drawing. In 1801–2 he went to Paris where he made a series of soft-ground etchings of views of Paris, published posthumously in 1803. On his return from Paris he resumed work on an enormous panorama of London (*The Eidometropolis*) which he exhibited in 1802. The panorama is lost, but half a dozen sketches for it are in the BM. In his watercolours Girtin bridged the gap between the 18th-century stained drawing and the 19th-century watercolour painting: the *White House at Chelsea* (1800: London, Tate), one of his finest works, shows this transition and the poetic spirit which informs his work. He made several technical innovations, including the use of rather absorbent off-white cartridge paper, but his most radical change was the abandonment of the older monochrome underpainting in favour of a richer handling, with broad washes of strong colour often offset by dark blobs. There are works by him in Bedford (Higgins Mus.), Birkenhead, Birmingham, Brighton, Bristol, Cambridge (Fitzwm), Cardiff, Dublin, Edinburgh, Leeds, Lincoln, London (BM, Tate, V & A, Guildhall, Courtauld Inst.), Manchester (Whitworth), Newcastle, New York (Met. Mus.), Ottawa, Oxford, Sheffield, Swansea, Victoria NSW, York, and other British museums.

GISLEBERTUS was a French Romanesque sculptor who worked *c.*1125–35 at Autun cathedral in Burgundy, where he carved a tympanum *Last Judgement* (conspicuously signed), and also executed many capitals. His figures are characterized by vivid imagery, and by minutely pleated drapery in rhythmic folds and flutters. The fragments of the N. transept door include the famous *Eve*. There are affinities between the work at Autun and some of the sculpture at Vézelay, which suggest that he may have worked there before going to Autun, and his iconographic dependence on Cluny suggests close links with the Abbey there. Other places in Burgundy have works deriving from Autun, probably by his workshop.

GIULIO Romano (1492 or 1499–1546). Painter and architect and one of the creators of MANNERISM. From about 1515 until RAPHAEL'S death in 1520 Giulio was his chief assistant and was working on the frescoes in the Sala dell' Incendio in the Vatican, a fact which makes it unlikely that he was born in 1499. Before going to Mantua in 1524 Giulio completed some of Raphael's unfinished works, including the *Transfiguration* and the Vatican frescoes (Sala di Costantino), and he also painted an altarpiece for Sta Maria dell'Anima, Rome, and the *Stoning of S. Stephen* for Sto Stefano, Genoa (1523). All these works show an exaggeration of Raphael's style and also a melodramatic invention coupled with the influence of MICHELANGELO and these qualities are carried further in the frescoes in the Palazzo del Tè, designed by him for the Gonzaga of Mantua. The *Fall of the Giants*, occupying the whole of one room, is a piece of brutal illusionism deliberately designed to overwhelm the spectator who finds himself involved in the crushing of the Giants by the thunderbolts of Jove in the sky above. The whole of the room is painted from floor to ceiling to increase the illusion, and Vasari – who admired it greatly – tells us that the flames in the fireplace were intended to add to the effect of general destruction. This series was painted 1532–4, and there are other frescoes by him in Mantua. Florence, London, Naples, Paris, Rome, and Vienna also have works. *See also* PARMIGIANINO.

GIUNTA Pisano was, with BERLINGHIERO, one of the earliest Italian painters known to us as individuals. Giunta was active in Pisa *c.*1229–*c.*1254 and is known from three surviving crucifixes in Assisi, Pisa and Bologna. He is also known to have painted a crucifix in Assisi (dated 1236 but now lost) and he may have painted the dramatic *S. Francis* (Pisa). His style is more consciously realistic than that of Berlinghiero and he uses the modern CHRISTUS PATIENS type of crucifix.

GLAZING is the process of applying a transparent layer of oil paint over a solid one so that the colour of the first is profoundly modified. Thus, a transparent glaze of crimson over a solid blue will give effects of purple to mulberry colour, depending on the thickness of the glaze or the intensity of pigment used. It is thus the opposite of SCUMBLING and is impossible in direct, or ALLA PRIMA, painting. The use of glazes is now very rare, as it implies a deliberation and a craftsmanly approach to painting which is often thought inconsistent with inspiration: by a paradox the principal exponents of glazing are now probably the TACHISTES. The exact use made of glazes by different Old Masters is a highly controversial subject, since every time a picture is cleaned someone will claim that the 'Master's final glazes have now irretrievably vanished': occasionally this may be true, but it usually means that the dirty varnish layer has been regarded as a glaze in its own right. There is an added complication in that some glazes were undoubtedly put on with fugitive colours and have therefore vanished of their own accord: this has affected many pictures by Reynolds.

GLEIZES, Albert (1881–1953), was overwhelmed by CUBISM in 1910, and in 1912 published with METZINGER 'Du Cubisme', the first book on the subject (English translation 'Cubism', 1913). He was one of the flat-pattern cubists, and also produced abstract works. In 1917, when in America, he turned to religion, and many of his later works are a marriage of traditional Catholic themes with cubist ideas. He also wrote on religion and art. There are works in London (Tate), Paris (Mus. d'Art Moderne), New York (M of MA), and Toronto.

GLYPTIC see SCULPTURE.

GOES, Hugo van der (d. 1482), was the most important Ghent painter in the period after Jan van Eyck, and one of the most gifted of all the early Netherlandish painters. He was probably born at Ghent and was in the Guild there in 1467, becoming Dean in 1473/4 and 1475. About 1475 or a little later he completed the *Portinari Altarpiece* (Florence, Uffizi) for a Florentine resident in the Netherlands: the picture went direct to Florence and had little influence in the Netherlands, but it made a considerable impression on several Florentines, notably Ghirlandaio. It is unusual in Flemish work in that it is on a huge scale (over 8 ft high), and the great size is a positive gain to Hugo's composition, whereas to any other Flemish painter it would have been an embarrassment. The cool but rich colour and the virtuosity of the oil technique must also have been regarded with wonder in Florence. About 1475 (or perhaps 1477/8) Hugo joined his brother as a lay-brother in the Augustinian monastery at Roode Clooster, near Brussels; but he continued to paint, to receive noble visitors, and apparently to travel, since he went to Louvain to value the estate of Bouts in 1479/80 and, about 1481, went to Cologne. On this journey he was seized by madness (from a contemporary description, a form of religious melancholia) and he died, still insane, the following year. The *Portinari Altar* is rather exiguously documented as his, but all other attributions are based on it; his dramatic, almost *exalté* style is easily recognizable. There are two other very large pictures by him, both in Berlin, and other works in Baltimore, Bruges (Mus. and S. Sauveur), Brussels, Cassel, Edinburgh (NG, on loan from the Royal Coll.), Frankfurt (Städel), Leningrad, New York (Met. Mus.), Oxford (Christ Church), Philadelphia (Johnson), Vaduz (Liechtenstein Coll.), Venice (Correr), Vienna, and Wilton House, Wilts.

GOGH, Vincent van (1853–90), was the son of a Dutch pastor. He was first employed in The Hague, London, and Paris by the picture dealers for whom his brother Theo worked. He then taught in two English schools, worked in a bookshop in Holland, began studying for the

Church, and became a missionary in the coalmining district of the Borinage in Belgium, where he shared the poverty and hardships of the miners. He did not begin to become an artist until he was living in great poverty after his dismissal from the mission in 1880, and from then until 1886 he lived variously at Brussels, Etten, The Hague, Drenthe, Nuenen, and Antwerp, teaching himself to draw and paint, with occasional lessons in Brussels, from Antoine Mauve in The Hague, and at the Academy in Antwerp, which appear to have contributed little to his development. In 1886 he joined Theo in Paris and came immediately into contact with the works of the Impressionists, which Theo endeavoured to sell in the gallery devoted to modern art that he directed. He met Toulouse-Lautrec, Pissarro, Degas, Seurat, and Gauguin, and in 1888 went to Arles where he was later joined by Gauguin. In December 1888 he became insane, and from then until his death suffered intermittent attacks of mental trouble. During the intervals between them he continued to paint, both in the asylums at Arles and S. Rémy and after his removal to Auvers, where, in July 1890, he shot himself. His brother Theo, to whom most of his long and revealing letters were addressed, and who was his constant support, moral and financial, died six months later.

Van Gogh's Dutch period is characterized by his use of dark colour, heavy forms, and subject matter chiefly drawn from peasants and their work. He ignored Theo's advice to lighten his palette as the Impressionists were doing, but during his short stay in Antwerp he became more interested in Japanese prints and the work of Rubens. After his arrival in Paris a complete change took place in his palette and subject matter; he adopted the Impressionist technique, leaning briefly towards the pointillism of Seurat, and turned to flowers, views of Paris, and portraits and self-portraits which enabled him to experiment with these new ideas. After he went to Arles, he painted many landscapes and portraits in heightened colour and with a vivid, passionate expression of light and feeling, and after the arrival of Gauguin his work shows the influence of SYNTHETISM in the greater simplification of his forms and his use of less modulated colour. His paintings done at S. Rémy and Auvers are vivid in colour and with writhing, flame-like forms in the drawing, completely expressive of his tormented sensibility. His greatest influence was on MUNCH and the German Expressionists.

He left a vast volume of work, the largest amount of which is in the collection of Theo's son, Ir. V. W. van Gogh, at Laren in Holland, in the new Van Gogh Mus. in Amsterdam and in the Kröller-Müller Mus. at Otterlo in Holland. There are also works in Amsterdam (Stedelijk Mus.), Baltimore, Boston (Mus.), Cambridge Mass. (Fogg), Chicago, Copenhagen, Edinburgh (NG), Essen, Glasgow, London (Tate, Courtauld Inst.), Minneapolis, Moscow, New York (Met.

Mus., M of MA, Brooklyn), Paris (Louvre, Mus. Rodin), São Paulo, Washington (NG, Phillips), and many other museums.

GOLDEN SECTION (Golden Mean) is the name given to an irrational proportion, known at least since Euclid, which has often been thought to possess some aesthetic virtue in itself, some hidden harmonic proportion in tune with the universe. It is defined strictly as a line which is divided in such a way that the smaller part is to the larger as the larger is to the whole (AB cut at C, so that CB:AC = AC:AB). In practice it works out at about 8:13 and may easily be discovered in most works of art.

GOLTZIUS, Hendrik (1558–1617), was a Haarlem engraver and painter, who, with SPRANGER, BLOEMAERT, and WTEWAEL, was a leading Mannerist. He founded a school of engraving in Haarlem in 1582, but did not begin to paint until 1600, under Italian influence – he had been in Italy in 1590–1. His portraits, both painted and engraved, have a sober realism and grasp of character quite different from his fancy subjects, and occasionally they seem to foreshadow Hals, his fellow-townsman. His engravings, executed by himself or by others to his designs, are very numerous and of superb technique. He was also the first to use colour wood-blocks for landscape prints, and he made a number of CHIAROSCURO woodcuts of figure subjects. There are paintings in Amsterdam, Arras, Baltimore (Walters), Basle, Haarlem, The Hague, Leningrad, Munich, Paris (Louvre), Philadelphia, Providence RI, and Rotterdam.

GONÇALVES, Nuno (active 1450–72), was the most important Portuguese painter of the 15th century. His *S. Vincent Altar* for Lisbon Cathedral was destroyed in 1755, but another, of six panels dedicated to the same Saint (now in Lisbon Mus.), is reasonably attributed to him. It contains many portraits and may be dated *c.* 1465–7: the style is ultimately Flemish, based on BOUTS, but simpler and more austere. The influence of wood-carving is discernible in the treatment of the heads.

GONZÁLEZ, Julio (1876–1942), was, with LAURENS and LIPCHITZ, a Cubist sculptor. He was born in Barcelona, into a family of metal workers. The family moved to Paris in 1900 and González soon came in contact with Picasso, whom he had already met in Barcelona: in 1930–2 he taught Picasso the technique of ironworking. For many years a painter, González worked in the Renault factories during the First World War and subsequently devoted himself to sculpture in iron. He was influenced by ARCHIPENKO and produced a form of Cubist sculpture: in turn, his work has had great influence on British and US sculptors (e.g. Butler). His masterpiece is the *Montserrat* (1936–7: Amsterdam, Stedelijk Mus.) made for the Spanish Pavilion at an International Exhibition, but it is more naturalistic than most of his works – e.g. the *Woman doing her Hair* (1936: New York,

M of MA). Many of his works are in Paris (Mus. d'Art Moderne).

GORE, Spencer Frederick (1878–1914), was strongly influenced by SICKERT and late Impressionist painting, and from 1910 (when Roger Fry organized the first POST-IMPRESSIONIST Exhibition in London) he was deeply influenced by Cézanne and Gauguin. In 1911 he was the first president of the newly founded CAMDEN TOWN GROUP. There are works by him in the Tate, London.

GORKY, Arshile (1904–48), was born Vosdanig Adoian in Turkish Armenia, fled before the Turks in 1915 and finally arrived in the US in 1920. His life began in tragedy – his mother starved to death – and ended in suicide, following a cancer operation in 1946 and a car crash in which he broke his neck. He worked in New York from c.1925 and began to paint Cubist pictures in 1927: his earliest works are imitations of Cézanne, later of Picasso and finally of MIRÒ. His *Artist and his Mother* (c.1926–36: New York, Whitney Mus.) is an able pastiche of Picasso's figure style of c.1920. In 1935 and 1939 he painted two large murals on the theme of aviation, but both are lost. In 1940 he met MATTA, who inspired him with Surrealist ideas similar to those of Mirò. Other American museums with pictures by Gorky include Baltimore, Buffalo, Chicago, New York (M of MA), Oberlin Ohio, San Francisco, Tucson Ariz. University, and Utica NY (Munson-Williams-Proctor).

GOSSAERT or Gossart, Jan, *see* MABUSE.

GOTHIC is a term normally used to describe the architectural style of N. Europe from the early 12th century until the 16th, and, as such, has no place in this Dictionary. It is, however, often used to describe the other arts of the same period, particularly when emphasizing their transcendental qualities in contradistinction to Renaissance art. The phrase 'Late Gothic' is useful in this connexion, since it means that artists such as NOTKE, HOLBEIN the Elder, and even GRÜNE-WALD continued to practise a style which was not affected by Renaissance ideas, as late as the end of the 15th century and into the 16th. The genuine Gothic art of France in the 14th century influenced some Italians, notably Simone MARTINI, and the result of this was the stylistic offshoot known as INTERNATIONAL GOTHIC.

GOTTLIEB, Adolph (*b.*1903), was born in New York, and studied there and in Paris, Berlin, and Munich. With his close friend ROTH-KO, he became known as an abstract painter, exploring myth-laden and subconscious mental states through automatic painting. During the 1950s he developed his 'pictographs' – panels divided first into chequerboard compartments, and later into bands, containing Red Indian magic symbols (hands, eyes, snakes, arrows). In 1956 he evolved his symbols of the cosmos and chaos: large disks of colour over explosive black blots.

GOUACHE is opaque watercolour paint (known to many people as

Poster Paint). With gouache effects very similar to those obtainable in oil-painting may be got with less trouble, so that it is a useful means of making studies for a large picture in oils; although, like its kin DIS-TEMPER and TEMPERA, it has the defect of drying much lighter in tone than it seems when wet. The medium lacks the peculiar charm of pure watercolour, but has always been popular on the Continent. Paul SANDBY was one of the few British artists to use it extensively. *See also* BODY COLOUR.

GOUJON, Jean (active 1540–62), was a French sculptor who is also re-corded as an architect. His elongated, elegant figures are derived from Parmigianino, Rosso, and Cellini, but these influences are so completely assimilated that he possesses a striking personal style, which also shows the influence of classical sculpture, known possibly through a visit to Italy before 1540. He worked in Paris on the rood-screen for S. Germain l'Auxerrois (from 1544: Louvre), on the *Fontaine des Innocents* (1547–9: most of the reliefs are now in the Louvre), and on decorations for the Louvre, much restored during the 19th century. These include figures and reliefs on the exterior, and the caryatids of the Gallery in what is now the Salle des Caryatides. He disappears from sight in 1562. Besides the works now in the Louvre, there are works in Rouen (Cath., S. Maclou) by or attributed to him.

GOYA, Francisco de G. y Lucientes (1746–1828), was born near Sara-gossa and studied there until (apparently) his amours and knifings caused him to leave: in 1766 he was in Madrid working under BAYEU, whose sister he married. He was in Rome in 1771, but was back in Saragossa later in the year, working in the Cathedral. By 1775 he was in Madrid and from 1776 began producing tapestry cartoons for the Royal manufactory; this started his successful career and he became Deputy Director of the Academy in 1785, *pintor del rey* 1786, *pintor de cámara* 1789, and *primer pintor de cámara* (i.e. Principal Painter to the King) in 1799, so that his contemporaries certainly recognized his genius. In 1792, however, he was very ill and became deaf, which undoubtedly made him still more introspective, so that we find Goya the official portrait painter also producing works which, he said, were 'to make observations for which commissioned works generally give no room, and in which fantasy and invention have no limit'. This fantasy was typified in the series of etchings called *Los Caprichos*, produced 1796–8 and announced for sale in 1799 (eight more were added in 1803). These are savagely satirical attacks on manners and customs and on abuses in the Church, yet in 1798 he painted the frescoes of the cupola of S. Antonio de la Florida in Madrid (tech-nically fascinating, because apparently executed with sponges in dabs and wipings of colour). The dilemma in which Goya and other liberal Spaniards found themselves became acute in 1793 when Charles IV declared war on the new French Republic; for Charles was very reactionary and most liberals were then partly in sympathy with France. In 1808 the troops of Napoleon invaded Spain and drove out Ferdinand VII, replacing him with Joseph Bonaparte. Many Spaniards welcomed his liberalism, yet hated the foreigners – in particular the French troops, who behaved with almost 20th-century savagery. These atrocities were recorded by Goya in the series of etchings called *The Disasters of War* (1810–13: first published in full in 1863) and, above all, in the two paintings called *2 May* and *3 May 1808* (*c.*1814: Madrid, Prado). The French were driven out with the aid of Wellington (whom Goya painted in 1812) and in 1814 Ferdinand VII was restored. Goya was pardoned for having worked for Joseph Bonaparte and continued to work for the Spanish Court until 1824 when there was a fresh wave of reaction and he went to Paris and then settled in voluntary exile in Bordeaux. What seems so difficult to understand is how the Bourbons could continue to employ him, for his portraits of Charles IV and his family have been described as making them look like prosperous grocers; but in fact these portraits, and those of Ferdinand VII, make them appear brutish, moronic, and arrogant.

From 1819 Goya began to practise the new art of lithography and he produced some bull-fighting scenes as well as single prints and several more etchings and aquatints. There are good examples of his prints in the BM, London, in Madrid, and New York (Hispanic Soc.).

As a painter Goya began his decorative works very much under the influence of Tiepolo's Spanish frescoes, while his portraits are influenced by Mengs and, oddly, by English 18th-century portraits (he is known to have owned engravings): an intensive study of Velazquez, his predecessor as Court Painter, led to a breadth of style which ends as a kind of Impressionism. He had great influence on 19th-century French painting, especially on Manet, and he has been called the last of the Old Masters and the first of the moderns (whatever that may mean). There are pictures in Agen, Baltimore, Barnard Castle, Bayonne, Berlin, Besançon, Boston (Mus.), Budapest, Castres, Chicago, Cincinnati, Cleveland Ohio, Detroit, San Diego Cal., Edinburgh, Hartford Conn., Houston Texas, Kansas City, Lille, London (NG, Courtauld Inst., Wellington Mus.), St Louis, Madrid (Prado, Acad., and S. Antonio de la Florida), Minneapolis, Montreal, Munich, New York (Met. Mus., Frick Coll., Brooklyn Mus., and especially Hispanic Soc.), Northampton Mass. (Smith Coll.), Ottawa, São Paulo Brazil, Paris (Louvre), Seville, Toledo, Toledo Ohio, Valencia, Washington (NG and Phillips Coll.), and Worcester Mass.

GOYEN, Jan van (1596–1656), was, with Salomon van RUYSDAEL, the most important Dutch landscape painter of the realist school before Jacob van RUISDAEL. He spent a year in France as a young man and then worked under E. van de VELDE in Haarlem *c*. 1617 before settling in The Hague in 1634. He travelled extensively in Holland and also went to the neighbourhood of Antwerp and Brussels (a sketchbook exists of his Belgian trip): many of his pictures represent identifiable places. He speculated all his earnings on tulips and houses and died insolvent, in spite of his huge production, but a portrait of the family by his son-in-law, Jan STEEN, shows a very prosperous-looking group, complete with negro page. His earliest works, up to *c*. 1630, show the influence of Esaias van de Velde, with rather crowded compositions and strong local colours. About 1630 a marked change is observable in his style. His composition is simplified, with the horizon set very low in the picture, and a great breadth of handling and tonality is obtained by the use of near-monochrome, with the light green and yellow-brown which is typical of him (Houbraken, writing before 1718, said that the blues had faded out of his greens, leaving yellows – cf. PYNACKER). At this stage it is often difficult to distinguish his pictures from those of S. van Ruysdael (a Ruysdael of 1631 in London, NG, passed for years as by van Goyen, and reasonably so). Later on his colour becomes richer again, until, at his death, the poetic imagination of Jacob van Ruisdael carried Dutch landscape painting to fresh heights. Van Goyen made some etchings as well as very numerous drawings, some of which were certainly made for sale as independent works of art. He painted his own figures in his landscapes, the earliest of which dates from 1618: about 1,200 are recorded, so that he is well represented in museums.

GOZZOLI, Benozzo (*c*. 1421–97), was the assistant of Fra ANGELICO, but was entirely secular in outlook. His numerous frescoes give a picture of 15th-century life, the most famous being the *Medici family as the Magi* (*c*. 1459: Florence, Medici Palace). A typical panel is in London (NG).

GRAF, Urs (*c*. 1485–1527/28), was a Swiss draughtsman, engraver, and goldsmith. He painted only one picture, *War* (*c*. 1515: Basle), and possibly one other, the *S. George*, which is also in Basle. He was a vile man who frequently went off as a mercenary soldier and his drawings of the life of these brutes have a morbid fascination, enhanced by the sweeping rhythms of the pen stroke. He disappeared from Basle in 1527 – perhaps to take part in the Sack of Rome – and his wife remarried in 1528. The great majority of his drawings and engravings are in Basle.

GRAFF, Anton (1736–1813), was born in Switzerland, but was the leading German portrait painter of the 18th century. He was a younger contemporary of Reynolds, with whom he is often compared, but Graff really belongs to a later generation, since most of his portraits lack the trappings of the Grand Style, and he worked almost into the BIEDERMEIER period. He was in Augsburg by 1756 and removed to

Dresden in 1766 to teach at the newly founded Academy. He recorded himself as having painted some 1,240 portraits in his long career and his sitters included many of the most famous of his contemporaries – Lessing, Herder, Schiller (whom he records as having fidgeted the whole time). He also made some 322 portrait drawings in silver point, a very rare technique in the 18th century. Some fragments of an auto-biography were posthumously published in Zürich in 1815. There are pictures in many German museums, including Berlin, Dresden, and Leipzig.

GRAFFITO *see* SGRAFFITO.

GRANACCI, Francesco (1469/70–1543), was a Florentine painter of the generation immediately preceding MICHELANGELO whose friend he was from early youth. Like Michelangelo, Granacci was a pupil of Domenico GHIRLANDAIO, whose assistant he later became. Granacci was one of the assistants engaged by Michelangelo in 1508 for the beginning of the Sistine ceiling but, like the others, was dismissed after about one month. On his return to Florence Granacci fell under the influence of Fra BARTOLOMMEO, and his later works have elongated figures in an attempt at monumentality. The Dublin *Holy Family*, which is usually attributed to him, has also been attributed to Michelangelo and shows the approximation of their styles. Basically, however, Granacci was a Quattrocento artist and is thus very similar to such transitional painters as Ridolfo Ghirlandaio and FRANCIABIGIO. There are works by him in Florence and in Baltimore (Walters), Berlin, London (V & A), Munich, Oxford, San Francisco, Sarasota Fla, and Washington.

GRANDI, Ercole di Giulio Cesare, *see* ROBERTI.

GRAPHIC ARTS. The phrase is an importation into English from the German *Graphik* and is used to mean those arts which depend for their effect on drawing and not on colour: in other words the arts of drawing and engraving in all its forms.

GRAVELOT, Hubert (1699–1773), was a French book-illustrator and engraver. He came to London in 1733 after studying in Paris under BOUCHER, and returned to Paris in 1746, after having been Gainsborough's master. He came back to London and remained till 1755 and then finally returned to Paris: he is the most important link between the French School – especially the Watteau followers – and the British in the mid-18th century. He illustrated most of the important books published in London during the years he lived in England. His paintings are rare – they influenced HAYMAN, among others – but there is a fine one at Marble Hill, Twickenham, London. One in York is, perhaps, a copy.

GRAVER *see* BURIN.

GRECO. Domenikos Theotocopoulos (1541–1614), called El Greco, was born in Crete and probably received his early training there.

Crete then belonged to Venice, but it was a centre of the survival of Byzantine art in the 16th century, and it would be natural for a young artist who wished to receive further training to go to Venice for it, as Greco did. The references to his Italian years are very scanty, the most important being the letters of his friend, the illuminator Giulio Clovio. One, written in 1570, seeks the patronage of Cardinal Farnese for him: 'There has arrived in Rome a young Candiote, a pupil of Titian, who seems ... to have a rare gift for painting'.

One early 17th-century source, not very reliable, records him as working in Rome during the Pontificate of Pius V (1566–72) and says that he had studied under Titian, coming to Rome at a propitious moment and with a great opinion of himself – saying, when Pius proposed to cover the nudities in Michelangelo's *Last Judgement* (eventually done by Daniele da Volterra), that if the whole thing were demolished he would paint another as good and decorous into the bargain. This caused such resentment that Greco was forced to go to Spain, where he had to compete for Court favour with established painters such as TIBALDI, ZUCCARO, and others, whose intrigues caused him to retire and die in obscurity. There is an element of truth in all this, including his lack of success at Court, and he is known to have owned a copy of VASARI's *Lives* in which he wrote slighting comments on Michelangelo and Florentine art in general.

Greco's early works show his wide range of sources; Titian, Michelangelo, Bassano, Raphael, Dürer, the MANNERISTS of Central Italy, such as Pontormo and Parmigianino, and, underlying all these, his Byzantine heritage. It is not known why he went to Spain, but he is recorded in Toledo from 1577 until his death. Soon after his arrival he received his first major commission – the High Altar and two transept altars in San Domingo el Antiguo (1577–9). The High Altar has been dispersed but the transept altars remain. It astonishes by the completeness with which he has assimilated all the varied elements of his style and also by its great scale – *The Trinity* (now in the Prado) is nearly 10 feet high and the *Assumption* (now in Chicago) is over 16 feet. His next major commission (also 1577–9) was for the *Disrobing of Christ* (*El Espolio*), for Toledo Cathedral: it was refused and he had to bring a lawsuit, but the verdict of the assessors was enthusiastic and may explain the number of repetitions. Soon after this he made a bid for Court favour with his *Dream of Philip* (in the Escorial; sketch in London NG), a sort of counterpart to Titian's *Gloria, or Vision of Charles V*. It represents the adoration of the Name of Jesus, and is an allegory of the Holy League against the Turks. This was painted *c*.1580, and in 1581 Philip commissioned the *Martyrdom of S. Maurice and the Theban Legion*, delivered in 1584, and immediately refused by the King, whose secretary wrote: 'The picture does not please His Majesty, and that is no wonder, for it pleases few, although it is said that there is much art in it and its author understands much for there are excellent things of his to be seen.' Philip was devoted to the balanced, serene art of Titian and this highly Mannerist work, asymmetrical, violent in scale changes, disturbing, and acid in colour, was bound to clash with the King's tastes. Philip tried hard to attract major artists into his service, but he got only feeble exponents of a style one of whose greatest masters he rejected out of hand. Greco passed the remainder of his life in Toledo and his ecstatic and passionate style becomes heightened with time, often increasing with successive repetitions of a subject, and so personal that his pupils and assistants do not even attempt to follow his example except for occasional weak imitations by his son Jorge Manuel. The background of Mannerism in Italy lies partly in the Sack of Rome and the Counter-Reformation: in Spain the background to Greco is in the Wars with the Netherlands and in the long tragedy of the Expulsion of the Jews and the Moriscos from 1585 to 1609, which ruined Toledo and left whole districts desolate, with grass growing in the streets. It lies also in the 'Spiritual Exercises' of S. Ignatius, the founder of the Jesuits, which insist upon immediacy of experience, even of the events of the Passion, for the person practising the devotions. Greco's use of colour, often eerie and strident, with sharp contrasts of blue, yellow, shrill green, and a livid mulberry pink, the elongated limbs and nervous tension of his figures, the feeling that the draperies swathing them have a life of their own – all these suggest the intensity of the painter's mystical experience and the catharsis he found in his art. The finest collections of El Greco's works are in Spain; in the Escorial, the Prado in Madrid, and in the Museums and churches of Toledo. There are others in Barnard Castle (Bowes Mus.), Boston, Budapest, Cadiz, Cambridge Mass. (Fogg Mus.), Chicago, Cincinnati, Cleveland Ohio, Copenhagen, Detroit, Dresden, Edinburgh (NG), Hartford Conn. (Wadsworth Atheneum), Kansas City, London (NG), Los Angeles, Milan, Minneapolis, Modena, Montreal, Munich, Naples, New York (Met. Mus., Frick Coll., Hispanic Soc.), Oslo, Ottawa, Oxford, Palencia (Cath.), Paris (Louvre), Parma, Philadelphia, Princeton, Providence RI, Rochester NY, St Louis, San Diego Cal., San Francisco Cal., Saragossa, Sarasota Fla, Seville, Stockholm, Strasbourg, Toledo Ohio, Villanueva y Geltrú, Washington (Dumbarton Oaks, NG, and Phillips Coll.), and Worcester Mass.

GRECO, Emilio (b.1913), is a Sicilian sculptor. As a boy he worked for a tombstone maker, but while in the Army managed to attend art school in Palermo. His first one-man show in Rome in 1946 brought him immediate success. His principal works are bronze portrait busts, and life-size bronze female figures, tall, slender, posturing with great elegance, and often in sharp and witty parody of classical statues. His pen drawings express form through hatchings, with only an occasional fine contour.

GREUZE, Jean Baptiste (1725–1805), made his name in the Salon of 1755 with *A Grandfather reading the Bible to his Family*, a piece of Dutch-inspired narrative genre painting, extolling the simple virtues of the poor. Enormously popular works such as *L'Accordée de Village* (1761: Louvre) and the *Paralytic tended by his Children* (1763: Leningrad, Hermitage) exploit this Rousseauish field with skill and determination, winning him extravagant praise from DIDEROT, who later came to a juster appreciation of Greuze's talent. His excessive vanity so antagonized his fellow artists that his attempt in 1769 to secure election to the Academy as a History painter with the inadequate and ill-drawn *Septimius Severus reproaching Caracalla* met with a deservedly humiliating rebuff, and caused his withdrawal from all further Salons. He exhibited his works privately, enjoying a great vogue during the 1770s when much of his fame derived from the popularity of engravings after his works, fully exploited by a number of engravers, and, less profitably, by the artist, whose wife embezzled most of the proceeds. During these years a severe and Poussinesque composition and a more restrained use of accessory detail were combined with turgid colour, strong chiaroscuro, and a heightened rendering of the gamut of the passions, displayed in vivid facial expressions and gestures and in a mountingly high moral tone. He also painted some excellent portraits and charmingly tender studies of children. During the late 1770s and in the 1780s, to offset his dwindling popularity, adversely affected by Neoclassicism, he produced increasing quantities of titillating semi-draped figures of young girls, grossly deficient in drawing and of mawkish sentimentality, and numerous 'Expression Studies' arbitrarily named 'Sorrow' or 'Innocence' and so on. His life was embittered by his disastrous marriage to the pretty model of his early pictures who later degenerated into a sleazy drab, whom he eventually divorced. After the Revolution, which ruined him, he endured poverty and neglect, occasionally relieved by a charitable commission from Napoleon and his circle. He died unnoticed, having – like Fragonard – outlived his time and his reputation. The largest collections of his pictures are in the Louvre, London (Wallace Coll.), and Montpellier. His native Tournus has a Musée Greuze which contains two very early portraits and some drawings as well as a room devoted to his life. This contains interesting comparative material ranging from Poussin to Hogarth. There are paintings in most French provincial museums and in Baltimore, Berlin, Berne, Budapest, Dublin, Edinburgh, Glasgow, Leningrad, London (NG), Minneapolis, Moscow, Munich, New York (Met. Mus.), Rotterdam, Stockholm, Vienna, Waddesdon Bucks. (National Trust), and York. There are also many drawings in Russia, where he was very popular.

GRIEN, Hans Baldung, *see* BALDUNG.

GRIS, Juan (1887–1927), left Madrid in 1906 and settled in Paris, living near PICASSO. At first he broke up the objects in his pictures into many-faceted planes, but by 1911 he was using the analytical form of Cubism, and later used *collage* and synthetic forms, with an understanding and an originality that preserve him from inclusion among the more obvious Picasso followers. He did some work for Diaghileff in 1922–3, but found the world of ballet too hectic.

His 'Possibilités de la peinture' was given as a paper at the Sorbonne in 1924. There are works in New York (M of MA) and Paris (Mus. d'Art Moderne).

GRISAILLE is a painting executed entirely in monochrome, in a series of greys. Strictly speaking, a monochrome painting is one executed in any one colour, red, blue, or black; a *grisaille*, as its name implies, is in neutral greys only. A *grisaille* may be executed for its own sake as a decoration, or as a model for an engraver to work from, or it may be the first stage in building up an OIL PAINTING.

GROS, Baron Antoine Jean (1771–1835). His parents were both minor artists, and he became a pupil of DAVID in 1785. In 1793 he was in Italy and was introduced by Josephine into the entourage of Napoleon (whom he painted) in Milan after the Italian campaign; he was one of the committee which selected the looted works of art taken from Italy to France. His strength lay in large pictures illustrating the Napoleonic Saga, such as *Napoleon visiting the plague-stricken at Jaffa* (1804: Louvre) and battlepieces full of movement and colour. He was David's closest friend and fervent admirer, and after his death in 1825 assumed the leadership of the classicist school. He was made a Baron by Charles X for his dome of the Panthéon which he had originally planned as an apotheosis of Napoleon and had to convert into an apotheosis of the Restoration Bourbons. His late classicist pictures were received with derision, and partly in despair at his failure, partly because of his miserable married life, he drowned himself. His influence on GÉRICAULT and DELACROIX was important for the development of the Romantic Movement.

There are works in Algiers, Besançon, Bordeaux, Chartres, Cleveland Ohio, Grenoble, Malmaison, Moscow, Paris (Louvre, Carnavalet, Invalides), Toulouse, Valenciennes, Versailles, and elsewhere.

GROSZ, Georg (1893–1959), was the leading German satirical draughtsman of this century. He was trained at the Dresden Academy from 1909 and served in the army from 1914, but his dislike of authority resulted in a court martial for insubordination and he was nearly shot. In 1918 he was one of the founders of DADA in Berlin and in 1920 produced a book of satirical drawings – 'Gott mit uns' – as a result of which he was fined for insulting the German Army. In 1923 he was again fined for an insult to morality, and in 1928 for blasphemy. Fortunately for him, he began to exhibit in America in 1931 and in 1933 he went to New York, remaining in America until he revisited Germany in 1951. He returned to Berlin, with the intention of staying there, in 1959, but died soon after his arrival. His autobiography has been published in German and English. There are examples of his work in Berlin, Cologne, and Stuttgart, as well as Boston, Cambridge Mass. (Fogg), Chicago, and New York (M of MA).

GROTESQUE in its technical sense has nothing to do with its normal usage. It refers to the kind of ornament, sometimes also called Arabesque (though this is not really identical), which was used as a decoration in antiquity. This consists of medallions, sphinxes, foliage, and similar elements and the name Grotesque derives from the fact that these classical ornaments were rediscovered in places like the Golden House of Nero, in grottoes, and were thus named *Grotteschi*. Raphael was one of the first modern artists to use these motives. The word *grottesco* was first used in 1502, in the contract for PINTORICCHIO's Piccolomini frescoes in Siena – with which Raphael may have been concerned.

GROUND is the surface on which a painting is made. If on canvas, the ground is usually white oil paint, sometimes with a tinted layer on top; on panel the ground may be the same or GESSO. Some incompetent artists do not use a ground and paint direct on to the support – i.e. the bare canvas or wood. On canvas this practice is always, eventually, fatal. *See also* BOLUS GROUND.

GRÜNEWALD. Mathis Neithardt-Gothardt, called Grünewald (*c.*1470/80–1528), was a contemporary of Dürer, and his exact opposite. Little is known of his life – he is first documented in 1501 in Seligenstadt – but he may have been in Aschaffenburg before then and was perhaps born in Würzburg. From 1508 to 1514 he was Court Painter to the Archbishop-Elector of Mainz and then to Cardinal Albrecht, Elector of Mainz; but he seems to have had Lutheran sympathies and in 1526 he was in Frankfurt and 1527 in Halle, where he died. Unlike most of his German contemporaries he seems never to have designed any woodcuts or made etchings or engravings, and relatively few drawings by him have survived. The first datable work is the *Mocking of Christ* (formerly dated 1503: Munich) but his masterpiece is the large folding altar for a church in Isenheim (finished *c.*1515: Colmar, Musée), which shows how completely his outlook differed from that of Dürer. Dürer attempted to learn the Italian technical methods in order to penetrate into the serene world of the Italian and classical tradition: Grünewald seems to have been well acquainted with the Renaissance ideas in, for example, perspective and the definition of a given space, but he uses these Renaissance technical means simply to heighten the emotional impact made by his essentially Late Gothic religious imagery. The terrible figure of the

Crucified Christ in the *Isenheim Altar* is anti-Renaissance in its intensity, but the altarpiece as a whole combines a passionate expression of the Visions of S. Bridget with an Italian (or rather Renaissance) feeling for drawing, light, and colour. His few paintings are in Basle, Donaueschingen, Frankfurt (Städel), Freiburg i. B., Karlsruhe, Munich, Stuppach in Württemberg, and Washington (NG).

GUARDI, Francesco (1712–93), was a Venetian VEDUTA painter, whose free handling and atmospheric effects now appeal more than CANALETTO's meticulous views of Venetian architecture, which were the more highly valued until the Impressionists taught us to see transient effects of light. Most of Guardi's views of Venice – he painted little else – were produced as souvenirs for tourists, and a contemporary diarist records him as a disciple of Canaletto, working for an Englishman. He worked with his brother, Giovanni Antonio (1699–1760), and collaborated with him on some religious pictures, but Francesco's activity as a figure painter has only recently been clarified by the discovery of such works as the altarpiece at Roncegno in Valsugana, of *c*.1777, and five large decorative panels (one in Hull). Two *Allegories* (Liverpool) may be by either Francesco or Giovanni Antonio and in this they represent a large class. The only certain (and very mediocre) work by Giovanni is *The Death of S. Joseph* (E. Berlin): this was thought to have been destroyed in 1945, but reappeared (rather mysteriously) in 1965. Francesco's *vedute*, for which he got only about half Canaletto's prices, were produced in great numbers and have also been imitated ever since the 18th century. The vivacity and bravura of his little figures, and his pale, bright colour, may owe something to his brother-in-law, TIEPOLO. Most large galleries have works by him, but the following are dated sets of pictures: *Election of Doge Alvise IV Mocenigo*, 1763, based on engravings after drawings by Canaletto, in the Louvre (7), Brussels, Grenoble, Nantes (2), and Toulouse; *Pius VI's visit to Venice*, 1782, in Oxford and private collections; *Fêtes for the Archduke Paul of Russia and Maria Feodorowna* ('*I Conti del Nord*'), 1782, in Munich and private collections. Other dated pictures include *Faith* and *Hope*, 1747, in the Ringling Mus., Sarasota Fla: *Hope* was signed by Francesco and dated – but both signature and date have now disappeared and doubts have been expressed concerning their authenticity. There are also two signed views of Venice of exceptional size, unique in his work, at Waddesdon, Bucks. (National Trust).

GUERCINO (1591–1666) was born at Cento, near Bologna. His nickname means 'squint-eyed', his real name being Francesco Barbieri. He was first strongly influenced by Ludovico CARRACCI, but early overlaid his Carraccesque training with the strong chiaroscuro associated with the Caravaggesques, which he invested with a charm and softness unknown to its originator, though he later abandoned it for an even, characterless illumination more suitable for the didactic, mechanical Counter-Reformation altarpieces of his late Bolognese period. In 1621 he was in Rome working for Pope Gregory XV, and his masterpiece is the *Aurora* on the ceiling of the Casino Ludovisi, one of the finest Baroque illusionistic decorations. In the landscape parts he was helped by Tassi and the BRILS. He returned to Cento on the death of the Pope in 1623, and set up a studio, but on the death of RENI – who loathed him, and accused him of fishing in his ideas and copying his handling – he moved to Bologna in 1642 and took over the Reni religious picture factory.

There are examples in the Royal Collection (rich in fine drawings), Bologna (Mus. and churches), Berlin, Birmingham, Brussels, Budapest, Cambridge (Fitzwm), Cento, Detroit, Dresden, Dublin, Edinburgh, Florence (Uffizi, Pitti), Genoa, Greenville SC, Hartford Conn., Leningrad, London (NG, Dulwich, Lancaster House, Wellington Mus.), Madrid (Prado), Milan (Brera), Minneapolis, Modena, Munich, Naples, Oxford (Ch. Ch.), Parma, Paris (Louvre), Piacenza, Providence RI, Rome, Rouen, Sarasota Fla, Toulouse, Vaduz (Liechtenstein Coll.), Vicenza, and Vienna.

GUIDO da Siena was the all but mythical founder of the Sienese School. He signed a picture in the Pal. Pubblico, Siena, and dated it 1221, but there are other pictures, also in Siena, associable with him which are datable 1262 and in the 1270s. There are therefore two schools of thought: (i) that 1221 is correct, in spite of the evidently repainted surface of much of the picture. In this case (*a*) Siena precedes Florence in the development of Dugento painting, and (*b*) the other pictures mentioned are by Guido's followers, not by Guido himself. (ii) The other school (which contains few Sienese) holds that 1221 is an old tampering with an original date *c.*1261 – perhaps MCCXXI was altered from MCCLXI – and the other pictures are therefore his and contemporary. Recent X-rays give no grounds for believing this. Another theory, more reasonable, assumes that the picture was painted perhaps 1260/70, but was a copy and replacement of an older image, and the date 1221 was copied faithfully from this older image.

GUILD. In the Middle Ages tradesmen formed themselves into Guilds for economic, religious, and social purposes, and often several different trades would unite in a single guild; at Florence, for example, painters belonged to the Doctors' and Apothecaries' Guild (*Medici e Speziali*). Much of our knowledge of early painting comes from Guild records, since all painters had to join unless they were in the personal service of the ruling prince. Only a Master could set up in business, take pupils, and employ JOURNEYMEN, and to become a Master it was necessary to submit a masterpiece to the

Guild as evidence of competence. The Guild officers also supervised the number of apprentices and the conditions of work and often also materials. Some Guilds bought in bulk for members, others allowed only panels stamped with their seal to be used for painting on. The tendency to uniformity of practice and to a 'Trade Union' mentality led to painters like Leonardo and Michelangelo insisting on the freedom and originality of the artist and his status as a professional man and a scholar (and gentleman). This new conception of the inspired being, instead of the honest tradesman, led to the decline of the Guilds and the rise of the ACADEMIES, which took over the all-important function of teaching. As one might expect, the power of the Guilds lasted longer in N. Europe than in Italy. As late as 1655 the Guild at Malines made itself ridiculous by trying to prevent Jan Cossiers from completing a commission, painted in his Antwerp studio, *in situ* in Malines – on the grounds that he was not a resident and was therefore forbidden to work in their town. A similar situation arose in Toronto in 1960.

GÜNTHER, Ignaz (1725–75), was the great Bavarian sculptor of the Rococo period, who used its light and gay forms to create deeply religious images. Most of his work is in painted wood and is in Munich and its neighbourhood.

GUTTOSO, Renato (*b*.1912), was born in Sicily and is the leading Italian (or European) exponent of SOCIAL REALISM. He studied Law and began to paint only in 1931. His works attacked Fascism and the Nazis (especially in his bitter drawings 'Gott mit uns'), and his style is necessarily realistic, but the influence of Picasso is evident. There are works in London (Tate), New York (M of MA), Prague, and Sydney NSW.

GUYS, Constantin (1802–92), was a draughtsman who chronicled the wars and the fashions of Europe in the 19th century. He travelled enormously and took part in the Greek War of Independence and the Crimean War (which he reported as correspondent of the 'Illustrated London News'), but he is best known for his witty drawings of soldiers, horses and courtesans. Baudelaire wrote a long essay on him as *le peintre de la vie moderne*. Paris (Mus. Marmottan) has a series of drawings by him which belonged to Monet.

H

HALF-TONES are all those tones between the lightest and the darkest. Thus, there is the illogical situation that a series of distinct tonal values can all be described as 'half-tones'. A half-tone block is used in process engraving and obtains the tonal varieties by dots, as may be seen in a newspaper photograph.

HALS, Frans (1581/5–1666), was born in Antwerp of Flemish parents, but spent most of his life in Haarlem. He was a pupil of Karel van MANDER (1600–3), and entered the Haarlem Guild in 1610. His earliest dated work (*Jacobus Zaffius*, 1611: Haarlem) was painted in Haarlem, but by 1616 he was probably in Antwerp and may have been in contact with Rubens, who visited him in Haarlem in 1624. His great gift was for portraiture, and especially for catching the fleeting expression, and he is best known for the huge but lively groups of the companies of Archers and Musketeers raised during the Wars against Spain, the earliest of which was painted in 1616. These groups solve the very difficult problem of composing a picture out of a number of figures all of whom demand the same prominence (since all the sitters subscribed), thus precluding the classical solution of subordinating the minor figures. Hals used a very virtuoso technique to enliven the whole picture surface and each portrait is caught in a fleeting gesture or expression. The whole is perhaps a little like a school photograph but that is what the sitters wanted, and the very informality caused his work to be a great influence on Manet and the Impressionists. In his single figures his dazzling skill sometimes runs away with him – as in the *Laughing Cavalier* (1624: London, Wallace Coll.) – and he never quite achieved the sympathy and insight of his greater contemporary Rembrandt. During the years 1624–8 he was strongly influenced by the UTRECHT School and adopted the type of genre portrait common to Terbrugghen and Honthorst. He used these largely for technical experiments, making his drawing even more simplified and his handling appear almost monochromatic and *alla prima*: he did in fact employ a very limited colour-range and used greys a great deal, but all the bravura of the handling is a deal less spontaneous than it appears at first sight. After the Peace of 1648 the Military Companies were disbanded, but their place was taken, for artists, by the great group portraits commissioned by Regents and Governors of Charities. Hals painted several of these, particularly in his last years when he was destitute and dependent on charity for himself and his wife: these have greater feeling for character and greater humanity than many of his earlier groups, and they are also strangely closer to the late Rembrandt in handling.

Both his brothers were painters, but only Dirk (1591–1656) achieved any independence, though his subjects and style were similar to Frans'. All seven of his sons were also painters, though of little significance. His pupils probably included BROUWER, Jan MOLE-NAER and his wife Judith LEYSTER, A. van OSTADE, and WOUWER-MAN, while Jan de BRAY owed much to Hals' development of the Regent groups. Hals had a large workshop, and as many as twenty versions of some works are known. The most important collection, including five Officer groups and three of Governors, is in the Hals Museum at Haarlem. Other works, by him or from his studio, include those in the Royal Coll. and in Amsterdam (Rijksmus.), Antwerp, Baltimore, Berlin, Birmingham (Barber Inst.), Boston (Mus.), Brussels, Cape Town, Cassel, Chicago, Cincinnati, Cleveland Ohio, Cologne (Wallraf-Richartz Mus.), Denver, Detroit, Dresden, Edinburgh (NG), Frankfurt (Städel), The Hague, Hartford Conn., Houston Texas, Hull, Kansas City, London (NG and Kenwood), Munich, New York (Met. Mus. and Frick Coll.), Ottawa, Paris (Louvre), Richmond Va, San Diego Cal., St Louis, Sarasota Fla (Ringling), Stockholm, Toledo Ohio, Toronto, Vienna, Washington (NG), Yale, and elsewhere.

HAMILTON, Gavin (1723–98), was a Scots laird who graduated at Glasgow and then went to Rome and trained as a painter in the 1740s. After practising as a portrait painter in Britain in 1753/4 he returned to Rome for good and became well-known as a dealer and antiquary and as a member of the NEOCLASSIC school centred round Mengs and Winckelmann. He was painting Poussinesque historical compositions by 1758 and is thus one of the original exponents of the doctrine preached by DAVID some 15 years later. He employed the engraver Cunego to make his compositions more widely known (as Raphael had employed Marcantonio), and he also obtained many commissions for vast historical compositions as *douceurs* in connexion with his activities as an antique dealer. There is a picture ascribed to him in Edinburgh (NG), but his most influential works are in the Villa Borghese in Rome.

HANDLING (Fr. *facture*; Ital. *fattura*) is the name given to the most personal part of a work of art, the actual execution. The general features of composition, of subject, of drawing or colour, can be used to assign a picture or other work to a given School or period; the handling of the paint, pencil, clay, or other medium is personal to the artist and is what the forger tries hardest to imitate. Just as a man's signature is highly personal and executed without thinking about it, so a painter will handle shapes and planes and even come to see them in terms of his own BRUSHWORK.

HARPIGNIES, Henri (1819–1916), was a French landscape painter who was principally influenced by Corot and the BARBIZON painters.

In his old age his failing eyesight forced him to generalize in a manner not unlike the late Corot. He was popular in England and there are four pictures by him in the NG, London.

HARTUNG, Hans (b.1904), was born in Leipzig and began as an Expressionist, but became an abstract painter about 1922: in 1925 he saw works by KANDINSKY, which confirmed him in this trend. He has lived in Paris since 1935, fought in the Foreign Legion and lost a leg at Belfort (1944), and is now a French citizen. His works are a mesh of calligraphic brushstrokes, usually dark on a light ground, which an admirer has described as 'a blend of the exacting discipline that governs French art with what is best and most distinguished in Germanic poetry'. The effect is often similar to the works of KLINE, the American, for whom no such background has been claimed. His paintings have no titles, but are distinguished by numbers, thus: T54–16 means Toile (i.e. canvas), 1954, number 16. There are examples in Basle, Grenoble, London (Tate), New York (Guggenheim), Paris (Mus. d'Art Moderne), and Philadelphia.

HATCHING is shading carried out in parallel lines; cross-hatching is shading in two layers of parallel lines, one layer crossing the other at an angle.

HAYDON, Benjamin Robert (1786–1846). British historical painter. Like BARRY, Haydon attempted to be a pure history painter in the Grand Style adumbrated by Reynolds in his 'Discourses'. His life was a tragi-comedy of high endeavour and High Art which ended in imprisonment for debt, and suicide. His tireless propaganda forced the Government and nobility to accept the novel idea that the patronage of the arts was socially desirable, and he was partly responsible for the Government's purchase of the Elgin Marbles in 1816. There are pictures in London (NPG and Tate), but his best memorial is his 'Autobiography and Memoirs'.

HAYMAN, Francis (1708–76), was a scene-painter and illustrator who became one of the Founder-Members of the RA in 1768 and was later its first Librarian. He painted several small portrait groups which influenced Gainsborough (who may have worked under him), but his most famous pictures were the decorations for the fashionable Vauxhall Gardens, begun in the mid 1740s. Some of these survive in the Tate and V & A London, and show the strong French element in his style, perhaps derived from his friend GRAVELOT: indeed the Quadrille (Birmingham) was engraved in 1743 as 'by Hayman, designed by Gravelot'. In 1748 he went to Paris with HOGARTH, and with him, was 'clapt into the Bastille' as a spy. Like HIGHMORE he illustrated the novels of Samuel Richardson – Southampton has a scene from 'Clarissa Harlowe' – while Sir Robert Walpole in the Painter's Studio (London, NPG) and his Finding of Moses (1746: London, Coram Foundation, formerly Foundling Hospital) are other aspects of his work. In 1760 he led the Society of Artists in the negoti-ations which resulted in the foundation of the Royal Academy.

HECKEL, Erich (1883–1970), studied architecture in Dresden in 1904, where he met KIRCHNER and SCHMIDT-ROTTLUFF, with whom he founded the BRÜCKE in 1905. A trip to Italy in 1909 was a great influence on him, and so were FEININGER, MACKE, and MARC, whom he met in 1912 and who introduced him to the DELAUNAY form of Cubism. He served in the army medical corps, 1915–18, and met Ensor and Beckmann in Belgium. From 1918 he lived in Berlin until he fled to Switzerland in 1944, after no fewer than 729 of his works had been removed from German museums. From 1949 to 1956 he taught at Karlsruhe, but finally returned to Switzerland. There are pictures by him in Berlin, Cologne, Detroit, Hagen, Harvard University, and New York (M of MA).

HEDA, Willem Claesz. (1594–1682), was a Dutch painter of still-life subjects, usually in cool greyish colour against a plain background, with elaborate goblets of wine and pewter vessels. There are examples in Amsterdam (Rijksmus.) and other Dutch museums, Dresden, Karlsruhe, Munich, and elsewhere.

His son Gerrit (c. 1620–before 1702) was also a still-life painter in a similar vein. There are works in Amsterdam (Rijksmus.), London (NG), Munich, Oxford (Ashmolean), Rotterdam, and Worcester Mass.

HEEM, Jan Davidsz. de (1606–84), worked at Utrecht and Leyden before the religious troubles drove him to settle in Antwerp. Usually his pictures contain a profusion of flowers, or fruit, oysters, etc., with elaborate goblets, but occasionally he painted a 'Melancholia' type of still-life, with a figure surrounded by books, papers, and pictures. He was the most brilliant still-life painter in a family of them; his father David (1570–1632) worked in Utrecht, and his son Cornelis (1631–95) worked in Leyden and Antwerp. There are works in Amsterdam (Rijksmus.), Berlin, Brussels, Darmstadt, Dresden, Edinburgh (NG), The Hague, London (NG, Wallace Coll.), Munich, Oxford, Toledo Ohio, Vienna, and elsewhere, by one or other member of the family.

HEEMSKERCK, Maerten van (1498–1574), worked with SCOREL in Haarlem 1527–9 and learned most of the Italianate manner from him before going to Italy in 1532 himself. Before he left he gave his *S. Luke painting the Virgin* to the Haarlem Guild (now in Haarlem, Hals Mus.): this is almost a parody of the Italian manner, as conceived by a Northerner at second hand. In Rome he made a large number of drawings (1532–5) of the antiquities and works of art, and two of his sketchbooks (Berlin) are invaluable evidence for the monuments of antiquity as they existed in the 16th century as well as for such things as the building of New S. Peter's. He settled in Haarlem in

1537 and worked there for the rest of his life except for a flight to Amsterdam (1572–3) while the Spaniards were besieging Haarlem. He painted a number of fine portraits, like those of Scorel, as well as Italianate religious pictures. There are works by him in Amsterdam (Rijksmus.), Barnard Castle (Bowes Mus.), Berlin, Brussels, Cambridge (Fitzwm, *Self-portrait with the Colosseum in the background*), Cassel, Ghent, The Hague, Lille, Linköping Cath. Sweden, New York (Met. Mus.), as well as in Haarlem and elsewhere.

HELST, Bartholomeus van der (1613–70), was a fashionable Amsterdam portrait painter and one of the founders of the Guild there (1653). He was probably a pupil of ELIAS and was influenced by both Hals and Rembrandt. There are works by him in Amsterdam, Berlin, Brussels, Cambridge (Fitzwm), Detroit, Dublin, The Hague, London (NG and Wallace Coll.), New York, Paris, Philadelphia (Johnson Coll.), Vienna, and elsewhere.

HEPWORTH, Barbara (*b*.1903), is a British abstract sculptor. She is a direct carver in wood and stone and has only recently turned to modelled forms, mostly partly cut in plaster before being cast in bronze. In 1931 she began piercing holes in her sculpture and has since exploited hollowed-out forms. She was trained in Leeds, where she met Henry MOORE, and was later also influenced by BRANCUSI. From 1938 she has carved abstract forms in which the large masses are set off by string or wire, giving an effect like a musical instrument. Her works can be seen in the open at Harlow New Town, Essex, Hatfield, or the Royal Festival Hall and Dulwich Park, London, where she has also made large-scale decorative works for several new buildings, e.g. State House, Holborn (1963). There are works in Aberdeen, Birmingham, Bristol, Coventry, Leeds, London (V & A and Tate), Manchester, Wakefield, as well as several American and European museums.

HERRING, John F. (1795–1865), was a stage-coachman who turned animal painter. After driving local coaches for four years he drove the 'High Flyer' between London and York until he devoted himself entirely to painting racehorses. He worked for many years in the Doncaster district and painted thirty-three successive winners of the St Leger before settling in Newmarket, and, in 1833, in London. He exhibited at the RA from 1818 to 1846 and worked for George IV and Queen Victoria. His works were very popular in the United States through engravings. His son John Frederick Herring the Younger worked in the same style and died as recently as 1907.

HEYDEN, Jan van der (1637–1712), was the first painter in Amsterdam to paint townscapes, although this was being done in Haarlem by the BERCKHEYDES. Van der Heyden began as a still-life painter and at the end of his life he took it up again, but his architectural subjects date mostly from the 1660s. He painted walls and masonry with minute skill, but his topography is often wilful. His pictures are often said to have figures by A. van de VELDE – who died in 1672. From *c.*1670 he designed fire-engines and street lighting, both of which activities made him very rich: his 'Fire-engine Book', with etchings by him, was published in 1690. There are works by him in the Royal Coll., in Amsterdam, Berlin, Dresden, Edinburgh, Florence (Uffizi: *Amsterdam Town Hall*, 1667, which has been in Florence at least since 1672), Glasgow, The Hague, Hamburg, London (NG, Wallace Coll., Wellington Mus., and Dulwich), Paris (Louvre), Philadelphia, Rotterdam, Vaduz (Liechtenstein Coll.), Vienna, Waddesdon, Bucks. (National Trust), Washington (NG), and elsewhere.

HICKS *see* PRIMITIVE.

HIGHMORE, Joseph (1692–1780), was an English portrait painter, contemporary with HOGARTH, who retired in 1761, when Reynolds had established himself. Apart from portraits Highmore also painted some illustrations to literature, the most famous being a Hogarth-like series from 'Pamela', by his friend Samuel Richardson (there are twelve in all, completed by 1745 and now divided between Cambridge (Fitzwm), London (Tate and V & A), and Melbourne). In 1732 he travelled in the Low Countries to study Rubens and van Dyck, and in 1734 he visited Paris: the French influence is very clear in the *Pamela* series, but it is important to remember the influence of Richardson on French writers, and especially on the *comédie larmoyante*. In 1746, inspired by Hogarth, he presented a history picture to the Foundling Hospital, where it still hangs. He was originally bred to the law, and in his later years published various writings on art. Other pictures are in the Royal Coll., Cambridge, Cardiff, Hull, Liverpool, London (NPG, Tate, Dulwich), Oxford and Waddesdon, Bucks. (National Trust).

HILDEBRAND, Adolf von (1847–1921), was the leading German sculptor of the classic tradition in the late 19th century. He went to Rome in 1867 and met the writer Konrad Fiedler, as well as the painter MARÉES, who had a decisive effect upon him. In 1872 he returned to Italy for five years, and in 1873 helped Marées on his frescoes in Naples. His most famous work is the Wittelsbach Fountain in Munich, begun in 1891; but he is probably better known as a writer, whose book on aesthetics, *Problem der Form*, first published in 1893, had reached its 9th edition by 1914. This was written under the influence of Fiedler, but became one of the most famous books on aesthetics ever published in Germany. Hildebrand's realist strain is seen in his portrait busts and monuments, which include one to Brahms. There are works in Berlin, Dresden, Frankfurt, Munich, and other German galleries.

HILLIARD (Hillyarde), Nicholas (*c.*1547–1619), is the first great British artist about whom we know a few details. He was the son of a gold-smith and was himself trained in, and practised, that art although he was painting miniature portraits by 1560. He may have been in Geneva (aged 10) in 1557, as one of a family of Protestant refugees, at about the same time as a goldsmith from Rouen called OLIVER. He is recorded in the Goldsmiths Company in 1570 and in the same year he painted his first dated portrait of Queen Elizabeth, to whom he had probably already been appointed Limner and Goldsmith: in the latter capacity he designed a Great Seal for her. He was certainly in France between 1576 and 1578 and was probably the Nicholas Belliart who was attached to the Duc d'Alençon, the Queen's suitor. About 1600 he composed a treatise 'The Arte of Limning' (first published in 1912), in the course of which he records conversations with the Queen and, in particular, their agreement that portrait-painting should be done without shadows: '. . . best in plaine lines without shadowing, for the lyne without shadowe showeth all to a good jug-ment, but the shadowe without lyne showeth nothing'. About this time he was in financial difficulties, perhaps partly caused by his old-fashioned insistence on line without modelling, for his pupil Isaac Oliver was by now a serious rival to him. In 1617 he was actually imprisoned, although it seems to have been as a surety for someone else. His miniatures are always intended to be thought of as jewels, to be held in the hand and in this his goldsmith's training was no doubt decisive. There are no known oil paintings which can be attributed to him with any confidence, but a small group of portraits shows his style: the so-called 'Pelican' portrait of Queen Elizabeth (Liverpool) and the 'Ermine' portrait at Hatfield House are the best-known. There are works by him in the Royal Coll., and in London (V & A) and in Cambridge (Fitzwm), Cleveland, London (NPG, Nat. Marit. Mus.), New York (Met. Mus.), and Oxford (Bodleian Library). His son, Laurence Hilliard (1582–after 1640), was also a limner.

HISTORY PAINTING, in fully developed academic theory, is the noblest form of art and consists of generalized representations of the passions and intellect as symbolized in classical history or myth-ology or in subjects taken from Christian iconography. The word 'history' was usually meant to refer to ancient history and mythology, but the Christian story was admitted as conformable to the highest flights of imaginative art. Modern history, and particularly subjects which involved modern dress instead of nondescript drapery, was admitted only in the late 18th century in England (WEST's *Death of Wolfe* is one of the classic examples) and even later elsewhere. The theory of history painting was pushed to extremes by men like HAYDON, who died of it, but it was also truly responsible for some of the greatest works of such masters as Raphael and Poussin.

HITCHENS, Ivon (b. 1893), is the son of a painter, and studied at the

Royal Academy Schools. In 1940, he went to live in Sussex, and his main subject matter is the richly wooded landscapes around his home, expressed in non-naturalistic, almost abstract and tachiste terms, usually in long rectangular format. He has also painted flowers and figures; these culminated in his enormous (69 × 20 ft) mural for the English Folk Song and Dance Society (1954), and for the University of Sussex (1963). There are characteristic works in many British museums, including Aberdeen, Birmingham, Cambridge (Fitzwm), Edinburgh (M of M A), London (Tate, V & A), Nottingham, and in Adelaide, Buffalo, Gothenburg, Melbourne, Montreal, Oslo, Ottawa, Paris (Mus. d'Art Moderne), Seattle, Toledo Ohio, Toronto, and Wellington NZ.

HOBBEMA, Meindert (1638–1709), was the friend and pupil of Jacob van RUISDAEL, whom he met in Amsterdam before 1659. His earliest pictures are dated 1658 (Detroit) and 1659 (Frankfurt and Grenoble) and not only are some of his works virtually indistinguishable from Ruisdael's, but they also occasionally painted the same views, e.g. the pair in Amsterdam and Washington. In 1668 he married the maid of the Burgomaster of Amsterdam, and through the influence of one of his wife's fellow-servants he obtained a minor post in the Excise, and from then onwards he seems to have painted much less. It used to be thought that his most famous work, the *Avenue at Middelharnis* (London NG), was dated 1669 and was his swan-song, but the date is now read as 1689, and there are pictures of 1671 (also in the NG) and 1689 (Bridgewater Coll.), so he presumably continued to paint but omitted to date his pictures. In any case it is difficult to understand how a man of such gifts could bring himself to stop painting and spend 40 years gauging wine in casks. Unlike Ruisdael he painted quiet landscapes, usually with watermills, with none of the romantic quality or the splendid clouds and skies of Ruisdael's pictures. Although his work was little prized in his own time it was very much sought after by English collectors of the 18th and 19th centuries and exerted great influence on English landscape painting: for this reason the best collection of his works is in the NG, London. There are others in the Royal Collection and Amsterdam, Antwerp, Berlin, Brussels, Cambridge (Fitzwm), Cape Town, Chicago, Cincinnati, Detroit, Frankfurt (Städel), Glasgow, The Hague, Indianapolis, London (Wallace Coll. and Dulwich), Minneapolis, Munich, New York (Frick Coll., Historical Soc., and Met. Mus.), Ottawa, Paris, Philadelphia, Rotterdam, Washington, and Vienna.

HODLER, Ferdinand (1853–1918), was, with BÖCKLIN, the leading Swiss painter of the 19th century. He visited Madrid (1878–9) and Paris (1891), where he was influenced by Corot and Courbet, but he ultimately developed a very linear, flat style, much closer to PUVIS de Chavannes. About 1891 he was much influenced by Symbolist ideas, by ART NOUVEAU, and, like many others, by the Rosicrucians. From the mid-1890s he concentrated on large-scale historical and mythological works, such as those for Jena University (1907) and Hanover Town Hall (1910). There are works by him in Zürich and other Swiss and German museums.

HOFER, Carl (1878–1955), is usually classed as an Expressionist, but his art is profoundly French in its adherence to classical ideals. He first went to Paris in 1900, after which he worked for two years under THOMA in Karlsruhe and then spent five years in Rome (1903–8). He returned to Paris, 1908–13, except for two trips to India, and was interned in France 1914–17. He became a Professor in Berlin in 1918, was dismissed in 1933, and reinstated in 1945. An air-raid in 1943 destroyed many of his works, and he set himself to paint some again from memory. His sober classicism, influenced by MARÉES, and above all by CÉZANNE, is very similar to that of DERAIN. He wrote an autobiography and also a book, published posthumously, on discipline in art. There are works in Cologne, Detroit, and Harvard University.

HOFMANN, Hans (1880-1966), was born in Bavaria. He studied in Munich, and in Paris from 1904–14, partly in the PURRMANN and MATISSE circle. He taught in Munich from 1915 until he emigrated to America in 1932. In New York, he became an influential teacher and exponent first of Expressionist and Fauve ideas, then of abstract painting which changed, during the 1950s, into vigorous ABSTRACT IMPRESSIONISM, in which he used dribbles and splodges of paint to create strongly coloured and free patterns of explosive force. He was a formative influence on POLLOCK.

HOGARTH, William (1697–1764), was apprenticed to a goldsmith but began engraving c.1720. He studied at the St Martin's Lane Academy, but never really achieved any proficiency as a draughtsman: he was, however, well aware of the need for academic training and later promoted another Academy in St Martin's Lane which was the principal forerunner of the Royal Academy. He began painting small groups and conversation pieces and by 1729, when he married THORNHILL's daughter, he had begun to make a name. The *Beggar's Opera* (several versions exist, one in the Tate Gall.) was perhaps the most successful of these, and it was probably the transition from portraiture to his best-known works, the moralities. Hogarth himself said 'I then married, and commenced painter of small conversation pieces, from twelve to fifteen inches high. This having novelty, succeeded for a few years . . . I therefore turned my thoughts to a still more novel mode, *viz*. painting and engraving modern moral subjects, a field not broken up in any country or any age . . . . I therefore wished to compose pictures on canvas, similar to representations on the stage; and farther hope, that they will be tried by the same test, and criticised by the same criterion. . . . I have endeavoured to treat my subjects as a dramatic writer; my picture is my stage, and men and women my players, who by means of certain actions and gestures, are to exhibit *a dumb show.*' The first of these moral subjects was the *Harlot's Progress*, showing the downfall of a country girl at the hands of the wicked Londoners (several of whom were recognizable). The comparison with 'Moll Flanders' shows how close Hogarth's links were with contemporary literature. The original paintings were probably executed in 1731/2 (they are now lost) but the popularity of the series depended on the engravings made from them in 1732; this was so great that they were frequently pirated and Hogarth ultimately got a Copyright Act passed in 1735 which was of great benefit to artists and engravers alike. The next series was the *Rake's Progress* (1735: paintings in the Soane Mus., London) and it was followed by the *Marriage à la Mode* (1743–5: London, NG) and the *Election* (1754: Soane Mus.). He visited Paris in 1743 and again in 1748 and was strongly influenced by French Rococo, but the influence was perhaps strongest early in his career, e.g. in *Before* and *After* (Cambridge, Fitzwm) and other pictures of the 1730s. He was in fact rabidly anti-French (his chief characteristics seem to have been pugnacity and self-assertion) and his xenophobia was not helped by the fact that, in 1748, in company with HAYMAN, he was arrested as a spy for drawing the fortification at Calais, celebrated in his picture *O the Roast Beef of Old England!* ('*Calais Gate*') (1748: London, NG). His efforts in the Italian Grand Manner had little success, although the *Pool of Bethesda* and *Good Samaritan* (1735–6: London, S. Bartholomew's Hospital) were certainly better received than the *Sigismunda* (1759: Tate Gall.) which he painted to show that he could treat a tragic subject in as grand a manner as a Bolognese picture of the same subject which was sold at auction for a price higher than Hogarth thought right. This was painted at the end of his life and was savagely attacked by John Wilkes who had recently been roughly handled by Hogarth in an engraving.

His fame was, and is, most firmly based on the engravings of his moral subjects, which have to be read, detail by telling detail, rather than contemplated as works of art; nevertheless, all through his life he was capable of pieces of superb painting. He continued to paint portraits, the most successful being those of sitters of his own type, e.g. the *Captain Coram* (1740: the Foundling Hospital, London). This was painted for the great charitable institution which Coram founded and of which Hogarth himself became a Governor. Not only is the portrait itself important as an adaptation of the Baroque state portrait to a middle-class sitter, but Hogarth managed to persuade a number of other artists, including HAYMAN and HIGHMORE, to join with him in presenting a history picture each to the Foundling

Hospital. These were shown to the public for the benefit of the Hospital, but the Exhibition was so popular that it led ultimately to the establishment of public exhibitions in London and thus to the Royal Academy. Hogarth also wrote a treatise on aesthetics, 'The Analysis of Beauty' (1753), and an Autobiography, the MS. of which is in the BM, and was printed in J. Burke's edition of the 'Analysis' (Oxford, 1955).

There are pictures in the Royal Collection and in Birmingham, Bristol, Buffalo, Detroit, Edinburgh (NG), Liverpool, London (NG, NPG, Tate, Nat. Marit. Mus., Dulwich, Soane Mus., and Coram Fdn, i.e. the Foundling Hospital), Manchester, Minneapolis, Montreal, New York (Met. Mus. and Frick Coll.), Northampton Mass., Oberlin Coll. Ohio, Ottawa, Philadelphia, St Louis, Toledo Ohio, Vancouver, Washington (Corcoran and Nat. Coll.), Worcester Mass., and in many English provincial galleries.

HOLBEIN, Hans the Elder (c. 1465–1524), was a Late Gothic painter with a large workshop in Augsburg in which his sons Hans the Younger and Ambrosius worked. By 1514 the shop had broken up, and Holbein senior moved to Isenheim probably by 1517. His major work was the *S. Sebastian Altar* (1515/17: Munich) but there is also a *Death of the Virgin*, signed and dated 149–, in Budapest, and a sketchbook, mostly of portrait drawings, in Berlin, which includes a double portrait of his two sons.

HOLBEIN, Hans the Younger (1497/8–1543), was probably the most accomplished and penetratingly realist portrait painter the North has produced. He began in his father's shop, but by 1515 he and his brother were in Basle working for a local painter. He was soon working for publishers, notably for Froben, through whom he probably met Erasmus about 1515/16. His early portraits (*Burgomaster Meyer* and his *Wife*, 1516, and *Bonifacius Amerbach*, 1519: Basle) show his gift for characterization, and his religious works (*Dead Christ*, 1521, Basle; *Solothurn Madonna*, 1522, Solothurn) show him either grimly realist or decorative rather than devotional. In 1517 he left Basle, visited Lucerne, and probably went to Italy; he returned to Basle after the death of his brother in 1519, became a citizen in 1520, and married. He was commissioned to paint the Council Chamber with frescoes of justice scenes, civic virtues, and law-givers in 1521, but the work was interrupted by the disturbances connected with the Reformation and by his absences and was not finished until 1530. He illustrated the Luther Bible and published the 'Dance of Death', 1523/4, and the 'Alphabet of Death', 1524. Both these add the bitterness of the Peasants' War to the medieval theme, and the Dance is dropped in favour of Death depicted as the harvester of every class of man. The 'Dance of Death' was published in Lyons, and ran to ten editions in twelve years.

His international reputation as a portraitist was established by three portraits of Erasmus in 1523 which were strongly influenced by M A S-SYS. In 1526, possibly because the continued religious troubles were affecting his business, he left Basle and travelled via Antwerp (where he met Massys) to London, bringing introductions from Erasmus to Sir Thomas More and Archbishop Warham. He stayed for eighteen months, during which time he painted the large group of the More family (now only known from copies and sketches) and may have been temporarily employed by the Crown on decorations. He returned to Basle until 1532, but the religious strife was now more acute (a document of 1530 shows him anxious about the meaning of the Communion Service), and even an offer by the Town Council of a pension could not retain him. When he arrived back in London in 1532 More was in disfavour, and from 1532 to 1536 he worked mainly for the Merchants of the Steelyard (the wool staple and the Hanseatic League) on half-length portraits of amazing virtuosity. He probably entered the Royal service after painting *The Ambassadors* (1533: London, NG) – a tour-de-force of representation and iconographical allusion. One of his chief works for Henry VIII was the dynastic group (1537) of Henry with his Queen, Jane Seymour, and Henry VII and Elizabeth of York (burnt in 1698; part of the cartoon is in London, NPG). The figure of Henry served as a model for the many versions of the King, who also employed Holbein as a goldsmith's designer and on painted and architectural decorations, and sent him abroad to paint prospective brides (the *Duchess of Milan*, 1538, London, NG; *Anne of Cleves*, 1539/40, Paris, Louvre). His late practice of painting from drawings instead of from the sitter was strengthened by the requirements of extensive Court portraiture. His portraits – life-sized and in miniature – became more linear in style and more hieratic in treatment than his early works, partly through their emphasis on detail, partly because working only from drawings led him to be less sensitive in handling and perception. None of his decorations or goldsmith's work in England has survived, though drawings and miniature versions exist. A pair of organ shutters in Basle, and many drawings for the now destroyed Council Chamber decorations and house façades in Basle and Lucerne, are the only records of his large decorative works, which were strongly influenced by Italian – particularly Milanese – style.

The largest collections of Holbein's works are in Basle and the Royal Coll. (there are 85 of the drawings for portraits at Windsor). Other works, by him or his studio, include those in Berlin, Boston (Mus. and Gardner), Brunswick, Darmstadt, Detroit, Dresden, Florence (Uffizi), Frankfurt (Städel), Freiburg im Breisgau (Cath.), The Hague, Karlsruhe, Liverpool, London (NG, NPG, V & A, Wallace Coll., Guildhall), Los Angeles, Munich, New York (Met.

Mus., Frick Coll.), Ottawa, Paris (Louvre), Parma, Philadelphia (Johnson), Rome (Gall. Naz.), St Louis, Stuttgart, Toledo Ohio, Vienna, Washington (NG), and Zürich.

HOLLAR, Wenceslaus (1607–77), was born in Prague but was the most important illustrator and topographer working in England in the 17th century. He travelled in Germany after leaving Bohemia in 1627 and was taken into the service of the Earl of Arundel in Cologne in 1636. He was captured by the Parliamentarians at the siege of Basing House in 1645 and left England for Antwerp in the same year but returned in 1652 and, after the Restoration, was appointed 'H.M. Scenographer and Designer of Prospects'. His work consists of etchings and watercolour drawings dealing with almost everything that could interest the 17th-century Englishman: they are principally illustrations to books but include maps, portraits, the series of Women's Costumes, plates of contemporary events, and, above all, the series of views of London before the Great Fire of 1666 and the plates of buildings like St Paul's, as well as reproductions of works of art, all of which are now invaluable historical material.

HÖLZEL, Adolf (1853–1934), was a German painter who went to Paris in 1882. He began to experiment with what he called 'coloured sounds' in 1917–18, and from 1923 produced many pastels of abstract compositions. His school at Dachau, opened in 1893, numbered NOLDE, SCHLEMMER, and BAUMEISTER among its pupils. There are works by him, including stained-glass windows, in Cologne, Hanover, and Stuttgart.

HOMER, Winslow (1836–1910), was, with EAKINS, one of the most influential of late 19th-century American painters. After two years in England and Paris (1866) he earned a living as an illustrator – he recorded the Civil War – and this sense of actuality remained in all his works even after 1875, when he devoted himself to painting. In the 1880s and 1890s he revolutionized American painting by his quasi-Impressionist style allied to Courbet-like studies of the sea and shooting and fishing subjects appealing to the American male. He was also affected by the Japanese craze which arrived in Europe in the 1860s and is visible in his work in the 70s. He is represented in the NG, Washington, and many other US museums.

HONDECOETER, Melchior (1636–95), was the last and best of a family of Dutch painters. He specialized in still-life and scenes of birds, many of them exotic, and his speciality was the representation of a farmyard, or a courtyard, with a great number of different birds. He was the pupil of his father Gysbert (1604–53) and of his uncle J. B. WEENIX. He worked at The Hague and Amsterdam and his numerous pictures include examples in the Royal Collection, Amsterdam (Rijksmus.), Boston, Brussels, Cologne, Derby, Glasgow, The Hague, London (NG and Wallace Coll.), Lyons, Munich, New York

(Met. Mus.), Nottingham, Paris (Louvre), and Vienna (Akad.).

HONE, Nathaniel (1718–84), was a Dubliner who painted portraits in the English provinces (often in miniature or in enamel), until a fortunate marriage allowed him to spend two years (1750–52) in Italy. After this he settled in London and became a Founder-Member of the RA, exhibiting regularly from 1769 until his death. In 1775, however, he submitted *The Conjuror*, which represented a conjuror, remarkably like Sir Joshua Reynolds, who points with a wand to prints after Michelangelo, Maratta, Pietro da Cortona and others, clearly implying plagiary; there was also a young woman, and Angelica KAUFFMANN (whose exact relationship with Reynolds was a matter of interested debate) felt herself impugned. She petitioned the Council and the picture was rejected: it was subsequently exhibited elsewhere. The picture (now in Dublin) was rediscovered in 1944, and it is clear that the imputations were not without foundation. Other pictures by Hone are in London (NPG *Henry Fielding*, 1762; RA, V & A), Belfast, Birmingham (Barber Inst.), Cardiff, Dublin, Leeds, Manchester, and Oxford.

HONTHORST, Gerard van (1590–1656), was one of the leading masters of the UTRECHT School. He was trained under BLOEMAERT and was in Rome c.1610/12–1620, where he was much influenced by Caravaggio (who died in 1610). SANDRART, who was Honthorst's own pupil, said that he was also much influenced by Caravaggio's follower MANFREDI. He worked for the Marchese Giustiniani, who had been Caravaggio's patron, and for him he painted the *Christ before the High Priest* (London, NG). This has the characteristic Northern Caravaggesque device of using one candle as the sole source of light, the direct rays being shielded by the figures. His night scenes were very popular and earned him the nickname in Italy of 'Gherardo delle Notti': he had 'much of ye manor of Caravaggioes colouringe; wh^ch is nowe soe much esteemed in Rome' (letter from Lord Arundel, 1621). He settled in Utrecht until 1628, when he visited England and painted the huge *Charles I and Henrietta Maria with the Liberal Arts* (Hampton Court), which marks the transition from his early Caravaggesque style and genre or mythological subjects to his second, Court, style based on realistic portraiture in a version of the elegant van Dyck manner. He succeeded MIEREVELD as Court Painter at The Hague (1637), and his later works are in a style very like Miereveld's. His brother Willem (1594–1666) worked with him. There are pictures in the Royal Coll. and in Alkmaar, Amsterdam, Berlin, Cologne, Dresden, Florence (Uffizi), Glasgow, Greenville SC, The Hague (a series of Court portraits), Haarlem, London (NG, NPG), Munich, Ottawa, Paris (Louvre), Rome (Borghese and churches), Utrecht, Vienna, and elsewhere.

HOOCH (Hoogh), Pieter de (1629–after 84), was the Dutch genre painter who came nearest to VERMEER in his feeling for the play of light. His first datable work is *Delft after the Explosion* (1654) and for the next decade or more he worked mainly in Delft, so that he must have known Vermeer. He chooses the same kind of subject – an interior with two or three figures engaged in some household task – and he occupies himself with rendering the fall of sunlight on surfaces, his favourite effect being that of a dark foreground with an open door leading through into a second room which is brightly lit. As in the case of Vermeer this interest in light is an ultimate legacy, via the UTRECHT School, of Caravaggio. De Hooch moved to Amsterdam in 1667. The works of the Amsterdam period are poorer in quality and also different in subject: unlike his simple interiors of the Delft period they are now rather bogus scenes of High Life, such as hardly existed in Holland, based on adaptations of the grand new Town Hall of Amsterdam or of Italian architecture. There are pictures in the Royal Collection and in Amsterdam, Berlin, Boston, Cape Town, Cincinnati, Cleveland Ohio, Copenhagen, Detroit, Dublin, London (NG, Wallace Coll., and Wellington Mus.), Los Angeles, Minneapolis, New York (Met. Mus.), Paris (Louvre), Philadelphia, Rome (Borghese and Gall. Naz.), St Louis, Stockholm, Toledo Ohio, Vienna (K-H Mus. and Akad.), Waddesdon, Bucks. (National Trust), and Washington (NG and Corcoran).

HOPPNER, John (c. 1758–1810), was one of the principal followers of Reynolds and a rival to LAWRENCE. He was a student at the RA in 1775, became Portrait Painter to the Prince of Wales in 1793 and RA in 1795. There are works by him in the Royal Coll. and in London (NG, NPG, Tate, V & A, and RA), New York (Met. Mus.), Ottawa, Washington (NG), and many other museums.

HORTUS CONCLUSUS (Lat. enclosed garden). The phrase is taken from the Song of Songs (iv. 12: *Hortus conclusus soror mea, sponsa . . .* A garden enclosed is my sister, my spouse . . .) and is used to describe paintings of the Madonna and Child in a garden with a fence round it, and often with a fountain inside it (*Hortus conclusus, fons signatus . . .* A spring shut up, a fountain sealed). Occasionally there are also several female Saints present, as in one of the finest examples, the *Paradise Garden* by an unknown German master of about 1415 (Frankfurt, Städel). The *Virgo inter Virgines* type has the female Saints, but need not have the fenced garden.

HOSKINS, John (d. 1665), was, according to his earliest biographer, 'bred a Face-painter in Oil but afterwards taking to *miniature*, he far exceeded what he did before'. His earliest miniatures date from c. 1620, so he was probably born at the end of the 16th century and some of his early works show some influence from HILLIARD and OLIVER. Nevertheless, he was probably the first 'who gave the strength and freedom of oil to miniature', although this was actually said of his nephews and pupils, Alexander and Samuel COOPER. Hoskins was Limner to Charles I and naturally came under the influence of van DYCK whose style he adapted to miniature. There are examples in the Royal Collection, Amsterdam (Rijksmus.), Cambridge (Fitzwm), London (V & A, Ham House and Wallace Coll.), and Oxford.

HOT COLOUR, TONE. Colours which tend to be reddish in hue. The phrase has generally a pejorative sense, implying that the balance of colour or tone is unduly inclined to the red end of the spectrum. It is sometimes due to BOLUS grounds.

HOUDON, Jean-Antoine (1741–1828), was the most celebrated French sculptor of the 18th century. He was a pupil of LEMOYNE and PIGALLE before going to the École royale des Élèves protégés (where his father was for many years the concierge) with a Rome Prize in 1761. He went on to Rome in 1764 and made his name with his simple and classical *S. Bruno* (1766) in Sta Maria degli Angeli. In 1769 he was back in Paris and an associate of the Academy; he became a full Academician in 1777 with his *Morpheus* (now in the Louvre). He narrowly escaped imprisonment during the Revolution and continued to work under the Empire. He retired in 1814 but continued to teach at the École des Beaux-Arts until 1823, when he became senile. Among his better-known works are the *Girl Shivering* (1783: Montpellier), the *Diana* (1780: Gulbenkian Coll., and 1790: Louvre), and the *Minerva* in the Institut, Paris, which is reproduced on all the Institut's publications. His portraits are, however, his most numerous as well as his finest works and they include many of the greatest men of his time, among them the seated *Voltaire* of 1781 in the Comédie Française (there are several other *Voltaire*s, including one in terracotta in Cambridge (Fitzwm) and one in London, V & A, and another in the Comédie, where there is also a *Molière*); his *Franklin* led to a commission from the State Parliament of Virginia for a statue of Washington. Houdon went to the US in 1785 to execute it and spent 14 days at Mount Vernon. The marble was completed by 1791 (although it is signed and dated 1788) and is in Richmond, Va; perhaps ironically, there is a bronze copy in London, outside the NG. There is a *Franklin* in New York (Met. Mus.) – the original plaster is in St Louis – and a *Diderot* in the Louvre, two busts in the Wallace Coll., London, and many others in France and in Gotha and elsewhere.

An unusual work is the *Anatomical Man*, a flayed figure done in the French Hospital in Rome, a cast of which was once in every art school.

HOURS of Turin. A manuscript (the 'Très Belles Heures') begun by JACQUEMART de Hesdin *c*.1385/90 but left unfinished at his death and divided *c*.1412/13, so that the unfinished parts went to Count

William of Holland (*d.* 1417), elder brother of Jan van EYCK's patron. This part, finished by various artists by the middle of the 15th century, was later subdivided between the Prince Trivulzio (Milan) and the Royal Library, Turin: the Turin parts were burnt in 1904 and the Trivulzio portion has now passed to the Mus. Civico, Turin. Hulin de Loo was the only scholar to study both portions and he declared that some 25 of the miniatures were by the van Eycks; controversy now rages – and presumably always will – over the exact attributions, since some of those destroyed had close links with the mature style of Jan van Eyck.

HUBER, Wolf (*c.* 1490–1553), was a painter and designer of woodcuts, who, after ALTDORFER, was the most important member of the DANUBE School. He was in contact with Altdorfer by ·c. 1510 and may have been his assistant; certainly he shares Altdorfer's feeling for the poetry of landscape, as may be seen in his drawings of pure landscape as well as his pictures. From 1515 he worked in Passau, where he was much disliked by the local painters. There are pictures by him in Dublin, Munich, and Vienna, and drawings in London (BM and University College).

HUDSON RIVER SCHOOL. A school of American landscape painting, highly Romantic in feeling and glorifying the wonders of Nature as visible in the American landscape. The type begins soon after 1800 with the landscapes of Washington ALLSTON, but the name is properly applied to the period from 1825, when COLE settled in New York, until the 1870s. DURAND was a typical painter of the school.

HUDSON, Thomas (1701–79), was the son-in-law of Jonathan RICHARDSON I and inherited the same kind of stereotyped face-painting practice. He is best-known as Reynolds's master (1740–3) but he painted a considerable number of portraits 1745–60, after which he virtually retired, probably because Reynolds was getting the business. He is well represented in London (Tate, Nat. Marit. Mus., Dulwich, NPG, Foundling Hospital), in Bristol, Edinburgh (NG and NPG), Manchester, New York (Met. Mus.), Waddesdon, Bucks. (National Trust), and elsewhere.

HUNT, William Holman (1827–1910), was in the RA Schools in 1844, and there met MILLAIS and ROSSETTI with whom he founded the PRB in 1848. He went to Egypt and the Holy Land in 1854, 1869, and 1873 to paint Biblical scenes with accurate local settings and types, and was the only member of the group to remain in any way faithful to PRB principles. His best-known work is perhaps *The Light of the World* (versions in Oxford, Keble Coll. and London, St Paul's Cath.). In 1905 he published 'Pre-Raphaelitism and the Pre-Raphaelite Brotherhood', the best documented memoir of the movement. He was given the OM in the same year. There are works in Birmingham, Liverpool, London (Tate), Manchester, Ottawa, Oxford (Ashmolean, Jesus College), and Port Sunlight.

HUYSUM, Jan van (1682–1749), was a Dutch flower-painter, son of the flower-painter Justus van Huysum (1659–1716), many of whose works are confused with his more famous son's. His flower pictures are very highly detailed, rich and crowded in composition and sometimes set against a light background (an innovation made by him). There are examples in many museums. He also painted a few landscapes and mythologies (a *Rape of Proserpine*, London, Wellington Mus., is ascribed to him) and there is a *Self-portrait*, probably unique in his work, in Oxford.

His younger brother, Jacob (1687–1740), who often imitated him, worked in England and died in London.

I

ICON (*Ikon*, Gk, image) originally meant a picture of Christ or a Saint
on a panel, as distinct from a wall-painting. These icons were extremely limited in subject matter and the actual forms and shapes
were prescribed and maintained unchanged for centuries in the Greek
Orthodox world: thus, the earliest surviving examples may date from
the 6th to 7th century but are virtually indistinguishable from those
painted as late as the 17th century or even later. An *Iconostasis* is a
screen dividing the sanctuary of a Greek Orthodox church from the
lay part and is covered with icons. *Iconoclasm* is the destruction of
images, the most famous outbreak being the Iconoclastic Controversy
of the 8th century. *Iconography* and *Iconology* are the knowledge of
the meanings to be attached to pictorial representations: thus, a
lamb with a flag is a simple problem in Christian iconography, but
many of the more complicated Baroque allegories, in which Christian
and pagan mythological figures are used side by side, may now be
almost beyond interpretation. Some knowledge of iconography is
essential to a full understanding of medieval and Renaissance art;
the frescoes of Giotto or Piero della Francesca being only partially
intelligible to those who regard them as no more than coloured shapes.

There is also an older meaning of Iconography, namely a collection of portraits, as in van Dyck's *Iconography*.

IDEAL ART. 'Any work of Art which represents not a material object,
but the mental conception of a material object, is in the primary sense
of the word, ideal; that is to say, it represents an idea, and not a
thing. Any work of Art which represents or realizes a material object
is, in the primary sense of the term, un-ideal' (Ruskin). According to
Plato the only realities are ideas, and everything perceptible to the
senses is merely an imperfect realization of the primary idea: thus, the
idea of a dog is the true dog and all dogs in the visible gutter merely
approximate to the idea of dogness. From this arises a perennial
theory that the true function of art is to mirror those Ideal forms that
are the sole realities, approaching them by way of the physical
phenomena which are their distorted images. The story, told by
Pliny, which served for centuries as the basis of this Ideal Art, tells
how Zeuxis had to paint a *Venus* and, after inspecting all the most
beautiful girls in Crotona, he selected five and painted the mouth of
one, the legs of another, and so on: the theory being that a sum of
perfect parts must add up to a perfect whole. Later, a similar story
was told of Raphael; the point of it is the same but he is made to add,
significantly, that not only must he see many beautiful women, but
he must also have a *certain idea* in his mind. This theory is obviously

not impregnable, but such is the hold of PROPORTION, classic harmony, and geometry on the human mind that for centuries (but most vocally in the NEOCLASSIC period) artists have sought to select, to refine, and to ennoble various details of the human figure into a whole which should express all these ideals and symbolize the highest aspirations of the mind. Naturally, this has meant an exclusive concern with the nude ('The human figure concealed under a frock-coat and trowsers is not a fit subject for sculpture. I would rather avoid contemplating such objects.' John GIBSON). Nevertheless, fallacious or not, the theory has produced many of the greatest works of art in existence and its perennial quality is perhaps best illustrated by the fact that it is still, under a new guise, one of the most fertile theories of aesthetics; for many forms of abstract art depend upon it, and the works of BRANCUSI, MALEVICH, or MONDRIAN ultimately spring from Platonic Idealism.

ILLUSIONISM is the virtuoso use of pictorial techniques such as perspective and foreshortening to deceive the eye into taking that which is painted for that which is real. The principal moments when this was practised were the Late Antique period (at Pompei and elsewhere) and the Italian Baroque, when it was common to use sculptural and architectural means to heighten the impression of actuality, e.g. by using plaster figures in three dimensions attached to a frame so that the painted and carved figures are indistinguishable. One of the first pieces of illusionism is, however, the Camera degli Sposi at Mantua by MANTEGNA, completed in 1474. When such technical skill is lavished on things like a fly painted on a frame or a view through a non-existent window the French term *trompe-l'œil* is often used, while the Italian word *quadraturista* is sometimes used for the professional painter of illusionist decorations (*quadrature*).

IMAGO PIETATIS (Lat. Image of Pity). A representation, most popular in the late Middle Ages, of the Dead Christ standing upright in the Tomb. He is sometimes surrounded by symbols of the Passion and sometimes supported by the Virgin, Saints, or Angels, but in any case the stress is laid on the suffering involved in the Redemption. The PIETÀ expresses the same basic idea in less symbolical terms.

IMPASTO is a word, Italian by origin, used to describe the thickness of the paint applied to a canvas or panel. When the paint is so heavily applied that it stands up in lumps with the tracks of the brush clearly evident it is said to be 'heavily impasted'.

IMPRESSIONISM was the derisive name given to the most important artistic phenomenon of the 19th century and the first of the Modern Movements. The name was derived from a picture by MONET, *Impression, Sunrise* (1872: Paris, Musée Marmottan), which represents the play of light on water, with the spectator looking straight into the rising sun. The occasion of the derision was the first Impressionist

Exhibition, held in 1874, when Monet, RENOIR, SISLEY, PISSARRO, CÉZANNE, DEGAS, Guillaumin, BOUDIN, Berthe MORISOT, and others held an independent exhibition. In fact, the true aim of Impressionism was to achieve ever greater naturalism, by exact analysis of tone and colour and by trying to render the play of light on the surface of objects. This is a form of sensualism in which traditional ideas of composition and drawing – that is, putting a line round a concept – were bound to suffer. Impressionist interest in colour and light was at least partly due to the researches into the physics of colour carried out by scientists like Chevreul; and the idea that an object of any given colour casts a shadow tinged with its complementary (though known already to Delacroix) suggested one of the principal ways in which they animated the surface of their canvases. The flickering touch, with the paint applied in small, brightly-coloured dabs, and the lack of firm outline, combined with the brightness of the colour, even in the shadows, and the generally high key undoubtedly alienated the public. In the course of time these technical devices became petrified into a quasi-scientific method of applying paint (NEO-IMPRESSIONISM) which was supposed to give the maximum of truth – optical truth – to Nature: it also led naturally to POST-IMPRESSIONISM; that is, to a purely artistic and anti-naturalistic movement. The great decade of Impressionism was 1870–80, but most of the major figures, such as Monet, Pissarro, and Sisley, continued to produce masterpieces in a more or less Impressionist style for many more years. Degas, Renoir, and Cézanne were only dubiously Impressionists even in the 70s (many of the original group felt that Cézanne was more than they could swallow) and they very soon moved away from it. Cézanne said that he wanted 'to make of Impressionism something solid and durable, like the art of the Museums', thus clearly defining the main weakness of the movement, its lack of intellectual rigour. Nevertheless, most painting of the last 100 years has been profoundly affected by it, and even the R A and the Salon would nowadays be lost without it. There is a special Musée de l'Impressionnisme in Paris; but the very nature of the movement, with its emphasis on painting landscapes out of doors and catching the fleeting impression, meant an enormous output of pictures so that they are not difficult to find. The eight Impressionist Exhibitions were held in 1874, 1876, 1877, 1879, 1880, 1881, 1882, and 1886.

IMPRIMITURA (Ital.). The priming or GROUND, often tinted, laid on canvas or panel.

INC. (Lat. *incidit*, he cut it) on an engraving refers to the engraver, or more commonly etcher: *see also* SCULP.

INGRES, Jean Auguste Dominique (1780–1867), was born at Montauban. His father, a mediocre artist, recognized his son's abilities and sent him to Toulouse Academy (1791) and on to DAVID in Paris in 1797. He won the Prix de Rome in 1801 with the *Ambassadors of Agamemnon* which was praised by FLAXMAN, who had a great influence on him. He earned a living by portraits until 1806, when he finally went to Italy intending to stay three or four years and remaining eighteen. His Rivière family portraits (1805: Louvre), with their stress on sinuous line forming a silhouette that both contains and explains the form, established a type that he developed and perfected, but hardly modified. Works sent back from Rome were bitterly criticized, and the fall of Napoleon forced him to seek a precarious livelihood making pencil drawings of visitors to Rome. In 1820 he settled in Florence and completed the *Vow of Louis XIII*, commissioned for Montauban Cathedral and exhibited in the 1824 Salon with enormous success. This work placed him in the front rank and established him as the official opponent of the ideas expressed by DELACROIX, and the main prop of a rigid classicism in opposition to the Romantic Movement. While his main works were portraits – which he professed to dislike, and in which he both influenced and was influenced by the earliest photographs – he also painted subject pictures and poeticized Oriental scenes providing an excuse for voluptuous nudes. His wall-paintings were not happy; the *Golden Age* (1842–9) was abandoned and has deteriorated, leaving only the superb nude studies made for it. In 1834 he returned to Rome as Director of the French Academy, having applied for the position in a fit of pique over the reception accorded his *Martyrdom of S. Symphorian*. After his return to Paris in 1841, his intransigent opposition to any ideas but his own, backed by his academic standing, gave him an influence which he used blindly, not only against Delacroix, but also against younger rebels against what had become in the hands of his imitators, entrenched in mediocrity, a stereotyped academicism. His own style hardly changed and to the end he pursued his piercingly exact vision, his sinuous line, and his worship of Raphael; while his deliberately charmless handling stresses his supreme draughtsmanship. He said 'Drawing is the probity of art' and 'Drawing includes everything except the tint': opposed views were those of Théophile Sylvestre '... he is a Chinese painter lost ... amid the ruins of Athens' and Delacroix's 'His art is the complete expression of an incomplete intelligence'. He became a Member of the Institute in 1825, a Grand Officer of the Legion of Honour in 1855, and a Senator in 1862. None of his many pupils except CHASSÉRIAU achieved lasting reputation: his real continuator was DEGAS.

There is a large Musée Ingres at Montauban and other works are in Aix-en-Provence, Algiers, Antwerp, Baltimore, Bayonne, Brussels, Cambridge Mass. (Fogg Mus.), Chantilly, Cincinnati,

Florence (Uffizi), Hartford Conn., Kansas City, Leningrad, Liège, London (NG, V & A), Lyons, Montpellier, Northampton Mass., New York (Met. Mus., Frick Coll.), Paris (Louvre, Carnavalet, Invalides), Philadelphia, Rouen, Stockholm, Toulouse, Versailles, Washington (NG), and elsewhere.

INNES, James Dickson (1887–1914), was a Welsh landscape painter with a powerful sense of design and a feeling for strong colour. He first worked in the Wilson Steer brand of Impressionism, and was then strongly influenced by Augustus JOHN. His premature death invites speculation whether he might not have developed into an English *Fauve*.

There are works in Aberdeen, Cardiff, Leeds, London (Tate), and Manchester.

INTAGLIO (*Cavo-rilievo*) consists of cutting forms out of a surface so as to form a kind of relief in reverse. The commonest example is an engraved seal-ring, hence the opposite term is often Cameo. For Intaglio processes, *see* ENGRAVING.

INTERNATIONAL GOTHIC. Towards the end of the 14th century there arose a new approach to Nature which first found expression in the Court art of France and Burgundy (*see* BROEDERLAM, LIMBOURG), but which rapidly spread to Italy, Germany, and Bohemia. As a style it remained fundamentally Gothic, for the new realism was confined to details, particularly to details of landscape, of animals, and of costume. This form of realism has almost nothing in common with the slightly later realism, classical and naturalistic in inspiration, practised by MASACCIO and DONATELLO. Aspects of both may, however, be detected in the work of GHIBERTI. In Italy the principal exponents of International Gothic were GENTILE da Fabriano and PISANELLO: a comparison between the *Madonna* by Gentile in the Royal Coll. and the Masaccio *Madonna* in the NG, London; or the Gentile *Adoration* in the Uffizi, Florence, and Masaccio's Brancacci Chapel will make clear the difference of intention as well as of style. The influence of International Gothic remained active for many years, and was even revived towards the end of the 15th century.

INTIMISME. A form of Impressionist technique applied to the depiction of everyday life in domestic interiors rather than to landscape. The work of BONNARD and VUILLARD is usually meant.

INTONACO *see* FRESCO.

INV., INVENIT (Lat. he invented it) often appears on an engraving as the credit title of the original author of the design, which may have been drawn (DEL.), engraved (INC. or SCULP.), and published (EXCUDIT) by other people.

ISABEY, Eugène-Gabriel (1803–86), was the son of the miniature-painter Jean-Baptiste (1767–1855). Eugène made a dramatic debut at the Salon of 1824 with marine and landscape paintings, gaining a medal. He went to Algiers in 1830 with the French navy as a marine-painter, but the Romantic influence on his colour came from Delacroix. He visited England several times and BONINGTON probably inspired him to employ watercolour. He was the painter of many of the events of the reign of Louis-Philippe (pictures in Versailles and the Royal Coll.). Other works are in the Louvre, and in Bayonne, Boston, Cardiff, Cleveland Ohio, Douai, London (NG, Wallace Coll.), Nancy, New York (Met. Mus.), Orleans and York.

ISENBRANDT (Ysenbrandt), Adriaen (d. 1551), was a painter active in Bruges from 1510. He is said to have been a pupil of Gerard DAVID and for this reason a diptych of the *Madonna of the Seven Sorrows* (Bruges, Notre Dame, and Brussels Mus.) has been ascribed to him: around this not very certain attribution a large accretion of early 16th-century Bruges School work has accumulated under his name, a good example being the *Adoration of the Magi* in Birmingham. To make it worse, some of these were once attributed to MOSTAERT by Waagen; hence *Der Waagen'sche Mostaert* or *The Pseudo-Mostaert* = 'Isenbrandt'.

ITALIANIZERS are Northern artists, generally Dutch or Flemish, who adopt as far as possible a style based on Italian models or who import Italian motives into their repertory. The word is often used of 17th-century Dutch landscape painters like ASSELYN, BOTH, and BERCHEM, but it is also used of 16th-century Flemings like MABUSE or van ORLEY, although these are usually called ROMANISTS.

IVES, James, *see* CURRIER.

J

JACOBELLO del Fiore (*d.*1439) was a Venetian painter who was active from 1394. He broke away from the Byzantine tradition typified by PAOLO Veneziano which dominated Venetian art until the end of the 14th century, but was in turn influenced by the International Gothic style of the early 15th century. Most of his works are in Venice but the earliest signed and dated work by him is of 1407 (formerly US private coll.).

JACQUEMART de Hesdin (*d.c.*1411) was the Painter to the Duke of Berri from 1384 until 1411, when he was succeeded by the LIMBOURG brothers. He made the 'Grandes Heures du Duc de Berri' (Paris, Bibliothèque Nationale), as well as the 'Très Belles Heures' (Brussels, Bibliothèque Royale), but is principally remembered as having started what became the HOURS of Turin.

JAMESONE, George (*d.*1644), was an Aberdeen painter who was trained in Edinburgh, and not, as a highly improbable tradition would have it, by Rubens. He painted portraits in a style not unlike that of Cornelius JOHNSON – i.e. basically a Flemish manner. He was painting in Aberdeen in 1619/20; in 1633 he painted Charles I in Edinburgh and also visited Italy; and from 1634 he worked mainly in Edinburgh. There are pictures by him in Edinburgh (NG, NPG) and a number in Aberdeen (Gall. and especially the University Collection).

JANET see CLOUET.

JANSENS (JANSSENS), Cornelius, see JOHNSON.

JAWLENSKY, Alexej (1864–1941), was a Russian painter, originally an officer in the Imperial Guard, who spent most of his life in Germany, although the major Western influence on his style was MATISSE. He studied in Munich from 1896, meeting KANDINSKY there, although he did not join the BLAUE REITER group. Later, with Kandinsky, KLEE, and FEININGER he formed a group known as the Blue Four. He settled in Wiesbaden in 1921 and his later works became more abstract, more Byzantine, and more expressive: he himself said that 'art is nostalgia for God'. There are many works in Wiesbaden and in Pasadena Cal.

JEAN de Boulogne see BOLOGNA.

JOHN, Augustus Edwin, OM (1878–1961), was born at Tenby in Wales. He was trained at the Slade, taught at Liverpool (1901–2), and joined the NEAC in 1903, gaining early recognition through his superb draughtsmanship. He was strongly influenced by PUVIS de Chavannes and Post-Impressionism, 1910–14, and made many cartoons for large decorations, only one of which (Johannesburg) was executed. His brilliant portraits derive from the grand manner tradition enlivened by a semi-Impressionist handling, colour high in tone, and a very un-Impressionist solidity of drawing. He travelled much in England and France, often gipsy-fashion, and was always a passionate opponent of academism, in art and life. He became an RA in 1928, later resigned with *éclat*, but was re-elected in 1940. There are works in Aberdeen, Birmingham, Brighton, Buffalo, Cambridge (Fitzwm), Cardiff, Detroit, Dublin, Glasgow, Leeds, Leicester, London (Tate), Manchester, Melbourne, Ottawa, Oxford, Sheffield, Stockholm, Swansea, Sydney, Toronto, Washington (NG), and elsewhere.

His sister Gwen (1876–1939) was also a painter, studied at the Slade and in Paris, and lived mostly in France – much with the Dominican Sisters at Meudon. In feeling her pictures are the antithesis of her brother's: retiring, delicate, grey in colour; and of an almost neurotic sensibility. There are examples in Cardiff, London (Tate and NPG, a *Self-portrait*), Manchester, and elsewhere.

JOHNS, Jasper (*b.*1930). With RAUSCHENBERG, he was one of the main formative influences on the New York variety of POP ART. He uses painting, collage, assemblages of objects, plastic metal, bronze, either separately or in combination, as in the bronze *Beer Cans* of 1961, with their painted labels. There is an example in London (Tate).

JOHNSON (Jonson), Cornelius (also called Jansens, Janssen van Ceulen) (1593–1661), was born in London of Netherlandish parents and became one of the most notable portrait painters in England before the arrival of van DYCK in 1632. He painted in a straightforward but sensitive Dutch manner sometimes indistinguishable from that of MYTENS, but he tended to confine himself to bust portraits set in an oval, although there is a fine family group in London (NPG). After 1632 he came under van Dyck's influence until, in 1643, the Civil War caused him to retire to Holland, where he adopted a more Dutch manner, closer to that of MIEREVELD. There are works by him in Amsterdam (Rijksmus.), Bath (Holbourne Mus.), Boston, Dublin, The Hague, Liverpool, London (NPG, Tate, BM, V & A (Ham House), and Dulwich), and New York (Met. Mus.).

JONGKIND, Johan Barthold (1819–91), was a Dutch landscape and marine painter, who, along with BOUDIN, was a precursor of Impressionism and a formative influence on MONET (who wrote to Boudin in 1860 that Jongkind 'is quite crazy'). He met Boudin in 1862 and exhibited at the SALON des Refusés in 1863. He spent most of his later life in France, living in squalor near Grenoble and ending in madness like van Gogh. He never painted in oils out of doors, working from drawings and watercolours made on the spot, but the results are very like those of the early Impressionists.

JOOS van Cleve (Cleef) (*c.*1485–1540/1) became a Master in Antwerp in 1511. He is usually identified with the MASTER OF THE DEATH OF THE VIRGIN, but there are wide discrepancies between the portraits and the religious pictures attributed to him (or them). Joos was a contemporary of MASSYS, and many of the portraits attributed to him are in a cool, realistic style not unlike that of Massys or even Holbein and Mabuse; they are perhaps closest to Barthel BRUYN. Joos seems to have been to Genoa and is reasonably supposed to have worked at the Court of François I of France *c.* 1530: certainly many portraits of François and his Queen exist and are attributed to him, but there are no portraits ascribed to him which are signed or satisfactorily documented; the *Self-portrait*(?) in the Royal Coll. is recorded in the 1639 Inventory of Charles I's collection 'Sotto Cleve done by himself . . .' (see below), but the features are those of Joos as known from 16th- and 17th-century engravings. Other pictures attributed to Joos van Cleve are in the Royal Coll. and in Antwerp, Berlin, Boston, Brussels, Cambridge (Fitzwm), Cologne (Wallraf-Richartz), Detroit, Dresden, Edinburgh, Florence (Uffizi), London (NG, Courtauld Inst.), Madrid, Manchester New Hampshire, Michigan (University), Munich, New York (Met. Mus.), Paris (Louvre), Philadelphia (Johnson), Toledo Ohio, Vienna, Washington (NG, Corcoran), and Worcester Mass.

His son Cornelis (1520–67), known as 'Sotte Cleve', was also a painter and visited London *c.*1554, hoping for Royal patronage. He was, however, anticipated by MOR and he went mad in 1556.

JOOS van Gent (van Wassenhove), called Justus of Ghent (active 1460–after 1475), became a Master in Antwerp in 1460 and in Ghent in 1464. There he met Hugo van der GOES (whom he sponsored in the Guild in 1467) and is recorded up to 1469, but by 1475 he had gone to Rome. In 1473–4 'Magistro Giusto da Guanto' was in Urbino, painting the *Institution of the Eucharist* (Urbino), the commission for which was originally given to PIERO della Francesca, while the predella is by UCCELLO, who was paid for it 1465–9. Among the works attributed to him are a *Crucifixion* (Ghent, Cath.) and a series of 28 *Famous Men* (*c.*1476: half in Paris, Louvre, and half in Urbino), the hands (at least) of the Duke of Urbino in Piero della Francesca's *Brera Madonna*, and other works in the Royal Coll., London (NG), New York (Met. Mus.), and Urbino. Two formerly in Berlin were destroyed in 1945. The *Famous Men* and the Duke's hands (and some of the other pictures) have been ascribed to P. BERRUGUETE, in spite of a specific mention in a 15th-century Italian writer of the *Famous Men* as by 'a Netherlander'. Joos is the only Netherlandish painter known to have worked in Urbino.

JORDAENS, Jacob (1593–1678), was born and died in Antwerp where he worked as an assistant to RUBENS. After Rubens's death he finished the incomplete works ordered for Spain, van DYCK's pretensions making it impossible to negotiate with him. He is an example of the pervasive effect of Rubens's style, for he uses a boisterous, restless type of Baroque derived from Rubens, but without his taste and control, or his imagination and versatility in design and colour. He worked for the House of Orange on portraits and decorations during the 1630s, and his late works include large genre scenes of drinking bouts – *Le roi boit* in Brussels is an example – full of overtones of BROUWER and STEEN. There are works in Antwerp, Belfast, Bristol, Brunswick, Brussels, Budapest, Cassel, Cleveland Ohio, Dresden, Karlsruhe, Lille, London (NG, Wallace Coll.), Madrid, New York (Met. Mus.), Paris (Louvre), Stockholm, and Stonyhurst College, Lancs. (*The Four Doctors of the Church*).

JOURNEYMAN (from Fr. *journée*, a day). An artist who had completed his apprenticeship but was not yet a Master in a GUILD. He earned his living as a day-labourer in the shops of various Masters (often making it difficult to distinguish between the products of shop A and shop B when he crossed the road to work in the other shop for a change). Some painters spent their WANDERJAHRE in this fashion; others never set up for themselves.

JUGENDSTIL *see* ART NOUVEAU.

JUSTUS of Ghent *see* JOOS van GENT.

K

KALF, Willem (1619–93), was a Dutch still-life painter who worked in Rotterdam, Paris, and Amsterdam. The depth and brilliance of his colour and the sureness of his touch suggest the influence of Vermeer. Usually his pictures contain elaborate gold, silver, and glass vessels, fruit, a Turkey carpet, against a dark ground with, often, a watch in the front of the group. There are works in Amsterdam (Rijksmus.), Berlin, Cleveland Ohio, Dresden, Frankfurt (Städel), Munich, Oxford, Paris (Louvre), Rouen, Vienna, and elsewhere.

KALRAET, Abraham, see CALRAET.

KANDINSKY, Wassily (1866–1944), was born in Moscow but trained in Munich, after abandoning a legal career. He painted his first purely abstract work in 1910 (one such is in the Tate Gallery, London), and was therefore one of the founders of 'pure' abstract painting. In 1911 he was one of the founders of the BLAUE REITER group and in 1912 he published a book which was translated into English in 1914 as 'The Art of Spiritual Harmony'. He returned to Russia 1914–21 and then went back to Germany and taught at the Bauhaus from 1922, again coming into contact with KLEE. In 1933 he went to France. New York (Guggenheim Mus.) has many works, and so have Munich and Russian museums.

KAUFFMANN, Angelica (1741–1807), was a Swiss decorative painter. She seems to have been an accomplished musician and painted an allegory of herself hesitating between the Arts of Music and Painting (1760: later versions exist). Having chosen painting she went to Rome in 1763, where she painted a portrait of WINCKELMANN (1764: Zürich, Kunsthaus) which helped to make her name. In 1765 she went to Venice and was in London the following year, where she remained until 1781. She became friendly with REYNOLDS (there were rumours of a romantic attachment) and imitated his style in her portraits. She was a Founder-Member of the RA in 1768. Her rather anaemic little decorative history pieces were widely engraved and the engravings used in the manufacture of *objets d'art*: from this has grown the habit of associating all decorative painting in all houses of the Adam period with her, although in fact only 4 such panels are known (two in the RA). Later, when she lived in Rome, her portraits became more Neoclassic in feeling. There are pictures in Brighton, Edinburgh (NG), London (NPG, Kenwood), Manchester, New York (Met. Mus.), Plymouth, and elsewhere. See also HONE.

KEEPING see VALUES.

KENT, William (1685–1748), is celebrated as an architect, landscape gardener, interior decorator, and furniture designer. He studied painting in Rome in 1714/15, and there met Lord Burlington, his most constant and influential patron. He completed, in 1719, the paintings which RICCI had left unfinished in Burlington House (now the Royal Academy) and the commission to decorate Kensington Palace was given to him in 1723 instead of to THORNHILL. This was virtually his last work in painting and led to the savage satire by HOGARTH (Thornhill's son-in-law) in which Lord Burlington is shown as a builder's labourer and Raphael and Michelangelo gaze, awe-struck, on the figure of Kent *triumphans*. In Rome he decorated the vault of S. Giuliano dei Fiamminghi.

KETTLE, Tilly (1735–86), was an English portrait painter who was the first to seek his fortune in India. He was born in London and was influenced at the beginning of his career by Reynolds, as may be seen in the portraits he painted in Oxford in 1762 and 1763. In 1769 he went to India, where he had a great success, and remained there until 1776. On his return to London he found competition greater than he expected and his extravagant living forced him to return to India in 1786, but he died in the desert near Basra. There are pictures by him in London (Tate, NPG, V & A, Nat. Marit. Mus., Dulwich, and Courtauld Inst., which has an important double portrait painted in India), Oxford, and Versailles. There are also works said to be still in India.

KEY. A painting is said to be high or low in key according to the average of the tone and colour values: thus an Impressionist picture is high in key, all the tones being kept nearer white than black and all the colours being pale and bright. Very low keyed pictures, such as those by the followers of Caravaggio, are TENEBRIST.

KEYSER, Thomas de (1596/7–1667). An Amsterdam portrait painter of the ELIAS generation, he first influenced REMBRANDT (e.g. Keyser's *Constantine Huyghens*, 1627; London NG) and was then influenced by him. Later works include small equestrian portraits with landscape backgrounds, often by other painters. Other works are in Amsterdam, Haarlem, The Hague, New York, Paris, Philadelphia, Raleigh NC, Toledo Ohio, and elsewhere.

KINETIC (Gk 'moving') ART is based on the idea that light and movement can create a work of art. Objects may be made to gyrate, and make interesting patterns of light and shadow as they do so; elaborate assemblages of moving pieces of metal, glass, or any other material may be combined with changing effects of coloured lights to create shadows and reflections. The mobiles of CALDER or CHADWICK are simple forms of kinetic art; more complicated forms often incorporate an electric motor, like the constructions by Bryan Wynter made of painted cards reflected in a concave mirror, Pol Bury's activated plastic hairs or wooden balls and cubes, or Julio Le Parc's random effects of glinting light made by moving squares of coloured metal hanging on nylon threads. GABO's *Standing wave* (1920: London, Tate) is an early use of the idea, and links kinetic art with CONSTRUCTIVISM.

KIRCHNER, Ernst Ludwig (1880–1938), was a German Expressionist painter who was an original member of the BRÜCKE. From 1917 Kirchner lived in Switzerland suffering from tuberculosis until his eventual suicide in 1938. Many of his pictures were confiscated by the Nazis, but the best collection is now in Stuttgart. He also made a large number of woodcuts and some sculpture. Kirchner formulated the programme for the Brücke in 1906 and wrote its obituary in 1913, although his close friend HECKEL was the most enterprising member. It is said that Kirchner occasionally deliberately dated some of his pictures too early in order to claim priority. There are works by him in Edinburgh and New York and other American museums as well as those in Germany.

KIT CAT (Kitkat). A canvas, size 36 × 28 inches, which is adapted to a portrait showing the head and one hand. *See* KNELLER.

KLEE, Paul (1879–1940), was a Swiss painter and etcher, whose art of free fantasy, perhaps the most poetic of modern times, is best defined in his own words as 'taking a line for a walk'. He was trained in Munich and went to Italy (1901–2), after which he returned to Switzerland and began etching. His early graphic work was influenced by Blake and Beardsley as well as Goya, and, later, ENSOR. He worked in Germany from 1906 until 1933, teaching for many years at the celebrated Bauhaus in Weimar and Dessau, and later at Düsseldorf Academy. He was an impassioned teacher and many of his 'Pedagogical Sketchbooks' and theoretical writings have been published. From 1911 he was associated with the BLAUE REITER artists, and was especially close to KANDINSKY, FEININGER, and JAWLENSKY (they were known, from 1924, as the 'Blue Four'). In 1914 he went to Tunisia with MACKE, an experience which revealed a new world of colour to him. From the 1920s he was famous, and no fewer than 102 works of his were confiscated from German galleries by the Nazis. There are works in most galleries of modern art now, and there is a Klee Foundation in Berne.

KLIMT, Gustav (1862–1918), was the principal Austrian *Jugendstil* (ART NOUVEAU) painter, and one of the founders of the Vienna Sezession (1898), although he resigned in 1903. He was essentially a decorator and, from 1883 to 1892, he shared a studio for decorative painting with his brother and another artist: they did decorations in the Kunsthistorisches Museum, Vienna, in 1891. From *c.*1898, after a barren period of about six years, he was influenced by Japanese art and by contemporary English painters like BURNE-JONES and Alma-Tadema. A more realist style characterized his ceilings for Vienna University (1900–3), which were very unpopular. He was perhaps most successful as a designer for the applied arts (e.g. mosaic), but he was also a great influence on SCHIELE and KOKOS-CHKA. There are works in Vienna (Oesterreichische Galerie).

KLINE, Franz (1910–62), was one of the leading representatives of the post-war American movement which has had so great an influence in the 1950s and 60s. He was an exponent of ABSTRACT EXPRESSION-ISM who was deeply influenced by oriental calligraphy and whose colour schemes were normally limited to black, white, and grey. He is well represented in American museums and there is a picture in the Tate Gallery, London.

KNAPTON, George (1698–1778), was a pupil of Richardson and went to Italy for seven years in 1725. He was a Founder-Member of the Society of Dilettanti in 1736, and painted between 1741 and 1749 twenty-three portraits of fellow members (all but one in fancy dress) which brought him into contact with the principal patrons of his day. From about 1737 he used pastel a good deal, a medium which pro-voked Vertue to remark 'Small pains and great gains in this darling modish study'. He was the master of COTES.

There are examples in the Royal Collection (including the huge group of Prince Frederick and his family, of 1761, in London, Marl-borough House), Birmingham (City Art Gall.), Cambridge (Fitzwm), London (Dulwich), and Sheffield.

KNELLER, Sir Godfrey (1646 or 1649–1723). Born in Lübeck, Kneller was trained in Amsterdam under Rembrandt's pupil BOL, and he may even have come into contact with the aged Rembrandt himself. He then went to Italy and finally arrived in England c. 1676, rapidly becoming the leading portrait painter. He was made Principal Painter jointly with RILEY in 1688 and succeeded to the whole office when Riley died in 1691; in 1692 he was knighted and in 1715 he became the first painter in England to be made a baronet. There is a gap in his career between 1678 and 1682 and it has been conjectured that he was then abroad again. His first works in England are entirely in the style of Bol but they later take on some of the softness of MARATTA: by 1683 Kneller had established his mature style and from then on there are hundreds of documented portraits by him, many signed and dated. Of these a great many are careless and mechanical in handling, and some are simply based on LELY's style and poses; yet his best works show a great grasp of character and are painted *alla prima* in a free and vigorous technique which became the normal English style for many years to come – in fact, until the more French manner of Allan Ramsay superseded it. Part of his influence is due to his large employment of assistants, part due to Kneller's Academy, founded in 1711, which was the first attempt at an ACADEMY in England. His best works are the 42 portraits, now in the NPG, London, known as the Kit Cat series. These all date from 1702–17 and are a standard size (36 × 28 inches, known later as Kit Cat), showing the head and one hand. They represent the members of a Whig club and were painted for the secretary. A direct comparison with Lely may be made in the two series of *Beauties*, at Hampton Court, and the *Admirals*, in the National Maritime Mus. There is a picture at Lübeck dated 1668 and one in the Tate Gall. of 1672: others are in the Royal Coll. and London (NG, NPG, and Tate) and elsewhere.

Kneller's conceit was vast. He is said to have swallowed the suggestion that things might have been better managed had the Deity consulted him at the Creation, but the suggestion was made by Pope, who was a hunchback, and Kneller replied unkindly that *some* things would have been better made.

KOCH, Joseph Anton (1768–1839), was an Austrian landscape painter, born in the Tyrol, who was fundamentally a Romantic artist, but, like many others, was influenced by Neoclassic principles. In 1791 an English patron financed a trip to Italy, and in Rome he met CARSTENS and THORWALDSEN (1795). His first known landscape, of a waterfall, is of 1796 (Hamburg) and is of the POUSSIN type, but his fully Romantic style is seen in works like the *Schmadribachfall* (1805/11: Leipzig; version 1821/2 in Munich). He worked in Vienna 1812–15 before returning to Rome, where he took part in the decoration of the Casa Massimo (1834–9) by the NAZARENER. He died in Rome. His landscapes are of the Italianate type deriving from Poussin which were popular in the early 19th century, and he said himself that he wanted to give landscape 'an elemental character such as one may imagine when reading the Bible or Homer'. There are works by him in Berlin, Cologne, Copenhagen, Düsseldorf, Karlsruhe, Munich, Vienna, and other Austrian and German galleries.

KOKOSCHKA, Oskar (*b.*1886), is an Austrian painter who developed, between 1908 and 1914, a highly imaginative Expressionist style. He taught at the Dresden Academy from 1919, was influenced by painters who had worked in the BRÜCKE group, and from 1924 to 1931 travelled widely in Europe, North Africa, and the Near East. He lived in Vienna from 1931 to 1934, and in England from 1935 to 1953. His portraits, landscapes, and, chiefly, town views, often seen almost in bird's-eye view, are vivid in colour and of a restless energy of drawing; he has also painted many allegories, inspired by legends or, more commonly, by ideological themes; one of these, in London, is a large ceiling decoration. There are works in Edinburgh (NG), London (Tate), New York (M of MA), and many other museums of modern art.

KOLLWITZ, Käthe (1867–1945), was one of the most powerfully emotional German artists of this century. She married a doctor in 1891 and settled in Berlin in a slum where she lived until she was bombed out in 1943. She soon began to make etchings, woodcuts, and lithographs mainly of the Mother and Child theme and often with left-wing intentions. Most of her best works are tragic and many of them are specifically pacifist – her son was killed in 1914 and her grandson in 1942. In 1927 she made a journey to Russia, but was subsequently disillusioned. In 1933 she was expelled from the Academy and in the following years made eight large lithographs called *Death*. In her later years she also made some bronzes of which the most important is a war memorial at Essen in Flanders.

KONINCK, Philips de (1619–88), may have been a pupil of Rembrandt before learning landscape painting from his brother Jacob de Koninck. He painted several rather unpleasing genre scenes in the manner of Brouwer, some not very distinguished portraits, and some superb panoramic views of the flat landscape and luminous skies of Holland. The figures in these are sometimes his own and sometimes by Lingelbach or Adriaen van de Velde. His very numerous drawings are in most big museums and have frequently been confused with Rembrandt's – a further possible confusion is between Philips and Salomon Koninck. There are pictures in the Royal Coll. and in Amsterdam (Rijksmus.), Berlin, Cape Town, Frankfurt (Städel), Glasgow (Univ.), The Hague, London (NG, V & A), Munich, New York (Met. Mus.), Oxford, Philadelphia (Mus.), Rotterdam, and elsewhere.

KONINCK, Salomon (1609–56), was an Amsterdam painter who, from the early 1630s, imitated Rembrandt, especially in his small figures and groups of bearded old men. Like Philips de Koninck – to whom he may have been distantly related – many of his drawings have passed as Rembrandt's. There are works in Amsterdam (Rijksmus.), Berlin, The Hague, Liverpool, Vaduz (Liechtenstein Coll.), and elsewhere.

KONRAD (Conrad) von Soest was the principal Westphalian painter of the early 15th century. His only certain work is the signed polyptych in Niederwildungen Parish Church, obscurely dated, but probably 1404. This shows the influence of the SOFT STYLE, and, more precisely, contemporary Franco-Burgundian work. Other works attributed to him are in churches in Soest and Dortmund.

KOONING, Willem De (*b.*1904), was born in Rotterdam, but has lived in the US since 1926. He was trained under the influence of De STIJL, but has since become a leading Action Painter. His works have a brutal quasi-realism similar to that of the Dutchman APPEL. He painted a mural for the New York World's Fair of 1939 and there are pictures by him in Buffalo and New York (M of MA).

KORTEGAARDJES, a Dutch word, from Fr. *corps de garde*, used to describe the guard-room scenes popular in the 17th century, which show soldiers engaged in drinking, gambling, quarrelling, and similar military occupations.

KRICKE, Norbert (*b.* 1922), is a German sculptor who is fascinated by the movement of water. His *Water Forest*, 9 feet high, in the grounds of the Gelsenkirchen Opera House (1957), is made of plexiglass, through which water circulates. He has also made compositions in wire, e.g. at Münster Theatre (1959).

KRÜGER, Franz (1797–1857), was the leading painter of the BIEDER-MEIER style in Berlin, where he was Professor at the Academy and Court painter. He specialized in horses, portraits, and ceremonial pictures very similar to those of his contemporary C. VERNET, whom he met on a visit to Paris in 1846. He also met DELACROIX and was influenced by him. Many of his portrait drawings were published as lithographs after his death. Most of his works are in Berlin.

KULMBACH, Hans Süss von (*c.* 1480–1522), was a Nuremberg painter who, with SCHÄUFFELEIN, was the best and closest of DÜRER'S followers. He formed his style on Dürer's with a leaning towards the Venetians (who had so profoundly influenced Dürer himself), as transmitted to him by Jacopo de' BARBARI. He probably went to Cracow in 1510/11 and was certainly there 1514–16. There are works by him in Berlin, Cracow, Dublin, Florence (Uffizi), Hanover, Leipzig, Munich, New York (Met. Mus.), Nuremberg, Turin, Vaduz (Liechtenstein Coll.), and Vienna.

KUPKA, Frantisek (Frank, Franz) (1871–1957), one of the founders of abstract art, was trained in Prague and Vienna before going to Paris in 1894/5. He practised as a spiritualist medium, as well as a Fauve painter, but *c.* 1911 he began to evolve an abstract style under the influences of KLIMT, ORPHISME, and the Section d'Or Cubists led by Jacques VILLON: his *Planes by Colours* (1911: Paris, Mus. d'Art Moderne) is comparable with KANDINSKY'S abstract water-colours and ante-dates the work of MALEVICH and MONDRIAN. Kupka also wrote a book on artistic creation. There is a Kupka Mus. in Prague (some 50 pictures) and other works are in London (Tate), New York (M of MA), and Paris (Mus. d'Art Moderne).

L

LAER, Pieter van, *see* BAMBOCCIO.

LAGUERRE, Louis (1663–1721), was a French painter who, after working for some time under Lebrun, came to England in 1683/4. He worked for VERRIO at Christ's Hospital in 1684, and, with a French architectural painter called Ricard, decorated the Chapel, the Painted Hall, and several State Rooms at Chatsworth, 1689–94. He worked in many country houses, including Burghley and Blenheim (his best work) and also at Marlborough House in London. In his last decade, he suffered from the competition of THORNHILL, who learned much from him.

LAM, Wifredo (or Wilfredo) (*b.* 1902), was born in Cuba of Negro and Chinese parents, and studied in Havana, Madrid, and Paris. He lived in Spain, 1923–38, and afterwards in Paris, where he became a Surrealist. He returned to Cuba in 1942, and then went to the US. His pictures make use of folklore and include totems and jungle scenes. There are examples in London (Tate) and New York (M of MA).

LANCRET, Nicolas (1690–1743), was, with PATER, the principal imitator of WATTEAU. After failing as a history painter he was influenced by Gillot's theatrical scenes, as Watteau had been, and he spent the rest of his life painting *fêtes galantes*. He is well represented in the Wallace Coll., London, and in Waddesdon, Bucks. (National Trust).

LANDSEER, Sir Edwin (1802–73), the celebrated painter of sentimental animal subjects, was an infant prodigy who first exhibited at the RA at the age of twelve. He was the son of an engraver and his eldest brother devoted his life to making engravings of his pictures, examples of which were once to be found in practically every public house in England. At the beginning of his career he was an excellent painter of animals who owned STUBBS's drawings for the 'Anatomy of the Horse', but he very soon discovered that by giving animals, and especially dogs, quasi-human expressions he was able to touch the hearts of a large public. He was entranced by his first visit to Scotland in 1824 and very soon began to move in the highest society, particularly on deer-stalking expeditions; he was Queen Victoria's favourite painter and the life-long friend of the Duchess of Bedford. Landseer was elected ARA at the earliest possible age (24), RA in 1831; he refused the Presidency in 1865, as he had already refused a knighthood in 1842 (though he accepted in 1850). His best-known work is the group of lions at the foot of the Nelson monument in Trafalgar Square, London, made in 1858. It has been observed that many of his pictures of animals have an unpleasant substratum of cruelty; in 1869 his mind gave way and he died four years later hopelessly insane. There are many pictures by him in the Royal Collection and others in Birmingham, Liverpool, London (Tate, NPG, RA, V & A, Kenwood), and elsewhere. The *Stag at Bay*, one of his numerous Highland subjects, is now in a private collection in Dublin.

LANFRANCO, Giovanni (1582–1647), was born in Parma, where he was a pupil of Agostino CARRACCI, and was also much influenced by the domes by Correggio. He was in Rome in 1612, and about 1616 decorated the ceiling of the Casino Borghese in a manner derived entirely from the Farnese Gallery. He developed Correggio's SOTTO IN SÙ type of illusionism to an extravagant point, and painted several domes and apses in Roman and Neapolitan churches in this manner. To him DOMENICHINO lost part of the commission for the decoration of S. Andrea della Valle, a slight he resented so bitterly that – so the story goes – he weakened part of the scaffolding, hoping that Lanfranco would break his neck. From 1633/4 to 1646 he was in Naples, and in 1641–3 painted the dome of the S. Gennaro chapel in the Cathedral, which by its more up-to-date illusionism and greater showiness appealed far more to local tastes than Domenichino's works there. His dome is based on Correggio's type of illusionism and replaces one actually begun by Domenichino. He died in Rome, where his last work was the apse of S. Carlo ai Catinari.

Apart from Rome and Naples, there are works in Berlin, Dresden, Dublin, Florence (Pitti), London (Foundling Hospital), Marseilles, Oxford (Ashmolean), Paris (Louvre), Parma, and Vienna.

LAOCOÖN. The famous antique statue, now in the Vatican, was discovered in 1506. The 16th-century restorations have recently been removed so that most reproductions no longer show it as it is. It represents the death agonies of Laocoön and his two sons, crushed by the serpents. The horrible naturalism of this late Hellenistic work led to erroneous ideas about the nature of Greek art and to a long controversy over whether Laocoön was really suffering in noble silence (WINCKELMANN, 1755) or (as he obviously is) howling with pain; part of this controversy was Lessing's 'Laocoön' published in 1766, and dealing with the relationship between painting and poetry.

LARGILLIERRE (Largillière), Nicolas de (1656–1746), was born in Paris but passed his youth in Antwerp and, from *c.*1674, spent some years in England as LELY's assistant. He was thus almost a Flemish painter when he returned to Paris in 1682. He became a member of the Academy in 1686 and ultimately its Director. His principal rival was RIGAUD, but he specialized in portraits of the wealthy middle classes, leaving the aristocrats to Rigaud. There are typical examples in London (NG, Wallace Coll.), New York (Met. Mus.), and Paris (Louvre). The *S. Geneviève* (Paris, S. Étienne) is the only survivor of the large *ex-voto* type of picture that he painted for the Corporations. He also painted a few pictures of still-life.

LASTMAN, Pieter (1583–1633), was an Amsterdam history painter who went to Italy *c*. 1604 and was influenced by Caravaggio – which makes him akin to the UTRECHT School – and by ELSHEIMER. He was back in Amsterdam by 1607. His real importance lies in the fact that LIEVENS was his pupil in 1617 and REMBRANDT in 1624/5. There are good examples in Amsterdam, Dublin, London (NG), and Providence RI.

LA TOUR, Georges de (1593–1652), worked all his life in Lorraine. He painted religious and genre subjects in a style that stems ultimately from Caravaggio although it seems more likely that he derived from the UTRECHT School than directly from Caravaggio or his Italian followers. In his later works he adopts a form of indirect lighting from a candle or other concealed source of light, which is close to Dutch Caravaggisti like HONTHORST. In his last works he evolves a figure style in which all masses are reduced to the simplest, almost geometrical, shapes, arranged in static calm which is itself an expression of French classicism. His religious subjects seem to be connected with a contemporary religious revival in Lorraine which was particularly associated with the Franciscans. There are works by him in Berlin, Cleveland, Detroit, Épinal, Grenoble, Hartford Conn., Kansas City, Le Mans, Middlesbrough, Nancy, Nantes, New York (Met. Mus. and Frick Coll.), Paris (Louvre), Rennes, Rouen, Stockholm.

LATOUR, Maurice Quentin de (1704–88), was, with PERRONNEAU, the most celebrated French pastellist of the 18th century. He was born in S. Quentin and went to Paris as a young man; after visits to London and other places he settled in Paris 1724–84. He soon found that the vogue for pastel portraits started by Rosalba CARRIERA in 1719/20 was still capable of exploitation and he devoted the rest of his life to it. His portraits are characterized by an extreme vivacity of handling – sometimes rather vulgar – and a firm grasp of character. As a very old man the study of politics drove him crazy, and he retired to S. Quentin, where the largest and best collection of his works is to be found: it includes many studies and sketches which are sometimes superior to the finished portraits.

LAURANA, Francesco (*c*. 1430–1502?), was Dalmatian by birth (at La Vrana, near Zadar) but Venetian by nationality although he worked much in Sicily and France. He was in France 1461–6 and in Sicily in 1467 – two *Madonnas* still there are dated 1471 – returning to France in 1477 for six years. He must have gone back to France once more (*c*. 1498?), since he died there before 12 March 1502. He is best known as the sculptor of a series of busts of enigmatic-looking women, now in several French provincial museums as well as in Berlin, Florence (Bargello), Paris (Louvre), Vienna, and Washington (NG). He worked on the Triumphal Arch at Naples in 1453, and may have been there 1483/98.

LAURENS, Henri (1885–1954), was a Cubist sculptor whose works are often of still-life subjects and are coloured, thus approaching COLLAGE: from 1911 he associated with Picasso, Braque, Léger, Gris, and other Cubist painters and thus, like LIPCHITZ, evolved a Cubist sculpture. From the late 1920s his work became more realistic, particularly when he treated Greek mythological themes. He also illustrated several books. There are works in London (Tate) and Paris (Mus. d'Art Moderne).

LAUTREC *see* TOULOUSE-LAUTREC.

LAWRENCE, Sir Thomas (1769–1830), was born in Bristol but was so precocious that, at the age of ten, he was in practice as a portrait draughtsman in crayons in Oxford: at 17 he wrote to his mother '. . . excepting Sir Joshua, for the painting of a head I would risk my reputation with any painter in London'. In 1787, however, he was a student at the RA Schools for a short time and exhibited at the Academy of that year. From then on he was enormously successful, being made ARA in 1791, appointed Painter to the King on the death of Reynolds in 1792, and elected RA in 1794; he became President of the RA in 1820, having been knighted five years earlier. He had a European reputation as a portrait painter, partly because of the very real glitter and force of his best works, partly because he was commissioned by the Regent (later George IV) to paint all the great personalities of the struggle against Napoleon, making a kind of triumphal progress through Vienna and Rome to do so. His income was huge, but he was always heavily in debt, which probably explains the empty flashiness of his worst work. He formed a superb collection of Old Master drawings – probably one of the best ever made – and his will offered it to the nation on very easy terms: by a piece of quite exceptional Governmental imbecility it was refused, and many of the finest drawings dispersed. Fortunately, a part was later bought for Oxford (Ashmolean). The best collection of his works is in the Waterloo Chamber at Windsor Castle, which houses the set of European sovereigns and statesmen painted for George IV. Other works are in museums all over the world, including Chicago, London (NG, NPG, BM, Tate, V & A, Wallace Coll., RA, Dulwich, Guildhall, Soane Mus., Kenwood, and Wellington Mus.), Ottawa, Paris (Louvre), San Marino Cal., the Vatican, Vienna, and Washington (NG, Corcoran, and Phillips).

LAY FIGURE. A jointed wooden figure, often life-size, which can be used either to arrange drapery on or as a guide to a complicated pose. It is said to have been invented by Fra Bartolommeo, but no doubt small clay figures or manikins were in use much earlier.

LAY-IN. In the traditional method of OIL PAINTING, as opposed to ALLA PRIMA methods, the painter began by making an exact drawing on his canvas. This was then 'laid in' in monochrome, so that the whole tonal effect – but not the colour – was worked out in full. This 'dead colour' was usually a brown, grey, or greenish tint, occasionally a dull red. The purpose was to get the whole design and tonality worked out, so that the painter could then concentrate on the colour values.

LEAL, Valdés, see VALDÉS.

LEAN see FAT.

LE BRUN, Mme Vigée, see VIGÉE.

LEBRUN, Charles (1619–90), was the virtual dictator of the arts in France under Louis XIV, until the death of his protector Colbert. He was the type of the artist-politician and as early as 1641 he gained Richelieu's patronage by an allegorical portrait of King Louis XIII. He was a pupil of VOUET and went to Rome, probably with Poussin, in 1642; he studied partly under Poussin and partly from the works of the Roman Baroque decorators, such as PIETRO da Cortona. He returned, without permission, in 1645, as he was bored with Rome. In 1647 he exhibited an altarpiece for Notre Dame (a MAI), which began his success, and in 1648 he had so far taken over Vouet's position that he was one of the leaders in the foundation of the ACADEMY in 1648. He was to be Rector, Chancellor, and Director of it. He began the decorations for Vaux-le-Vicomte, for the minister Fouquet, in 1658. After Fouquet's fall Colbert recognized Lebrun's talent as well as the advantages of a centralized institution as an instrument of policy, and advanced Lebrun, who became director of the huge undertakings at the Gobelins factory as well as *premier peintre* in 1664 (though he may have held the post since 1658). In 1665 Bernini arrived in Paris, where he seems to have been critical of Lebrun's gifts. This may have some connexion with the sabotaging of Bernini's plans for the Louvre and the general failure of his visit: on the other hand, Lebrun was elected to the Academy of S. Luke in Rome in 1675 and made Director in the same year (and in 1676). For the French Academy he laid down a strict system of rules and even wrote a treatise on the expression of the passions. His most important paintings are at Versailles, where he decorated the *Galerie des Glaces* (1679–84) and the *Salons de la Guerre* and *de la Paix* (completed 1686). After the death of Colbert in 1683 Lebrun, though promoted Director of the Academy in that year, was gradually superseded by MIGNARD. There are paintings by him in Bristol, London (V & A, Dulwich), Montreal, Munich, Nottingham, Ottawa, Paris (Louvre), Prague, Venice, and many French provincial museums. There are about 2,000 drawings by him in the Louvre.

LEGA, Silvestro (1826–95), like FATTORI, fought in 1848–9 and was a leading member of the MACCHIAIOLI c.1860. Unlike Fattori, however, Lega carried his political opposition to the French to the length of disliking French art: nevertheless, his masterpiece *The Pergola* (1868) is unthinkable without the example of COROT and the beginnings of Impressionism. He suffered from eye trouble from 1880 and was blind for some years before his death, in great poverty, in Florence. There are works in Florence, Milan, and Rome.

LÉGER, Fernand (1881–1955), met BRAQUE and PICASSO in 1910 and eventually from his early block-like figures evolved, by c.1917, a form of curvilinear CUBISM, dependent on the dynamic shapes of machinery and their geometrical bases: cones, cylinders, cogged wheels, pistons, and brilliant metallic surfaces. These forms also influenced his massive, robot-like figures, and increased the effect of his clear greys and his strong, unbroken colours. He designed for the Swedish Ballet in 1921–2, and in 1924 made the first abstract film, 'Le Ballet Mécanique', from actual objects, not animated abstract drawings as had been used by Eggeling and Richter some seven years earlier. Among his last works were the huge murals for the UN building in New York. He also made a set of stained-glass windows for the Sacré Cœur, Audincourt, nr. Belfort (Doubs).

There are works in Edinburgh, London (Tate), New York (M of MA), Paris (Mus. d'Art Moderne), and there is a Musée Léger at Biot, Côte d'Azur.

LEHMBRUCK, Wilhelm (1881–1919), was a German sculptor trained in Düsseldorf, where he was a contemporary of MACKE. He went to Italy in 1905 and lived in Paris 1910–14. He was influenced by both RODIN and MAILLOL, but his own forms are more elongated, and his masterpiece, the *Kneeling Woman*, of 1911, has a Gothic expressiveness. He committed suicide in 1919. There are many works in his native Duisburg and others in Auckland N.Z., Buffalo, London (Tate), New York (M of MA), Otterlo, and several German museums.

LEIBL, Wilhelm (1844–1900), was a Cologne painter who was the leader of German Realism in the late 19th century. He met Courbet in Munich at the time of Courbet's exhibition in 1869, and later spent six months in Paris before the outbreak of the Franco-Prussian War (1870). His technical experiments included the use of tempera to obtain an enamel-like surface, and the minuteness of his handling can be seen in his masterpiece *Three Women in a Village Church* (1881: Hamburg). He lived in Bavarian villages and used peasant models, thus exerting a great influence on THOMA and the School of Munich. Many German museums possess examples, including Berlin, Cologne, Hamburg, and Munich.

LELY, Sir Peter (1618–80), was born in Germany of Dutch parents –

his real name was van der Faes – and studied in Haarlem under Pieter de Grebber, becoming a Master in the Haarlem Guild in 1637. No works of this Dutch period are known, but he was certainly in London ten years later, and the earliest works produced in this country are still more or less in the style of de Grebber: they are history and subject pieces, even religious pictures, which he continued to paint throughout the Commonwealth. By 1647, however, he had painted the King as well as the Royal children and the double portrait of Charles I and the Duke of York (1647: Syon House, Middx) inspired Lovelace's poem 'See what a clouded majesty . . .'. With the Restoration Lely at once began the production of that huge flood of portraits which made him the most influential of English 17th-century painters; more important even than van Dyck, to whose position he succeeded when he became Principal Painter to Charles II in 1661. From then until his death he maintained a large studio turning out hundreds of portraits painted in an International Baroque style and exactly catching that atmosphere of sensual languor which most of Charles's Court saw themselves as possessing. The two poles of his art are represented by the sleepily voluptuous *Beauties* of Charles II's Court (Royal Coll., Hampton Court) and the splendidly masculine *Admirals* (Nat. Marit. Mus.). These represent the twelve Admirals under the command of the Duke of York (later James II), for whom the set was painted to commemorate the victories in the Second Dutch War. Pepys records (18 April 1666): 'To Mr Lilly's, the painter's; and there saw the heads, some finished, and all begun, of the Flaggmen in the late great fight . . .'. There are other pictures by him in the Royal Coll. and in Birmingham, London (NG, NPG, Tate, Courtauld Inst., Dulwich, Guildhall, and Ham House), Manchester, New York (Met. Mus.), Ottawa, York, and elsewhere.

LE MOYNE (Le Moine), François (1688–1737), continued, in the age of WATTEAU, the Grand Manner of LEBRUN. He did many decorations at Versailles, and his *Time revealing Truth* in the Wallace Coll., London, painted just before he committed suicide, shows the pure 17th-century style unaffected by Watteau, although it does show the triumph of RUBÉNISME. Boucher was his pupil.

LEMOYNE, Jean Baptiste (1704–78), was the son of a sculptor. He won the Rome Prize in 1725 but never made the journey. His *Baptism of Christ* (1731: Paris, S. Roch) is his most famous religious work, but he is best known for his splendid portrait busts and as a teacher – his pupils included Falconet, Pigalle, Pajou, and Houdon. There are works in Paris (Louvre, Jacquemart-André, and Comédie Française), Versailles, Stockholm, Toledo Ohio, Vienna, and many French provincial museums.

LE NAIN. There were three painter brothers of this name, all born in Laon. Antoine (c. 1588–1648) was in Paris from 1629 and his two brothers Louis (*c.* 1593–1648) and Mathieu (*c.* 1607–77) from 1630. All three were elected members of the Academy on its foundation in 1648. The snag is that there are about 15 signed and dated pictures – but no signature has any initial and all the dates are in or before 1648; i.e. there is no certain means of telling one from another. However, there is a group of small pictures, mostly on copper, with small figures painted in strong colours: these are usually associated with Antoine. Another group is much larger in scale, painted in cool greyish tones, sometimes (like Antoine's) of peasant families but also sometimes of religious subjects: these are called 'Louis' and are perhaps the most valuable artistically. Louis is supposed to have been to Rome. Any remaining tend to get ascribed to Mathieu. Pictures by one or other are in Berlin, Boston, Bristol, Cardiff, Glasgow, Hagerstown Md, Hartford Conn., London (NG, V & A), New York (Met. Mus.), Paris (Louvre), San Francisco (Legion of Honor), Springfield Mass., and several French provincial museums.

LENBACH, Franz von (1836–1904), studied at Munich before going to Rome in 1858–9. In 1863 he returned to Rome with BÖCKLIN. He visited Spain in 1867 before settling in Munich in 1868, where he became a successful portrait painter working in a style derived from Rembrandt and Reynolds. He painted some 80 versions of Bismarck. There is a Lenbach Gallery in Munich, and other German galleries have examples: his *Lord Acton* is in London (NPG).

LEONARDO da Vinci (1452–1519) was one of the greatest of the Universal Men produced by the Renaissance. His intellectual powers were such that he anticipated many later discoveries in anatomy, aeronautics, and several other fields, as well as being one of the greatest of Italian artists. He has always been counted as one of the three great creators of the High Renaissance of the 16th century, yet he was born in 1452 and was thus a contemporary of Perugino and Signorelli and much older than either Michelangelo (*b.* 1475) or Raphael (*b.* 1483). The intellectual powers which allowed him to overcome the 'dry and hard manner' (as Vasari called it) of the Quattrocento were, however, so diffused over an enormous range of interests that he brought hardly any major enterprise to a conclusion: he almost discovered the circulation of the blood, he invented the first armoured fighting vehicle, projected several aircraft and helicopters and anticipated the submarine, but not one of these discoveries was completed; and in the same way he left thousands of notes and drawings but only a handful of paintings, and still fewer completed ones.

He was born at Vinci, the illegitimate son of a Florentine notary, but was brought up in his father's house and trained as a painter, traditionally under VERROCCHIO. He is said to have painted the left-hand angel in Verrocchio's *Baptism* (Florence, Uffizi), as a result of which Verrocchio gave up painting. On stylistic grounds there is every reason to accept the truth of the story, and Verrocchio may well have felt that he could stick to sculpture if he could have so good a painter in the firm; for it is certainly true that Leonardo was living in Verrocchio's house in 1476, presumably as his assistant, since in that year an anonymous accusation of homosexuality which was made against him says so. He had already become a Master in the Guild in 1472, and his earliest datable work is a drawing of an Arno landscape (1473) which already shows his interest in rock-formation and the structure of the earth. There are also some drapery studies, made in the 1470s, which show him breaking new ground, for earlier painters had been content to invent a formula for the folds in drapery and stick to it all their lives, but it is typical of Leonardo that he should have made a special study of fold-structure. In the 70s he was also experimenting with the technique of oil painting, as may be seen in the *Madonna* in Munich, in which the detail of the dewdrops on the crystal vase astounded his contemporaries, and in the *Ginevra de' Benci* (probably 1474: Washington, NG), which may originally have had hands, like the Verrocchio bust of a lady with flowers. This half-length with the hands shown would thus be a new type of portrait, looking forward to the *Mona Lisa*. In 1481 his reputation must have been considerable, for he was commissioned to paint a large *Adoration of the Kings* for the monks of S. Donato a Scopeto, near Florence. The composition of this work is of great importance as summing up all the aims of the later 15th century in creating a surface pattern which should also be a pyramidal form in depth, compact yet dynamic. Many drawings of this period exist, but the picture (now in the Uffizi) was never finished and the payments to Leonardo ceased in 1481. Nothing is known of his activities until he is documented in Milan in 1483, where he may have gone in the previous year. A draft letter exists, in which Leonardo offered his services to Lodovico Sforza, Il Moro, Duke of Milan, and in which he claimed at great length to be a highly skilled military engineer, ending with the words: 'In peace I believe that I can give you as complete satisfaction as anyone in the construction of buildings, both public and private .... I can further execute sculpture in marble, bronze or clay, and in painting I can do as much as anyone, whoever he may be. Moreover, I would undertake the commission of the bronze horse, which will endow with immortal glory and eternal honour the auspicious memory of your father and of the illustrious house of Sforza ...'.

Soon after his arrival he probably painted the *Lady with an Ermine* (now in Cracow) which almost certainly represents Cecilia Gallerani, the mistress of Lodovico Il Moro (Gallerani is almost Greek for 'ermine'): this picture shows the same stylistic characteristics as those attributable to his earlier Florentine period, a point which it is important to bear in mind when considering the problems raised by the two versions of the *Virgin of the Rocks* in Paris (Louvre) and London (NG). Briefly, the problem may be stated thus: Leonardo rarely finished one work, so that it is not likely he would have painted two versions, almost, but not quite, identical, of a picture for which only one set of documents seems to exist. These documents run from 1483 to 1506 and they seem to refer to a picture which must be identified with the NG one, the history of which is known in detail. Nevertheless, the Louvre version is indubitably the earlier – i.e. more Florentine – in style, which corresponds with a date *c.*1483 for the commission. Leonardo remained in Milan until 1499, working on a few artistic projects and several scientific ones but principally acting as resident genius at the Court. Originally he had intended to carry out the elaborate bronze equestrian monument to Francesco Sforza, father of Lodovico Il Moro, but the project got no further than a huge clay model of the horse without its rider. It was never cast, and perished early in the 16th century, but there are some superb drawings of horses connected with it. Leonardo was a famous horseman and he seems to have projected a book on the anatomy of the horse while he was working on the Sforza Monument. One other major work was carried out at this time – the *Last Supper* in Sta Maria delle Grazie, Milan, on which he was working in 1497. Owing to his slow methods and his desire for experiment he worked on the plaster in oil instead of fresco, with the result that the painting was already a wreck in his own lifetime. Nevertheless, this is the first work of the High Renaissance, with its stress on the psychology of the Disciples and the tension of the moment when Christ announces that one of them is about to betray Him, a subtlety of interpretation quite foreign to the 15th century. The stories of Leonardo's slowness in working on this wallpainting and his search for psychological expressiveness justify the claims made by a later generation which regarded Leonardo as the originator of the idea of the artist as a contemplative and creative thinker, the equal of the philosopher, and not a mere artisan who was paid to cover so many square yards of wall a day. Certainly all the 16th-century ideas on the dignity of the artist can be traced back to the example set by him.

In 1499 the French invaded Milan, the dynasty fell, and Leonardo left the city, returning to Florence in 1500 and working in 1502–3, with what seems a cynical detachment, as a military engineer for Cesare Borgia. During his second Florentine period he did a great deal of dissection and made himself into incomparably the finest anatomist of his day, but he also worked on three major artistic projects. The most important was the commission given by the city to its two greatest artists, Leonardo and Michelangelo (who disliked each other intensely). This was for two gigantic wall-paintings, to commemorate Florentine victories, in the Council Chamber of the new Republic. Neither was ever finished. Leonardo's was to represent the Battle of Anghiari, but no more than the central group was ever painted; and this was apparently in some wax medium, in imitation of an antique technique, which failed miserably. Work was begun in 1503 and stopped in 1505. During these years he was also working on a number of versions of the Madonna and Child with S. Anne, seeking a solution to the problem of creating a single compositional form from two adult figures and one or more children. The two survivors are probably the first and last of the series, the one in London (NG) being probably begun in Milan and taken to Florence, and the one in the Louvre dating from c.1506. One of his few finished works is the celebrated portrait of the wife of a Florentine official, known as *Mona Lisa* or 'La Gioconda'. This was painted between c.1500 and c.1504, and, apart from its accretions of fame as a *femme fatale*, is important as a type of portrait and as a feat of oil-technique, particularly in its SFUMATO effects.

In 1506 Leonardo returned to Milan and was made *Peintre et Ingénieur* to Francis I of France in 1507: he died in France, at Cloux near Amboise, in a château given him by the King. His last years were spent mainly in scientific pursuits but he also projected another equestrian monument, this time to Trivulzio, the commander of the French troops, but the idea got no further than drawings. His last painting, probably done before he moved to France in 1517, was the *S. John* (c.1514/15: Paris, Louvre). In this androgynous object the defects of Leonardo's qualities are painfully apparent: the search for solidity of modelling has led to inky shadows and the total suppression of colour in favour of chiaroscuro; and the search for subtlety of facial expression has led to the smirk with which Leonardo's Milanese followers have made us all too familiar.

A treatise on painting, for which many notes were made, was never written by Leonardo, but it was published from the notes for the first time in 1651 (and recently in full). Incomparably the finest collection of his drawings is in the Royal Library, Windsor Castle. There are other paintings by him in Leningrad, Milan (Ambrosiana), and the Vatican.

LÉPINE, Stanislas (1835–92), was a pupil of Corot and the friend of Boudin, Jongkind, and the Impressionists. He spent his life painting views of Paris in a style derived from Corot and Impressionism. There is a good example in Glasgow.

LE SUEUR, Eustache (1616/17–55), was, from 1632, a pupil of Vouet, whom he closely followed. He worked at the Hôtel Lambert, first on a *History of Cupid* for the Cabinet d'Amour, 1646–7, then in the Cabinet des Muses, 1647–9, where he turns more consciously towards Raphael and Poussin, the great influences on the later part of his career. Poussin, whom he may have known in 1640–2, dominates the *Life of S. Bruno* series painted for the Charterhouse of Paris (*c*.1648: Louvre), and in his last works his imitation of Raphael (though he never went to Rome) turns him into a dully derivative artist. There are works in Paris (Louvre) and French provincial museums.

LE SUEUR, Hubert (active 1610–43), worked first in France, where he was sculptor to the King by 1610, and is mentioned as working in 1624. He was in England by 1629, when he made figures for the catafalque of James I, and soon after was employed to make the monstrous tombs of the Duke of Lennox and Richmond, and the Duke of Buckingham, in Westminster Abbey. His equestrian statue of Charles I at Charing Cross, begun in 1630, is an effective *pastiche* of the Henri IV on the Pont Neuf in Paris, but, like all his works, suffers from his pedestrian style and his emptiness of form. Charles I seems to have been aware that his sculptor was far below his painter, van Dyck, in quality. There are works in the Royal Collection, and in London (V & A), Oxford (St John's College, Schools Quadrangle, Bodleian Library).

LEWIS, Wyndham (1884–1957), was an English painter and writer who flourished on controversy. He was the founder of VORTICISM, which derived from Cubism and Futurism, and edited its paper 'Blast'. He is supposed to have painted the first English picture to be influenced by Cubism, in 1912. The Vorticist group amalgamated itself with the LONDON GROUP – but Lewis soon resigned. He wrote a number of novels and satires, and is represented as a painter in Edinburgh, London (Tate), Manchester, and elsewhere.

LEYDEN, Lucas van, *see* LUCAS.

LEYDEN, Nicolaus Gerhaert von, *see* GERHAERT.

LEYSTER, Judith (1609–60), and her husband, Jan MOLENAER, whom she married in 1636, were Haarlem painters and were probably pupils of Frans HALS. They painted groups of people laughing and drinking which are strongly influenced by, if not entirely derived from, Hals, against whom Judith brought a lawsuit for the enticement of an apprentice from her workshop into his. Her *Lute-playing Fool* (Amsterdam, Rijksmus.) – a very UTRECHT SCHOOL subject – for many years passed as a Hals. There are works by her in Amsterdam (Rijksmus.), Dublin, The Hague, London (NG), Philadelphia, Stockholm, and elsewhere.

LIBER STUDIORUM *see* LIBER VERITATIS.

LIBER VERITATIS (Lat. book of truth) was the name given by CLAUDE to the collection of 195 drawings after his own paintings which he assembled as a record of authentic works. The number was later made up to 200 by the addition of five drawings not related to paintings: the entire collection, for centuries the property of the Dukes of Devonshire at Chatsworth, is now in the BM. They were engraved in mezzotint by R. Earlom in 1777, with a note based on BALDINUCCI'S account of the origin of the drawings. This collection inspired TURNER to compile his own *Liber Studiorum: Illustrative of Landscape Compositions, viz., Historical, Mountainous, Pastoral, Marine, and Architectural* ... (1807 onwards). These were compositions drawn, and partly engraved, by Turner, intended to form a corpus of landscape types, quite different in intention from Claude's index to his paintings. Turner was particularly stringent in his demands on the engravers' skill and the *Liber* may have raised standards in this respect.

LICHTENSTEIN, Roy (*b.* 1923), is a leading American POP artist. His usually large pictures are based on the magnification of details from advertisements of every-day objects – a foot on a pedal-bin, a hand holding a sponge, a cooker with food in the open oven – and strip cartoons – *Blonde waiting* (1964) or *Whaam* (1963: London, Tate). His technique imitates the coarse screen process of cheap newspaper printing, and his stylized forms translate his commonplace sources into simple but powerful patterns, expressed in strong primary colours, or in black and white. Some of his imagery is sub-Picasso in origin, and he has also experimented with curiously dazzling effects of coloured plastics, and brass and enamelled metal sculpture.

LIEBERMANN, Max (1847–1935), was the principal Impressionist painter in Germany. In 1874 he went to BARBIZON and was much influenced by MILLET. He returned to Germany in 1878 and painted rather sentimental genre scenes until the 1890s when he began to work more and more in the Impressionist manner. When the Berlin SEZESSION was founded in 1899 Liebermann became its President. He is well represented in German museums (though out of favour under the Nazis) and in London (Tate) and New York (Met. Mus.).

LIEVENS, Jan (1607–74), of Leyden was the friend and contemporary of REMBRANDT. He was a pupil of LASTMAN in Amsterdam and then shared a studio with Rembrandt in Leyden in the later 1620s: many works of this period show one influencing the other. Lievens went to England, probably in 1632 after Rembrandt moved to Amsterdam, but he was in Antwerp by 1635, where he was influenced by the courtly style of van Dyck. He returned to Holland in 1639 and became a successful painter of portraits and allegories. There are works in Amsterdam, Berlin, Besançon, Brighton, Copenhagen, Dublin, Edinburgh (NG), The Hague (Mauritshuis and Huis ten Bosch), Leyden, Lille, London (NG), Nancy, Ottawa, Paris (Louvre), Rotterdam, and Vienna.

LIMBOURG, Pol, Hennequin, and Herman de. Pol was the eldest of the brothers, but the first mention of any of them occurs in the accounts of the Duchy of Burgundy for 1400/1 (probably May 1400): there the story is told of Herman and Jacquemin (Hennequin), 'young children' who had been sent as apprentices to a Flemish goldsmith in Paris. The plague broke out and they were on their way home when they were caught up in a war and imprisoned in Brussels. The Duke of Burgundy paid the ransom, presumably because they were related to his painter Jehan MALOUEL. Immediately after this they began working for the Duke and from 1411 they were the Court Painters of the Duke of Berri, for whom they made the most splendid of all his fabulous collection of manuscripts, the 'Très Riches Heures du Duc de Berri' (Chantilly, Musée Condé), one of the greatest achievements of the INTERNATIONAL GOTHIC style. It is now known that all three were dead by 1416, when their heirs claimed property in Bourges.

LIMNING. An old-fashioned word, now coming back into use, for portrait painting 'in little' – i.e. miniatures.

LINEAR COMPOSITION. A composition which depends for its effect on the pattern made by the outlines of the forms represented (whether naturalistic or not) rather than on the masses of tone and colour, which tell as shapes rather than edges.

LINGELBACH, Johannes (1622–74), was an Amsterdam painter of Italianate landscapes and BAMBOCCIATE. He often painted figures in landscapes by others, e.g. Hobbema and Wynants.

LINNELL, John (1792–1882), painted miniatures, landscapes, and Bible illustrations. He was disliked by many fellow-artists and Constable is usually blamed for spreading the gossip about sharp practice in dealing which caused his constant rejection at RA elections. His son-in-law PALMER loathed him, and his one saving grace was the help he gave to Blake, whom he met in 1818. There are works by him in Brighton, Cambridge, and London (Tate and V & A).

LINOCUT see ENGRAVING.

LIOTARD, Jean Étienne (1702–89), was a Swiss pastellist who worked in Paris from 1725, went to Italy in 1738 and there met two English noblemen who took him to Constantinople, where he adopted Turkish dress and a beard which he retained afterwards for the notoriety they brought him. He was in England from 1753–5 painting portraits which Walpole described as 'too like to please', but their liveliness of colour and expression had great success and much influenced Cotes. He worked in Holland after his English visit, and returned to London from 1772 to 1774, but without his earlier success. There are works in Amsterdam (Rijksmus.), Dresden, Geneva (many of his best works), London (V & A), Vienna, and elsewhere.

LIPCHITZ, Jacques (1891-1973), was born in Lithuania but went to Paris in 1909. His sculpture shows the influence of CUBISM – he met Rivera and Picasso in 1913 – but by c. 1925 he had evolved a personal style of openwork sculpture (*sculptures transparentes*). In 1941 he went to America, where he spent most of the rest of his life, but in 1946 he was commissioned to make a *Madonna* for one of the new French churches, at Plateau d'Assy. The Barnes Foundation, Merion Pa, has many works bought in 1922 by Dr Barnes: others are in Amsterdam (Stedelijk), Edinburgh (NG Modern Art), London (Tate), New York (M of MA), Ottawa, Paris, and many U.S. museums.

LIPPI, Filippino (1457/8–1504), was the son of Fra Filippo and completed his father's works (or at least cleared up his estate) in Spoleto, after which – at the age of about 12 – he set off alone for Florence on 1 January 1470. He was with BOTTICELLI in 1472 but the first certainly datable work by him is the *Annunciation* (1483/4: S. Gimignano) on two *tondi*. This long gap, coupled with the existence of a group of pictures which are close to both Filippino and Botticelli, led to the creation of AMICO di Sandro, but the group has now been redivided between the two. His first major commission was to complete the fresco cycle in the Brancacci Chapel in the Carmine, Florence, which had either been left unfinished by Masaccio or had been partially destroyed. This he probably painted about 1484 and in 1486 he completed one of his best known and most typical paintings, the *Vision of S. Bernard* (Florence, Badìa), which shows his restless, fluttering line and bright colour. Between 1487 and 1502 he painted a fresco cycle in the Strozzi Chapel in Sta Maria Novella, and another one in Rome. This was the cycle in the Caraffa Chapel, S. Maria sopra Minerva (1488–93), and his years in Rome gave him the opportunity to study antique remains: ever afterwards he introduced bits and pieces of antiquity into all his pictures, whether suitable or not. There are many panels datable in the 1490s and the last years of his life, but, like Botticelli, his style went out of date in his life-time: it is sometimes called 'Quattrocento Mannerism'. There are pictures by him in Berlin, Chantilly, Cleveland Ohio, Copenhagen, Edinburgh (NG), Florence (Accad., Uffizi, Pitti, Horne Mus., S. Spirito), Genoa, London (NG), Munich, New York (Met. Mus.), Ottawa, Oxford (Ch. Ch.), Toledo Ohio, Washington (NG), and elsewhere.

LIPPI, Fra Filippo (*c.*1406–69), was probably the only direct pupil of Masaccio. He was an orphan and was put into the Carmine in Florence in 1421, presumably to get him out of the way although he was temperamentally unfitted to be a monk. In the 1420s Masaccio was painting the Brancacci Chapel there and in 1430 (after Masaccio's death) Fra Filippo is first recorded as a painter. The hypothesis that he was Masaccio's pupil is much strengthened by the fresco fragments, datable *c.*1432, of the *Relaxation of the Carmelite Rule* which are his earliest works: they reflect the influence of Masaccio to the exclusion of almost everything else. In 1434 Fra Filippo had left the Carmine and was in Padua, but his work there has disappeared. The first picture by him which bears a date is the *Tarquinia Madonna* (1437: Rome, Gall. Naz.), and this shows that Masaccio's influence is being gradually superseded by that of Donatello and of Flemish painting.

The *Barbadori Altarpiece* (Paris, Louvre) was also begun in 1437 and shows him using the new SACRA CONVERSAZIONE type of composition, with the old divisions of a triptych modified into a unified composition, the kneeling figures at the sides being used to form a pyramidal shape which stretches across the old divisions. His frescoes at Prato are perhaps his major achievement, and show him developing a progressively more dramatic style, with great interest in the problem of rendering movement, with by now no trace of Masaccio. The Prato cycle was begun in 1452 and was still incomplete in 1464: these years include Lippi's trial for fraud (1450) and his abduction of the nun Lucrezia (and the consequent birth of Filippino). The Medici family, his constant patrons and friends, obtained him a dispensation to marry Lucrezia – but he does not seem to have been suitably grateful. In spite of his activities, his late works are infused with religious feeling and are far more lyrical than the early ones. The series of *Nativities* (Berlin and Florence) are examples. His last works were the frescoes in Spoleto Cathedral, but from the beginning in 1466 until his death there in 1469 he seems to have been in bad health and most of the work was done by pupils and assistants. The final receipts are signed by his son Filippino who was then about 12. BOTTICELLI was probably also Fra Filippo's pupil in the 1460s. There are works by him in Baltimore, Berlin, Empoli, Florence (Uffizi, Pitti, Pal. Medici, and S. Lorenzo), London (NG, Courtauld Inst.), Milan (Castello), Munich, New York (Met. Mus.), Oxford, Prato (Mus.), Rome (Pal. Venezia), Washington (NG), and elsewhere.

LISS (Lys), Johann (*c.* 1597–1629/30), was a German painter who seems to have trained in the Netherlands, perhaps under GOLTZIUS, and in Paris, before settling in Venice by 1621. He died there of the plague. His Roman BENTNAME 'Pan', given on his visit *c.* 1622, sufficiently expresses his robustly Rubensian art, crossed with Venetian colouring, and his preferred subjects. There are examples in Berlin, Bremen (Kunsthalle, Roseliushaus), Budapest, Cassel, Dresden, Florence (Uffizi), The Hague (Bredius Mus.), London (NG), Nuremberg, Pommersfelden (Schloss Schönborn), Venice (Accad. and S. Niccolò dei Tolentini), and Vienna (K-H Mus. and Akad.).

LITHOGRAPHY *see* ENGRAVING.

LOCAL COLOUR is the actual colour of an object, uninfluenced by reflected light or colour: thus, the local colour of lips is pink although they may appear brown in certain lights.

LOCHNER, Stefan (*d.* 1451), was active in Cologne from at least 1442 and is the major master of the Cologne School, an important representative of the SOFT and pretty style associated with INTERNATIONAL GOTHIC. He seems to have been trained in the Netherlands, at least under the influence of the MASTER OF FLÉMALLE (he was a contemporary of Roger van der Weyden) and perhaps also of the LIMBOURG brothers. His masterpiece is the *Patron Saints of Cologne* ('*Das Dombild*') in Cologne Cath. Other works include the dated one (1447) in Darmstadt and others in Cologne (Wallraf-Richartz Mus. and Archiepiscopal Mus.), Frankfurt (Städel), London (NG), Munich, and Nuremberg. The Gulbenkian Coll., Lisbon, has one dated 1445.

LOMAZZO, Giovanni Paolo (1538–1600), was a Milanese painter, trained under Gaudenzio FERRARI, whose career was cut short at the age of 33, in 1571, by blindness. He devoted his later years to writing, mainly on the theory of art, and his treatise 'L'Arte della Pittura', first published in Milan in 1584, has been described as 'the Bible of Mannerism'. It was translated by the Oxford physician and amateur engraver, Richard Haydocke, as early as 1598, and this edition, with 13 of Haydocke's own engravings, must have been known to Shakespeare. It has the additional interest of mentioning English artists such as HILLIARD and OLIVER, who are not in the original Italian edition. He also wrote the 'Idea del Tempio della Pittura' (Milan, 1590) and some poems. There is a self-portrait in Milan (Brera).

LOMBARDO, Pietro (*c.*1435–1515), and his sons Tullio (*c.*1455–1532) and Antonio (*c.*1458–1516?) were the major Venetian sculptors and architects of their time. Pietro, who came from Lombardy, was first recorded in Padua in 1464 (Roselli tomb in the Santo, 1467), but his style suggests that he had already been in Florence. He settled in Venice probably *c.*1467, and with his sons ran the principal sculpture workshop; they executed many tombs, the Mocenigo tombs in SS. Giovanni e Paolo, finished by 1481, being the most important. He also worked at Treviso, and made Dante's tomb in Ravenna. His style is characterized by rather thick-set figures of markedly Antique derivation, soft modelling, and a certain hesitancy in form and movement. Tullio's career depended upon his father's, but in style he is more emphatic, dramatic, and even more influenced by the Antique. Antonio was also strongly classical in inspiration, reflecting the tastes of his patrons, but he finally dwindled into decorative work for the Este of Ferrara. Tullio and Antonio did most of the decorative sculpture and statues for S. Maria dei Miracoli, which their father built (1481–89), and they also did the odd perspective reliefs on the lower part of the façade of the Scuola di S. Marco. Besides numerous works in churches in Venice and in Treviso Cathedral, there are examples by Tullio in New York (Met. Mus.), Northampton Mass. (Smith Coll.) and Vienna (K-H Mus.).

LONDON GROUP. Founded in 1913, the London Group arose from a fusion between the CAMDEN TOWN GROUP and the VORTICISTS, together with some other artists. The first president was GILMAN and the members included SICKERT and Wyndham LEWIS. The Group still exists.

LONGHI, Alessandro (1733–1813), was the son of Pietro Longhi, and a well-known portrait painter. His reputation was established as early as 1760 and two years later he published a book on Venetian painters of his own times ('Compendio delle Vite . . .' 1762) which is an important source-book. There are pictures in Venice and in London (NG), Boston, New York (Met. Mus.), Toledo Ohio, and elsewhere.

LONGHI, Pietro (1702–85), was a Venetian genre painter, whose scenes of every-day patrician life in Venice are of value to the historian. The comparison with Hogarth is often made, but it is not really valid, since Longhi entirely lacks Hogarth's biting satire. These pictures are very numerous and were often repeated by pupils or imitators and are therefore very common: the largest collection is in the Querini-Stampalia Gall., Venice. Others are in London, New York (Met. Mus.), and Washington (NG).

LOO, van. A family of painters of Flemish descent working in France, of whom the most important were Jean Baptiste, Carle, and Louis Michel. Jean Baptiste (1684–1745) was the eldest, but was the fourth generation of the family to be a painter. He was born in the south of France and worked there until he went to North Italy and on to Rome in 1714. From 1720 he was settled in Paris, becoming a Member of the Academy in 1731. He established himself as a portrait painter in the circle of the Regent, and also painted a version of the state portrait of Louis XV. In 1737 he moved to London, for reasons which are not clear; he had an immediate success, and was patronized by the Prime Minister, Sir Robert Walpole. He had great facility in catching a likeness, and by 1738 VERTUE wrote: 'The English painters have had great uneasines it has much blemishd their reputation – and business'. According to van Loo's own account, Walpole said he would have made him Painter to the King, but this was impossible since no foreigner could hold the post. In 1741 Vertue recorded his complaints about the English climate, and in 1742 he retired to his native Aix. His work had considerable influence on his English rivals such as HUDSON and HOGARTH. There are works by him in Aix, Brussels, Glasgow, Leningrad (Hermitage: a portrait of Walpole), London (NPG), New York (Hist. Soc.), Paris (Louvre and churches), Turin, Versailles, and Worcester (Town Hall).

Carle (1705–1765) was Jean Baptiste's brother and pupil and went with him to Rome in 1714, and back to Paris in 1720. After study in Paris he returned to Rome in 1727, and worked in Turin for two years before returning to Paris in 1734. He was elected to the Academy in 1735, and became the most famous member of the family in France, being appointed Principal Painter to the King in 1762, and Director of the Academy in 1763. There are works by him, principally decorations, in many French museums and also in Barnard Castle (Bowes Mus.), Florence (Uffizi), Glasgow, Leningrad (Hermitage), London (Wallace Coll.), Madrid, New York (Met. Mus.), Paris (Louvre, Notre Dame, and churches), Potsdam, Quebec, Stockholm, and Vienna.

Louis Michel (1707–71) was the son of Jean Baptiste and the brother of three further painters. Like his uncle Carle, who was only two years his elder, he was Jean Baptiste's pupil in Turin and Rome, and he won a prize at the Academy in Paris in 1725. With his uncle he went to Rome 1727–32, but in 1736 he became Court Painter in Madrid where he painted many portraits. He was a Founder-Member of the Academy in Madrid in 1752, but returned to Paris in 1753, and made many versions of the state portrait of Louis XV for presentation to the Courts of Europe. In 1765 he succeeded his uncle as Director of the special school of the French Academy known as the École des Élèves protégés (*see* COYPEL). There are works by him in Copenhagen, Leningrad, London (Wallace Coll.), Madrid (Prado and Acad.), Paris (Louvre), Versailles, and other French museums.

LORENZETTI, Pietro (active 1306?–45) and Ambrogio (active 1319–47), were brothers, Pietro probably being the elder. They were Sienese painters who extended the side of Duccio's art that was concerned with rendering solidity of form and emotional depth: in this they were opposed to Simone MARTINI and were influenced by the sculpture of Giovanni PISANO (as Duccio himself was) and also by contemporary work in Florence by Giotto and his immediate followers. Like some of their Florentine contemporaries such as DADDI they form a stylistic link between Duccio and Giotto, between the Schools of Siena and Florence. Pietro was perhaps Duccio's pupil, but his earliest work, the polyptych in the Parish Church, Arezzo, which was commissioned in 1320, shows an independent style already, even though it has Ducciesque characteristics and is comparable with the polyptych by Simone Martini at Pisa, also of 1320. Pietro's beginnings are much complicated by two facts, the interpretation of which is controversial. Firstly, there is a payment from Siena Town Council for a picture in 1306: it was made to 'Petruccio di Lorenzo', whom most scholars would now identify with Pietro. Secondly, the *Sta Umiltà* panels in Florence (Uffizi) were recorded in the 19th century as dated – but the date could be read as 1316 or 1341 (i.e. MCCCXVI or MCCCXLI). Stylistically, the later date is now thought more likely. There are several frescoes and other panel pictures by Pietro, the most notable being the frescoes at Assisi (S. Francesco, Lower Church), the *Carmine Altar* (1329: Siena, Pinacoteca), and the *Birth of the Virgin* (1342: Siena, Opera del Duomo). The Assisi frescoes show the impact of the art of Giotto on him, and they are probably the most tragically grand and simple works produced by a Sienese in the 14th century. The *Birth of the Virgin* is probably later – the date of the Assisi frescoes is very controversial – and, by comparison with the more complex *Presentation* by his brother (also 1342: Florence, Uffizi), it seems very simple, yet it has great narrative power and it shows Pietro as a colourist. The setting is reminiscent of his brother's *Presentation*, but simpler and less accurate in its perspective, and it is thought that Ambrogio was the more inventive of the two. He may have been in Florence *c.*1318 and the earliest work attributed to him, a *Madonna* of 1319, at Vico L'Abate (now in Florence, Mus. Diocesano), is much more influenced by Florentine ideas than by Sienese. He entered the Guild at Florence in 1327 and was in the city again in 1331–2, so that he was in constant touch with the art of Giotto and his followers. His most important works are the frescoes of *Good and Bad Government* in the Town Hall of Siena (1337–9). There is a large allegorical fresco, a sort of political manifesto, which shows the influence of Giotto in the bulky forms of the allegorical females, but the two most interesting are those representing Good Government in the Town and in the Country, where the streets of Siena are represented in perspective of astonishing mastery at that date, and the great panoramic landscape in the *Country* with its small figures riding through the peaceful countryside (the bandits have been hanged by the Good Government) is perhaps the first landscape in modern art to be used as an essential component of a composition, both reflecting and creating a mood. Ambrogio is last recorded in 1347, and it is probable that both brothers died in the Black Death of 1348 which ravaged Siena with particular severity and killed off most of the artists – hence the rapid decline in the second half of the 14th century.

There are works by one or both in Baltimore (Walters), Berlin, Borgo San Sepolcro, Budapest, Cambridge Mass. (Fogg), Cleveland Ohio, Cortona, Dijon, Fiesole, Florence (Uffizi, Horne Mus., Sta Lucia), Frankfurt (Städel), Le Mans, London (NG), Massa Marittima, Milan (Poldi-Pezzoli), New York (Met. Mus.), Philadelphia (Johnson), the Vatican, Washington (NG), Yale, and elsewhere. The so-called 'UGOLINO-LORENZETTI' had no real existence and was not another member of the family.

LORENZO Monaco (i.e. Lorenzo the Monk) (*c.* 1370/2–1422/5, probably 1425) was a Sienese who settled in Florence and took vows in the Camaldolensian monastery of S. Maria degli Angeli, which was famous as a school of manuscript illuminators: Don Lorenzo is also known to have painted illuminations. He was a follower of Agnolo GADDI and the Sienese strain in late Trecento art, but he was also influenced by GHIBERTI, and, like him, by INTERNATIONAL GOTHIC. His principal works are the *Coronation of the Virgin* (1413 Florentine Style, i.e. 1414: Florence, Uffizi), painted for his own monastery, and a similar *Coronation* (London, NG), probably also for a Camaldolensian house. Both these are traditional Trecento altarpieces, with gold backgrounds and flat figures, bright in colour and occupying no space in the picture. What is probably his last picture is the *Adoration of the Magi* (Florence, Uffizi) and this shows a complete change to the International Gothic style – dark colour, realistic detail and landscape background, and an attempt at depth, though with very elongated figures. He is thus important as one of the introducers of the style into Florence before the arrival of GENTILE da Fabriano. There are other works in Florence (Accad., Uffizi, Bargello, Mus. di S. Marco, and churches) and in Amsterdam, Baltimore (Walters), Berlin, Cambridge (Fitzwm), Edinburgh (NG), London (NG, Courtauld Inst.), New York (Met. Mus.), Paris (Louvre), Philadelphia (Johnson), Siena, Toledo Ohio, the Vatican, Washington (NG), Worcester Mass., Yale University, and elsewhere.

LORRAIN(E), Claude, see CLAUDE.

LOTTO, Lorenzo (*c.*1480–1556), was probably born in Venice. He worked in Treviso, Bergamo, Venice, and Ancona, and in 1509 was painting in the Vatican, though what he did there and how long he stayed is unknown. He settled in the monastery of the Santa Casa at Loreto in 1552, becoming a lay brother in 1554.

His early works are strongly influenced by Giovanni Bellini, but after his removals to Bergamo and Venice he develops a chameleon-like quality, reflecting Botticelli, Fra Bartolommeo, Raphael, Correggio, Giorgione, Titian, and even something of Dürer and Holbein, though always with an intensely personal quality and with a steady development from the detailed, episodic vision of the 15th century to the broader handling of the 16th century. His account book (a rare survival), kept from 1538 onwards, suggests a troubled and difficult character and little material success.

His principal frescoes are in and near Bergamo, and there are works by him in the Royal Coll., Ancona and the surrounding district, Bergamo (Accad. Carrara and churches), Berlin, Brescia, Budapest, Cambridge Mass. (Fogg), Cleveland Ohio, Dresden, Edinburgh (NG), Florence (Uffizi), Jesi, Leningrad, London (NG), Loreto, Madrid (Prado), Milan (Brera, Castello, Poldi-Pezzoli), Munich, Naples, New Orleans, Oxford (Christ Church), Paris (Louvre), Philadelphia (Johnson), Princeton, Recanati (Mus. and churches), Rome (Borghese, Barberini, Capitoline, Castel S. Angelo, Doria Gall.), Sarasota Fla, Treviso, Venice (Accad., Correr, and churches), Vienna, Washington (NG), and elsewhere.

LOUIS, Morris (1912–62). American painter, working mostly in Washington. His speciality was the large canvas of fine material, on to which bright, pure colours were floated like patches of stain, without visible brushstrokes.

Lucas van Leyden (1494 or perhaps 1489–1533) is said to have been precociously capable in 1508: the evidence for this is a supremely competent line-engraving, *The Drunkenness of Mohammed*, which is signed 'L 1508'. He was the pupil of his father, by whom no works are known, and Cornelis Engelbrechtsz., with whose paintings his are confused: almost nothing is known about the Leyden school. He married in Leyden in 1515, met Dürer in Antwerp in 1521, and may have entered the Guild there in 1522. He visited Mabuse in Middelburg, and travelled in Flanders with him in 1527, when Lucas gave banquets for local painters. His paintings are characterized by fluid, calligraphic brushwork and surprising colour. His numerous woodcuts and engravings lean heavily on Dürer; they display sensitive, brilliant draughtsmanship and the inventiveness in subject common in the North. The volume of his *œuvre* belies van Mander's stories of his dilettante travelling, working in bed, and wining and dining in yellow silk clothes. There are works in Amsterdam, Boston (Mus.), Bremen, Brunswick, Brussels, Leningrad, Leyden, London (NG), Munich, Nuremberg, Paris (Louvre), Philadelphia (Johnson), and elsewhere.

Luini, Bernardino (*c.* 1481/2–1532), was one of the most popular Milanese painters in the early 16th century, principally because he succeeded in vulgarizing the style of Leonardo (as indeed all his Milanese followers tried to do). He was certainly active by 1512, but there is a picture in the Musée Jacquemart-André, Paris, which is dated 1507 and is the work of a Bernardino: partisans for and against the attribution to Luini may be found. Before his domination by the style of Leonardo he seems to have been influenced by Bramantino and other Milanese and to have painted gay and enjoyable works like the fresco fragments in Milan (Brera), Pavia, Paris (Louvre), and London (Wallace Coll.), all from a villa at Monza. His very numerous works are mostly in Milan (Brera, Castello, Poldi-Pezzoli, Ambrosiana, and churches), but there are others in the Royal Coll. and in Berlin, Boston, Cambridge Mass. (Fogg), Chiaravalle nr Milan (the fresco *Madonna* dated 1512), Cleveland Ohio, Como (Cath.), Detroit, Florence (Uffizi), London (NG, Wallace Coll., Wellington Mus., Courtauld Inst.), Lugano (S.M. degli Angeli), Minneapolis, Ottawa, Paris (Louvre), Pavia (Mus., Certosa), Philadelphia (Johnson), Sarasota Fla, Saronno nr Milan (S. Maria dei Miracoli), Vienna, Washington (NG), and elsewhere.

Lukasbrüder *see* Nazarener.

Lurçat, Jean (1892–1966), was the only great tapestry designer for generations. He began as a painter and was influenced by Cézanne and by Cubist ideas, but after being wounded in 1914 he began to work on tapestries in 1917. He lived for years in Spain and eventually abandoned Cubism. From 1937 he worked as designer at Aubusson,

and from 1939 for the Gobelins; in the post-war period he did much
to revive this art, many of his tapestries being woven for the French
Government to use in Embassies abroad. Other examples are in
Beaune, Cambridge (Churchill College), London (the BBC), and
Strasbourg. There are paintings by him in Paris (Mus. d'Art Moderne),
Melbourne, Toledo Ohio, and Washington (NG). He also wrote a
book on tapestry design.

LYON, Corneille de, *see* CORNEILLE.

M

MABUSE, Jan Gossaert called (*d.c.*1533), probably came from Maubeuge in Hainault, and is first documented in the Antwerp Guild in 1503. His early style derives from Gerard David, Hugo van der Goes, and Dürer, but he introduces flamboyant, over-abundant detail, amounting almost to a *horror vacui*. In 1508 he went to Italy, and after this his works display florid Italianized detail, particularly in the architectural settings, and borrowed poses, with no understanding of the essentials of the Italian Renaissance. He became an important ROMANIST, and was the first to introduce into Flanders classical subjects with nude figures. There are works in the Royal Collection, and in Antwerp, Barnard Castle (Bowes Mus.), Brussels, Berlin, London (NG, Courtauld Inst.), Ottawa, Palermo, Paris (Louvre), Prague, Toledo Ohio, Vienna, and elsewhere.

MACCHIAIOLI, I (Ital. *macchia*, a stain or blot). A group of Italian painters working mainly in Florence *c.*1855/65, who, in revolt against academism, exploited the individual blob or touch of paint (cf. TACHISME). Influenced by COROT and by COURBET's Realism, some produced landscapes and genre subjects (the best among these were LEGA, FATTORI, and SIGNORINI), while others turned out pseudo-Romantic costume history pieces (Vito d'Ancona, Costa). The only ones influenced much by Impressionism were Degas's friends De NITTIS and ZANDOMENEGHI, and BOLDINI who became a glossily fashionable portraitist in Paris. Diego Martelli, who was painted by Degas (Edinburgh, NG), was their chief critic and apologist.

MACKE, August (1887–1914), was a German painter deeply influenced by contemporary French painting, particularly by DELAUNAY's very bright colour used in conjunction with near-Cubist ideas. Associated with MARC and KANDINSKY in the BLAUE REITER, and influenced by Futurist ideas, he remained a more visual and representational artist than these associations suggest. In 1914 he went to Tunisia with Klee. He was killed in France. There is a good collection of his work in Munich (Städtische Gal.).

MADONNIERI. A Venetian word, applied to anonymous producers of devotional Madonna images, often of no artistic value.

MAELWEL *see* MALOUEL.

MAES, Nicolaes (1634–93), was a Dordrecht painter who became a pupil of Rembrandt *c.*1648. From then until about 1665 he painted genre and portraits in a Rembrandtesque manner and some genre subjects rather like those of P. de Hooch. About 1665/6 he went to Antwerp and was much impressed by the modishness of Flemish portraiture in the French taste: this elegance he took back with him and applied to his Dutch sitters. There are examples in Amsterdam (Rijksmus.), Antwerp, Barnard Castle (Bowes Mus.), Boston, Brussels, Dordrecht, The Hague, London (NG, Wallace Coll., Wellington Mus.), New York (Met. Mus.), Ottawa, Oxford (a *Still-life*), Toledo Ohio, Washington (NG), and elsewhere.

MAESTÀ (Ital. majesty) is an abbreviation for the Madonna and Child enthroned in Majesty and surrounded by Saints and/or Angels. The subject is most common in the Dugento and Trecento and the best-known example is the *Maestà* by Duccio, painted for the High Altar of Siena Cathedral 1308–11.

MAGNASCO, Alessandro (1677–1749), painted extremely melodramatic landscapes, usually with storm-tossed trees and frenetic monks, in an 18th-century version of Salvator ROSA's 'savagery'. Some of Marco RICCI's works are almost indistinguishable from his.

MAGNELLI, Alberto (1888–1971), was an abstract painter of the type of LÉGER and MONDRIAN, practising what is sometimes called 'Concrete Art'. He was born in Florence, but went to Paris c. 1910, and came in contact with the Cubists and Futurists. Later he met Picasso and Léger. He began painting abstract pictures in Florence in 1915, but reverted to figurative forms until he returned to France, settling in Paris in 1933. In 1958 he was awarded the Guggenheim Prize. There are works in Paris (Mus. d'Art Moderne) and several other museums in Europe, and in the US.

MAGRITTE, René (1898–1967), was a Belgian Surrealist painter who was trained in Brussels and travelled in France, Britain, Germany, and Holland. He lived near Paris, 1927–30, and came into contact with the French Surrealist movement, although he painted some Impressionist-style pictures during the Second World War. He lived in Brussels and painted murals for Belgian public buildings. His pale and dryly painted works have a dream-like clarity. There are examples in Chicago and New York (M of MA), and London (Tate).

MAHLSTICK (Maulstick). A short stick with a padded knob used as a rest for the right hand when painting detailed passages.

'MAI'. A large altarpiece, commissioned by the Goldsmiths' Guild of Paris from one of the major painters of the day, and presented by them to the cathedral of Notre Dame on 1 May. The custom seems to have died out at the beginning of the 18th century, and very few of these pictures have survived.

MAIANO, Benedetto da, *see* BENEDETTO.

MAILLOL, Aristide (1861–1944), was a French sculptor whose works are devoted almost exclusively to the female nude. He returned to the ideals of Greek art of the 5th century B.C. in a reaction against RODIN's fluid forms, changing silhouettes, and dramatic content, although it was Rodin who helped to make his name. By contrast,

Maillol stressed the static and monumental qualities of the human figure. He sometimes made use of the 'fragment' device, but never sought the dramatic contrasts of the partly unfinished figure. From 1889 he was friendly with BOURDELLE, although he did not begin sculpture until 1895; from 1900 he had links with the NABIS and became a life-long friend of Matisse. In 1908 he went to Greece. One of his most famous works, the Cézanne Monument, commissioned in 1912 for Aix, was formally rejected by the city in 1925 and was finally placed in the Tuileries in Paris. He is represented in the museums of modern art in London, Paris, and New York.

MALERISCH. This German word, meaning *painterly, pertaining to a painter*, was given a special sense by the great Swiss art historian Heinrich Wölfflin. In this technical sense it is used to denote the opposite of linear; that is, a feeling for form which does not see in terms of outline or drawing, but in patches of coloured light and shade, or painting in which the edges of the forms merge into one another or into the tone of the background. Titian and Rembrandt are among the most *malerisch* of painters, Botticelli or Michelangelo among the least.

MALEVICH, Kasimir (1878–1935), was a Russian artist who, not content with Cubism, invented SUPREMATISM and painted the picture which should have ended all abstract pictures – a white square on a white ground (c. 1918: New York, M of MA). From c. 1904 in Moscow he was aware of modern French painting, mainly from the splendid Shchukin collection; about 1912 he went to Paris for a month, and came back a Cubist. He claimed to have invented Suprematism as a purer form of Cubism in 1913, but it was more probably in 1915. After the Revolution he had a violent disagreement with CHAGALL over aesthetics: part of his 'Decree A in art. Vitebsk, 15 November 1920' reads '1. The fifth dimension is established . . . 18. To summon an economic council (of the fifth dimension) for the liquidation of all the arts of the old world . . .'.

MALOUEL (Maelwel), Jean (d.1419), was a Dutch painter working in Gelderland in 1386, but who had gone to Paris by 1396. He became Court Painter to the Dukes of Burgundy in 1397 and was succeeded by Bellechose in 1415. Malouel is known to have painted five works for Dijon in 1398 but no work certainly by him can now be identified. On the other hand, the large round *Pietà* (Paris: Louvre) which dates from 1400/10 is probably either by him or by Bellechose. Another picture in the Louvre, the *Martyrdom of S. Denis*, has been identified with one of the five Dijon altarpieces of 1398, but it seems more likely that it is a picture completed in 1416 by Bellechose. It has been suggested that the *S. Denis* was begun by Malouel and completed by Bellechose but this is pure guesswork.

Henri Bellechose was born in Brabant but worked mostly in Dijon.

He is known to have worked for the Dukes of Burgundy at Dijon 1415–25 and he died at Dijon 1440/4.

MANDER, Karel van (1548–1606), was a Flemish painter who was in Rome in 1575 and in Vienna in 1577. He settled in Haarlem where he opened an academy with Goltzius and Cornelis van Haarlem which propagated Italianizing tendencies in the North. He is most celebrated for his 'Schilderboek', published in 1604 – a poor imitation of Vasari's 'Lives', which, despite its gossipy inaccuracies, is the best early source on Northern painters.

MANDORLA (Ital. almond). An almond shaped glory of light which is shown as enclosing the whole figure of the Resurrected Christ or of the Virgin at the Assumption.

MANESSIER, Alfred (b. 1911), is a French abstract painter who differs from many others in that some, at least, of his pictures have a specifically religious intent. He made a retreat at the Trappist monastery at Soligny and has designed stained-glass windows for churches in Bresseux (Jura), Arles, and Basle (1953). His picture of the Crown of Thorns (Paris, Mus. d'Art Moderne) is clearly based on a meditation on the Passion, but the connexion between his *Salve Regina* and the great 11th-century Latin antiphon is less evident (though probably susceptible of exegesis by the Dominicans of S. Germain-des-Prés). There are pictures by him in Basle, Brussels, London (Tate), New York (Guggenheim), Oslo, Paris, Pittsburgh, Stockholm, and Turin.

MANET, Édouard (1832–83). His well-to-do bourgeois father reluctantly allowed him to study under COUTURE 1850–6. He then reacted very strongly against the academic history painting of his teacher and began his career as an artistic rebel with the *Absinthe Drinker* (1859: Ny Carlsberg Mus., Copenhagen), a scene from the seamier side of life. His brilliant technique, founded on the opposition of light and shadow with as little half-tone as possible, on painting directly from the model with intense immediacy, and on a restricted palette in which black was extremely important, helped him to create a new style; yet one founded on Velazquez, Goya, and Hals. His early works include many Spanish subjects inspired by troupes of dancers visiting Paris and he did not actually visit Spain until 1865. These Spanish pieces include numerous bull-fighting scenes, *Lola de Valence* (1862: Louvre) and the *Guitarist* (1860: private coll.), his only successful Salon exhibit before *Le bon Bock* (1873: Philadelphia). He had previously travelled in Italy, Holland, Flanders, and Germany.

His work was frequently rejected by the SALON jury (he played an important part in the 1863 Salon des Refusés) and, if hung, was ill-received by critics, his friend Zola being almost alone in defending him. After 1870, due partly to the influence of Berthe MORISOT, he adopted the Impressionist technique and palette, abandoning the use of black and his genius for analysis and synthesis for a lighter, sweeter, colour and a freer handling. He also tended more to sentimental subjects, such as *Washing Day* (1875: private coll.), *Chez le père Lathuile* (1880: Tournai), lacking the sober gravity of his earlier works – the *Déjeuner sur l'herbe* (1863: Louvre, sketch in Courtauld Institute, London), *Olympia* and *The Fifer* (1865 and 1866: both Louvre). He always longed for official recognition and refused to take part in the Impressionist exhibitions organized by Degas. Although he was friendly with Monet, Renoir, Sisley, and Pissarro he bitterly resented being coupled with them in newspaper criticisms as the leader of 'Manet's gang'. At the end of his life he was given the Legion of Honour and the vilification of his works abated, chiefly because Impressionist handling and colour were beginning to affect academic painting. The tragedy of his life was that he was the perfect academic painter, unrecognized and rejected by the body whose dying traditions he alone could have revivified.

Apart from those mentioned already the following cities have works: Baltimore, Berlin, Berne, Boston, Bremen, Budapest, Buenos Aires, Cardiff, Chicago, Copenhagen, Dijon, Dresden, Essen, Frankfurt (Städel), Glasgow (Burrell Coll.), Hamburg, London (NG, Tate, Courtauld Inst.), Lyons, Mannheim, Melbourne, Merion Pa (Barnes Foundation), Moscow, Munich, Nancy, New York (Met. Mus. and Frick Coll.), Oslo, Philadelphia (Johnson Coll.), Providence RI, St Louis, São Paulo, Stockholm, Toledo Ohio, and Washington (NG and Phillips).

MANFREDI, Bartolommeo (*c.* 1580–1620/1), was a Mantuan follower of Caravaggio, who seems not to have been above a little Caravaggio-faking immediately after the latter's death in 1610. His greatest claim to fame lies in the fact that it seems to have been he – and not Caravaggio – who popularized subjects such as cardsharpers and soldiers in guard-rooms, with half-length figures on a largish scale. These were the works which influenced the Northerners in Rome (Honthorst and other UTRECHT painters, as well as French and Germans) and there are cases where the early writers mention such painters as being followers of Manfredi rather than of Caravaggio. It is also recorded that his works were exported to Holland. There are no signed or fully documented works by him, and most of what are now regarded as characteristic examples of his style were, at one time or another, called Caravaggios. There are examples in Brunswick, Brussels, Chicago, Dresden, Florence (Uffizi, Pitti), Rome (Gall. Naz.), and Vienna.

MANIÈRE CRIBLÉE *see* DOTTED PRINT.

MANNER. Usually now used as a pejorative alternative for 'style': my friends have style, yours merely manner (cf. MANNERISM).

The original Italian term *maniera* meant personal style, 'handwriting', and the word manner is usually used in this sense in 18th-century criticism – 'a fine, free manner'.

MANNERISM is a term developed in the present century to describe the artistic manifestations, principally Italian, of the period *c.* 1520–1600. During these years many major works were produced which cannot be called RENAISSANCE or BAROQUE without rendering these terms meaningless. The word *maniera*, from which Mannerism is derived, was used by Vasari (himself a notorious practitioner) to describe the schematic quality of much of the work produced, based on intellectual preconceptions rather than direct visual perceptions. Much of Mannerism consists of deliberately flouting the 'Rules' deduced from classical art and established during the Renaissance. This presupposes an educated spectator; otherwise there is no point in breaking the rules. The effect is more obvious in architecture, since the Rules there are both more simple and more rigid, and the works of GIULIO Romano show him to have been a major Mannerist architect although less important as a painter.

The principal characteristics of a Mannerist work of art include an insistence on the primacy of the human figure, which, however, is set in strained poses, wilfully distorted and elongated, while the muscles are sometimes also grossly overemphasized. The composition is usually forced and unclear, with the principal subject set in a corner or in the background, with great discrepancies of scale between the figures and with the perspective treated more often as a piece of virtuosity than as a contribution to the lucidity of the narrative. The colour of a Mannerist picture is always vivid and often harsh, since it is intended to heighten the emotional effect rather than describe the forms; many Mannerists also have a preference for 'shot' colours, red blending into orange, yellow into green, and so on. It is essentially an unquiet style, subjective and emotional, and was therefore well fitted to be rediscovered and defined during the 1920s, but it is certainly wrong – as Marxist critics do – to equate it wholly with the disturbed political and social conditions prevailing in Central Italy after the Sack of Rome in 1527. These conditions, however influential, were more or less permanent; but it is fair to say that these disturbances, and particularly the unsettling effect of the Reformation (with its doctrine of private judgement) and the Counter-Reformation (with its repressive and didactic aspects), led to the abandonment of the serenity and calm classicism of the High Renaissance, of the art of Bramante and Raphael, and much of Mannerism is a conscious artistic revolution against the qualities summarized in Raphael: it is even possible to see Michelangelo's *Last Judgement* as a renunciation of the ideas underlying his own Sistine Ceiling. By about 1520 it was clear that the very perfection of Raphael was an impasse for his successors, leading only to pointless emulation; and his most gifted pupil, Giulio Romano, therefore turned to an exaggeration of facial expression, gesture, and lighting, derived partly from Raphael himself (the *Transfiguration*) but even more from Michelangelo, in an attempt to conquer entirely new fields of emotional expressiveness. The overwhelming greatness of Michelangelo is another major factor. His single-minded and sculptural devotion to the male nude led to many minor painters eschewing the painting of landscapes and accessories in a desire to storm the artistic heights of DISEGNO, with all its difficulties of anatomy, composition, and *contrapposto*.

On the whole, Mannerism is a style best adapted to neurotic artists such as Pontormo, Rosso, and Parmigianino, all of whom produced major works, as well as such great masters as Michelangelo, Tintoretto, and El Greco. There were also many very dull painters who strained every nerve to be neurotically interesting, but produced only frenziedly gesticulating and twisted figures in insipidly repetitive *contrapposto* derived from Michelangelo. It should be observed, however, that Mannerism had relatively little effect in Venice, where the political conditions which favoured the style in Central Italy did not obtain. From Vasari and Pellegrino TIBALDI elegant petrifaction set in – as in the splendidly null Court portraits of Bronzino – and the style eventually died of inanition at the hands of the Cavaliere d'ARPINO. It was succeeded by a wave of returning confidence and vitality coupled with a return to Nature in the BAROQUE. (For Antwerp Mannerism *see* ANTWERP.)

MANTEGNA, Andrea (*c.* 1431–1506), was a pupil and adopted son of the archaeologist-painter SQUARCIONE, and is first recorded in the contract for the decoration of the Ovetari Chapel in the Eremitani Church (destroyed 1944) in Padua, where he completed a fresco cycle in 1459 with four scenes from the Life of S. James, an *Assumption* and a *Martyrdom of S. Christopher* (which alone survives). In these, as in his *Madonna and Saints* (*c.* 1456/9: Verona, S. Zeno) and in all his other works, his forms appear to be made of tinted stone or bronze, a result of the powerful influence of DONATELLO. The *S. Zeno Madonna* is extremely important as an early example of a SACRA CONVERSAZIONE treated as a group of figures in a single, comprehensible space instead of as a triptych or other form of subdivided space. The *S. Sebastian* (*c.* 1460: Vienna) is referred to by Vasari as in his 'stony manner' and it also shows the painter's interest in the details of classical antiquity, an interest that made him a leading expert on archaeology and tended to swamp his paintings. In 1460 he left Padua and settled as Court Painter at Mantua. There he painted the frescoes of the *Camera degli Sposi* (finished in 1474) in the Castello as a memorial to the Gonzaga family, whose portraits on the walls appear to the spectator to be in an extension of the room-space; while on the ceiling is a view of a balcony with figures looking down, beneath an open sky, into the room. This is the first completely illusionistic SOTTO IN SÙ decoration of the Renaissance but the idea was not exploited again until CORREGGIO and not fully developed before the Baroque. Other works executed for the Gonzaga include the *Triumph of Caesar* (*c.* 1486–94: Hampton Court, the Royal Coll.) and the *Madonna della Vittoria* (1495–6: Louvre). He painted the *Parnassus* (Louvre) for Isabella d'Este, and a chapel in the Vatican (*c.* 1490: destroyed). The BELLINI were his brothers-in-law. There are other works by him in Berlin, Copenhagen, Dresden, Dublin, Florence, London, Madrid, Milan (Brera, Castello, Poldi-Pezzoli), Naples, New York, Tours, Venice, Vienna, Washington, and elsewhere.

MANZÙ, Giacomo (*b.* 1908), the leading Italian sculptor, was born of poor parents in Bergamo and apprenticed to a wood-carver in 1919: after military service he went to Paris, *c.* 1927, and settled in Milan in 1930, where the Archbishop gave him his first large commission, for the Catholic University chapel. Among modern sculptors he has been influenced by Medardo ROSSO, RODIN, and MAILLOL, but it is probable that DONATELLO has been the greatest factor, both in his exploitation of very low relief and in the feeling for drama in religious imagery. In 1939 and during the war years he made many religious works, including eight reliefs of Christ, and these culminated in the great bronze doors for St Peter's, Rome, and for Salzburg Cathedral. The commission for St Peter's was the subject of an international competition in 1949 and was given to Manzù in 1950: they were consecrated in 1964. The subject of the panels is Death in various forms. The doors of Salzburg Cathedral were completed in 1958. Manzù is also a painter and has illustrated several books. There are works by him in Antwerp (Middelheim Park), Bristol, Cleveland, London (Tate), Milan (S.M. in Chiesa Rossa), New York (M of MA), Rome (Gall. Moderna and S. Eugenio), and Turin.

MAQUETTE (Fr. small model). Used only of sketches in clay, wax, etc., for sculpture. A BOZZETTO.

MARATTA (Maratti), Carlo (1625–1713), was the last representative of one aspect of Baroque art and the first Neoclassic: his ideal was a return to the calm and noble style of Raphael and the Carracci and he was opposed to the more dramatic style of PIETRO da Cortona or BACICCIA. Not surprisingly, he was a pupil of Andrea SACCHI and, like him, a fine portrait painter although most of his works are altarpieces. His enormously long career began in 1645 and he made his name in 1650 with a *Nativity* for S. Giuseppe dei Falegnami, Rome; he was still painting in 1706 and continued to teach for some years after that. Much of his work looks forward to the 18th century, as for example the *Robert, 2nd Earl of Sunderland in antique costume*, which was painted in 1661 (Althorp, Earl Spencer). There are pictures by him in many of the churches and galleries of Rome, in the Royal Coll., and in Ancona, Berlin, Brussels, Cambridge (Fitzwm), Cassel, Chatsworth, Dresden, Dublin, Florence (Pitti), Greenville SC (Bob Jones University), Hanover, Leeds, Leningrad, Lille, London, Madrid, Munich, Naples, Paris, Stockholm, Toledo Ohio, Vaduz (Liechtenstein Coll.), Versailles, Vienna, and elsewhere.

MARC, Franz (1880–1916), was a German Expressionist painter, associated with MACKE and KANDINSKY in the BLAUE REITER. His chief subjects were animals, and his variants on the theme of the Blue Horse are perhaps his best known works. He met DELAUNAY in Paris in 1912 and his last works (1914) are more abstract. He was killed at Verdun. There is a good collection of his work in Munich (Städtische Gal.).

MARÉES, Hans von (1837–87), was a German landscape painter who went to Italy in 1864. In 1869 he visited Spain, France, and Holland with the writer on art, Konrad Fiedler, his future biographer. He served in the Franco-Prussian War of 1870–1, but was able to return to Italy in 1873 and began his most famous work, the frescoes in the Aquarium at Naples. He spent the rest of his life in Italy, and, like BÖCKLIN and FEUERBACH, he was essentially a German Romantic who longed for Italy: unlike LEIBL, he was untouched by the Realist movement and all that it implied. In spite of his interest in wall-painting and the success of his Naples frescoes he never succeeded in obtaining another monumental commission. The style of the frescoes is similar to that of his great French contemporary, PUVIS de Chavannes. There are oil paintings by Marées in Berlin, Hamburg, and Munich. *See also* HILDEBRAND.

MARGARITO(NE) of Arezzo, active about 1260–90 (*d.* 1293?), was one of the few Italian painters of the mid 13th century who are known to us from signed works, such as those in Arezzo, Siena, London (NG), and Washington. The London example was acquired in 1857 'to show the barbarous state into which art had sunk even in Italy previously to its revival' (under CIMABUE and GIOTTO).

MARIESCHI, Michele (1710 not 1696–1743), was a Venetian painter whose works have often been confused with those by other members of the same family. He was working in Saxony before 1735, and on his return to Venice was much influenced by CANALETTO; the vivacious quality of his own handling probably made him an influence on GUARDI. His early works seem mostly to be architectural CAPRICCI, but after his return from Germany the VEDUTE are much more accurate representations of Venice. He made a series of twenty-one etchings of views of Venice, published in 1741 as *Magnificentiores . . . Urbis Venetiarum Prospectus. . .* Paintings by him are in Bristol (the only signed one), Cambridge (Fitzwm), Dublin, London (NG and Guildhall), Philadelphia, Stockholm, Venice, and Vienna (Akad.).

MARIN, John (1870–1953), was an American painter, best-known for his semi-abstract watercolours, often of the sea. He began as an architect, but in 1905 he went to Paris, where he was influenced by WHISTLER. He returned to the US from Europe in 1911, and in 1913 he took part in the ARMORY SHOW. New York (Met. Mus.), Washington (Phillips), and many other American museums have works.

MARINETTI, Filippo (1876–1944), was an Italian poet and publicist closely associated with the FUTURIST movement, which he is said to have named. His career reached its apogee in friendship with Mussolini.

MARINI, Marino (b.1901), is one of the leading Italian sculptors, although he began as a painter and continues to produce paintings and graphic work. He was trained in Florence and Paris and travelled extensively before settling in Milan. His bronze and wood sculpture includes many versions of the horse-and-rider theme, all of which show his great interest in archaic Greek art. Most major European and American museums have examples.

MARINUS van Reymerswaele (active 1509?–after 1567?) was a painter of three themes, all more or less caricatural. He painted a number of straightforward S. Jeromes, all derived from Dürer's picture of 1521 (Lisbon) but stressing the crabbedness of scholarship. The other two themes are interdependent: two exceedingly ugly and covetous Tax Gatherers and a Banker and his wife (the banker counting his profits). The Banker is closely related to MASSYS' picture of the same subject, and it may be that the Tax Gatherers derive from Massys' borrowings from the caricatures of Leonardo da Vinci. There are about 30 versions of the Tax Gatherers (the best is in London, NG; another has the date 1552) and what nobody has so far explained is why so many people should want to own a picture of tax men (and excessively ugly ones at that) gloating over their imposts. There are also examples in the Royal Coll. and in Antwerp, Berlin, Ghent, Madrid, Munich, and Vienna.

MARMION, Simon (active 1449–d.89), was a painter and illuminator who worked in Amiens and Valenciennes. The most important painting attributed to him is the S. Bertin Altarpiece (c.1459: Berlin and London, NG); other paintings attributed to him are in London (NG), New York (Met. Mus.), Paris (Louvre), Philadelphia (Johnson), Rome (Gall. Naz.), and Strasbourg.

MARQUET, Albert (1875–1947), exhibited at the original FAUVE show in 1905, but never shared either the ideas or the style of the other participants. He developed into a good latterday Impressionist, specializing in simple landscapes and town views, executed with an undemanding technique, but with a nice perception of tonal values. He was a great friend of MATISSE.

MARSHALL, Benjamin (1768–1835), was a British sporting painter who travelled in Italy, but who was principally influenced by STUBBS, and, in his brushwork, Raeburn. In 1819 he was crippled in a coach smash. He also wrote on horse racing, which was almost exclusively the subject of his pictures. There are examples in the Royal Coll. and in Leicester, London (Tate), San Marino Cal., and Toronto.

MARTIN, John ('Mad') (1789–1854), was the most spectacularly melodramatic history painter of the early 19th century. He exhibited at the RA from 1811 and soon attained fame with his *Joshua commanding the Sun to stand still* (1816) and others in the next few years. He developed a type of enormous canvas, crowded with tiny figures set in fantastic architecture and beneath lowering skies that now seems merely Hollywood, but which seems to have influenced the French Romantics. He chose subjects like the *Destruction of Herculaneum* (1822: Manchester) or *The Great Day of His Wrath* (c. 1853: London, Tate), and the public taste soon faded, to be revived by the *Coronation of Queen Victoria* (1839: Tate). He also illustrated Milton's 'Paradise Lost' in 1827. The Balston Coll., now in London (V & A), is very large.

MARTINI, Simone (c. 1284–1344), was a Sienese painter, the pupil of DUCCIO, who developed the use of outline for the sake of linear rhythm as well as the sophisticated colour harmonies implicit in Duccio. He was also deeply influenced by the sculpture of Giovanni PISANO, and even more by French Gothic art. His first work was a large fresco of the *Maestà* (1315, reworked 1321) painted for the Town Hall of Siena as a counterpart to the huge *pala* by Duccio in the Cathedral. This shows the formative influence of Duccio on him, but there is already a perceptible Gothic influence in it which is much strengthened in his next work, the *S. Louis of Toulouse* (1317: Naples). At this date Naples was a French kingdom, ruled by Robert of Anjou, who sent for Simone and commissioned him to paint a new kind of picture: Robert's claim to the throne of Naples was not impeccable, and he therefore caused Simone to paint a large votive image of the newly canonized S. Louis of Toulouse (a member of the French Royal house) shown in the act of resigning his crown to Robert. From this time on, Simone's is essentially a Court art, refined and elegant, and much influenced by France. The type of *Madonna* evolved by Simone was of great importance in Sienese painting and may be seen in his Pisa polyptych (1320) and in several others. In 1328 Simone painted another fresco for the Town Hall, Siena, this time a commemorative equestrian portrait of the mercenary soldier Guidoriccio da Fogliano. It is one of the earliest of such commemorative images, and contains a vast panoramic landscape with the tents of the soldiers in the background. At some date not yet established Simone went to Assisi and painted a fresco cycle in S.

Francesco, of scenes from the life of S. Martin, which again show both the interest in French Gothic art and the sense of chivalric pomp that distinguish Simone. His best-known, and perhaps his finest, work is the *Annunciation* (1333: Florence, Uffizi) which was painted in collaboration with his brother-in-law Lippo Memmi (*d.*1357). Lippo often worked with him, but in this case they both signed the picture. It is perhaps the most splendid example of pure craftsmanship produced in Siena in the 14th century, with its elaborate tooling of the burnished and matt gold, but it is also an almost abstract essay in pure line and two-dimensional pattern, at the furthest possible remove from either Giotto or even their Sienese contemporary Ambrogio LORENZETTI. In 1340/1 Simone went to France. It seems that he went on official business, and not as a painter, to the Curia at Avignon, where the Papacy was then established, and in this Franco-Italian enclave he spent the rest of his life. There he painted the jewel-like *Christ returning to His Parents after disputing with the Doctors* (1342: Liverpool), a most unusual subject that probably once formed half of a diptych. In Avignon he met Petrarch and became friendly with him, illustrating a Virgil codex for him (Milan, Ambrosiana); he also painted frescoes in Notre Dame des Doms, of which the *Sinopie* remain. They are probably datable in 1341. His influence on French 14th-century painting is hard to assess, but a century later the Sienese (so Ghiberti informs us) regarded him as their greatest painter. There are works in Antwerp, Berlin, Birmingham (Gall. and Barber Inst.), Boston (Gardner Mus.), Cambridge (Fitzwm), Cambridge Mass. (Fogg), Leningrad, London (Courtauld Inst.), Naples, New Haven Conn. (Jarves Coll.), New York (Met. Mus.), Orvieto (Cath.), Ottawa, Paris (Louvre), Siena (S. Agostino), the Vatican, Washington (NG), and elsewhere.

MASACCIO (1401–probably 28) was born Tommaso di Ser Giovanni di Mone and nicknamed 'Masaccio' (Hulking Tom). He was the first and arguably the greatest of the succession of great masters in 15th-century Florence; certainly the greatest in that he achieved so much in a lifetime of 27 years. He is first recorded as a painter in 1422, when he entered the Guild in Florence, which disproves the tradition that he was MASOLINO's pupil, since Masolino did not register with the Guild (and therefore could not take pupils) until 1423. A recently-discovered altarpiece of 1422 may prove important in this connexion, but the attribution to Masaccio is still under discussion. The first major work by Masaccio for which documentary evidence exists is the Pisa Polyptych, painted for the Carmelite Church in Pisa in 1426, but now dismembered and largely lost. The central panel, of the *Madonna and Child*, is now in the NG, London, and shows that, at the age of 25, Masaccio had already developed his austere and heroic style in opposition to the INTERNATIONAL GOTHIC then being so successfully practised in Florence by GENTILE da Fabriano. This new style, in its realism, sobriety of gesture, narrative power, and the economy with which it creates its effects of space, light, and solidity of form, is akin to Giotto's, and is comparable among contemporaries only with the humanist and intellectual art then being developed by the much older DONATELLO in sculpture and Brunelleschi in architecture. For this reason Masaccio has always been regarded as one of the founders of modern painting. Between the end of 1425 and his death, probably at the end of 1428, Masaccio certainly painted a fresco of the *Trinity* in Sta Maria Novella, Florence, and his major surviving work, the frescoes in the Brancacci Chapel of the Carmelite Church in Florence (Sta Maria del Carmine). The Chapel was decorated with scenes from the Lives of the Apostles and may have been begun by Masolino in 1425, but a large part of the frescoes, including the earlier ones, perished in the 18th century. Those that survive are by three hands – a 15th-century source says that the Chapel was 'painted by three masters, all good but he (Masaccio) was marvellous' – and the puzzle is to sort out the shares. The parts by Filippino LIPPI are half a century later and easily distinguishable, and approximate agreement has now been reached over the remainder, it being generally accepted that the *Expulsion* on the entrance arch, the *Tribute Money*, parts of the *Raising of the Praetor's Son* and all *S. Peter enthroned, S. Peter's shadow healing the sick, S. Peter giving alms*, are by Masaccio, while the *Baptism of the Neophytes* is probably by him, but is sometimes contested. The remainder of the original commission is by Masolino. Again, Masaccio's style is fully realistic and uncompromisingly grand, which probably explains why these frescoes long served as an art school without enjoying general popularity. Indeed, much of later 15th-century painting flatly contradicts the principles enunciated in the Brancacci Chapel. Parts of the frescoes may still have been incomplete when Masaccio went to Rome and died there. The remaining parts of the Pisa Polyptych are in Naples, Pisa, Vienna, and Berlin. Other works by or attributed to him are in Berlin, Boston (Isabella Gardner Mus.), Florence (Uffizi and Horne Mus.), London (NG), Montemarciano, and Washington (NG).

MASO di Banco, active in the second quarter of the 14th century, was perhaps the greatest of Giotto's followers, and the only one to retain something of Giotto's amplitude of form; indeed, some of his figures are even more massive than Giotto's. The only work that can be attributed to him with certainty is the fresco cycle of *S. Sylvester and the Emperor Constantine* in Sta Croce, conveniently placed for comparison with Giotto. Other works are attributed to him – in Assisi, Berlin, Budapest, Edinburgh, Florence, and elsewhere – but it is now agreed that he is not identical with GIOTTINO, and a good many revisions will be necessary.

MASOLINO (*c.*1383/4–1447?) was not the master of MASACCIO, as Vasari thought, but rather his pupil for a short time, in spite of the great difference of age. Masolino may have worked under Ghiberti on the First Baptistry Doors (1403/7), and this would explain his normal INTERNATIONAL GOTHIC style. He entered the Guild of Painters in Florence in 1423 – there is nothing to explain what he was doing 1407–23 – and in the same year painted a *Madonna* (Bremen) which shows the influence of late Trecento art, and Lorenzo Monaco in particular. In 1427 he went to Hungary, but it is probable that he worked in the Brancacci Chapel in Sta Maria del Carmine in the interval; there he came under the influence of Masaccio to such an extent that it is not easy to distinguish them. He may also have worked in the Brancacci Chapel after Masaccio's death (1428) and before he went to Rome *c.*1430 to decorate a chapel in S. Clemente for Cardinal Branda Castiglione, for whom he later worked in Castiglione d'Olona, near Como, one of the frescoes being dated 1435: the frescoes in the Collegiata and the Baptistry are very markedly less Masacciesque than those in the Brancacci Chapel and it would seem therefore that Masolino reverted in his last years to the style he had practised as a young man. The two wings of *Saints* (London, NG), belonging to an altarpiece of which the most important panels are in Naples, are now generally thought to be one by Masolino and the other by Masaccio. There are other works in Detroit, Empoli, Munich, Naples, New York (Met. Mus.), Philadelphia (Johnson), Todi, the Vatican, and Washington (NG).

MASSES. In art criticism, the masses are the largest, simplest, and most fundamental shapes to which the component parts of a painting, a piece of sculpture, or a building can be reduced. To think (or see) in masses means the ability not to be distracted by unimportant detail and to concentrate on the forms which must be completely realized for a satisfactory aesthetic effect. Such an effect may be totally different from a naturalistic representation.

MASSYS (Matsys, Metsys), Quentin (1464/5–1530), was born at Louvain but became a Master in the Antwerp Guild in 1491. His earliest certain work is the *S. Anne Triptych* (1509: centre in Brussels, wings in the Liechtenstein Coll.), a large work painted in clear, pale, cool colour, with a subject – the Kinship of the Holy Family – traditional in the North. Many of his works introduce landscape backgrounds of fantastic wooded and rocky mountains, some of which may have been painted by PATENIER, and the type became common among Antwerp painters. His use of *contrapposto* and of florid architectural detail of a debased classical type suggest some knowledge of Italian art, and he also knew a version of Leonardo's *Madonna and Child with S. Anne* (Louvre). He may have visited Italy between 1514 and 1519. In the latter year he built himself a house in Antwerp with a frescoed façade and polychromed statue, which was visited by Dürer in 1520, although he failed to find Massys at home. He painted genre subjects such as the *Banker and his Wife* (1514: Louvre) which may have a recondite religious or moral significance, and is connected with other contemporary paintings of bankers, moneylenders, or tax gatherers (cf. MARINUS), and the *Ill-matched Pair*, with caricature types and an equivocal moral lesson. This is probably connected with Prodigal Son subjects and is the ancestor of the Flemish tavern scene picture. Besides his portraits of sitters seen against a landscape, Massys introduced a new type, derived from paintings of S. Jerome, of the scholar in his setting of desk, books, and papers, and used this form appropriately for his *Erasmus* (1517: Rome, Gall. Naz.) and his *Egidius* (Longford Castle Coll.), both of which look forward to portraits by van Orley and Holbein. There are works by him in Antwerp, Berlin, Brussels, Chicago, Detroit, Edinburgh, Frankfurt (Städel), Lisbon, London (NG), Lyons, Madrid (Prado), Munich, New York (Met. Mus.), Ottawa, Paris (Louvre, Jacquemart-André), Philadelphia (Johnson), Poznan, Vaduz (Liechtenstein Coll.), Venice (Doge's Pal.), Vienna, Worcester Mass., and Yale.

MASTER OF 1456 *see* FOUQUET.

MASTER OF THE AIX ANNUNCIATION. A triptych of the *Annunciation* and two *Prophets* was completed in 1445 and placed in the Église des Prêcheurs, Aix-en-Provence. The *Annunciation* is still there, but one of the wings is now in Brussels and the other is divided into two parts, one in Amsterdam (Rijksmus.) and the other in Rotterdam. The style of the altarpiece shows many points of contact with Flemish art, and others with the art of Naples; various identifications have been suggested, but it is likely that the painter was a Frenchman, and Jean Chapus, who lived in Aix and was working for King René of Anjou in 1437 and 1448, seems to fit the bill.

MASTER OF S. BARTHOLOMEW (active in the late 15th and early 16th centuries). A German painter whose name derives from an altarpiece formerly in S. Columba, Cologne, and now in Munich. Two other altarpieces by him are still in Cologne and probably date from *c.*1500, although the S. Bartholomew Altar itself is perhaps as late as 1510. The painter was probably a Cologne man, but his earliest works show the influence of the Netherlands, especially Roger van der WEYDEN and the school of Utrecht, so that it is sometimes suggested that he may have worked in Utrecht *c.*1470. This influence is seen in a *Virgin and Child with S. Anne*, now in Munich. His work is characterized by bright enamel-like colour; there are examples in Berlin, Brussels, London (NG and Courtauld Inst.), and Paris (Petit Pal. and Louvre: based on Roger van der Weyden's Escorial *Deposition*).

MASTER OF S. CECILIA. An unknown Italian painter active before 1304, influenced by GIOTTO, who painted the *S. Cecilia Altarpiece*

(Florence, Uffizi). The most important attribution to him is the beginning and end of the fresco cycle of S. Francis at Assisi. In recent years attempts have been made to attribute the whole cycle to him, an honour for which he seems unfitted.

MASTER OF THE DEATH OF THE VIRGIN. A painter, active 1507–37, who is named from two altarpieces of the *Death of the Virgin* in Cologne and Munich. He is often identified with JOOS van Cleve, and certainly he influenced BRUYN.

MASTER OF FLÉMALLE. A name given to the painter of some pictures in Frankfurt (Städel) which are (wrongly) supposed to have come from Flémalle. He is also supposed to have painted another fragment in Frankfurt, the *Mérode Altar* now in New York (Met. Mus.), the *Werl Altar* dated 1438 in the Prado, Madrid, pictures in the NG, London, and some other works. His style is slightly earlier than that of Jan van Eyck, but almost as revolutionary in its naturalism. An *Entombment* (private coll., London), thought to be his earliest work, is probably earlier than any surviving painting by Jan and seems to show a style not compatible with that of any other painter. Various attempts have been made to identify him, the most satisfactory being that which equates him with CAMPIN and the least satisfactory that which identifies him with Roger van der WEYDEN, whose style is certainly similar but more subtle – and there is evidence that Roger was Campin's pupil.

MASTER OF S. GILES (active *c.*1500) was a Flemish painter (or Flemish-trained painter) who worked in France. He is named after the two *Scenes from the Legend of S. Giles* in London (NG): two other panels, now in Washington (NG), have been connected with the S. Giles ones, but they seem to come from another altarpiece by the same hand. Other pictures attributed to him are in Berlin, Boston, Brussels, Chantilly (Musée Condé), and Paris (Louvre).

MASTER OF THE HOUSEBOOK (*Meister des Hausbuchs*) was a Rhenish or Dutch painter, draughtsman, and engraver active in the last quarter of the 15th century. He is named from a series of drawings in the so-called *Hausbuch* in Schloss Wolfegg; many of the drawings show scenes of everyday life and so do the engravings (about 90 are known) attributed to him. By far the best collection of the engravings is in Amsterdam Print Room, and he was therefore once known as the *Master of the Amsterdam Cabinet*. Because of this, and because he seems to fit into the Bosch-Bruegel tradition, he is often thought to have been Dutch and various identifications have been suggested: the latest is Erhard REUWICH, who worked on the Middle Rhine *c.*1480. A few paintings are also ascribed to him, including the *Pair of Lovers* (Gotha) and one in Frankfurt (Städel), but his work as an engraver was historically far more important.

MASTER OF THE LIFE OF MARY, Master of the Life of the Virgin,

Meister des Marienlebens (active *c.*1463/5–*c.*1480/90) was a Cologne painter whose name derives from a series of 8 panels of *Scenes from the Life of the Virgin*, formerly in S. Ursula, Cologne, and now divided between Munich (7) and the NG, London (1). The altarpiece is known to have been the gift of a Councillor who was active *c.*1460, while a *Crucifixion with Nicholas of Cusa as Donor* (Cues, Hospital church) seems to date from *c.*1465. The Master may have been trained in the Netherlands, since his style is based on Roger van der WEYDEN and, especially, BOUTS, with skinny figures, rather small in scale and lost among their surroundings. The Master of the Lyversberg Passion may be identical with the Master of the Life of Mary, while the Master of Werden is probably only an aspect of his studio.

MASTER OF THE LIFE OF THE VIRGIN *see* MASTER OF THE LIFE OF MARY.

MASTER OF THE LYVERSBERG PASSION. A German painter responsible for a Passion series (now in Cologne), which was at one time thought to be the work of the MASTER OF THE LIFE OF MARY. The relationship between the two masters is very close indeed, but is not necessarily that of identity.

MASTER OF MÉRODE *see* MASTER OF FLÉMALLE.

MASTER OF MOULINS (active *c.*1480–*c.*99) has been identified with PERRÉAL and a number of other painters including, most recently, Jean Prévost (active 1470–*d.*1504), a Lyons painter who collaborated with Perréal. The Master, one of the great French 15th-century painters, much influenced by Hugo van der Goes, takes his name from a triptych of the *Madonna and Child with Angels and Donors* in Moulins Cathedral datable *c.*1498/9. Other works attributed to him are in Autun (Mus.), Brussels, Chicago, Glasgow, London (NG, Wallace Coll.), Munich, and Paris (Louvre).

MASTER OF THE OSSERVANZA *see* SASSETTA.

MASTER OF OULTREMONT *see* MOSTAERT.

MASTER OF TŘEBOŇ *see* MASTER OF WITTINGAU.

MASTER OF THE VIRGO INTER VIRGINES. The Virgo Master was a Dutch painter active *c.*1470–*c.*1500 who was influenced by BOSCH and GEERTGEN and who ranks with them as an artist, although almost nothing is known about him. He was perhaps working in Delft 1490/95, where he seems to have influenced woodcut book-illustrations for which he may have made the designs. His name is derived from the *Madonna and Child with Four Female Saints* (*Virgo inter Virgines*) in Amsterdam (Rijksmus.). There are important pictures by him in Barnard Castle (Bowes Mus.), and Liverpool, and others in Berlin, Brussels, Chicago, Florence (Uffizi), Glasgow (Burrell Coll.), St Louis, Milan (Brera), New York (Met. Mus.), Philadelphia, Rotterdam, Vienna, and elsewhere.

MASTER OF WERDEN. The painter of a series of panels, in the NG,

London, which have now been reattributed to the Studio of the
MASTER OF THE LIFE OF MARY.

MASTER OF WITTINGAU (Master of the Třeboň Altarpiece). In the
NG of Prague there are three double-sided panels representing three
Passion scenes and three sets of Saints, from an altarpiece in a church
at Třeboň (Wittingau) in Czechoslovakia. They date from about 1390
and represent the next stage in Bohemian painting after Master
THEODORIC, being related to the SOFT STYLE. The Master may have
gone on working until c. 1420.

MATHIEU, Georges (b. 1922). French ABSTRACT IMPRESSIONIST
painter who began exhibiting in Paris in the late 1940s, in association
with HARTUNG, De KOONING, GORKY, POLLOCK, and others.

MATIÈRE (Fr. material). The matière of a picture is simply paint.

MATISSE, Henri (1869–1954), was the principal artist of the FAUVE
group. He was a pupil of the academician Bouguereau for a few
months in 1892, and from 1892 to 1897 was a pupil of Gustave
Moreau, in whose studio he met Rouault, Marquet, Manguin,
Camoin, and Piot. He copied in the Louvre, and was strongly
influenced by Impressionism, and his Dinner Table (La Desserte) of
1897 shows him working close to Bonnard and Vuillard. In 1901 he
first met Vlaminck in the company of Derain, whom he already knew.
He tried the Divisionist technique about 1899, but turned to Cézanne
by 1901–3, painting in strongly modelled form and dark tones to offset
the rather superficial quality of Signac's bright colour. The influence
of Signac was renewed in 1904 when Matisse stayed with him in the
South of France, and this renewed contact probably started the train
which led to the explosion of colour of the Fauve movement. This
came in 1905, but in the midst of the general abuse Matisse acquired
patrons in the Stein family who encouraged him, bought pictures and
encouraged other Americans to buy, and later the Russians Shchukin
and Morosov became his chief patrons. Exhibitions in Germany
followed and in 1908–10 Matisse (or, rather, PURRMANN) ran a
school which was thronged by American, German, and, above all,
Scandinavian pupils. By this time Picasso had appeared on the
scene, and after all the years of preparation for the leadership of
modern painting, Matisse found that the artistic centre of gravity had
shifted to CUBISM. In 1910 Matisse saw the exhibition of Near
Eastern art at Munich, and it is clear that this highly decorative and
brilliantly coloured art had a deep and lasting influence on him,
particularly in his development of flat patterns with arabesques,
flowered backgrounds, and in his use of brilliant and pure colours
either juxtaposed or separated only by thin white lines or contours
(anti-cernes). He travelled widely in Europe and North Africa (and
also visited America and Oceania), and in 1914 went to Nice for the
winter, to remain for most of the rest of his life on the Riviera, where

he painted the long series of Odalisque and still-life subjects which are his main *œuvre*. He had done a certain amount of sculpture from the start of his career, but it never assumed an importance equal to that of his painting; he also made several illustrated books, notably editions of Ronsard and Baudelaire, done at the end of the Second World War. His last major work was the decoration of the interior of the Chapel of Dominican nuns at Vence, and in his last years he used a mixture of cut-outs in coloured paper with gouache and crayons to overcome the handicaps of age and illness.

Matisse's works are to be found in nearly every museum of modern art throughout the world. The two largest collections are the Moscow collection, made up of paintings bought by Shchukin and Morosov, and that at the Barnes Foundation at Merion Pa, which contains, among other important works, the huge murals of the *Dance* done in 1932–3.

MATSYS *see* MASSYS.

MATTA (i.e. Roberto Sebastiano Matta Echaurren) (*b*. 1912) is a Chilean painter, now living in Paris, who began as an architect (1934) under Le Corbusier. From 1938 to 1947 he was a Surrealist, and is still a Freudian. He went to the US in 1939, where he met DUCHAMP. There are works by him in London (Tate) and New York (M of MA).

MATTEO di Giovanni (*c*. 1435–95), a Sienese painter, was a pupil of VECCHIETTA. In Borgo San Sepolcro he completed in 1465 the polyptych of which the central panel (*Baptism of Christ*, London NG) was by PIERO della Francesca. His linear and decorative style also shows the influence of POLLAIUOLO. There are works in Birmingham (Barber Inst.), London (NG), and Siena (Mus. and Cath.).

MATTOIR *see* ENGRAVING 2 (d).

MAULBERTSCH (Maulpertsch), Franz Anton (1724–96), was the major Viennese painter of the 18th century, becoming a member of the Academy in 1759 and Professor in 1770. There is no record of his having been to Italy, although it seems highly likely that he did so. Almost all his works are frescoes and altarpieces in Austrian, Hungarian, and Czech churches, which combine a certain Rembrandt influence with a very marked similarity to contemporary Venetian decorative painters such as PITTONI. There are sketches by him in Vienna (Barockmus.) but most of his works are still in the churches for which they were painted.

MAZO, Juan Bautista del (*c*. 1612/16–67), was the pupil of VELAZQUEZ, whose daughter he married in 1634. He had an appointment in the Royal Household by 1646 and succeeded to his father-in-law's position as Court Painter in 1661. His close relationship to Velazquez has led to the attribution to him of several pictures not considered good enough for Velazquez: his own style is not sufficiently distinguished to prevent this. There are very few certain works by him, but one is the *Queen Mariana* of 1666 (London, NG). The *Artist's Family* (Vienna) is almost certainly his, and there are other pictures in Madrid (Prado). A good example of the Velazquez-type portrait is the *Admiral Pulido Pareja* (London, NG) which is now attributed to Mazo.

MEDICI E SPEZIALI. The Florentine GUILD of Doctors and Apothecaries to which the painters belonged. This seems to have been on account of their using rare minerals like lapis lazuli, which were part of the druggist's stock-in-trade.

MEDINA, Sir John Baptist (*c.* 1655/60–1710), was a portrait painter of Spanish descent, born in Brussels, who worked in London – in the style of KNELLER – from 1686 until 1688/9 when he went to Edinburgh and introduced the Kneller style there with a stock of ready-painted figures requiring only the faces. He was knighted in 1706 and left a prosperous portrait business to his son. AIKMAN was his pupil. There are 31 portraits by him in the Royal College of Surgeons, Edinburgh, and others in Edinburgh (NPG), Glasgow, Florence (Pitti), and Providence RI.

MEDIUM. The liquid used to bind powdered colour to make paint. By extension, the various techniques of painting: thus, the oil medium is oil painting; powdered colour mixed to a thick consistency with oil, usually linseed. Other media are size (for distemper), egg yolk (for tempera), and gum arabic (for watercolour or pastel). In a more general sense it is possible to talk of pen-and-ink or pencil as media.

MEISSONIER, Jean-Louis-Ernest (1815–91), belonged to the circle of Mme Sabatier which included Baudelaire and Sir Richard Wallace (hence the 16 Meissoniers in the Wallace Collection). He was a painter of historical genre subjects, treated with Hollywood 'historical correctness', and most of his small pictures closely resemble 17th century Dutch works, not only in the minuteness of handling. His larger canvases are less microscopic and now have a Wardour Street appearance. He was the first artist to receive the Grand Cross of the Legion of Honour, but this may have had something to do with his choice of Napoleonic subjects. The Louvre has 39 of his pictures, including the *Campagne de France*, 1814 and the *Siege of Paris*, 1870. Others are in Bordeaux, Boston, Brussels, Chantilly and New York (Met. Mus.).

MELOZZO da Forlì (1438–94) was famous in the 16th century as the inventor of extreme foreshortening – SOTTO IN SÙ. Most of his works exist in such fragmentary condition that it is impossible to be sure if this is correct, but it is clear that he was connected with PIERO della Francesca. His *Platina appointed Vatican Librarian* (1477: Vatican) shows his knowledge of perspective and a certain link with Piero. Some fragments of an important fresco are in the Vatican, but his dome (1493/4) in S. Biagio, Forlì, was destroyed 1939/45. There are frescoes at Loreto.

MEMLINC (Memling), Hans (c. 1430/40–94), was born in Seligenstadt, near Frankfurt-am-Main, but was traditionally – and very probably – a pupil of Roger van der WEYDEN. His art is purely Netherlandish, and he seems to have spent his life in Bruges, where he became a citizen in 1465 and was one of the largest taxpayers by 1480. He painted calm and devotional pictures, full of the gentle piety which is one aspect of the later Middle Ages, and also some fine portraits, such as the *Diptych of Martin van Nieuwenhove* (1487: Bruges, Hospital Mus.), which show a type of half-length that may have been known to Italians such as Perugino or even Giovanni Bellini. (A portrait in Venice was for long attributed to ANTONELLO da Messina.) His religious pictures add nothing to what he took from the styles of Roger van der Weyden and Dieric BOUTS. The *Donne Triptych* (formerly Chatsworth, now London, NG) was for long believed to date from 1469, but is more probably of 1477: his earliest dated work is of 1472 (Ottawa), but a picture in Turin, painted for the Portinari, Hugo van der GOES's patrons, may date from c. 1470, and a *Last Judgement*, also painted for an Italian in Bruges, was captured at sea in 1473. It is now in Danzig (Gdansk). The *Passion Altar* in Lübeck was formerly dated 1491 on the frame. There are several dated works in Bruges (Hospital Mus., including the *Shrine of S. Ursula*, consecrated 1489, and Mus.); other works are in the Royal Collection and Antwerp, Berlin, Boston, Brussels, Chicago, Cincinnati, Cleveland Ohio, Cologne, Copenhagen, Florence (Uffizi), Frankfurt (Städel), Granada (Capilla Real), The Hague, Lisbon, London (NG, Wallace Coll.), Madrid (Prado), Melbourne, Montreal, Munich, New York (Met. Mus.), Paris (Louvre, Jacquemart-André), Philadelphia (Johnson), Toledo, Turin, Vicenza, Vienna (K-H Mus. and Akad.), and Washington (NG).

MENGS, Anton Raffael (1728–79), the most celebrated exponent of NEOCLASSICISM, was the son of the Dresden Court Painter who named him Anton (after Correggio) and Raffael (= Raphael) and brought him up with excessive severity to be a great painter. The boy was taken to Rome in 1741 and soon developed into something of a prodigy, specializing in pastel portraits. He was made Court Painter at Dresden in 1745, but his real career began in 1755, when he met WINCKELMANN, who praised him highly and whose theories Mengs adopted in return. He wrote a treatise on Beauty in Painting (published in 1762), which was apparently borrowed by an Englishman named Daniel Webb who published it as his own in 1760, when it had a considerable success. Mengs's first major work in Rome was the ceiling of S. Eusebio (1757–8), which cannot be called Neoclassical, but after this he went to see the antiquities then being excavated at Herculaneum, drew them, and returned to Rome to paint his best-known work, the *Parnassus* (1761: Rome, Villa

Albani), which breaks completely with the Baroque tradition of illusionism and treats a ceiling as if it were a relief, composed from drawings after the Antique, and seen orthogonally – i.e. as if it were at the spectator's eye-level, and not SOTTO IN SÙ. In 1761 he went to Spain as Court Painter and began decorating the Royal Palaces; when TIEPOLO arrived he found Mengs formidably entrenched, but Mengs's ceilings are markedly less Neoclassic in face of the competition from Tiepolo. In 1771 he returned to Italy and worked in the Vatican 1772–3. He went back to Spain 1773–7 and died in Rome. He had met VIEN in Rome, and like him, he was not really more than a precursor for the full Neoclassicism of DAVID, who arrived in Rome in 1775. Mengs was a fine portrait painter, and in this he was close in style to his principal rival, BATONI. There are works by him in Dresden and in Cardiff, Chicago, Liverpool, London (NPG, Wellington Mus.), Madrid (Prado), Manchester, Milan, Naples, Oxford (All Souls College), Paris (Louvre), and Vienna.

MENZEL, Adolf (1815–1905), was one of the leading German painters of the 19th century. He was trained in Berlin and took over his father's business as a lithographer in 1832, thus beginning a long career as an illustrator. Perhaps his most important graphic works are the drawings for the Life of Frederick the Great (1840–42), which were admired by Degas. In 1839 he saw some pictures by Constable in Berlin and in the 1840s and 50s he made a series of paintings which are very free in handling and seem to anticipate Impressionism, although later he rejected the theory. There are pictures by him in many German museums and in London (Tate).

MERYON, Charles (1821–68), ranks with Piranesi as the greatest of architectural etchers. He was the illegitimate son of an English doctor and a dancer at the Opéra and began his career in the French Navy, spending 1842–6 in the South Pacific. There are some drawings of exotic scenes and ships, but his reputation rests on the great series of views of Paris, described by Victor Hugo as 'visions', which he began c.1850. The series ranges from straightforward vedute through Romantic horror (the Gargoyle of Notre-Dame, the Morgue) to uncomfortable fantasies like the Ministry of Marine with flying Devils. The series was not popular, and Meryon was very difficult in his personal character: he spent 1858–9 in an asylum and also the last two years of his life, believing himself to be Christ. All his etchings date from 1849 to 1866. He also drew Dr Gachet, later to befriend van Gogh in his madness.

MERZ see SCHWITTERS.

MEŠTROVIČ, Ivan (1883–1962), was the greatest Yugoslav sculptor. He was the son of Dalmatian peasants and began as a woodcarver, later serving an apprenticeship to a mason. He studied in Vienna until 1904 and his early works, reflecting the Yugoslav patriotic movement, soon brought him fame. The freedom of his handling gave his work a certain kinship to that of RODIN. He went to America in 1947 and died there. There are examples of his religious works and also of his portraiture in London (Tate), and others in American museums, Belgrade, and in Zagreb.

METSU, Gabriel (1629–67), was a Dutch painter, born in Leyden but mainly active in Amsterdam, of interiors and genre subjects, representing nice, clean, and well-behaved people. He also painted a few portraits, religious subjects and perhaps some still-life. He was probably a pupil of DOU and was slightly influenced by Rembrandt, but on the whole he closely resembles Ter Borch and de Hooch and his works can be confused with theirs. In his best works, such as the *Sick Child* (Amsterdam, Rijksmus.), he approaches Vermeer. There are works by him in the Royal Coll. and in Aix, Amsterdam, Berlin, Boston, Brussels, Cape Town, Cheltenham, Dresden, Florence (Uffizi), The Hague, Leningrad, London (NG, Wallace Coll.), Montpellier, Munich, New York (Met. Mus.), Oxford, Paris (Louvre), Rotterdam, Stockholm, Venice, Vienna (Akad., K-H Mus.) and Washington (NG).

METZINGER, Jean (1883–1956), became a Cubist painter and, with GLEIZES, published in 1912 'Du Cubisme', the first book on the movement (English edition, 1913). He used the flat-pattern type of Cubism in rather bright colour. There is an example in London (Tate) and several in Paris (Mus. d'Art Moderne).

MEZZO-RILIEVO *see* RELIEF.

MEZZOTINT *see* ENGRAVING.

MICHEL, Georges (1763–1843), was employed by the Louvre on the cleaning and restoration of, principally, Dutch pictures, and the influence of Dutch 17th-century landscapes is clearly visible in his own works. He rarely moved away from his native Paris, and declared that no painter needs more than four square miles in which to find all the subjects he desires. Michel's simple pictures of muddy lanes, stormy skies, and unprettified fields and heaths are probably late works; they presage the landscape based on the observation of nature alone, exploited by the BARBIZON School, and his concentration on tone rather than colour links him with COROT. There are works in Besançon, Berwick-on-Tweed, Cambridge (Fitzwm), Edinburgh, Glasgow, Hanover, Leningrad, London (NG and V & A), Paris (Louvre), Strasbourg, and elsewhere.

MICHELANGELO Buonarroti (1475–1564) was born at Caprese, in Florentine territory, where his father was resident magistrate. A few weeks after Michelangelo's birth the family returned to Florence, and, in 1488, after overcoming parental opposition he was formally apprenticed to Domenico GHIRLANDAIO for a term of three years. Later in life Michelangelo tried to suppress this fact, probably to make it seem that he had never had an ordinary workshop training, for it was he more than anyone else who introduced the idea of the 'Fine' Arts having no connexion with the craft which painting had always previously been. In fact his stay in the Ghirlandaio shop must have been very short, for it was probably later in the same year that he was transferred to the School set up in the Medici Garden under the direct patronage of Lorenzo de' Medici, 'Il Magnifico', and supervised by BERTOLDO; nevertheless, it must have been Ghirlandaio who taught him the elements of fresco technique, and it was probably also in that shop that he made his drawings after the great Florentine masters of the past (copies after Giotto and Masaccio; now in the Louvre, in Munich, and in Vienna). In 1492 his patron Lorenzo de' Medici died. The next few years were marked by the expulsion of the Medici and the gloomy Theocracy set up under Savonarola, but Michelangelo avoided the worst of the crises by going to Bologna, and, in 1496, to Rome. There he carved the first of his major works, the *Bacchus* (Florence, Bargello) and the St Peter's *Pietà*, which was completed at the turn of the century. It is highly finished and shows that he had already mastered anatomy and the disposition of drapery, but above all it shows that he had solved the problem presented by the representation of a full-grown man stretched out nearly horizontally on the lap of a woman, the whole being contained in a pyramidal shape: in this it is the consummation of everything the sculptors of the 15th century had striven to attain. The *Pietà* made his name and he returned to Florence in 1501 as a famous sculptor, remaining there until 1505. During these years he was extremely active, carving the gigantic *David* (1501–4: now in the Accad.), the *Bruges Madonna* (Bruges, Notre-Dame) and beginning the series of the *Twelve Apostles* for the Cathedral which was commissioned in 1503 but never completed (the *S. Matthew* now in the Accad. is the only one which was even sketched in). At about this time he also painted the *Doni Tondo* (Florence, Uffizi). After the completion of the *David* in 1504 he began work on the cartoon for a huge fresco in the Council Hall of the new Florentine Republic, as a pendant to the one already commissioned from Leonardo da Vinci. Both remained unfinished and the grandiose project of employing the two greatest living artists on the decoration of the Town Hall of their native city came to nothing. Of Michelangelo's fresco, which was to represent an incident in the Pisan War, we now have a few studies by him and copies of the only fragment of the whole which was actually begun as a full-scale cartoon (the best copy is the painting in Lord Leicester's Coll., Holkham, Norfolk). This cartoon, which is known as the *Bathers*, was for many years the resort of every young artist in Florence, and, by its exclusive stress on the nude human body as a sufficient vehicle for the expression of all emotions which the painter can depict, had an enormous influence on the subsequent development of Italian art – especially MANNERISM – and therefore on European art as a whole. This influence is more readily detectable in his next major work, the ceiling of the Sistine Chapel. In fact, however, the *Battle of Cascina* was left incomplete because the Signoria of Florence found it expedient to comply with a request from the masterful Pope Julius II, who was anxious to have a fitting tomb made in his lifetime. The Julius Monument was, in Michelangelo's own view, the Tragedy of the Tomb. This was partly because Michelangelo and Julius had the same ardent temperament – they admired each other deeply – and very soon quarrelled, and partly because, after the death of Julius in 1513, Michelangelo was under constant pressure from Popes and Princes to abandon his contractual obligations and work for them while equally under pressure from the heirs of Julius, who at one time went so far as to accuse him of embezzlement. The original project was for a vast free-standing Tomb with forty figures but this was substantially reduced in the second contract (1513), drawn up after Julius's death; under this contract the *Moses*, which is the major figure on the extant Tomb, was prepared as a subsidiary figure. Two others, the *Slaves* in the Louvre, were made under this contract but were subsequently abandoned. The third contract (1516) was followed by a fourth (1532) and a fifth and final one in 1542, under the terms of which the present miserably mutilated version of the original conception was carried out by assistants, under Michelangelo's supervision, in S. Pietro in Vincoli (Julius II's titular church) in 1545. Michelangelo was then 70 and had spent nearly 40 years on the Tomb.

Meanwhile, the original quarrel of 1506 with Julius was made up and Michelangelo executed a colossal bronze statue of the Pope as an admonition to the recently conquered Bolognese (who destroyed it as soon as they could, in 1511). In 1508, back in Rome, he began his most important work, the ceiling of the Sistine Chapel in the Vatican for Julius, who, as usual, was impatient to see it finished. Dissatisfied with the normal working methods and with the abilities of the assistants he had engaged, Michelangelo determined to execute the whole of this vast area virtually alone. Working under appalling difficulties (amusingly described in one of his own sonnets), most of the time lying down and never able to get far enough away from the ceiling to be able to see what he was doing, he completed the first half (the part nearer to the door) in 1510. There followed a longish break, while new scaffolding was prepared. The whole enormous undertaking was completed in 1512, Michelangelo being by then so practised that he was able to execute the second half much more rapidly and freely. It was at once recognized as a supreme work of art, even at the moment when Raphael was also at work in the Vatican

Stanze. From then on Michelangelo was universally regarded as the greatest living artist, although he was then only 37 and this was in the lifetimes of Leonardo and Raphael (who was even younger). From this moment, too, dates the idea of the artist as in some sense a super-human being, set apart from ordinary men, and for the first time it was possible to use the phrase *il divino Michelangelo* without seeming merely blasphemous.

The Sistine Ceiling is a shallow barrel vault divided up by painted architecture into a series of alternating large and small panels which appear to be open to the sky. These are the Histories. Each of the smaller panels is surrounded by four figures of nude youths – the Slaves, or *Ignudi* – who are represented as seated on the architectural frame and who are not of the same order of reality as the figures in the Histories, since their system of perspective is different. Below them are the Prophets and Sibyls, and still lower, the figures of the Ancestors of Christ. The whole ceiling completes the chapel decoration by representing life on earth before the Law: on the walls are frescoes, painted in 1481–2, representing the Life of Moses (i.e. the Old Dispensation) and the Life of Christ (the New Dispensation). The Histories begin over the altar and work away from it (though they were painted in the reverse direction): the first scene represents God alone, in the Primal Act of Creation, and the story continues through the rest of the Creation to the Fall, the Flood, and the Drunkenness of Noah, representing the human soul at its furthest from God. The whole conception owes much to the Neoplatonist philosophy current in Michelangelo's youth in Florence, perhaps most in the idea of the *Ignudi*, perfect human beauty, on the level immediately below the Divine story. Below them come the Old Testament Prophets and the Seers of the ancient world who foretold the coming of Christ; while the four corners have scenes from the Old Testament representing Salvation. The Prophet Jonah is above the altar, since his three days in the whale were held to prefigure the Resurrection. On the lowest and darkest parts – and very freely paint-ed – are the human families who were the Ancestors of Christ. There can be no doubt that the splendour of this conception and the size of the task distracted Michelangelo from the Tomb, but he at once returned to it as soon as the ceiling was finished, from 1513 to 1516, when he returned to Florence to work for the Medici.

His new master was Pope Leo X, the younger son of Lorenzo de' Medici, who had known Michelangelo from boyhood and who now commissioned him to complete the façade of S. Lorenzo, the family church in Florence. Michelangelo wasted four years on this and it came to nothing. In 1520 he began planning the Medici Chapel, a funerary chapel in honour of four of the Medici – two of them by no means the most glorious of their family. The chapel is

attached to S. Lorenzo. Leo X died in 1521 and it was not until after
the accession of another Medici Pope, Clement VII, in 1523 that this
project was resumed. Work began in earnest in 1524 and at the same
time he was commissioned to design the Laurenziana Library in the
cloister of the same church. Both these buildings are turning-points
in architectural history, but the sculptural decoration of the chapel
(an integral part of the architecture) was never completed, although
the figures of Giuliano and Lorenzo de' Medici set over their tombs,
above symbols of Time and Mortality – *Day* and *Night*, *Dawn* and
Evening – eternally symbolize the Active and the Contemplative Life
and are among his finest creations. The unfinished *Madonna* was
meant as the focal point of the chapel. In 1527 the Medici were again
expelled from Florence, and Michelangelo, who was politically a
Republican in spite of his close ties with the Medici, took an active
part in the defence of Florence up to the capitulation in 1530, although
in a moment of panic he had fled in 1529. After the reinstatement of
the Medici he was pardoned and set to work once more on the Chapel
which was to glorify them until, in 1534, he left Florence and settled
in Rome for the 30 years remaining to him. He was at once commissioned to paint his next great work, the *Last Judgement* on the
altar wall of the Sistine Chapel, which affords the strongest possible
contrast with his own Ceiling. He began work on it in 1536. In the
interval there had been the Sack of Rome and the Reformation, and
the confident humanism and Christian Neoplatonism of the Ceiling
has curdled into the personal pessimism and despondency of the
Judgement. The very choice of subject is indicative of the new mood,
as is the curious fact that the mouth of Hell gapes over the altar
itself. It was unveiled in 1541 and caused a sensation equalled only
by his own work of 30 years earlier. Most of the ideas of Mannerism
are traceable implicitly or explicitly in the *Judgement* and, more than
ever, it served to imprint the idea that the scope of painting is strictly
limited to the exploitation of the nude, preferably in foreshortened –
and therefore difficult – poses. Paul III, who had commissioned the
Judgement, immediately commissioned two more frescoes for his own
chapel, the Cappella Paolina; these were begun in 1542 and completed
in 1550. They represent the *Conversion of S. Paul* and the *Crucifixion
of S. Peter*. Michelangelo was now 75 years old, but since 1546 he
had been increasingly active as an architect; in particular, he was
Chief Architect to S. Peter's and was doing more there than had been
done for 30 years. This was the greatest architectural undertaking in
Christendom, and Michelangelo did it, as he did all his late works,
solely for the glory of God. In his last years he made a number
of drawings of the Crucifixion, wrote much of his finest poetry,
and carved the *Pietà* (now in Florence Cathedral) which was
originally intended for his own tomb, as well as the nearly abstract

Rondanini Pietà (Milan, Castello) charged with emotional intensity which contemporaries recognized as Michelangelo's *terribilità*, and in which the very forms of the Dead Christ actually merge with those of His Mother. He was working on this *Pietà* within a few days of his death, in his 89th year, on 18 February 1564. There is a whole world of difference between it and the 'beautiful' *St Peter's Pietà*, carved some 65 years earlier. Unlike any previous artist, Michelangelo was the subject of two biographies in his own lifetime. The first of these was by VASARI, who concluded the first (1550) edition of his 'Vite' with the Life of one living artist, Michelangelo. In 1553 there appeared a 'Life of Michelangelo' by his pupil Ascanio Condivi (there is an English translation by C. Holroyd 1903); this is really almost an Autobiography, promoted by Michelangelo to correct some errors of Vasari and to shift the emphasis in what Michelangelo regarded as a more desirable direction. Vasari, however, became more and more friendly with Michelangelo and was also his most devoted and articulate admirer, so that the very long Life which appears in Vasari's second edition (1568), after Michelangelo's death, gives us the most complete biography of any artist up to that time and is a trustworthy guide to the feelings of contemporaries about the man who can lay claim to be the greatest sculptor, painter, and draughtsman that has ever lived, as well as one of the greatest of architects and poets. He is the archetype of genius.

Apart from the works mentioned above there are others in Florence (Accad., Bargello, Casa Buonarroti – the house of his family, which contains relics of him – and Pal. della Signoria) and in Bologna (S. Domenico), London (NG and RA), and Rome (Sta Maria sopra Minerva). There are also about 500 drawings by him, the majority of which are in the Royal Coll., Florence (Uffizi and Casa Buonarroti), London (BM), Oxford, and Paris.

MICHELOZZO Michelozzi (1396–1472), though most famous as an architect, was the collaborator of Ghiberti and DONATELLO. He worked with Ghiberti from *c.* 1417 on his bronze Doors and was in partnership with Donatello 1423–38, during which time he was mainly responsible for the architecture and the decorative sculpture in their joint works. During 1427 the partners were engaged on three major commissions, the Monuments for Antipope John XXIII (Florence, Baptistry), Cardinal Brancacci (Naples, S. Angelo a Nilo), and Bartolommeo Aragazzi. Most of the sculpture on the Aragazzi Monument was Michelozzo's, and pieces of it survive in Montepulciano and in the V & A, London. He also made the *Baptist* for the Silver Altar (1452: Florence, Cath. Mus.).

MIEREVELD, Michiel Jansz.(1567–1641), was a prolific portrait painter, who was born and died in Delft, but was in The Hague in 1625 and became Painter to the Princes of Orange. His portraits are mostly small in size, often busts only, and always sober in handling. There are examples in Amsterdam (Rijksmus.), Boston, Delft, The Hague, London (NG, NPG, Wallace Coll.), Manchester, New York (Met. Mus.), Rotterdam, and elsewhere.

MIGNARD, Pierre (1612–95), was the rival of LEBRUN but an exponent of the same Academic theories. Like Lebrun he was a pupil of VOUET but he went to Rome in 1636 and remained there until 1657, forming his style on the approved models of the Carracci, Domenichino, and Poussin. He returned to Paris on the orders of Louis XIV and decorated the dome of the Val-de-Grâce (1663), but his principal importance was as portrait painter to the Court. He revived the earlier Italian type of allegorical portrait, and a good example is the *Marquise de Seignelay as Thetis* (1691: London, NG). He was strongly opposed to the *Académie royale* and, in spite of his own stylistic origins, championed the Venetian or 'colourist' school (*see* RUBÉNISME); this, however, was probably only to oppose Lebrun. When Lebrun died in 1690 Mignard was at once made *premier peintre*, and, on the King's orders, the Academy had, in one sitting, to appoint Mignard Associate, Member, Rector, Director, and Chancellor of the body he had so long opposed. There are pictures by him in the Royal Coll., London (NPG), and many French museums.

MILLAIS, Sir John Everett (1829–96), was in the RA Schools in 1840 – an infant prodigy. In 1848, he, HUNT, and ROSSETTI founded the PRB, and in 1853 he was elected an ARA. In 1854 he married Ruskin's former wife, and his friendship with Ruskin was broken off; Millais developed into a fashionable and technically brilliant academic painter of portraits, costume history, and genre pieces, forsaking his original PRB theories, and went on to become RA, President of the RA, and a baronet.

There are works in Cambridge (Fitzwm), Birmingham, Liverpool, London (Tate, NPG, Guildhall), Manchester, and Oxford.

MILLES, Carl (1875–1955). Probably the greatest of Swedish artists, Milles was one of the most famous sculptors since Rodin, by whom he was much influenced at the beginning of his career. Milles started to emigrate to Chile in 1897, but got no further than Paris, where he stayed for eight years. His strong feeling for architecture distinguishes him from Rodin, and most of his best works are fountains, in which the figures must be seen against the water and sky as part of an architectural whole. Much of his best work is in the USA where he soon became famous. There is a fountain by him in Kansas City, his last work, and another forms part of the Metropolitan Mus., New York.

MILLET, Jean François, called Francisque (1642–79), worked in

Paris from 1659, painting landscapes in the style of Gaspar POUSSIN. He had relatives of the same name, and it is not clear what is by him: a good example of what is usually associated with his name is in London (NG). Three etchings are now attributed to him.

MILLET, Jean François (1814–75), was the son of a peasant. He was trained under a local painter at Cherbourg and then in Paris (1837) under Delaroche. His earliest works are pastiches of the pastorals of the 18th century and rather erotic nudes, but he also painted portraits for a time. The influence of DAUMIER seems to have been decisive, and in 1848 he exhibited at the Salon a peasant subject, *The Winnower* (destroyed: two versions are in Paris, Louvre). From *c.* 1850 his choice of subject-matter led to accusations of Socialism (e.g. *The Sower*, Salon of 1850). In 1849 he moved to BARBIZON and remained there for the rest of his life, painting scenes of peasants and their labours and also some ordinary landscapes and marines. The *Angelus* (1857–9: Louvre) shows him with an unusually sentimental approach. His works are particularly well represented in Boston, and in America generally. There are also works in several French museums and in Cardiff, Edinburgh, Glasgow, London (NG, V & A), and Vienna.

MINIATURE. A painting in little, usually a portrait, executed in gouache or watercolour. The 16th-century type of miniature, as exemplified in the work of HILLIARD or OLIVER, was normally executed in body colour on playing cards or on vellum, the material used by the medieval illuminator. This type of portrait, with its allegories and symbolism, is a direct descendant of manuscript illumination. In the hands of men like COOPER, in the 17th century the portrait miniature became more closely allied to contemporary oil painting (some miniatures were actually executed in oil, usually on metal). In the 18th century the whole character of miniature painting was changed by the introduction of ivory as a ground and support; this could be left as a white ground and was most effective in conjunction with transparent watercolour. COSWAY used this technique.

MINO da Fiesole (1429–84) was a Florentine sculptor who was traditionally a pupil of his contemporary DESIDERIO da Settignano, but was in Rome by 1454, where he did several works for churches. His principal Tombs are those in Fiesole and Florence, particularly the Tomb of Count Ugo in the Badia, Florence, of 1469–81: this shows both the delicacy and virtuosity of his marble carving and also the influence of the Antique on him. He also made a number of strongly characterized busts, the earliest dated portrait bust of the Renaissance being his *Piero de' Medici* (Florence, Bargello) of 1453, and one of the best being that of Niccolò Strozzi (1454; Berlin). There are works by him in Florence (Bargello), London (V & A and Courtauld Inst.), Paris (Louvre), and Washington (NG).

MIRÒ, Joan (*b.* 1893), is a Surrealist painter of Spanish origin who lived for some time in the US. In 1925 he took part in the First Surrealist Exhibition, and, with DALI, was recognized as the leading Spanish Surrealist. His work has tended to become abstract, although he says: 'For me a form is never something abstract; it is always a sign of something. It is always a man, a bird, or something else. For me painting is never form for form's sake'. He designed the ballet 'Jeux d'Enfants' in 1932. There are works in several US museums, London (Tate), Paris (Mus. d'Art Moderne), and elsewhere.

MISERICORDIA, MADONNA DELLA (Ital. Madonna of Pity). A representation of the Madonna standing erect and sheltering under her outspread mantle a number of people, usually members of a *Confraternità della Misericordia* or other charitable organization.

MIXED METHOD. Oil glazes over TEMPERA underpainting.

MOBILE. A form of sculpture invented in 1932 by CALDER, and named by DUCHAMP. Essentially a mobile consists of a series of shapes cut from wood or sheet metal and connected by wires or rods of metal so that a gentle touch will cause the whole to revolve like a planetarium, giving an ever-changing sequence of planes, solids, and colours in three-dimensional movement. The interior decoration of the 1950s and 1960s has been much affected by coloured shapes linked with wire.

MOCHI, Francesco (1580–1654), was an Italian sculptor whose *Annunciation* group in Orvieto Cathedral, finished in 1609, has been called the first piece of Baroque sculpture. He made two equestrian statues in Piacenza, but his best-known work is the *S. Veronica* in S. Peter's (1629–40: *see* BOLGI).

MODELLING. (i) The three-dimensional representation of forms, by means of some plastic material, usually modelling clay. The opposite of carving. *See* SCULPTURE. (ii) The representation of three-dimensional forms on a two-dimensional surface, in such a way that they appear solid. Thus it is usual to speak of the modelling of a hand or figure, meaning the apparent solidity of it, or the painter's comprehension of the form.

MODELLO, MODELLETTO. Italian words used to describe a small version of a large picture, not strictly speaking a preliminary sketch, which was shown to the person or body commissioning the large work for approval before the final design was put in hand. Many such small versions, often quite highly finished, still exist, e.g. by TIEPOLO. Most *modelli* are in oil paint or a combination of chalk, ink and paint such as BAROCCI's *Madonna of the Rosary* (Oxford, Ashmolean). A very beautiful chalk drawing by Camillo Procaccini (NY) shows a cut-out figure pasted over another and obviously introduced as a modification of the original design. *See also* BOZZETTO.

MODERSOHN-BECKER, Paula (1876–1907), was the most important German woman artist of her day and one of the main precursors of

EXPRESSIONISM. She was born in Dresden and trained in Berlin (1896–8) before settling in the artists' colony of Worpswede, near Bremen. She went to Paris in 1900 and again in 1903, 1905, and 1906: these visits brought her under the influence of Gauguin and the Fauves (who exhibited in 1905). The simplification of form and colour and the stress on line were introduced by her into Germany, making her a link with the development of the BLAUE REITER and BRÜCKE groups. There are several works in Bremen and in other German museums. She was a friend of the poet Rainer Maria Rilke, who wrote a biography of her, and her portrait of him is in a private collection.

MODIGLIANI, Amedeo (1884–1920), was known as 'Modi' for short, from which by natural corruption the French referred to him as *un peintre maudit* – and those who were like him were equally accursed. He was born in Leghorn of a distinguished Italian-Jewish family and had his first training in Italy before going to Paris in 1906. He spent the rest of his life there, working at first in a manner influenced by Toulouse-Lautrec, but his *Cellist* of 1910 won him recognition and shows that his real style was based on African sculpture, Cézanne, and Picasso and, above all, his Italian heritage. He was a superb draughtsman, and all his work contains echoes of Botticelli, of Sienese Trecento painters, and of some of the Mannerists, so that he is truly the greatest Italian artist of the 20th century, and not a French painter at all. He was handsome, amorous, and addicted to drink and drugs. He said, 'I am going to drink myself dead', and he did. There are paintings or sculpture by him in Buffalo, Chicago, London (Tate, V&A, Courtauld Inst.), New York (M of MA), Paris (Mus. d'Art Moderne), Philadelphia, São Paulo, Washington (Phillips), and elsewhere.

MOHOLY-NAGY, László (1895–1946), was a Hungarian law-student who, after the First World War, studied art in Berlin and by 1923 was teaching at the BAUHAUS. In 1928 he went to Berlin. He emigrated to Amsterdam in 1934, lived in London 1935–7, and then settled in Chicago, where he was head of the New Bauhaus (later called the Institute of Design) 1937–9. His greatest importance was as a teacher, writer, and experimenter, especially with new materials, such as plexiglass, and he also used semi-industrial techniques. His constructions, called Space Modulators, have interchangeable elements. As early as 1919 he came under the influence of MALEVICH, and in the early 1920s he was associated with SUPREMATISM, CONSTRUCTIVISM, De STIJL, and DADA. At the Bauhaus he edited the Bauhausbücher and he also did much film and stage design, including the sets for H. G. Wells's 'Shape of Things to Come' in London; the last book he published in his lifetime was called 'The New Vision'. There are works by him in Cologne, Harvard University, and New York (Guggenheim).

MOLENAER, Jan Miensz. (c.1609/10–68), was a Haarlem genre painter, active from 1629, who married Judith LEYSTER in 1636. He spent his time in Haarlem and Amsterdam and his earlier works, like those of his wife, are strongly influenced by HALS. The later pictures are more like the genre scenes of A. van OSTADE. There are works by him in Amsterdam, Berlin, Boston, Brussels, Frankfurt (Städel), Haarlem, The Hague, London (NG), Stockholm, and Vienna.

MONACO, Lorenzo, see LORENZO.

MONDRIAN, Piet (1872–1944), was a Dutch painter who went to Paris in 1911 and abandoned his realistic landscapes for Cubist ones. In 1914 he returned to Holland but he lived in Paris 1919–38, then in London, and he went to New York in 1940, where he exerted great influence on the development of the New York School. His form of Abstraction was a peculiarly rigorous one known as Neo-Plasticism, which consists principally of restricting forms to purely geometrical shapes, set at right angles to the horizontal or vertical axes and coloured in the three primary colours, and white, black, or grey. The only enlivening touch he permitted himself was in his titles – *Boogie-Woogie*, for example. As might be expected, he was a prolific writer (often in De STIJL) and his 'Plastic Art and Pure Plastic Art' (1937) summarizes his theories.

MONET, Claude (1840–1926), was the leading member of the IMPRESSIONIST group, and the one who longest practised the principles of absolute fidelity to the visual sensation and painting directly from the object, if necessary out of doors. Cézanne is said to have described him as 'only an eye, but my God what an eye!' and this description is certainly true in that his constant search for verisimilitude led at times to a neglect of form. He was born in Paris but went as a child to Le Havre. There he met BOUDIN – whose work he did not then like – and was persuaded by him to become a landscape painter (1856/8); at this time he also bought his first Japanese prints, then newly coming into Europe. In 1859 he went to Paris to study, meeting PISSARRO in the ATELIER Suisse. From 1860 to 1862 he was in Algeria as a conscript, but in 1862 he met Jongkind – who influenced him considerably – and returned to Paris, where he met most of the major artists of his own time; in 1862 Bazille, Sisley, and Renoir, in 1864 Courbet, in 1865 Cézanne and Whistler, and in 1866 Manet, whose work he had earlier admired. Then and for many years to come he was extremely poor. In 1870 to escape the Franco-Prussian War he came to London, where he painted some views, and, in 1871, with Pissarro he visited the National Gallery and the V & A, where they studied Turner and Constable, but, according to Monet himself, were not tremendously impressed. He returned to Paris via Holland and in 1872 visited Le Havre, where he painted *An Impres-*

sion, which, when exhibited in 1874 at what is now known as the First Impressionist Exhibition, was used derisively to name the whole movement IMPRESSIONISM. During the 1870s and 1880s he gradually became known and for the last thirty years of his very long life he was generally regarded as the greatest of the Impressionists. From about 1890 he began to paint series of pictures of one subject, the first being the *Poplars* and the *Haystacks*, representing them under various conditions and at different times of day; other series are those of *Rouen Cathedral* (1892–5), of the *Thames* (these were certainly finished in France, as he had by now given up the original practice of painting exclusively from nature) (1899–1904), the second *London* series (1905) and the *Venice* series (1908), and, most famous of all, the *Water-lilies* painted in the elaborate garden he had made for himself. He painted these over and over again, but the most important are the large ones begun in 1916 and retained by him until his death. They were painted for the State and are in a special museum (Paris, Orangerie). It has recently been claimed that these shimmering pools of colour, almost totally devoid of form, are the true starting-point of abstract art, or at least certain forms of it, particularly that now called ABSTRACT IMPRESSIONISM. They were, however, painted after CUBISM had been invented and can be seen equally as the logical outcome of Monet's lifelong devotion to the ultimate form of naturalism, truth of retinal sensation. He was enormously prolific, and many museums possess works: three very rich collections are Paris (Mus. de l'Impressionnisme and Mus. Marmottan, which now has 45 paintings bequeathed by Monet's son), and Boston.

MONNOYER, Jean Baptiste (1636–99), called 'Baptiste', was a Franco-Flemish flower painter who was trained in Antwerp, but became a member of the Academy in Paris in 1665 and worked for Louis XIV. It is said that he was annoyed by his son Antoine, an inferior flower painter, who was allowed to alter some of his works, and in a fit of pique he went to London *c.*1685. There he worked for the Duke of Montagu's new (and very French) town house (many of these pictures have passed by inheritance to the Duke of Buccleuch), and he remained in London until his death. His flowerpieces are rich and splendid, yet painted with the greatest regard for botanical accuracy: they frequently appear in English sale-rooms under his nickname 'Baptiste'. He also published books of engravings of flowers. Apart from those in English private collections and French provincial museums there are paintings by him in Munich and New York (Met. Mus.).

MONOCHROME. A painting or drawing executed in any one colour. *See* GRISAILLE.

MONOTYPE. A single print, not strictly an engraving at all, made by painting, with oil-paint or printer's ink, on an untouched copper plate, and printing on paper in the normal way. The only reason for doing this instead of painting direct on the paper is the quality of texture given by the pressure of printing. It is also possible to follow some of the indications left on the plate and repeat the process with slight variations. The technique was practised by CASTIGLIONE and DEGAS, among others.

MONRO, Dr Thomas (1759–1833), was a London physician and amateur draughtsman who befriended or patronized many artists, including Turner and Girtin, De Wint, J. R. COZENS, and Cotman. According to FARINGTON (*Diary*, 1794 and 1798) Turner and Girtin were employed by Dr Monro to draw at his house in the evenings, and in the winter evenings his house was like an Academy, being full of young painters whom he encouraged to use it as a studio. Some of his own drawings are in London (V & A, Courtauld Inst.).

MONTAGE is the sticking of one layer over another especially as in photomontage when photographs of objects are applied to a photograph of an unusual or incongruous background. The technique was much used by the Cubists, who frequently stuck newspaper cuttings on to their canvases: it is now much exploited by advertising agents. *See* COLLAGE.

MONTAGNA, Bartolommeo (*d.*1523), was the principal painter of Vicenza in the late 15th century. He is first documented in 1459 and is recorded as living in Venice in 1469. He was then presumably training as a painter, since he is first mentioned as such in Vicenza in 1474. His works are markedly influenced by Giovanni BELLINI, the VIVARINI, and ANTONELLO, especially his SACRA CONVERSAZIONE of 1499 (Milan, Brera). There are examples in Vicenza, and in Amsterdam (Rijksmus.), Baltimore (Walters Gall.), Bergamo, Berlin, Budapest, Columbus Ohio, Dublin, Glasgow, Liverpool, London (NG and Courtauld Inst.), Milan (Brera, Poldi-Pezzoli and Castello), Naples, New York (Met. Mus.), Ottawa, Oxford, Paris (Louvre), Philadelphia (Johnson), Rome (Borghese), San Francisco, Springfield Mass., Venice, Verona, Washington (NG), Williamstown Mass., and Worcester Mass.

MONUMENTAL. The most overworked word in current art history and criticism. It is intended to convey the idea that a particular work of art, or part of such a work, is grand, noble, elevated in idea, simple in conception and execution, without any excess of virtuosity, and having something of the enduring, stable, and timeless nature of great architecture. The word may properly be applied to the Pyramids, the paintings of Poussin or Piero della Francesca, and some few other works of art. It is not a synonym for 'large'.

MOORE, Henry, O.M. (*b.*1898), is the most eminent living British sculptor. He was trained in Leeds – where he met Barbara HEPWORTH –

and in London, winning a travelling scholarship to Paris and Italy in 1925. He was one of the advocates of direct carving and has always used his material to express natural forms in terms of stone or wood. His earliest major work was the *North Wind* (1928) for the London Underground building and it has been followed by several commissions for architectural sculpture, e.g. the Time-Life building in London (1952–3), and works in the open air in London, Paris, Rotterdam, and Arnhem. From 1940 he made many drawings of the underground air raid shelters and of coal miners, while his *Madonna* statue for S. Matthew, Northampton, was completed in 1944. His international reputation dates from 1948, when he was awarded the sculpture prize at the Venice Biennale, and he is now well represented in museums, particularly the Tate, London, and Ontario, Canada.

MOR, Anthonis (Antonio Moro) (*c.*1517/21–76/7), was an Utrecht portrait painter, the pupil of SCOREL, who became the Court Painter of the Spanish Netherlands and superimposed the grand air of Titian's portraits on to his own acute Dutch sense of character and polished technique. He was working for Cardinal Granvella in 1549 and visited Rome soon afterwards. In 1554 he painted Queen Mary Tudor (Madrid, Prado), presumably in London and to celebrate her marriage with Philip of Spain. His portraits had enormous influence on the development of a Court style of portraiture in both Spain and the Netherlands, but the presence of a Holbein tradition in England meant that he had no influence here, and in any case he could have had little opportunity in what must have been a very short visit. He was Court Painter to Philip II of Spain by 1560 and the Spaniard SÁNCHEZ COELLO was his pupil. There are pictures by him in Amsterdam (Rijksmus.), Berlin, Brussels, Cambridge (Fitzwm), Dresden, Florence (Uffizi), The Hague, London (NG, NPG), Madrid (Prado), Munich, New York (Met. Mus.), Ottawa, Paris (Louvre), Sheffield, Vaduz (Liechtenstein Coll.), Vienna (K-H Mus.), and Washington (NG).

MORALES, Luis, 'El Divino' (active 1547–86). Morales is the most typical Spanish Mannerist, whose style was formed by a combination of the Flemish-Italianate painters such as MASSYS, and the Italian artists who influenced them, principally LEONARDO and his Milanese followers. Morales seems to have studied under a Dutch painter called Sturmio who worked in Spain, but the final result is a highly personal style. He is first documented in 1547, but there is a *Madonna* attributed to him which is dated 1546. He spent most of his life in Badajoz where there are still works by him, although he may have worked in Madrid for Philip II in 1564. He thus precedes EL GRECO as an exponent of extreme Mannerism in Spain. Outside Spain and Portugal there are works by him in Berlin, Cardiff, Catania, Dresden, Dublin, Florence (Uffizi), Leeds, Leningrad (Hermitage), London

(NG), Mexico City, Minneapolis, New York (Hispanic Soc.), Oxford, Paris (Louvre), and Rome (Gall. Naz.).

MORANDI, Giorgio (1890–1964), was an Italian still-life painter. He never left his native country, but (apart from such Italian masters of the 15th century as Piero della Francesca) Cézanne and Chardin were the painters most akin to his withdrawn and meditative spirit. He lived in Bologna and painted some landscapes and flowerpieces, but most of his works are simple arrangements of bottles, treated in austere brownish tones approximating to monochrome. The PITTURA METAFISICA of CHIRICO, purged of its bombast, influenced him. He was also a celebrated etcher – again mainly of bottles – and made some 90 plates, mostly dating from 1921–4 and 1927–33. There are pictures by him in Birmingham, Edinburgh (M of MA), Hamburg, London (Tate), and Toledo Ohio.

MORAZZONE, Pier Francesco Mazzuchelli, called Morazzone (1571 or 73–1626), was, with G. B. CRESPI and G. C. PROCACCINI, the leading Milanese painter of the early 17th century. Like Crespi, he was in Rome in the 1590s, where frescoes by him survive in S. Silvestro in Capite. Even more than Crespi and Procaccini, however, he based his art on Gaudenzio FERRARI, and his principal works are also for chapels on the Sacro Monte at Varallo, Varese, and Novara. At the time of his death he was painting frescoes in Piacenza Cathedral, completed by Guercino.

MORBIDEZZA (Ital. softness). A term much used in 18th-century criticism to indicate a softness of edges and a fusion of tones which is characteristic of CORREGGIO: hence the 18th-century mockery 'the Correggiosity of Correggio' as a cant phrase suitable for the would-be connoisseur. Its use is not now recommended.

MOREAU, Gustave (1826–98), painted elaborate Biblical and mythological fantasies in a detailed, almost encrusted, technique. His importance – except for his slight influence on Surrealism – lies in his tolerant and intelligent teaching at the École des Beaux-Arts in Paris from 1892 to 1898, when ROUAULT, MATISSE, and MARQUET were his pupils. He left his collections to the State as a Museum, of which Rouault was to be the Curator.

MORETTO of Brescia (c. 1498–1554) worked mainly in the Brescia and Bergamo districts until he visited Milan and Verona in the 1540s. His religious works are of a warm, late Bellini and Giorgionesque type; his portraits are outstanding, showing the influence of Lotto and Titian, and developing types that Titian did not use until much later. He was probably the first to introduce the full-length portrait into Italy as an independent subject, not part of a religious work (cf. the *Nobleman* dated 1526 in the NG, London) – an idea developed from German examples, notably from CRANACH, although CARPACCIO may have been one of the first to use it. MORONI was his pupil.

There are works in Bergamo, Brescia (Mus., churches), Budapest, Cambridge Mass. (Fogg Mus.), Detroit, Frankfurt (Städel), London (NG), Milan (Ambrosiana, Brera, Castello), New York (Met. Mus.), Paris (Louvre), Philadelphia (Johnson), the Vatican, Venice (Accad.), Verona, Vienna, and elsewhere.

MORISOT, Berthe (1841–95), was the first woman to join the IMPRESSIONISTS – the other was Mary CASSATT. She met Fantin-Latour in 1859, and in 1860 was encouraged by Corot, who influenced her early work. In 1868 she met MANET and in 1874 married his younger brother Eugène. She exhibited in all but one (1879) of the Impressionist Exhibitions. Her great importance lies in her influence on Manet, for it was partly through her that he came to adopt the Impressionist palette and to abandon black of which he was so great a master. She could never persuade him into joining the group, but their close family tie made it even more difficult for him to dissociate himself from them. After about 1885 she was very strongly influenced by Renoir. There are works in Boston (Mus.), London (Tate), Paris (Mus. de l'Impressionnisme), and Washington (NG).

MORLAND, George (1763–1804), was an exponent of picturesque rustic genre painting who based himself on Dutch and Flemish 17th-century models such as BROUWER. Like them, he refused to work for individual patrons and preferred to sell through an agent, thus altering the whole basis of patronage in 18th-century England. His very numerous works were popularized through engravings, many of which were executed by William Ward, brother of James WARD, Morland's own brother-in-law, and imitator. The son of a painter, Henry Morland (c. 1730–97), he exhibited drawings at the RA at the age of ten (1773), and his first oil-painting was shown there in 1781. From then on he lived wildly, and in 1799 was arrested (as a French spy) while on the run from his creditors; after which he was in the King's Bench Prison until 1802. He died in prison after producing an enormous amount of scamped work to pay his debts. His reputation immediately declined and his place was taken by WILKIE. Among his most purely Dutch works are the *Industry* and *Idleness* (Edinburgh, NG), while the *Stable* (1791: London, NG) is one of his best rustic subjects. Other works are in London (Tate, V & A, Kenwood) and Birmingham, Bristol, Glasgow, Leeds, Leicester, Manchester, New York (Met. Mus.), Nottingham, Ottawa, Port Sunlight (Lever Gall.), Rouen, Wellington NZ, Wolverhampton and York.

MORO *see* MOR.

MORONI, Giovanni Battista (c. 1525–78), was a pupil of MORETTO, and was also much influenced by Lotto. His religious works are dull and derivative, but he excels as a painter of quiet family portraits and, like his master, he blends the realism of Holbein with the feeling for style of the Venetians to produce the placid, intimate, human portrait style of the Lombards. His portraits also have a grey tonality, unlike any contemporary Italian work, and curiously anticipatory of Whistler's delicacy. There are works in Baltimore, Bergamo (Mus. and churches), Berlin, Boston (Mus.), Brescia, Budapest, Detroit, Florence (Pitti, Uffizi), London (NG), Milan (Ambrosiana, Brera, Castello), Minneapolis, New York (Met. Mus.), Ottawa, Paris (Louvre), Philadelphia (Johnson, Wilstach, Widener), Princeton, Sarasota Fla, Vienna, Worcester Mass., and elsewhere.

MORRIS, William (1834–96), met BURNE-JONES when at Exeter College, Oxford. He then studied architecture under Street, but abandoned it to become a painter under the influence of ROSSETTI. In 1861 he founded the firm of Morris and Co., to produce wallpapers, furniture, tapestries, and stained-glass windows (many designed by Burne-Jones), carpets and furnishing materials in a style entirely different from that of contemporary Victorian decoration, but one which, nevertheless, tended towards a different kind of *horror vacui* and the use of equally dark and heavy colours. He is particularly important for the development of the private press, and did much with his Kelmscott Press, founded in 1890, to raise the standards of book design and printing, although he favoured a revival of medieval black-letter where Lucien Pissarro's Eragny Press (1896) concentrated on modern type faces. His poems and other writings are anti-industrialist and support a socialist theory for the regeneration of man by handicraft. There are drawings and a painting in the Tate and the V & A, London, the latter also having a room entirely decorated with Morris products.

MORSE, Samuel (1791–1872), was an American painter and first President of the National Academy (1826), but is better known as the inventor of the electric telegraph (hence Morse code). After leaving Yale in 1810 he went to London and trained under ALLSTON and WEST: his ambitions as a History painter led him to exhibit a *Hercules* at the RA, but on his return to America in 1815 he had to live by portrait painting. He invented the telegraph in 1832 and painted relatively little after that. His best-known portraits are the *House of Representatives* (Washington, Corcoran) and *Lafayette* (1825: Brooklyn Mus.).

MOSAIC. One of the oldest and most durable forms of mural decoration, mosaic was in constant use from the earliest times up to about the 13th century, when it was largely superseded by fresco and other forms of painting which are both much cheaper and much more adaptable to a realistic style. Recently, however, the very stylization inherent in mosaic has led to its revival as a decorative art. The technique is simple but laborious. A cartoon is drawn on the wall to be decorated and a small area covered with cement. Previously small cubes (called *tesserae*) have been chipped from slabs of coloured stone, marble, and coloured or gilt glass; the *tesserae* are then stuck into the cement. Great care was taken in the best early mosaics to ensure that all the *tesserae* were not perfectly flat and level, since an uneven surface catches the light and reflects it in different ways according to the angle of incidence and the material used for the *tesserae*. Mosaic was much used for the decoration of Early Christian and Byzantine churches and there are splendid cycles in Rome, Ravenna, Venice, and Sicily as well as in Greece. The great 13th-century revival in Rome preceded the realistic movement in painting (CAVALLINI, GIOTTO) and the art was still practised in Venice in the 15th century (e.g. by UCCELLO in St Mark's).

MOSER, Lucas, is known only from the Magdalen Altar in the church at Tiefenbronn, near Pforzheim, which is signed and dated 1431 and has an inscription roughly translatable as: 'Cry, Art, cry and lament loudly, nobody nowadays wants you. So alas, 1431'. In fact, the style of the picture is markedly modern and forms a German counterpart to the realism of WITZ or van EYCK and CAMPIN.

MOSTAERT, Jan (*c.*1475–1555/6), was a Haarlem painter who is recorded, on fair evidence, as having painted a *West Indian Landscape* as well as having worked for the Regent of the Netherlands. A picture at Haarlem (Hals Mus.) is presumably the landscape, and a group of pictures showing stylistic affinities with GEERTGEN – i.e. 'Dutch', rather than Flemish – can be considered as his. He must be distinguished from the 'Waagen'sche Mostaert', who is now identified with ISENBRANDT: on the other hand, the Master of Oultremont is probably identical with Mostaert. There are pictures ascribed to him in Amsterdam (Rijksmus.), Brussels, Cologne, Liverpool, London (NG), Paris (Louvre, Petit Pal.), Philadelphia (Johnson), St Louis, Sarasota Fla, Worcester Mass., and elsewhere.

MOTHERWELL, Robert (*b.* 1915), is an American Abstract Expressionist painter who began by studying philosophy at Harvard. He has said: 'Without ethical consciousness, a painter is only a decorator.' After a visit to Europe in 1938 he exhibited with the Surrealists in New York (1939) and later associated with POLLOCK, De KOONING and ROTHKO (with whom he founded an art school). He was editor (1944–57) of the important 'Documents of Modern Art' series.

MÜLLER, Otto (1874–1930), was a member of the BRÜCKE who experimented with techniques involving the use of distemper and beeswax rather than oil paint. The flatness inherent in this medium, and his passion for Egyptian art, led to striking simplifications of form which influenced the other members of the group. He studied lithography in Breslau from 1890 to 1895 and was trained at the Dresden Academy before going to Berlin in 1908, where he met HECKEL and subsequently joined the Brücke. He was much influenced by the sculptor LEHMBRUCK as well as by Gauguin, and his decorative paintings of gipsies and skinny nudes are less brutal than the works of most of his contemporaries. There are examples in Berlin, Cologne, and Harvard University.

MÜLLER, William James (1812–45), was a landscape painter, born at Bristol of German extraction, who was much influenced by Constable and Cox. He visited Egypt in 1838–9, and was one of the first English artists to paint Arabian subjects. In 1842–3 he was a member of an expedition to Asia Minor in search of antique marbles. The largest collection of his work is in Bristol, but there are others in London (BM, Tate Gall., V & A).

MULTSCHER, Hans (c. 1400–before 67), was active in Ulm for some 40 years, principally as a sculptor. His sharp sense of realism, noticeable in his sculpture, is even more marked in the first documented picture by him, the eight panels of the *Wurzach Altar*, of which the central part is lost (1437: Berlin). These panels belong to the same slightly crude realist school as MOSER's *Tiefenbronn Altar* or even the work of WITZ. A second altarpiece, including 8 paintings, was commissioned in 1456 and completed in 1459: it was for Sterzing (S. Tyrol) and is now in the Museum there.

MUNCH, Edvard (1863–1944), a Norwegian painter, was one of the forerunners of EXPRESSIONISM, whose most formative years were spent in Paris and Berlin, where a large Exhibition of his work, as early as 1892, was a formative influence on much German painting, since the repercussions led to the foundation of the Berlin SEZESSION in 1899. Formally, he was much influenced by van GOGH and GAUGUIN but his subjects (especially his *Frieze of Life* project) deal with basic themes of love and death, for which he sought pictorial equivalents. He was friendly with Strindberg, and his art, though sometimes powerful, is always neurotic and frequently hysterical. His graphic works were perhaps even more influential than his paintings. About 1,000 of his pictures are in the Munch Mus., Oslo, but there is also one in London (Tate).

MURAL *see* WALL-PAINTING.

MURILLO, Bartolomé Esteban (1617–82), was born in Seville where he passed the greater part of his life. He started as a painter of the kind of pictures that are sold at fairs (in Spain a bad painting is called a *pintura de feria*, and a good one, irrespective, a '*Murillo*'), but no certain example survives. He visited Madrid, perhaps in 1648, and stayed there for about three years, being apparently helped by Velazquez. His change of style from his earliest works in the cloister of San Francisco in Seville, dated 1646, to his later style could not have been effected without a knowledge of Rubens, van Dyck, Titian, and Velazquez. He also studied BAROCCI in the Royal Collection. In 1660 he was one of the founders, and the first President, of the Seville

Academy. The Spaniards mark off his stylistic progression by his changes in the use of colour. First, the rather hard naturalism of the early beggar-boy pictures, with their hints of Ribera and Velazquez; then the *estilo frio* of the early religious subjects, cool, detached, with only a little idealization; then the *estilo cálido* of the type of the *Madonna del Rosario* (Madrid, Prado), above all a devotional image, with idealized forms, a certain Baroque flutter to the draperies, a certain artificiality, but with warmth, charm, and quiet religious feeling; then the *estilo vaporoso* of his late works, where all tends towards the softening and sweetening of style and colour, to the sentimental emotionalism of a pious image. His later beggar-boy scenes also exploit this sentimental attitude, and he found a ready market for these glamourized, picturesque urchins in fancy dress rags, exuding the charms of Bohemianism and serving to exorcize poverty by robbing it of its power to inspire pity and horror. He had a large shop with many assistants, and his simple undemanding pictures enjoyed huge popularity, so much so that 'Murillos' were painted until well into the 19th century, as a style in art, not primarily as forgeries. His best works are of moderate size, when he is versatile and inventive in composition, but his large decorations in the Hospital de la Cáridad in Seville (1671–4) are involved compositions without clear organization and with an uneasy blend of the naturalistic and the idealized.

There are works by him in Amsterdam, Baltimore, Berlin, Boston, Budapest, Cadiz, Cambridge Mass. (Fogg Mus.), Chicago, Cincinnati, Detroit, Dresden, Genoa, Hartford Conn. (Wadsworth Atheneum), Indianapolis, Kansas City, Leningrad, Liverpool, London (NG, Dulwich, Wallace Coll., Wellington Mus.), Madrid, Minneapolis, Munich, New York (Met. Mus.), Notre Dame Univ. Indiana, Ottawa, Paris, Philadelphia (Widener), Raleigh N. Carolina, Rome (Corsini Gall.), St Louis, San Diego Cal., Seville (Mus. and churches), Sheffield, the Vatican, Vienna, and Washington.

MYTENS, Daniel (c.1590–before 1648), was trained in The Hague, probably under MIEREVELD, but was in England by 1618 and was working for the Crown soon after that. He was appointed Painter to Charles I in 1625 and painted a number of portraits, including several full-lengths, which had a great success before the arrival of van DYCK in 1632. In 1626 and 1630 he re-visited the Low Countries, perhaps to refresh his knowledge of Rubens and van Dyck. Some of his works are difficult to distinguish from JOHNSON's, but his masterpiece is the full-length *Duke of Hamilton* (on loan to Edinburgh NG) which was painted in 1629 and therefore shows most of the elegance associated with van Dyck before his arrival in England. From c.1635 Mytens seems to have lived in Holland. There are works by him in the Royal Coll. (including portraits of Charles I and his Queen that

show why van Dyck's success was immediate) and in Leeds, London
(NPG, Tate, Nat. Marit. Mus.), New York (Met. Mus.), Ottawa, and
St Louis.

N

NABIS, Les (from Hebrew, prophet), was the name taken by a small group of French artists, including BONNARD, VUILLARD, and MAILLOL, between *c.*1889 and 1899. They were attracted by GAUGUIN's advice to paint in flat, pure colours; and one of them, Maurice Denis, 'uttered one of the great battle-cries of modern art' when he said: 'Remember that a picture, before being a horse, a nude, or some kind of anecdote, is essentially a flat surface covered with colours assembled in a certain order.' They reacted sharply away from the naturalism implicit in Impressionism, but their links with the Symbolist writers meant that they attached considerable importance to subject-matter. The best painters of the group, Bonnard and Vuillard, eventually reverted to a modified Impressionist style known as INTIMISME.

NAIN, Le, *see* LE NAIN.

NANNI di Banco (*c.*1384–1421) was a Florentine sculptor who was working with his father on the Cathedral in 1406/7 and received the commission for a *Prophet* on the Porta della Mandorla (1407/8), the companion figure being by DONATELLO. In 1408 he and Donatello again shared a commission for the Cathedral (Donatello: *David*; Nanni: *Isaiah*). His best-known works are the four *Saints* (*Quattro Santi Coronati*) in a niche on Orsanmichele, where there are others by him, and the *Assumption* over the Porta della Mandorla of the Cathedral. His early death cut short a career which promised to rival Donatello's and in some respects, such as the use of classical exemplars, Nanni may have been in advance.

NARRATIVE painting is not quite conterminous with GENRE, since it implies a literary element not always found in genre painting. A narrative picture implies the choice of a moment in the story so that the spectator will know (or can guess) what has happened and what is about to happen – *When did you last see your father?*

NASH, Paul (1889–1946), was trained at the Slade School and served in the 1914–18 War at the front before being appointed an Official War Artist in 1917. He was again appointed in the Second World War. His poetic imagination was rather stimulated by Surrealism and he exhibited with the Surrealists in their Paris Exhibition, 1938. He did much work as a designer and book-illustrator. There are paintings by him in Belfast, Blackpool, Durban, Leeds, Leicester, Liverpool, London (Tate, Imperial War Mus.), Manchester, Ottawa, Sheffield, and Toronto.

His brother, John Nash RA, was born in 1893 and is also represented in the Tate Gall.

NATTIER, Jean Marc (1685–1766), began his career as an engraver of the Rubens *Marie de' Medici* cycle in Paris but later became established as the painter of the ladies of Louis XV's Court. There are works in Versailles and Paris (Louvre and Jacquemart-André), French provincial museums and London (NG, Wallace Coll.), New York (Met. Mus., Frick Coll.), Stockholm, Toledo Ohio, and elsewhere.

NATURE MORTE (Fr. STILL-LIFE).

NAY, Ernst Wilhelm (*b*. 1902), was born in Berlin but now lives in Cologne. He was trained under HOFER at the Berlin Academy (1925–8), and then went to Paris, where he was influenced by Picasso. He was in Rome, 1930–1, and with MUNCH in Norway, 1936–7. He was fortunate in being able to continue painting when he was stationed at Le Mans in northern France, 1942–4, and, beginning from Nolde and the Expressionists, he developed towards abstraction. There are works in Cologne.

NAZARENER. In 1809 two young painters, OVERBECK and Pforr, founded a quasi-religious order, the *Lukasbrüder*, in Vienna with the intention of regenerating German religious art in imitation of the works of Dürer, Perugino, and the young Raphael. Both went to Rome in 1810 and began working in the deserted monastery of Sant' Isidoro, where they were soon joined by others, the most important of whom was CORNELIUS. Several, including Overbeck, became Catholics and the group became known mockingly as 'Nazarenes'. As an experiment in medieval workshop practice they painted jointly some frescoes (1816–17: now in Berlin) and decorated the Casa Massimo in Rome (1819). Their ideas were known and admired in England, e.g. by DYCE, and influenced the Pre-Raphaelites; they also influenced INGRES.

NEAC (New English Art Club). The New English was founded in 1886 as a challenge to the complacent conventionalism of the Royal Academy (*see* SEZESSION), by a group of artists who were either French-trained or admirers of the French elective jury system. WHISTLER was admired by most of them, and he actually sat on the jury for a while before his inevitable resignation. STEER was an original member and SICKERT joined in 1886, and within a few years the Club tended to become an appanage of the Slade School, reflecting its tradition of draughtsmanship in the work of members like JOHN. The CAMDEN TOWN GROUP was founded in 1911, by GILMAN, GORE, and SICKERT, but in the winter of 1910/11 the Post-Impressionist Exhibition in London led to schism in both groups and the foundation of a new group, influenced by Cézanne, Gauguin, and van Gogh rather than the Impressionists. This was the LONDON GROUP, presided over by Gilman, and consisting of most of the Camden Towners, the VORTICISTS, and a few others. The NEAC still exists.

NEER, Aert van der (1603/4–77), was a Dutch landscape painter who specialized in moonlight effects, usually showing the canals around Amsterdam, where he lived. He seems to have had difficulty in making a living and took to keeping a wineshop 1658–62, but he was no more successful at this and returned to painting. He also painted some winter scenes, rather in the manner of Hendrik Avercamp; but his moonlights are unique. There are typical examples in Amsterdam (Rijksmus.), London (NG, Wallace Coll.), and New York (Met. Mus.).

His son Eglon Hendrik (1634–1703) painted a few landscapes but is best known as a genre painter in the manner of Metsu. He is represented in Boston, London (NG, Wallace Coll.), New York (Met. Mus.), and elsewhere.

NEOCLASSICISM is the name given to the movement which originated in Rome in the middle of the 18th century and spread rapidly over the civilized world. It arose partly in reaction against the 'excesses' of BAROQUE and ROCOCO – the former of which was also largely a Roman movement – and partly from a genuine desire to recreate the art of Greece and Rome, a desire much stimulated by the chief prophet of the movement, WINCKELMANN. From 1748 the discoveries at Herculaneum and Pompeii gave impetus to the movement – it has been argued that they created it – but, even more important, they provided some evidence of what ancient art actually looked like. This knowledge was disseminated by publications like 'Le Antichità di Ercolano' (1757 and later), plates from which were much used as models by MENGS and many others. Even Winckelmann knew practically nothing of Greek originals; and one main reason for the tendency of the Neoclassic movement in the 18th century to equate the Antique with Roman art, where the 19th century equated it with the purer style of the Greeks (as they would have expressed it), lies in the great discoveries of the archaeologists in the late 18th century and early 19th century.

Neoclassicism differs from all the earlier Classic revivals in that for the first time, artists consciously imitated antique art and knew what they were imitating, both in style and in subject matter. This is particularly true of sculpture, which survives in much greater quantity and in better preservation than either painting or architecture. This is one reason for the adaptation of bas-reliefs as pictures, in sharp reaction against the composition in depth of Baroque artists. The imitation of ancient subject matter was carried very far – as by DAVID, whose *Horatii* drew an ancient moral for modern circumstances – and is a different matter from the earlier type of History painting, where a subject such as the *Death of Caesar* was an excuse for dramatic grouping, not an incitement to tyrannicide.

Some of the principal exponents of various forms of Neoclassicism

were BARRY, CANOVA, FLAXMAN, HAMILTON, MENGS, PIRAN-
ESI, THORWALDSEN, VIEN, and WEST.

NEO-IMPRESSIONISM has, properly speaking, little to do with
Impressionism. In its purest form, as it is found in SEURAT, it involves the use of Divisionism (*see* OPTICAL MIXTURES) and a
strict, formal composition; both were too cerebral and too consciously
applied by the artist to have much relation to the fleeting colour
effects and the accidental, 'snapshot' composition of Impressionism.
Neo-Impressionism was first seen in an exhibition held in 1884 in
Paris by the *Salon des Artistes Indépendants*, where Seurat exhibited
the *Bathers at Asnières* (London, Tate), and in 1886 Seurat, SIGNAC,
and PISSARRO all showed works based on Seurat's theories at the last
Impressionist exhibition, hence the tendency to regard the movement
as an offshoot of Impressionism. According to Signac it 'guaranteed
all the benefits of luminosity, colour, and harmony by the optical
mixture of pure pigments (all the colours of the prism and all their
tones); by the separation of differing elements (local colour, the
colour of the light, and their interactions); by the balancing of these
elements and their proportions (according to the laws of contrast, of
gradation, and irradiation); by the selection of a size of touch
proportionate to the size of the picture.'

The theory had a strong but passing effect on van Gogh during his
years in Paris (1886–8), on Gauguin *c.* 1886, on Toulouse-Lautrec
c. 1887, and on Segantini *c.* 1891; other adherents include Maximilien
Luce (1858–1941), Henri-Edmond Cross (1856–1910), Charles An-
grand (1854–1926), Albert Dubois-Pillet (1846–90), and Théo van
Rysselberghe (1862–1926).

NEUE SACHLICHKEIT (Ger. new objectivity). About 1920 a reaction
against EXPRESSIONISM took place in Germany and the phrase *die
neue Sachlichkeit* was coined in 1923 to distinguish a new attention to
realistic representation of actual objects in a detailed way – thus also
reacting against the muzziness of Impressionism. The movement
petered out, but the new feeling for the subject is distantly related to
SURREALISM. *See also* DIX.

NEW ENGLISH ART CLUB *see* NEAC.

NEWMAN, Barnett (1905–70). American painter, born in New York. He
is best known for his very large canvases, many from six to nine feet
high, painted from the 1940s onwards. These often consist of a single
strong colour, modified only by changes of direction in the brushstrokes, or bisection by one or more vertical streaks.

NICHOLSON, Ben and William. Sir William (1872–1949) was an English
painter, especially of still-life, who is best known for his woodcuts of
Victorian types and characters and for having contributed much,
with his brother-in-law James Pryde (1866–1941), to the development
of the poster. The two were known as the Beggarstaff Brothers.

Nicholson is well represented in London (Tate) and in Cambridge (Fitzwm).

His son, Ben (*b.* 1894), O M, is the best-known British abstract painter and the first winner of the Guggenheim Award. His paintings and reliefs (plain and coloured) are geometrically inspired and derive from the austerer forms of Cubism and from Mondrian. Of his own *Au Chat Botté* (Manchester) he wrote: 'About space-construction: I can explain one aspect of this by an early painting I made of a shop window in Dieppe. . . . The name of the shop was "Au Chat Botté" . . . the words themselves had also an abstract quality – but what was important was that this name was printed in very lovely red lettering on the glass window – *giving one plane* – and in this window were reflections of what was behind me as I looked in – *giving a second plane* – while through the window objects on a table were performing a kind of ballet and forming the "eye" or life-point of the painting – *giving a third plane.*' He is represented in Edinburgh (NG Modern Art), London (Tate), Manchester, New York (M of M A), Toronto, and elsewhere.

NIELLO is a branch of goldsmiths' work which was of great importance in the early development of line ENGRAVING. A *niello* is a small plate of silver or gold which has a pattern engraved on it, the pattern being then filled with *niello*, a mixture of lead, silver, copper, and sulphur. This composition is fused into the lines of the pattern and the plate is then polished, so that the pattern is in black on a burnished ground. Sometimes the goldsmith would test his work by making a sulphur cast from the *niello* or by printing from it on to paper: from this it is a short step to making engravings for the sole purpose of being printed on paper. A few such impressions and sulphur casts still exist.

NITTIS, Giuseppe De (1846–84), was trained in Naples, but was expelled in 1863 and went to Florence, where he came in contact with the MACCHIAOLI. From Florence he went to Paris, where he spent the rest of his life except for a visit to London in 1875. He was much influenced by the Impressionists, particularly by DEGAS, like his contemporary, ZANDOMENEGHI; he exhibited in the First (1874) Impressionist Exhibition, to help give it respectability. His *vedute* are similar to those of SIGNORINI, who was his friend and companion on the trip to Britain. The largest collection of his works is in his native Barletta (190 pictures bequeathed by his widow), but there are others in Florence, Paris, Philadelphia (Wilstach), and Rome.

NOCTURNE. A night-piece. The term was first used by WHISTLER, who frequently gave his paintings musical titles, but the idea of painting landscapes as night scenes goes much further back, and most of A. van der NEER'S works are of this kind.

NOLAN, Sidney (*b.*1917), is recognized as the leader of the modern Australian school. He was born in Melbourne and trained there. His grandfather was a policeman who told stories of the 'Kelly Era', and Nolan has painted a series of works on the theme of the semi-mythical outlaw in his home-made armour, which express the violence of his deeds and death and the hallucinatory quality of the Outback with a visionary intensity. Another Australian folk hero, Mrs Fraser, has also figured in his private mythology, as has the better-known Leda, more accessible in symbolism but equally the vehicle for his multi-layered exploration of the significance of form, colour, and emotional content. The series of the carcasses of sheep in the Outback has an almost Surrealist quality. Nolan first saw modern European painting in 1939, and in 1940 had his first one-man show, of abstract works. In 1951 he visited Europe, and in 1958–60 worked in the US. There are works in Australian museums and in Bedford, Liverpool, London (Tate), and New York (M of MA).

NOLDE, Emil (1867–1956), was a German Expressionist painter of landscapes, Biblical scenes, and figure subjects based on a private mythology. He shared in the BRÜCKE movement in 1906–7, and in 1913–14 travelled through Russia, China, Japan, and Polynesia, where he was impressed by the demoniac quality of primitive art and religion. He was persecuted by the Nazis, although many of his ideas were close to theirs. His pictures have a particularly ferocious quality, distorted drawing, violent colour, and a tormented technique. He also worked in etching, lithography, and woodcut. There is a Nolde Foundation at Seebüll, on the German-Danish border.

NOLLEKENS, Joseph (1737–1823), was an English sculptor who, from 1759–70, worked in Rome where he also dealt in antiques and fragments which he restored and sold to English tourists. He became an ARA in 1771, an RA in 1772, and enjoyed a very considerable reputation. His able and lifelike busts ensured him a position in sculpture almost equal to that of Reynolds in painting; his character, mercilessly delineated by his pupil J. T. Smith in the first 'debunking' biography 'Nollekens and his Times' (1828), is that of a grasping man only outdone in miserliness by his wife. He made the bust of Dr Johnson in Westminster Abbey, where there are also several tombs by him, and there are works in the Royal Collection, Cambridge (Fitzwm), Edinburgh (NPG), London (V & A, Wellington Mus., and Kenwood), and Oxford. There are said to be over 70 replicas of his bust of *Pitt*, which contributed handsomely to his fortune of £200,000.

NORTHCOTE, James (1746–1831), was pupil and assistant of Reynolds (1771–5), and he studied in Rome (1777–80). He was a tame follower of Reynolds's portrait style, and his history pictures – mostly for Boydell's Shakespeare Gallery – are full of figures from the Antique and the Italian grand manner, roughly transplanted into an alien land

and made to toil humbly at unsuitable tasks. He wrote a biography of Reynolds and some gossipy reminiscences.

NORWICH SCHOOL. This was the only regional School of painting in England which had an internal cohesion comparable to the Italian local Schools. Its two great masters were COTMAN and CROME, and it began at a meeting at Crome's house in Norwich on 19 February 1803, when his friends, patrons, and pupils formed the Norwich Society 'for the purpose of an Enquiry into the Rise, Progress and present state of Painting, Architecture, and Sculpture, with a view to point out the Best Methods of study to attain to Greater Perfection ...'. From 1805 it became an Exhibiting Society and was joined by Cotman in 1807. Among the many minor artists the sons of Crome and Cotman, Joseph Stannard (1797–1830), James Stark (1794–1859) a pupil of Crome in 1811, John Thistle (1777–1839) the brother-in-law of Cotman, and Vincent are the best known. All are well represented in Norwich Museum.

NOTKE, Bernt (c. 1440–1509), was the most important painter and woodcarver active in the late 15th century in the Baltic area. He was recorded at Lübeck in 1467 and was specifically exempted from the regulations of the Guild, so he may have been of higher social status than most German artists of his time. His main work, the High Altar for Aarhus Cathedral in Denmark, was being worked on in 1478/9 and was completed by 1482. The paintings are probably his, but the sculpture may be by his assistants. In 1477 he had carved the great cross for Lübeck Cathedral in polychromed wood with a combination of Late Gothic pathos and light-hearted elegance. The spiky elegance, coupled with an extreme realism of detail, is best seen in his most famous work, the huge statue of S. George killing the Dragon, completed in 1489 (Stockholm, S. Nicholas). This was an important commission given by a leading Swedish statesman and was intended as a national memorial to a victory over the Danes. Notke appears to have spent several years in Stockholm and he also made the High Altar for Reval Cathedral (1482/3).

NOVECENTO (Ital. nine hundred). The 20th century, i.e. the nineteen hundreds. It was also the name given to a movement, founded in 1926, which became associated with Fascism on account of its 'back-to-the-great-Italian-past' character.

O

OBJET TROUVÉ *see* FOUND OBJECT.

OCHTERVELT, Jacob (*c.*1635–1708/10), was a Dutch genre painter much influenced by Pieter de HOOCH, and, through him, by Vermeer. The NG, London, has typical examples of his work.

ODALISQUE is a female slave. In art it is a name for a type of voluptuous nude (sometimes wearing baggy trousers), such as Ingres or Matisse delighted in.

ŒUVRE (Fr. work). The *œuvre* of an artist is the total of his output, and an *Œuvre Catalogue* is, therefore, an attempt to record every single painting, or drawing, or statue, by a given artist.

OFFSET *see* COUNTERPROOF.

OIL-PAINTING is the most usual technique for painting pictures of some size and importance. Basically, it consists of covering a slightly absorbent surface (usually primed canvas) with one or more layers of pigment ground in just enough oil to make the mixture pleasantly sticky. The oil used is normally linseed, but poppy or nut oils have also been used, since they remain workable for long periods. On the other hand, 'dryers' are sometimes mixed with linseed oil to speed up the drying processes. The use of oil mixtures for house and decorative painting probably goes back to antiquity, but the 'invention of oil-painting' – i.e. the technique adapted to the painting of pictures – is traditionally credited to the EYCKS. This is not true, but it does seem certain that a much improved technique, probably based on better-quality oil, was introduced into Flanders early in the 15th century. Italian painters were slow in catching up, and a picture like the *S. Sebastian* by the POLLAIUOLO brothers (1475: London, NG) shows that they were still far from proficient towards the end of the century.

There are two principal ways of painting pictures in oil. One, known as ALLA PRIMA or 'direct' painting, consists of just putting the paint on and hoping it comes out right. If this fails the proper cure is to take another canvas and start again. The second, more elaborate, technique is the one favoured by the Old Masters. This involves a good deal of planning ahead, since the canvas is first drawn on, then covered with one or more layers of monochrome so that the whole picture is virtually complete except for the colour; this is then applied in layers, so that the underlying layers show through to a predetermined extent, while the colours themselves are modified by their application as transparent films (GLAZES) or as opaque paste (SCUMBLES), much extra effect being gained from IMPASTO and BRUSHWORK. This technique, in the hands of a master craftsman such as Rembrandt, Rubens, or Titian, is capable of almost unlimited subtlety and variety; which is why oil-painting has practically superseded all its rivals, although ACRYLIC paints may now provide formidable competition.

OLIVER, Isaac (*d*.1617), was brought to England as a child in 1568 to escape the persecution of the Huguenots. He learned the art of miniature painting from HILLIARD and became his chief rival by about 1595. He may have gone abroad in 1588, and he was certainly in Venice in 1596 – when he described himself as a Frenchman – and he must have seen a good deal of Italian art, principally that of Parmigianino, for he had ambitions, unlike Hilliard who painted only portraits, towards history painting in miniature. One of his three wives was a GHEERAERTS and he was popular at the Court of James I. He is well represented in the Royal Coll. and in the V & A, London. His son Peter (1594?–1647) completed some of his works.

OP or OPTICAL ART is based on the idea that the painter or sculptor can create optical effects that persuade the spectator to see visual illusions. The patterns made by Vasarely and Bridget Riley are themselves static, but the spectator is so dazzled by them that they appear to move. The complex layers of clear and coloured perspex arranged by Eric Olsen or Francisco Sobrino create illusions of space and depth. The fields of inclined and painted nails by Gunther Uecker, or Sue Fuller's string compositions derive more obviously from GABO'S CONSTRUCTIVIST objects, which early exploited the optical effects created by light and shadow within complex surfaces. Most op, kinetic, and constructivist art is technically very accomplished, since much of the effect depends on the contrast of simple shapes and the weird optical effects generated by them.

OPIE, John (1761–1807), was launched in London in 1781 as the 'Cornish Wonder', an untutored natural genius, by John Wolcot, doctor, sometime pupil of Wilson, satirist ('Peter Pindar') and skilful impresario. The young Opie's talent lay in painting peasant types in strong chiaroscuro, and he is best with old people and children, whom he treats with Rembrandtesque effects of light: 'Ah!' said Reynolds to Northcote, newly back from Italy, 'there is *such* a young man come out of Cornwall ... like Caravaggio, but finer!' His large compositions for Boydell's Shakespeare Gallery, popular in engravings, were influential in establishing the costume-history piece, but once his Tenebrist vision was smothered by elegant face-painting, he declined into insipidity. His second marriage, in 1798, to the novelist Amelia Alderson led to his painting more 'literary' subjects. From 1799 he had a studio in Norwich and knew CROME. He became an RA in 1787, was made a Professor at the RA in 1805, and gave a series of lectures, published posthumously in 1809. There are works in London

(Guildhall, Tate, NPG), Aberdeen, Birmingham, Brighton, Bristol, Cardiff, Exeter, Glasgow (City Mus.), Leeds, Norwich, Plymouth, Southampton, Truro, and elsewhere.

OPTICAL MIXTURES. According to the colour-theory of NEO-IMPRESSIONISM, it is possible to obtain brighter secondary colours, such as green, by making a series of blobs of both primaries (which in the case of green would be blue and yellow) so that the blue and yellow blobs are very closely intermingled but not actually mixed. In this way, the colours mix in the spectator's eye at a certain distance from the picture, giving a much brighter and cleaner green than is obtainable by actual mixing of the pigments on the palette. For this reason, the Neo-Impressionists painted their pictures entirely in small dots or commas of colour, either the colours of the spectrum used pure, or blended only with white, and they varied the size of the blob according to the size of the picture and the distance at which it was to be seen, relying always on distance to make the mixture in the spectator's eye. The Neo-Impressionists disliked the term Pointillism, preferring Divisionism as a description of their technique: a full description is given in SIGNAC's book 'De Delacroix au Néo-Impressionnisme' (Chap. I). The Impressionists had already used a known variant of the technique, by juxtaposing different shades and tones of one or more colours, so as to enhance the brilliance and shimmering quality of their colour. Optical greys are also obtained in this way, and are claimed to be superior to mixtures with black pigment in them; they were essential to Impressionism, the theory of which does not recognize the existence of black in Nature. Many of Degas's pastels show the use of optical mixtures – not in the rigid manner of the Neo-Impressionist theory, but in a much more elaborate form than that employed by the Impressionists, and he frequently used superposed scumbles to achieve depth of colour.

ORCAGNA, Andrea (c. 1308–68), was a painter, sculptor, and architect active in Florence in the mid 14th century, one of the first major figures to arise after Giotto, whose ideals he did not entirely share. The first document to mention him (1343) speaks of his 'many defects and faults'. He was admitted to the Guild of Painters in 1343/4 and Stonemasons in 1352. His only certain painting is the large altarpiece in the Strozzi Chapel of S. Maria Novella, Florence (1354–7). This shows a wiry sense of form and a rejection of the sense of spatial depth that had been one of Giotto's greatest achievements: in its place Orcagna creates a much more hieratic art, in which gold backgrounds play an important part, probably directly related to a change in religious feeling after the Black Death of 1348. His main work in sculpture is the Tabernacle, with a relief of the *Death and Assumption of the Virgin* (signed and dated 1359), in Orsanmichele, Florence. In

1368 an altarpiece of *S. Matthew* (Florence, Uffizi) was completed by his brother Jacopo di Cione on account of Orcagna's illness and almost certainly he died in that year. His brothers Nardo (active 1343/6–*d*.1365/6) and Jacopo (active 1365–98) di Cione were the most influential painters in Florence at the end of the 14th century. The fresco of the *Inferno* in the Strozzi Chapel does not seem to be by the same hand as the altarpiece (i.e. it is not by Orcagna) – and Ghiberti ascribes it to Nardo. There are many works which are vaguely Orcagnesque and seem to date from the end of the 14th century: these are usually attributed to Jacopo. Pictures by one or the other are in the Royal Collection and in Berlin, Budapest, Florence (Accad., Uffizi, S.M. Novella, and other churches), Liverpool, London (NG, V & A), New York (Met. Mus., Hist. Soc.), Philadelphia (Johnson), St Louis, the Vatican, Washington (NG), and Yale University.

ORLEY, Bernard (Barent) van (*c*.1488–1541), was a Brussels painter, head of a large workshop. He was called in his own day the Raphael of the Netherlands, from his garbled imitation of Italian Renaissance ideas and forms, derived from his knowledge of the Raphael tapestry cartoons, which were woven in Brussels *c*.1516/19, and from two conjectural visits to Italy. He was Court Painter to the Spanish Governors of the Netherlands; was one of the principal ROMANISTS; was a prolific designer of tapestries and stained glass, and executed occasional portraits in the Massys and Holbein style. There are examples in the Royal Collection (tapestries), Antwerp, Brussels, Detroit, Munich, Toronto, Turin, Vienna, Waddesdon, Bucks. (National Trust), and elsewhere.

OROZCO, José (1883–1949), was a Mexican painter who used an Expressionist style for his frequently huge decorations (often in fresco or in imitations of fresco achieved with modern building materials). Most of his works have strong political overtones, and, like RIVERA, he executed many commissions for revolutionary governments.

ORPHIC CUBISM, ORPHISME. A term invented in 1913 by Apollinaire to describe 'the art of painting new structures out of elements that have not been borrowed from the visual sphere but have been created entirely by the artist himself, and have been endowed by him with the fullness of reality. It is pure art.' This art was attributed to DELAUNAY, who was mainly concerned with the primacy of colour over form. He thus achieved a fusion of CUBISM, Futurism, and the independent colour of Fauvism to produce a precursor of pure Abstract painting. Through KANDINSKY and KLEE his ideas exerted great influence in Germany. He also used the spectrum to produce what he called the Law of Simultaneous Contrasts.

Orphic Cubism is so called because it was regarded as more oracular and esoteric (and therefore 'purer') than ordinary Cubism.

OSTADE, Adriaen van (1610–84), was a Haarlem genre painter who was a pupil of Frans Hals, though it is difficult to see any influence of Hals in his interiors with drunken peasants or conversations between hags. In the 1640s he was influenced by Rembrandt (the *Slaughtered Pig*, 1643, Frankfurt, Städel, is a case in point), but the principal influence seems to be that of BROUWER, in the sense that both painted the same kind of peasant scenes. He painted about 1,000 pictures, so that he is well represented in museums. Jan Steen was his pupil.

OSTADE, Isack van (1621–49), was the younger brother and pupil of Adriaen. In his short life he painted a large number of pictures, some of genre subjects like his brother's, but the best are of landscape: there are good winter scenes by him in London (NG, Wallace Coll., and Kenwood).

OTTOCENTO (Ital. eight hundred). The 19th century, i.e. the eighteen hundreds.

OUDRY, Jean Baptiste (1686–1755), was one of the greatest French painters of hunting, animal, and still-life subjects, particularly those with game and dead beasts in the open air. He was a pupil of his father and of Largillierre, and was influenced by DESPORTES, his only equal in his chosen genre. After painting portraits, still-life and flower subjects, he concentrated from *c.*1720 on animals, hunts and landscapes, with occasional portraits. He was appointed Court Painter to Louis XV, and painted the royal hounds, and from 1726 onwards he worked for the Beauvais tapestry factory. After he became manager (in 1734) he designed the illustrations to the Fables of La Fontaine that brought the factory world fame. He also worked for the Gobelins from 1736, and designed for it the *Hunts of Louis XV*. His works show a careful attention to detail, but also have a largeness of handling in light and shade and feeling for colour. There are works in Barnard Castle (Bowes Mus.), Caen, Cambridge Mass. (Fogg), Compiègne, Copenhagen, Fontainebleau, Leningrad (Hermitage), London (Wallace Coll.), Marseilles, Moscow, New York (Met. Mus.), Paris (Louvre, Carnavalet, Mus. des Arts Décoratifs, Petit Pal.), Schwerin (the largest collection: 43), Stockholm, Toledo Ohio, and elsewhere.

OUWATER, Albert van (mid 15th century). All that is known about this painter is that he was a Haarlemer who was the master of GEERT-GEN tot Sint Jans, and that he made a painting of the *Raising of Lazarus* which is unmistakably the one in Berlin under his name (or perhaps the Berlin picture is a copy of a lost original). By deduction from Geertgen's activities it is possible to assume that Ouwater was contemporary with the other major 15th-century Haarlem painter, BOUTS the Elder. It is also thought that he may have been born *c.*1435, that he was in Haarlem in 1467, and that he may have designed for the new craft of woodcut illustrations. A tiny fragment in New York (Met. Mus.) is also attributed to him.

OVERBECK, Johann Friedrich (1789–1869), was the most important of the NAZARENER group, which he founded with another painter, Pforr, in 1809. From 1810 he lived almost entirely in Rome and painted in a purely 'Quattrocento' style; like INGRES, he idolized Raphael. He became a Catholic in 1813. He exerted considerable influence on the PRE-RAPHAELITES through BROWN and DYCE. There are works in Assisi (S.M. degli Angeli), Basle, Berlin, Cologne (Cath.), Munich, and elsewhere.

OVILE MASTER *see* 'UGOLINO-LORENZETTI'.

OZENFANT, Amédée (1886–1966), was a French painter who, with the architect Le Corbusier, invented PURISM. From about 1924, the human figure began to creep back into his works, culminating in two huge paintings entitled *Life*. In 1937 he founded a school in London, but moved the following year to New York, where he spent some 10 years. He is represented in the museums of modern art in London, New York, and Paris. His book 'Art' (English edition 1931, as *'Foundations of Modern Art'*) had considerable influence.

P

P., PINX., PINXIT (Lat. he painted), following a name on a painting or, more commonly, an engraving after a painting, refers to the authorship of the original picture.

PACHECO, Francisco (1564–1654), was a Spanish painter and writer on art. He was the master of CANO and VELAZQUEZ, who was also his son-in-law. Pacheco worked mostly in Seville and is not known to have visited Italy, although he had a large collection of engravings including some after Michelangelo, Veronese, Dürer, and Lucas van Leyden. In 1611 Velazquez became his pupil, and in the same year he made a trip to Madrid and Toledo where he visited GRECO. In 1618 he was appointed Censor of Paintings to the Inquisition and in 1619 was made a Painter to the King. His book 'El Arte de la Pintura' took thirty years to write and was completed in 1637/8. It was published in 1649, but a new and fuller edition appeared in 1956. Pacheco claimed to have painted 150 portraits by 1647. Most of his works are in Seville, but there is one in Williamstown Mass.

PACHER, Michael (c. 1435–98), was the principal Tyrolean painter and was active also as a wood-carver, but his sculpture is more Gothic in style than his paintings. As his geographical position would imply, Pacher is a sort of half-way house between the Gothic qualities of German 15th-century painting and the more intellectual interests of the Italians – in his case, Mantegna seems to have been the principal influence. There is an altarpiece by him in Munich and other works in Cologne (Schnütgen Mus.) and Vienna (Belvedere), and a panel of his school in London (NG), but the majority of his works remain in the parish churches for which they were painted or carved, his masterpiece being the S. Wolfgang altarpiece completed by 1481.

PAINTERLY *see* MALERISCH.

PAINTING TECHNIQUES *see* ACRYLIC, ENCAUSTIC WAX, FRESCO, GOUACHE, OIL-PAINTING, PASTEL, SIZE COLOUR, TEMPERA, WATERCOLOUR.

PAJOU, Augustin (1730–1809), was a French sculptor who was a pupil of J. B. LEMOYNE and studied in Rome 1752–6. He is best known for his decorative sculpture in the Opera House at Versailles (1768–70) and for his numerous portraits – *Lemoyne* (1758) and *Buffon* in the Louvre, *Descartes* and *Bossuet* in the Institut. He worked much for Mme du Barry. In 1777 he was appointed Keeper of the King's Antiquities and in 1792 he served on a Revolutionary Committee on the Conservation of Works of Art. His *Psyche abandoned* (1791: Louvre) is a piece of Neoclassic sentiment.

PALA. An Italian word for a large altarpiece: unlike an ANCONA a pala may consist of one picture only. A 'Pala of a unified type' is one in which all the action (if any), and all the figures, are represented as inhabiting one single space, which is treated as a consistent pictorial continuum. In most POLYPTYCHS each scene, or even each Saint, has its own space.

PALIOTTO is Italian for an *antependium* or altar frontal, i.e. the hanging which covers the front of an altar. These are normally of cloth, the colour agreeing with the liturgical colour of the day, but there are examples of carved, painted, or enamelled frontals. They are often very ancient, and the most famous is perhaps the golden one in St Mark's, Venice, which is 13th-century, or that in Sant' Ambrogio, Milan, of the 9th century.

PALMA Giovane (1544–1628) was the grand-nephew of Palma Vecchio. In 1570 he entered TITIAN's studio and completed the *Entombment* intended for Titian's own tomb. He began in a style related to Roman Mannerism, but developed towards the style of TINTORETTO. There are works by him in most Venetian churches and galleries, in the Royal Coll. and in Florence (Uffizi), London (NG), Madrid, Milan (Brera), Munich, Naples, Rouen and Vienna.

PALMA Vecchio (Jacopo Palma) (*c.*1480–1528) was a Venetian painter who was a pupil of Giovanni Bellini and was much influenced by Titian, as well as by Giorgione and Lotto. He is chiefly remembered as the painter of a particularly splendid type of blonde, said to be characteristically Venetian in her ample charms. For this reason, many of his works are *Sacre Conversazioni* with several female Saints. His masterpiece is perhaps the *S. Barbara and other Saints* in S.M. Formosa, Venice, but there are other works in Venice and in the Royal Coll. and Berlin, Budapest, Cambridge (Fitzwm), Chicago, Detroit, Dresden, Florence (Uffizi), Glasgow, London (NG and RA), Milan (Brera), Paris (Louvre), Philadelphia, Rome (Gall. Naz., Borghese, Capitoline), San Marino Cal. (Huntington), Sarasota Fla, Vienna, Worcester Mass., York, and elsewhere.

PALMER, Samuel (1805–81), was a painter of pastoral landscape and the most important follower of BLAKE, whom he met in 1824. He was very precocious and exhibited at the RA from 1819. His 'Shoreham Period' (1826–35) was the moment of perfect balance between inner and outer vision – a landscape charged with fecundity and Christian symbolism, expressed in terms of observed detail. This 'primitive and infantine feeling' (his own words) for landscape began to fade *c.*1832; in 1838 he married the daughter of John LINNELL and visited Italy, and his son later wrote of these events 'After the Shoreham and Italian periods, the whole of my father's life became a dreadful tragedy'. His early work has influenced modern Romantic painters, e.g. SUTHERLAND: examples are in London (BM, V & A, and Tate), Cambridge (Fitzwm), Oxford (Ashmolean Mus.), and elsewhere.

PANINI (or Pannini), Giovanni Paolo (*c.* 1692–1765/8), was the first painter to specialize in ruins, treating them as Roman VEDUTE of a special kind. He was working in Rome by *c.*1717, but the earliest surviving dated picture is of 1727 (London, Wellington Mus.); in 1729 he was concerned in a Fête given by Cardinal de Polignac in honour of the birth of the Dauphin and this began a long connexion with France and the French Academy in Rome. Paintings of the Fête are in the Louvre (1729) and Dublin (1731). His views of modern Rome, as well as his *capricci* based on the better-known ruins, had an enormous vogue among tourists and examples are to be found in most galleries. PIRANESI, though more of an archaeologist, was influenced by him, and so was CANALETTO.

PAOLO Veneziano (*d. c.*1362) was the principal painter working in the Byzantine style in 14th-century Venice. In 1358 he and his son Giovanni jointly signed a *Coronation of the Virgin* (New York, Frick Coll.) which is the last known work by him, but another *Coronation* (Washington, NG) attributed to him is dated 1324. His son Luca was also a painter and the father and both sons jointly signed the cover which they made for the PALIOTTO, the *Pala d'Oro*, in S. Mark's in 1345.

PAOLOZZI, Eduardo (*b.*1924), was born in Edinburgh of Italian parents. He worked in Paris 1947–50, where he was influenced by Klee and knew GIACOMETTI. He was one of the main impulses behind the development of POP ART in London in the mid 1950s and now specializes in large, abstract, metal sculptures.

PAPIER COLLÉ (Fr. stuck paper) is a form of COLLAGE built up from layers of paper stuck on a ground such as canvas.

PARIS, THE SCHOOL OF (*L'École de Paris*). Since about 1900 Paris has been the Mecca of young painters of every nationality, Picasso being perhaps the most obvious example. The term now means little more than contemporary painting, predominantly non-figurative, without regard to national schools: Eastern European and German refugees, Spanish and American painters can all be included in the term, and De STAEL, HARTUNG, and RIOPELLE equally with SOULAGES, MANESSIER, or DUBUFFET are covered by it. The phrase tends to mean different things to French writers, who would like to imply hegemony.

PARMIGIANINO, Francesco (1503–40), was one of the most sensitive and elegant of the early Mannerists. He was born in Parma and was commissioned to decorate the S. transept of Parma Cathedral as early as 1522 and was painting frescoes in S. Giovanni Evangelista there in 1522/3: as this church contains frescoes by CORREGGIO the principal influence on his style was Correggio, soon followed by Pordenone and Raphael. He was in Rome by late 1523 and was captured in the Sack of Rome (1527) while working on the *S. Jerome* (now London, NG). He was able to escape to Bologna and travelled to Verona and Venice before returning to Parma in 1530. The last ten years of his life were spent in painting frescoes in Sta Maria della Steccata, Parma, and quarrelling with the overseers of the works; although he was supposed to start in 1531 he did so little that, finally, in 1539 the authorities sacked him and had him imprisoned for breach of contract. They then approached GIULIO Romano, who, at first, attempted to evade the commission, since Parmigianino had written begging him not to act against the interests of a fellow artist. In the event, the overseers were dissatisfied with Giulio as well. The next year Parmigianino died, and it is an adequate description of his neurotic temperament to quote Vasari: 'having his thoughts filled with alchemy . . . [he] changed from the delicate, amiable, and elegant person that he was, to a bearded, long-haired, neglected, and almost savage or wild man . . . he was there interred naked, as he had wished, and with a cross of cypress placed upright on his breast in the grave'. His work, both in painting and perhaps even more through his etchings, which had wide currency, was very influential in Italy and also in N. Europe. His figures have long necks and hands and seem almost swooning in their ecstasy, much of which is truly Counter-Reformation in taste. The so-called *Madonna with the long neck* (*c.*1535: Florence, Uffizi) is one of the best examples. His portraits, when he had a congenial sitter, have deep spiritual insight (especially, perhaps, the early *Self-portrait* in Vienna, in which he saw himself distorted in a convex mirror). There are paintings by him in the Royal Coll. and in Berlin, Bologna (Pinacoteca, S. Petronio), Copenhagen, Detroit, Dresden, Florence (Uffizi, Pitti), Frankfurt, Glasgow, Madrid (Prado), Milan (Ambrosiana), Naples, Parma (Gall., S. Giovanni Evang., Madonna della Steccata, Canonica di Bardi), Rocca di Fontanellato nr Parma, Rome (Borghese, Doria Pal.), Vienna, York.

Parmigianino was, after Dürer, one of the earliest painter-etchers – i.e. to use the medium for making works of art of his own. His compositions were also very widely reproduced as engravings and as CHIAROSCURO WOODCUTS, for which he was probably among the first to make designs.

PASCIN, Jules (1885–1930), was born Julius Pincas in Bulgaria, but settled in Paris and called himself Pascin. He was trained in Vienna and Munich and worked for the famous satirical paper *Simplizissimus* before going to Paris in 1905, where he settled soon afterwards. He spent the 1914–18 War in the US and became an American citizen, but returned to Paris in 1922 and lived there until he hanged himself on the opening day of his one-man show in 1930. His pictures are all of equivocally young girls in sprawling poses, a sort of Lolita *avant la lettre*, and have much in common with certain French 18th-century painters (BOUCHER) and engravers; perhaps for this reason he is not well represented in public galleries, although there are examples in Paris (Mus. d'Art Moderne), Minneapolis, Southampton, and Toledo Ohio.

PASMORE, Victor (b.1908), was one of the members of the EUSTON ROAD group in the late 1930s. He was unable to paint full time until 1938, but from then until 1947 he painted the most subtle landscapes and interiors seen in England since Steer or Whistler. The later scenes of the Thames were almost Oriental in their tonal subtlety and hinted at the abstraction which he embraced in 1947: since the 1950s he has made constructions in the manner of GABO, usually of simply coloured wood and Perspex. He has been a most influential teacher, first in Newcastle and then in London, of a course based on abstract principles of design. There are works by him in many British and Commonwealth galleries: he was concerned also with the New Town at Peterlee, Durham.

PASTEL is a medium consisting of dry powdered colour mixed with just enough gum (usually gum arabic) to bind it. The mixture is allowed to set in moulds, forming very fragile sticks about the size of a finger. These sticks, when rubbed on paper, disintegrate so that the powder adheres to the paper; but one of the great drawbacks of the medium is the ease with which the powder falls off again or smudges. The softest pastels give an effect which is virtually that of painting, the whole surface of the paper being covered by the pigment layer, but it is also possible to use much harder, grittier pastels (like the chalk used in schools) to get an effect more closely related to drawing. The first method was used by such French masters as Quentin LATOUR or CHARDIN; the second is more usual for making studies instead of finished works. DEGAS, perhaps the greatest of pastellists, tended to use the medium as a form of drawing rather than painting, but he also had various technical tricks (such as soaking the paper in turpentine) which have helped to preserve his pastels, although they incur the wrath of the purists.

PASTICHE, PASTICCIO. An imitation or forgery which consists of a number of motives taken from several genuine works by any one artist recombined in such a way as to give the impression of being an independent original creation by that artist.

PATENIER, Patinier, or Patinir, Joachim (d.c.1524), is documented in the Antwerp Guild in 1515. Dürer, who owned a picture by him, mentions him as a landscape painter, attended the festivities at his second marriage in 1521, and drew his portrait. His small landscapes have something in common with Antwerp Mannerism in that they are cool in colour and very blue in the distances, and they represent fantastic scenery with jagged mountains, farmlands dotted with villages and ruins, rocky shores, and little figures of saints, hermits, and country people. They offer a wonderful mixture of fantasy and naturalistic detail that presages the more naturalistic landscapes of Bruegel. Sometimes the figures are by others; in one case at least by MASSYS, who became the guardian of Patenier's children in 1524. There are only four signed works to serve as a basis for attributions to him: in Antwerp, Karlsruhe, Vienna, and recently discovered, in a Belgian private coll. Other works are in Basle, Berlin, Cambridge (Fitzwm), London (NG), Madrid (Prado), Minneapolis, New York (Met. Mus.), Oxford, Paris (Louvre), Philadelphia (Mus. and Johnson), Rome (Borghese), York, and elsewhere.

PATER, Jean Baptiste Joseph (1695–1736), was an imitator of WATTEAU, whose only pupil he was. Apparently they separated on account of Watteau's extreme irritability, but in his last days Watteau repented of this, sent for Pater, and gave him his final lessons. Pater soon wore out his own talent in repetitions of *fêtes galantes*, typical examples of which are in the Wallace Coll., Kenwood, London, and Waddesdon, Bucks. (National Trust).

PATINA is the greenish incrustation on the surface of old BRONZE. It is esteemed for its own sake, and the word has had its meaning extended to cover all forms of mellowing with age. When a picture has had the dirt cleaned off its surface it is often described as having 'lost its patina'.

PEALE. A family of American painters and naturalists. The two earliest members were Charles Willson Peale (1741–1827) and his brother James (1749–1831). Charles was a saddler and woodcarver who had lessons from COPLEY, went to London 1767–69 and worked under WEST, returning to settle in Philadelphia. He painted a number of portraits of the leading figures in the Revolutionary War including the earliest (1772) of Washington. In 1786 he founded the Peale Museum and from then on was principally concerned with the scientific aspect of his museum – e.g. in 1806 he exhibited the skeleton of the first American mastodon. He began to paint again at the age of 74 and died at 86, his death being brought on by carrying a trunk for a mile on his way to court his fourth wife. He wrote an autobiography, and his three wives gave him seventeen children who were ambitiously christened, the boys including Raphaelle, Rembrandt, Titian, Rubens, and the girls being christened Angelica Kauffmann, Rosalba Carriera, and Sophonisba (after an Italian woman painter). Raphaelle (1774–1825) painted some very fine and austere still-lifes, not at all Dutch in feeling but far closer to Spanish 17th-century work. He was the best painter of the family, but his attempt with Rembrandt Peale to run the family museum was a failure; he was unhappily married and eventually took to drink. Rembrandt (1778–1860) also painted still-life and some very fine, detailed portraits (*Rubens Peale with a Geranium Plant*). He visited England in 1802–3 and worked under West and painted a number of French statesmen in Paris 1808–10 for his father's museum. He settled in New York in 1822 but revisited Europe in 1829/30, and finally returned to Philadelphia in 1831. He was one of the first American artists to practise lithography and he also painted one of the best-known portraits of Washington, the so-called Port-hole Portrait painted in 1823, twenty-four years after Washington's death. The original is now in the Capitol, Washington, in the Vice-President's room, but about eighty replicas are known. Rubens (1784–1865) and Titian the Elder (1799–1881) were also painters, but less important.

Charles Willson's brother James was a miniaturist in Philadelphia and may have been one of the first painters of still-life in America. He had seven children, five of whom were painters, but they were less eccentrically named than their cousins. There are works by one or other of the Peales in many American museums including Baltimore, New York (Historical Soc.), Philadelphia, Washington (NG), and Worcester Mass.

PEARCE (Pierce), Edward (d.1695), was a prolific and able wood and stone carver, who worked on decorative sculpture for country houses and churches, for Wren's City churches (he made the wooden model of the copper dragon for the vane of St Mary-le-Bow), the Guildhall, St Paul's Cathedral, Hampton Court, several City Companies, and Clare College, Cambridge. His bust of Wren (1673: Oxford, Ashmolean) shows him with a gift for the restrained Baroque current in England, and a ready eye for liveliness of character. There are works in the Royal Collection, and London (NPG, London Mus.).

PECHSTEIN, Max (1881–1955), was one of the leading German Expressionists. He was trained in Dresden and in 1906 became a member of the BRÜCKE group, founded the year before by KIRCHNER, SCHMIDT-ROTTLUFF and others. In 1907–8 he went to Italy and Paris and in 1914 was able to go to the South Seas, to the island of Palau, where his works were very obviously influenced by GAUGUIN's example. In 1915 he was arrested by the Japanese and sent to Nagasaki, returning to Germany via New York. He served in the German Army until 1918. In 1934 he was expelled from the Prussian Academy and forbidden to exhibit: after 1945, like Schmidt-Rottluff, he became a Professor in Berlin. There are works in several German museums as well as Baltimore, Los Angeles, and Toledo Ohio. His autobiography was published posthumously.

PEDIGREE see PROVENANCE.

PEINTURE À L'ESSENCE see DEGAS.

PELLEGRINI, Giovanni Antonio (1675–1741), was a Venetian decorative painter who was a pupil of Sebastiano RICCI and one of the most important of TIEPOLO's predecessors. Like PITTONI, he worked for many foreign patrons and travelled widely. He was first recorded as a painter in 1703 and soon after this he married the sister of Rosalba CARRIERA, who mentions him in her diary on several occasions. In 1707 Lord Manchester went on an embassy to Venice; he commissioned a picture to celebrate the event from CARLEVARIS and brought Pellegrini and Marco Ricci back to London with him in 1708. Pellegrini soon had considerable success and became a Director of Kneller's Academy in 1711. VERTUE says that Pellegrini 'painted prodigious quick, had a very noble and fruitfull invention' which may be seen in the decorations at Kimbolton Castle (now a school), done for Lord Manchester, or in the decorations at Castle Howard (1709: mostly destroyed in 1941). In these decorative series Pellegrini shows that he was a true precursor of Tiepolo in the lightness and gaiety of his touch which contrasts with the duller history painting of Pittoni. In 1713 he went to Germany and Flanders, returning to England in 1719 when, according to Vertue, he was less successful because Marco Ricci had sent for his uncle Sebastiano, who was generally agreed to be a better painter. Pellegrini also painted a splendid ceiling for the Bank of France (since destroyed) in Paris and worked in Prague, Dresden, and Vienna. There is a sketch of 1710 in London (V & A) which may represent his design for the cupola of St Paul's for which, according to Vertue, 'he made several designs and a moddle for painting the Cupulo at St Paul's, for which he was paid tho' he had not the cupolo to paint'. There are works by him in Barnard Castle (Bowes Mus.), Berlin, Birmingham, Boston, Dresden, The Hague, Leeds (*Hector* from Kimbolton), London (NG), Paris (Louvre), Vienna, and elsewhere.

PENCIL in 18th-century usage means 'brush' and *Pencilling* means BRUSHWORK.

PENCZ, Georg (*c.*1500–50), was a German painter first recorded in the Nuremberg Guild in 1523. About two years later, along with the engravers B. and H. S. Beham, he was banished from the city for expressing anarchistic and atheistic ideas. He may have been a pupil of DÜRER and, like him, was profoundly influenced by Venetian art. His best works are his portraits, which are very like those of AMBERGER; that is, a combination of Dürer and Venice. Pencz almost certainly visited Italy, and may have studied in Rome, since his mythological pictures show the influence of Raphael, while a ceiling painting in Nuremberg seems to derive from GIULIO Romano's work at Mantua. In the 1540s his portraits are less obviously Italianate and probably owe something to Holbein and Massys, both of whom he is known to have copied. He was also active as an engraver, and some copper engravings signed G.P. are dated between 1534 and 1547. There are pictures by him in Berlin, Brunswick, Cologne, Copenhagen, Darmstadt, Dresden, Dublin, Florence, and Munich, as well as Nuremberg.

PENTIMENTO (Ital. *pentirsi*, to repent). When a painter changes his mind in the course of a picture and alters, say, the position of a leg, it sometimes happens that the old form will begin to show through in a ghostly way; this ghost is a *pentimento*. It is sometimes inferred that, because there are *pentimenti* visible, a painting must be an original – since it shows the artist changing his mind – and not a copy. The validity of this argument is open to doubt. The word may also be used to denote several attempts to fix a contour with precision in a drawing.

PERMEKE, Constant (1886–1952), was the leading Belgian Expressionist painter. He was the son of a painter and was trained in Bruges before settling in the village of Laethem-St Martin, which was an artists' colony, where he met several other Expressionists. He was there 1902–12 and was called up in 1914, but was wounded in the same year and spent the rest of the war in England. About 1920 he was slightly influenced by Cubism, but on the whole he was a latter-day MILLET whose deep sympathy for farmers and fishermen is evident in his best work. In 1929 he settled at Jabbeke, near Ostend, where his house is now a museum. Other works by him are in Antwerp, Brussels, Edinburgh, London (Tate), Rotterdam, and São Paulo.

PERMOSER, Balthasar (1651–1732), was the leading Late Baroque sculptor in Dresden, where he helped to create the Zwinger. He was trained in Salzburg *c*.1663 before going to Italy for fourteen years. He arrived there *c*.1675 and went to Venice, Rome, Florence, and other cities; in Florence he carved the façade of S. Gaetano (*c*.1684) and worked for the Grand Duke Cosimo III, who tried to secure him as Court Sculptor. Permoser, however, went to Dresden as Court Sculptor in 1689. He spent the rest of his life there, except for several trips to Berlin, a visit to Italy in 1697–8 and another in 1725, when, at the age of 74, he walked to Rome. He returned in 1728. As might be expected from his strong Italian leanings, he was much influenced by Bernini, but, like the other Northerners PUGET, DONNER, and SCHLÜTER, he introduced an element of restrained classicism – though this is not very obvious in his most famous work, the *Apotheosis of Prince Eugene* (1718–21: Vienna, Lower Belvedere). Most of his Dresden works were damaged in 1945, but are now under repair. There are others in Bautzen, Freiberg i. S., and a small *Deposition* is in London (V & A).

PERRÉAL, Jean (*c*.1455–1530), used to be identified with the MASTER OF MOULINS. He was Court Painter to the Bourbons and later worked for Charles VIII of France and his successors, Louis XII and François I. He was in Italy several times 1499/1505 and in London in 1514, to paint Princess Mary Tudor and supervise her new dresses. He also designed Tombs, notably those (unexecuted) at Brou (1509–12). The most important attributions to him are the *Louis XII* in the Royal Coll. and a miniature in London (BM).

PERRONNEAU, Jean Baptiste (1715?–83), was a French portrait painter in oil and pastel. From *c.*1755 he journeyed all over Europe, dying in Amsterdam. He was the only rival to LATOUR as a pastellist in the later 18th century, and the popular *Girl with a Kitten* (1745: London, NG) shows his charm.

PERSPECTIVE. A quasi-mathematical system for the representation of three-dimensional objects in spatial recession on a two-dimensional surface, i.e. for the creation of an independent pictorial space as a microcosm of nature. As normally practised now, perspective is a sophisticated version of the COSTRUZIONE LEGITTIMA invented in the early 15th century, perhaps by Brunelleschi, and improved by Alberti, UCCELLO, and PIERO della Francesca. The basic assumption of all perspective systems is that parallel lines never meet, but that they appear to do so; and that, further, all parallel lines going in any one direction meet at a single point on the horizon known as a Vanishing Point. The early systems were based on a single, central VP; all other parallels were automatically assumed to be parallel to the picture plane and therefore exempt from the assumption that they must meet at some point in the distance. This system is perfectly satisfactory as an aesthetic system, i.e. for the creation of an independent order of reality, a picture-world distinct from the real world; but it is inadequate for an exact representation of physical reality. In order to obtain this greater naturalism – with all the possibilities of illusionism it implies – a system was evolved which uses two VPs on the horizon, and more if necessary to obtain up-hill and down-dale effects. A further refinement is the use of Measuring Points, which allow of the exact representation of objects to scale. All this can be learnt by any moderately mathematically-minded art student in a few hours; for this very reason, many artists are no longer interested in verisimilitude of space and prefer either to renounce the representation of the third dimension altogether (as most abstract artists do), or else to create a spatial illusion of their own, stressing the independence of the world created by the artist from the laws which govern appearance in the physical world.

Aerial Perspective deals with the changes in tone and colour values which are observable in objects receding from the spectator. Owing to the density of the atmosphere all tone contrasts are muted and all colours tend towards blue in proportion to their distance from the observer. Thus, mountains in the background are always bluish. The difference between the atmospheres of Northern Europe and the Mediterranean accounts for the greater interest in aerial perspective to be found in the North, particularly among the Impressionists.

PERUGINO (*c.*1445/50–1523) may have been a pupil of PIERO della Francesca late in the 1460s, after which he went to Florence and probably worked in the shop of VERROCCHIO, where in the early 1470s LEONARDO was also active. He was in Rome in 1479 and is recorded in the 1481 contract for the frescoes in the Sistine Chapel (along with BOTTICELLI, GHIRLANDAIO, and Cosimo Rosselli), where his *Charge to S. Peter* demonstrates his qualities of simplicity, order, and clearly articulated composition. The influence of his friend SIGNORELLI strengthened his draughtsmanship, that of Flemings like MEMLINC suggested the landscape background for his portraits as well as their general composition, and to the persistence of Piero's influence is due the use of architectural and landscape settings for his figure compositions. The *Pietà* (Florence, Accad.) set centrally in a receding arcade, and above all the *Crucifixion with Saints* (Florence, Sta Maria Maddalena de' Pazzi), a fresco of 1496 with an extensive landscape linking the three apparent divisions of the wall, are perfect examples of his quiet, pietistic art, with gentle, rather sentimental figures with drooping postures, tip-tilted heads, and mild rounded faces – a type he repeated all his life with, in his later years, dull and routine repetitiveness.

From *c.*1500 to *c.*1504 RAPHAEL was a pupil in his shop and may have helped with the fresco cycle in the Sala del Cambio at Perugia, Perugino's largest (but not best) work in fresco. Raphael's own early work in S. Severo at Perugia was later – after his death in 1520 – completed by his master. In 1506 Perugino retired to Perugia, since his style was now hopelessly outmoded in Florence, where, however, it had served to counter-balance the confusion of late Quattrocento style. It was to be the herald of the High Renaissance.

Apart from Rome, Florence, and Perugia there are works by him in Baltimore, Brussels, Cambridge (Fitzwm), Cerqueto nr Perugia (the earliest work, of 1478), Chicago, Edinburgh, Frankfurt, London (NG), Lyons, Munich, Nancy, New York (Met. Mus.), Paris (Louvre), Philadelphia, Vienna, and elsewhere.

PESELLINO (*c.*1422–57) is confused in the old sources with his own grandfather, Giuliano Pesello, who was a painter and probably taught Pesellino; he was certainly influenced by Fra Filippo Lippi and the only documented work by Pesellino, the *Trinity with Saints* (1455–7: London, NG, part on loan from the Royal Coll.), was in fact completed after his death by Fra Filippo's workshop. There are works attributed to him in Berlin, Boston (Gardner), Cambridge Mass. (Fogg), Dresden, Florence (Uffizi, Sta Margherita), London (Courtauld Inst.), Milan (Poldi-Pezzoli), New York (Met. Mus., Hist. Soc.), Paris (Louvre), Philadelphia (Johnson), Toledo Ohio, Washington (NG), Worcester Mass., Yale Univ., and elsewhere.

PEVSNER, Antoine (1886–1962), was GABO's elder brother. He was born in Russia and trained in Kiev, where the Byzantine works had a profound effect on him. In 1911 he went to Paris and was influenced by Cubist ideas, but in 1914 he joined his brother in Norway and in 1917 they returned to Revolutionary Russia, hoping for a revolution in the arts. He was made a professor and worked with TATLIN and MALEVICH, going on to CONSTRUCTIVISM. The growing dissatisfaction of the Soviet authorities with abstract art drove him back to Paris in 1923. There are works by him there (Mus. d'Art Moderne) and also in London (Tate) and New York (M of MA).

PHOTOGRAPHIC ETCHING *see* ENGRAVING 2c.

PIAZZETTA, Giovanni Battista (1683–1754), was a Venetian painter, son of a woodcarver, who studied under G. M. CRESPI in Bologna and was probably influenced by him to take up genre subjects. He settled in Venice by 1711, and after his death his family petitioned the State for a pension, claiming that his 'constant studies and his pursuit of glory rather than gain had reduced him to poverty and hastened his death'. His works are comparatively few, and though appearing to be executed with speed and facility were the product of careful deliberation and infinite pains. He made many drawings for collectors and as book illustrations in order to support his family; his work was much influenced by Rembrandt's etchings and his paintings evolve from Baroque contrasts of chiaroscuro towards a freer and more fluid Rococo handling. Piazzetta's influence on the young TIEPOLO was very great and it was Tiepolo who completed the transition to the Rococo. Most of his paintings are in Venice, including his only ceiling decoration, the *Glory of S. Dominic*, painted before 1727 (SS. Giovanni e Paolo). Other works are in Boston, Cologne, Chicago, Cleveland Ohio, Detroit, Dresden, Dublin, Florence (Uffizi), London (NG), Milan (Brera), Padua, Vicenza, and elsewhere. His drawings are well represented in the Royal Collection at Windsor Castle.

PICABIA, Francis (1879–1953), was born in Paris. He has some claim to have painted the first abstract picture – a watercolour of 1908/9, now in Paris (Mus. d'Art Moderne) – which would antedate KANDINSKY. In 1912 he joined the Section d'Or Cubists, subsequently running through Dadaism and, from 1924, Surrealism: he also painted precisely representational nudes for sale in Algiers. He visited America on several occasions and exhibited at the ARMORY SHOW. There are works in Chicago and Leeds as well as Paris (Mus. d'Art Moderne).

PICASSO, Pablo Ruiz y (1881–1973), was born in Malaga, the son of an art teacher. The boy showed exceptional talent at an early age, and the artistic current flowing into Barcelona (where the family had settled) from France and Northern Europe stimulated him into trying out the personal languages of Munch, Toulouse-Lautrec, Renoir, and other northern lights. In 1900 he visited Paris for a short time, and returned in 1901 to join the cohort of young Bohemians attracted to the capital by the stimulating and exciting atmosphere then prevailing in the arts.

Lautrec, Gauguin, van Gogh, Steinlen, late Impressionism flit across his canvases in a bewildering medley and leave behind a passion for blue, which became the dominant colour for his portrayal of the squalid tragedy of the Paris streets – the beggar, the harlot, the sick child, the hungry. Through this welter of contemporary influences ran the steady current of the things he had grown up with: the elongated forms of Catalan Gothic sculpture and Italian Mannerism, the simplified colour and straightforward approach of Velazquez, Zurbarán, and Goya. These also inform his pictures of actors, mountebanks, and harlequins, whose tender fawns and pinks replace the earlier drab and sad colours. Until then nothing unusual had transpired: even his interest in Iberian sculpture in 1906, and the radical simplification of form and colour it led to, gave little hint of the position when the FAUVE outbreak was at its height. Picasso took no part in this. He was questioning the whole basis of painting and was therefore unable to follow still further the road from Impressionism to the dissolution of form and its translation into colour and imaginative feeling. Picasso's reply to Matisse's 'Composition is the art of arranging in a decorative manner the various elements at the painter's disposal for the expression of his feelings' was to turn to Cézanne, whose *petite sensation* never had any truck with pure decoration and whose composition was based on the rigorous discipline of the relations of form and space on a two-dimensional surface. Picasso's *Demoiselles d'Avignon* (New York, M of M A) of 1907 was begun in the vein of his harlequin series, but ended as a semi-abstract composition, in which the forms of the nudes and their accessories are broken up into planes compressed into a shallow space. The influence of Negro sculptures, which first appears in the *Demoiselles*, also fitted in with his quest for the expression of form and helped, by the bizarre nature of their forms, to release him from the tyranny of the representational tradition in art. In 1907 he met BRAQUE, who had drifted into the Fauve circle and out of it again, and by 1909 they found that they faced the same problems and were striving to solve them in the same way. Both rejected decorative arabesques and bright, sensuous colour and were striving to devise a pictorial language which would define volumes and their relationships without destroying the flat surface of the picture, and without descending to the imitation of accidental and superficial appearances. Together they evolved what is now called Analytical Cubism.

By 1912, colour had begun to creep back among the greys, olive greens, and drab browns, and actual objects – a piece of cane seating, a newspaper heading – were imported so as to stress by their complaisant acquiescence in becoming an element in a design the modest role of Nature in the Ideal, and also to serve as an example of the way in which Nature may be re-created. COLLAGE was a natural extension of this. Objects could be literally reconstituted with bits of wood, wire, paper, and string, their forms distorted by the artist into a flat composition whose inherent third dimension is alluded to at the same time as it is suppressed – although Picasso, having started this hare, did not course it, any more than he did that of SURREA-LISM, born from the juxtaposition of recognizable objects and re-constituted forms.

At the moment when the War broke out in 1914, Braque and Picasso were separated by a quarrel (the breach was never healed) and both had consistently held aloof from the host of minor artists who had by now realized that Cubism was the coming thing and had climbed aboard the bandwagon – Gleizes, Metzinger, Delaunay, Marcoussis, Duchamp-Villon, Picabia, La Fresnaye, and Derain. From 1915 he had shown his interest in Ingres' drawings by precise and restrainedly stylized pencil drawings, and his connexion with the Diaghileff Russian Ballet in Rome in 1917 led to works showing a return to traditional vision, with parallel works in a glitteringly sophis-ticated Cubist idiom. Finally, contact with the Antique and with Roman classicism ushers in a series of paintings and drawings of monumental female nudes, at first almost motionless and then, by 1923, galvanized into terrifying movement which distorts them into frightening caricatures before dissolving them, via calligraphic curves and lines, into the convulsive and repellent distortions of the *Three Dancers* of 1925. For the next ten years Picasso developed these distorted and disquieting figures through what is generally called the Metamorphic phase, in which he was perhaps somewhat influenced by Mirò and Tanguy. By the early 1930s he was rather taking the wind out of Matisse's sails with a series of nudes – odalisques almost – which combine brilliance of colour with flat pattern of a violent intensity; soon after he began the series of bull-fighting subjects which culminated in the imagery present in *Guernica* (1936: on extended loan to M of MA, New York). This huge composition, prompted by the Spanish Civil War, expresses in complicated iconography and personal symbolical language, comprehensible after careful study, the artist's abhorrence of the violence and beastliness of war. This dark mood persisted in the dislocated forms and frightening imagery of his work during the Second World War. He remained in Paris during the Occupation and gradually acquired by his aloofness the stature of a symbol of resistance, but from 1946 to his death he lived mainly in the South of France. During these years he experimented with ceramics and also painted a large mural for UNESCO in Paris.

No man has changed more radically the nature of art. Like Giotto, Michelangelo, and Bernini he stands at the beginning of a new epoch. Most museums of modern art throughout the world have examples.

PICKENOY (Picquenoy) *see* ELIAS.

PICTURE PLANE. The extreme front edge of the imaginary space in the picture. It lies immediately behind the glass of the frame and is the plane at which the world of the spectator and of the picture make contact.

PICTURESQUE (Ital. *pittoresco*, pertaining to a painter). Originally (in the 18th century) this meant that a landscape looked as though it came straight out of a picture (by CLAUDE or Gaspar POUSSIN), but the original meaning has been reversed so that it now means that a scene is pictorially worthy to be transferred straight to canvas (it is used in this sense by the sophisticated only with a derogatory implication). In the 18th century, particularly in connexion with landscape gardening, there arose a long, complicated, and dreary controversy over The Picturesque (satirized by Jane Austen in 'Sense and Sensibility' and 'Northanger Abbey'), but it served some purpose in that it established a new kind of Beauty, midway between Burke's Sublime and Beautiful (this latter we would call Pretty), which was dependent for its effect on roughness, irregularity, and a certain amount of deformity. The different types are contrasted in Thomson's 'Castle of Indolence':

> Whate'er Lorraine light-touched with softening hue,
> Or savage Rosa dashed, or learned Poussin drew.

The idea was much expanded by the Romantics of the 19th century.

PIERCE *see* PEARCE.

PIERO della Francesca (de' Franceschi) (1410/20–92), long neglected, is now probably the most popular painter of the Quattrocento. This is due to the mathematical perfection of his forms and to his superb sense of interval, the whole giving a timeless and serene air to his works, increased by his pale and soft colours. A generation brought up on Cubism and the intellectual rigour of Cézanne has the right to appreciate Piero. He is first recorded in 1439, when he was in Florence with DOMENICO Veneziano, painting frescoes in Sant' Egidio which are now lost. He came from the small town of Borgo San Sepolcro in Umbria, and the experience of Florentine art, in the works of Domenico Veneziano, Andrea del Castagno, Uccello, and Masaccio, must have been decisive in his artistic education. In 1442 he was back in Borgo – he had a deep affection for his native place and spent as much time as possible there – and was then serving as a Town Councillor, which would indicate a certain maturity. The Compagnia della Misericordia, a charitable foundation in Borgo, commissioned a polyptych of the *Madonna della Misericordia*, showing the Madonna protecting humanity (and in particular the members of the Compagnia) under her mantle, from him in 1445 for delivery in 3 years: it was not finally paid for until 1462 and the execution may therefore have dragged on for years. Piero always seems to have worked with the greatest deliberation, and other cases are known of his taking several years over a work: he even seems to have developed, at Arezzo, a technique which allowed him to work slowly in fresco.

The length of time taken over the Borgo *Madonna* makes it difficult to know what his early style was like, but the *Baptism* in London (NG) is accepted as an early work, showing traces of Florentine (and Sienese) influence, yet standing for a calm and classic stillness totally opposed to all that the Florentines then sought. A *S. Jerome* at Berlin, signed and dated 1450, is unfortunately too damaged for use in stylistic comparisons, but a damaged fresco of 1451 in S. Francesco at Rimini, *Sigismondo Malatesta and his Patron Saint*, shows Piero's love of symmetry and of counterchanged patterns in the two dogs. By this time he had probably painted some frescoes, now lost, in Ferrara, the influence of which is discernible in the local School. About 1452 Piero began the work on which his fame chiefly rests, the fresco cycle in the choir of S. Francesco at Arezzo depicting the story of the True Cross. The narrative is highly complicated, being based on several different accounts in the Golden Legend, and it is not made easier to follow by the fact that Piero, presumably for artistic reasons, has treated the story in a cavalier way and arranged, for example, the two battle scenes out of order in the story but facing each other at the bottom of each of the side walls, thus forming one of the symmetries he loved. The frescoes were almost unknown for centuries and suffered from neglect, but at least they were not repainted much and therefore give a good idea of Piero's mature style, and of what he owed to Domenico Veneziano and to Florence. In 1459 Piero was in Rome, by which time the Arezzo frescoes were presumably finished. The work in the Vatican which Piero is known to have done has vanished, but a *S. Luke* in Sta Maria Maggiore is, perhaps optimistically, ascribed to him. The ascription is not made any more plausible by the fact that two of his masterpieces are likely to date from this time – the fresco of *The Resurrection* in Borgo and the diptych with the portraits of his friends and patrons the Duke and Duchess of Urbino (Florence, Uffizi). The portraits have been associated with a poem of 1465, but look stylistically rather later (*c.* 1472?). They show strong influence from Flemish painting in the use of the oil technique, perhaps due to the presence of Flemish pictures in Italy. Later on, Joos van Ghent worked at Urbino. The curious *Flagellation of Christ*, which again shows Flemish influence, was also painted for Urbino. Various explanations of the subject and date have been advanced. All this time Piero was working on a large altarpiece, parts of which survive. It was commissioned for Borgo San Sepolcro in 1454 and completed fifteen years later: the centre panel was probably a *Madonna* but is now lost; on either side were *SS. Augustine, Michael, John* (?), and *Nicholas of Tolentino* (now in Lisbon, London (NG), New York (Frick Coll.), and Milan (Poldi-Pezzoli)). The last two pictures Piero painted are the *Madonna with the Duke of Urbino as Donor* (Milan, Brera), known as the *Brera Madonna*, which is datable between *c*.1472 and *c*.1475, and the unfinished *Nativity* (London NG). It is sometimes said, on exiguous evidence, that the hand (or even the head) of the Duke in the *Brera Madonna* is by BERRU-GUETE. In any case, it seems clear that Piero stopped painting in the 1470s – the last document to record him as a painter is of 1478, concerning a lost fresco – although he lived on until 1492. One explanation for this is that he became increasingly interested in perspective and mathematics, for he wrote two treatises, 'De prospectiva pingendi' and 'De quinque corporibus regularibus', and it is also likely that his sight failed, for he seems to have been blind in his last years. His chief pupils were PERUGINO and SIGNORELLI, both of whom reacted against his style. There are other works by him in Arezzo, Boston (Gardner), Monterchi nr Borgo, Oxford (Ch. Ch.), Perugia, Sansepolcro, Urbino, Vaduz (Liechtenstein Coll.), Venice (Accad.), and Williamstown Mass.

PIERO di Cosimo (*c*.1462–1521?) was a pupil of Cosimo Rosselli and probably assisted him on his frescoes in the Sistine Chapel of the Vatican, *c*.1481. He was much influenced by Signorelli and Leonardo da Vinci and his mature works differ entirely from Rosselli's in that they are mostly rather obscure, but very poetically felt, mythologies. He was famous in his own day as a designer of the *Trionfi* processions, especially for his gruesome *Triumph of Death* of 1511. In his later years he became a recluse. There are pictures by him in Berlin, Chantilly, Florence (Uffizi, Pitti, Horne Mus., Innocenti), The Hague, Hartford Conn., London (NG, Wallace Coll., Dulwich), Munich, New York (Met. Mus.), Ottawa, Oxford, Paris (Louvre), Philadelphia (Johnson), Rome (Borghese, Gall. Naz.), Sarasota Fla, Toledo Ohio, Washington (NG), Worcester Mass., Yale, and elsewhere.

PIETÀ (Ital. pity). A representation of the Dead Christ supported on His Mother's lap, with or without other mourning figures. The idea originated in 14th-century Germany (Ger. *Vesperbild*) and is an expression of Northern piety which stressed the human relationship between Christ and the Virgin, and which here drew a parallel with the Madonna holding the infant Christ on her lap. The earliest example (*c*.1320?) is at Veste Coburg. These early German works emphasize the sufferings of Christ by distortion and exaggeration: in Michelangelo's *St Peter's Pietà* (*c*.1500), for the first time, the Northern expressiveness is combined with the Hellenistic qualities of form and beauty. *See* IMAGO PIETATIS.

PIETRO Berrettini da Cortona (1596–1669), painter and architect, was one of the founders of the Roman High Baroque, comparable with BERNINI in sculpture. His first works were painted for the Sacchetti family and are now in the Capitoline Gallery, Rome, along with other works of his, but he was soon taken up by the powerful Barberini family – the family of Urban VIII – for whom he painted frescoes in Sta Bibiana, Rome (1624–6), followed by his greatest work, the ceiling in the Barberini Palace (now the Galleria Nazionale, Rome). This is a huge fresco representing an *Allegory of Divine Providence and Barberini Power*, begun in 1633 and completed in 1639: a sketch for it is now exhibited with it, but its authenticity is open to doubt. The fresco is a huge illusion, like the ceilings of LANFRANCO or GUERCINO, with the central field apparently open to the sky and scores of figures seen *al di* SOTTO IN SÙ apparently coming into the room itself or floating above it. While working on this Pietro also went to Florence and began a series of similar frescoes in the Pitti Palace; he also began a series of frescoes in the Chiesa Nuova, Rome, which was not finished until 1665 (the *modello* for the cupola is now in Hartford, Conn., Wadsworth Atheneum). Towards the end of his life he devoted much of his time to architecture, but he published a Treatise on Painting in 1652 under a pseudonym and in collaboration. He refused invitations to both France and Spain. With the help of numerous pupils, of whom Ciro FERRI was the most important, he painted many other frescoes and easel pictures in Rome and Florence. Outside Italy there are works by him in the Royal Collection, and in Berlin, Bristol, Chatsworth, Madrid, Munich, Paris, Sarasota Fla, Toledo Ohio, and Vienna.

PIGALLE, Jean Baptiste (1714–85), was a French sculptor, a pupil of LEMOYNE, who failed to win a scholarship to Rome, went at his own expense in 1736, nearly starved, and was rescued by G. Coustou II. He returned to France in 1739 and worked for churches and for Mme de Pompadour, for whom he made the *Love and Friendship* (1758) now in the Louvre (the plaster is in Baltimore). His major works include the Tomb of Maréchal de Saxe in S. Thomas, Strasbourg (1753–76), and his *Nude Voltaire* (1776) in the Institut, Paris. He also made the base of BOUCHARDON's equestrian *Louis XV*.

PILON, Germain (c.1531–90), was a French sculptor who worked in marble and bronze. His early style (e.g. in the three Graces of the Monument for the Heart of Henri II, 1560: Louvre) is based on the elongated, Mannerist elegance of Primaticcio's plaster decorations at Fontainebleau. Later, his work becomes more fluid and more realist at the same time; his softly flowing forms invest with poignancy the relaxed recumbent marble figures of the dead Henri II and his Queen, Catherine de' Medici, in their tomb, while above on the canopy the living figures of the monarchs are sharply characterized in bronze

(1563–70: S. Denis). His marble relief of Valentine Balbiani has a strange rippling quality which stresses the dead woman's angular, skeletal forms beneath the taut skin and the loose curling hair. Pilon seeks to create emotion through the marriage of virtuosity of handling and dramatic intensity. His use of Michelangelo and Pontormo is apparent, but never obvious or derivative. He also made portrait medals and busts, chiefly of the French Royal family, during the 1570s. Most of his works are in Paris (Louvre and S. Denis), but there is a bronze bust of Charles IX in London (Wallace Coll.).

PINTORICCHIO (Pinturicchio), Bernardino (c. 1454–1513), was active in Perugia in 1481, but before that he was probably in Rome assisting Perugino with the frescoes in the Sistine Chapel (1481/2). The influence of Perugino remained dominant for the rest of his life. His principal works are the fresco cycles in the Borgia Apartments in the Vatican (1492–c. 1495) and in the Piccolomini Library of the Cathedral of Siena (1503–8). His numerous works include those in Baltimore (Walters), Berlin, Boston (Mus., Gardner), Cambridge (Fitzwm), Cambridge Mass. (Fogg), Cleveland Ohio, Dresden, London (NG), New York (Met. Mus.), Oxford, Paris (Louvre), Perugia, Philadelphia (Johnson), Rome (churches), San Marino Cal. (Huntington), Siena (Mus. and Cath.), Spello (Mus. and churches), Spoleto (Cath.), and Washington (NG).

PIOMBO, Sebastiano del, see SEBASTIANO.

PIRANESI, Giovanni Battista (1720–78), was a Venetian architect who went to Rome in 1740 and became the recorder of Roman antiquities in hundreds of etchings. His feeling for the poetry of ruins, his romantic archaeology, and his intensely dramatic exploitation of the contrasts of light and shade possible in etching exerted great influence on 18th-century architecture, and even more on the whole visual approach to Antiquity and the Decline and Fall. His most original works are the *Carceri d'Invenzione* (begun c. 1745, reworked 1761) of imaginary and megalomaniac prisons, but he was far more famous for his *Vedute*, 135 etchings of ancient and modern Rome, published from 1745 onwards, and for his violent archaeological polemics (pro-Roman and anti-Greek). The *Vedute* continued to be printed long after his death and formed the basis of the mental image of Rome possessed by thousands who never went there, and, with PANINI, he created a lasting picture of Rome, as Canaletto and Guardi created one of Venice. In his lifetime (1771) Horace Walpole spoke of '... the sublime dreams of Piranesi, who seems to have conceived visions of Rome beyond what it boasted even in the meridian of its splendour. Savage as Salvator Rosa, fierce as Michael Angelo, and exuberant as Rubens, he has imagined scenes that would startle geometry, and exhaust the Indies to realise.'

PISANELLO, Antonio (probably 1395–1455/6), was the major Italian exponent of INTERNATIONAL GOTHIC in succession to GENTILE da Fabriano, who was very probably his master. He was trained in Verona, probably under STEFANO da Verona, and then went to Venice where he seems to have succeeded Gentile in painting a series of frescoes in the Doge's Palace (1415/22: all destroyed); he also succeeded Gentile in Rome, at the Lateran Basilica (1431/2: also destroyed). These were probably works in the International style, and the fact that he succeeded Gentile makes it seem likely that he was regarded as his heir. The earliest extant major work by Pisanello is the *Annunciation* (1423/4: Verona, S. Fermo) and in it, as in the later *S. George and the Princess* (1437/8: Verona, S. Anastasia), his courtly interests and narrative gifts are clearly shown. In 1438 he made his first datable portrait medal, and it is as a medallist and draughtsman that he is best known. In 1448/9 he made a set of medals of Alfonso of Aragon, King of Naples, and he is known to have been there. The Vallardi Codex (Paris, Louvre) is one of the most important surviving collections of 15th-century drawings, and contains not only Pisanello's own drawings – studies of animals, costume, antiques, sketches for pictures and copies of other drawings – but also what seem to be drawings by pupils and by other artists kept in case they came in handy one day. His wonderful studies of animals reveal how sharp his observation was in this typical International Gothic interest, and his portraits confirm this (Bergamo and Paris). The closeness of his ties with Burgundy is demonstrated by the *Profile of a Girl* (Washington, NG) which is still undetermined between him and the Franco-Flemish School *c*.1420. The only other paintings by him are in London (NG) and some fresco fragments rediscovered in Mantua in 1968: a good set of his medals is in the V & A Museum.

PISANO, Andrea (*c*.1290–1348), appears for the first time in 1330, when he began work on the bronze Doors of the Baptistry of Florence. This presumably indicated that he was already a sculptor of some renown, and his name perhaps indicates that he was trained in Pisa. He finished the bronze Doors in 1336, and the type of Gothic relief and the general disposition of the relief fields conditioned the form of GHIBERTI's first Baptistry Doors more than half a century later. The only other work associated with him is a series of reliefs, and possibly some statues on the Campanile of Florence Cathedral, where Andrea succeeded Giotto (*d*.1337). Giotto may have designed some of the reliefs, and Andrea's bronze Door certainly contains reminiscences of Giotto's work in the Peruzzi Chapel. In 1347 Andrea became head of the works at Orvieto Cathedral, where he was succeeded by his son Nino Pisano (*c*.1315–68?), also a sculptor, by whom there is a signed *Madonna* in Florence (S.M. Novella).

PISANO, Nicola (*c*.1220/5 or earlier–84?) and his son, Giovanni (*c*.1245/50–after 1314), were the creators of modern sculpture, preceding such painters as GIOTTO in the 'rebirth of the arts'. They are documented between 1258 and 1314 and there is a considerable body of work certainly attributable to them, either individually or in collaboration, including the four great Pulpits which are their main claim to fame. The first of these is the work of Nicola alone and is signed and dated 1260. It stands in the Baptistry at Pisa, and, by its affinity to antique sarcophagi such as the one in the Campo Santo at Pisa, clearly proclaims that its creator was using antique art as a model, and was attempting to create a Christian art with the realism and dignity of Late Roman sculpture, thus distinguishing it from the art of the Gothic North of Europe. The place of Nicola's birth is unknown, but there is some evidence for the view that he must have imbibed this feeling for Roman art in South Italy, where the Emperor Frederick II (*d.*1250) was engaged in a deliberate revival of Roman grandeur. Between 1265 and 1268 Nicola was engaged on the Pulpit in Siena Cathedral, but he had several assistants including ARNOLFO and his own young son Giovanni, who was engaged on the understanding that he would come to Siena and would stay there and be patient in his work. Opinion is divided on the relative shares of these masters, since there is a noticeable increase in French Gothic influence in the relief panels with New Testament scenes and in the rest of the work. Much the same is true of the Fountain in the Piazza at Perugia, which is signed by both and dated 1278. This was Nicola's last major work, the last two pulpits being certainly by Giovanni alone. The French influence in them, as in much of his other work, has led to the hypothesis – for which there is no evidence – that he paid a visit to France at some point in his career. The pulpit in S. Andrea, Pistoia, was completed in 1301 and traditionally took 4 years to make. It shows what is perhaps the highest point of the French influence on Giovanni's style; for the last and greatest of the Pulpits, that in Pisa Cathedral, is considerably closer in spirit to his father and seems to show that Giovanni was working towards a new and personal synthesis of Gothic and classical elements. This pulpit was commissioned in 1302 and completed in 1310, although it is signed and dated 1311. There is also a curious and cryptic inscription alluding to the difficulties and tribulations experienced by Giovanni in the course of the work.

Giovanni was also active as an architect and worked much at Siena Cathedral, where many of the figures on the façade were carved by him (a fragment in London, V & A). As early as 1284 he was exempted from all taxes on account of his work at the Cathedral. Other works by him include an ivory *Madonna* (*c.*1299) in Pisa Cathedral, and *Madonnas* in Padua (Arena Chapel: *c.*1305) and Prato Cathedral.

PISIS, Filippo de (1896–1956), was an Italian painter who worked in

Ferrara and Paris. He was influenced by CHIRICO and Pittura Metafisica in 1918–19, but he lived in Paris 1920–40 and then based his style on the fluent, quasi-Impressionist brushwork of Manet and GUARDI, whom he especially imitated in his views of Venice and other towns. There are works in the Modern Museums of Florence, Milan, Rome, Turin, and Venice.

PISSARRO, Camille (1831–1903), was born in St Thomas in the West Indies, the son of a Creole mother and a father of Portuguese-Jewish descent. He worked as a clerk in his father's general store until in 1852 he ran away to Venezuela with a Danish painter, after which his reluctant parents resigned themselves to his becoming an artist. He arrived in Paris in 1855, in time to see the great exhibition at the World Fair (when COURBET exhibited his rejected pictures independently). Soon after he met COROT, by whom he was deeply influenced, although by 1866 Corot disapproved of the way that the younger landscape painters were going, and was particularly severe about Pissarro's connexion with Courbet and Manet. He met MONET in 1859, and in 1863 several of his pictures were in the SALON des Refusés. From 1866–9 he worked at Pontoise on landscapes painted entirely in the open, but he could sell almost nothing and he and his family lived in the most cruel poverty. In 1870 he fled before the German invasion, first to Brittany and then to London, where eventually news reached him that his house in Louveciennes had been used as a butchery by the invaders, and his store of 200 to 300 pictures used as duckboards in the muddy garden. In 1872 Cézanne joined him in Pontoise and worked with him, with a radical effect on his own style. In 1874 he took part in the first IMPRESSIONIST Exhibition: he was the only one who exhibited in all eight, and it was he who introduced first Gauguin, then Seurat and Signac into the Impressionist exhibitions, with consequent disruption among the group. He was much influenced from 1884 by Seurat's theories of OPTICAL MIXTURE, which he used until 1888, when he declared that the method 'inhibits me and hinders the development of spontaneity of sensation'. From 1895 the worsening of his eye-trouble forced him to give up working out-of-doors, and he painted many town views from windows in Paris; he died blind.

His production was enormous and in all techniques – chiefly oil-painting, but he also used pastel, gouache, drawing in all media, etching, and lithography. Of all the Impressionists he was the most consistent; he never compromised, he did his best to compose the bitter quarrels which broke out around him, he never blamed any for their defections, intolerance, impatience, and occasional spites. In return, they gave him respect and admiration for his principles as much as for his art. There are paintings by him all over the world, in almost every museum of modern art. His son Lucien (1863–1944) followed in his father's stylistic footsteps. He lived in England, where he founded the Eragny Press (named after his father's final home) in 1896 and exerted great influence on book-illustration and printing in this country. His daughter, known as Orovida (1893–1968), was also a painter.

PITATI, Bonifazio de', *see* BONIFAZIO.

PITTONI, Giovanni Battista (1687–1767), was, with PELLEGRINI, one of the principal Venetian Rococo painters on a lower level than TIEPOLO. He was influenced by Tiepolo and by Sebastiano RICCI and was highly regarded by his contemporaries. He entered the Guild in Venice in 1716, and in 1758 succeeded Tiepolo as President of the Venetian Academy. Much of his work was done for German, Polish, and Russian patrons and it is likely that his basic sentimentality and the brightness of his colour appealed to them. There are many works by him in Venice and others in Berlin, Dresden, Edinburgh, Florence (Uffizi), Paris (Louvre), and Vicenza.

PITTURA METAFISICA (Ital. metaphysical painting) was the result of CHIRICO's dissatisfaction with the mechanical aspect of Cubism, which he experienced in Paris. In 1917, in Ferrara, he was in the Italian army and met CARRÀ, with whom he founded *Pittura Metafisica*. The movement did not last long, but it influenced de PISIS and MORANDI.

PLASTER CASTING is an intermediate stage in the production of a piece of sculpture which is often the last process actually to be carried out by the sculptor himself. Once his model has been cast in plaster it can be regarded as a finished work, rather fragile in nature, or it can be executed in bronze, lead, or any other metal, or, with a POINTING MACHINE, it can be mechanically reproduced in marble or stone.

Any work of sculpture which is not a piece of direct carving in some hard substance is normally carried out in clay or wax. If, say, a head has been modelled in wax it can be left at that; if in clay it will dry up and crumble to pieces unless it is either kept permanently damp or transformed into Terracotta or Plaster. Terracotta is really no more than baking the clay, in the same way as a common flower-pot is produced. The result is the same in texture and usually varies in colour from grey-brown to brick red. A plaster cast is rather more complicated, but the basic process is simple enough. First, a mould has to be made. The clay head is first divided into two or three parts by strips of zinc, usually stuck like a fringe round the side of the head at ear level (figures and more complex shapes may require multi-part moulds), the purpose being to ensure that the two halves of the mould lift off easily. Some plaster of Paris is now mixed up and tinted with dye, and as soon as it is firm and creamy it is thrown at the head, so that it sticks to the whole surface and forms a coating about $\frac{1}{8}/\frac{1}{4}$ in. thick. This is then thickly coated with untinted plaster and left to harden, the two halves being pulled apart when the plaster has set (the head in clay often gets damaged in this process). The mould is now cleaned out and the inside brushed over with oil and soft soap to prevent the cast from sticking to it. Next, the halves of the mould are re-united and tied together and fresh plaster is poured into it from the open base, swirled around to drive it into all the crevices, and then allowed to harden. The mould is now destroyed by chipping it away with mallet and chisel, the purpose of the thin layer of tinted plaster being to warn the sculptor when he is nearing the surface of the cast. When all the plaster has been removed the finished cast is revealed and it can then be left white, painted or bronzed over, or handed to the bronze-founder or mason for reproduction in bronze or marble. *See* BRONZE and POINTING MACHINE.

PLASTICITY. The quality of appearing three-dimensional. A painting is said to have great plasticity if it gives the impression that the figures are fully modelled and are capable of moving freely in the pictorial space. Plasticity is often obtained by emphasizing the tonal contrasts and by keeping the greater part of the picture in shadow.

PLATE MARK. The indentation made by printing an intaglio plate on paper (*see* ENGRAVING 2, *Intaglio*).

PLEIN AIR (Fr. open air). The feeling that a picture really gives the impression of the open air, a quality much sought by the Impressionists. In a more restricted sense it applies to landscapes actually painted out of doors, with the intention of catching this quality. This practice is relatively recent, at least as far as finished pictures are concerned (but *see* CLAUDE), and it was this concern for a non-aesthetic quality which underlies the remark said to have been made by Degas, that Monet's pictures always made him turn up his coat collar.

PLEYDENWURFF, Hans (*c.* 1420–72), was the major Nuremberg painter immediately before WOLGEMUT and DÜRER. He became a citizen there in 1457, and introduced the realism of the Netherlands, especially that of BOUTS. In 1462 he completed the altarpiece for the high altar of S. Elizabeth in Breslau, where fragments still remain. He may also have worked in Cracow. His son Wilhelm (*d.* 1494) was also a painter and woodcut maker, and worked in the shop of Wolgemut, who married Pleydenwurff's widow.

POCHADE (Fr.). A sketch, usually a small one in oils made in front of some actual landscape with the intention of working up a large picture from it.

POINTILLISM *see* OPTICAL MIXTURES.

POINTING MACHINE. A mechanical device for reproducing a PLASTER cast in stone or marble without the exercise of any artistic skill on the part of the carver. It was originally developed by the ancient Greeks but was perfected in the 18th and 19th centuries and became very popular among academic sculptors of the later 19th century, since it allows the sculptor to work in clay or wax and leave all the dirty work to professional masons. The whole idea is repugnant to most modern sculptors, who feel that the form taken by the finished work should be conditioned by the material from which it is carved (e.g. a carving in wood ought to take account of the grain): for this reason most modern sculptors prefer to carve direct, working only from a sketch and not even using a model made of clay, which would be unglyptic.

A pointing machine works by triangulation from three points selected on the surface of a full-size model – e.g. top of the head, tip of the nose, cheek-bone – and these are measured against a given frame, usually of wood, and repeated on the marble block, so that the carver can cut to the depth measured on the machine. Further points can then be measured against the original three. Normally, a skin of stone is left, so that the sculptor himself can give the final touches. Several plaster models, with the metal 'points' still in them, are preserved in the CANOVA museum at Possagno.

POLIAKOFF, Serge (1906–1969), was born in Moscow, of a well-off family. He emigrated in 1919 and for many years earned a living as a guitarist, settling in Paris and beginning to paint in 1930. He worked in London at Chelsea and the Slade School 1935–7 and returned to Paris, meeting KANDINSKY in 1937 and DELAUNAY in 1938. From then on he painted abstract pictures, and, later, was influenced by the more mathematical art of MALEVICH. He also made colour lithographs.

POLLAIUOLO (Pollaiolo, Pollajuolo), Antonio (c.1432–98) and Piero (c.1441–96), were brothers who ran one of the most advanced and successful workshops in Florence in the second half of the 15th century. They worked as painters, sculptors, engravers, goldsmiths, and designers of embroidery, and their knowledge of anatomy and the new technique of oil-painting together with the study they made of the problems of representing violent action placed them at the head of the scientific painters immediately preceding Leonardo. It is now customary to assume that all the best work was done by Antonio, and all the bad by Piero. This view receives considerable support from the fact that documented work by Piero – a set of *Virtues* in Florence, Uffizi (one other was by BOTTICELLI), and an altarpiece (1483) in San Gimignano – is very poor. On the other hand, a signed engraving by Antonio of a *Battle of the Nude Gods* is of very high quality indeed, and fully justifies the praise early lavished on him as a draughtsman and anatomist; yet no painting can be certainly ascribed to him. The influence of DONATELLO and of Andrea del CASTAGNO is paramount in their work, and Piero (not Antonio) is said to have been Castagno's pupil for a short time. Their most ambitious works are the *S. Sebastian* (1475: London, NG) and the Tombs of Popes

Sixtus IV (1493) and Innocent VIII (1492–8), both in St Peter's. Other works are in Berlin, Florence (Uffizi, Bargello, Cathedral Mus., S. Miniato, Villa Gallina), London (NG, BM), Milan (Poldi-Pezzoli), Naples, Staggia nr Siena, Turin, Washington (NG: a *Portrait* more usually attributed to Castagno), and Yale.

POLLOCK, Jackson (1912–56), the chief American exponent of ACTION PAINTING, made studies for his apparently unpremeditated works, done on continuous lengths of canvas tacked to the floor, and later cut up with selective care. He abandoned the use of brushes in 1947, pouring the paint straight on to the canvas, but in 1953 he began to employ brushes again. He said of his paintings (1951): 'I don't work from drawings or colour sketches. My painting is direct. . . . I want to express my feelings rather than illustrate them. . . . When I am painting I have a general notion as to what I am about. I *can* control the flow of paint: there is no accident, just as there is no beginning and no end.' He used metallic paints and ordinary commercial synthetic enamel and plastic paint, with results that are already unfortunate. There are examples in London (Tate), Rio de Janeiro and many US museums.

POLYCHROMATIC SCULPTURE is sculpture which, like most sculpture before the 16th century, has been painted in naturalistic colours to heighten its life-like effect.

POLYMER *see* ACRYLIC.

POLYPTYCH. A picture or relief, usually an altarpiece, which is made up of two or more panels. Two panels form a diptych, three a triptych, five a pentaptych: more than three are usually called simply a polyptych. A typical Italian 14th–15th-century polyptych consists of a large central panel of the *Madonna*, with perhaps two *Saints* on either side and an *Annunciation* on top. The PREDELLA would then consist of narrative scenes from the Lives of Saints 1 and 2, with a scene from the Life of Christ – perhaps the *Adoration of the Magi* – in the middle and then scenes from the Lives of Saints 3 and 4.

PONTORMO, Jacopo (1494–1556), was born at Pontormo, near Empoli. He went to Florence and was influenced by Leonardo, Piero di Cosimo, and Albertinelli, before working under Andrea del Sarto *c.*1512, when he met ROSSO, with whom he was to be one of the creators of MANNERISM. He was working on his own by about 1513, in Sta Maria Novella and SS. Annunziata in Florence, and in 1518 he painted the *Madonna*, still in S. Michele Visdomini, Florence, which is one of the first Mannerist pictures; profoundly influenced still by Andrea del Sarto, but with a new unease, an agitation which sharply distinguishes it from the complacency of Andrea's Madonnas. Pontormo was a profoundly religious painter and this probably underlies the forms he chose. He came to the notice of the Medici family and was commissioned by them to decorate their Villa at

Poggio a Caiano (1521) which he did with a gay and light fresco. His next frescoes were the Passion cycle in the Certosa near Florence (1522–5), disturbing, thoroughly Mannerist, and containing such un-Florentine ideas as borrowings from Dürer, whose angularities of form expressed profound religious ideas. While working on these frescoes Pontormo was assisted by BRONZINO, who was more or less his adopted son, though a totally different kind of artist. What is perhaps his supreme masterpiece, and one of the central pictures in the development of early Mannerism, is the *Deposition* painted about 1525 as the altarpiece for a chapel in Sta Felicita, Florence, where there are also frescoes by Pontormo and Bronzino. Here the darkness of the chapel probably dictated the very light tone and bright colours, but the crowding and agitation of the figures powerfully reinforce the direct emotional effect of the sharp, pale colours. In the drawing the influence of Michelangelo is patent, and this was to become more marked after 1530 when Pontormo was in contact with Michelangelo. Little is known about his later years, principally because the frescoes in S. Lorenzo, on which he worked 1546–56, have all gone and are known only through the drawings. He was a great draughtsman even in an age of great draughtsmen, and there is a huge collection of his drawings in Florence, Uffizi. His character was strange, sensitive, withdrawn, and highly neurotic: his Diary (1555–6) shows him obsessed with his work, his solitariness (often shunning even Bronzino), and above all the state of his bowels. There are works in Amsterdam (Rijksmus.), Baltimore, Cambridge Mass. (Fogg), Carmignano nr Florence, Chicago, Dublin, Florence (Uffizi, Pitti, Accad., Pal. Vecchio, Medici Mus., Innocenti Mus.), Frankfurt, Hanover, London (NG), Lucca, Milan (Castello), Munich, Naples, Oxford (Christ Church), Paris (Louvre, Jacquemart-André), Philadelphia (Johnson), Pontormo, Rome (Borghese, Gall. Naz.), San Francisco, Sansepolcro, Vienna, Washington (NG), and Yale.

POP ART appeared in England in the late 1950s, and in America in the 1960s, though the two streams claim to have developed independently. It consists of the use, as sources, of artifacts, photographs, advertising and strip cartoons, often blown-up to enormous size, and painted usually in a hard-edged technique and garish colour, or of disparate objects and detritus assembled in a manner reminiscent of Surrealism. Its English originators were PAOLOZZI and Hamilton, and its main figures were R. Smith and Blake, with a further wave which includes Hockney, Kitaj, and Phillips. In New York, Pop Art was inspired by Jasper JOHNS and RAUSCHENBERG, and its chief adherents are Warhol, LICHTENSTEIN, Wesselmann, and Oldenburg. In California, it developed rather as a reaction against ABSTRACT IMPRESSIONISM.

PORDENONE, Giovanni Antonio (1483/4–1539), was a North Italian painter who was influenced by the Venetians – especially Titian and Giorgione – and also by German art, particularly in its more violent aspects. This fusion leads to a kind of Mannerism in his style as early as the 1520s. He may have gone to Rome *c*.1515–16, as there is a Raphaelesque phase in his art just then. In 1519/20 he was painting a dome in Treviso in the illusionistic manner introduced by Mantegna, but his dome precedes the one by Correggio, whose influence is, however, discernible in the dome at Piacenza (*c*.1530). For a brief moment Pordenone presented a serious challenge to the supremacy of Titian himself, and he eventually settled in Venice, but his frescoes in Treviso Cath. (1520) do not compare very well with the *Annunciation* by Titian, painted as the altarpiece for the chapel. His principal works are in Cremona, Piacenza, Treviso, and Venice: others are in the Royal Coll. and in London (NG), Milan (Brera), Philadelphia, Prague, Sarasota Fla, and Vienna.

POST-IMPRESSIONISM is a rather vague term applied to the movement which developed in reaction against both Impressionism and Neo-Impressionism and had as its chief aim either a return to a more formal conception of art or a new stress on the importance of the subject. The most important figures covered by the term are van Gogh, Gauguin, and Cézanne. It was given currency in England by the Exhibition arranged by Roger Fry in the winter of 1910–11, called 'Manet and the Post-Impressionists', which caused much heartburning in London art circles and led to the formation of the LONDON GROUP.

Le post-impressionnisme has now come into use in French as the equivalent term.

POTTER, Paulus (1625–54), one of the most famous Dutch animal painters, was the son of a painter and very precocious – his first works are of 1640, and his most famous picture, the life-size *Bull* (The Hague), is signed and dated 1647. On the whole, however, his smaller pictures are better. There are works by him in the Royal Coll. and in Amsterdam, Berlin, Brussels, Copenhagen, Dresden, Dublin, London (NG and Wallace Coll.), Munich, Paris (Louvre), Philadelphia, and elsewhere.

POURBUS, Pieter (1523–84), worked mainly in Bruges where he followed, in his religious works, the florid Italianizing style of Lancelot Blondeel, whose daughter he married. His portraits are stiff and formal affairs, but equal to those of his contemporaries Mor or Joos van Cleve. There are works in Antwerp, Bruges (Mus. and churches), Brussels, London (Wallace Coll.), New York (Met. Mus.), and elsewhere.

Frans I (1545–81), his son and pupil, painted religious pictures and portraits. He worked mainly in Antwerp, where he was also the pupil of Frans FLORIS, whose niece he married. His religious works are usually in the Italianizing style of Floris, but markedly Reformed Church in content; his portraits are close to the sober style of Mor. There are works in Berlin, Brussels, Dresden, Ghent (Mus. and S. Bavon), London (Wallace Coll.), Rotterdam, Vienna, and elsewhere.

Frans II (1569–1622), son of Frans I, worked for the Court of the Spanish Regents of the Netherlands in Brussels, and in 1600 became Court Painter to the Duke of Mantua, being there at the same time as Rubens. He also worked in Innsbruck, Naples, and Turin, and in 1609 became painter to Marie de' Medici at the French Court. His is the most international style of any member of the family. There are works in the Royal Collection and in Amsterdam (Rijksmus.), Berlin, Leeds, Madrid (Prado), Munich, Paris (Louvre), Vienna, and elsewhere.

POUSSIN, Gaspard (1615–75). His name was Dughet but he adopted the name of his illustrious brother-in-law Nicolas, whose pupil he was from about 1630–3. He lived and worked in Rome and its surroundings and attempted, not entirely unsuccessfully, the difficult feat of combining the landscape style and principles of POUSSIN and CLAUDE. He was immensely popular during the 18th century so that most of the older galleries and collections have examples, although these are always attributions, for apart from some frescoes in S. Martino ai Monti in Rome nothing can positively be assigned to him.

POUSSIN, Nicolas (1594–1665), was born in Normandy and after some training went to Paris about 1612. Little is known about him before 1621 when he was employed with Philippe de CHAMPAIGNE on decorations in the Luxembourg Palace. His style was probably based on the second School of FONTAINEBLEAU, modified by the Antique and Italian Renaissance works in the French Royal Collection. In 1624 he went to Rome and in his early struggling years there worked in the studio of Domenichino, whose lucid composition and cool colour affected him strongly. In 1628 he obtained a commission for an altarpiece for St Peter's, the *Martyrdom of S. Erasmus* (now in the Vatican), a work painted in competition with Le VALENTIN and not wholly successful since it involved a compromise between Baroque eloquence and Poussin's less dramatic style.

About 1629–30 he had a serious illness. This marks a change in his style, for he now stopped trying to compete with the increasingly popular opulent Baroque and turned to smaller works and to patrons from the upper middle class. He made many experiments in these early Roman years, one being his short interest in Venetian art which led, for instance, in the Louvre *Inspiration of the Poet*, to a combination of classical form and Venetian colour of the most supreme beauty. He turned from religious to classical subjects, to mythologies, and to Tasso. But this elegiac phase was short-lived, and by 1633 he was working on compositions filled with figures grouped in dramatic poses chosen to make the narrative plain; the influence of Venetian colour gave place to a more rigid use of local colour, and Raphael and the Antique are paramount. Poussin used the device of the miniature stage with small draped wax models to try out effects of gesture, grouping, and lighting.

In 1640 he was persuaded to return to Paris to work for the King and Cardinal Richelieu. This brought him into uneasy competition with most of the artists working for the Crown, of whose work he was outspokenly critical, and in particular with VOUET, but the artistic climate of Paris and the conditions of his employment were highly uncongenial and in 1642, after just over 18 months, he made an excuse to return to Rome which he never again left. In 1642 he finished the first set of the *Seven Sacraments*, of which the *Baptism* is now in Washington (NG). His trip to France enabled him to make new contacts among bourgeois patrons, such as Chantelou, for whom he had worked in Rome and who was his host in Paris (as he later was to Bernini) and for whom the second set of the *Seven Sacraments* (Edinburgh NG, on loan from the Duke of Sutherland) was painted between about 1644 and 1648. These patrons were highly educated, intellectual men of strict piety, and the classical themes he now chose were the heroic and stoical ones of Roman moral victory and sacrifice paralleling the dramas of Corneille, or dramatic Biblical themes where the action turns on the psychological impact of the moment. The late works are essays in solid geometry, with facial expressions eliminated and immobile figures. By comparison with his early works they are frigid and cerebral, but they are the logical exposition of his theories: a picture must contain the maximum of moral content expressed in a composition which shall convey its intellectual content; the pattern must be pleasing in itself and not conflict with the two-dimensional quality of the picture plane; the colour must offer no sensuous charm to lessen the unity of vision. Nowhere is this severe attitude expressed with more finality than in his landscapes which exemplify his utter dissimilarity to CLAUDE. This doctrine of the subordination of colour led to the quarrel between the Poussinists and the RUBENISTS.

There are works in Berlin, Boston (Mus., Fogg), Chantilly, Chicago, Cleveland Ohio, Copenhagen, Detroit, Dresden, Glasgow, Hartford Conn. (Wadsworth), Kansas City, Leningrad, London (NG, Dulwich, Wallace Coll.), Madrid, Minneapolis, Montreal, Munich, New York (Met. Mus.), Ottawa, Paris (Louvre), Philadelphia, Providence RI, Rouen, Sarasota Fla (Ringling), Stockholm, Toledo Ohio, Toronto, Vaduz (Liechtenstein Coll.), the Vatican, Vienna, and Washington (NG).

POUSSINISME *see* RUBÉNISME.

POZZO, Andrea (1642–1709), was the most skilful of all perspective experts and *quadraturisti*. He was born and trained in the north of Italy and became a Jesuit lay brother in 1665 (he is often given the courtesy title 'Padre') and wanted to abandon painting but was made to continue by his superiors. From 1681 to 1702 he was in Rome and his masterpiece of illusionism and SOTTO IN SÙ (which only works from one point in the nave) is the ceiling of the Jesuit church of S. Ignazio (1691–4). This is an allegory of the missionary activity of the Society of Jesus, and Pozzo himself explained it in a letter to Prince Liechtenstein (1694: published as a pamphlet in 1828). In 1702 he went to Vienna, where he died, and he introduced similar ideas there, which were of great importance in the development of Austrian Rococo. His influence was spread by his treatise 'Perspectiva pictorum ...' (1693–8), which was translated into English in 1693 and is said to have decided Reynolds to become a painter; the book was even translated into Chinese, by Portuguese Jesuits in 1737.

PRB, PRE-RAPHAELITE BROTHERHOOD. The mysterious initials first appeared following ROSSETTI's signature in an exhibition in 1849. They were the outcome of talks between HUNT and MILLAIS in 1848, although the choice of the expression 'Pre-Raphaelite' was largely fortuitous. It had already been said of the NAZARENER that they sought to emulate the painters earlier than Raphael, and this was more or less the idea of the original Brotherhood (Hunt, Millais, Rossetti, and his brother William, Collinson, Woolner the sculptor, and Stephens) – they knew very little about Italian painting earlier than Raphael, but they did know that they thought Raphael himself over-praised and they did not like Bolognese and Roman 17th-century painting, which they thought insincere. From the first the movement was very literary (a periodical called 'The Germ' ran for four numbers) and the painters insisted on the importance of a serious subject and on a highly elaborated symbolism and freshly thought-out iconography. The technical means, such as bright colour, extreme detail, study of outdoor motives on the spot, and the famous method of working into a wet white ground – all these were no more than means, although they had great influence on later painters who had no connexion with the movement, such as Ford Madox BROWN. In 1850 Rossetti revealed the meaning of the initials and at once a great storm broke; the principal accusations being that they set themselves up as better than Raphael, that they were secret Romanists (i.e. linked with the Oxford Movement), and that they were blasphemers. This last point was made – in an exceptionally savage and unperceptive attack – by Dickens, the victim being Millais' *Christ in the House of His Parents*, better known as *The Carpenter's Shop* (RA 1850: London, Tate). In the next year, however, Ruskin came to their defence and their success was assured. Shortly after this the group, which had never had any avowed theoretical basis, dissolved: Millais to become the typical successful RA and PRA, Rossetti to found a sort of second Brotherhood at Oxford with MORRIS and BURNE-JONES, and Hunt alone, working in Palestine on religious pictures, to maintain the original ideas. From the mid-1850s they were well supported by the new middle-class patrons. There are good collections of their works in Birmingham, Manchester, Oxford, and London (Tate).

PREDELLA. An Italian word for the small strip of paintings which form the lower edge or socle of a large altarpiece (*pala*). Such a POLYPTYCH consists of a principal, central panel with subsidiary side and/or top panels, and a *predella:* the *predella* usually has narrative scenes from the lives of the Saints who are represented in the panels above. Because of the small size of *predelle* – they are not usually more than 10–12 inches high, though often relatively very wide – they were frequently used for pictorial experiments that the painter did not wish to risk making in the larger panels. The first datable example seems to be that in Simone Martini's *S. Louis of Toulouse* (1317: Naples).

PRE-RAPHAELITE BROTHERHOOD *see* PRB.

PRETI, Mattia (Il Cavaliere Calabrese) (1613–99), was in Rome *c.*1630 but had presumably already absorbed the influence of Caravaggio in Naples, since he came from Calabria. He also visited Venice and Emilia, where he was influenced by GUERCINO and LANFRANCO. His easel pictures are more Caravaggesque than his frescoes, which show the influence of Guercino and Lanfranco, in Rome (1650–1: S. Andrea della Valle and in S. Carlo ai Catinari) and Modena. He was in Naples 1656–60 and spent most of the rest of his life in Malta, where he went in 1661 to decorate S. John's in Valletta. Other works are in Aix-en-Provence, Greenville SC, London (NG), Naples, Toledo Ohio, and Toronto.

PRÉVOST *see* MASTER OF MOULINS.

PRIMARY COLOURS are the three colours, red, blue, and yellow, from which, in theory, all others can be obtained. A secondary colour, such as green or orange, is obtained by the mixture of two primaries, and a tertiary colour (and in theory black as well) from three. White and black are not primary colours.

PRIMATICCIO, Francesco (1504/5–70), was the head of the First School of FONTAINEBLEAU and a universal impresario – painter, sculptor, architect, interior decorator. He learned these arts under GIULIO Romano in the Palazzo del Tè at Mantua, from 1525/6 until 1532, when he was summoned to France by François I and began to work at Fontainebleau, where he met ROSSO. From 1540 till 1542 he was in Rome buying for François, and on his return he found that Rosso was dead and Cellini had arrived (Cellini later threatened to kill him 'like a dog'). With Niccolò dell'ABBATE he worked on the (lost) decorations of the Galerie d'Ulysse at Fontainebleau, and in 1546 he was again in Rome to get casts made, including Michelangelo's *Pietà* in St Peter's, while in 1563 he revisited Bologna, his native town, and met Vasari there. There are works by him in Barnard Castle (Bowes Mus.), Bologna, Chantilly, Florence (Uffizi), Glasgow, Montpellier, Paris (Louvre, Cluny Mus.), Pittsburgh, and Toledo Ohio, but his main contribution is the combination of painted and high relief stucco decoration evolved at Fontainebleau and still partially preserved there.

PRIMING. The first coat on which all subsequent paint layers (including the GROUND) are applied. For oil-painting on canvas, the sized canvas is usually primed with white lead, either plain or slightly tinted.

PRIMITIVE. A word which is now almost meaningless, being applied to (i) painters, particularly of the Netherlandish and Italian Schools, working before *c*.1500 – i.e. Netherlandish painters of the late 14th and all the 15th centuries, and all Italian painters between Giotto and Raphael. They have no obvious connexion with (ii) the naïve, unsophisticated, unspoilt vision consistent with amateur, or 'Sunday' painter, status, admired for its connotations of genuineness and purity of artistic impulse, and freedom from the trammels of professionalism, tradition, technique, and formal training. This type of Primitive varies from the genuine American Primitives of the early 19th century such as Edward Hicks (1780–1849), the Quaker painter of *The Peaceable Kingdom*, to charwomen (SERAPHINE), peasants, and fishermen in modern Europe. The Douanier ROUSSEAU is their *chef d'école*, but the American 'Grandma' Moses may provide greater thrills for the sophisticated pursuit of the innocent eye.

PROCACCINI, Giulio Cesare (1574–1625), was one of the painters of the *Martyrdom of SS. Rufina and Seconda* (Milan, Brera), which is one of the key-pictures of Lombard Mannerism. The other two were G.B. CRESPI ('Il Cerano') and MORAZZONE. Giulio was born in Bologna, the younger brother of the painter Camillo (*c*.1560–1629), but the family settled in Milan *c*.1590, where Giulio began his career as a sculptor. He later worked as a painter in Modena (1613–16), where he was influenced by Correggio and Parmigianino, and in Genoa (1618), where he came in contact with Rubens. Most of his works are in Milan, but examples are in Berlin, Edinburgh, Oxford (Ch. Ch.), Paris, Turin, Vienna, and Worcester Mass.

PROFIL PERDU (Fr. lost profile) is that view of a head in which the profile is lost because the whole head is turned so far away that only the outline of the cheek is visible. By extension, the *profil perdu* of any object is what is seen of it when it is more than half turned away from the spectator.

PROOF. Usually this means a print of any kind of engraving, made either by the artist himself or under his supervision and for his own satisfaction or information, before he hands the plate over to a professional printer. Some proofs – e.g. some of Turner's *Liber Studiorum* – were extensively worked on by the artist before he was finally satisfied. A *Proof before all Letters* is one made before an engraving was handed over to the lettering engraver for the title, dedication, etc. to be added: they are naturally rare, and, as they are also supposed to be made while the plate is still very new, they command higher prices than ordinary prints. This has led to the Artist's Proofs racket – i.e. the first 10 or 20 prints of a run, signed or marked in some special way (REMARQUE PROOFS), and sold at advanced prices.

PROPORTION. The relation of one part to a whole or to other parts. In the arts it usually means a will-o'-the-wisp search for significant mathematical relationships between the parts of the human body. Such a search certainly began in classical times – the evidence is in much Greek sculpture – and the codified rules given in Vitruvius's 'Treatise on Architecture' (early in the 1st century A.D.) led to much theorizing in the Renaissance. Leonardo da Vinci and Dürer were the two artists who devoted the most energy to these studies ('There is no excellent beauty that hath not some strangeness in the proportion. A man cannot tell whether Apelles or Albert Durer were the more trifler; whereof the one would make a personage by geometrical proportions: the other, by taking the best parts out of divers faces to make one excellent': Bacon, 'Of Beauty'). In practice, the normal human body is about 7 or $7\frac{1}{2}$ times as tall as the height of its own head, and the total height is also roughly equal to the width of the outstretched arms. In IDEAL ART, therefore, it is usual to make the height equal to the full width of the arms; and further to gain mathematical harmony by elongating the body so that the total height becomes 8 heads. This gives a body which can be inscribed in squares and circles and also the convenient divisions so beloved of classically-minded artists – e.g. the groin becomes the exact half, the legs can be again halved at the knees, and so on. *See also* GOLDEN SECTION.

PROVENANCE (Fr. source, origin). The provenance of a work of art is its pedigree. A complete record of its ownership is its provenance, and it is the duty of a cataloguer to establish, as far as humanly possible, the provenance of a work of art. In some cases – e.g. the Sistine ceiling – no doubt is possible, but the exact pedigree of a picture by Vermeer is a matter of great importance, especially to the dealer trying to sell it. The English form 'provenience' is occasionally advocated, but it has a stilted sound and is not usual.

PRUD'HON, Pierre Paul (1758–1823), was born at Cluny. The Bishop of Mâcon sent him to Dijon Academy in 1774 and in 1780 he went to

Paris, where he worked for engravers. In 1784 he won the Rome Prize offered by the States of Burgundy; in Italy he became a friend of Canova and did almost no work, but his pictures show the influence of Raphael, Correggio, and Leonardo. In 1787 he returned to Paris and earned a precarious living drawing for engravers and in the provinces painting portraits. He was almost unaffected by the current Neoclassicism in painting – DAVID called him the Boucher of his day – and he became almost the only competitor to David and his pupils, through the warm patronage of both Napoleon's Empresses to whom he was dra ving master and Court Painter. He gave his, mostly female, sitters an ndefinably romantic and mysterious air, but his faulty technique and free use of bitumen has caused the deterioration of much of his work, particularly his large decorations. He designed all the furniture and decorations for the Empress Marie Louise's bridal suite, and cradles for the King of Rome, and his considerable influence on interior decoration was, unlike his painting, strongly classicist and Greek revival. From 1803 he found relief from his disastrous marriage, made in haste at 19, in a liaison with his favourite pupil, Constance Mayer, many of whose pictures he designed or worked on, but the shock of her suicide in 1821 eventually killed him.

There are works in Amsterdam (Rijksmus.), Chantilly, Chartres, Dijon, Lille, London (Wallace Coll.), Lyons, Montpellier, New York (Met. Mus., Hist. Soc.), Paris (Louvre, Carnavalet, Jacquemart-André), St Louis, and Versailles.

PRYDE *see* NICHOLSON.

PUGET, Pierre (1620–94), was a French sculptor whose controlled Baroque made no appeal to the classicizing taste of Louis XIV, and whose intransigent character was unacceptable to Colbert. He worked much in Italy and was a pupil of PIETRO da Cortona (1640–3). Despite his successful *Milo of Crotona* of 1683, his hopes of Court patronage were frustrated, and other works for the King were refused. There are examples in Toulon (caryatids, Hôtel de Ville, 1656–7), Genoa (S.M. in Carignano), Marseilles, New York (Met. Mus.), Paris (Louvre), and Quebec (Laval University).

PUNCH *see* STONE CARVING.

PURISM. In 1918 OZENFANT and Édouard Jeanneret (better known as the architect Le Corbusier) published 'Après le Cubisme', in which they accused the Cubists of turning to mere decoration. Purism, which they therefore invented, was to be an art unsullied by decoration, fantasy, or individuality, and inspired by the machine as a form of creation from which all unnecessary detail has been eliminated. Such is the waywardness of man that this arid doctrine produced no art at all: only to the architecture of Le Corbusier has it proved of any consequence.

PURRMANN, Hans (1880–1966), studied in Germany before going to

Paris in 1906, where he met and greatly admired MATISSE. In 1908 Purrmann organized a school to which Matisse gave his name: it petered out in 1910/11, as Matisse gave less and less time to it. Purrmann also organized several Matisse exhibitions in Germany which greatly influenced the Expressionists. In 1943 he was forced to retire to Switzerland. There are works in Basle, Berlin, Cologne, Karlsruhe, and Munich.

PUTTO (Ital. boy). A chubby naked boy: an AMORINO.

PUVIS de Chavannes, Pierre (1824–98), attempted to recreate something of the monumental Italian fresco style in his huge decorative canvases painted in oil, but kept flat and pale in colour and simplified in the drawing to give something of the effect of fresco. He decorated many Town Halls and other official buildings in France, the most famous being the Panthéon, Paris (1874–8, 1898, *Life of S. Geneviève*), and the Hôtel de Ville, Paris (1889–93). He was particularly admired by the artists grouped under POST-IMPRESSIONISM and NEO-IMPRESSIONISM as a painter of symbolical and allegorical decorations who respected the plane of the wall and composed his murals in simple areas of colour and with a rhythmic linear pattern. He decorated the Library at Boston in 1893–5, and there are other works by him in Birmingham (Barber Inst.), Budapest, Chicago, Dresden, Frankfurt (Städel), London (NG), Melbourne, New York (Met. Mus.), Paris (Louvre, Petit Pal., Mus. des Arts Décoratifs, Cluny Mus.), St Louis, Washington (NG), and many French provincial museums.

PYNACKER, Adam (1622–73), was a landscape painter from Delft who spent three years in Italy, but was back in Delft by 1649. He moved to Amsterdam c.1658. His landscapes are very like those of BOTH but are often hard and bluish, with silver tree-trunks and blue foliage. There is a particularly fine one in Dulwich which has a curious blue where one would expect green in the foliage; this is due to the use of fugitive yellow pigments which have faded out of the greens. There are examples in Amsterdam, Boston, Copenhagen, Florence (Uffizi), Hamburg, London (Wallace Coll.), Munich, Nottingham, Paris (Louvre), and Vienna (K-H Mus. and Akad.).

PYNAS, Jan (1583/4–1631) and Jacob (1590–1650 or later), were brothers who were both in Rome c.1605 and returned to Holland with a new kind of history painting, much influenced by Italian ideas and also by ELSHEIMER: their principal importance is that they passed these ideas on to Rembrandt, who may have been Jacob's pupil for a few months. There are works by them in Amsterdam (Rembrandt House), Hartford Conn., Paris, and Philadelphia (Johnson).

Q

QUADRATURISTA. A painter of *quadrature*. *See* ILLUSIONISM.

QUADRO RIPORTATO (Ital. carried picture). A term applied to easel paintings seen in normal perspective, which have been inserted into a ceiling decoration so that the effect is not the same as the ILLUSIONISM of *quadrature*.

QUARTON, Enguerrand (c.1410–66 or later), sometimes wrongly called Charonton, was a French painter working in Avignon. There are two documented works by him, in Chantilly (Musée Condé) and in Villeneuve-lès-Avignon (Hospice): the latter is a large *Coronation of the Virgin*, completed in 1454, which is one of the most important surviving 15th-century French paintings. It is unique in that the contract for it survives and contains the joint theological views of the priest who commissioned it and the painter himself, who reserved the right – which he exercised – to treat the picture as seemed best to him: 'Contract of 24 April 1453 between Dominus Jean de Montagnac and Master Enguerrand Quarton, of the diocese of Laon, painter. (1) There should be the form of Paradise, and in that Paradise should be the Holy Trinity, and there should not be any difference between the Father and the Son; and the Holy Ghost in the form of a dove; and Our Lady in front as it will seem best to Master Enguerrand; the Holy Trinity will place the crown on the head of Our Lady. (2) . . . Item: In paradise below should be all the estates of the world . . . After the heavens, the world in which should be shown a part of the city of Rome . . . the church of S. Peter at Rome . . . On the other side of the sea, will be a part of Jerusalem . . . the cross of Our Lord, and at the foot . . . a praying Carthusian. On the left side will be Hell. . . .'

The greatest of all 15th-century French pictures – the *Pietà* from Villeneuve-lès-Avignon now in the Louvre – has also been attributed to Quarton.

QUATTROCENTO (Ital. four hundred). The 15th century, i.e. the fourteen hundreds. *Quattrocento Mannerism* is a phrase sometimes used to describe the agitated and nervous style of a Botticelli or a Filippino Lippi, the assumption being that it is a 15th-century precursor of MANNERISM.

QUELLIN, Arnold (1653–86), was the son of Artus I. He was born in Antwerp but settled in London in 1680, where he died at the age of 33. He worked with Grinling GIBBONS (1682–6) and probably did much of the work for which Gibbons was paid – e.g. the *James II*, outside the NG, London. Their major joint work was the Catholic chapel in Whitehall Palace, designed by Wren in 1685–6 for James II, which Evelyn visited on 29 December 1686: 'Nothing can be finer than the magnificent Marble work and Architecture at the End, where are 4 statues representing st. Joh: st. Petre, st. Paule, and the Church, statues in white marble, the worke of Mr Gibbons. . . .' The Chapel was demolished in 1695, but some fragments survive at Westminster Abbey and in Burnham Church, Somerset. The Thynne Monument (1682/4), in Westminster Abbey, is Quellin's and there are other works in London (Guildhall and Soane Mus.).

QUELLIN, Artus I (1609–68), was one of the leading sculptors in the Netherlands in the 17th century. He was the son of the sculptor Erasmus Quellin and the father of the sculptors Artus II and Arnold. He studied in Rome, where he was much influenced by the classical Baroque of DUQUESNOY and ALGARDI, and on his return to Antwerp in 1639 he combined these influences with that of Rubens. In this he resembled Philippe de CHAMPAIGNE, his contemporary and fellow-Netherlander. In 1650 he moved to Amsterdam and spent 14 years working on the Town Hall (now Royal Palace), employing many assistants; this was his major work and many sketches for the decorations there are now in Amsterdam (Rijksmus.). Other works are in Antwerp (S. Andreas), and Brussels (Cath.).

QUERCIA, Jacopo della (1374/5–1438), was the greatest Sienese sculptor and a contemporary of Ghiberti and Donatello. He took part in the 1401 Competition for the First Baptistry Doors (won by Ghiberti) in Florence, but his entry is lost and the earliest work attributed to him is the Tomb of Ilaria del Carretto (c. 1406) in Lucca Cathedral. This is now fragmentary, but it seems to show a knowledge of Northern motives, and it is often said that Jacopo must have had some knowledge of the Burgundian School around SLUTER. The sarcophagus is also decorated with *putti* carrying garlands, perhaps the earliest modern use of a classical Roman motive. In 1409 he was commissioned to make a public fountain, the Fonte Gaia, for his native Siena, and he executed it 1414–19 (he seems always to have been dilatory): it is now dismembered in the Palazzo Pubblico, Siena. Between 1417 and 1431 he was working on reliefs for the Baptistry of Siena on which both Ghiberti and Donatello also worked. Indeed, the *Salome* relief by Donatello was originally commissioned from Quercia; in 1425 all three sculptors had to return money advanced to them, on account of their unsatisfactory progress. From 1425 Quercia was also working on another commission, the stone reliefs outside S. Petronio, Bologna, which occupied him until his death. These reliefs in particular show an almost Donatellesque vigour of handling and were much admired by Michelangelo. Other works by Quercia are in Bologna (S. Giacomo), Ferrara (Cath.), Lucca (S. Frediano), and S. Gimignano.

R

RAEBURN, Sir Henry (1756–1823), was the portrait painter who has recorded the personalities of the 'Athens of the North', the lawyers and scholars of the great age of Edinburgh, and also some of the more picturesque representatives of the Highland lairds before the depopulations and emigrations. Raeburn was left an orphan at an early age and was apprenticed to a jeweller *c*.1772, when he probably began to paint miniatures. Very little is known of his early career, but in 1776, at the age of 20, he was commissioned to paint a full-length portrait in oils of George Chalmers, for Dunfermline Town Council (to whom it still belongs). This clearly betrays his lack of professional training; equally, it is an astonishing performance under the circumstances. In 1780 he married a well-off widow and was able to devote himself to painting, but there are few datable works of this period. Traditionally, the *Rev. Robert Walker skating* (Edinburgh, NG) was painted in 1784. In this year Raeburn went to London, where he met Reynolds, and on to Italy. He was back in Edinburgh by 1787, totally uninfluenced by his Italian experience, but much influenced by Reynolds, becoming the leading Scots painter. In the course of the 1790s he developed a virtuoso handling of paint, generally drawing straight on to the canvas with his brush (there are no drawings known by him). This executive skill often over-reaches itself, and the celebrated 'square touch' which he developed in the first years of the 19th century can render the beefy common sense of one of the great Law Lords (*Lord Newton*, 1806/11), while at other times it is merely insensitive. Perhaps his best-known work is *The Macnab* (1803/13), where the sitter himself was enough to startle any painter out of a rut – particularly in the age of Scott. Hoppner died in 1810 and Raeburn went to London, apparently with the intention of taking over Hoppner's house and practice, but he decided against this and returned to Edinburgh, where he reigned alone. Nevertheless, from 1810 he exhibited regularly at the RA and visited London again in 1815 when he was elected RA. In 1822 George IV made his celebrated State Visit to Edinburgh and Raeburn was knighted and appointed King's Limner for Scotland.

Many of Raeburn's portraits are still in the families for which they were painted, but there are several in Edinburgh (NG and NPG of Scotland, University, and RSA) and in Aberdeen, Baltimore, Boston, Chicago, Cincinnati, Cleveland Ohio, Detroit, Glasgow, Kansas City, London (NG, Tate, NPG, RA, Osterley Park (V & A), Courtauld Inst. and Kenwood), Melbourne, Montreal, Newcastle, New York (Met. Mus., Frick Coll., and Brooklyn), San Marino Cal. (Huntington), Toronto, Washington (NG, Nat. Coll., and Corcoran), and elsewhere.

RAMSAY, Allan (1713–84), was the Scottish counterpart to Reynolds and Gainsborough, with something of the learning of Reynolds and some of Gainsborough's grace. He was the son of the author of 'The Gentle Shepherd' and received his first training in Edinburgh and London; unlike his English contemporaries, however, he underwent a full Italian training as a pupil of Imperiali and SOLIMENA (1736–8): Solimena's work was known in Scotland by 1731, which may explain Ramsay's choice of master. He settled in London and was 'much cried up by the Scotch Gentry': worse, his style was far more elegant and Frenchified than the face-painting practised by Kneller's successors. VERTUE noted in 1739 that: 'Ramsay still accustomes himself to draw the faces in red lines shades &c. finishing the likeness in one red colour or mask before he puts on the flesh Colour, which he proposes as a method to make the flesh clear & transparent – and such a method was used in Italy, by Cavaliere Luti & others. & so did Titian he says. (but is doubted this last) however when the faces are painted 4. 5. or 6 times over little or nothing of that first red is to be seen – certain it is that hitherto. the manner he paints in, neither like the valuable Manner of Dahl Kneller. Lilly [i.e. Lely], Riley. Dobson Vandyke. Rubens. or Titian – however it is rather lick't than pencilld. neither broad, grand, nor Free, has more of the finishd labourd uncertain – or modish French, German &c. dutch way – his good fortune has been much improved in this years worke.' His Italian Grand Manner portraits precede Reynolds's by several years but he had not Reynolds's ambition and spent much time in travel – he visited Italy four times – and in conversation, in which Dr Johnson himself admitted his prowess. In 1755 he published anonymously 'The Investigator, a Dialogue on Taste', which championed Greek and Gothic and was sharply attacked by PIRANESI. In 1759 Horace Walpole acutely observed: 'Mr Reynolds . . . is bold and has a kind of tempestuous colouring, yet with dignity and grace; the latter [Ramsay] is all delicacy. Mr Reynolds seldom succeeds in women, Mr Ramsay is formed to paint them.' During the 1760s he was appointed painter to George III, to Reynolds's chagrin, but he produced only a series of Royal images, mostly executed by assistants, for Government buildings. His best works are in Edinburgh (NG, NPG), including hundreds of the drawings which were the foundation of his pictures, again in contrast with English practice. Other works are in London (NPG, Tate Gall., Courtauld Inst., V & A, Foundling Hospital), Birmingham, Glasgow, Liverpool, Ottawa, and elsewhere.

RAPHAEL (1483–1520) was the youngest of the three great creators of the High Renaissance and was the most eclectic of great artists. He was the son of the painter Giovanni SANTI, and his real name was Raffaello Sanzio. His father died in 1494 and Raphael's earliest years are obscure, but by 1500 he was working in the shop of PERUGINO, probably on the frescoes at Perugia; and in this year he received his first recorded commission, now lost. Probably at this time he painted the *Knight's Dream* (London, NG). He was thus a prodigy, but, what is more extraordinary, in 1500 he was 17 while Leonardo da Vinci was 48 and Michelangelo 25; and yet in less than 10 years the provincial youth, who had not had their advantage in being born and brought up in Florence, was generally admitted to be their equal. The decade 1500–1510 not only saw the emergence of Raphael as a great master, it also saw the creation of the High Renaissance, in which Raphael played a leading part and which hardly survived him.

His early works show the influence of Perugino and not much else, as in the *Mond Crucifixion* of c.1502/3 (London, NG), but the *Betrothal of the Virgin* (*Lo Sposalizio*), his first signed and dated work (1504: Milan, Brera), although derived from a Perugino, already shows powers of composition and draughtsmanship far in advance of Perugino. At this point in his career Raphael went to Florence, where he must have found that all he knew was old-fashioned and provincial. He began at once to learn all he could from the Florentines, and a whole series of drawings and paintings demonstrates how rapidly he assimilated all they could teach him. From Leonardo's cartoons of the *Virgin and Child with S. Anne* he developed a series of small *Madonnas* (e.g. those in Florence, Paris, and Vienna); from the *Mona Lisa* he learned a new portrait type which he used for his *Maddalena Doni* (Florence, Pitti), while Leonardo's experiments in chiaroscuro are the reason for the dark background in the *Madonna del Granduca* (Florence, Pitti). Michelangelo's influence is principally to be found in a new severity and power in drawing, but the *Deposition* (1507: Rome, Borghese) contains several Michelangelesque motives, not all of them digested. Raphael seems also to have come into close contact with Fra BARTOLOMMEO at this time.

Probably towards the end of 1508 Raphael went to Rome, perhaps because he had heard that the Pope, Julius II, was having new apartments decorated. By 1509 he was certainly employed in the first of these rooms, the Stanza della Segnatura, and he rapidly became the principal master employed in the Vatican, with the sole exception of Michelangelo who was then painting the Sistine Ceiling. At 26 Raphael was in the front rank, and there he remained for the rest of his short life. The Stanza della Segnatura is the first of the series of relatively small rooms, known collectively as the Stanze, which Raphael and his pupils and assistants decorated for Julius II and Leo X. It was painted between 1509 and 1511, the theme of the room being the human intellect. The two principal frescoes represent Philosophy and Theology and are known respectively as the *School of Athens* and the *Disputa*, or *Disputation concerning the Blessed Sacrament*. These two frescoes, balanced and serene, calm, and classically poised, are perhaps the best examples of the High Renaissance at its apogee. The second Stanza, that of Heliodorus (the Stanza d'Eliodoro), has a different theme – Divine intervention on behalf of the Church – and in keeping with this more dramatic theme, the style is more dramatic and colourful. This may also be due to the fact that the Stanza was painted between 1511 and 1514 and Michelangelo's Sistine Ceiling was unveiled in 1512. The principal subjects are the *Expulsion of Heliodorus from the Temple*, the *Liberation of S. Peter*, and the *Miracle of the Mass at Bolsena*. The remainder of the decorative scheme – the Stanza dell'Incendio and the Sala di Costantino – was almost entirely executed by Raphael's numerous and well-trained assistants, and the exact amount of Raphael's responsibility is a matter of controversy. The principal reason for this is that Raphael was increasingly overwhelmed with work, not only in commissions for pictures from the Pope and from Kings and Princes, but also in that he succeeded Bramante (*d.*1514) as architect of the new St Peter's, and he was also engaged on innumerable other tasks. The most important of these were the frescoes in the Farnesina, Rome, and the tapestry cartoons designed in 1515–16 and intended to be used for tapestries to hang below the 15th-century frescoes on the walls of the Sistine Chapel. The surviving tapestries are still in the Vatican, and the original cartoons for seven of them are in the V & A, London (loaned from the Royal Coll.). At this time he also supervised the execution of the series of Old Testament scenes in the Logge of the Vatican: these were completed in 1519, but no more than the general design can be attributed to Raphael. The *Sistine Madonna* (Dresden) probably dates from *c.*1513 and is unusual in that it is all by Raphael himself and yet it is not known why he should have spent so much trouble on it, apparently for a small religious community in Piacenza. It has been suggested that it was carried at Julius II's funeral. It shows, by comparison with any of his Florentine *Madonnas*, how his style had become larger and simpler and also how the very conception of the Madonna had changed, from the simple naturalism of the 15th century to the superhuman being which the 16th century thought more appropriate to the Mother of God – hence the figure floating in the clouds.

The last major work on which Raphael was engaged was the *Transfiguration* (Vatican), commissioned in 1517 but still unfinished when he died in 1520. It was completed after his death, partly at least by his heir and most important pupil, GIULIO Romano, and it is controversial to what extent the MANNERISM discernible in the picture is due to Giulio. The basic design (including the twisted figure of the woman) and all the drawings, however, are certainly by Raphael and it seems likely that his art was on the point of taking a new direction. When he died at the age of 37, Raphael occupied a unique social position, on terms of friendship with Cardinals and Princes, a position never before attained by an artist. The (baseless) rumour current at his death that the Pope had intended to make him a Cardinal is the most eloquent proof of the change that had come over the status of the artist, a change wrought principally by Leonardo, Michelangelo, and Raphael.

There are pictures by him, in addition to those already mentioned, in Baltimore, Bergamo, Berlin, Bologna, Boston (Gardner Mus.), Brescia, Budapest, Chantilly, Città di Castello, Cracow, Detroit, Dresden, Florence (Pitti and Uffizi), Leningrad, Lisbon, London (NG and Dulwich), Madrid, Milan (Ambrosiana and Brera), Munich, Naples, New York, Paris, Perugia, Princeton NJ (Univ. Gall.), Rome (Borghese and Doria Gall., Accad. di S. Luca, S. Agostino, S.M. della Pace, S.M. del Popolo), Vaduz (Liechtenstein Coll.), the Vatican, and Washington.

RAUSCHENBERG, Robert (b.1925), was associated with his friend Jasper JOHNS in New York in the early 1960s in the creation of POP ART. His works include paintings, collages, and combinations of disparate objects – *Monogram*, 1959, consists of a stuffed goat girdled by a tyre on a painted base.

RAYONISM (Rayonnism, Rayonnisme) was a short-lived Russian off-shoot of CUBISM. 'Rayonism is concerned with the special forms which may arise from the intersection of reflected rays from different objects, forms selected by the artist at will', according to its inventor, the painter Larionov, in 1913.

RAYSKI, Ferdinand von (1806–90), was trained in Dresden before joining the army in 1825; he served as an officer for four years. He then began to paint portraits of the Saxon nobility, and in 1835 he visited Paris. From 1839 he was settled in Dresden, with a strong connexion both for portraits and animals among the local gentry. His style was based on Dutch 17th-century portraits brought up to date by reference to contemporary Frenchmen such as DELACROIX. He visited England in 1862. Most of his works are in Dresden.

READY-MADE *see* DUCHAMP, Marcel.

REALISM as an aesthetic watchword does not go any further back than COURBET, and in the visual arts, as in literature, it generally signifies the search for the squalid and depressing as a means of life-enhancement. It is in fact the total repudiation of IDEAL ART (which in the mid 19th century was necessary). It should not be confused with Naturalism, which is no more than the simple-minded pleasure in being able to make an accurate transcript of nature – 'a speaking likeness' – nor should it be confused with its cousin german SOCIAL

REALISM. Some English painters – notably Bratby, Greaves, and Middleditch – practise a style which some critics have seen fit to call Neo-Realism.

RECESSION is the name given to the ability to make the objects in a picture appear to recede into the depth of the imaginary picture space. It is most readily obtained by the use of linear and aerial PERSPECTIVE.

REDON, Odilon (1840–1916), created two entirely different types of picture: colourful, semi-Impressionist vases of flowers, animals, or landscapes, and highly imaginative drawings, lithographs, and paintings of fantastic subjects such as plants with human heads, phantoms and figments from dreams, visions, and nightmares. He maintained stoutly that the fantasy pictures were only possible because of his contact with reality. His work became known in Paris between 1879 and 1882, and he was hailed as one of the principal Symbolist painters, particularly by the literary Symbolists. He was a great friend of Mallarmé.

REFUSÉS see SALON.

RELIEF sculpture is that which is not free-standing, and, in having a background, approximates to the condition of painting. There are several names to indicate the varying depth of projection, ranging from *alto – rilievo*, or high relief – which is almost detached from the ground – through *mezzo-rilievo* to bas-relief (*basso-rilievo*) and further still to *rilievo stiacciato* (or *schiacciato*) which is scarcely more than scratched. *Cavo-rilievo* is the same as intaglio, that is, relief in inverse, sunk into the surface instead of embossed upon it.

REMARQUE PROOFS are PROOFS with a scribbled drawing or other mark in the margin to indicate a supposed superiority to ordinary proofs.

REMBRANDT van Ryn (1606–69) was born in Leyden, the son of a miller, at the time when Holland became an independent nation. After about a year at Leyden University he was apprenticed for three years to an obscure painter named Swanenburgh, but this was followed by a much more important six months in Amsterdam (1624/5) with Pieter LASTMAN, who was the means of his introduction to the rhetoric of early Baroque and perhaps also the channel by which the influences of CARAVAGGIO and ELSHEIMER reached him. He may also have spent some time with the PYNAS brothers. In 1625 he returned to Leyden where he set up in company with Jan LIEVENS, an association that lasted until Rembrandt's move to Amsterdam in 1631/2. By 1628 he was sufficiently well-known to have DOU as his pupil. The earliest works known to us are dated 1626, and in them – e.g. the *Clemency of Titus* (Utrecht Mus.) – the influence of Lastman is still dominant. Many paintings of the Leyden period show great interest in light and represent scholars in lofty rooms, or are studies of old age; examples are the Melbourne *Scholars disputing*, 1628, the *Scholar in a lofty Room* (London, NG), and *Rembrandt's Mother as the Prophetess Hannah* (1631: Amsterdam, Rijksmus.). At the end of 1631 or early in 1632 he moved to Amsterdam and set up as a portrait painter, attracting attention in 1632 with the *Anatomy Lesson of Dr Tulp*, a group portrait of the Amsterdam Guild of Surgeons (The Hague, Mauritshuis). This made his name and for the next ten years he prospered, producing highly finished likenesses, often in pairs, such as '*Maerten Daey*' and his *Wife* (1634: private coll., Paris), *Jan Pellicorne and his Son* and his *Wife and Daughter* (*c*.1635/7, both in London, Wallace Coll.), or the *Unknown Man* of 1641 in Brussels and its pendant, the *Woman with a Fan* in the Royal Coll. In 1634 he married Saskia van Uylenborch, who brought him a considerable dowry as well as good connexions, and Rembrandt promptly began to live well beyond his means; the *Portrait of himself with Saskia* (*c*.1634: Dresden) shows them in a mood of blatant opulence. There are many portraits of Saskia, painted, drawn, and etched (e.g. *Saskia as Flora*, 1635, London NG), but in 1642 she died, leaving him with a son, Titus. In the same year his great group portrait, the *Company of Capt. Frans Banning Cocq* (Amsterdam, Rijksmus.), better-known as the *Night Watch*, was painted. It was one of several such commemorative groups of the volunteer militia enlisted to defend Amsterdam. Each man paid according to the prominence given to his portrait, some finding themselves subordinated to the exigencies of Rembrandt's art in a way which HELST or KEYSER, or even HALS, would never have attempted.

After 1642 Rembrandt's business declined and the inevitable bankruptcy followed in 1656. It used to be thought that this was because of the revolutionary character of the *Night Watch*, but it now seems certain that Captain Cocq and his men were perfectly content with their picture. Meanwhile he was living with Hendrickje Stoffels, who, with his son Titus, 'employed' him from 1660 onwards, thus affording some relief from creditors. During these years he turned to Biblical subjects, creating a Protestant iconography, to landscape and to studies of the Jews among whom he lived. He had been painting religious subjects from the start of his career, and had painted a series of Passion scenes for Prince Frederick Henry, 1633-9 (now in Munich), and such exuberantly Baroque works as the *Blinding of Samson* of 1636 (Frankfurt), but the later works are deeper in emotional content and far less superficially dramatic. The same contrasts can be seen in his etchings – compare the *Annunciation to the Shepherds* of 1634 with the 'Hundred Guilder Print' (*Christ Healing*) of *c*.1649 – and the landscapes which he drew and etched in the 1640s compared with the romantic ones of the period from *c*.1635 when he was much influenced by SEGHERS. His portraits of the

1650s and 1660s include such masterpieces of psychological penetration painted to please himself as the *Jewish Merchant* of *c*.1650 (London, NG), the *Old Jew in an Armchair* (1652: London, NG) and the portrait of *Jan Six* (1654: still in the family coll., Amsterdam), as well as portraits like the *Man* (1663: Washington), the *Man with a Magnifying Glass* (New York, Met. Mus.), and the *Woman with a Plume* (Washington), both painted in the 1660s and clearly commissioned works.

The long series of self-portraits, datable between 1629 and 1669, records every stage of his career, every moment of disillusion, with ever-deepening self-analysis. In his last years he continued to receive some important commissions, such as the *Anatomy Lesson of Dr Deyman* (1656: Amsterdam, Rijksmus.), or the *Conspiracy of the Batavians*, commissioned in 1661 for the Amsterdam Town Hall but removed at once for alterations (and now in Stockholm Nat. Mus.); both these now exist only as fragments. In 1662 he completed the group of the *Staal Meesters*, the Syndics of the Guild of Drapers, and this, the greatest of all Dutch group portraits, is now in the Rijksmuseum, Amsterdam. Later still he painted the *Family Group* now in Brunswick, and these very late works impressed the aged Hals so much that Rembrandt's influence is perceptible in his last works. It is an influence which has never died out. Rembrandt's output was prodigious, and there are about 650 paintings by him (of which some 60 are self-portraits) as well as about 300 etchings and 1,500–2,000 drawings. He maintained for many years a large teaching studio, and among his numerous pupils were BOL, FLINCK, EECKHOUT, KONINCK, and Aert de GELDER. There are paintings by Rembrandt in the Royal Coll., and in Aix-en-Provence, Amsterdam, Antwerp, Baltimore, Bayonne, Berlin, Boston, Brunswick, Brussels, Cape Town, Cambridge (Fitzwm), Cambridge Mass. (Fogg), Cassel, Chicago, Cincinnati, Cleveland Ohio, Cologne, Copenhagen, Detroit, Dublin, Edinburgh, Florence, Frankfurt, Glasgow, The Hague, Kansas City, Leningrad, Leyden, Liverpool, London (NG, Dulwich, Kenwood, V & A, Wallace Coll.), Madrid, Melbourne, Milan, Minneapolis, Munich, New York (Met. Mus., Frick Coll., Historical Soc.), Ottawa, Paris (Louvre, Jacquemart-André), Philadelphia (Johnson Coll.), Raleigh N. Carolina, Rotterdam, San Francisco, Sarasota Fla (Ringling Mus.), Stockholm, Toledo Ohio, Toronto, Utrecht, Vienna, Washington, and Worcester Mass.

RENAISSANCE (Fr., or Ital. *Rinascimento*, rebirth). Usually defined as the 'revival of art and letters under the influence of classical models in the 14th–16th century' (OED). As early as 1550 Vasari used the word *rinascita* to describe this rebirth, which he knew to have culminated in his own days, but it probably received the wide currency it now has from Jacob Burckhardt's 'Civilization of the

Renaissance in Italy', first published in 1860. In the visual arts the term is now used with some care, if any degree of precision is desirable. It is felt that the influence of classical models is not easy to distinguish in Italy, where the classical tradition is virtually unbroken, and a term which can be made to cover Giotto at one end and Titian at the other is too vague to be useful in any discussion of style (the case is even worse in English architectural history, where 'Renaissance' is still made to cover Elizabethan buildings, Wren, and the Adam brothers). It is therefore agreed that Giotto may be said to have begun the Renaissance in the other sense, that of according a new dignity to man and his works, but that the classical ideals hardly came into play before the first years of the 15th century, when the humanist ideals of Alberti were indistinguishable from those of MASACCIO, Brunelleschi, and DONATELLO, and, to a lesser extent, Ghiberti. The period from c.1420 to 1500 is therefore now generally called the Early Renaissance and the term High Renaissance is reserved for the tiny span of time when a pure, classical, balanced harmony was attained, and when artists of the first rank were in absolute control of their techniques, able to render anything they wanted with the maximum of fidelity to nature. It is this mastery of technique which, with the elimination of superfluous detail, is one of the distinguishing marks between Early and High Renaissance. The High Renaissance lasted from c.1500 to about 1527, the date of the Sack of Rome, and it includes the earlier works of MICHELANGELO, all the Roman works of RAPHAEL, and most of LEONARDO's work. The later work of Michelangelo is dedicated to different ideals, and the style of the period 1530/1600 is now generally known as MANNERISM, while the style of the 17th century, in accordance with yet other ideals, is BAROQUE. All these have a passion for classical models as a distinguishing mark, so that the Renaissance style must also have the classical qualities of serenity and harmony – qualities which were lost sight of in the period of the Counter-Reformation or the Thirty Years War.

RENI, Guido (1575–1642), was a Bolognese painter who enjoyed the highest reputation in the 17th and 18th centuries until it was blasted by Ruskin. In spite of his sentimental religiosity his pictures are now returning to favour, on account of their combination of CARAVAGGIO and the CARRACCI. To the surprise of his fellow-countrymen he remained a life-long virgin; this, however, he compensated for by a passionate addiction to gambling. He was a pupil, with Albani and Domenichino, of the Fleming CALVAERT until his conversion to the manner of the Carracci c.1594. About 1600/3 he went to Rome for the first time, where he was influenced to some extent by the naturalism of Caravaggio (who, typically, is said to have threatened to kill him); his own style, however, depends much more on the Raphaelesque classicism of the Carracci Academy and is best seen in the *Aurora* (1613–14: Rome, Casino Rospigliosi). This is a ceiling fresco that makes no attempt at SOTTO IN SÙ illusionism (cf. GUERCINO'S *Aurora* of 1621–3), but is treated exactly as an easel picture seen in the normal way; it also contains some conscious quotations from the antique. Apart from a trip to Naples in 1622 he worked in Rome, and, mainly, in Bologna. There are many works by him in Bologna and Rome (Capitoline, Borghese, Quirinal Palace, S. Gregorio Magno and other Roman churches) and others in London (NG and Dulwich), Auckland NZ, Birmingham, Cambridge (Fitzwm), Chicago, Dresden, Dublin, Glasgow, Greenville SC, Leeds, Munich, Naples, Paris (*Deeds of Hercules* set, 1617/21, in the Louvre, and the *Job*, 1622–36, recently rediscovered in Notre Dame), Prague, Sarasota Fla, the Vatican, and Vienna.

RENOIR, Pierre Auguste (1841–1919), was one of the greatest of the painters affected by IMPRESSIONISM. He worked from the age of 13 in a china factory and his early training as a painter on porcelain predisposed him towards the light palette of Impressionism. In 1861 he spent some time in the teaching studio of the academician Gleyre, where he met MONET, BAZILLE, and SISLEY. He also went to the Louvre often, and was particularly interested in Watteau, Boucher, and Fragonard: all his life he was conscious of the need to study art in museums, and dissatisfied with the purely visual aspects of Impressionism. The main influence on his early career was COURBET, until about 1868, and during this time he used heavy impasto and rather dark colour. In 1868 he and Monet worked together on the Seine, and as a result of painting continually out-of-doors – and of Monet's influence – his colour became lighter and higher in key, and his handling freer, the whole canvas being managed in patches of coloured light and shadow without any definite drawing. He exhibited in the first three Impressionist exhibitions, and then in the seventh; after 1877 he was successful in getting some of his portraits into the Salon, and was unwilling to risk the market that this offered for the sake of the often disadvantageous advertisement provided by the group shows. In 1879 (and again in 1882) he visited North Africa, was in Guernsey in 1880, and made his first of several trips to Italy in the winter of 1881–2; he later travelled widely, visiting London, Holland, Spain, Germany, studying in museums, and he deeply admired Raphael and Velazquez – more even than Rubens, to whose art his own was so much indebted. After his first Italian journey his drawing became much firmer, his Impressionism much less the spontaneous result of purely visual stimuli than the conscious use of colour to recreate Nature and form, and this in turn involved departure from Monet's form of Impressionism – direct painting before the object – by the adoption of a more elaborate technique, with preparatory drawings and successive sessions on the canvas while the figure and its setting was worked up: '*Il faut meubler la toile*', was his way of putting it. Where his early works include portraits, landscapes, flowers and groups of figures in settings of café, dance-hall, boats, or riverside landscapes, his late works are mostly nudes, or near nudes. The warmth and tenderness of pink and pearly flesh entranced him and gave him full scope for his favourite colour schemes of pinks and reds, and the exploitation of a chosen colour-scheme is in itself an un-Impressionist idea: '*Il faut avoir*', he said '*le sentiment des fesses et des tétons*'.

In 1906 he settled in Cagnes in the south of France, but he was already crippled with arthritis, which finally rendered him completely helpless, so that his last pictures were painted with brushes stuck between his twisted fingers. He also 'made' a certain amount of sculpture – 'dictated' rather, since the clay was worked by an assistant who added or removed on his instructions, to create rather Maillol-like figures of impressive simplicity and solidity. In his last years he saw a good deal of Matisse, who lived nearby, and he was interested in and sympathetic to the ideas behind Fauvism. He painted about 6,000 pictures: there is a large collection in Paris (Mus. de l'Impressionnisme), and there are works in Berlin, Boston (Mus.), Budapest, Cambridge Mass. (Fogg), Chicago, Cologne (Wallraf-Richartz), Essen, Glasgow, London (NG, Tate, Courtauld Inst.), Rouen, São Paulo, Stockholm, Toronto, and Washington (NG, Phillips). America is particularly rich in Renoirs, since they were bought there when the artist was still unappreciated in Europe.

REPLICA. An exact copy of a picture, made by the painter of the original or at least under his supervision. It is often used to describe two or more paintings, exactly alike, when one is in doubt which (if any) is the prime original.

REPOUSSOIR (Fr. *repousser*, to push back) is used to describe a figure or other object placed in the extreme foreground of a picture, usually at the right or left edge, with the object of deflecting the spectator's eye into the centre of the picture. A *repoussoir* figure often aids in this by gesticulating in the required direction.

REREDOS (Retable). The structure behind an altar, sometimes resting on it, like a ledge, and sometimes standing clear of it. The very large groups of carvings, common in medieval Germany, are properly referred to as reredoses or retables, rather than altarpieces, which term is perhaps best reserved for paintings.

RETHEL, Alfred (1816–59), was, with CORNELIUS, the major early 19th-century German painter on a monumental scale. He was influenced by the NAZARENER, but worked on a much larger scale. He visited Italy in 1844–5 and again in 1852–3, but his career was cut short by madness in 1853. His major works were the frescoes for the

Town Hall, Aachen, projected from 1840, begun in 1847, and left incomplete. He also made a woodcut series of the *Dance of Death* (1849), in imitation of Holbein.

RETROUSSAGE is a term used in etching to describe the action of passing a pad of muslin lightly over an inked plate with the intention of dragging some of the ink out of the lines and smearing it across the plate.

REUWICH, Erhard, active in Mainz *c.*1475–*c.*1500, is often identified with the MASTER OF THE HOUSEBOOK. B. von Breydenbach's 'Peregrinationes in terram sanctam' (Mainz, 1486) mentions him as an Utrecht painter who accompanied Breydenbach on his travels, making a drawing of Venice on the spot in 1483. The woodcuts in the book (as well as a view of Venice, of 1486) are attributed to him, and by stylistic comparison, the Housebook Master's engravings and paintings have been added to his *œuvre*.

REYMERSWAELE (Roymerswaele) *see* MARINUS.

REYNOLDS, Sir Joshua (1723–92), is, historically, the most important figure in British painting. He was born at Plympton St Maurice in Devon, where his father was headmaster of the Grammar School and a former Fellow of Balliol: this is worth mentioning because it shows that Reynolds was born and brought up in an educated family at a time when most English painters were hardly more than ill-educated tradesmen. Reynolds himself became the close friend of Dr Johnson, Goldsmith, Burke, and Garrick, and it is probably true that he did more to raise the status of the artist in England through his learning and personal example than by his actual quality as an artist. He was apprenticed to HUDSON in 1740, in London, but in 1743 he left his master and returned to Devonshire; from 1743–9 he was in practice on his own in London and Devonshire, before leaving for Italy in 1749. As early as 1746 he painted the *Eliot Family Group*, based on a famous van Dyck at Wilton House, and this already shows the fundamental basis of his art – the deliberate use of allusion to the Old Masters or Antique sculpture as a classical allusion might have been used by an 18th-century speaker or writer. This appeal to the educated eye, above and beyond the needs of mere likeness, is the essence of his own style and the reason for the rise in public esteem for the visual arts which is so marked a feature of his age. In 1749 he had the chance to go to Italy with Commodore (later Admiral Viscount) Keppel, who was also to become one of his best friends. Up to this time the main influences on his style had been Hogarth, Ramsay, and to a moderate extent only, Hudson; he now spent two years (1750–2) in Rome, where he made a really prolonged study of the Antique, of Raphael and, above all, of Michelangelo. Here he learned the intellectual basis of Italian art (just as WILSON was doing), and this was something that scarcely any other British painter, with the possible exception of

Ramsay, had done up to then, even in Rome itself. In fact, Reynolds's own practice as a portrait painter was more profoundly influenced by the few weeks he spent in Venice on his way home in 1752. He never ceased to exhort his students to master the principles of the Grand Style, and in fact he regarded Venetian art, and portrait painting, as of less importance. In 1753 he set up in London, met Dr Johnson, and began rapidly to make a name. He sought consciously to marry the Grand Style with the needs of face-painting (and earning a living), and he succeeded so well that he was soon employing assistants, although the Kneller school was not converted ('Shakespeare in poetry, and Kneller in painting, damme!' as one of them observed). Only Ramsay and Cotes were rivals of any significance, but by 1768, when the Royal Academy was founded, it was obvious that Reynolds was the only possible choice for the President. He was knighted in 1769 and made DCL at Oxford (an honour that would have been unthinkable for a painter only a generation earlier) and Mayor of his native Plympton in 1772. The works of the years following 1768 show him at his most classical and most learned, determined to use the Academy as an instrument to forge a British School of History painters to stand beside those of Rome or Bologna. To this end he composed and delivered at intervals (1769–90) the fifteen Discourses which are the most lucid and sensible exposition of the Academic position that, by well-directed labour, it is possible to learn the Rules of Art and to use the inventions and ideas of one's predecessors to create a new style of one's own. During these years Reynolds exhibited regularly at the Academy exhibitions and usually showed a skilful blend of large portraits treated in a historical manner, history pictures proper, and some curious combinations of the two, such as *Dr Beattie* (*The Triumph of Truth*) (Aberdeen Univ.) or *Three Ladies adorning a Term of Hymen* (London, NG), both in the RA of 1774. This idea had been exploited by him as early as 1760/1 in his *Garrick between Tragedy and Comedy*, a thoroughly 'learned' picture which he exhibited in 1762 at the Society of Artists, the Academy's precursor. He won the victory in general terms, although many ladies still preferred to be painted in a fashionable gown by Gainsborough to the 'nightgowns' which Sir Joshua insisted on, as less subject to the vagaries of fashion and more nearly classical in type. In 1781 he made a journey to Flanders and Holland and was profoundly influenced by the force and freedom of Rubens's handling, and from then until his sight failed in 1789 his works are less consciously classical and painted with greater warmth and feeling. The overwhelming majority of his vast output consists of portraits, which include almost every man and woman of note in the second half of the 18th century. Unlike Gainsborough, he employed many pupils and assistants and his work also differs from Gainsborough's in being frequently badly preserved on account of his bad technical procedures. The faces of his sitters are often deathly pale because the carmine has faded out completely. Most of his sitter-books still exist and thus nearly all his works are documented: practically every major museum in Britain and America contains one or more, and others are as far afield as Leningrad and São Paulo, Dresden and Adelaide, Budapest and Ottawa.

RIBALTA, Francisco (1565–1628), was a Catalan painter whose first known work is the *Christ nailed to the Cross* of 1582 (Leningrad, Hermitage). This is a crude work in the Mannerist tradition, but after Ribalta settled in Valencia in 1599 his style seems to have undergone a considerable change. He was one of the first of the 17th-century Spanish Realists, and his mature works have an austere, almost grim, sobriety, combined with dramatic lighting which seems to show CARAVAGGIO's influence. It seems that he had actually studied in Italy, as he copied a Caravaggio, but his earliest Caravaggesque paintings are not earlier than 1615, by which date other Spaniards had been influenced by Italian TENEBRISM. In his last works there is an affinity with the style of RIBERA. The *Vision of Fr Simon* (1612: London, NG) is a good example of his devotional style, although it does not yet show Caravaggio's influence. His son Juan – who died in the same year, 1628 – was also a painter. There are works in Madrid (Prado) and Valencia.

RIBERA, Jusepe or José (1591–1652), was born near Valencia and may possibly have studied under Ribalta before going to Italy, where he travelled, became a member of the Accademia di S. Luca in Rome, and settled in Naples by 1616. The style of his early works shows a blending of Spanish realism with a degree of idealization derived from the Carracci, expressed in the strong chiaroscuro of Caravaggio, of whom in his own day he was considered to be a follower. This invests his often brutal subjects with a powerful but unsubtle forcefulness, now accentuated by the darkening of his colours through his use of bitumen and bolus grounds. His etchings are frequently better composed than his paintings of related subjects in that they are free of these excessive contrasts of light and shadow. By the mid 1630s his style had changed to a greater softness and the blocks of light in a sea of dark gave place to suaver colour and more even handling, perhaps reflecting the influence of Velazquez, who was in Naples in 1630. The tales of his bloodthirsty opposition to the competition in Naples of Guido RENI and DOMENICHINO are probably apocryphal. He enjoyed the patronage of successive Viceroys and his works were very popular in Spain, since they exploited the essentially Spanish subjects of Counter-Reformation painting – half, or less frequently, full length figures of strongly characterized male saints or rapt female ones, occasional mythologies in which even

Venus is fully clothed, tender Nativities, scenes from the Passion or the lives of the saints, full of emotion and devotion. In his late years his reputation was diminished by his reduced output and slowness of execution, due to his ill-health, in turn probably affected by the *éclat* of the seduction of his daughter by Don Juan of Austria, a natural son of Philip IV of Spain, who was sent to Naples to quell the Masaniello rising in 1647. The large school of Neapolitan Tene-brist painting probably owes more to Ribera than to Caravaggio, since it develops along his lines, to the point that when it is impossible to decide whether a work is Spanish or Italian, the answer is usually to call it Neapolitan.

There are many works by him in Madrid (Prado, Academia), and in Naples (Pinacoteca, Palazzo Reale, Cathedral, Mus. di S. Martino, Mus. Civico), and also in Bilbao, Berlin, Boston (Mus.), Brussels, Budapest, Cambridge Mass. (Fogg Mus.), Dresden, the Escorial, Hartford Conn. (Wadsworth), Leeds, London (NG, Wellington Mus.), Milan (Poldi-Pezzoli), Montreal, New York (Hispanic Soc., Met. Mus.), Paris (Louvre), Philadelphia, Rome (Doria, Gall. Naz.), Rouen, Salamanca (Immaculate Conception), Toledo Ohio, Vitoria, Worcester Mass., and Yale.

RICCI. There were two, Sebastiano and his nephew Marco, both Venetians. Sebastiano (1659–1734) was the first of the itinerant Vene-tian painters (cf. CANALETTO, BELLOTTO, TIEPOLO), working in Bologna, Rome, Modena, Florence, and Parma, before going to Vienna, where he worked in the Schönbrunn Palace. In 1712 he went to England with his nephew, and both left in 1716 after Sebastiano failed to get the commissions to decorate the dome of St Paul's and Hampton Court Palace, both of which went to THORNHILL. His major English work is the *Resurrection* painted in the apse of Chelsea Hospital Chapel; it has a light, quick rhythm and a decorative feeling quite new after the ponderous and tasteless works of VERRIO. He left the decoration of Burlington House incomplete (it was finished by KENT) when he returned to Venice, and on the way home he stopped in Paris and visited Watteau, some of whose drawings he copied. There are 21 paintings by Sebastiano in the Royal Collection, including a *Finding of Moses* originally attributed to Veronese. This stresses the fact that Sebastiano had been so well trained in the Vero-nese tradition that his works could pass as by the 16th-century artist: his stay in London was enlivened by several rows over his abilities as a *pasticheur*. His translations of Veronese into 18th-century style were an important influence on the young Tiepolo. Marco (1676–1730) was a pupil of Sebastiano's, and probably worked with him in Florence, 1706–7. He may also have visited Rome and Milan, where he perhaps knew MAGNASCO, who influenced him. He went to England in 1708 with PELLEGRINI, with whom he worked on stage scenery, and in 1710 he seems to have gone back to Venice to fetch his uncle. They returned together in 1712, travelling via the Netherlands, and remained for about four years, arriving back in Venice *c*.1717. The remainder of his life is ill-documented: he appears to have worked for Sebastiano on landscape backgrounds for large religious works and to have executed small landscapes in tempera on leather. His landscapes are often *capricci*; they are usually lively and free in handling. He was one of the first of the Venetian etchers of the 18th century, and his *Experimenta* were published posthumously in 1730.

There is a large number of drawings by both Riccis in the Royal Collection, and many of the older galleries have paintings by them.

RICCIO, Andrea (1470/5–1532), was a Paduan sculptor who is supposed to have been a pupil of Bellano, who was himself an assistant of DONATELLO. Riccio was trained as a goldsmith, which may account for the very delicate handling of his small bronzes. He was working in Padua by 1496/7 and his most famous work is the Paschal candlestick in the Santo at Padua of 1507/15. His bronze statuettes are in most major museums, and reflect the humanist tastes of Padua in the 15th and 16th centuries.

RICHARDS, Ceri (1903-71), was a Welsh painter whose abstract pictures are often based on themes taken from poetry (Dylan Thomas: 'Do not go gentle into that good night ...') or music (Debussy, *La Cathédrale engloutie*), or based on earlier paintings, such as the *Lion Hunt*, after Delacroix. He painted a huge decoration for the Shakespeare Festival, 1964, and decorated the Chapel of the Blessed Sacrament in Liverpool Cathedral (1967). There are works by him in Aberdeen, Cardiff, Edinburgh (M of MA), London (Tate), Manchester (Whitworth), Ottawa, Swansea (Gallery and Parish Church), and Toledo Ohio.

RICHARDSON, Jonathan (1665–1745), a pupil of Riley, *c*.1688–91, and inheritor of his teacher's stiff and solemn manner, was the principal portrait painter of the period between Kneller and Hudson. In 1711 he and Kneller founded the St Martin's Lane Academy, from which eventually sprang the RA Schools. He had a considerable influence through his books 'The Theory of Painting', 1715, and the guidebook widely used by Grand Tourists, which he wrote with his son, Jonathan the Younger (1694–1771), in 1722. His son also painted, but is better known for his writings on connoisseurship.

There are works in Oxford and Cambridge Colleges, Edinburgh (NPG), Leeds, London (NPG), and elsewhere.

RICHIER, Germaine (1904–59), was a French sculptress, who also made engravings, book-illustrations, and ceramics. She worked with BOURDELLE 1925–9 and then, under the influence of Surrealism, she began to make spindly figures similar to those by GIACOMETTI (who had also been a pupil of Bourdelle). She lived in Switzerland

1939–45, but in 1950 was commissioned to make a crucifix for the new and controversial church at Assy (Haute-Savoie), which has works by Braque, Matisse, Lipchitz, and other leading artists. There are works in museums in Amsterdam, Basle, Brussels, London (Tate), Minneapolis, Paris, Rome, Stockholm, and Zürich.

RIEMENSCHNEIDER, Tilman (c. 1460–1531), was, with STOSS, the leading German sculptor of the Late Gothic style. From 1483 he worked in Würzburg where he kept a very large shop which produced scores of carvings, mostly in wood, of dramatic and emotional subjects such as the Lamentation over the Dead Christ. He also worked in stone. Apart from Würzburg, there are examples in Berlin, Cleveland Ohio, London (V & A), Munich, Providence RI, and many German churches.

RIGAUD, Hyacinthe (1659–1743), was awarded the Prix de Rome in 1682 but did not go to Italy. He was the principal official painter to the Court of Louis XIV and also worked under Louis XV: like his friend and rival LARGILLIERRE he expresses the pomp of le Roi Soleil in his great State portraits, and occasionally the character of his sitters. His non-official portraits show the influence of Rembrandt. He had a very active studio and few of his pictures – on the evidence of his account books – can be wholly his own work. There are examples in Versailles, Paris (Louvre), and French provincial museums and in Dresden, Florence (Uffizi), London (NG, NPG, Wallace Coll., Dulwich, Kenwood), Melbourne, Munich, Naples, New York (Met. Mus.), Ottawa, Stockholm, Toledo Ohio, Vienna, and elsewhere. He painted an average of 35 portraits a year for 62 years.

RILEY, John (1646–91), was the leading English portrait painter in the short interval between the dominations of Lely and Kneller. Nothing is known of Riley's work before 1680, but by 1688 his fame was so well grounded that he was appointed Principal Painter to William and Mary jointly with Kneller; nevertheless, his best works may well be the portraits of humble people, such as the Bridget Holmes, a nonagenarian Housemaid, in the Royal Coll., or the Scullion at Christ Church, Oxford. There are other pictures by him in the Royal Coll., London (Tate, Dulwich), Oxford (Ashmolean and Bodleian Library), and Waddesdon, Bucks. (National Trust).

RILIEVO see RELIEF.

RIOPELLE, Jean Paul (b. 1923), is the leading Canadian abstract painter, although he has lived in Paris since 1947. His work shows the influence of Kandinsky, Mirò, and Pollock.

RIVERA, Diego (1886–1957), was a Mexican painter who worked in Paris during the years that brought Cubism to birth, and he knew most of the principal artists in that movement. He held aloof from it, however, and eventually returned to Mexico (in 1921), where, like OROZCO, he was powerfully affected by politics. His first teacher, in

Mexico City, had been a pupil of Ingres and Rivera's art was always more revolutionary in content than in style. His 'Mexican' art is largely dependent on a vocabulary evolved from a mixture of Gauguin with Aztec and Mayan sculpture. In his large commissions for the decoration of public buildings Rivera used *buon fresco*, a technique that he revived, as he also revived the use of ancient encaustic methods. His mural in the Rockefeller Centre, New York, was replaced by one by BRANGWYN on account of the introduction of a portrait of Lenin rather than for any objection to the style.

ROBBIA, Luca della (1400–82), was ranked by contemporaries as one of the great innovators at the beginning of the 15th century, along with Ghiberti and Donatello, who were much older, and Masaccio, who was his contemporary but had a very short life compared to Luca's very long one. His first major work was the *Cantoria* or *Singing Gallery* for the Cathedral in Florence (1431–8: now in the Cath. Mus.), which was commissioned from him before its companion was ordered from Donatello. This shows his use of antique examples, but it has also his warm and cheerful humanity, quite unlike the drama and grandeur of Donatello. Much later, between 1464 and 1469, he made the bronze doors of the Cathedral Sacristy, and again the comparison with Donatello's Sacristy in S. Lorenzo can hardly be avoided. Early in his career – perhaps even before 1430 – Luca discovered a means of applying the vitrified lead glazes used by potters to sculpture in terracotta, and he exploited this discovery in a number of smallish works with figures in white against a clear blue background. He was also able to use a large number of colours in this way, but he restricted them to architectural and decorative works (e.g. the entrance of the Pazzi Chapel, Florence). To some extent this discovery was the ruin of his art (but not so much as is commonly supposed), for he was able to found a flourishing family business which later undertook some very large and highly coloured commissions. His nephew, Andrea della Robbia (1435–1525), carried on the business and is best known for the *Foundling Children* on the façade of the Spedale degli Innocenti, Florence (1463–6). His sons, Giovanni (1469–after 1529) and Girolamo (1488–1566), and other sons for a short time as well, all carried on the tradition well into the 16th century.

There are works by Luca in Berlin, Florence (Bargello, Cath., Campanile, Sta Trinita, Sta Croce (Pazzi Chapel), and other churches and palaces), Impruneta, London (V & A), New York (Met. Mus.), Paris (Louvre, Cluny Mus., Jacquemart-André), Peretola nr Florence, Pescia, Toledo Ohio, Urbino (S. Domenico), Vienna, and Washington (NG).

ROBERT, Hubert (1733–1808), went to Rome in 1754 and spent 11 years in Italy, where he became a friend of PIRANESI and PANINI, whose type of Romantic ruin-painting he introduced to France. In

1761 he went to South Italy and Sicily with FRAGONARD and the Abbé de Saint-Non, and he and Fragonard influenced each other profoundly in style, though not in subject matter. He returned to Paris in 1765, became a member of the Academy and painted decorative compositions for a number of great houses; later, his range widened and he painted views and street-scenes in Paris. He became Keeper of Louis XVI's pictures and was later one of the first Curators of the Louvre. He is represented in the Louvre and many French provincial museums and also in Baltimore, Barnard Castle (Bowes Mus.), Boston, Bristol, Cambridge (Fitzwm), Chicago, Detroit, New York (Met. Mus.), and elsewhere.

ROBERTI, Ercole d'Antonio de' (c. 1448/55–96), was active in Ferrara from 1479 and from 1486 was Court Painter to the Este family there, He may have been a pupil of COSSA and worked with him in Bologna before settling in Ferrara, but he was also influenced by the Ferrarese TURA and above all by Giovanni BELLINI, although he is not known to have had any contacts with Venice. The only work reasonably certainly his is a large altarpiece of 1480/1 (Milan, Brera) by 'Ercole', but his highly personal style, with its nervous sensibility and deep pathos in such works as the Liverpool *Pietà*, is easily recognizable: nevertheless, much confusion has been caused by the introduction of Ercole di Giulio Cesare de' Grandi, who is said to have died in 1531. This man may well have existed and may even have been a Bolognese painter, and was conceivably influenced by Ercole Roberti – only there is no evidence at all for any work by him. Other works by Roberti are in Berlin, Bologna (Pinacoteca, University), Chicago, Dresden, Ferrara, London (NG), Paris (Louvre), Philadelphia (Johnson), the Vatican, and Washington (NG).

ROCOCO. Immediately after the death of Louis XIV of France in 1715 there was a reaction of relief against the excessive splendours and pomps of Versailles and the whole ceremonious *Roi Soleil* way of life. One of the results was to transfer the centre of French life back to Paris and to build new town houses which were both smaller and much more comfortable than the Baroque palaces. Rococo – which comes from a French word *rocaille*, meaning rock-work – is basically a style of interior decoration, and consists principally in the use of C scrolls and counter-curves, and, in its fullest form around 1730, asymmetrical arrangements of curves in panelling and elsewhere. Porcelain, and gold and silversmiths' work of the first half of the 18th century exemplify the tendencies admirably. The characteristics of small curves, prettiness, and gaiety can also be found in painting and sculpture of the period – Watteau and Boucher, and even, in a very modified form, in Hogarth. Nevertheless, England did not take to Rococo and in France it fell out of fashion in the 1740s to be decisively superseded by the earnest ideals and Republican Roman virtue of NEOCLASSICISM, which was largely propagated by Germans. Yet the one country in which the Rococo produced numerous great works of art (and not merely amusing interiors) was Germany, or rather, Germany and Austria. There, in the Catholic South, the style produced scores of absurdly beautiful churches and statues, by artists like Ignaz GÜNTHER, which are elegant, modish, and deeply moving. Guardi, Tiepolo, and Goya all produced masterpieces, but Rococo had relatively little currency in Italy and Spain.

RODIN, Auguste (1840–1917), was the most celebrated sculptor of the late 19th century, achieving during his lifetime a fame which has done much to obscure his real qualities. He worked as a mason from about 1864, and in 1871 was sent to Brussels to do the decorative figures on the new Stock Exchange building, on which he eventually worked as a free-lance. He supplemented his technical training by studying in museums and became interested in Michelangelo, to whom he was probably led by his admiration for PUGET. In 1875 he visited Italy, and soon after began working on his first independent freestanding figure, *Bronze Age* (1877). Its lifelike quality, accuracy of proportion and anatomy, and rendering of movement gave rise to the tale that it had been made from a cast taken from a live model. Though the absurd accusation was later dropped, the figure received no real recognition until it was shown in London in 1884. This put Rodin into much the same position of anti-academism as the Impressionists and their successors, although he never had to face opposition as vehement and entrenched as they did. Most of his public commissions were unlucky: the base of the *Claude Lorraine* monument in Nancy was altered to suit the town council; the town council of Calais refused to erect his *Burghers* (1884–6; replica outside the Houses of Parliament, London) according to his design; his only equestrian statue, *General Lynch*, was destroyed before erection in Santiago by a Chilean revolution (a small bronze of the model is now in Santiago); his *Thinker* was not erected as he wished and was savaged by a vandal with a chopper; his *Hugo* was produced in several versions to meet endless objections and was finally not put up as planned; his *Balzac* monument was refused by the commissioning committee in 1893 and only erected much later; his *Gate of Hell*, commissioned in 1880 as a door for the École des Arts Décoratifs, was still unfinished at his death.

This door, inspired by Ghiberti's so-called *Gates of Paradise* for the Baptistry in Florence, contained a large number of figures which provided him with a fount of ideas which he used over and over in larger independent statues and groups in bronze and marble. He employed many marble-cutters and cast-makers to make replicas, which he often completed himself. He was the creator of a new form in sculpture – the fragment as a finished work, usually a head and trunk, but sometimes a pair of hands only – and he also employed a variant of Michelangelo's unfinished figures, giving to some parts a waxy delicacy of finish, while leaving others parts buried in the hardly touched block. His great influence was through the possibilities opened up by his use of fragments, through his expression of emotion and movement, his use of symbolism and distortion, and the amazing sensitiveness of his modelling. This is seen particularly in his male portraits which combine vivid characterization with a deliberately free handling.

There is little point in listing museums containing works, since there are, for instance, 150 or more replicas of the *Bronze Age*, but the Musée Rodin in Paris and the Tate Gall., London, have perhaps the most examples. There is also a Rodin Mus. in Philadelphia.

ROHLFS, Christian (1849–1938), was the son of a farmer, but a leg injury enabled him to study art at Weimar, where he lived until *c*.1900, painting in an Impressionist manner. An exhibition of works by van Gogh (his younger contemporary) at Hagen in 1902 was a major influence on him, as was his friendship with NOLDE from *c*.1905. He then began to practise a gentle form of Expressionism, and, like MÜLLER, he abandoned oil paint in favour of tempera and watercolour (from 1911). He painted several series of buildings – the church at Soest and Erfurt Cathedral – but his finest works are the delicate flowerpieces, mostly painted when he was nearing 80. Many of these were painted at Ascona, on Lake Maggiore, where he spent most of the years 1927–37. There are works by him in Cologne, Dresden, Essen, Hagen in Westphalia, Harvard University, Karlsruhe, Mannheim, and Paris (Mus. d'Art Moderne).

ROMANISTS were the Northern artists who went to Italy and returned filled with the idea of rivalling Raphael and/or Michelangelo. The name is principally given to painters of the first half of the 16th century, such as MABUSE, van ORLEY, or Maerten van HEEMSKERCK, all of whom imported a quasi-Renaissance style into Northern Europe.

ROMANO, Giulio, *see* GIULIO.

ROMANTIC *see* CLASSIC.

ROMBOUTS, Theodor (1579–1637), was an Antwerp painter who became a Master in the Guild there in 1601, but he went to Rome *c*.1616 and stayed until *c*.1625, where he immediately became strongly influenced by Caravaggio. Like the members of the UTRECHT School he took his Caravaggism home to the Netherlands, but on settling in Antwerp again he changed his style under the fresh influence of Rubens and van Dyck. There are pictures in Antwerp, Ghent, Karlsruhe, Lawrence (Kansas Univ. Mus.), Lille, Madrid, Munich, Paris, and Vaduz (Liechtenstein Coll.).

ROMNEY, George (1734–1802), was, with Gainsborough and Reynolds, the most famous English portrait painter of the later 18th century, before the rise of Lawrence. He was, however, artistically very inferior to any of these, even as a portrait painter. He was born in Lancashire and practised in the North until 1762, when he moved to London. He visited Paris in 1764 and in 1773 he took the serious step of abandoning his London practice (Reynolds was then at the height of his powers, and Gainsborough arrived in London in 1774) to go to Italy, where he stayed till 1775. In Rome he was infected with a longing for the Grand Style, and much of the rest of his life was spent in making sketches for vast historical pictures, some of which were begun on canvas, and painting prosaic portraits, which he did with skill if without passion: John Wesley noted in his Journal (5 Jan. 1789) that he 'struck off an exact likeness at once, and did more in one hour than Sir Joshua did in ten'. He is best known for his Lady Hamilton pictures. He met her in 1781 and seems to have had some kind of liaison with her (his wife having been left in the North), and he could paint portraits of her in more or less *déshabille*, imagining them to be history pieces if called *Lady Hamilton as Circe* or some such title. Many hundreds of his execrable drawings exist, mostly scribbles for historical compositions or illustrations to the poems of Hayley, with whom he was in close contact: in this way he had some importance as a Neoclassic and as a link with FLAXMAN, FUSELI, and BLAKE. He rarely exhibited his works, and never at the RA. In his last years he became senile and returned to his wife to die. At one time his pictures were popular in America and many are in museums there: representative works are in Boston, Edinburgh (NG), London (NG, Tate, NPG, Wallace Coll., Courtauld Inst., Dulwich, and Kenwood), Manchester, New York (Met. Mus.), Ottawa, San Marino Cal., Waddesdon, Bucks. (National Trust), and Washington (NG).

ROSA, Salvator (1615–73), painter, etcher, poet, actor, and musician, is the 19th century's idea of the Romantic artist. He was traditionally a bandit for a while, but this story, unfortunately, seems to have been invented in the 19th century. He was very precocious as a painter of landscapes near his native Naples and of battle-pieces, and is said to have attracted the notice of LANFRANCO. He went to Rome in 1635 but contracted malaria, and had to return to Naples in 1636; in 1639 he returned to Rome and settled there, painting battles, marines, and landscapes: in the same year, however, he was rash enough to compose and recite a lampoon on Bernini. He arrived safely in Florence in 1640 and did not go back to Rome until 1649, when he set up as a religious and historical painter but met with less success. His landscapes are infused with the Pathetic Fallacy, thus having a 'poetic' quality quite different from that of Poussin or Claude, and one that appealed deeply to the Age of Reason, so that he was immensely popular in England in the 18th and 19th centuries: indeed the celebrated lines

> Whate'er Lorraine light-touched with softening hue,
> Or savage Rosa dashed, or learned Poussin drew

(Thomson, 'The Castle of Indolence') more or less sum up the 18th-century connoisseur's equipment.

He began etching only in 1660 but was very successful and completed over 100 plates. His very numerous pictures are in all older galleries, but there are good examples in Florence (Pitti), Glasgow, London (NG and Wallace Coll.), New York (Met. Mus.), Oxford (Ch. Ch.), Paris (Louvre), Rome (Gall. Naz.), and Sarasota Fla.

ROSALBA *see* CARRIERA.

ROSLIN, Alexandre (1718–93), was a Swedish portrait painter who worked much in Paris and who is stylistically indistinguishable from a French painter. He arrived in Paris in 1752, revisited Stockholm in 1774, going in 1775 to St Petersburg and returning to Paris, via Warsaw and Vienna, in 1779. There are pictures by him in London (NG), Paris (Louvre), and Stockholm.

ROSSELLI, Cosimo (1439–1507), was a Florentine painter who ran an important workshop despite his being one of the most uninspired and pedestrian of the better-known painters of his day, and gifted particularly in irrelevant and trivial details. Part of the contract for the 1481 fresco cycle in the Sistine Chapel in the Vatican was with him, and he appears to have been given a large share of the work. Among his pupils were Piero di Cosimo and Fra Bartolommeo. There are works by him in Baltimore (Walters), Berlin, Birmingham (Barber Inst.), Boston (Mus.), Cambridge (Fitzwm), Florence (Accad., Uffizi, Mus. di S. Marco, and churches), Liverpool (Walker), Lucca (Cath.), Oxford (Ashmolean), Paris (Louvre), Philadelphia (Johnson), San Marino Cal. (Huntington), and elsewhere.

ROSSELLINO, Bernardo (1409–64) and Antonio (1427–*c*.79), were brothers. Bernardo was active as an architect as well as a sculptor, and both seem to have done a certain amount of decorative work. Bernardo's principal work is the Tomb of the Florentine Chancellor Leonardo Bruni (1444/50: Florence, Sta Croce), which derives directly from the Tomb of John XXIII by DONATELLO and in its turn sets the type of Tomb in a niche which was normal for the rest of the century. There are other works by him in Florence and in Empoli and Forlì. Antonio was his pupil and was also much influenced by Donatello, although, like MINO, DESIDERIO, and BENEDETTO da Maiano, he rejected the rugged side of Donatello and concentrated on grace and beauty of line. He is best known for his Madonna reliefs, but he also made portrait busts and a Tomb which derives from his brother's, but is a grander affair: it is that of the Cardinal-Prince ,of Portugal (1461–6: Florence, S. Miniato al Monte). There are works by him in Berlin, Empoli, Faenza, Florence (Bargello, Sto Spirito), London (V & A), Naples, New York (Met. Mus.), Pistoia (Cath.), Prato (Cath.), Toledo Ohio, Vienna, Washington (NG), and elsewhere.

ROSSETTI, Dante Gabriel (1828–82), poet and painter, was the son of an Italian political refugee in London. He was taught drawing by Cotman and after a few unsuccessful months with Ford Madox BROWN he went to Holman HUNT in 1848. Under his guidance he painted his first major work, the *Girlhood of Mary Virgin*, the first picture exhibited (March 1849) with the initials of the PRB. His adherence to the tenets of the Brotherhood was, however, very short-lived. His subjects were drawn mostly from Dante and from a medieval dream world also reflected in his verse. In 1850 he met Elizabeth Siddal, who also posed for Hunt and MILLAIS, and from 1852 onwards she developed under his inspiration into an artist of poetic and neurotic intensity. His best work was produced during the years of their uneasy association. They married in 1860; in 1862 she died of narcotics and he became virtually a recluse and eventually a chloral addict. In 1857 he was concerned (with MORRIS, BURNE-JONES, and others) in the decoration of the Oxford Union and he did one painting directly on a whitewashed wall. It perished immediately. His poor technique and his use of studio assistants are obvious in many of his later works. Birmingham, Cambridge (Fitzwm), Cambridge Mass. (Fogg), Dublin, Liverpool, London (NG, NPG, Tate, V & A), Manchester, Ottawa, and Wilmington Delaware have examples.

ROSSO, Giovanni Battista ('Rosso Fiorentino') (1494–1540), was a friend and contemporary of PONTORMO and, like him, worked under Andrea del Sarto, and was one of the founders of MANNERISM. He worked in Florence from 1513 to 1523, when he went to Rome and stayed there until the Sack (1527), after which he wandered around Italy until 1530 when he went to Venice and then, in the same year, to France for François I. He worked at Fontainebleau with PRIMATICCIO and was thus one of the founders of the Fontainebleau style and had a great influence on French painting. According to Vasari he committed suicide, which would have been in keeping with his neurotic temperament, but he seems in fact to have died a natural death. His *Deposition* (Paris, Louvre) was painted in France and its dead Christ with His livid body and reddish hair is typical of his later emotional style. There are works by him in Arezzo, Berlin, Bradford, Florence (Uffizi, Pitti, SS. Annunziata, S. Lorenzo), Frankfurt, Liverpool, London (NG), Los Angeles, Naples, Pisa, Rome (Borghese), Siena, Volterra, and Washington (NG).

ROSSO, Medardo (1858–1928), was one of the leading Italian sculptors of the late 19th century, although he was a painter until 1883 and only turned to sculpture as a result of reading Baudelaire's 'Curiosités esthétiques'. He was fascinated by the play of light on surfaces – an essentially Impressionist preoccupation – and, like RODIN, he translated this into sculpture, although he differed from Rodin in preferring the single view-point. His favourite medium was wax, since this has a colouristic effect as well as allowing very slight modulations of the surface. He did, in fact, exert some influence on Rodin as well as on later Italian sculptors (e.g. MANZÙ), but his fame has been largely confined to Italy, since his stay in Paris (1884–6) was disastrous. There are works by him in Paris (Petit Pal. and Mus. Rodin) as well as in Italian museums, particularly Rome (Gall. Naz. d'Arte Moderna) and the Rosso Museum in Barzio (Como).

ROTHKO, Mark (1903–70), was born in Russia but went to America in 1913. He began painting in 1926 and was originally influenced by the European Surrealists who settled in the US after 1940. His characteristic works, however, are large abstract pictures which consist of horizontal bands of colour with muzzy edges. There are examples in London (Tate), New York (M of MA), and other American museums.

ROTTLUFF, Karl Schmidt, see SCHMIDT.

ROTTMAYR, Johann Michael (1654–1730), was the leading Austrian Baroque painter. According to his own account, he went to Venice in 1675 and worked there for thirteen years in the studio of Johann Carl Loth (known in Italy as Carlo Lotti): no works of his are known from this period, but his style is certainly Italianate (Correggio and cf. Pittoni) with a trace of French influence. He returned to Salzburg c.1688 and lived in Vienna from 1696, but was often away painting ceilings all over Austria. His large ceiling in the Karlskirche, Vienna (1726–30), is very close to Correggio, but other late works show some influence from Rubens. There are many ceilings still in existence in Vienna, Melk, and elsewhere, and paintings in Munich, Nuremberg, Passau Cathedral, Sarasota Fla, and Vienna (Oesterreichische Gal.).

ROUAULT, Georges (1871–1958), had already completed his apprentice-ship to a stained-glass window maker when he entered, in 1891, the École des Beaux-Arts, where he was a pupil of MOREAU from 1892 to 1895. He became the first Curator of the Musée Moreau in 1898. His early works show Moreau's influence, but by 1903 he had abandoned his dark and overworked oil-paintings of Biblical subjects for the series of *Prostitutes*, *Clowns* (from 1904, 1907, and again during the 1930s), and *Judges* (from 1908). These usually have heavy dark contours enclosing areas of violent colour, and express the painter's loathing of vice, hypocrisy, cruelty, and complacency. Although he exhibited at the famous FAUVE show in 1905, he re-mained aloof from all groups and systems of aesthetics, and developed one of the purest forms of Expressionism. Before 1908 he worked mostly in watercolour and gouache, only returning to oil-painting after about 1918: he also executed a large amount of graphic work. His series of etchings, originally made for two books *Guerre* and *Miserere* from 1916 to 1927, were eventually published in 1948 under the title *Miserere*, and he also made lithographs and coloured etchings. His themes remained within the limits of his three series, religious subjects – chiefly of the Passion (Rouault was a devout Catholic) – landscapes of bleak and hostile country, and an occasional bouquet of flowers. He worked for the Diaghileff Ballet in 1929, executed tapestry cartoons in 1933, and in 1945 designed stained-glass windows for the church of Plateau d'Assy (Haute Savoie). There are works in most museums of modern art.

ROUBILIAC, Louis François (?1705–62), was born in Lyons. He came to England *c.*1732, and in 1737 carved the statue of Handel for Vauxhall Gardens (now London, V & A: terracotta at Cambridge, Fitzwm) which made his name. From 1745 he taught sculpture at the St Martin's Lane Academy, precursor of the Royal Academy schools, and he worked for a short time as a modeller at the Chelsea china factory *c.*1750. His was probably the finest sculpture done during the 18th century in England: his busts have a vivid look of life, allied to a great style in presentation and a superb technique. His monument to Lady Elizabeth Nightingale (1761: Westminster Abbey) has been decried as theatrical; despite its allusions to the circumstances of her death, the skeletal figure of Death issuing from the tomb to strike at the living owes much to Bernini's monument to Alexander VII in St Peter's in Rome. Roubiliac had visited Italy in 1752. He executed a number of other tombs in Westminster Abbey (including the very fine and influential one of the Duke of Argyll, 1748), a statue of Newton, and a large series of fine busts for Trinity College, Cambridge, and there are other works in the Royal Collection, Greenwich (Nat. Marit. Mus.), Leeds, London (NPG, RA, V & A), and elsewhere.

ROUSSEAU, Henri, called 'le Douanier' (1844–1910), was an amateur or 'Sunday' painter with a direct, simple and hauntingly naïve vision who painted some unusually large and complicated pictures of elaborately fanciful and picturesquely exotic subjects in a matter-of-factly pedestrian technique and strong colour. He served as a Regimental bandsman – according to his own account, in Mexico in 1861–7, which provided him with his fantastic settings – and as a Sergeant in the Franco-Prussian War of 1870–1. He entered the Paris municipal Customs service (hence 'le Douanier'), and began painting about 1880, exhibiting at the Indépendants from 1886. A dinner in his honour was given in Picasso's studio in 1908, and this gesture has played its part in the transmogrification of 'le Douanier' into a symbol of sophisticated interest in the pseudo-Primitive and in the opening of the floodgates of both the psychological and the sentimental school of writers on art. He seems to have combined a certain peasant shrewdness and bland self-esteem with gullible simple-mindedness; he kept a school where he taught elocution, music, and painting, wrote two plays, got himself involved, though guiltlessly, in a trial for fraud, and finally died, it is said, as a result of a disappointment in love in pursuit of a third wife. There are works in London (Tate, Courtauld Inst.), New York (M of M A), Paris (Louvre), Zürich, and elsewhere.

ROUSSEAU, Théodore (1812–67), was a French landscape painter, the friend of MILLET and DIAZ, who settled at BARBIZON in 1844. His aims, style, and development are characteristic of the Barbizon School, of which he was one of the principal members. Like others in the group he suffered great hardship as a result of his attempts to introduce a non-Academic landscape style, although this did not make him any more understanding or friendly to the Impressionists in later years. From 1863 he was deeply interested in Japanese art. There are pictures by him in Boston, Glasgow, London (NG, V & A, Wallace Coll.), New York (Met. Mus.), Ottawa, and many French and US museums.

ROWLANDSON, Thomas (1756–1827), was the finest of the draughtsmen and caricaturists who portrayed life and manners in 18th- and early 19th-century England. He was born in London, went to Paris for two years at 16 and studied there, and was at the RA Schools before and after his stay abroad. He started as a painter of serious subjects and portraits, but was an inveterate gambler, and after dissipating the fortune inherited from his French aunt, earned a living and paid his debts with a flood of drawings of popular and low-life subjects, full of rollicking humour and an outsize sense of the ridiculous. His gift for exuberant and flowing line is more French – and Rococo – than English, but his handling of tone is typically English in the delicacy of its effects, which often enhance by contrast the robustness of his subjects. Much of his work was produced for the print-publisher Ackermann. Most English museums have examples.

ROYAL ACADEMY *see* ACADEMY.

RUBÉNISME was the most important artistic movement in France at the end of the 17th century, reaching a climax in the work of WATTEAU. In 1671–2 there was a violent argument in the Academy of Painting (known as the Quarrel of Colour and Design), concerning the relative importance of colour in painting. The Poussinistes regarded it as a mere decorative adjunct to the formal essentials of drawing and design, as typified in the works of Raphael, the Carracci, and the Frenchman Poussin (thus cunningly introducing a patriotic note). The strong suit of the Colourists was naturalism: painting is an imitation of appearances, and, they said, colour was the most convincing means of imitation. This theory depends on Titian as much as Rubens, but the fact of the existence in Paris of the great Rubens cycle of the *Life of Marie de' Medici* coupled with the undoubted naturalism of most Flemish painting led to the Party of Colour becoming transformed into Rubénistes. In 1672 LEBRUN himself had officially settled the matter once and for all: 'The function of colour is to satisfy the eyes, whereas drawing satisfies the mind' – that is, he merely repeated the classic theory of DISEGNO. The critic Roger de Piles published a Life of Rubens in 1677; in 1699 he was elected an Honorary Member of the Academy, thus marking the final victory of Rubénisme, and he then republished his earlier 'Dialogue sur le Coloris' (1st ed. 1673). Thus, by the beginning of the 18th century the way was prepared for Watteau and also for the new ideas in ROCOCO.

RUBENS, Sir Peter Paul (1577–1640), was born at Siegen in Westphalia. He came of an Antwerp family which returned there by 1589 and in 1591 he became for six months the pupil of a landscape and decorative painter called Verhaecht, who had been to Italy. He was then, for four or five years, in the studio of Adam van Noort before becoming a pupil of Otto van Veen, a travelled and scholarly painter, until 1599. He entered the Guild in 1598 and in 1600 went to Italy and became Court Painter to Vincenzo Gonzaga, Duke of Mantua. In 1603 he accompanied an embassy taking horses and pictures from Mantua to Philip III in Madrid, where he admired the Titians and Raphaels in the Spanish Royal Collection. From 1604 to 1608 he was in Mantua, Rome, Genoa, and Milan, and was working in Rome when he received news of his mother's illness. He reached Antwerp too late, and was about to return to Mantua when he was appointed Court Painter to the Spanish Governors of the Netherlands, an appointment he held to his death. He settled in Antwerp, where he built himself an Italianate palace, married Isabella Brandt in 1609, and started on what was perhaps the most energetic and fruitful career in the history of art and one which made him the most important artist in Northern Europe and the greatest Northern exponent of the Baroque.

In Italy he had studied the artists of the High Renaissance, particularly Titian and Michelangelo, and after his return to Flanders his first works show how deeply he was influenced by Caravaggio. After the success of the *Raising of the Cross* (1610), he evolved in the *Descent from the Cross* (1611–14: both Antwerp Cathedral) a less passionately dramatic style so that numerous assistants could work under him to fulfil the multitude of commissions that poured in. His letters prove how carefully he controlled the execution of his designs, and in most cases he did the final work on a picture himself to restore to it something of the unity of the first sketch; the amount of personal execution was a question of price. His chief assistants were of the first ability; the young van DYCK entered his studio about 1617, and JORDAENS and SNYDERS were for many years employed by him. Without the methods he devised for the division of labour his vast output over so many years could never have been achieved, much less maintained, at so high a standard. His practice was to make smallish sketches, very free in handling, usually on panels with a light streaky buff or grey ground, the loose drawing touched in with indications of the local colours. Some of his tapestry designs are larger, more closely worked out, and more fully coloured.

His major commissions include the decoration, begun in 1620, of the Jesuit Church in Antwerp, calling for 39 ceiling paintings and three altarpieces, which last alone survive, the rest having been burnt in 1718: the Medici cycle painted for the Luxembourg Palace in Paris (1622–5: now in the Louvre); the ceiling of the Banqueting House in Whitehall (his only surviving ceiling) completed for Charles I in 1635; the huge scheme of decoration for the Torre de la Parada commissioned by Philip IV of Spain, on which he was working at his death. Besides these there were countless altarpieces, portraits, hunting scenes, landscapes, religious pictures, scenes from classical mythology and history, allegories, tapestry designs, book illustrations, and designs for triumphal processions.

He was employed on diplomatic missions by the Governors of the Netherlands – to Holland in 1627 (when he visited Utrecht and met HONTHORST), to Spain in 1628 (when he made copies of the Titians he had admired in 1603, and became friendly with Velazquez), to England in 1629 (when he was knighted by Charles I), and these missions served as a distraction after the death of Isabella Brandt in 1626. In 1630 he married again. The 16-year-old Hélène Fourment became the theme and inspiration of his late mythologies and the subject of many portraits. Since gout was now limiting his activity in the workshop he could devote more time to the personal side of his art in which his domestic life, hitherto kept in the background, played a dominant part. After his death, his widow wanted to destroy some of his more intimate portraits of her, such as the one in a fur cloak, now in Vienna.

Almost all the older galleries, and most of the more recent ones, contain works attributed to Rubens, which may be entirely autograph or more or less autograph workshop productions.

RUDE, François (1784–1855), was the major French sculptor of the early 19th century, whose principal work is the relief of the *Volunteers of 1792* (better known as the *Marseillaise*), on the Arc de Triomphe in Paris (1833–6). The romanticism of Delacroix is coupled in his work with the classical outlook as well as the Napoleonic enthusiasm of DAVID, whom he accompanied to Brussels 1814–27. His bust of

David (1831) is in the Louvre, and his wife Sophie (1797–1867) was a painter and pupil of David. Rude went to Italy in 1842. His works are in Brussels and Paris and in a Rude museum in his native Dijon.

RUISDAEL, Jacob van (1628/9–82), was the greatest of the Dutch realist landscape painters and exerted a huge influence on the development of European landscape painting in the 19th century, although in his own day he was less popular than Italianate painters such as BERCHEM (who may occasionally have painted figures in Ruisdael's landscapes). He was born in Haarlem, where the realist landscape was first developed in the early 17th century, and may have been a pupil of his father, Isack, about whom little is known. Later he probably worked with his uncle Salomon van RUYSDAEL (whose son, also a landscape painter, was also named Jacob). His early works represent views in the neighbourhood of Haarlem with great fidelity, so that many are still recognizable. About 1650 he travelled in East Holland and probably in Western Germany as well, where he saw mountains for the first time. He settled in Amsterdam *c*. 1655 and lived there until his death, although he was buried in Haarlem. In 1676 he took a medical degree at Caen and he seems to have practised as a surgeon in Amsterdam while continuing to paint, but the latest date on any of his pictures is 1678. It is now known that the story of his poverty and death in the Haarlem Poorhouse refers to Jacob Salomonsz. RUYSDAEL.

His later works have a much more Romantic approach and are more dramatic in handling; some even imitate the kind of mountain landscape popularized by A. van EVERDINGEN. His finest works, however, are generally agreed to be the typical Dutch panoramas with the sun breaking fitfully through the clouds and lighting up patches of the duneland. It has been said that 'he never painted a hot day', and his temper was indeed melancholic and grave; yet unlike his uncle or Jan van GOYEN who sought breadth and used monochromatic effects to get it, he employs strong local colours and gains his atmospheric effects by means of the luminosity of his skies and the vast sweep of his clouds. HOBBEMA was the most important of his many pupils and imitators. He is thought to have painted well over a thousand pictures, so that practically every major gallery has one, but the best collection is in the NG, London.

RUNGE, Philipp Otto (1777–1810), was a German painter who studied in Copenhagen 1799–1801. After this he went to Dresden where he became the most important early German Romantic painter. In Dresden he met FRIEDRICH and Goethe, who was interested in Runge's theory of colour. He began a series of *The Times of Day* which reflect his highly subjective and emotional approach to landscape as a revelation of Nature. He was a naïve, almost primitive, painter and his rather austere Romanticism was influenced by English artists, principally FLAXMAN and BLAKE. It is therefore sharply distinguished from the (by comparison) voluptuousness of the later French Romantics. There is a biography of him by his elder brother which gives an account of his ideas. Most of his works are in Hamburg, but there are others in Berlin, Hartford Conn., and Vienna.

RUSKIN, John (1819–1900), was the most influential art critic of 19th-century England. He was the son of well-off parents, who encouraged his precocious artistic and literary gifts, and he was able to travel all over Europe between 1833 and 1888. He met TURNER in 1840, and in 1843 published the first volume of 'Modern Painters', a work designed to establish Turner's supremacy over all other landscape painters. The remaining four volumes, published at intervals up to 1860, were less single-minded and contain a highly personal aesthetic. His many other books deal with architecture, politics, social reform, mineralogy and other subjects, but his advocacy of Gothic – particularly Venetian Gothic – architecture had results so horrible that he himself bitterly repented it: 'there is scarcely a public-house near the Crystal Palace but sells its gin and bitters under pseudo-Venetian capitals copied from the church of the Madonna of Health or of Miracles ... my present house ... is surrounded everywhere by the accursed Frankenstein monsters of, indirectly, my own making'. His view of art as an expression of morality, his identification of good art with medieval art, his violent diatribes against Palladian architecture, his powerful and timely support of the Pre-Raphaelites, his sensational attack on Whistler leading to the libel suit, his disastrous marriage to Effie Gray in 1848 and its annulment in 1854 (after which she married Millais), as well as his Utopian agricultural schemes and his hatred of industrialism – all illustrate his complex and many-sided character. He became very famous, and his involved, contradictory, and highly emotional prose gave his art criticism an impact so enduring that not only is he still a folk-memory in the English attitude to the arts, but there has lately been a revival of interest in his theories. He died insane.

He was a meticulous draughtsman, particularly of architecture and plant forms, and there are large collections of his drawings in Oxford (where he was the first Slade Professor) and at Bembridge School. Many British and American museums possess examples.

RUYSCH, Rachel (1664–1750), was a Dutch woman painter of flowers and still-life. There are works by her in Amsterdam, Brussels, Dresden, Florence (Uffizi and Pitti), Glasgow, The Hague, London (V&A), Melbourne, Munich, New York (Met. Mus.), Oxford, Preston, Toledo Ohio, and Vienna (Akad.).

RUYSDAEL, Salomon van (c. 1600/2–70), was one of the leading Dutch realist landscape painters of the first half of the 17th century, the brother of Isack and uncle of Jacob van RUISDAEL (the fully signed pictures always have this difference in spelling). He is first recorded in the Haarlem Guild in 1623 but the earliest dated picture is of 1627 (Vienna), and the early works are all of the simplest landscape themes, many of them approaching very closely to the work of Jan van GOYEN, especially those with ferry boats, an expanse of water, and a few trees on the bank in an even grey light. He lived in Haarlem, and was a Mennonite, prosperous and esteemed: his son, Jacob Salomonsz. (1629/30–81), was also a landscape painter who is known to have worked up to at least 1668 and who died in the Haarlem Poorhouse. There are representative pictures by Salomon in the Royal Coll. and in Amsterdam, Antwerp, Baltimore, Barnard Castle (Bowes Mus.), Basle, Berlin, Brussels, Cambridge (Fitzwm), Cambridge Mass. (Fogg Mus.), Cologne, Copenhagen, Detroit, Dresden, Dublin, Frankfurt, Grenoble, The Hague (Mauritshuis and Bredius Mus., which has a *Still-Life* of 1662), Hamburg, Leicester, Leipzig, Leningrad, Liverpool, London (NG), Melbourne, Merion Pa (Barnes Foundation), Minneapolis, Munich, New York (Met. Mus.), Oslo, Ottawa, Paris (Louvre and Mus. des Arts Décoratifs), Philadelphia, Providence RI, Rotterdam, Sarasota Fla (Ringling Mus.), Stockholm, Strasbourg, Vienna, Worcester Mass., and York. There is a picture by Jacob Salomonsz. in London (NG), but the few signed works bear only a monogram JvR which can lead to confusion with his cousin Jacob's pictures.

RYDER, Albert Pinkham (1847–1917), was the most original and poetic late 19th-century American Romantic painter, and the counterpart to Edgar Allen Poe, whom he admired. He was born in New Bedford, Mass., a whaling port from the world of Moby Dick, and all his life he was haunted by the sea, although he actually lived in squalor in New York. His marine and landscape paintings have a visionary and brooding quality and were very fine in colour, but his deficient technique and the loading of layers of rich, enamel-like pigment have caused them to deteriorate badly. He travelled to Europe, but seems to have been unaffected by it. There are works by him in many American museums, including Chicago, Cleveland Ohio, Detroit, New York (Met. Mus.), St Louis, Toledo Ohio, and Washington (NG, Corcoran, and Phillips): it is said that many forgeries also exist.

RYSBRACK, John Michael (1694–1770), was the son of an Antwerp landscape painter, Peter, who worked for a time in England. Rysbrack worked first for Gibbs the architect, but from about 1730 he shared with ROUBILIAC the position of most eminent sculptor in England, until the advent of SCHEEMAKERS in 1741 somewhat affected his business. He was more severely classical than Roubiliac, e.g. in his bust of Sir Robert Walpole in a toga. In 1747 he began his celebrated *Hercules* (now at Stourhead) which embodied a variant of the theory of ideal beauty, in that the artist composed it by using as models boxers and wrestlers, from whom he selected the best parts. He executed a number of tombs in Westminster Abbey (including Sir Isaac Newton's), and there are works by him in the Royal Collection, Cambridge (Fitzwm and Senate House), London (NPG, Wallace Coll., BM, V & A, Nat. Marit. Mus., St Martin-in-the-Fields), Oxford (Radcliffe Camera, Christ Church, Ashmolean).

S

SACCHI, Andrea (1599–1661), was the chief representative of the classic strain of ALGARDI and POUSSIN in Roman Baroque painting. He was a native Roman, trained first under ALBANI and then, while still in his teens, in Bologna he came under the influence of Lodovico CARRACCI. Back in Rome he was patronized by the great Barberini family, for whom he painted the *Divine Wisdom* in the Barberini Palace (*c*.1629–33) in a much less Baroque style than PIETRO da Cortona's ceiling in the same Palace. Sacchi's *Vision of S. Romuald* (1640: Vatican) is still more classic in feeling and this classicism was handed down to the 18th century through his chief pupil, MARATTA. Apart from Rome there are works by him in Berlin, Cardiff, Dresden, Madrid, Ottawa, Philadelphia, and Vienna.

SACHLICHKEIT, Die neue, *see* NEUE SACHLICHKEIT.

SACRA CONVERSAZIONE (Ital. holy conversation) is the name given to a representation of the Madonna and Child with Saints, in which the sacred personages are aware of each other or are united by some common action. This type of representation replaced the earlier form of altarpiece in which each figure occupied one panel of a POLYPTYCH: in a *Sacra Conversazione* the barriers have been broken down and all the figures have moved into a single, unified space. The earliest examples occur in the work of FRA ANGELICO and his contemporaries, Fra Filippo LIPPI and DOMENICO Veneziano. Donatello's altar in the Santo at Padua seems to have introduced the idea, in three-dimensional form, to the North and MANTEGNA'S S. Zeno altarpiece (1459) forms the link between the Florentine examples and the important altarpieces, all of *c*.1475, by PIERO della Francesca, ANTONELLO, and Giovanni BELLINI, which create a single, unified space for the figures and for the spectator.

SAENREDAM, Pieter (1597–1665), was a Haarlem painter who specialized in church interiors, rendered in cool silvery tones with an occasional gleam of sunlight. He never went to Italy, but a few of his pictures were painted from the drawings made in Rome in 1532/5 by Maerten van HEEMSKERCK. He seems to have made very elaborate preparatory drawings, including fully worked out perspective projections and diagrams. There are examples in Amsterdam (Rijksmus.), Copenhagen (the earliest dated work, 1626), Glasgow, Haarlem (Hals Mus. and Bisschoppelijk Mus.), Hamburg, London (NG), Munich, Orléans, Philadelphia (Johnson), Rotterdam, Utrecht, Worcester Mass., and elsewhere.

SALON. During the 17th century exhibitions of works by members of the French Royal Academy were held in the Salon d'Apollon in the

Louvre, hence the name. Originally occasional, it was biennial from 1737 to the Revolution, and then annual, being thrown open to all artists and the jury abolished, although it was soon re-established to limit the huge entry. Since there was no other public exhibition of any standing, the jury (composed almost exclusively of members of the Institut) obtained a stranglehold, using its enormous power to exclude any painter of whom it did not approve. In 1863 the scandal and the protests over the number of works refused were so great that Napoleon III ordered a special exhibition of them, known as the *Salon des Refusés*. So bitter was the official opposition and so uncomprehending was the mass of the public, incapable of independent judgement, that no such exhibition was held again, nor was the rigour of the jury modified. Among the principal exhibitors were MANET, BOUDIN, FANTIN-LATOUR, JONGKIND, PISSARRO, WHISTLER, while CÉZANNE also exhibited and COURBET had the distinction of being rejected from both exhibitions. The present huge yearly Salon is organized by the Société des Artistes Français and has been since 1881, but there are now several other 'Salons' – e.g. d'Automne, des Indépendants – which cater for different types of art.

SALVIATI, Francesco (1510–63), was a Florentine Mannerist and a close friend of Vasari. He worked on various decorative schemes in Rome, Venice, and Florence and went to France in 1554. He was a pupil of Andrea del Sarto and was much influenced by Michelangelo, Pontormo, and the Venetians: out of this mixture he was able to produce some fine portraits as well as allegories. There are works in Florence (Uffizi, Pitti), London (NG), New York (Met. Mus.), Paris (Louvre), Springfield Mass., Turin, Vienna, Washington (NG), Worcester Mass., and elsewhere.

SÁNCHEZ COELLO, Alonso (1531/2–88), was the pupil and successor of MOR as Court portrait painter to Philip II of Spain. He received his education in Flanders and Portugal, and his style is based upon the withdrawn dignity with which Mor invested his sitters; but he was also much influenced by TITIAN (who was Philip II's favourite painter). He began his career in Portugal and painted a few altarpieces, but he is principally known for his portraits, and he worked for the Court at Valladolid from 1557. His portraits, especially the full-lengths, became models for imitation since they perfectly express the rigidity of Spanish Court etiquette, or at least the more pleasing side of it. The dignity and gravity of his style was admirably adapted to these royal icons which were sent as presents to the numerous connections of the Hapsburgs. He is said to have painted S. Ignatius Loyola in 1585, but this, which would have been a fascinating document, is unfortunately lost. There are four pictures by him in the Royal Collection, and others in Bamberg, Berlin, Boston (Gardner Mus.), Brussels, Dublin, the Escorial, Madrid (Prado), Munich, New

York (Hispanic Soc.), San Diego Cal., Vienna (K-H Mus.), and Wisconsin University.

SANDBY, Paul (1725–1809), and his brother Thomas (1721–98), were topographical draughtsmen employed by the Crown, and Paul was sent to the Highlands of Scotland to work on the Ordnance Survey made after the 1745 Rising. He portrayed landscape not only with accuracy and feeling, but also with a sensitive eye for atmosphere. He studied figure drawing, etched, and introduced aquatint into England. From about 1752 he lived in London, and he worked a good deal at Windsor, where Thomas was Deputy Ranger of Windsor Forest. He was a founder-member of the RA. From 1770, he visited Wales several times, and was one of the first watercolour painters to appreciate Welsh scenery. He usually painted in transparent washes, and often drew in watercolour as distinct from tinting a pencil drawing; he also painted in gouache, and many of his large series of Windsor (in the Royal Library) use this medium, which in his hands almost rivals oil paint. Gainsborough referred to him as 'the only man of genius' who had painted 'real views from Nature in this country'; that is, who did not rearrange the material into picturesque compositions à la Gaspar or Claude, or work up his topography (for instance, at Windsor) according to the example of Canaletto's views. Besides the unrivalled series in the Royal Collection, there are examples in London (BM, V & A, Tate and Courtauld Inst.). Thomas was also a founder-member of the RA, and its first Professor of Architecture. He painted many watercolours, very similar to Paul's, but was also the designer of Virginia Water, near Windsor.

SANDRART, Joachim von (1606–88), was a German painter who accompanied his master HONTHORST to London in 1627, before going on to Italy 1628–35, where he met many famous artists and went sketching with CLAUDE, POUSSIN, and BAMBOCCIO. His paintings are forgotten but his book, 'Teutsche Akademie' (1675–9, Latin ed. 1683), was the first of a long line of German art-historical books and is a source of great importance for many 17th-century painters. There is a *Self-portrait* in Frankfurt (Historisches Mus.).

SANGUINE. A reddish-brown chalk used for drawing.

SANSOVINO, Andrea (1467/71–1529), was a Florentine sculptor who was trained under Antonio POLLAIUOLO and BERTOLDO but developed under the influence of Raphael and the Antique. He went to Portugal in 1491, sent by Lorenzo de' Medici, worked on the Baptistry in Florence 1493–6, and returned to Portugal until 1499: nothing is known of his activity there. On his return to Italy he worked in Rome 1505–12 and his most famous works are the two large and complex Tombs in Sta Maria del Popolo to Cardinal Ascanio Sforza (1505) and Cardinal Girolamo della Rovere (1507). These large wall-tombs with recumbent effigies and standing figures of

Virtues set the type of monument normal in the 16th century. Most of his later years were spent in Loreto. His *Baptism* (1502–5: Florence, Baptistry) was completed by DANTI after 1568. Other works are in Berlin, Florence (Bargello), and Genoa (Cath.).

SANSOVINO, Jacopo (1486–1570), was the pupil of Andrea Sansovino and took his name. He worked as a sculptor and architect in Florence and Rome before going to Venice in 1527, where he became City Architect and is principally famous as the designer of the Library of S. Mark and other buildings. His most famous work in sculpture is the pair of gigantic statues of *Mars* and *Neptune* at the head of the steps in the Doge's Palace. Other works are in Venice, Padua (Il Santo), Florence (Bargello) and elsewhere.

SANTI, Giovanni (*c.*1430/40–94), is important for two reasons, neither connected with his pictures. First, he was the father of Raphael; second, he wrote a rhymed Chronicle which mentions a number of 15th-century artists. There are pictures by him in Urbino, where he worked, and in Berlin, London, Milan, the Vatican, and elsewhere.

SARACENI, Carlo (1579–1620), was a Venetian painter who went to Rome *c.*1598, where he later came under the influence of CARA-VAGGIO and ELSHEIMER; in particular, he imitated Elsheimer's effects of light in small-scale pictures (often on copper) so that they have been confused. Elsheimer and Caravaggio both died in 1610, and Saraceni seems to have succeeded to their market; indeed his *Death of the Virgin* was commissioned to replace Caravaggio's (a signed version belongs to Ampleforth Abbey, on loan to Barnard Castle (Bowes Mus.), and Rome, S.M. della Scala has another version). By 1613 he was working for the Mantuan Court, and, *c.*1619, he went to Venice, where he began a painting for the Doge's Palace, completed after his death by a pupil. There are works by him in Berlin, Bologna, Detroit, Dijon, Dresden, Hartford Conn., Munich, Naples, Padua, Prague, Rome (Capitoline and churches, especially his masterpiece, *The Miracle of S. Benno*, 1618, in S.M. dell' Anima), Vienna, and Venice (Accad. and Redentore).

SARGENT, John Singer (1856–1925), was an American virtuoso portrait painter who settled in London and painted High Society in Edwardian and Georgian times. He was born in Italy of American expatriate parents and was trained in Florence and Paris, settling in London in 1884/5 and continuing the *bravura* tradition of LAWRENCE, crossed with Velazquez. He visited the US frequently and painted some large-scale decorations in Boston Public Library (1890) and the Museum of Fine Arts (1916–25), but he is best known for his portraits, and for his brilliant watercolours. In 1880 he had visited Spain and the technical skill and simple colour schemes of most of his portraits reflect Velazquez, seen through the eyes of MANET and Courbet: Sargent's *Mme Gautreau*, painted in Paris in 1884, shows all this, but was a *succès de scandale* and was one of the causes of his leaving Paris for London. His huge output means that his portraits are almost everywhere in Britain and America. His superficial brilliance is very like that of BOLDINI.

SARTO, Andrea del, *see* ANDREA.

SARTORIUS, John N. (*c.*1755–1828), was a British painter of fox hunts and horse races. There is a typical example in San Marino Cal.

SASSETTA, Stefano di Giovanni (*c.*1400, perhaps 1392–1450), was, with GIOVANNI di Paolo, the major Sienese 15th-century painter. Like all his Sienese contemporaries, he was quite happy to continue the style of the 14th-century masters, but he was also aware of new trends coming from the North, and the INTERNATIONAL GOTHIC style makes itself felt in his work and is perceptible in the influence on him of painters like MASOLINO or GENTILE da Fabriano. He is first recorded as painting an altarpiece in 1423–6 (parts of it survive, in Siena, Barnard Castle (Bowes Mus.), Budapest, and the Vatican): it has a sense of space that is not improperly associable with the work then being painted in Florence, even with MASACCIO's Brancacci Chapel. Sassetta did not develop into a realistic painter, as that would have been understood in Florence, but his essentially mystic character uses the new forms to give a blend of tradition and modern actuality. The best example of this is the altarpiece painted in 1437–44 for S. Francesco, Sansepolcro (where PIERO della Francesca would have seen it). The altarpiece is now dismembered, the central panel of *S. Francis in Glory* belonging to the Berenson Coll. in Florence, but the greater part of it is in London (NG) and Paris (Louvre). An altarpiece dated 1436 in the Chiesa dell' Osservanza, Siena, is now thought to be the work of an imitator, known as the Osservanza Master (there are other works by him in Pienza Cath. and in London, NG). Other pictures by Sassetta are in Berlin, Boston, Chantilly (part of the *S. Francis* altar), Cleveland Ohio, Cortona (S. Domenico), Detroit, Florence, London (NG), New York (Met. Mus., Frick Coll.), Siena, Washington (NG), Yale Univ., and elsewhere.

SAVOLDO, Giovanni Girolamo (active 1508–after 1548). He was a Brescian who worked mainly in Venice, where he was deeply influenced by GIORGIONE and TITIAN, yet he is first recorded in the Guild at Florence, in 1508. His large altarpiece of 1521 (Treviso, S. Niccolo) is entirely in the Bellini-Giorgione tradition; he may also have worked in Milan *c.*1532/35. His works have a wonderful sense of light effect, and his night scenes are half a century earlier than CARAVAGGIO. The writer Pino was his pupil and records that he painted but few works. In 1548 Aretino referred to him as 'decrepit', and he probably died soon afterwards. There are pictures by him in the Royal Coll. and in Amsterdam, Berlin, Brescia, Cleveland, Dublin, Florence (Uffizi), London (NG, Courtauld Inst.), Milan (Brera),

New York (Met. Mus.), Paris (Louvre), Rome (Borghese and Capitoline), Turin, Venice, Vienna, and Washington.

SCHADOW, Gottfried (1764–1850), was one of the leading German Neoclassic sculptors. He was in Rome 1785–7 and was much influenced by his friend CANOVA before returning to Berlin, to become Court Sculptor in 1788. He spent the rest of his life there. His works include many monuments in Berlin churches, the first major one being to the boy Graf von der Marck (1790). He also made the Quadriga on the Brandenburg Gate and numerous busts, including one of Goethe (who had earlier criticized Schadow for his excessive realism), and others for the Bavarian Valhalla. His monuments to Frederick the Great (1793) and Blücher (1819) are at Stettin and Rostock, but his projected equestrian Frederick the Great was never realized. His son Rudolf (1786–1822) was also a sculptor – there is a work at Chatsworth, Derbyshire – and another son, Wilhelm (1788–1862), was a painter and a member of the NAZARENER.

SCHÄUFFELEIN, Hans Leonhard (c. 1483–1539/40), was a painter and designer of woodcuts. As a painter he was much influenced by DÜRER, his master, but his woodcuts are both more original and more important than his pictures. He often signed his works HS and a little shovel (Schäuffelein). There are paintings by him in Basle, Berlin, Chatsworth, Dresden, Gateshead, Hamburg, Munich, Nuremberg, Vienna, and Nördlingen, where he lived from 1515.

SCHEEMAKERS, Peter (1691–1781), was the son of an Antwerp sculptor, and first worked in Cologne, but was so determined to get to Rome that he walked there. After a short stay he went to London, where he worked for BIRD, and he was then in partnership with DELVAUX, with whom in 1728 he went again to Rome. His first success was in 1740 with his Shakespeare monument in Westminster Abbey, and the reputation he gained somewhat obscured RYSBRACK'S. Scheemakers gave his works a very detailed finish and a high polish which, aided by his habit of undercutting his rivals' prices, brought him much business. He began to retire in 1753, but worked here until 1771, when he returned to Antwerp.

There are many tombs by him in Westminster Abbey, in parish churches all over England, and one in Boston Mass. There are also works in many of the greater houses and gardens in England, and some busts at the Trinity Colleges of Cambridge and Dublin.

SCHIELE, Egon (1890–1918), was an Austrian Expressionist painter, the contemporary of KOKOSCHKA, and, like him, influenced by KLIMT, as well as by HODLER. He began to exhibit early and was profoundly affected by Freudian psychology, which he endeavoured to apply to portrait painting. He died in the influenza epidemic of 1918. There are works in Vienna (Oesterreichische Gal.), The Hague, and Minneapolis.

SCHILDERSBENT see BENTNAME.

SCHLEMMER, Oskar (1888–1943), was a pupil of HÖLZEL. He taught at the BAUHAUS, 1920–9, where he had a great influence. He taught in Breslau and Berlin until 1933, after which he had to live in retirement until his death. He did a great deal of theatrical design, and his paintings have the slightly desiccated air of those Bauhaus products that were emphatically machine-made. There are paintings in Basle, Cologne, Harvard University, and New York (M of M A).

SCHLÜTER, Andreas (1660/4–1714), was the leading North German Baroque architect and sculptor, whose position in Berlin was in its way analogous to that of Bernini in Rome. He arrived in Berlin from Poland in 1694 and, after short trips to France (1695) and Italy (1696), he began the decorative sculpture for the Zeughaus (largely executed by others) and also his masterpiece, the equestrian statue of the Great Elector. This was begun in 1696, cast in bronze in 1700, set up in 1703, and completed by the *Slaves* made by others from his designs, in 1708/9. It is strongly influenced by similar Italian works, such as the Farnese monuments in Piacenza by MOCHI, and the TACCA *Four Moors* in Leghorn. The monument is now in Berlin-Charlottenburg. His statue of Friedrich III was begun in 1697, and cast in 1698, but was not set up (in Königsberg) until 1802. Early in the 18th century Schlüter was engaged in several architectural undertakings, but they were attended by misfortune and he was sacked in 1706. He accepted an invitation to St Petersburg in 1714, but died there soon after his arrival. There are several pieces of his sculpture in Berlin (churches and public buildings) and also in Homburg-Hessen.

SCHMIDT-ROTTLUFF, Karl (*b.*1884), was born Karl Schmidt in the village of Rottluff in Saxony. He became one of the leaders of German Expressionism, especially in the graphic arts (there are some 700 engravings and lithographs by him). He studied architecture in Dresden, where he met KIRCHNER, and in 1906 he met NOLDE. In 1905 he was one of the founders of the BRÜCKE. He went to Norway in 1911 and settled in Berlin in that year, where he met FEININGER. During the 1920s his art became rather more naturalistic, although still much influenced by Negro art and by Cubism and with great stress on the outline. He was particularly persecuted by the Nazis, being expelled from the Prussian Academy in 1933 and, in 1941, forbidden to paint at all and supervised by the Nazi police. After 1945 he was reinstated and lived in East Germany. There are pictures by him in London (Tate) and New York (M of M A), and once again in German galleries (Berlin, Hamburg).

SCHNORR von Carolsfeld, Julius (1794–1872), was a German painter and illustrator who was in Italy 1818–25 and joined the NAZARENER in their decoration of the Casa Massimo in Rome (1819). His contribution consisted of a combination of 15th-century Italian frescoes and Raphael but it was successful enough to get him a commission in Munich from the King in 1825. This, and later commissions, occupied him until 1867. He became a professor in Dresden in 1846 and was also Director of the Dresden Gallery. His Bible illustrations were also published in an English edition in 1860. Many German galleries have examples.

SCHONGAUER, Martin (first recorded 1465–*d.* 1491), was a Colmar painter and engraver who was much influenced by Roger van der WEYDEN and other Netherlandish painters. His only reasonably certain painting is the *Madonna of the Rosehedge* (1473: Colmar, S. Martin), an over life-size figure which shows the influence of his Flemish models. There are 115 engravings by him, all signed MS, and these were of great importance in the development of the art in Germany: it is well-known that Dürer went to visit him, only to find that he had died. Some fragments of a wall-painting of the *Last Judgement* have been discovered in S. Stephan, Breisach, where Schongauer lived from 1488/9. There are pictures ascribed to him in Basle, Berlin, Boston (Gardner), Colmar (Mus.), Frankfurt (Städel), London (NG), Munich, and Vienna.

SCHOOL. This word is susceptible of a variety of meanings and no precise demarcation between them is commonly accepted. In its widest sense – Italian School, British School – it means no more than that an experienced eye can detect the country of origin of a particular picture without being able to identify the painter, or indeed to give more than a vague explanation of the processes by which this conclusion was reached. A more limited sense attaches to the term when it is applied to a smaller territorial area, usually in Italy: in this sense an experienced eye can again distinguish with considerable accuracy and speed between a work painted in Florence, say in the 15th century, and one of the same approximate date painted in Venice. The characteristics of such Schools – whether of Florence, Siena, Naples, or of Bruges and Antwerp – are recognizable and could perhaps be imprecisely formulated in words. There seems no point in trying to do so here, as the essential marks of such stylistic varieties are purely visual. Anyone who wishes to distinguish Florentine from Sienese pictures can do so in one way and one way only – looking at them as often and as hard as possible. A more easily defined use of the word occurs in connexion with a painter instead of a place, e.g. School of Raphael. This can be sub-divided into two meanings, according to the intention of the person using it; a good and useful meaning being that a picture has all the characteristics of one by Raphael except genius. In this case, it is licit to assume that it was painted by assistants in Raphael's studio, more or less under his supervision (and probably according to the amount the buyer was offering). A less valid use of the word is as a synonym for 'copy after' or 'imitation of'. It has been suggested in recent years (e.g. in the National Gallery Catalogues) that *School* is best reserved for a geographical designation, while *Style of . . .* should be used to indicate relationship to a particular painter and this distinction would help to clarify the term.

SCHUTTERSTUK *see* DOELENSTUK.

SCHWIND, Moritz von (1804–71), was an Austrian Romantic painter, influenced by CORNELIUS and Nazarene ideas. He painted the German Middle Ages, with Teutonic Knights in armour, and also designed for the crafts. His frescoes in Karlsruhe Gallery date from 1840. In 1857 he visited London and Manchester (for the great Old Master exhibition) and later designed stained glass for Glasgow Cathedral and for S. Michael, Paddington, London. There are pictures by him in many German galleries.

SCHWITTERS, Kurt (1887–1948), was a poet and abstract painter, best known as the inventor of *Merz*, a form of DADA. He was influenced by KANDINSKY and the Dadaists, and, after studying in Dresden, he began to experiment with abstract pictures in 1918, using COLLAGES with pieces of torn-up paper attached to them. One such piece had the letters MERZ in red capitals torn from the advertisement of a Bank (*Commerz und Privatbank*) and from this circumstance he described his assemblages as Merz, and *c.* 1920 he began his first Merzbau, a huge construction which expanded so that it nearly filled a house (it was destroyed in 1943). He was particularly fond of rubbish – bits of lino, bus tickets, worn-out shoe soles – as a typical Dadaist gesture in creating art from non-art: in a rather Wagnerian way he said: 'my ultimate object is to combine art and non-art in a *Merzgesamtweltbild*'. In 1929 he first visited Norway, and in 1937 he emigrated there and made his second Merzbau (destroyed 1951). In 1940 he escaped from Norway to Britain, where he died leaving a third Merzbau unfinished at Ambleside, Westmorland (moved to Newcastle University, 1965). There are works by him in London (Tate) and New York (M of MA) and there is to be a Schwitters Museum in Oslo. Three of his works are in Kendal, near his home.

SCOREL, Jan van (1495–1562), was trained in Amsterdam but had gone to Utrecht by 1517. In 1519 he set off on a journey to Germany and went to Nuremberg and visited Dürer, but, it seems, Dürer was so preoccupied with Lutheranism that Scorel found him useless as a teacher. By 1520 he was in Carinthia, where he painted a triptych still in Obervellach Parish Church. He went on to Venice, where he was influenced by Giorgione and Palma Vecchio, and then on to Jerusalem with a pilgrimage, returning to Venice in 1521 and going down to Rome where he had the good fortune to arrive in the

Pontificate of Hadrian VI, the Utrecht Pope. He was appointed inspector of the Belvedere, painted the Pope, was made Canon of Utrecht, and was deeply influenced by Michelangelo and Raphael. After Hadrian died Scorel went back to Utrecht (1524), and Haarlem, where M. van HEEMSKERCK was his pupil in 1527. In 1540 he went to France and in 1550 restored the Ghent Altar. Many of his large religious works were destroyed by the Iconoclasts in the 16th century, but there are works in Haarlem and Utrecht (including group portraits of *Pilgrims to Jerusalem*) and in Amsterdam (Rijksmus.), Basle, Berlin, Birmingham, Bloomfield Hills Mich., Bonn, Breda, Brussels, Cassel, Detroit, Florence (Pitti), Lisbon, Oxford (Ch. Ch.), Padua, Palermo, Rome (Gall. Naz., Spada), Rotterdam, Stuttgart, Venice (Cà d'Oro), Vienna, and York. His portrait by his pupil MOR hung over his tomb: it now belongs to the Society of Antiquaries in London.

SCORZO, ISCORZO. An Italian word for a figure in sharp FORE-SHORTENING.

SCOTT, Samuel (*c.*1702–72), was one of the earliest English marine and topographical painters. He worked in the manner of the van de VELDES, painting naval battles, colonial forts, and Thames shipping until CANALETTO'S success in London (he arrived in 1746) caused Scott to work in his manner on similar views. There are several scenes by the two men which are nearly identical and it seems that, at least once, Canaletto worked from Scott's drawings. There are pictures in London (Guildhall, Tate, and Nat. Maritime Mus.), and Bath.

SCOTT, William (*b.*1913), was born in Scotland but trained in Belfast and then at the Royal Academy. He visited Italy and lived in France before the Second World War, when he served in the Royal Engineers and learned lithography. In 1953 he went to America, where he met POLLOCK, KLINE, and ROTHKO; as a result his work, described before 1951 as hermetically sexually symbolic, is now more abstract and greyer in colour. In 1958–61 he painted a mural for Londonderry Hospital and many galleries have pictures, including Belfast, Edinburgh, London (Tate and V & A), Paris (Mus. d'Art Moderne), and Rome.

SCROTS (or Stretes), Guillim, a Netherlander, was appointed painter to Mary of Hungary, Regent of the Netherlands, in 1537, and was employed by Henry VIII from 1545/6 to 1553. His portraits, which are Italianate and Mannerist in type, are important in the development of the full-length portrait – a form which became commoner in England than it was on the Continent at the same period. *Henry Howard, Earl of Surrey* (the best version belongs to the Duke of Norfolk), dated 1546 but probably painted after his execution in 1547, is reasonably attributed to Scrots. Other attributed portraits are in the Royal Coll. and in London (NPG).

SCULP. (Lat. *sculpsit*, he engraved it) on an engraving refers to the name of the engraver. In 17th-century English 'sculptures' means engravings: cf. Evelyn's 'Sculptura, or the History and Art of Chalcography and Engraving in Copper' ... 1662. *Incidit* also refers to the engraver.

SCULPTURE is the art of creating forms in three dimensions or in RELIEF. Basically, there are two opposed conceptions of sculptural form: glyptic, which means carved, and consists essentially in removing waste material until the form is freed from the matter in which it was imprisoned (this Neo-Platonic conception was Michelangelo's) and its opposite, in which form is created from nothing, by building up in some plastic material. Carving and modelling are thus two separate and complementary aspects of sculpture, the present tendency being to exalt direct carving and the feel of the material at the expense of modelling, which involves using clay or wax as a preliminary material for translation into plaster, bronze, lead, or even stone (*see* BRONZE, PLASTER, POINTING MACHINE, STONE CARVING).

SCUMBLING is the opposite of GLAZING. It consists of working an opaque layer of oil paint over another layer of a different colour or tone so that the lower layer is not entirely obliterated, giving an uneven, broken effect. The two processes of glazing and scumbling together demonstrate the range of effects, from transparency to opacity, possible in the oil medium; effects which ensured its universal adoption.

SEBASTIANO del Piombo (*c.*1485–1547) was a Venetian painter who was perhaps trained under Giovanni BELLINI but was certainly deeply influenced by GIORGIONE. When Giorgione died (1510) Sebastiano may have completed some of his unfinished works: his style at this date can be seen in his *Salome* (1510: London, NG). In 1511 he went to Rome and began working in the Villa Farnesina, in contact with the Raphael circle. He seems to have quarrelled with Raphael and soon became a partisan of Michelangelo, who influenced him deeply and even provided him with drawings to work from (e.g. the *Pietà* in Viterbo and the *Flagellation* in S. Pietro in Montorio, Rome). His gigantic *Raising of Lazarus* (1517–19: London, NG) shows the Michelangelo influence at its height and was painted in more or less open competition with Raphael's *Transfiguration*. In 1531 he received a Papal sinecure (known as 'il Piombo', hence his name) and he painted rather less, but continued to produce admirable portraits which combine the virtues of his Venetian training with the Roman discipline in form: an example is *Cardinal Pole* (*c.*1537: Leningrad). There are other works by him in Arezzo, Basle, Berlin, Budapest, Cambridge (Fitzwm), Dublin, Florence (Uffizi, Pitti), London (NG), Madrid, Naples, New York (Met. Mus.), Paris (Louvre), Parma, Philadelphia

(Johhnson), Rome (Doria Gall., S.M. del Popolo), Sarasota Fla, Venice (Accad. and churches), and Vienna.

SECCO (Ital. dry). A method of wall-painting sometimes used as a substitute for FRESCO and sometimes to retouch parts of a fresco. The wall is soaked with lime-water, but the plaster has already set, so the pigments are applied with some binding medium. It is easier than true fresco, since there is no need to work fast, but it is far less permanent. Occasionally one sees a wall-painting in which the heads and hands are well-preserved but the draperies have virtually disappeared. This is because the heads and hands are in true fresco and the ornamented draperies were painted *a secco*.

SECTION D'OR *see* GOLDEN SECTION.

SEGANTINI, Giovanni (1858–99), was an Italian painter of Alpine landscapes and subject pictures. He used a method not unlike that of NEO-IMPRESSIONISM to get the maximum effect of the bright mountain light. There is a Segantini Museum in St Moritz.

SEGHERS, Hercules (1589/90–1638 or earlier), a Dutch landscape painter and etcher, was a pupil of G. van CONINXLOO in Amsterdam and continued the fantastic mountain landscapes of Momper and Savery, but in a far more realistic and at the same time romantic way. Some of his landscapes represent actual places and it has been argued that he must have been to Italy and in the Alps. He was much influenced by ELSHEIMER and was himself probably the most important influence on Rembrandt's landscapes. Rembrandt owned eight of his paintings and actually reworked an etching of his. Seghers was a virtuoso etcher and frequently used coloured paper or tinted the proofs to increase the romantic light effects. There are over 50 etchings known; his rare paintings include those in Amsterdam, Berlin, Detroit, Florence, The Hague (Bredius Mus.), London, Philadelphia (Johnson Coll.), and Rotterdam.

SEICENTO (Ital. six hundred). The 17th century, i.e. the sixteen hundreds.

SEISENEGGER, Jakob (1505–67), painted portraits of the Emperor Charles V in 1530 and again in 1532 in Bologna, where the copy made by Titian so excelled the original full-length that Titian henceforth painted the Emperor's state portraits. There are pictures by Seisenegger in Vienna and one in London (NG).

SEPIA. A brown pigment, like BISTRE, made from cuttlefish.

SÉRAPHINE (i.e. Séraphine Louis) (1864–1934) was a domestic servant at Senlis, near Paris, whose talent was discovered in 1912 by the German critic Wilhelm Uhde, who had a special interest in modern primitives. Unlike most of them, however, she was not a naïve realist (like Vivin, whom Uhde also discovered), but painted only plants and flowers of the greatest complexity and richness of colour, reminiscent of Indian Numdah rugs and Persian miniatures, as well as the stained-glass windows that were certainly familiar to her. She became insane in 1930 and died in an asylum. There is a characteristic example in Paris (Mus. d'Art Moderne).

SERIGRAPHY, or Silk-screen printing, is not, strictly speaking, a technique of ENGRAVING. The basic principles are those of a stencil, in that it is a method by which paint is brushed over a screen so that the colour penetrates those parts of the screen that have not previously been masked. By using successive masks on the same screen it is possible to produce prints in several colours, and also to obtain colour mixtures by printing one colour over another – for instance, printing blue over yellow to make a green. The screen itself is made of fairly fine silk, and the masks are usually either of paper, or made by painting an impervious lacquer on the screen itself; paint is brushed on and soaks through the silk in the parts which have not been masked. The process was originally developed for commercial purposes, since it is possible to use unskilled labour to make prints once the masks have been prepared. In recent years, however, first in America and later in Europe, the technique has been greatly developed as a method of making large numbers of artist-produced prints which can be sold at fairly low prices, although each print is, like a lithograph, an original work of art. One of the advantages to the artist is that, by very slight, but easily – even accidentally – made changes in mask or paint density, variations are achieved in the prints which can remove serigraphy from the more mechanical processes of printing such as those employed in lithography.

SÉRUSIER, Paul (1863–1927). The year of his birth is sometimes given as 1864 or 1865. He met GAUGUIN in Brittany in 1888, and was deeply influenced by the ideas of SYNTHETISM: Gauguin gave him one lesson – 'How do you see those trees? They are yellow? Well, paint them yellow. The shadow is bluish? Make it pure ultramarine. . . . Red leaves? Use vermilion.' In Paris, Sérusier was, with DENIS, BONNARD, and VUILLARD, one of the founders of the NABIS. He visited Italy and Germany, and, in 1897, went to the Benedictine monastery at Beuron in Germany, where he was much influenced by their theories of religious art. His own 'ABC de la Peinture' was first published in 1921. There are works in London (Tate), Ottawa, Paris (Mus. d'Art Moderne), Stuttgart, and Warsaw.

SETTECENTO (Ital. seven hundred). The 18th century, i.e. the seventeen hundreds.

SETTIGNANO, Desiderio da, see DESIDERIO.

SEURAT, Georges (1859–91), studied at the École des Beaux-Arts, when he read Chevreul's book on the theory of colour (first published in 1839, and republished in 1889). Later he studied the paintings of Delacroix at S. Sulpice in Paris, and Delacroix's theory as it is ascertainable from his Diaries, for precedents for the theories he was himself elaborating. He was also much influenced by the aesthetic theories based on the observations of a scientist, Charles Henry, and the conclusions of David Sutter's writings on the phenomena of vision, published in 1880. These led him to evolve first the theory of Divisionism (*see* OPTICAL MIXTURES) and then a method of painting by the use of colour contrasts in which the areas of shadow are broken down into the complementaries of adjacent areas of light, the light itself being broken down into local colour, the colour of the light and of reflections, so that for instance bright yellow-green grass will contain reflections from the sky and from other nearby objects, and shadows in it will tend towards reddish-purple; or the shadows in a reddish-orange dress will be preponderantly greenish-blue. He also evolved a formal type of composition, based on the Golden Section, on the proportion and relation of objects within the picture space to one another and to the size and shape of the picture, on the balance of verticals and horizontals, and on figures placed across the picture plane or at right angles to it. Where the Impressionists stressed the flickering quality of light and figures caught in movement, Seurat aimed at a static quality. His *Bathers at Asnières* (*La Baignade*: London, Tate), exhibited in 1884 at the Salon des Artistes Indépendants in Paris, was not so thorough-going an exposition of his theories as the *Sunday on the Island of La Grande Jatte* (Chicago) exhibited in 1886 at the last Impressionist exhibition, and the term NEO-IMPRESSIONISM was established for Seurat and the group round him by 1886. He was for long opposed to any popularization of his theories, since he believed that by robbing them of novelty it would also rob them of their effect, but in 1890 he consented to the publication of a *résumé* of his theory. His early death, however, meant that his ideas were developed only by followers and imitators.

There are works in Brussels, Chicago, Edinburgh, Glasgow, Indianapolis, Liverpool, London (NG, Tate, Courtauld Inst.), Merion Pa (Barnes Fdn), New York (M of MA), Otterlo (Kröller-Müller), Paris (Louvre), and elsewhere.

SEVERINI, Gino (1883–1966), was living in Paris when the original Manifesto of FUTURIST Painting appeared in 1910. He signed it, but thought that it showed his fellow-countrymen in a provincial light, and he induced them to pay more attention to Cubism. He himself was much influenced by Seurat and Neo-Impressionist theories. In his last years he decorated several churches in Switzerland with frescoes and mosaics in a more Neoclassical manner, and his book *Du Cubisme au Classicisme* (1921) shows the trend of his thought. His *Suburban Train arriving in Paris* (1915: London, Tate) is one of a group of Futurist works painted in Paris 1914/18. Others are in Amsterdam (Stedelijk) and New York (Guggenheim).

SEZESSION (Ger. secession). The *Sezessionen* were groups of artists in

Germany and Austria who resigned from established academic bodies and exhibiting societies in order to forward the aims of various modern (usually Impressionist) movements. The most important were those of Munich (1892), Berlin, headed by LIEBERMANN and partly due to the scandal over the MUNCH Exhibition of 1892 (1899), Vienna (1897), and Darmstadt. In due course the Expressionists seceded in their turn.

SFUMATO (Ital. evaporated, cleared like mist) is a word used to describe the transitions of colour or, especially, tone from light to dark by stages so gradual as to be imperceptible. LEONARDO attached great importance to this as a means of obtaining that effect of relief which he regarded as essential to the art of painting, and in some of his works the softness of contour and the darkness of the shadows have now combined to spoil much of the effect intended. In his notes on painting he says that light and shade should blend 'without lines or borders, in the manner of smoke'.

SGRAFFITO (Ital. scratched). A decorative technique in which tinted plaster is covered with a thin layer of white plaster (or vice-versa), the top layer then being scratched with a design, revealing the lower layer. The technique was employed for arabesques and similar decorations in 16th-century Italy, but it can usually be seen in a rudimentary form on any whitewashed wall, and has been exploited in this sense by modern painters such as DUBUFFET. A much earlier form of the technique, found in Italian panel paintings, consists of a gold ground with opaque colour over it, so that scratching the surface provides gold lights.

SHAHN, Ben (1898–1969), was born in Lithuania, but went to the US in 1906 and became a characteristically American exponent of SOCIAL REALISM. His use of photographic realism of detail and some of the technical devices of advertising set him apart from most modern American painters, but his art was always a vehicle for his ideas. The Sacco and Vanzetti case (when two immigrant anarchists were judicially murdered) led to the production of a series (1931–2) of biting comments, mostly drawings. Naturally, he was much influenced by ROUAULT and RIVERA, collaborating with the latter on the Radio City murals in 1933. Other murals are in the Bronx Post Office, New York (1938–9), and the Social Security Building, Washington (1940–2). He also wrote on art.

SHOP WORK see WORKSHOP PRODUCTION.

SICKERT, Walter Richard (1860–1942), was, with Wilson STEER, the most important of the British Impressionists – and it is highly characteristic of him that he can hardly be included in any definition of Impressionism, since he worked at the bottom of the tone scale, and his light effects gleam out from sombre colours and tones. Towards the end of his life his palette lightened considerably, when he painted scenes (never on the spot) in Bath and Brighton and also made a series of pictures based either on newspaper and other photographs or on Victorian magazine illustrations. He was profoundly influenced by Whistler and Degas, sharing something of their dispassionate wit, and was equally far from being a typical Impressionist. He was at various times connected with the stage and most of his best works are scenes of London music halls and their audiences, although he also had great feeling for the shabbier parts of London, Dieppe, and Venice. The open air and the countryside had no appeal for him. In 1911 he founded the CAMDEN TOWN GROUP (with Islington it was one of his favourite boroughs) and he later belonged to the LONDON GROUP (which absorbed the Camden Town one), the NEAC and the RA, from which he resigned resoundingly. He was one of the few modern painters to make extensive use of studio assistants and his technical procedures are very like those of the Old Masters. He also etched and wrote a great deal (not all of it sense). He is well represented in London (Tate, Courtauld Inst. and Islington Public Library) as well as Rouen, many British galleries (especially Liverpool), and Dieppe, Melbourne, New York (M of M A), Ottawa, Sydney, Toledo Ohio, and Yale.

SIGNAC, Paul (1863–1935), was a follower of SEURAT, whose ideas he enthusiastically advocated, and whose style he imitated with more energy than perception. He was the most vocal theorist among the Neo-Impressionists and his book 'De Delacroix au Néo-Impressionnisme', published in 1899, is the text-book of the movement.

SIGNIFICANT FORM. A phrase invented by Clive Bell to define the specifically aesthetic element in a work of art. That is aesthetically valid ('significant') which is an expression of form: that is formally effective which is significant. A neat example of arguing in a circle.

SIGNORELLI, Luca (c. 1441/50–1523), was traditionally a pupil, with PERUGINO, of PIERO della Francesca. He is first documented in 1470 and some fragments in Città di Castello, of 1474, are his earliest datable works. Although his earliest works (including two sides of a processional banner in the Brera, Milan) show some influence from Piero they already show the very marked influence of the POLLAIUOLI in the use of figures with exaggerated muscular development in violent action. This Florentine stress on outline as a means of conveying drama, and the use of characteristic gesture, link him with Donatello on the one hand and Verrocchio on the other; as may be seen in his frescoes in the Casa Santa at Loreto. He was in Rome in the early 1480s and probably worked on the Sistine Chapel frescoes with Perugino, Botticelli, Rosselli, and others. His masterpiece is the fresco cycle in Orvieto Cathedral, begun by Fra Angelico in 1447, which he was commissioned to complete in 1499. The frescoes depict with vivid realism the End of the World, the Coming and Fall of

Anti-Christ, and the Last Judgement. His gifts as a draughtsman are fully revealed in the sharp foreshortenings of the figures, their strained poses, the perspective, the hardness of outline, and the imaginative power with which, for example, he peoples Hell, not with pathetically grotesque creatures half-beast, half-fantasy, but with vigorous, muscular devils, passionately engaged in fiendish cruelties and entirely human in form, though with the hideous colour of rotting flesh. His use of the nude figure for dramatic ends, his interest in classical antiquity and his *terribilità* presage, and influenced, Michelangelo. His later works never again reach this pitch of intensity, probably because the Orvieto frescoes were painted at the time of the French invasions and while Savonarola's threats of doom and the coming of Anti-Christ were in all men's minds. He was in Rome again *c*.1508, and again in 1513, but he stood no chance against Raphael and Michelangelo and he settled in Cortona as a good, provincial master with a large shop, producing hard, repetitive, and old-fashioned altarpieces. Vasari claimed to be his great-nephew. There are works in Altenburg, Arezzo, Baltimore (Walters), Bergamo, Berlin, Borgo San Sepolcro, Boston (Mus.), Cortona (Mus. and churches), Detroit, Florence (Uffizi, Horne Mus.), Liverpool, London (NG), Milan (Brera, Poldi-Pezzoli), Monte Oliveto Maggiore, Munich, Naples, New York (Met. Mus.), Orvieto (Cath., Mus., Library, S. Rocco), Paris (Louvre, Jacquemart-André), Perugia (Mus., Cath.), Philadelphia (Johnson), Toledo Ohio, Umbertide (Sta Croce), Urbino, Venice (Cà d'Oro), Washington, Yale, and elsewhere.

SIGNORINI, Telemaco (1835–1901), was an Italian painter and etcher who was a representative of *Verismo*, the Italian form of the Realist movement of the 19th century. He joined the MACCHIAIOLI and was also much influenced by the French Impressionists. He met COROT in Paris in 1861, and travelled to London and Edinburgh with De NITTIS – like his friend he was much influenced by DEGAS and Toulouse-Lautrec. His 'Memoirs' (1893) are the chief source of information about the Macchiaioli. There are works by him in Florence, Milan, Rome, Turin, and Venice.

SILK-SCREEN *see* SERIGRAPHY.

SILVA, Vieira da, *see* VIEIRA da Silva.

SILVER POINT. A technique of drawing much favoured in the 15th and 16th centuries but now almost entirely disused. The drawing is made on a sheet of paper which has been prepared by coating it with opaque white (to which a slight tint of colour is usually added), with a piece of silver wire held in wood like the lead in a modern pencil. The silver point produces a silver-grey indelible mark which will not smudge and the drawing can be heightened, if desired, with Chinese white. Gold or lead may be used in place of silver, all giving the effect of a modern pencil but rather more subtle and with the advantage of indelibility, which makes the draughtsman think before he puts down a line.

SIMONE Martini *see* MARTINI.

SINOPIA. A reddish-brown earth colour often used for the under-drawing of a FRESCO. Frequently used to mean the drawing itself.

SIQUEIROS, David Alfaro (1896-1974), was a Mexican painter imprisoned and exiled many times during his violent career as a political revolutionary in Mexico and Spain. His art stems from RIVERA and OROZCO, with whom he worked on projects for huge mural paintings expressing political ideas in a strained yet realist style, and he was also affected by the darker aspects of Surrealism and Mexican folk art and ethnography. His best work is in Mexico.

SISLEY, Alfred (1839–99), was a French Impressionist painter of English descent. With MONET he was one of the purest of the IMPRESSIONISTS and was practically exclusively a landscape painter: unlike Monet, however, he did not dissolve the forms of the landscape into a sort of coloured mist in his search for colour and light. In 1856–7 he was sent to England to learn the language and to begin a commercial career but in 1862 he entered the École des Beaux-Arts, where he met Monet, Renoir, and Bazille. He exhibited at the SALON des Refusés in 1863 and at the First Impressionist Exhibition (1874) and some of the later ones. During the Franco-Prussian War he went to England (1871) and he returned in 1874, when he painted at Hampton Court and in the London suburbs. There are pictures by him in most modern museums, including Aberdeen, Boston, London (Tate Gall., Courtauld Inst.), Ottawa, Paris (Mus. de l'Impressionnisme), and Washington (NG).

SIZE colour. A method of painting in which the powdered pigment is mixed with hot glue-size. It is quick and simple but easily damaged and is now used almost exclusively for scene-painting. Ordinary distemper is a form of size colour.

SKETCH. A sketch is the rough draught of a composition or part of a composition, made in order to satisfy the artist himself on certain points of scale, composition, lighting, etc. It is the trial run – or one of many – for the full-scale work but it must be carefully distinguished from a STUDY. A sketch by a landscape painter is usually a small and rapid note of the effect of light on a given scene, and it is intended for future reference and reworking if necessary. The quality of some artists' sketches is however so high that what they would have considered their important works are now often undervalued: Rubens and Constable are examples. Constable's sketches, in particular, have been responsible for many subsequent artists painting such rapid notations – and then exhibiting them as works of art. Rubens's sketches were often made as guides to his assistants in the layout and first stages of a grand composition. These compositions were often executed almost entirely by the assistants, hence the preference now accorded to the original sketches.

SLEVOGT, Max (1868–1932), was, with CORINTH and LIEBERMANN, one of the leading German Impressionists. He was trained in Munich before going to Paris in 1889 and then to Italy; later he travelled widely in Denmark, Holland, and Egypt (1913–14, where he painted landscapes filled with blazing light). His Impressionist style began *c.*1900, at the same time as he made a name as an illustrator. He worked for 'Simplizissimus' and the Art Nouveau periodical 'Jugend', as well as illustrating many books. His most famous paintings are the series of the singer *D'Andrade as Don Giovanni* (*c.*1902–3), but his last work, a fresco of Golgotha in the Friedenskirche at Ludwigshafen (1932), may be his masterpiece. He painted other frescoes and there are pictures by him in many German museums.

SLUTER, Claus (active *c.*1380–*d.*1405/6), was the greatest realist sculptor of Northern Europe at the turn of the 15th century and preceded both Jan van Eyck and Donatello, the two 15th-century artists most akin to him in spirit. He worked principally for the Dijon Court of Philip the Bold, Duke of Burgundy, but he was himself of Dutch origin and probably worked in Brussels before arriving in Dijon, where he was assistant to the Duke's sculptor, Jean de Marville, 1385–9, when he became Court Sculptor himself. He worked on the sculptural decoration of the Duke's foundation, the Chartreuse de Champmol, 1391–6/7 and from 1395 to 1403 was engaged on his masterpiece, the *Well of Moses*, a well-head with six full-length Prophets around it. This survives, but the upper part, a *Calvary*, is known only from a fragment of the *Crucified Christ* (Dijon, Musée Archéologique). The grandeur of style of the *Moses* and its sharply characterized pose and features mark it as something quite new and totally different from the INTERNATIONAL GOTHIC or SOFT STYLE then current. Sluter also worked on the Tomb of Philip the Bold, but this had been begun under his predecessor in 1384 and was continued by his own successor, his nephew Claus de Werve (*d.*1439), who completed it in 1411. The most famous part of it is the series of Pleurants or Weepers, small mourning figures round the sides, of the greatest realism. One of these is in Cleveland Ohio (Mus.); the surviving parts of the Tomb are in Dijon (Mus.).

SMET, Gustave De (1877–1943), was, with PERMEKE, one of the leading Belgian Expressionists. He was trained in Ghent and settled at the artists' colony of Laethem-Saint-Martin in 1901. Up to 1914 he painted in an Impressionist manner, but became an Expressionist while a refugee in Holland. There are works in Amsterdam (Stedelijk), Antwerp, Basle, Brussels, Ghent, Grenoble, The Hague, Liège, and Rotterdam.

SMIBERT, John (1688–1751), was an Edinburgh painter who worked in Italy 1717–20 and went to America with Berkeley (later Bishop Berkeley) in 1728 in an attempt to settle the Bermudas. His portrait of Berkeley is in London (NPG). In 1730 he settled in Boston and painted portraits which recall those of Jervas – i.e. they are not very good imitations of the KNELLER style. He was one of the first landscape painters in America. There are works in Edinburgh (NPG) and many American museums, including Boston.

SMITH, David (1906–65). American sculptor. In 1925, he worked in a car factory, where he learned techniques later useful in his sculpture. In New York, he associated with GORKY, De KOONING, and DAVIS, producing paintings to which he attached 'found objects'. In 1933, he began working in welded steel, his chief and preferred medium, making large abstract constructions. In Italy in 1962, he made the *Voltri* series for the 4th Festival at Spoleto.

SMITH, Sir Matthew (1879–1959), first went to Paris in 1910 and was in contact with Matisse for a month or two, at Matisse's school, which closed in 1911. The influence of the FAUVE movement was decisive and he spent much time in France up to 1939; the richness of his colour and the opulence of his forms have always made him seem more of a French than an English painter. There are pictures by him in Coventry, Leeds (Temple Newsam), London (Tate), Manchester, Ottawa, and other museums.

SNYDERS, Frans (1579–1657), was a pupil of Pieter Bruegel the Younger. He travelled in Italy in 1608–9 and on his return settled in Antwerp, where he was much employed by RUBENS on the still-life and animal parts of his hunting and other pictures. He also worked with JORDAENS, and on his own account produced many vigorous hunting scenes and large still-life subjects of great complexity. He married a sister of the de VOS brothers.

There are examples in the Royal Collection, and in Antwerp, Berlin, Boston (Mus.), Brussels, Cape Town, Dresden, Edinburgh (NG), The Hague, London (NG, Kenwood), Madrid, Munich, Ottawa, Paris (Louvre), Toronto, and elsewhere.

SOCIAL REALISM is the painting of the contemporary scene, usually from a Leftish viewpoint. The movement probably goes back to COURBET (and owes much to literary examples, e.g. Zola): it is now fairly current in the US (SHAHN, the ASHCAN School) and in Britain (Bratby, Jack Smith, and the New, or 'Kitchen Sink', Realists). GUTTOSO is perhaps the leading European exponent. It must be distinguished from *Socialist Realism*, which is the official Party Art of the USSR and the Communist Party generally. This is the dreariest kind of academic art, glorifying the Party or the Peasant and other stock figures. A victim has said of it: 'Impressionism is painting what you see, Expressionism is painting what you feel, and Socialist Realism is painting what you hear.'

SODOMA. Giovanni Antonio Bazzi, called 'Il Sodoma' (1477–1549), was one of the best-known Sienese painters of the early 16th century. He was born at Vercelli and trained under the minor Lombard G. M. Spanzotti (1490–7) and was probably in Milan between 1497 and 1501, when he arrived in Siena. He must have seen the work of Leonardo da Vinci in Milan and again in Florence c. 1504. Between 1505 and 1508 he completed a series of 31 frescoes in the Benedictine monastery of Monte Oliveto, near Siena, where Signorelli had begun the scenes from the life of S. Benedict. Sodoma became the leading artist of Siena, but Vasari – who is very severe on Sodoma's general beastliness – points out that this was not really deserved and much of his work is very uninspired. The obvious interpretation of his nickname seems to be belied by the tax-return (perhaps not wholly serious) that he filled in c. 1531: 'I have an ape and a talking raven, which I keep in a cage so that he can teach a theological ass to talk. ... I possess three beastly she-animals, which are women, and I have also thirty grown-up children, which is a real encumbrance ... and as twelve children exempt a man from taxation I recommend myself to you. Farewell.' In recent years it has come to be realized that the great Sienese artist of the period is not Sodoma but BECCA-FUMI. Sodoma painted in the Vatican in 1508 (part of the ceiling of the Stanza della Segnatura, subsequently given to Raphael to complete) and some fine frescoes in the Villa Farnesina in Rome in 1512. He is well represented in Siena and Florence and in London, Paris, New York, and many other galleries.

SOEST, Konrad von, see KONRAD.

SOFT-GROUND ETCHING see ENGRAVING.

SOFT STYLE is a name given to the style found principally in Germany at the end of the 14th and beginning of the 15th centuries. It is very closely related to INTERNATIONAL GOTHIC, and, as the name implies, is characterized by soft and gentle rhythms, especially in the flow of drapery, and by a sweet and playful sentiment. The principal subject is the Madonna playing with the Christ Child and these are sometimes called *Schöne Madonnen* – 'Beautiful Madonnas'. Sculpture and the earliest woodcuts show the style even more clearly than painting.

SOLIMENA, Francesco (called L'Abate Ciccio) (1657–1747), was the major late Baroque painter in Naples and was extremely famous in the 18th century, being described in 1733 as 'by universal consent the greatest painter in the world'. He acquired great wealth, lived in a Palace, became a Baron, and was in constant demand by Kings and Princes. He was a celebrated teacher, and his pupils included such diverse artists as CONCA and Allan RAMSAY, although his style was most faithfully continued by Francesco de Mura. He formed his style on that of Luca GIORDANO but modified it profoundly by the classical tendencies of MARATTA and Pietro da Cortona, as well as Lanfranco and Mattia Preti. He settled in Naples in 1674 and his principal works there are in the churches (all damaged in 1939/45) of S. Paolo Maggiore (1689–90), the Gesù Nuovo (1725), and S. Domenico Maggiore. Many of his best works are the sketches for large compositions in Naples (Mus.) and there are many others in Neapolitan churches as well as in Abingdon Berks., Barnard Castle (Bowes Mus.), Dresden, Florence (Uffizi), The Hague, Leeds, Liverpool, London (Courtauld Gall.), Madrid, Milan (Brera), New York (Met. Mus.), Northampton, Oxford, Paris (Louvre), Rome (Gall. Naz.), the Vatican, Venice (Accad.), Vienna, and York.

SOMER, Paul van (c. 1577/8–1622), was an Antwerp painter who settled in London in 1616. He was, with MYTENS and JOHNSON, one of the best portrait painters in England before the arrival of van Dyck. He soon began to work for the Court, and his earliest datable work, *Queen Anne of Denmark with her horse and dogs* (1617: Royal Coll.), is perhaps the best. There are others in London (NPG and Tate).

SOPRA PORTE, Superporte. Grand words for overdoors; i.e. paintings, usually landscapes, specially composed to fit the space above a doorway.

SOTTO IN SÙ (Ital. from below upwards). A term applied to the extreme of illusionistic perspective which shows figures painted on a ceiling so foreshortened as to appear actually floating in space above the spectator. It is first found in a developed form in MANTEGNA (1474) and was taken up by CORREGGIO and Roman Baroque painters such as LANFRANCO and PIETRO da Cortona and, later, POZZO.

SOULAGES, Pierre (b. 1919), is, with HARTUNG, one of the leading abstract painters of the SCHOOL of Paris. He has travelled in the US and Japan and is well represented in American museums. His paintings have no titles, but are referred to by the date of completion – e.g. *23 mai 1953* (London, Tate).

SOUTINE, Chaïm (1894–1943), was born near Minsk but managed to get to Paris in 1913, where he met MODIGLIANI, CHAGALL, and other *peintres maudits*. He was much influenced by EXPRESSIONISM and developed a style depending greatly on impasto; this is most noticeable in his slaughterhouse pieces. There are many works in America – Dr Barnes bought 100 in 1923 – for instance, the M of MA, New York, and Washington (NG and Phillips). The Barnes pictures are now in Merion, Pa.

SPENCER, Sir Stanley (1891–1959), was one of the most original of modern painters; original in iconography rather than formally, with a kind of naïve religious feeling that is probably closer to Blake than to anyone else. He was trained at the Slade School 1908–12 and served in Macedonia in the First World War from 1915 to 1918: his experiences in the RAMC were to be transformed in the next decade into the series of mural decorations in Burghclere Chapel, Hants. He made designs for such a series of pictures, culminating in a *Resurrection of the Soldiers* as an altarpiece, in 1922–3, and in 1926–7 the chapel was built as a memorial to a man killed in the War, and the paintings carried out between 1926 and 1932: at this time he was also painting his huge *Resurrection, Cookham* (1922–7: London, Tate), Cookham being his native village, where he spent most of his life. During the War of 1939–45 he painted a series of *Shipyards*, officially commissioned, in Port Glasgow. After 1945 he returned to the Resurrection theme in a series of large-scale religious works. He was elected ARA in 1932, but resigned in 1935 after a controversy over two of his more imaginative pictures. In 1950 he returned as RA and in 1959, just before his death, he was knighted. There is a Spencer Gallery at Cookham and pictures by him in Aberdeen, Belfast, Birmingham, Cambridge (Fitzwm), Hull, Leeds, London (Tate, Imperial War Mus.), Manchester, New York (M of MA), Ottawa, Oxford, Sheffield, Southampton, Toronto, and elsewhere.

His brother Gilbert (*b.* 1892) is also a painter.

SPINELLO Aretino (active 1373–*d.* 1410/11) came, as his name implies, from Arezzo but was probably trained in Florence, perhaps under Agnolo GADDI. So far from being the last flicker of the Giotto tradition Spinello seems to have returned, about the end of the Trecento, to the massive style of Giotto and was thus a precursor of Masaccio. There are works by him in Arezzo (Mus. and churches), Budapest, Cambridge Mass. (Fogg), Chicago, Copenhagen, Florence (Uffizi, Accad., churches), Liverpool, London (NG), New York (Met. Mus.), Oxford (Christ Church), Paris (Louvre, École des Beaux-Arts), Pisa (Mus., churches), Providence RI, St Louis, Siena, the Vatican, Washington (NG), and elsewhere. His son, Parri Spinelli (*d.* 1452), worked with him.

SPITZWEG, Carl (1808–85), was perhaps the most characteristic BIEDERMEIER painter. He was self-taught and worked as a newspaper illustrator before becoming a painter: it was probably this training which prevented him from falling into the pretentiousness which afflicted his friend SCHWIND. He travelled extensively – Italy, Paris, London, Antwerp – and was deeply impressed by both DELACROIX and the BARBIZON painters, but was not tempted into the Grand Style. His *Poor Poet*, of which three versions exist, is a good example of his homely, anecdotal, style. There are pictures in Berlin, Berne, Hamburg, Hanover, and Munich.

SPOLVERO. A kind of auxiliary CARTOON (from Ital. *spolvero*, fine dust). The purpose of the *spolvero* was to preserve the cartoon for the guidance of the assistants working on the final painting, since the *spolvero* was pricked through and pounced with charcoal dust. For this reason it is doubtful whether any have survived.

SPRANGER, Bartholomeus (1546–1611), was an Antwerp painter who worked in Paris (c.1565) at the same time as PRIMATICCIO and N. dell' ABBATE, and in Rome (c.1567–75) as an assistant to Taddeo ZUCCARI, and in Vienna, for the Emperor Maximilian II, in 1575. He later worked for Rudolf II in Prague, where he died. He was a typical representative of late Mannerism, using numerous nude figures in unlikely attitudes to fill his compositions, which derive ultimately from Correggio and Parmigianino. The engravings of GOLTZIUS made his works very widely known. He is well represented in the Vienna Gallery, but there are other examples in Antwerp, Brussels, Chicago, Cleveland, London (NG), Munich, Paris, and elsewhere.

SQUARCIONE, Francesco (1397–1468), was a Paduan, first recorded as a painter in 1429. Although he seems to have been active as a painter all his life, he is principally famous on account of his pupils. It is said that he had 137, some of whom he seems to have adopted. The most famous was MANTEGNA who quarrelled violently with him and left his house in 1448. ZOPPO was also a pupil. He is said to have had a house full of casts of antique sculpture and to have made journeys to Rome and even to Greece in pursuit of antiquities. Only two works are known by him, a polyptych of 1449–52 in Padua (Mus.) and a signed *Madonna* in Berlin. Both demonstrate the extreme dryness of his style and his archaeological interests, and these, coupled with Donatello's influence, go far to explain Mantegna's early style.

SQUARED (for transfer). A drawing is said to be squared (up) when it has been covered with a network of squares. These squares can be numbered, and the same number of squares of a larger size can then be drawn on a wall or canvas: the contents of each small square can then be rapidly transferred to the corresponding large one, thus giving an enlarged version of the original drawing, more or less mechanically.

STABILE. Sculpture that keeps still. The opposite of MOBILE.

STAËL, Nicholas de (1914–55), was born in St Petersburg but was brought up and educated in Brussels. He went to Paris in 1933 and became one of the leading abstract painters, coming under the influence of BRAQUE, whom he met during the war. His later works mark a return to a kind of representation in which the forms, though mostly abstract, were recognizably landscapes, still-life, or other real objects. He committed suicide in 1955. There are works by him in Edinburgh, New York (M of MA), London (Tate), Ottawa, and Paris (Mus. d'Art Moderne).

STAFFAGE. This word, pronounced as French, is used in both English and German to describe the figures and animals which animate a picture intended essentially as a landscape or *veduta*; in other words, figures which are not really essential and could be added by another painter. In the highly specialized world of the Dutch painters of the 17th century this was very often the case, so that a landscape painter like WYNANTS never did his own *staffage*; whereas a CANALETTO or a GUARDI always did.

STAINED GLASS consists of designs or figure subjects made from pieces of coloured glass held together by strips of lead, which themselves form the outlines of a design partly independent of the coloured patches. It was apparently a Byzantine invention but soon became a distinctively Western and medieval art form, first appearing in the West at Augsburg in the early 11th century. By 1100 the French were leading exponents and the art was introduced to England in the second half of the 12th century. Splendid examples of the early period exist at Canterbury, while York has the best later windows. The coloured glass was made in one of two ways: by adding metallic oxides to molten glass, thus causing it to be coloured all through, or by fusing thin layers of coloured glass on to plain. The former is called 'pot metal' and the latter 'flashed'. Ruby red was usually obtained by flashing: pot metal varies very much in colour according to the temperature, and great variations often exist in the same window. Details were painted in matt enamel on the glass and then fused to it by reheating. In the later Middle Ages much *grisaille* glass was produced; that is, plain glass with enamel drawing on it and sometimes silver-stain was added. This is a strong yellow obtained by painting on a silver preparation and then heating it. It was introduced soon after 1300 and was often used to obtain the most elaborate patterns. The art continued to flourish until well into the 16th century (King's College Chapel, Cambridge) in England and on the continent, especially in Germany and Switzerland, but it gradually gave way to the bastard form of painted glass, which is simply a translation of oil-painting. The windows by Sir Joshua Reynolds at New College, Oxford, are good examples. The medieval methods have been used for the new Coventry Cathedral. A 20th-century variant is to set the glass in concrete instead of lead. CHAGALL has also made a series of twelve important stained-glass windows for a synagogue in Jerusalem.

STANZE (Ital. rooms). The suite of rooms in the Vatican decorated by RAPHAEL.

STANZIONE, Massimo (1585/6–1656), was one of the leading Neapolitan painters of the Caravaggio School. He was working in Rome by 1617 where he would have seen the Farnese Gallery by Annibale CARRACCI. His style is similar to that of SARACENI in that it is a more graceful and elegant form of Caravaggism than that practised by his fellow Neapolitan RIBERA, although Ribera exerted some influence on him. Stanzione has been called the Neapolitan Guido RENI which aptly summarizes his semi-Bolognese classicism. Most of his pictures are in Naples, but there are works in Dresden, Florence (Uffizi), Frankfurt (Städel), and London (NG).

STATE is the name given to the stages in the development of an engraving or etching. When the artist has finished his work and pulls the first proofs these constitute the first state; if he decides to add a line here or burnish one out there then each successive alteration will constitute a fresh state. Many of Rembrandt's etchings run to seven or eight, each marking some definite artistic change, but it is an unfortunate temptation for cataloguers to invent new states, and for artists to meet the demand by introducing meaningless alterations. It should be noted that the twentieth state is not necessarily a poor impression, if only two or three prints have been pulled of each of the preceding states; equally, a plate can be worn out in its first state. *See* PROOF, REMARQUE.

STEEL ENGRAVING, STEEL-FACED. The comparative softness of copper limits the number of prints that can be taken from an engraving, and, in the second quarter of the 19th century, steel plates came into use. These, however, are very hard on the engraver and a satisfactory solution was soon found by steel-facing the completed copper plates. This is done by electrolysis, depositing a microscopic film of steel on the surface of the plate, which hardens it sufficiently to allow the printing of large editions, without interfering with the finest work on the plate.

STEELL, Sir John (1804–91), was a Scottish sculptor who studied in Rome. Chantrey urged him to settle in London, but he preferred to stay in Scotland, where he soon became the foremost sculptor, received a Court appointment in 1838, and was knighted in 1876. His *Scott* in the Scott Monument was probably the first marble statue commissioned in Scotland from a Scot. He also introduced bronze-founding into Scotland and his large equestrian *Wellington* in Edinburgh was aptly described as 'The Iron Duke in bronze by Steell'. There are many other works in Edinburgh, and in London (Nat. Marit. Mus.).

STEEN, Jan (1626–79), was a Dutch painter of humorous subjects from the life of the peasantry and middle classes in a variety of styles, like those of BROUWER, OSTADE, and DOU. Even his Biblical subjects are treated as incidents in 17th-century Holland, but his pictures mostly represent tavern scenes or visits to respectable households. He worked in The Hague, and Delft, where he leased a brewery, Haarlem, and Leyden, where he kept a tavern. He was the son-in-law of van Goyen, in whose manner he painted a few landscapes, and he also painted some portraits. About 700 paintings by him exist and most galleries have one.

STEER, Wilson (1860–1942), was the son of a portrait painter. He studied in Paris, 1882–3, and in the late 1880s discovered Degas and the Impressionists, particularly Monet. From then on his work reflects these influences, which are very strong in his landscapes, these being Constable revivified by Impressionist technique, although he made occasional excursions into Gainsborough. There are works in Aberdeen, Bradford, Cambridge (Fitzwm), Edinburgh, Leeds, Liverpool, London (Tate), Manchester (City and Whitworth), Ottawa, Oxford, Southampton, and elsewhere.

STEFANO da Zevio (or da Verona) (*c.*1375–1451) was the principal Veronese painter in the INTERNATIONAL GOTHIC style. He was much influenced by GENTILE da Fabriano and was probably the master of PISANELLO, continuing a sort of proto-Pisanello style as late as 1435 in his signed and dated *Adoration of the Magi* (Milan, Brera): on the other hand, the *Madonna of the Quail* (Verona) may be by him or by Pisanello. Most of his works are in Verona (Mus. and churches), but there are others in Rome (Pal. Venezia), Mount Holyoke Mass., and Worcester Mass.

STEVENS, Alfred (1817–75), was born in Blandford Forum, Dorset, the son of a decorator. He was befriended by a clergyman who lent him things to copy, so that at 15 he was a competent portraitist in the Reynolds tradition. His patron collected £60 and approached Landseer, but Landseer's premium was £500, so in 1833 the boy was put on a ship for Naples. No arrangements had been made for him and no further funds were provided; he knew no Italian, got involved in political intrigues, and fell among thieves. He spent 18 months in and around Naples, and in 1835 walked to Rome, keeping himself by painting and drawing portraits. He found Rome in an uncongenial political uproar, so went on to Florence, where he remained four years, copying in the Uffizi for a living and producing for dealers what were virtually forgeries. In 1839 he was in Milan and Venice, studying Titian, and in 1840 was in Rome, where he met Thorwaldsen and worked in his studio until he returned to England in 1842. He failed even to get a mention in the 1842 Houses of Parliament competition, worked for industrialists on products exhibited in the 1851 Great Exhibition, and in 1856 had his first success with the Wellington monument in St Paul's Cathedral, although the equestrian statue of the Duke was not erected until 45 years after the artist's death. He worked in houses now destroyed and on mosaics in St Paul's Cathedral (finished 1864). He painted occasional portraits, but his principal surviving works are drawings, chiefly in sanguine, the main inspiration for which was Raphael.

There are large collections of his work in Liverpool and London (Tate) with most of his surviving paintings and sculpture, and Cambridge (Fitzwm), Oxford, and Sheffield have many drawings.

STIACCIATO *see* RELIEF.

STIJL, De, was a Dutch magazine (1917–28) devoted to boosting
MONDRIAN and Neo-Plasticism in general; it subsequently sank
into the hands of DADAISTS. The ideas advocated by it are also
sometimes called De Stijl, and these have had a marked influence on
the architecture of Gropius and others of the BAUHAUS movement,
and on commercial art – poster designing, packaging, printing –
particularly in Germany at first, but later spreading all over the
world.

STILL, Clyfford (b. 1904). American painter best known for his abstract
canvases, often in heavy oil impasto, which consist of jagged shaped
islands of contrasting colour, like rock formations.

STILL-LIFE does not emerge as a subject in its own right until the
16th century; before that it appeared in religious pictures and portraits as part of the setting. It is a Northern rather than a Southern
art-form, with its greatest currency in Flanders and Holland and its
least in England. After the Reformation, when religious painting
virtually disappeared in the Protestant North, it became popular and
was developed along various lines, the chief being the *Vanitas* type,
a collection of objects chosen and arranged to remind the spectator
of the transience and uncertainty of life; the symbolic type, where the
objects portrayed have a significance beyond their individual appearance, and one heightened by their association; into this latter category come many still-life subjects which at first sight appear no more
than members of the third type – collections of objects arranged to
display the painter's virtuosity. The *Vanitas* is named from Ecclesiastes
(i. 2), 'Vanitas Vanitatum . . .' and is easily recognized – hour-glasses,
skulls, mirrors, butterflies, flowers, guttering candles, books, speak
an immediate and universal language. The type was probably
derived from the *Memento Mori* representations of S. Jerome, popular in Utrecht, whereas in the theological University city of Leyden
the still-life alone could be made to carry the moral. The second type
is more difficult but usually contains bread in some form, wine,
water, and other recondite references to the Passion, the Trinity,
the iconography of saints or the Virgin. The last category is self-
evident but often difficult to distinguish from the symbolic one.

This also applies to flower pieces. Many are merely luxuriant
bouquets; many are also composite works containing flowers
blooming at different times of the year, thus suggesting Time or the
Seasons; many of the flowers may have hidden religious or literary
meanings.

There are also large still-life pieces of the 'furniture picture' type
– kitchen interiors, with quantities of raw and cooked food, flowers,
guns, dogs, and cookmaids. The earliest flower piece seems to be the
vase of flowers on the back of a portrait by Memlinc in the Thyssen
Coll., though this probably had a devotional emblematical meaning;

and the earliest dated pure flower piece is German, of 1562. The type
seems to have developed from Herbals in the mid 16th century. The
earliest known still-life is by the Venetian-trained Jacopo de' BAR-
BARI, dated 1504, in Munich, but there is a *Madonna* of *c.*1470, by a
follower of Roger van der Weyden, which has a niche containing still-
life objects painted on the back (Rotterdam); this, however, is almost
certainly symbolic in intent, since the objects are those often associated with the Annunciation. The towel, basin, and ewer all figure in
the *Annunciation* on the wings of the Ghent Altar. Even earlier is a
similar still-life by T. Gaddi (1332–8), but this is a representation
of a credence table – i.e. it is a liturgical fitment. Still-life hardly
appears in Italian painting independently of a subject, except for
the small baskets of fruit by Caravaggio, done early in his career,
although notable exceptions are the fruit, flower, and fish-pieces of
the Neapolitan school in the 17th and 18th centuries and the musical
instruments painted by the Bergamasque Baschenis (1617–77). It is,
however, an essential feature of the pictures in wood veneers known
as *intarsie* and marble panels inlaid with *pietre dure* – onyx, lapis
lazuli, etc. – and also bulks large in Bassano's genre subjects, being,
in fact, usually allied to such pictures. Spain produced a rather
austere form, known as BODEGONES, and in France the 17th and
18th centuries saw, with Oudry and Chardin, highly developed forms
of the Northern furniture pictures and the virtuoso still-life, though
Oudry verges on animal painting and Chardin eschews *objets de luxe*
in favour of kitchen utensils and simple arrangements of food and
drink.

STIPPLED DRAWING is one modelled in light and shade by hundreds
of tiny dots and flecks, sometimes also STUMPED, an elaborate
technique giving a result not unlike a photograph and consequently
very popular in 19th-century art schools. Stipple engraving: *see*
ENGRAVING.

STOMER, Matthias (1600–after 1650), was a Dutch Caravaggesque,
whose style has much in common with the UTRECHT School. He
was born in Amersfoort and was a pupil of HONTHORST, presumably
soon after 1620. He entered the Guild in Rome in 1630, but was in
Naples in 1631 and seems to have spent the rest of his life in Sicily
and South Italy, never returning to Holland. There are pictures by
him in Baltimore, Berlin, Birmingham, Brussels (Musée de S. Jean),
Caccamo in Sicily (S. Agostino: dated 1641), Catania, Copenhagen,
Darmstadt, Greenville SC, The Hague (Bredius Mus.), Leeds,
Madrid, Monreale, Munich, Naples, Ottawa, Padua, Palermo (S.M.
del Rosario and palaces), Paris, Prague, Providence RI, Stockholm,
Turin, Vaduz (Liechtenstein Coll.), Valletta Malta, and Worcester
Mass. The Caccamo picture was stolen in 1971.

STONE CARVING is of incalculable antiquity, and the basic tools employed by the modern sculptor are fundamentally the same as those used by the Greeks of the 6th century B.C. It is possible to reproduce a model made in wax or plaster mechanically by means of the POINTING MACHINE, but many sculptors have always preferred direct carving, since the material conditions the final form. A block of stone is usually more or less rectilinear, and the outlines are first drawn on all the faces of it as a rough guide. The first blocking-out of the form is done with a stonemason's hammer, or *boucharde*, which has a heavy steel head covered with pyramidal points. Next, a punch, which is simply a pointed bar of steel, is used with a mallet to knock off large chips of stone. The forms are then defined with more precision by means of a claw chisel, which has three, four, or more teeth, giving a furrow-like effect to the surface of the stone. When the statue is virtually complete, but still furrowed all over by the claw marks, the sculptor takes an ordinary cold chisel and begins to define the forms as closely as possible. If a polished surface is desired it can be obtained by using files and abrasive powders. A drill is often used, and was particularly popular with Baroque sculptors to produce small points of shadow, in the hair or in an eyeball, to give vivacity to the expression.

STOPPING OUT *see* ENGRAVING.

STOSS, Veit (1440/50–1533), was, with RIEMENSCHNEIDER, the leading German Late Gothic sculptor. He went to Cracow in Poland (where he is known as Wit Stwosz) in 1477, where he carved his masterpiece, the High Altar for the Church of S. Mary (1477–89), an enormously complicated shrine, full of figures and some 40 feet high. He also worked in stone, and other works by him are in the Cathedral and Museum at Cracow. In 1496 he returned to Nuremberg, and in 1503 attempted to exculpate himself from a criminal charge by forging a document, as a result of which he was sentenced to be branded on both cheeks and forbidden to leave Nuremberg. He also made some engravings and was active as a painter. Other works are in Cleveland Ohio, Nuremberg, and Florence (SS. Annunziata).

STREETER (Streater), Robert (1624–80), appointed Sergeant-Painter to Charles II in 1663, is best known for his ceiling (1669) of the Sheldonian Theatre, Oxford, painted with an elaborate allegory of the Triumph of Truth and the Arts. It is the most high-flown Baroque composition painted by an Englishman before Thornhill, and it inspired the immortal lines: '. . . future Ages must confess they owe To Streeter more than Michael Angelo' (R. Whitehall, *Urania*, 1669).

STRETES *see* SCROTS.

STRIGEL, Bernhardin (*c.*1460/61–1528), was a German painter mainly of portraits who became Court Painter to the Emperor Maximilian I. All attributions to him are based on the *Cuspinian Family* (private coll.) which has an inscription dated 1520 and giving Strigel's name.

There are, however, two pictures (Vienna, K-H Mus.) of *Maximilian and his Family* and the *Virgin and Child with S. Anne and other Saints* which are apparently of about 1515 but came from the same complex as the *Cuspinian Family*. Other pictures are in Baltimore, Berlin, Boston, Denver Col., Munich, New York (Met. Mus.), Nuremberg, Stuttgart, Vienna (K-H Mus.), Washington (NG), and York.

STROZZI, Bernardo (1581–1644), was a Genoese painter who became a Franciscan friar at the age of 17 (hence his nicknames 'Il Cappuccino' and 'Il Prete Genovese'). From 1607 his art was powerfully affected by Rubens, who was in Genoa then. In 1610 he left his convent to support his mother and spent the rest of his life as a painter although he was made a Monsignor in 1635. From 1630 he lived in Venice and Venetian art was the other great influence on his work. There are pictures by him in the Royal Collection and in Baltimore, Berlin, Birmingham, Cardiff, Cincinnati, Cleveland, Dayton Ohio, Dresden, Dublin, Florence (Uffizi), Genoa, Greenville, SC, Hartford (Wadsworth Atheneum), Kansas City, London (NG), Milan (Brera), New York (Met. Mus.), Ottawa, Oxford (Ashmolean and Christ Church), Paris (Louvre), Rome (Gall. Naz.), St Louis, Venice, Vienna, Washington, Worcester Mass., and elsewhere.

STUART, Gilbert (1755–1828), was born in America but went to Scotland *c.* 1770. After returning to America he came back to London in 1775 and studied under his fellow-countryman WEST. After escaping from his creditors by working in Dublin 1787–93 he returned to America and became famous as a portrait painter. His *Washington* exists in three main types, versions being in every major American collection. The Tate Gall., London, has his *West* and others, and the NPG also has portraits.

STUBBS, George (1724–1806), painted portraits for a living while studying anatomy in York, where he lectured to medical students. His earliest works are illustrations for a textbook of midwifery (1751). In 1754 he went to Rome not to study Italian art but to prove to himself that this was unnecessary, since 'Nature is superior to art'. Returning via Ceuta he saw a lion devouring a horse, a sight which haunted him for the rest of his life and which became one of his most admired subjects. He then lived in a desolate Lincolnshire farmhouse, dissecting horses and drawing them, but during the 1760s he lived in London and worked as an animal painter while preparing his 'Anatomy of the Horse', published in 1766. In 1780 he became an ARA, but was never elected RA because of a dispute with the Academy. From 1795 until his death he worked on a book on the comparative anatomy of Man, Tiger, and Fowl. The text and 125 drawings were discovered in 1957 in the Public Library, Worcester Mass.

Most of his paintings are oils on canvas, but from 1770 he experimented with enamel, fired on copper plates, or on Wedgwood china plaques (a *Self-portrait* on a Wedgwood plaque is now in London, NPG). Stubbs is far more than an animal painter or a horse portraitist: all nature was his field, and his amazing accuracy of representation is the servant of a highly developed pictorial imagination. There are examples in Bath (Holburne Mus.), Glasgow (Hunterian), Leeds, Liverpool, London (NG, BM, Tate, RA), Manchester, Melbourne, Port Sunlight, Yale, and elsewhere.

STUDY. A drawing or painting of a detail, such as a figure, a hand, or a piece of drapery, made for the purpose of study or for use in a larger composition. A study should never be confused with a SKETCH, which is a rough draught of the whole, whereas a study may be very highly wrought but does not usually embrace more than a part of the composition.

STUMP. A cigar-shaped roll of paper, sharply pointed at each end, which was used to rub charcoal or chalk drawings so as to obtain very delicate transitions of tone. A stumped drawing looks very like a photograph, hence the decay of the technique.

STYLE CRITICISM requires an exact knowledge of the characteristics of any given School as well as the personal style of any particular artist. Given such a knowledge, it is possible to analyse the style of a work of art so that a convincing attribution may be made to a specific artist and even to a particular moment in his career. Further, given a precise knowledge of many works by many masters of any one country or period, it is possible to make general deductions about the style of that country or period as reflected in its practitioners. The proper practice of stylistic analysis is more difficult than it is sometimes made to seem.

SULLY, Thomas (1783–1872), was born in England but went to America as a child. He studied under STUART in Boston before working with WEST in London in 1809. He returned to America and settled in Philadelphia in 1810 but revisited England in 1837–8 to paint Queen Victoria at the request of the St George's Society of Philadelphia. Sully painted her at Buckingham Palace and said that 'she was very affable, like a well-bred lady of Philadelphia or Boston'. This finished picture is still in Philadelphia but the original study is in New York (Met. Mus.) and another version is in London (Wallace Coll.). Sully kept an index of his works from 1801 which runs to 2,631 items, most of which are in America. His 'Hints to Young Painters' was published posthumously.

SUPER-REALISM *see* SURREALISM.

SUPREMATISM was a hyper-orthodox form of CUBISM, invented in 1913/15 by MALEVICH (who later wrote a book about it) as an absolutely pure geometrical abstract art. To the uninitiated it is scarcely distinguishable from analytical Cubism: to the really initiated it must be distinguished from CONSTRUCTIVISM and from the abstract paintings of MONDRIAN.

SURREALISM, which was born of a union between the COLLAGE and CONSTRUCTIVIST aspects of CUBISM, and the nihilism of DADA, claims a long artistic ancestry in the art of Bosch, Arcimboldi, Fuseli, Goya, Redon, and any other artist who has expressed the weird and fantastic. After the demise of Dada in 1922, André Breton gathered up the remnants of the group, took over the word *surréaliste* from Apollinaire (who had used it in 1917), and defined it as 'Pure psychic AUTOMATISM, by which it is intended to express verbally, in writing or in any other way, the true process of thought. It is the dictation of thought, free from the exercise of reason, and every aesthetic or moral preoccupation.' The object was to free artists from the normal association of pictorial ideas and from all accepted means of expression, so that they might create according to the irrational dictates of their subconscious mind and vision. Surrealism developed in two directions: pure fantasy, and the elaborate reconstruction of a dream-world. The first produced FOUND OBJECTS, either alone or composed – a bottle dryer, a bicycle wheel, or a birdcage filled with sugar-cubes and a thermometer, a random assortment of bric-à-brac – automatic drawing, Ernst's FROTTAGES and abstract works charged with meaning by a strange title – Klee's *Twittering machine*, or Picabia's *Catch as catch can*. The second took the form of highly detailed likenesses of objects, straight or distorted, or three-dimensional abstractions, in a fantastic and unexpected juxtaposition, or in a setting of a hallucinatory kind: CHIRICO, Tanguy, DALI, Man Ray's photographs, and much of Picasso's painting and sculpture from the late 1920s develop this type, the feverish search for the unexpected being well rendered by Lautréamont's simile: 'Beautiful as the chance encounter of a sewing machine and an umbrella on an operating table.' In 1925 the fifth number of 'La Révolution Surréaliste', edited by Breton, associated the movement with Communism, but the Communists, as a political party, would have none of it. The movement has had as much currency in literature and drama as in the visual arts, and despite its own particular strait-jacket, has had a liberating influence. Its ideas of strange juxtapositions have been widely commercialized – particularly in sophisticated window-dressing – and, its initial force now spent and its edge dulled by surfeit, it survives as a respectable ghost of hauntingly incoherent incantations, and even threatens to become academic.

SUTHERLAND, Graham, OM (*b.*1903), one of the best-known of living British painters, began as an etcher and engraver and painted little before 1935. He was appointed an Official War Artist in 1941 and his semi-abstract scenes of desolation after bombing exactly expressed the atmosphere of such a scene. He is primarily a painter of the mood of landscape, but exceptions are the *Crucifixion* and the related subjects and studies of about 1946, and his portraits. The *Crucifixion* was commissioned by Canon Hussey for S. Matthew's, Northampton, where there is also a Henry Moore statue of the *Madonna and Child*, and his religious works have become more important with the huge tapestry for Coventry Cathedral (1962: most of the studies are in Coventry Mus.) and the *Crucifixion* for S. Aidan's, East Acton, London, of 1963. Sutherland's portraits include the *Maugham* (1949), *Beaverbrook* (1951), and the *Churchill*, not so far seen in public. There are pictures in Birmingham, Darlington, Hull, London (Tate, Imperial War Mus.), Manchester, Melbourne, Nebraska Univ., New Brunswick, New York (M of MA), Ottawa, Paris (Mus. d'Art Moderne), Southampton, Toronto, and elsewhere.

SWEERTS, Michael (1624–64), was a Brussels painter who went to Rome in or before 1646, when he was a member of the Academy, charged with the difficult task of collecting the dues owed to the Guild by the Netherlandish immigrant painters. He remained in Rome until 1652 at least, and in 1656 opened a school in Brussels. In 1661, as a lay brother he began a journey to the East with an unsuccessful religious mission. He died in Goa. His Roman works are good examples of BAMBOCCIATE, but after his return north his works approximated more closely to Dutch genre painting as practised by Pieter de HOOCH, or portraits similar to those by VERMEER. There are works by him in Amsterdam, Detroit, Haarlem, The Hague, Hartford Conn., Leningrad, London (Wallace Coll.), Milan (Castello), Munich, Oberlin Ohio, Paris (Louvre), Rome (Capitoline and Accad.), Rotterdam, and Worcester Mass.

SYNTHETISM, or Cloisonnisme, is synonymous with Symbolism. The movement was originally a literary one, starting in 1886 with Rimbaud's 'Illuminations'. In 1889 GAUGUIN and other artists from Pont-Aven exhibited their works as 'Synthetist' painters, their object being the expression of ideas, mood, and emotion and the complete rejection of naturalistic representation. Their pictures were painted in brilliant colours, separated by black lines, and sought to be both decorative and the abstractions, or syntheses, of the ideas which inspired them. The chief members of the group were Gauguin and Émile BERNARD (who claimed to have invented Synthetism); Odilon REDON developed the purely personal and fantastic side of Symbolism and strongly influenced the NABIS. Linked with the group, though not part of it, were Gustave MOREAU and PUVIS de Chavannes.

T

TACCA, Pietro (1557–1640), was a pupil of Giovanni da BOLOGNA and succeeded him as Sculptor to the Tuscan Grand-Dukes. He also finished his master's equestrian statues in Florence (1608), Madrid (1606–13) and Paris (*Henri IV*, 1613, destroyed 1792). His masterpiece is *The Four Moors* (1615–24) on the base of the monument to the Grand-Duke Ferdinand I in Leghorn. He also made an equestrian monument to Philip IV in Madrid (1634–40) and monuments in Florence (S. Lorenzo). His works show the influence of Michelangelo, but look forward to the violence of Baroque movement.

TACHISME (Fr. *tache*, blot, stain) is very similar to ACTION PAINTING. The most notable exponent was POLLOCK, who now has a host of followers on both sides of the Atlantic, but KANDINSKY painted remarkably similar pictures before the First World War.

TACTILE VALUES. An illusion of tangibility. The inventor of the phrase, Bernhard Berenson, claimed that the representation of three-dimensional objects on a two-dimensional surface in such a way that one received a strong impression of physical tangibility is 'life-enhancing'. It is not clear why.

TAILLE-DOUCE (Fr.). Line ENGRAVING.

TAMAYO, Rufino (*b.*1899), is a Mexican painter who has, like RIVERA, founded his style on a mixture of his native prehistoric art and modern European art, chiefly Expressionism and Surrealism. He has worked a good deal in America, and in 1943 executed frescoes for Smith College Library, Northampton Mass. His use of sophisticated foreign elements has made him something of a prophet in his own land.

TANGUY, Yves (1900–55), was a French Surrealist, who began life as a merchant seaman and took up painting in 1924 after seeing a Chirico. Unlike Chirico, however, Tanguy's pictures rarely contain recognizable forms or buildings, but are lunar landscapes populated by amorphous beings, not unlike those of Ernst. From 1939 he lived in the US. There are works by him in Basle, Buffalo, Chicago, Hartford Conn. (Wadsworth), New York (Met. Mus., M of MA, Whitney), Paris (Mus. d'Art Moderne), and Philadelphia.

TAPIÈS, Antonio (*b.*1923), studied law before becoming the leading Spanish abstract painter. He began to paint in 1946 and went to Paris in 1950: his works mostly consist of puddled sand and paint, often with incised dashes, giving an effect not unlike the sea-shore after the tide has ebbed. There are examples in London (Tate) and New York (M of MA).

TATLIN, Vladimir (1885–1953?), was a Russian painter who, in 1913, switched to sculpture and founded CONSTRUCTIVISM. In the same year he met Picasso in Paris. Unlike many other Russian artists – GABO, PEVSNER, CHAGALL – he remained after the Soviet authorities abandoned their brief flirtation with 'advanced' art. Tatlin worked as a designer, especially for film and stage sets, but it is significant that the date of his death is difficult to ascertain. It was probably 1953, but 1956 is also given in reference books, and some writers speak of him as still alive.

TECTONIC *see* ARCHITECTONIC.

TEMPERA. This word really means any kind of binder which will serve to 'temper' powder colour and make it workable: in practice, however, it is confined to egg tempera, which was the commonest technique of painting until the late 15th century for the production of easel pictures. If you take a panel well prepared with GESSO and paint on it with powder colour which is mixed with fresh egg-yolk thinned with water the result will be a paint film which dries almost instantaneously (making reworking difficult) and is also tough and permanent. It dries several tones lighter than the wet paint. There are many modifications of this basic recipe, and some painters used the whole egg; illuminators of MSS often used only the white. From very early times it was noticed that powder colour could be mixed with some form of drying oil and would then form a rich and transparent film which could be used to modify the semi-opaque tempera layer. Probably the earliest use of this oil GLAZE was to shade off burnished gold or silver leaf, but from this the whole technique of OIL-PAINTING developed. For many years it was usual to paint most of a picture in tempera – which dries in minutes – and then to apply only the final touches in oil. One good reason for this is the fact that tempera, because of the speed with which it dries, has to be hatched and cross-hatched to obtain modelling: a final glaze of oil-colour will spread a unifying film, or, as painters say, 'pull it together'. No one really knows how long this 'Mixed Method' continued – it was certainly still practised by Rubens – but it is plain that the oil medium has such attractive qualities of its own, notably in IMPASTO, that it became the dominant partner. Rembrandt, whose lifetime overlaps with Rubens, seems always to have used oil alone. In the last few years a small number of painters have returned to the pure tempera medium (the paints can now be bought ready mixed), but a judicious use of the Mixed Method offers great scope for technical virtuosity and could well be revived. *See also* ACRYLIC.

TENEBRISM (from Ital. *tenebroso*, murky) is the name given to painting in a very low KEY, specifically to the works of those early 17th-century painters, mostly Neapolitan and Spanish, who were much influenced by CARAVAGGIO. They did not form any kind of organized group and the *Tenebristi* did not call themselves by that name.

Teniers, David I (1582–1649), was a painter of religious pictures, influenced by Rubens, and some landscapes with peasants similar to those by his son David II (1610–90), the most famous member of the family. Teniers the Younger became a Master in Antwerp in 1632/3 and worked there until 1651, when he settled in Brussels. He was the Court Painter to the Archduke Leopold Wilhelm, Regent of the Netherlands and one of the greatest of collectors, and Teniers became Keeper of his pictures. He was also Court Painter to the next Regent and was the main founder of the Antwerp Academy, opened in 1665. He painted almost every kind of picture, but predominantly genre scenes of peasant life. His earliest are in the manner of Brouwer, but he developed his own style and produced most of his best works in the decade 1640–50, before moving to Brussels. Many of his later works are largely by assistants, since the demand was enormous. He painted a few religious subjects and some of Witches' Sabbaths, and even apes and cats dressed up as humans, but historically the most interesting are the interiors of picture galleries, showing recognizable pictures in their 17th-century settings. As an art-historian he made many copies of the Archduke Leopold Wilhelm's pictures, 244 of which were engraved in 1660 under the title 'Theatrum Pictorium': most of the originals are now in Vienna and have thus an established history back to the mid 17th century. More than 2,000 pictures are attributed to him, and there are good examples in the Royal Coll. and in Amsterdam, Antwerp, Berlin, Brussels, Dresden, Edinburgh (NG), Glasgow, The Hague, Leningrad, London (NG, Wallace Coll. (an example of almost every kind of picture he painted), Dulwich, Wellington Mus.), Madrid, Munich, New York (Met. Mus.), Paris (Louvre), and Vienna (K-H Mus.). His son David III (1638–85), was also a painter and often imitated him.

Ter Borch (Terburg, Terborch), Gerard (1617–81), was the son of a minor painter and was very precocious. He was in Amsterdam and Haarlem 1632/4, when Rembrandt was making his name and Hals was working in Haarlem; in 1635 he visited England; in 1640 he was in Italy; he returned to Holland probably via France, and in 1646 he went to Münster in Westphalia (presumably to paint portraits of the dignitaries at the Congress of the Peace of Westphalia), and in 1648 he accompanied the Spanish Envoy to Madrid, returning to Holland in 1650. On account of these travels Ter Borch must have had first-hand knowledge of almost all the great 17th-century artists – Rembrandt, Hals, Velazquez, Bernini – and yet his style betrays no hint of this, for he is content to paint small portraits and genteel genre scenes, diligent in style, paying particular attention to the rendering of silk and satin. His most famous work is the *Peace of Münster, May 15, 1648* (London, NG), a group portrait of all the dignitaries at full length, on copper, $17\frac{1}{2}$ by $22\frac{1}{2}$ inches: all his other pictures are small portraits and portrait groups, usually full length, and scenes of well-to-do Dutch family life or else guard-room scenes. Most of his figures have a curious doll-like charm and the costumes and accessories recur so often in his portraits even down to identical folds, that it is possible he painted the pictures in advance and simply added heads and hands when necessary. His works are often similar to those of his junior, METSU, but his subtle treatment of colour and light were far exceeded by VERMEER. There are works by him in the Royal Coll. and in Aix, Amsterdam, Antwerp, Berlin, Boston (Gardner), Bremen, Budapest, Cape Town, Chicago, Cincinnati, Cologne, Copenhagen, Detroit, Deventer (Town Hall), Dresden, Dublin, Florence (Uffizi), Frankfurt (Städel), Haarlem, The Hague, Hamburg, Indianapolis, London (NG, V & A, and Wallace Coll.), Munich, New York (Met. Mus., Frick Coll., and Hist. Soc.), Paris (Louvre and Petit Pal.), Philadelphia, Richmond Va, Rotterdam, Rouen, Toledo Ohio, Vaduz (Liechtenstein Coll.: *Portrait of van Goyen*), Vienna, Washington (NG), and Wellesley College, Mass.

TERBRUGGHEN, Hendrick (1588–1629), was born in Deventer and became a pupil of BLOEMAERT before going to Italy 1604–14. He settled in Utrecht by 1616 and became one of the leading members of the UTRECHT School, but his style shows almost no influence of his master Bloemaert and, strictly speaking, little of that of Caravaggio except in the predilection for strong contrasts of light and shadow – and even that disappears in his later works, for the *Jacob and Laban* (1627: London, NG) is painted in much lighter and clearer colours and looks forward to VERMEER, who also turned *Caravaggismo* upside down. Some of Terbrugghen's religious subjects are taken from Caravaggio – the *Incredulity of S. Thomas* and the *Calling of S. Matthew* are reworkings of Caravaggio themes – but the iconography of others goes back to such Northern artists as e.g. Dürer. More typical works are nearer to MANFREDI, e.g. the *Lute Players* and the harlot and the clown of the *Duet* and similar pictures. There are pictures by him in the Royal Coll. and in Amsterdam (Rijksmus.), Augsburg, Basle, Berlin, Bordeaux, Cambridge Mass. (Fogg), Cassel, Cologne, Copenhagen, Deventer (Town Hall), Edinburgh (NG), Gotha, Gothenburg, Greenville SC, Le Havre, London (NG), New York (Met. Mus.), Oberlin Ohio, Oxford (Ashmolean), Paris (Louvre), Rome (Gall. Naz.), Sacramento Cal., Schwerin, Stockholm, Utrecht, and Vienna (K-H Mus.).

TERRACOTTA (Ital. baked earth) *see* PLASTER CASTING.

TERRIBILITÀ (Ital. terribleness). A word usually applied to Michelangelo and, by extension, to any art of austere and tragic grandeur.

TESSERAE. The cubes used in MOSAIC.

THEODORIC of Prague (active 1343?–68) was recorded in the Prague Painters' Guild in 1348. He was Painter to the Emperor Charles IV by 1359 and executed over 100 paintings for his Castle at Karlstein in Bohemia by 1365. He was the greatest of the Bohemian painters of the 14th century and began a severe and realistic style that influenced much later German and Bohemian painting.

THOMA, Hans (1839–1924), spent a few weeks in Paris in 1868 and was profoundly impressed by the Realist ideas of COURBET and the BARBIZON painters. In the 1870s he met LEIBL and BÖCKLIN and in 1874 he went to Italy, where he met MARÉES, and the Romanticism of these latter influenced his work in the direction of what now seems a deplorable sentimentality. He is very well represented in German museums, especially Karlsruhe (where he was Director), and there are other pictures in New York (Met. Mus.), Stockholm, Vienna, and Zürich.

THORNHILL, Sir James (1675/6–1734), was the only English decorator in the grand Baroque tradition. In the Dome of St Paul's (1715–17) incidents from the saint's life appear in eight grisaille panels picked out in gold, and the decoration does not obtrude on the painted architectural setting. His work at Greenwich Hospital, lasting from 1708 to 1727, includes the immense Painted Hall, the lower Hall, and Vestibule, and set him the problem of treating modern history subjects in a grand allegorical setting, which he solved with a display of the most Italianate illusionism. He does not appear to have had any direct contact with Verrio or Laguerre, yet both influenced him, though his ceiling of Queen Anne's Bedroom at Hampton Court (1715) is finer than anything of theirs. He travelled in the Netherlands in 1711, and in France in 1717; was knighted and made Sergeant Painter in 1720, Member of Parliament for his native town of Melcombe Regis in Dorset in 1722, Fellow of the Royal Society in 1723, and Master of the Painter-Stainers' Company. These offices and honours gave him a very different position from that usually accorded to artists and not reached again until the advent of Reynolds. He appeared at a time when grand decoration was required, and reaped the advantage of being the only English painter able to compete with the many foreigners then seeking work in England (Pellegrini, the Riccis, and Amigoni, besides Verrio and Laguerre) at a moment when anti-foreign feeling prevailed. His son-in-law, Hogarth, is an excellent example of this. His only big failure was when Kent was given the job of decorating Kensington Palace, through the influence of his patron, Lord Burlington.

There are also works at Chatsworth, Easton Neston, London (Tate, NPG), and elsewhere.

THORWALDSEN (Thorvaldsen), Bertel (1768, or, according to his own account, 1770–1844), is the only Danish artist to have attained international fame. He won a scholarship to Italy and went in 1796, living in Rome from 1797 until his triumphal return to Denmark in

1819; in 1820 he returned to Rome for another 18 years. He was one of the three great NEOCLASSIC sculptors, ranking above GIBSON, but rather below CANOVA. It was generally felt that he was less influenced by the Italian tradition than was Canova, but he is also rather more matter-of-fact: his works are calm and noble, or insipid copies of the Antique, according to taste. There is a complete collection – originals, casts, and copies – in the Thorwaldsen Mus. in Copenhagen, but there are others in Naples, Rome (especially S. Peter's: Tomb of Pius VII), Liverpool, and Minneapolis.

TIBALDI, Pellegrino (1527–96), was a painter, sculptor, and architect who was one of the leading Italian Mannerists of the late 16th century and whose work in Spain helped to spread the style there. His earliest painting is the large *Adoration of the Shepherds* (1548 not 49: Rome, Borghese) painted when he was 21. This shows the influence of Michelangelo and his followers, but Tibaldi was also influenced by PARMIGIANINO and Niccolò dell' ABBATE. He was in Rome by 1549/50, but returned to Bologna in 1553 when he began a series of frescoes of the story of Odysseus (Pal. Poggi, now the University) and the decorations in S. Giacomo Maggiore. From 1560 Tibaldi was connected with S. Charles Borromeo, Archbishop of Milan, for whom he also worked as an architect. In 1585 he was invited to Spain by Philip II, but he did not go until 1587. There he supervised the building and decoration of the Escorial, painting 46 frescoes in the cloister alone. In 1596, rich and ennobled, he returned to Milan where he died. There are other works by him in Amsterdam, Ancona, Bologna, Leningrad, Milan (Brera), and Vaduz (Liechtenstein Coll.: replica of the Borghese *Adoration*).

TIEPOLO, Giovanni Battista (Giambattista) (1696–1770), was the last of the great Venetian decorators, the purest exponent of the Italian ROCOCO, and arguably the greatest painter of the 18th century. He was trained under an obscure painter named Lazzarini but was really formed by the study of Sebastiano RICCI and PIAZZETTA among living painters and VERONESE among the older masters. He was received into the Fraglia (Guild) in 1717 but had already painted the *Sacrifice of Abraham* (1715/16: Venice, Ospedaletto), a dark picture very much in the manner of Piazzetta and the 17th century generally. In 1719 he married the sister of Guardi and at about this time his own lighter and looser style began to form. His first great commission for fresco decorations came in 1725, when he began the work in the Archbishop's Palace at Udine (completed 1728). These already show the virtuosity of his handling, the light tone and pale colours necessitated by fresco obviously helping him to break free from the dark Piazzettesque models he had previously followed. The Udine frescoes also show him developing as the creator of a world in steep perspective beyond the picture plane, with the architecture receding into dizzy distances. The highly specialized work of painting these architectural perspectives was done by Mengozzi-Colonna, who did this work for Tiepolo for most of his life. Following the Udine frescoes Tiepolo travelled widely in N. Italy, painting many more frescoes in palaces and churches, as well as altarpieces in oil which culminate in the gigantic *Gathering of the Manna* and *Sacrifice of Melchizedek* (c. 1735–40: Verolanuova, Parish Church), each of which is about 30 feet high. The frescoes of this period culminate in the *Antony and Cleopatra* series in the Palazzo Labia, Venice, which were probably finished just before 1750, when he left Venice for Würzburg. He was invited to decorate the ceiling of the Kaisersaal in the Residenz at Würzburg by the Prince-Bishop, Karl Phillip von Greiffenklau, and Tiepolo and his sons Giandomenico and Lorenzo arrived in Würzburg at the end of 1750 and remained there until 1753. He painted the staircase with frescoes, some overdoors, and some altarpieces as well as the Kaisersaal, and both his sons, as well as several other assistants, helped in the gigantic task. The Palace itself is a superb example of German Rococo architecture and the combination of architecture and painting into one vast and airy allegory – apparently referring to the Prince-Bishop as a patron, but including Barbarossa and German history – is perhaps the most successful even in Tiepolo's career. In 1755, after his return to Venice, he was elected first President of the Venetian Academy and in 1761 he was invited to Spain to decorate the Royal Palace in Madrid by Charles III. He arrived in 1762, with his sons and assistants, and painted the huge ceilings in the Palace in 4 years. In 1767 Charles commissioned seven altarpieces for Aranjuez but Tiepolo's last years in Spain were embittered by intrigues on behalf of MENGS, the representative of that Neoclassicism which was soon to condemn his kind of splendid and carefree painting as frivolous. He died suddenly in Madrid. His enormous output of frescoes and altarpieces was partly due to his habit of painting small *modelli* which, when approved by the client, could be carried out by his skilled assistants under his own supervision. Scores of these *modelli* and sketches survive, together with hundreds of drawings. He painted very few portraits – the best-known is the so-called *Querini* in the Querini Gall., Venice, but this may, in fact, be by his son Domenico. He also etched many plates. There are works in many churches, palaces, and galleries in Venice and in Amsterdam, Barnard Castle (Bowes Mus.), Bergamo (Cath., Accad.), Berlin, Boston (Mus. and Gardner), Budapest, Cambridge Mass. (Fogg), Chicago, Detroit, Dresden, Edinburgh (NG), Este, London (NG, Dulwich), Melbourne (NG), Milan (Brera and Poldi-Pezzoli), Montreal, Munich, New York (Met. Mus.), Ottawa, Paris (Louvre), Philadelphia (Johnson), Rovigo, St Louis, Stockholm (Nat. Mus. and Univ. Mus.), Strà (Villa Pisani), Stuttgart, Verona,

Vicenza (Villa Valmarana), Vienna (K-H Mus., Akad.), Washington (NG), and many other places.

His son Giovanni Domenico (1727–1804) was also a considerable painter in his own right, as well as his father's assistant and imitator. His frescoes in the Villa Valmarana (one is now known to be dated 1757) show that he had a different approach from his father's, less allegorical and more sardonic and matter-of-fact, with a delight in the activities of clowns and mountebanks. There are some pictures by him in London (NG), but there is a tendency to ascribe works to him which are not quite good enough for his father: if they are not really good enough for Domenico they get ascribed to Lorenzo (1736–76), about whose style little is known. He made some etchings after his father's pictures.

TINO di Camaino (c. 1285–1337) was a Sienese sculptor, perhaps the pupil of Giovanni PISANO. He was working in Pisa by 1311, and became head of the works at the Cathedral in 1315, when he was commissioned to make a Tomb for the Emperor Henry VII, parts of which survive in the Cathedral. In 1319–20 Tino was head of the works at Siena Cathedral and later worked in Florence before going to Naples in 1323/4 to make Monuments for the Angevin rulers. He stayed in Naples until his death, and he seems to have been in close touch with Giotto, who was Court Painter in Naples 1329–33, and also with the Sienese painter Pietro Lorenzetti, who became guardian of Tino's child: Tino's grave, but rather clumsy, figures have much in common with Lorenzetti's. There are works in Florence, Naples, Pisa, Siena, and in Berlin, Detroit, Frankfurt, London (V & A), Paris (Louvre), Turin, and Yale.

TINTORETTO, Jacopo (1518–94), was born in Venice. Little is known of his early years; he claimed to have been a pupil of Titian, and was probably associated with Schiavone and Paris BORDONE. He was a master in 1539, but no work can certainly be ascribed to him before about 1545. Titian was his model, and he aimed at the Mannerist conception of the ideal through a synthesis of Michelangelo's drawing with Titian's colour, which in his case succeeded, chiefly because his drawing is nothing like Michelangelo's and his colour is nothing like Titian's.

In his early works he composes his figures across the picture in a frieze, with elegant elongated forms and all the devices of placing the principal incident deep into the picture, dispersing the interest over the whole canvas, or using *repoussoir* figures in front and at the sides, opposing diagonals and contrasts of light on dark and dark on light. He made his reputation in 1548 with the *S. Mark rescuing a slave* (Venice, Accad.), a large and crowded composition with daring foreshortening, brilliant colour, and a concentration on one moment and incident. Later he evolved compositions based on an exploding centre or on rapidly receding diagonals, full of figures in violent movement. After the fires in the Doges' Palace in 1574 and 1577, Tintoretto and Veronese were the principal artists commissioned to renew the interior, and for this Tintoretto painted the gigantic *Paradise* for the main hall.

Like Titian, Tintoretto kept a huge workshop, his chief assistants being his sons Domenico and Marco, and his daughter Marietta. The system in the Tintoretto workshop differed from that in use in the Titian and Veronese workshops in that instead of limiting his assistants to close versions, copies, or preparatory work on a commission, he employed them mainly on enlargements and extensively altered variants of his original compositions. Besides his work for the State, he worked for most of the larger Confraternities and he began his long association with the Scuola di S. Rocco in 1564, becoming a member in 1565. In 1576 he contracted with the Confraternity for a regular stipend (which was paid; his State pension was often in arrears) in return for which he undertook to complete the decoration of the entire building. This was finished in 1588. The Scuola di S. Rocco consists of a huge lower hall with paintings over 12 feet high illustrating the Life of the Virgin, an upper hall of the same size with paintings over 16 feet high of the Life of Christ, with a further large room adjoining it with scenes from the Passion. They display to the full his extraordinary use of the unexpected viewpoint, contrasts of scale, unusual movement, and visionary effects of colour and flickering light. Vasari disapproved of him, and tempered his admiration by saying that Tintoretto treated art as a joke – which is a measure of the difference between Central Italian Mannerism and the Venetian kind.

There are few mythologies in his *œuvre*, for he had none of Titian's classical interest, neither does he approach Titian's range and inventiveness in portraits. After his death, painting in Venice dwindled in significance, not to revive until Piazzetta or to see similar glories until Tiepolo.

Most of the major galleries of the world possess an example, but it is impossible to see him properly except in Venice, and in particular in the Scuola di S. Rocco.

TISCHBEIN, Johann Heinrich Wilhelm (1751–1829), was one of a family of painters and was the pupil of his uncles in Hamburg. He went to Holland in 1771 and began to work as a portrait painter, having a great success at the Court in Berlin after 1777. He became dissatisfied with portraiture and went to Munich where he studied Dürer and the early German painters, going on to Italy in 1779. In 1783 he was in Rome for the second time and began to paint history pictures, but in 1786 he met Goethe, and in 1786/88 he painted the *Goethe in the Campagna* (Frankfurt, Städel) on which his reputation chiefly rests. In 1789 he became Director of the Naples Academy and from 1791 supervised the engravings of the Greek vases belonging to Sir William Hamilton which were so important in the spread of NEOCLASSICISM. He returned to Germany in 1799. There are works by him in Berlin, Hamburg, Weimar, and other German museums.

TISSOT, James (1836–1902), was born in Nantes but settled in England after the Franco-Prussian War of 1870. He spent 10 years in Palestine, working on his pictures of the Life of Christ, but he is now remembered as the most charming illustrator of Victorian life. There are good examples of this in London (Tate).

TITIAN (Tiziano Vecelli) (c. 1487/90–1576) was the greatest of Venetian painters and, in some senses, the founder of modern painting. Traditionally he lived to be 99; but this is highly improbable, since it makes him born in 1477 and therefore older than GIORGIONE who seems to have been the decisive innovator in the early years of the 16th century. Certainly Giorgione is the only painter mentioned in the documents concerning the frescoes on the Fondaco dei Tedeschi (1508), although Titian traditionally painted those on the less important façade. All these frescoes have now perished, but Titian's earliest style is certainly involved with Giorgione's. Titian seems to have been a pupil first of Gentile BELLINI and then of his brother Giovanni; but long before Giovanni's death in 1516 Titian had been decisively influenced by Giorgione, who, though not his master in any strict sense, was his real teacher. Giorgione's early death, in 1510, led to the completion of some of his works by Titian and SEBASTIANO del Piombo, and to consequent critical confusion: the Dresden *Venus* and the *Noli Me Tangere* (London, NG) may be two such Giorgione/Titians. In 1511 Titian was painting frescoes in Padua, but the unexpected death of Giorgione and the removal of Sebastiano to Rome in 1511 left Titian without a rival in Venice except the very aged Giovanni Bellini: on his death in 1516 Titian succeeded him as Painter to the Republic, and in the same year he began his *Assumption* for the Frari Church in Venice. This was completed in 1518 and laid the foundations of his fame. It is an enormous picture, in the 'modern' style, and marks the beginning of the High Renaissance in Venice. The *Pesaro Altar* (1519–26), in the same church, contains further innovations and shows Titian now firmly established and in possession of a fully developed personal style. In 1532 he met the Emperor Charles V at Bologna, where he painted a copy (1532–3: Madrid, Prado) of a full-length portrait of Charles by his Austrian Court Painter SEISENEGGER, as a result of which he was ennobled and made Court Painter in 1533. Subsequently Titian became a personal friend of the Emperor – an unheard-of honour for a painter of the 16th century, comparable only with Michelangelo's relationship with the Popes. During the 1540s Michelangelo's influence on Titian can be noted and some Mannerist elements infiltrate into his style – these, and also a new interest in classical antiquity, are partly attributable to his visit to Rome in 1545–6, when he painted a shatteringly revealing portrait of Paul III and his nasty Farnese grandsons apparently engaged in a family quarrel (Naples). He visited the Imperial Court at Augsburg in 1548–9 and again in 1550–1 and his portraits of these years established the type of official portrait which was later to be exploited by Rubens, van Dyck, and many others. After the abdication of Charles V in 1555, Titian continued to work for his successor, Philip II of Spain, who, however, employed him less as a portraitist than as a painter of *poesie* (Titian's own word); that is, more or less erotic mythologies which, at first sight, accord ill with the Counter-Reformation ideals of Philip II. During these years the old painter developed a very free handling, almost anticipating Impressionism in its disregard for contours and its concentration on the rendering of form as patches of colour. In the 1560s there were many criticisms of his failing powers, but in fact he was developing a sublime late style, best seen in the *modelli* he produced and from which his numerous assistants (who included his son Orazio) fabricated 'finished pictures'. The *Entomb-ment* (Venice, Accad.) was left unfinished at his death and was completed by PALMA Giovane, who has left the following descrip-tion of Titian's technique: 'He laid in his pictures with a mass of colour which served as a groundwork for what he wanted to express. I myself have seen such vigorous underpainting in plain red earth [*terra rossa*, probably Venetian red] for the half-tones, or in white lead. With the same brush dipped in red, black, or yellow he worked up the light parts and in four strokes he could create a remarkably fine figure. . . . Then he turned the picture to the wall and left it for months without looking at it, until he returned to it and stared critically at it, as if it were a mortal enemy. . . . If he found something which displeased him he went to work like a surgeon. . . . Thus, by repeated revisions he brought his pictures to a high state of perfec-tion and while one was drying he worked on another. This quin-tessence of a composition he then covered with many layers of living flesh. . . . He never painted a figure *alla prima*, and used to say that he who improvises can never make a perfect line of poetry. The final touches he softened, occasionally modulating the highest lights into the half-tones and local colours with his finger; sometimes he used his finger to dab a dark patch in a corner as an accent, or to heighten the surface with a bit of red like a drop of blood. He finished his figures like this and in the last stages he used his fingers more than his brush.'

There are works in the Royal Collection and in Ancona, Antwerp, Baltimore, Berlin, Besançon, Boston (Mus. and Gardner Mus.),

Brescia, Cambridge (Fitzwm), Cassel, Chicago, Cincinnati, Cleveland Ohio, Copenhagen, Detroit, Dresden, Dublin, Edinburgh (NG: loan from Lord Ellesmere), the Escorial, Florence (Pitti and Uffizi), Indianapolis, Kansas City, Kremsier, Leningrad, Lentiai nr Belluno, Lille, London (NG and Wallace Coll.), Madrid (Prado), Melbourne, Milan (Brera, Ambrosiana and Castello), Minneapolis, Munich, Naples, New York (Met. Mus., Frick Coll.), Omaha Nevada, Ottawa, Padua (Scuola del Santo and Mus.), Paris (Louvre), Philadelphia, Prague, Rome (Mus. Naz., Borghese, Capitoline), Rotterdam, San Diego Cal., San Francisco, St Louis, São Paulo, Treviso (Cath. and Mus.), Urbino, the Vatican, Venice (Accad. and widely elsewhere), Verona (Cath. and Mus.), Vienna (Akad. and K-H Mus.), Washington (NG, Nat. Coll. and Corcoran), Yale, and elsewhere.

TOBEY, Mark (*b.*1911), was born in Centerville Wis., and originally worked as a commercial artist. He taught at Dartington Hall School, in England, 1931–8, but visited Japan and China in 1934. He was much influenced by Chinese calligraphy (taking lessons from a Chinese artist) and was also one of the first American intellectuals to become interested in Zen. From 1935 he painted abstract pictures in what is called 'white writing', based on Chinese calligraphy: the effect is reminiscent of, but more fastidious than, the calligraphy of POLLOCK. These white squiggles have been described by an admirer as: 'looping over layers of interpenetrating space . . . holding icons in a shifting web'. Since 1939 he has lived in Seattle. There are works in London (Tate) and New York (M of MA).

TOCQUÉ, Louis (1696–1772), was a French portrait painter who was the pupil and son-in-law of NATTIER. He admired Rigaud and Largillierre and adapted their styles, and Nattier's, to the requirements of his own time. He worked in Paris except for a trip to St Petersburg and Copenhagen (1756–9), and a second trip to Copenhagen in 1769. There are examples in Boston, Copenhagen, London (NG), Paris (Louvre), and Versailles.

TONDO (Ital. round). A circular picture. They became fashionable in Italy in the mid 15th century, although earlier examples are known.

TONE VALUES *see* VALUES.

TORRIGIANO, Pietro (1472–1528), was a Florentine sculptor who, in youth, broke the nose of Michelangelo and for this has been hated by all Florentines ever since. Cellini tells how Torrigiano, who worked in England 1511–18 on the Tombs of Lady Margaret Beaufort, Elizabeth of York, and Henry VII in Westminster Abbey, returned to Florence *c.*1519 and offered him a job in England. 'He had stories every day of his brave deeds among those brutes of Englishmen', but in spite of the prospects Cellini, after hearing how Torrigiano broke Michelangelo's nose, 'felt such a hatred for him that far from wanting to go to England with him I could not bear to look at him'. Torrigiano did return to England – his masterpiece is the Tomb of Henry VII – and then went to Seville. There, according to Vasari (who also hated him for breaking Michelangelo's nose), he fell into the hands of the Inquisition and starved himself to death from sheer spleen. There is a bust of *Henry VII* in London (V & A).

TORSO. The trunk of the human body. Usually applied to a statue which lacks head, arms, and legs: the *Belvedere Torso* is a celebrated antique statue in the Vatican.

TOTENTANZ *see* DANCE OF DEATH.

TOULOUSE-LAUTREC, Henri Marie Raymond de (1864–1901), had the misfortune to break both his legs in childhood, as a result of which he was stunted in his growth. In 1882 he began to study art seriously in Paris, and by 1885 had a studio in Montmartre. He exhibited at the Salon des Indépendants from 1889 and with Les XX in Brussels, and in 1891 his first posters brought him immediate recognition. He made his first colour prints in 1892, and held a one-man show in Paris in the following year. In 1894 he went to Brussels, and in 1895 made his first of several visits to London, where he knew Oscar Wilde and Beardsley. He held a second exhibition in 1896, and visited Holland, Portugal, and Spain, but in 1898 his health began to suffer from drink. In 1899 he spent three months in a clinic recovering from an attack of DTs, and during his convalescence he worked on a series of drawings of the circus. After his recovery, he resumed his old life, but in 1901 he broke down completely and was taken to his mother's country house, where he died.

His first teacher had encouraged him to paint animals, particularly horses; after he began studying in Paris he met Émile Bernard and van Gogh, and he was deeply influenced by the technique and subject matter of Degas, and by Japanese prints, the influence of which was all-pervasive in Impressionist circles. His subject matter was centred narrowly round the life he led: some portraits, many painted out-of-doors, scenes from dance-halls and cafés in Montmartre, such as the Moulin Rouge, or from Aristide Bruant's cabaret 'Le Mirliton', figures of actresses, female clowns, circus artists seen backstage, and a great number of nudes, either *à la* Degas – washing, dressing – or seen sitting around in brothels, waiting for customers. He loathed posed models; these naked women just walking or sitting about provided him with models in movement and under no restraint either in pose or behaviour, and to study them he lived for some time in *maisons closes*.

His technical range was very wide. He was a superb draughtsman with a gift for conveying rapid movement and the whole atmosphere of a scene with a few strokes. Most of his paintings are in spirit-thinned oil-paint on unprimed cardboard, using the neutral buff tone of the board as an element in the design. He executed a large number of posters in lithography, with masterly handling of highly simplified line, large areas of flat colour, and a unique concentration on the eye-catching quality of the design. He also made small lithographs, either for menu-heads, programmes, book-covers or the like, or as single prints or series from his usual subject-matter. Occasionally he used watercolour and pastel, and towards the end of his life his use of oil-paint tended to become heavier, more impasted, with more solidly painted backgrounds. He was not interested in light as were the Impressionists, but only in form and movement, and most of his works are devoid of chiaroscuro; for him, light illuminated, never enveloped. He subscribed to no theories, was a member of no artistic or aesthetic movement, and the works in which he records what he saw and understood contain no hint of comment – no pity, no sentiment, no blame, no innuendo.

There are works in most museums of modern art; Albi (his birthplace) has a notable collection, and the following may be particularly mentioned: London (Tate, Courtauld Inst.), Paris (Mus. de l'Impressionnisme), and Washington (NG).

TOUR, de la, *see* LATOUR.

TRAINI, Francesco, was first recorded in 1321. He was a Pisan painter much influenced by the Sienese LORENZETTI and by Giovanni PISANO's pulpit in Pisa Cathedral. He signed an altarpiece (Pisa Mus.) in 1345, and a *Glory of S. Thomas Aquinas* in Sta Caterina, Pisa, may be the picture referred to in a document of 1363. Much the most important work attributed to him is the *Triumph of Death*, a series of frescoes in the Campo Santo in Pisa. These were almost entirely destroyed in 1944, but the destruction of the top layer exposed the SINOPIE which have a strength of draughtsmanship reminiscent of Giotto. Some have now been reconstituted.

TRECENTO (Ital. three hundred). The 14th century, i.e. the thirteen hundreds.

TRIPTYCH. A tripartite POLYPTYCH. Usually the central panel is twice the width of the wings, so that they can be folded over it to protect it. A common form of triptych, as an object of private devotion, is to have a *Madonna* as the centre and one's patron Saints on the wings: the backs of the wings, which become visible when the triptych is shut, usually bear the owner's coat of arms.

TROMPE L'ŒIL (Fr. deceive the eye) *see* ILLUSIONISM.

TROOST, Cornelis (1697–1750), was the contemporary of Hogarth and is often called 'the Dutch Hogarth', but his work lacks the biting satire of the Englishman. Troost was born in Amsterdam and made his name with traditional group portraits, but soon evolved small conversation pieces very like Hogarth's. He also painted scenes from theatrical performances and vaguely moral genre scenes (the *Drink-*

ing Scenes in The Hague), and worked in pastel. There are examples in the Royal Collection and in Berlin and Dublin as well as in Holland.

TROY, Jean François de (1679–1752), was a French painter, first of classical subjects like LE MOYNE, then of *fêtes galantes* and hunting scenes, and of the elaborate breakfasts and picnics that accompanied them. He also designed two large series of Gobelins tapestries – the *History of Queen Esther* and *Jason and Medea* – and painted some religious subjects, such as Susanna, that afforded opportunities for the nude. He was the son of François de Troy (1645–1730), a Toulouse portrait painter who sent him to Italy at the age of 14. The influence of Venice was permanent. From 1738 to 1751 he was Director of the French Academy in Rome, and, when he was replaced, died of grief at the thought of leaving a young Roman woman with whom he had just fallen in love. His style incorporates the colour and realism of Rubens' hunts, Snyders' animals and still-life, with the pastoral quality of the best Watteau followers – i.e. he is a particularly good example of RUBÉNISME. There are pictures in Paris (Louvre, Carnavalet and S. Étienne du Mont), Toulouse, Versailles and other French provincial museums, Florence (Uffizi), Leningrad, London (NG, V & A, Wallace Coll.), New York (Met. Mus.), and Rotterdam.

TRUMBULL, John (1756–1843), was an American artist who fought in the War of Independence, after which (1780) he travelled to London and Paris and worked with WEST. He painted principally portraits and historical pictures of the War of Independence, well represented in American museums. His *Battle of Bunker's Hill, 1775*, was painted in London in the studio of the loyalist West; rather to his surprise no English engraver would reproduce it. His 'Autobiography' was published in 1841 (and again in 1953).

TURA, Cosmè (Cosimo) (before 1431–95), was the first great Ferrarese painter. He worked there from 1451 for the Este Court, but much of his production has been lost. The main influence on his style was MANTEGNA, and perhaps also Mantegna's own inspirer Donatello, and the wiry quality of the forms and the austerity of feeling persists in all the Ferrarese painters of the 15th century – Cossa, Costa, and above all Ercole ROBERTI. Curiously, the very different world of Piero della Francesca also plays a strong part in Tura's stylistic evolution, most probably through the frescoes, now lost, which Piero painted in Ferrara some time before 1450. His brittle and metallic sense of form hardly changed during his lifetime, but he was succeeded as Court Painter by Roberti in 1486 and died poor. There are works in Ajaccio, Bergamo, Berlin, Boston (Gardner), Caen, Cambridge (Fitzwm), Cambridge Mass. (Fogg), Ferrara (Pinacoteca and Cath.), Florence (Uffizi), London (NG), Milan (Brera, Poldi-Pezzoli), Modena, Nantes, New York (Met. Mus.), Paris (Louvre), Philadelphia (Johnson), San Diego Cal., Venice (Accad., Correr), Vienna, and Washington (NG).

TURNER, Joseph Mallord William (1775–1851), was the son of a barber and born in Maiden Lane, Covent Garden. His talent was precocious. He was admitted to the Royal Academy Schools in 1789 and first exhibited at the RA in 1791; throughout his life he was much indebted to the RA, which recognized his genius and supported him against many of the arbiters of taste. He became an ARA in 1799, RA in 1802 – at the age of 27 – Professor of Perspective in 1807, and Deputy President in 1845. His extremely good head for business caused him to be appointed to audit the finances for many years. In 1792 Turner made the first of the sketching tours that were to take up so much of his time for the next half-century. Soon after this, for three years in the mid 1790s he worked with GIRTIN at Dr MONRO's house, Girtin drawing the outlines and Turner washing in the effects. After the death of Girtin Turner is said to have remarked 'If Tom Girtin had lived I should have starved': apart from the element of exaggeration in this, it is probably true that, at this stage, Girtin was the leader and Turner imitated him so closely that it is not always possible to distinguish the watercolours of the one from those of the other. Up to c. 1796 Turner was exclusively a watercolourist, working in the topographical tradition, but in 1796 or 1797 he exhibited his first oil-paintings at the RA; the two which he showed in 1797 being markedly influenced by Dutch 17th-century marine painting (the *Millbank, moonlight*, now in the Tate Gall., is close to the moonlight scenes of A. van der Neer). This influence was almost immediately succeeded by that of Wilson and Claude, and, early in the 1800s, he was composing in a grand manner learned ultimately from Claude. In 1802, with scores of other artists, he went to see the pictures looted by Napoleon which were then exhibited in the Louvre, and there he particularly admired Poussin. His next major work, however, was the *Calais Pier* of 1803 (now in the NG), which is very unlike Poussin, is thoroughly Romantic, and was generally condemned as unfinished. For many years after this Turner was bitterly attacked, principally by Sir George Beaumont, the artistic dictator of the day, and warmly defended, by Sir Thomas LAWRENCE among others. These attacks led to a decline in sales in his larger oil-paintings (*Crossing the Brook*, 1815: London, NG, is a case in point) and in 1816 his landscapes were actually called 'pictures of nothing, and very like'. Turner himself, in one of his few recorded epigrams, is said to have remarked of painting in general that it was 'a rum thing', but between 1806 and 1819 he did take steps to defend himself by publishing a series of engravings of different kinds of landscape under the title 'Liber Studiorum' (*see* LIBER VERITATIS). The series was not successful, principally because Turner was always very close with his money and underpaid the engravers. In 1819, encouraged by Lawrence, he made his first visit to Italy and from then on his oil-paintings tend more and more to the pale brilliance of colour which he had already achieved in watercolour and he begins to think in terms of coloured light, or, in Constable's phrase, 'tinted steam'. He returned to Italy in 1828 and to Venice in 1835 and again in 1840, the late Venetian watercolours and gouaches being among the most magical effects of light even in his work. By this time he was rather out of favour and public interest was turning to the detailed approach that culminated in the Pre-Raphaelites, when, rather to his surprise, Ruskin came to his defence with the first volume of 'Modern Painters' in 1843 (the full title is: 'Modern Painters: their superiority in the art of landscape painting to all the ancient masters proved by examples of the True, the Beautiful, and the Intellectual, from the works of modern artists, especially from those of J. M. W. Turner, Esq., RA'). By his will Turner left nearly 300 paintings and nearly 20,000 watercolours and drawings to the nation: his conditions have been scandalously disregarded but the principal collections remain those in London (NG, Tate Gall., and BM), with others in the V & A, Nat. Marit. Mus., and Kenwood, and in Auckland NZ, Boston (Mus.), Cambridge (Fitzwm), Cambridge Mass. (Fogg Mus.), Cardiff, Chicago, Cleveland Ohio, Dublin, Dunedin, Edinburgh (NG), Hartford Conn. (Wadsworth Atheneum), Indianapolis (Herron), Manchester (City Art Gall., and Whitworth), Melbourne, New York (Met. Mus., Frick Coll.), Ohio, Ottawa (NG), Oxford, Philadelphia, Sheffield, Washington (NG, Corcoran), and elsewhere.

U

UCCELLO, Paolo (1396/7–1475), is celebrated in the early sources as a master of perspective; indeed, the invention of it is sometimes wrongly credited to him. What is clear is that he became absorbed in the study of perspective (and, still more, foreshortening) and that it modified his style in his middle years, but he never used it for the naturalist purposes envisaged by MASACCIO and others. Uccello is first recorded as a *garzone* in 1407, in the shop where GHIBERTI'S First Baptistry Doors were being made, and this semi-Gothic style was to remain the foundation of his own. In 1415 he entered the Painters' Guild, but nothing is known of any paintings by him for about another 15 years. In 1425 he went to Venice and worked on mosaics in S. Mark's for about 5 years. He was certainly in Florence again in 1431, but he had been out of the city during the years when Masaccio created the new, naturalistic style which was later to influence him in a rather superficial way. In 1436 he was commissioned by the city to paint the fresco in imitation of an equestrian statue to the English mercenary soldier Sir John Hawkwood, known in Italy as Giovanni Acuto. This fresco is still in the Cathedral of Florence, but it was repainted by Uccello himself, since the first version failed to please. In it we see for the first time the intensive study of the new science of foreshortening, since the intention is to deceive the eye into thinking that the painted statue is a real one: in fact, Uccello never really carried out the full implications of a perspective setting, since the plinth and the effigy are seen from two disparate viewpoints, and this inconsistency is usual in all his works. He was able to make another experiment in foreshortening in the *Four Prophets* (1443) round the clockface in the Cathedral, and between 1443 and 1445 he designed stained-glass windows for it. About 1445 he went to Padua, and the *Giants* he painted there are supposed to have influenced MANTEGNA, but they are now lost. On his return, *c.*1445, he painted his most famous work, the *Deluge* in the Chiostro Verde of Sta Maria Novella, Florence, where he had already painted some Creation scenes (from *c.*1431). The *Deluge* (recently restored, previously almost lost) shows the impact of the new ideas on perspective at their most powerful, and it is often related to the treatise on painting by the humanist Alberti ('Della Pittura', 1435), where a system of perspective construction is explained and several subjects are suggested which are to be found in the *Deluge*. Similar ideas on foreshortening may be found in the three *Battles* (1454/7: Florence (Uffizi), London (NG), and Paris (Louvre)), which he painted for the Medici, but here the decorative aspect is far more important and in all his later works the decorative side of his early training comes back strongly. His last documented work is the *predella* for an altarpiece, commissioned by an Urbino Confraternity of the Holy Sacrament (1465–9: Urbino), *see* JOOS van Gent: a *Hunt* (Oxford, Ashmolean) which is equally decorative in character and fairy-tale in atmosphere is probably of the same date. In 1469, in filling in his tax return he said: 'I am old, infirm, and unemployed, and my wife is ill.'

Other works are in Chambéry, Dublin, Florence (S. Martino alla Scala), Paris (Louvre, Jacquemart-André), and Washington (NG).

UGOLINO da Siena (active 1317–27) was a close follower of DUCCIO. He painted the High Altar of Sta Croce, Florence, now dispersed: parts of it are in London (NG) and Berlin and Philadelphia (Johnson). Other pictures attributed to him are in Birmingham (Barber Inst.), Cleveland Ohio, London (Courtauld Inst.), St Louis, Siena, Washington, and Williamstown Mass.

'UGOLINO-LORENZETTI'. An invented name for an unknown artist midway between the styles of UGOLINO da Siena and the LORENZETTI. Also known as the Ovile Master, he has been tentatively identified with Bartolommeo Bulgarini, who is known to have been a painter.

UNDERPAINTING is the preliminary lay-in, usually in GRISAILLE, in which the drawing, composition, and tone values of a picture are worked out. It may sometimes include an indication of colour, but the purpose of underpainting is to get the design and tonal values established before tackling the colouristic problems, particularly if many GLAZES are envisaged. The underpainting of a specific area can mean, in a narrower sense, the preparation for a glaze – e.g. a solid yellow which is to be glazed with red and purple to get a richer effect of shot colours and in shadows.

UTRECHT SCHOOL. This is a fairly precisely defined moment in Dutch painting, early in the 17th century, when the influence of CARAVAGGIO made its impact on a whole circle of Utrecht painters, of whom the most important were BABUREN, HONTHORST, and TERBRUGGHEN. All three were in Rome in the period 1610/20, at the moment immediately after Caravaggio's death when his influence was at its highest and was then being exploited by MANFREDI. All three returned to Utrecht by the 1620s. They painted religious pictures – Utrecht is a Catholic centre – and also genre scenes of the Five Senses and brothel pictures, unlike Caravaggio's work (but like Manfredi's), though stemming from his relentless realism. Towards the end of the 1620s the effect began to wear off and Terbrugghen in particular began to lighten his palette (e.g. *Jacob and Laban*, 1627: London, NG) and to study light effects in a totally un-Caravaggesque way. Bylert, Bor, and Stomer were more or less influenced by Utrecht ideas, although Bylert changed his style and Stomer remained in Italy. The spread of Caravaggism through the Utrecht School was such that even Hals, Vermeer, and Rembrandt were affected by it.

UTRILLO, Maurice (1883-1955), was the son of Suzanne Valadon, herself a talented painter who was encouraged by Renoir, Degas, and Toulouse-Lautrec, for whom she posed as a model. He early developed into a confirmed drunkard and drug addict, spent many years in clinics and sanatoria, and his drinking bouts often ended in the police station. His mother made him learn to paint as a distraction and a form of therapy. His art shows nothing of this wild and melodramatic background. His paintings are almost all town views, often painted from picture-postcards; they show a sensitive understanding of tone, and are delicate and almost monochromatic in colour, with precise drawing and a strange feeling for the atmosphere of a particular street or building. His best works were produced between 1908 and 1916: success made him repeat himself. Most museums of modern art have an example.

UYTEWAEL *see* WTEWAEL.

V

VALDÉS LEAL, Juan de (1622–90), was a painter active in Seville where he helped to found the Academy in 1660. He was President 1663–6, but his difficult temperament made it impossible for him to get on with his fellow-artists. His style is dramatic and emotional to the point of morbidity and is seen at its best in VANITAS subjects such as the *Triumph of Death* and the *Sic Transit Gloria Mundi*, with their decomposing corpses. There are works by him in Cordova and Seville, and in Barnard Castle (Bowes Mus.), Dresden, Dublin, Grenoble, Hartford Conn., Kansas City, London (NG), Madrid (Prado), New York (Hispanic Soc.), Paris (Louvre), Washington (NG), and York.

VALENTIN, Le (Moïse Valentin, Valentin de Boullogne) (*c.* 1591 or 1594–1632), was a French painter, born at Coulommiers, but was perhaps the son of an Italian (neither his Christian name Moïse nor the de Boullogne seems to be correct); certainly he was, like Finsonius, more of an Italian than a Northern painter. He was in Rome perhaps as early as 1612/13, certainly by 1614, and was there strongly influenced by VOUET, whose pupil he may have been, and perhaps even more by MANFREDI and the Caravaggio influence he represents. Valentin became a friend of Poussin and his only documented work, the *Martyrdom of SS. Processus and Martinian* (1629/30: Vatican), was a pendant to Poussin's *S. Erasmus* in St Peter's. There are pictures attributed to him in Besançon, Cambridge (Fitzwm), Cologne, Dresden, Gateshead, London (NG), Munich, Paris (Louvre), Poughkeepsie NY (Vassar College), Rome (Gall. Naz.), Toulouse, Valletta Malta, Versailles, and Vienna.

VALUES (Fr. *valeurs*) are the gradations of tone from light to dark observable in any solid object under the play of light. Tone values are independent of local colour and are best perceived by half-closing the eyes so that colour effects are diminished (a photograph is an example of pure tonal effect). Since it is impossible to match the range from light to dark in nature with pigments ranging only from white to black, the greatest skill is necessary to determine where the transitional tones shall be modified, suppressed, or exaggerated so as to maintain pictorial unity. The problem is complicated by Colour Values, when the relative importance to the composition as a whole of each patch of colour has to be determined simultaneously with its tonal value, one often interacting on the other. 'Keeping' is an old-fashioned word, frequent in 18th-century criticism, signifying success in this operation.

VANDYKE *see* DYCK.

VANISHING POINT *see* PERSPECTIVE.

VANITAS *see* STILL-LIFE.

VAN LOO *see* LOO.

VANSOMER *see* SOMER.

VARIANT. Generally used to mean a version of a picture which has slight differences, perhaps intended by the artist. The assumption is that a variant is at least from the studio of the painter of the prime original, but it is often a convenient euphemism for a copy.

VARLEY, John (1778–1842), was an English watercolour painter of the transitional period between the topographical drawing and the painting in watercolours. He was helped at the beginning of his career by Dr MONRO, and in his turn helped and taught many other artists: he was also a close friend of Blake. He seems to have been very credulous and he wrote on astrology, in which he firmly believed. There are works in London (BM, Tate, and V & A). His brothers Cornelius (1781–1873) and William (*c.*1785–1856) were also painters and are represented in the V & A.

VASARI, Giorgio (1511–74), was born in Arezzo and trained in Florence, in the circle of Andrea del Sarto and his pupils Rosso and Pontormo, where, above all, he became a Michelangelo idolater. He spent his busy and productive life as a painter between Florence and Rome, but he was really a superb impresario rather than a painter himself, and perhaps because of his gifts in this direction his work as an architect ranks much higher than his painting. His principal paintings are in Florence (Pal. Vecchio frescoes and in galleries) and Rome (Sala Regia in the Vatican, and the so-called 100 days fresco in the Cancelleria), as well as in his own house in Arezzo, which is now a museum. Above all, however, his fame rests solidly on his book, 'Le Vite de' più eccellenti Architetti, Pittori, et Scultori Italiani ...', first published in 1550 and issued in a second, much enlarged, edition in 1568. This 1568 edition has been translated into most languages and is perhaps the most important book on the history of art ever written, both as a source-book and as an example for all the later Italian historiographers. By comparison the 1550 edition is little-known, but the differences between it and the second edition are not all in the latter's favour; in the first edition the plan is much clearer, for in it Vasari's intention is plain – to show how the arts died in the Dark Ages, after having been brought to a high pitch in Ancient Rome, and were then revived under Giotto the Tuscan, to progress in a steady rise in Tuscany, until the ultimate perfection was reached in his own day in the hands of the Tuscan Michelangelo. In the 1550 edition MICHELANGELO is the climax of the story and his is the only biography of a living artist. The later edition is less sure in design and includes a number of living artists, including Vasari's own autobiography.

VECCHIETTA (1412–80) was a Sienese sculptor who also worked as a painter and architect. He was a pupil of SASSETTA and the teacher of MATTEO di Giovanni. His style is expressive, naturalistic, and linear, with strong Florentine influences. His works are mostly in Siena, but there are others in Florence (Uffizi), Liverpool, New York (Frick), Paris (Louvre, Cluny Mus.), Pienza (Cath.), and Rome (S.M. del Popolo).

VEDUTA (Ital. view). A painting or drawing of a place, usually a town e.g. Venice or Rome. The accuracy of the delineation varies greatly: a *veduta ideata* is an imaginary view, while a CAPRICCIO is often architecturally accurate but fantastic in its juxtapositions. PANINI and PIRANESI, CANALETTO and GUARDI are the best-known *vedutisti*, but the genre was probably invented by Northern artists working in Italy, e.g. BRIL. *See also* BERCKHEYDE.
working in Italy, e.g. BRILL.

VEHICLE is synonymous with MEDIUM, as something to bind pigment or to thin stiff paint.

VELAZQUEZ, Diego Rodriguez de Silva (1599–1660), was born in Seville but was of Portuguese origin. Any training he may have had before entering PACHECO's Academy in Seville in 1613 may be disregarded; in 1617 he became an independent master and in 1618 married Pacheco's daughter. He worked in Seville until 1622 and his early paintings show his interest in the naturalistic representation of things seen in strong light. In 1622 he visited Madrid, and in 1623 returned there to become Court Painter. He was a slow worker, with a deliberate technique without bravura, and sober colour rather low in tone, and he used a plain background for many of his portraits so that the figure stands out as a silhouette. His court appointment gave him few opportunities for religious painting, mythologies were rare in Spain, and only occasionally did he execute subject pictures, except during his Italian journeys. He was little influenced by other artists, though he profited from the Titians in the Spanish Royal Collection and the visit of Rubens in 1628, which was his first contact with a great living painter, who was also a Court Painter, though one with an entirely different vision, temperament, and artistic education. Whether or not it was Rubens who inspired him to visit Italy, it was due to Rubens's influence that he obtained permission to go. He left in August 1629, visited Genoa, Venice, Rome, and Naples (where he met Ribera) and returned to Madrid in 1631. The *Topers* ('*Los Borrachos*'; in the Spanish Royal Collection by July 1629), with its character heads and still-life detail, suggests the influence of RIBERA's realism, and the subject pictures painted in Italy (*Joseph's coat brought to Jacob*, Escorial, and the *Forge of Vulcan*, Prado) show his preoccupation with the male nude and his fuller range of colour. The main effect of his Italian journey was to increase his breadth of vision, but without affecting its fundamentally realistic basis.

The surrender of Breda – an incident in the Dutch Wars of

Independence – took place in 1625. In 1634, Velazquez recorded the moment when the Marchese Spinola (whom he had known in Italy in 1629) received the surrender from Justin of Nassau, as one of a series of victory pictures (others were by Maino and Zurbarán) intended to accompany his equestrian portraits of Philip, his Queen, and his heir, Don Balthasar Carlos. Velazquez's composition may owe something to Tempesta's engravings after van Veen in the 'Bataviorum cum Romanis Bellum' of Tacitus, published in Antwerp in 1612, but his brilliant colour, panoramic landscape background and heightened realism transcend any derivation. Portraits painted after his return possibly owe their more brilliant colour to their being the record of the only joyous years in the King's dreary reign – the portrait of the King called *The Fraga Philip* (1644: Frick Collection, New York) has a richness reminiscent of Rubens.

In 1648 Velazquez accompanied the Embassy travelling to Italy to escort the new Queen, Marianna of Austria. He again visited Genoa, Venice, Rome, and Naples, and returned to Madrid in June 1651. His object had been to buy pictures for the Royal Collection, and he also executed several works during his stay: the portrait of Pope Innocent X (Doria Coll., Rome), and his only female nude, the so-called *Rokeby Venus* (London, NG), were the most outstanding. The finest of the portraits painted after the second Italian journey is that of the little Infanta Margareta Teresa with her retinue of ladies and dwarfs, called *Las Meninas* (1656: Prado), and in this work he reaches perhaps his highest point in the blending of realism with atmosphere and a deeply sensitive appreciation of character. During the 1630s and 1640s he had painted a series of portraits of the court dwarfs, playmates of the Royal children, for they interested him as character studies much as old age, wrinkles, and rags interested him in his imaginary portraits of *Aesop* and *Menippus* (both in the Prado), and as did, too, the ageing face of his sick and gloomy King, whom he painted all through his long reign, and who acknowledged the greatness of his painter by making him a Knight of the Order of Santiago in 1658. His chief assistant was his son-in-law MAZO, but he was far from his equal, and after Velazquez's death his position was held by a succession of dim foreigners, mostly French, until, late in the 18th century, Mengs and Tiepolo were followed by Goya.

There are unrivalled collections in Spain – in the Prado in Madrid and in the Escorial – but most major galleries have an example including Berlin, Boston (Mus. and Gardner Mus.), Budapest, Chicago, Cincinnati, Detroit, Dresden, Florence (Pitti), Kansas City, London (NG, Wallace Coll., Wellington Mus.), Montreal, New York (Met. Mus., Hispanic Soc., Frick Coll.), Paris (Louvre), Rouen, São Paulo, San Diego Cal., Toledo Ohio, Vienna, and Washington (NG).

VELDE, Adriaen van de (1636–72), was the son of Willem I van de

Velde, the brother of Willem II, and probably the nephew of Esaias. He was trained under his father and under WYNANTS and POTTER. It is doubtful whether he ever went to Italy, but he uses Italian motives and landscapes (e.g. in the Wallace Coll. *Jacob and Laban*); he also painted a few religious subjects without landscape (e.g. the *Annunciation* in Amsterdam), but most of his works are pastoral landscapes with figures or simply the figures in the landscapes of other painters. He painted figures for his elder brother Willem II, for his master Wynants, and for Ruisdael, Hobbema, and others, especially van der Heyden. This last died in 1712, yet nearly all his works are described as having Adriaen's figures, although dated pictures painted after Adriaen's early death prove that van der Heyden was quite capable of adding his own figures. There are pictures in the Royal Coll. and in Amsterdam, Antwerp, Berlin, Boston, Cambridge (Fitzwm), Dresden, Florence (Uffizi), Frankfurt, Glasgow, The Hague, Leipzig, London (NG, Wallace Coll., Dulwich), Munich, New York (Hist. Soc.), Paris (Petit Pal.), Philadelphia, Rotterdam, Vienna, and Washington.

VELDE, Esaias van de (*c.*1591–1630), was a painter of genre and battle pictures, but is best known for his realistic landscapes which presage those of his great pupil Jan van GOYEN. He worked in Haarlem 1610–18 and then in The Hague, where he was Court Painter to the Princes Maurits and Frederik Hendrik, until his death. There are pictures in Amsterdam (Rijksmus.), Berlin, The Hague, Leipzig, London (NG), Munich, Rotterdam, Stockholm, and elsewhere.

VELDE, Willem I van de (1611–93), and his son Willem II (1633–1707), both arrived in London in 1672 and remained there as official marine artists. It is extremely difficult to separate the works of the two, and a document of 1674 which provides for regular payment to the father for drawing sea-fights and to his son for colouring them suggests that they worked together. There are, however, some elaborate grisaille drawings on a large scale that are certainly the elder man's work, while there are over 600 pictures of marine subjects attributed to the younger, who is generally recognized as the greatest marine painter of the Dutch School as well as the father of all English marine painting. Most of their records of sea-fights were done from drawings made under fire from a small boat in the thick of the action: there is a very large and important collection of these in the Nat. Marit. Mus., London, which also has paintings. Other paintings are in the Royal Coll. and in Amsterdam (Rijksmus.), and London (NG, Wallace Coll., Kenwood, and Ham House).

VENEZIANO, Domenico, *see* DOMENICO.

VERMEER, Jan (1632–75), of Delft, was the most calm and peaceful of all the Dutch masters and the recognition of his greatness has been long delayed. Very little is known of his life and his pictures were completely forgotten until the mid 19th century. He was certainly influenced by Carel FABRITIUS, and may have been his pupil before becoming a Master himself in the Delft Guild in 1653. He married in the same year, was Dean of the Guild in 1663 and 1670 and died in 1675, leaving a widow and eleven children and an enormous debt to the baker, who held two pictures of his. In 1676 his widow tried to get them back, offering to pay off the debt over twelve years. Later that year she was declared bankrupt. It is certain that she and the children were Catholics, and this may explain the relative obscurity in which Vermeer lived. He was obviously a very slow worker, for only about 40 pictures are generally accepted as his and most of them are quite small. They usually represent domestic interiors with one or two figures writing, doing housework, or playing musical instruments; in reproduction they look exactly like works by Maes or Pieter de Hooch, but in the originals the splendour of the colour and the play of light, falling in little pearls of paint on everything in the picture, transform the everyday scenes into poetry totally unlike the sober prose of the average Dutch master. His best-known work, the *View of Delft* (The Hague), is slightly different in character, resembling the town-views of van der HEYDEN, and there are also some pictures, such as the *Allegory of Faith* (New York, Met. Mus.) or the *Allegory of Painting* (Vienna, K-H Mus.), which represents the painter in his studio, that go beyond the domestic interior. These form a link with a small group of totally different scenes. One, the *Procuress* (Dresden), is signed and dated 1656. Recently a painting signed and dated 1655 (the earliest recorded) has been discovered: it represents the unusual subject of *S. Praxedis mopping up the blood of the Martyrs* (New York, private coll.). These are clearly early works and show a link– though not a very strong one – with the UTRECHT School, as does the *Christ in the House of Martha and Mary* (Edinburgh, NG), presumably also early. The fourth and most puzzling is the *Diana and her Companions* (The Hague, Mauritshius) which is unlike all his other works and has, accordingly, been attributed to another Vermeer, an Utrecht painter (*c*.1630–88) who had been in Italy. (The signature on it, partially visible in 1895, is now almost illegible.) There are pictures by him in the Royal Coll., and in Amsterdam (Rijksmus.), Berlin, Boston (Gardner), Brunswick, Dresden, Edinburgh, Frankfurt (Städel), The Hague, London (NG, Kenwood), New York (Met. Mus., Frick Coll.), Paris (Louvre), Vienna (K-H Mus.), and Washington (NG).

Yet another Vermeer was Jan II (son of Jan I and father of Jan III), a Haarlem landscape painter (1628–91), whose works are very like those of J. van Ruisdael or P. Koninck: examples are in The Hague and Rotterdam, as well as Oxford (Ch. Ch.), and Paris (Louvre).

VERMEYEN, Jan Cornelisz. (*c*.1500–59), was a Dutch painter and tapestry designer who was probably a pupil of MABUSE. About 1525 he became Court Painter to Margaret of Austria, Regent of the Netherlands, at Malines and in 1535 he accompanied the Emperor Charles V to Tunis. This journey supplied him with scenes for later works, including tapestries designed 1545/8 for the Regent, Mary of Hungary. At present many portraits are ascribed to him on very little evidence, as an alternative to SCOREL, HEEMSKERCK, or LUCAS van Leyden. There are pictures in Amsterdam, Brussels, Florence, Haarlem, New York, Vienna (tapestry designs), and (as Style of 'Vermeyen') London, and elsewhere.

VERNET. A family of French painters of whom the best known were: Claude Joseph (1714–89) who painted landscapes in a sub-Claude manner and worked for many years in Italy, where he was a friend of Wilson. He was commissioned by Louis XV to paint the *Ports of France*, of which he executed 16. He also painted dramatic shipwrecks of a highly romantic and rather theatrical kind. His father and three brothers were also painters. Carle, son of Joseph (1758–1836), specialized in horses, racing, and battle scenes, the latter principally for Napoleon. Horace, son of Carle (1789–1863), also painted horses and battle scenes, as popular and facile as his father's. He remained an ardent Bonapartist, and his chief work was the huge Gallery of Battles at Versailles, painted for Louis Philippe. His sister married the costume-history painter Paul Delaroche.

VERONA, Stefano da, *see* STEFANO.

VERONESE, Bonifazio, *see* BONIFAZIO.

VERONESE, Paolo (*c.*1528–88), was born in Verona and trained under several minor artists. The chief influence on him was Titian although such diverse artists as Michelangelo, Giulio Romano, and Parmigianino all contributed to his formation. He worked in Venice, probably from 1553 onwards, when he began his ceilings for the Doge's Palace, with daring SOTTO IN SÙ perspective and Mannerist nude figures in complicated poses filling up the picture space. He is thought to have gone to Rome for the first time in 1560, and it was probably after this that he painted the frescoes in the Villa Maser (near Treviso), with their brilliant mixture of illusionism with Palladio's simple architecture. They are also important in the history of Venetian landscape painting.

He specialized mainly in huge pictures of Biblical, allegorical, or historical subjects which permitted of the introduction of vast crowds of accessory figures, filling the scene with light and colour, with splendid golden-haired women dressed in the height of fashion, with horses, dogs, apes, courtiers, musicians, soldiers, and magnificent buildings, but devoid of religious or dramatic content. His gorgeous pageantry is redolent of the magnificence and richness of 16th-century Venice; but the licence he took with sacred subjects (e.g. the *Feast in the House of Levi*, Venice, Accad.) got him into trouble with the Inquisition, which in 1573 called him to account for the profane incidents – dogs, German soldiers, and such things – introduced into a religious picture. It seems to have been a *Last Supper*, but, because of the objections of the tribunal, it was re-named. The concept of decorum is fundamental to all Counter-Reformation art, and may be summed up in the exchange between Veronese and the Inquisitor:

Veronese: I paint my pictures with such judgement as I have and as seems fitting.

Inquisitor: And does it seem fitting to represent the Last Supper with buffoons, drunkards, German soldiers, dwarfs, and similar scurrilities?

His repudiation of any impropriety and his claim to an absolute right of pictorial licence has remained one of the classic defences of the artist against the Philistine (even though the Inquisitor seems to have out-argued him). Most of his works are in Venice, but other examples are in the Royal Coll. and Amsterdam, Baltimore (Mus. and Walters Gall.), Berlin, Boston (Mus. and Gardner Mus.), Brussels, Budapest, Caen, Cambridge (Fitzwm), Cambridge Mass. (Fogg Mus.), Chicago, Cleveland Ohio, Detroit, Dresden, Dublin, Edinburgh, the Escorial, Florence (Pitti and Uffizi), Greenville SC, Hartford Conn., Kansas City, Leningrad, London (NG, Courtauld Inst., Dulwich, Westminster Hospital), Madrid, Melbourne, Milan (Brera), Modena, Munich, New York (Met. Mus. and Frick Coll.), Ottawa, Oxford (Ashmolean, Ch. Ch.), Padua, Paris (Louvre), Philadelphia, Prague, Rome (Borghese, Capitoline), San Francisco, St Louis, Sarasota Fla (Ringling), Toledo Ohio, Verona, Vicenza, Vienna, Washington (NG), and elsewhere.

VERRIO, Antonio (1639–1707), was a Neapolitan painter who was an Agréé of the French Academy in 1671, and probably came to England in the next year. From about 1675 to 1684 he worked at Windsor and Whitehall (though little survives), and succeeded Lely as Court Painter in 1684. After 1688 he worked chiefly at Chatsworth and Burghley, but from 1699 he was employed extensively at Hampton Court and Windsor by Queen Anne. His decorations are gaudy and banal; they represent the tail end of a Baroque tradition sufficiently novel in England to impress through pretentiousness, and blatant enough to dazzle eyes ignorant of the real thing. His greatest immortality is in Pope's 'On painted ceilings you devoutly stare, Where sprawl the saints of Verrio and LAGUERRE'.

VERROCCHIO, Andrea del (*c.*1435–88), was a Florentine painter, goldsmith, and sculptor. He was perhaps a pupil of Donatello, after whose death he ranked as the principal sculptor in the city. He executed many works for the Medici. His style as a sculptor is clearly established and is markedly different from that of Donatello, for

Verrocchio is intent upon lightness, grace, and elegance of pose and highly finished craftsmanship, completely missing the tragic power of Donatello. The *David* (before 1476: Florence, Bargello), if compared with Donatello's bronze *David*, shows this difference; even more is it visible in Verrocchio's last work, the equestrian monument to Bartolommeo Colleone in Venice (commissioned *c.* 1479, completed after Verrocchio's death), where all his effort has been directed to the rendering of movement and of a sense of strain and energy. The Donatello monument to Gattamelata in Padua was obviously the model he sought to surpass, but he misses the air of calm command. Verrocchio ran a large and prosperous shop, accepting orders for paintings as well as sculpture and goldsmith's work. In later years his principal assistant in painting was Lorenzo di CREDI, but he was also the master (and probably employer) of LEONARDO da Vinci, who is supposed to have painted an angel in the *Baptism* (Florence, Uffizi). There are works by him, in painting or sculpture, in Berlin, Budapest, Florence (Bargello, Cathedral Mus., Orsanmichele, S. Lorenzo, and the Pal. della Signoria), London (NG, V & A), New York (Met. Mus.), Paris (Louvre), Pistoia (Cath.), Sheffield (Ruskin Mus.), Toledo Ohio, and Washington (NG).

VERTUE, George (1684–1756), was an engraver and antiquary who is now remembered as the father of English art history. His voluminous, ill-written, and rambling notes on the arts in England, especially on his immediate predecessors and his contemporaries, are our principal source and have now been published *in extenso*. They were originally bought by Horace Walpole, and, reduced to order, served as the basis of his 'Anecdotes of Painting in England' (1762–71).

VESPERBILD *see* PIETÀ.

VIEIRA da Silva, Maria Elena (*b.* 1908), was born in Lisbon, but has become French and lives in Paris. From 1927, she studied sculpture with Bourdelle and Despiau, print-making with Hayter, and painting with Léger and Friesz. From Expressionist beginnings, she developed, during the 1930s, into an abstract painter, creating elaborate expanding linear patterns which seem to be based on intricate town plans or the intersecting wires of a suspension bridge.

VIEN, Joseph (1716–1809), was a French painter who was in Rome 1743–50; he probably knew the young MENGS at that time, when all Rome was excited by the antique Roman paintings newly discovered in Herculaneum and Pompeii, and by Greek classical architecture at Paestum. This revival of interest in the antique made him the more receptive to Winckelmann's Neoclassicist ideas on their publication in 1755 and 1764, an influence reinforced by his long and close association with the amateur archaeologist, the Comte de Caylus. His cold, prim, classical genre subjects depict Greek maidens of whom Diderot remarked that they induced 'no desire to be their lover, only their father or brother', yet he achieved enormous prestige, and was the chief teacher of the period; his most celebrated pupil was DAVID.

VIGÉE-LEBRUN, Louise Élisabeth (1755–1842), one of the most successful of all women painters, was the daughter of a pastellist named Vigée and married the dealer Lebrun. She was trained by her father and influenced by GREUZE, and got her great chance when she was summoned to Versailles in 1779 to paint Marie Antoinette. She became her friend as well as Painter to the Queen, was elected to the Academy in 1783, and kept a famous Salon. She was in fact a charming woman. She left France in 1789, at the outbreak of the Revolution, and went to Italy, Vienna, Prague, Dresden, and was in Russia 1795–1800 before returning to Berlin and, in 1802, to Paris. She had received permission to return but disliked society under Napoleon and left at once for England, where she stayed until 1805, before going to Switzerland and so back to France. In all these countries she had great success as a portraitist, excelling in portraits of women and children. She wrote her Memoirs, which give a picture of the times as well as an account of her works (they were first published in 1835–7: two English translations exist). Her portraits may be found in most of the places she worked in and there are other examples in London (Wallace Coll. and NG) and in New York (Met. Mus.), and Toledo Ohio.

VILLON, Jacques (1875–1963). His full name was Gaston Duchamp-Villon, and he was the brother of Marcel DUCHAMP and Raymond DUCHAMP-VILLON. He went to Paris in 1895 and became a friend of Toulouse-Lautrec, making satirical drawings for illustrated papers (later he earned his living as an engraver). He became a Cubist in 1911 and in 1912 organized the Section d'Or exhibition (see GOLDEN SECTION) with GLEIZES, METZINGER, LÉGER, and La Fresnaye. He visited the US in 1935 and began gradually to make a name, but in 1940, when he fled to the Tarn in southern France, he began painting landscapes which, though abstract, have a feeling for locality. Big exhibitions in 1951 and 1961 in Paris established his reputation. There are works in Paris (Mus. d'Art Moderne).

VILLON, Raymond Duchamp-, see DUCHAMP-VILLON.

VINCI, Leonardo da, see LEONARDO.

VINGT, Les, were 20 painters, including ENSOR, who formed an exhibiting society in Brussels in 1884 which lasted for ten years and showed non-Belgian artists such as Seurat (1887, *Grande Jatte*), Gauguin (1889), Cézanne, and van Gogh (1890), but rejected Ensor in 1889.

VISCHER. A Nuremberg family of bronzeworkers and sculptors, the most celebrated of whom, Peter I and II, were Dürer's contemporaries. The family workshop was started by Hermann (d. 1488), who was the father of Peter I (c. 1460–1529). Peter was trained by his father and became a Master in 1489, after which he travelled to Heidelberg and Cracow, but not to Italy, although the influence of Renaissance ideas can be seen in his work, though far less powerfully than in Dürer. The real problem concerns the exact shares of the various members of the family in their masterpiece, the Shrine of S. Sebaldus in Nuremberg. The first design (now in Vienna, Akad.) is signed by Peter I and dated 1488, but the actual work was begun, on a new design, in 1508, worked on for four years and then completed 1514–19. After 1512, Peter I was working on a Tomb at Innsbruck for the Emperor Maximilian, and it is likely that his sons, Hermann and Peter II, took an increasing share of the Sebaldus Shrine, especially in the second phase: nevertheless, the *Apostles* may be by him. The most important of his sons was Peter II (1487–1528), who may have visited Italy and who did the statuettes on the Sebaldus Shrine.

VITTORIA, Alessandro (1525–1608), was the pupil of Jacopo SANSOVINO and the most important sculptor in Venice in the late 16th century. He arrived in 1543 and was at first influenced by AMMANATI, but later, after 1560, more directly by Michelangelo. He did a great deal of decorative work in the Doge's Palace after the 1577 fire and there are religious works in Sta Maria de' Frari and other Venetian churches, but he is best known for his portrait busts, many in Venetian galleries. Other works are in Berlin, Chicago, London (V & A), New York (Met. Mus.), Rotterdam, Vienna, and Washington (NG). With his friends Titian and Tintoretto, and with the great architect Palladio, Vittoria was one of the leading artists of the Venetian Renaissance. The Villa Maser, near Treviso, is a splendid example of collaboration between Palladio, Veronese and Vittoria.

VIVARINI. A family of Venetian painters, consisting of Antonio (active 1440?–d. 1476/84), his brother Bartolommeo (active 1450–99), and Antonio's son Alvise (alive in 1457–d. 1503/5). Antonio was the partner of his brother-in-law, Giovanni d'Alemagna, whose name may imply that he was a German. Antonio signed a picture in 1440 (Parenzo, now Poreč) by himself, but he seems to have worked with Giovanni until 1450 (when Giovanni probably died), and then he went into partnership with his brother Bartolommeo. The pictures produced by both partnerships were influenced first by Gentile da Fabriano and then by Mantegna and Giovanni Bellini – i.e. the successive leaders of Venetian painting. There is a picture signed by Antonio alone and dated 1464 in the Vatican; one signed by Bartolommeo and dated 1459 in Paris, Louvre, as well as others up to 1491: it is doubtful whether it is worth the trouble to distinguish further. Alvise was the son of Antonio but perhaps the pupil of Bartolommeo: the important influences on him were ANTONELLO da Messina and Giovanni BELLINI. He was alive in 1457, but the earliest signed and dated work is of 1475; from 1488 he was employed by the State, and an altarpiece in Sta Maria de'Frari, Venice, was completed after his death by another Bellinesque, Marco Basaiti. There are examples of one or more of the family in London (NG, Courtauld Inst.), New York (Met. Mus.), Washington (NG), and Yale, as well as in the Accademia and the churches of Venice.

VIVIN, Louis (1861–1936), was a French modern primitive who worked in the Post Office, 1879–1922, and first exhibited at the Post Office Art Club in 1889. He was – like Séraphine – discovered by the German critic Uhde in 1925. His works consist largely of naïvely realist townscapes, and often seem to be inspired by picture-postcard views. There are works in Paris (Mus. d'Art Moderne).

VLAMINCK, Maurice (1876–1958), was one of the FAUVE group, and shared a studio with Derain. He wrote, played the violin, was a racing cyclist, and loved speed, crowds, and popular amusements. He admired van Gogh in 1901, Negro sculpture about 1904, Cézanne in 1907, and denounced CUBISM as over-intellectual and sterile. He painted chiefly landscapes of stormy weather, where the feeling is Expressionist and the dark shadows, strong light effects, and wild skies are rendered in a technique whose slashing brush-stroke and heavy impasto are largely derived from Courbet – an artist whom he resembled in some ways. Most museums of modern art have examples.

VLIEGER, Simon de (c. 1600–53), was one of the leading Dutch marine painters of the first half of the 17th century. He was a pupil of W. van de VELDE the Elder and the teacher of W. van de VELDE the Younger, and he also exerted a great influence on CAPPELLE who owned 1300 drawings and nine paintings by him. His principal paintings are of the sea and are representative of the period of Dutch marine painting which concentrated on the rendering of light effects in subdued local colours. He also made twenty etchings of landscapes and animals. He painted a great many pictures, and most museums have examples.

VORTICISM. A variety of CUBISM, exclusive to England, invented by Wyndham LEWIS.

VOS, Cornelis de (1584–1651), was an Antwerp portrait painter who occasionally worked for Rubens; some of his portraits have been mistaken for those of Rubens or van Dyck. He also painted large historical and allegorical works. There are examples in Antwerp, Berlin, Brussels, London (Wallace Coll.), Madrid, Munich, Philadelphia (Mus.), San Francisco (Legion of Honor), Vienna, York, and elsewhere.

His brother Paul (1596–1678) was a painter of lively hunting scenes and large still-life subjects with dead game, fruit, and live birds and animals. Their sister married SNYDERS, with whose art Paul's has much in common, and they were close friends of van Dyck.

Vos, Marten de (1531/2–1603), was an Antwerp painter of the last generation of Italianizers (*see* SPRANGER). He spent six years in Italy, in Rome and then in Venice, where he is said to have worked as a landscape assistant to Tintoretto. He brought the Venetian style back to Antwerp, where he returned in 1558, and there painted many altarpieces (especially after the destruction caused in the Spanish Fury of 1576) as well as some portraits. There are works in Amsterdam, Antwerp, Berlin, Brussels, Florence (Uffizi), The Hague, Paris (Louvre), Rouen, Stockholm, and Vienna.

Vouet, Simon (1590–1649), was in Italy between 1613 and 1627, when he returned to France to enjoy a successful career as a painter of large decorations and smaller, highly decorative religious and allegorical works. He derived from his years in Rome, and his visits to Venice, Naples, Genoa, and elsewhere, a form of temperate and classicized Baroque which he infused into French painting, and he also adapted to his own uses the cool colour of CHAMPAIGNE, the classical composition of POUSSIN, and the richness of Venetian handling. Poussin's return to Paris in 1640 put him on his mettle (particularly in view of Louis XIII's malicious remark which Poussin records with disingenuous satisfaction, and which may be freely translated as 'Here's one in the eye for Vouet'), but after 1642 his position remained unchallenged, except by LEBRUN.

There are works in the Royal Collection and Berlin, Brussels, Cambridge (Fitzwm), Chatsworth, Dresden, Florence (Uffizi), Fontainebleau, Genoa, Glasgow, Hartford Conn., Leningrad, London (NG), Madrid, Naples, Ottawa, Oxford, Paris (Louvre and many churches), Rome (S. Francesco a Ripa, S. Lorenzo in Lucina ,Corsini), Rouen, Sarasota Fla, Versailles, Washington (NG), and many French provincial museums.

Vries, Adriaen de (*c.*1560–1626), was one of the leading Late Mannerist sculptors whose career well exemplifies the internationalism of the period: he was born in The Hague, trained in Italy and worked mainly in Prague. He was trained as a bronzeworker under Giovanni BOLOGNA (a Fleming in spite of his name) and, from 1593, he worked for the Emperor Rudolf II in Prague, but he also made two Fountains in Augsburg (*Mercury*, completed 1599, and *Hercules*, 1602) and works for Bückeburg and Stadthagen. There are also examples in Edinburgh, London (V & A), Paris (Louvre), Stockholm, and Vienna.

Vuillard, Édouard (1868–1940), was an Intimist painter and decorator whose career closely paralleled that of his friend BONNARD. There are pictures by him in Boston, Bristol, Cleveland Ohio, Glasgow, London (Tate and Courtauld Inst.), Manchester (Whitworth), New

York (M of MA), Paris (Mus. d'Art Moderne and Petit Pal.), Toronto, and Washington (Phillips), and decorations in Paris (Comédie des Champs-Élysées, Palais de Chaillot) and Geneva (League of Nations).

W

WALDMÜLLER, Ferdinand Georg (1793–1865), was the leading Austrian artist of the early 19th century, painting BIEDERMEIER portraits and landscapes, which later approached the *plein-air* works of the BARBIZON group. He was trained at the Vienna Academy, and from 1829 was a professor there, but he was bitterly opposed to the teaching methods of his colleagues and wrote many pamphlets on the subject. For a time he was put on half-pay. He visited Italy in 1829 (the first of many visits), Paris in 1830, and in 1856 he started out for Philadelphia, but stopped in London, where, through the intervention of the British Ambassador in Vienna, he succeeded in selling 31 pictures to Queen Victoria, Prince Albert, and the Court. The best collection of his works is in Vienna (Oesterreichische Gal.), but many other Austrian and German galleries have examples; the pictures sold in London seem to have disappeared.

WALKER, Robert (c. 1605/10–56/8), is chiefly known for his portraits of Cromwell and his circle. The usual way of putting it is that DOBSON painted the Royalists and Walker the Parliamentarians. There are works in Leeds (Temple Newsam, a *Cromwell*), London (NPG), Oxford (Ashmolean), and elsewhere.

WALL-PAINTING, or mural, is a term used to describe any kind of wall decoration: it is not interchangeable with FRESCO.

WANDERJAHRE (Ger. wander years). In the North of Europe it was common for a young artist to complete his apprenticeship in his home town and then to spend several years as a JOURNEYMAN, wandering from one famous master's shop to another and working for a while in each until he returned home, submitted his masterpiece (in the literal sense) to his GUILD, married, and settled down. 'The Cloister and the Hearth' gives a picture of this life and Dürer's career affords another.

WARD, James (1769–1859), was a British landscape and animal painter whose early work was influenced by that of his brother-in-law George MORLAND. In 1803 his style was much affected by Rubens's *Château de Steen* (London, NG). His best work is the vast *Gordale Scar, Yorkshire*, which is one of many works by him in the Tate Gallery, London.

WARM COLOUR, TONE. Those colours and tones which are red, orange, or purplish in general effect. Not necessarily HOT, but the opposite of COLD.

WATERCOLOUR. The technique of painting with colour ground up with water-soluble gums (Gum Arabic, etc.). When moistened with plain water a transparent stain is obtained which is then applied in washes to white or tinted paper. The classical English method – and pure watercolour is almost an English monopoly – is to use the white paper as the highest lights and to apply transparent washes one over another to obtain gradations of colour and of tone: to the purists of this school the use of any form of BODY COLOUR is Frenchified and anathema. Nevertheless, the four greatest practitioners – J. R. COZENS, GIRTIN, COTMAN, and TURNER – all used procedures which vary from the norm defined above. The watercolours of Cozens are perhaps nearest to this norm, but he retained the monochromatic underpainting used by the earliest exponents as a legacy from oil technique. Turner not only used body colour freely, but also wiped partially dry colour with rags and sponges and scratched the surface of the paper with a knife to get extra lights: this last practice is now regarded with peculiar horror.

WATTEAU, (Jean) Antoine (1684–1721), was born in Valenciennes, a Flemish town which had recently become French. To a contemporary Watteau was *Vato, peintre flamand*, and this Flemish background probably explains his admiration for (and obscure affinity with) Rubens, whose healthy vitality expressed everything Watteau could only envy. He went to Paris *c.*1702 and worked as a hack painter before going to Gillot, a painter of theatrical scenes, in 1704/5. By then he had probably already contracted tuberculosis and was already exhibiting the symptoms of chronic restlessness which dominated the rest of his short life. By 1707/8 he had moved on to the decorative painter Claude Audran, who, as Keeper of the Luxembourg Palace, was able to give him access to the great Rubens cycle of the *Life of Marie de' Medici*: this was the main influence in the formation of his style, and the drawings he then made were used over and over again. In 1709 he revisited Valenciennes and painted a few military scenes in a Flemish manner, but on his return to Paris he was able to study the great Venetians, especially Veronese, and he then merged all these influences into a completely personal form of RUBÉNISME. In 1712 he was made an Agréé of the Academy and he should then have submitted a Diploma Work, but he delayed this until 1717 when he presented the *Embarkation for the Island of Cythera* (now in the Louvre: a later version in Berlin) and was received as a painter of *fêtes galantes*, the first to be so described. The difficulty felt by the Academy in classifying him is understandable, for, like Giorgione's, his pictures have a mood for a subject, a fleeting and melancholy sense of the transitoriness of all pleasure and all life. In 1719–20 Watteau was in London, perhaps to seek medical advice, but a London winter completed the ruin of his constitution and he returned to Paris to die. One of the last pictures he painted, the *Halt in the Chase* (London, Wallace Coll.), is in the same style as his previous works but the shop-sign he painted in 1720–1 for his friend the dealer

Gersaint (known as the *Enseigne de Gersaint*, now in Berlin) shows a new stylistic trend. The sign is bigger than his usual small size, and it represents the interior of Gersaint's shop, full of customers and assistants, with a greater degree of realism than was usual with Watteau. The new style was in fact a return to Flemish naturalism, owing much to Teniers (who had also influenced his early military scenes), but his death prevented any further development along these lines. His theatrical subjects are far less realistic, although they derive from the painstaking representations of Gillot. They usually show figures from the Italian or French Comedy in more or less melancholy and reflective attitudes. All Watteau's pictures – except the *Enseigne* – were composed by taking the required number of figures from the big bound volumes in which he kept hundreds of his superb drawings. Studies of figures, heads, hands, draperies were made in three-colour crayon – black, red, and white for the highlights – and were then used when needed. Many hundreds of these still exist, usually in better condition than most of his paintings, which have suffered badly from his atrocious technique. Because the same drawing may have been used over and over again all his pictures have a strong likeness, increasing the sense of half-attained intimacy. LANCRET and PATER were his principal imitators, but neither was gifted with his exquisite sensibility and his tender amorousness coarsens under their hands. There are several pictures by Watteau in the Wallace Coll., and others in Berlin, Birmingham (University, Barber Inst.), Boston, Chantilly, Cleveland Ohio, Dresden, Edinburgh (NG), Glasgow, Hartford Conn., Leningrad, London (NG, Soane Mus., and Dulwich Coll.), Madrid, New York (Met. Mus.), Paris (Louvre), Stockholm, Toledo Ohio, Troyes, Waddesdon, Bucks. (National Trust), and Washington (NG).

His nephew and great-nephew, Louis Joseph (1731–98) and François Louis Joseph (1758–1823), were both known as 'Watteau de Lille'. Louis was born in Valenciennes but went to Lille in 1755 and taught drawing from the nude there: this caused such scandal that he had to resign and did not return until 1775. He did not always imitate his uncle's works, often painting histories or religious pictures. His son worked in a style closer to his great-uncle's, and, like him, was influenced by Teniers. Lille has examples of both men.

WATTS, George Frederic (1817–1904), first exhibited, with success, at the RA in 1837, and in 1843 won a £300 prize in one of the competitions for the decoration of the Houses of Parliament. He left at once for Florence, where he stayed until 1847, leading the sheltered life of a tame genius in the household of the British Minister at the Tuscan Court, Lord Holland. In 1847 he again won a prize in a Houses of Parliament competition, this time for £500, and he started to paint large allegorical pictures while earning his living as a portraitist. His portraits of beauties and celebrities make a real attempt at more than a successful superficial likeness; in his series of famous men he strove to portray the whole man – character, personality, and appearance – and for this reason would only paint men he could like or admire. His decorations are either frankly decorative stories, such as his *Tales from Boccaccio* (1843–4: Tate), with areas of crude, warring colour, applied flatly within a strongly marked contour, or huge turgid allegories, expressing in trite, rather literary symbolism such moral imponderables as *Mammon, Progress, Destiny, Chaos, Love and Death*. The best known of these is probably *Hope*, which, it has been objected, could as easily portray *Despair*. He attempted to revive fresco painting, of which he had no proper knowledge, and in his allegories often used appalling technical methods which have resulted in considerable deterioration. He also executed some large pieces of sculpture; the best known are the *Physical Energy* in Kensington Gardens, and the huge *Tennyson* monument at Lincoln. He became an RA in 1867, twice refused a baronetcy, but accepted the Order of Merit in 1902. Watts was one of the last grand allegorical history painters in the Haydon tradition of 'High Art': a type of picture based on high-minded generalities or abstractions, expressed with idealized forms, and a striving for sublime feeling that results in a numbing divorce from reality, physical and intellectual.

There are examples in the Royal Collection, Bristol, Compton nr Guildford (Watts Museum in his former house), Dublin (Municipal Gall.), Edinburgh (NG), Leicester, Liverpool (Walker), London (Tate, NPG, V & A, Leighton House), Manchester, Munich, New York (Met. Mus.), Northampton, Ottawa, and elsewhere. A large mural, *Justice*, is in the New Hall, Lincoln's Inn (1853–9).

WEENIX, Jan (1640–1719), was the son of Jan Baptist Weenix, and was his father's pupil with his cousin Hondecoeter. He never visited Italy, but he painted Italianate scenes like his father's and pursued more single-mindedly the still-life with flowers, animals, and dead game subjects which he also took over from his father. He worked mainly in Amsterdam, but also at Bensberg and Düsseldorf for the Elector Palatine, for whom he executed a huge series of still-lifes (1702–16). There are works in Amsterdam (Rijksmus.), Augsburg, Cape Town, Dresden, The Hague, London (NG, Wallace Coll., Dulwich), Munich, Oxford, Toronto, and elsewhere.

WEENIX, Jan Baptist (1621–before Nov. 1663), was a pupil of BLOE-MAERT who was in Italy 1642–6 and returned, calling himself 'Giovanni Battista', to Holland to paint Italianate landscapes with ruins of ancient buildings and figures in modern dress, very reminiscent of the work of BERCHEM. Later in life he changed his style entirely and painted still-life and some portraits, his very detailed style being continued by his son Jan. There are typical works in

Amsterdam, Antwerp, Berlin, Dresden, Glasgow, Hartford Conn., London (NG, Wallace Coll., Kenwood), New York (Met. Mus.), Paris (Louvre), Rotterdam, Utrecht (including a *Descartes*), and Vienna.

WEEPERS. Small mourning figures on a tomb.

WEICHER STIL *see* SOFT STYLE.

WEST, Benjamin (1738–1820), came of Pennsylvania Quaker stock, and learned to paint in America. In 1760 he went to Italy, and spent three years in Rome, Florence, Bologna, and Venice. He enjoyed the prestige of novelty – American painters were unknown and the blind Cardinal Albani asked if he were not a Red Indian? He was much influenced by the Neoclassical style of MENGS and Gavin Hamilton, and evolved, partly through them and partly because of his lack of academic training, history pictures on a smallish scale (what Haydon dubbed 'Poussin size'). He set up as a portrait painter in London in 1763, working in a style close to Mengs, was a Founder-Member of the RA, and in 1769 began his long, and highly profitable, association with George III. His *Death of Wolfe* (RA 1771: Ottawa and many versions) marked a turning point in the painting of modern history pieces in England, since West, whose picture is, in fact, historically inaccurate, imposed a classical composition on figures in contemporary dress. He carried the idea further in his pictures of medieval history subjects, and established a fashion not only popular in England but widely imitated in France. Such was his prestige and his favour with George III that he succeeded Reynolds as President of the RA in 1792, but refused a knighthood because of his Quaker principles.

There are works in the Royal Collection, Leeds, London (Tate, V & A, Foundling Hospital, Nat. Marit. Mus.), and a great number of American Museums.

WESTMACOTT, Sir Richard (1775–1856), was the son of a sculptor, whose pupil he was before he went to Rome, where he worked under CANOVA. He was in Italy from 1793 to 1797, and on his way home was robbed and wounded by bandits. He enjoyed a large and successful practice in London, working for Queen Charlotte and at Brighton Pavilion for the Prince Regent, executing panels for the Marble Arch, the *Achilles* in Hyde Park as a memorial to Wellington, and the pediment of the British Museum. He became an RA in 1811, succeeded Flaxman as professor of sculpture at the RA Schools, and was knighted in 1837. He made a number of tombs in Westminster Abbey, including those of Fox (1810: Canova praised the negro highly) and Pitt the Elder, and in countless parish churches all over England.

WEYDEN, Roger van der, or Rogier de le Pasture (1399/1400–64), was the major artist of the mid 15th century in Flanders. He was almost certainly a pupil of Robert CAMPIN in Tournai, 1427–32, at the same time as DARET. Like Daret, he seems to have been older than most apprentices, since there is a record in 1426 of the Town Council of Tournai making a gift of wine to 'Master Roger'. One possible explanation for the fact that both he and Daret seemed to have started their apprenticeships at a much later age than usual may be found in the conservative and strict rules of the Tournai Guild. It is known that in 1432, immediately after he became a Master in the Guild, Daret was made Provost so it is possible that both men were apprenticed only in a technical sense. Nevertheless, the identification of Campin with the MASTER OF FLÉMALLE is fundamentally due to the close stylistic similarity between the work of Flémalle and the one documented altarpiece by Daret. This has led some scholars to assume that the stylistic similarity between the work of Flémalle and the work of Roger is to be explained by the fact that both men were one and the same person. More common, however, is the view that Roger's early work resembles the Flémalle group for the same reason as Daret's does – namely, that Roger and Daret were both Campin's pupils.

The problem would be greatly simplified if we had any real knowledge of Roger's early style, but in fact there are no works by him which are certainly documented. What is generally considered to be his masterpiece is the *Deposition* (Madrid, Prado) which is one of the great masterpieces of northern 15th-century painting. It is quite unlike the work of Jan van EYCK and has a depth of religious feeling, expressed in linear terms, quite different from the dispassionate realism of Jan: Roger's more emotional style was far more influential in Flanders and in Germany in the second half of the 15th century. Nevertheless, the *Deposition* is believed to be Roger's solely on the strength of a 16th-century attribution, and its date is put at about 1435 on rather slender evidence. There are, however, a few pictures generally attributed to him – the *Braque Triptych* in Paris, the Bladelin altarpiece in Berlin, the *Last Judgement* in the Hospice at Beaune in Burgundy – which can be given approximate dates in the 1440s and 1450s. The general feeling of this group of works is far more refined and sensitive than that associated with the realistic but rather plebeian style of Campin/Flémalle, so that there seems little reason to try to fuse the two groups of works. Equally, Roger's works are more concerned with human emotion than those of Jan van Eyck, which tend to concentrate on naturalistic detail in the creation of a miniature world. Roger's colour sense is also highly personal, with a tendency towards the use of gold and pale, bright colours which, in the 15th century, may already have seemed slightly old-fashioned.

Roger married a Brussels woman *c.*1426, and after completing his apprenticeship with Campin, settled in Brussels. He became, before

1436, the City Painter, and achieved a great reputation and a solid fortune. In 1450, the year of the Jubilee, he probably visited Rome and also Florence, since the *Entombment* (Uffizi), once in the Medici Collection, has strong affinities not only with Italian art generally but with Fra Angelico specifically, and the *Madonna with four Saints* (Frankfurt, Städel) not only bears the arms of Florence and contains the Medici patron saints, Cosmas and Damian, and SS. John Baptist and Peter, name saints of Cosimo's two sons, but also reflects in its composition the Italian SACRA CONVERSAZIONE type of Domenico Veneziano's S. Lucy Altar. Roger never held a Court appointment, as Jan did, but he nevertheless worked for many members of the Burgundian Court, such as Chancellor Rolin, for whose foundation, the Hospice de Beaune, he painted the *Last Judgement*, c. 1446 (still there); Peter Bladelin, Duke Philip's controller of finances and founder of Middelburg, for whose church the triptych of the *Nativity* (c. 1452: Berlin) was painted; Jean Chevrot, Bishop of Tournai (the *Seven Sacraments*, Antwerp, c. 1453). He also painted superb and sensitive portraits, such as *Charles the Bold* (Berlin), *Le Grand Bâtard* of Burgundy (Brussels), *Francisque d'Este* (New York, Met. Mus.). He appears to have invented the type of diptych with a Madonna and Child on one wing facing a praying portrait on the other, and though none survives intact, the *Philippe de Croy* (Antwerp) and *Madonna* (San Marino Cal., Huntington) and *Laurent Froiment* (Brussels) and *Madonna* (Caen) may be cited. This type of diptych became very popular and perhaps the best complete example is that by his pupil MEMLINC of Martin Nieuwenhove, while many were executed in the BOUTS workshop. His most closely datable work is the unusual *Braque Triptych* (c. 1452: Louvre), which displays all his characteristics of colour, feeling, and technique.

Other works are in Berlin, Boston, Brussels, Chicago, Detroit, Granada (Capilla Real), London (NG, and two silverpoint drawings in the BM), Paris (Louvre), Philadelphia (Johnson), Washington (NG), and elsewhere.

WHEATLEY, Francis (1747–1801), may have been a pupil of Zoffany, and began as a painter of small portraits and conversation pieces. From 1779–83/4 he worked in Dublin, and after his return to London gave up his small group portraits in favour of adaptations to the English taste of Greuze's type of genre subject, with overtones of the picturesque and deserving poor. His *Mr Howard relieving prisoners* (1787) and his celebrated *Cries of London*, engraved in 1795, are instances of this skilful blend of moral feeling and popular sentiment, and also show his clear, rather pale colour and his free, sensitive handling.

WHISTLER, James Abbott McNeill (1834–1903), was born in Lowell, Mass., and attended West Point Military Academy, 1851–4. Failing there, he worked as a Navy cartographer, which at least taught him the technique of etching, before going to Paris to study painting in 1855. There he met Fantin-Latour and Degas and was influenced by COURBET, as may be seen in *Au piano*, rejected by the Salon in 1859 and exhibited privately by Whistler, following Courbet's example. In 1859 he moved to London, but he continued to visit Paris frequently as well as going – for no known reason – to Valparaiso in 1866. In 1876/7 he had a quarrel (in which he was entirely in the wrong) over the decoration of the 'Peacock Room' in a London house (now in Washington, Freer Gallery) and in 1877 Ruskin wrote of his *Nocturne in Black and Gold* (now in Detroit) as 'flinging a pot of paint in the public's face'. Whistler sued him and won, in 1878, damages of a farthing but his own costs ruined him and he went to Venice in 1879 and 1880 to make a series of etchings, for his mastery of etching was never disputed even by bitter critics of his paintings and he hoped to recoup himself in this way. He lived as a dandy and had a deserved reputation as a mordant wit, well able to keep up with his friend Oscar Wilde: after one sally Wilde is supposed to have said admiringly 'I wish I had said that'. Whistler replied 'You will, Oscar, you will!'

The early influence of Fantin-Latour and Courbet was succeeded to some extent by that of Manet, who was one of Whistler's fellow-exhibitors in the Salon des Refusés of 1863, but an even more marked influence in the 1860s was that of Japanese art, then finding its way to Europe and being discovered by the more advanced Parisians. Strangely, there is also some influence discernible from English academic painters like Albert Moore, particularly in the colour 'arrangements' which are really studies in the juxtaposition of closely related tones and colours. Whistler liked to emphasize the aesthetic nature of his pictures in conscious reaction against the dominance of the subject in Victorian times, hence his choice of titles like *Symphony* or *Nocturne*. The best collections of his work are in Washington (Freer Gall.) and Glasgow University; other pictures are in Glasgow (Gall.), London (Tate), Ottawa, Paris (Louvre), and several American museums. His etchings are well represented in the Royal Coll., and London (BM and V & A).

WILHELM, Master (active 1358–*d*.72/8), was a Cologne painter by whom no works are known but who has been built up into a legendary figure to whom even LOCHNER's *Dombild* has been ascribed. He may have been identical with a painter named Wilhelm von Herle, but the legend was begun in the German Romantic era, and, though now dead in Germany, is still active in British and American auction rooms and elsewhere.

WILIGELMO was the sculptor responsible for most of the decoration of Modena Cathedral, in a very classical style, between *c*.1099 and *c.*1106. Similar sculpture at Cremona Cathedral is strongly influenced by his work but is probably not actually his. Wiligelmo's low-relief style is characterized by stocky, expressive figures of great narrative force.

WILKIE, Sir David (1785–1841), was the son of the minister of Cults, Fifeshire, and studied in Edinburgh. His first important work, painted when he was nineteen, was *Pitlessie Fair* (1804: Edinburgh NG) which is an accomplished essay in the manner of Teniers. In 1805 he entered the RA Schools in London and exhibited his *Village Politicians* in the RA of 1806. This made his name and led to his treating similar subjects in the style of Ostade or Teniers for some 20 years. He was elected ARA in 1809, RA in 1811, succeeded Lawrence as Painter to the King in 1830, and was knighted in 1836. He was a friend of HAYDON – although he had the sense not to attempt Haydon's High Art – and they went to Paris together in 1814 to see the pictures looted by Napoleon. Because of ill-health he spent 1825–8 in Italy, Austria, Germany, and Spain, and his new experience of Italian and Spanish art led to a great style change; Velazquez and Murillo being the principal influences on the new, broader manner and change of subject-matter, which included several histories. In 1840 he went to the Near East and died at sea on the way home: his burial at sea is the subject of an imaginative composition by Turner. There are examples in the Royal Coll. and in Cupar (Fife) Town Hall, Edinburgh (NG, NPG), London (Tate, Wallace Coll., Wellington Mus.), Munich, New York (Met. Mus.), Riga, and elsewhere.

WILSON, Benjamin (1721–88), was an English portrait painter, whose chief claim to fame lies in the easy confusion of his name with Richard Wilson's. Zoffany may have worked for him until *c.*1762, perhaps on theatrical scenes. From about 1770 Wilson seems to have devoted himself principally to science. There are examples in Leeds, London (NPG and Dulwich Coll.), and Manchester.

WILSON, Richard (1713 (or 14)–82), was the son of a Welsh clergyman who gave him a good classical education. This was probably decisive in his approach to landscape painting, which, for Wilson, has the classic overtones of the Italy of Claude and Gaspar Poussin. These two, with Cuyp, were acknowledged by Wilson as his inspiration. He came to London in the 1740s and soon built up a practice as a portrait painter (there are portraits by him in London (NPG, Tate Gall. (*Zuccarelli*, 1751), and Nat. Marit. Mus.) and in Edinburgh), but he was certainly painting landscapes by 1746, when he painted two for the Foundling Hosptial which are still there. The real turning-point in his career was his Italian period, when he decided to devote himself exclusively to landscape; a decision which may have been influenced by ZUCCARELLI and C.-J. VERNET. He was in Venice in 1750 and spent most of his Italian years in Rome and the Campagna, which left its mark on him as on so many other landscapists from Claude and Gaspar Poussin onwards. He returned to England, probably in 1757, and continued to paint Italian landscapes, which, considering their classicism of subject as well as of handling, should have been much more popular among the Grand Tourists than they were. The remainder of his output consisted of views in England and Wales treated in a markedly Italian and classical way (so much so, that it is not always possible to be sure what the scene represented is), and of commissioned views of country houses. His *Niobe* was exhibited at the Society of Artists in 1760 and during the 1760s he seems to have painted a series of Grand Manner mythologies, perhaps as an equivalent to the Grand Manner portrait then being introduced by Reynolds, whose success was in marked contrast to Wilson's neglect. He was one of the Founder-Members of the Royal Academy in 1768 and was appointed Librarian in 1776, when he had almost ceased to paint and was in need. At his best, in such designs as the *Snowdon* (Liverpool and Nottingham), Wilson achieved a pure classicism which depends on the austere beauty of the design and informs it with a glow of light learned from the Dutch as well as from Claude. These designs are of such nobility that they can stand numerous repetitions, which they often received, and their poetry is indeed Roman in inspiration: there could hardly be a greater contrast to the naturalness of Constable. Wilson's pictures often exist in many versions, so that most English galleries have at least one. The largest collection is in Cardiff (Nat. Mus. of Wales), and there are others in Adelaide, Auckland NZ, Baltimore, Berlin, Boston, Buffalo, Cambridge Mass. (Harvard Univ.), Chicago, Detroit, Dublin, Dunedin, Edinburgh (NG and NPG), Glasgow, Hanover, London (NG, NPG, Tate Gall., V & A, Royal Academy, Nat. Marit. Mus., Dulwich Coll., and Foundling Hosp.), Manchester, Melbourne, Minneapolis, Montreal, New York (Met. Mus.), Ottawa, Philadelphia, San Marino Cal., Stockholm, Vancouver, Washington (Nat. Coll.), and Worcester Mass.

WILTON, Joseph (1722–1803), was the son of a prosperous maker of ornamental plasterwork and *papier-mâché*, which enabled him to study under DELVAUX in Flanders and PIGALLE in Paris. In 1747 he went to Italy, working in Rome (where he met ROUBILIAC in 1752) and Florence until 1755. His *Dr Cocchi* (1755: London, V & A) is a very early example of the Neoclassical type of bust, with neither wig nor drapery, in the ancient Roman manner, but Wilton never developed these new ideas. He returned to London with Chambers the architect in 1755 and soon had a considerable practice, in which he was helped by Chambers, who often employed him to carve the ornamental detail and chimney pieces in his buildings (notably at Somerset House). Wilton was a Founder-

Member of the RA. He retired in 1786, and was appointed Keeper of the RA in 1790, having dissipated the large fortune inherited from his father, and that won by his own work. There are several tombs by him in Westminster Abbey (including General Wolfe's), and works in Edinburgh (NPG), London (V & A), and New York (Hist. Soc.).

WINCKELMANN, Johann Joachim (1717–68), was the first of the great German art historians and one of the founders of NEOCLASSICISM. He published his 'Gedanken über die Nachahmung der griechischen Werke . . .' ('On the Imitation of Greek Works . . .') in 1755, and later that year he moved from Dresden to Rome. The 'Gedanken' contains the phrase which sums up all his teachings about Greek art (which he scarcely knew from the originals, most of them being still undiscovered): *edle Einfalt und stille Grösse*, noble simplicity and calm grandeur. In 1764 he published his very influential history of ancient art, soon translated into French and English, and in 1768 he was murdered in Trieste for some medals he carried. His theories profoundly influenced many artists, but the one closest to him was MENGS.

WINT, Peter De, *see* DE WINT.

WITTE, Emanuel de (probably 1616/8–92), was a Dutch painter of church and house interiors and market scenes. His interiors usually stress shafts of light falling on pillars, tombs, or parquetry floors, and his open-air scenes have still-life detail in the foreground, as in his various fish-market pictures. He entered the Guild at Delft in 1636 (apparently aged 19), moved *c*.1650 to Amsterdam, and, by 1655, to Haarlem where he married his second wife. Despite the beauty of his interiors they brought him little success, while his second wife caused him great trouble – she and their daughter were convicted of theft – and he ended his own life. There are works in Amsterdam (Rijksmus.), Berlin, Brussels, Cape Town, Edinburgh, The Hague, Hartford Conn., London (NG, Wallace Coll.), Rotterdam, Toledo Ohio, and elsewhere.

WITZ, Konrad (1400/10–44/6), was the greatest Swiss painter before Holbein. He entered the Basle Guild in 1434, but he came from Germany and may have been attracted to Basle by the Church Council which convened there in 1431. About 1435 he probably began his major work, the large altarpiece of the Redemption (*Heilspiegelaltar*), parts of which have survived. His only signed and dated work is the *Christ walking on the Water* (1444: Geneva), which contains one of the earliest certainly datable views in modern art. The landscape is recognizably that of a particular point on the Lake of Geneva, not just a Swiss scene. His extremely realist style shows that he must have been in contact with his immediate predecessors in Flanders, Jan van Eyck and the Master of Flémalle, and with them he substituted a strongly realistic style for the Soft Style hitherto practised in Germany. His few known works are in Basle (Mus. and Mus. of History), Berlin, Dijon, Geneva, Naples, Nuremberg, and Strasbourg.

WOLGEMUT, Michael (1434–1519), a Nuremberg painter and designer of woodcut book-illustrations, was the master of Dürer. He probably went to Flanders *c*.1450, as the influence of BOUTS and Roger van der WEYDEN seems to have come to Nuremberg through him. Only two paintings can be given to him: the altarpiece in Zwickau (1476–9) and the one in Schwabach (1506–8), but the central panel of a triptych in Brighton is signed MW, and he also designed the woodcuts for two of the most famous 15th-century books, the 'Schatzbehalter' of 1491 and Schedel's 'Weltchronik' (1491–3).

WOLS (i.e. Alfred Otto Wolfgang Schulze) (1913–51) was born in Berlin and studied at the Bauhaus under MOHOLY-NAGY before going to Paris in 1933. He made a living as a photographer until he was interned in 1939, when he began to paint. He lived in desperate poverty in the South of France, 1940–5, and began to paint in oils only in 1946. His spiky abstractions are Tachiste in style.

WOODCUT (Wood Engraving) *see* ENGRAVING.

WOOTTON, John (*d*.1756), was one of the earliest English exponents of landscape in the style of Claude and Gaspar, and introduced this form into England after his visit to Italy during the 1720s. He combined his landscapes – which are often very large – with horse portraits, hunting scenes, and sporting conversation pieces, and occasionally even portrayed battles. There is a fine and representative hunt picture in London (Tate), a *Battle of Dettingen* in the National Army Mus., and a landscape in Manchester.

WORKSHOP PRODUCTION or a 'Shop Work' are descriptions of works of art which are produced by relatively unskilled or insensitive assistants from drawings or cartoons by a major artist, and more or less under his supervision. There are, for example, two *tondi* of the *Madonna and Child*, one in the NG, London, and one in the Chigi Coll., Rome, which are painted from the same cartoon by Botticelli – but which nevertheless betray the hands of two men, neither of whom was Botticelli.

WOTRUBA, Fritz (*b*.1907), is a Viennese sculptor whose work is based on the human figure, but treated in an abstract way. He usually employs coarse stone and works direct, but some of his work is in lead or bronze. He emigrated to Switzerland, 1939–45, but now teaches at the Vienna Academy. There are works by him in London (Tate), Vienna (City and State Galleries), Winterthur, and Zürich.

WOUWERMAN, Philips (1619–68), was a Haarlem painter who was a pupil of Hals but who painted genre scenes of horsemen, battles, and camp life much more akin to BAMBOCCIATE. He frequently disposed dozens, even hundreds, of small figures in his canvases and he had a special fondness for white horses. He often painted figures in the landscapes of other painters – e.g. Wynants, Ruisdael. There are about 1,200 pictures recorded, some of the largest collections being in Dresden, Leningrad, London (NG and Dulwich), and Vienna. His brothers Jan (1629–66) and Pieter (1623–82) were also landscape painters.

WRIGHT, John Michael (?1617–1700). Wright, whose first name is uncertain, was born in London but apprenticed to JAMESONE in Edinburgh in 1636 and seems to have gone to Italy by 1647: in 1648 he became a member of the Roman Academy of S. Luke, the only British member in the 17th century. In Rome he became an antiquarian and later worked as such for that great patron of the arts, the Archduke Leopold Wilhelm, Governor of the Netherlands. It is clear that he was a Catholic, yet he returned to Commonwealth England in 1656/8 and painted many portraits in a Dobsonesque manner, the most important being a series (of which only two survive) for the City of London; of which Evelyn observed in 1673 that 'Most of them are very like the persons they represent, though I never took Wright to be any considerable artist' and Pepys had earlier (1662) compared him with Lely, remarking 'Lord! the difference': Wright was, nevertheless, Painter to Charles II. He returned to Rome with an Embassy to the Pope in 1686, while Kneller built up his practice in London, and Wright died apparently in poverty. There are pictures by him in the Royal Coll., and in Aberdeen (University), Edinburgh (NPG), London (Tate, NPG, Guildhall, and Ham House), Manchester, Nottingham (part of the ceiling of Charles II's bedroom, from Whitehall Palace), and Oxford (Magdalen College).

WRIGHT, Joseph (1734–97), usually called Wright of Derby, was a pupil of HUDSON. He established himself at Derby where, except for a visit to Liverpool in 1769, he remained until he travelled in Italy in 1773–5. All his life he specialized in lighting effects and his candlelight pictures show affinities with those of Honthorst and others of the Utrecht School, and his moonlit landscapes recall Aert van der Neer as well as his contemporary Vernet. In Derby he found admirers among the pioneers of science allied to industry: Wedgwood and Arkwright were his patrons, and among his completely new subjects were representations of experiments made by candlelight, such as the *Orrery* (1766: Derby) and the *Experiment with an Air Pump* (1768: London, Tate).

In Italy he was not interested in the grandest art, but was deeply impressed by a fireworks display at Castel S. Angelo and an eruption of Vesuvius, both of which he painted on his return. He also evolved moonlit landscapes, first of Vesuvius, then of the Derbyshire countryside, his main interest being as much in the quality of the light as in the picturesque effect. He tried to replace Gainsborough at Bath in

1775, but in 1777 returned to Derby where he had a prosperous portrait connexion and opportunities for painting landscapes and subject pictures which eventually decline into sentimental genre. His best portraits were painted in the early 1780s, and *Sir Brooke Boothby* (1781: London, NG), lying reading Rousseau in a woody glade, is an adroit but sympathetic blend of Batoni with the new literary influences from France.

WTEWAEL, Joachim (1566–1638), was one of the leading Mannerists in Utrecht at the time of BLOEMAERT. He spent four years in Italy and France (St Malo 1588–90). His religious pictures and portraits are well represented in Utrecht, and there are others in Gateshead, London (NG), Ottawa, Oxford, Vienna, Waddesdon, Bucks. (National Trust), and Yale.

WYNANTS, Johannes (*c.*1625–84), was a Haarlem landscape painter who also kept an inn, but was still always in debt. His rather limited art consisted of landscapes with low hills in the background and a sandy road in the foreground winding past trees in the middle distance. There is usually a dead tree in the foreground as well as a figure group. These figures are never by Wynants himself, but usually by Wouwerman, Lingelbach, or Wynants' own pupil Adriaen van de VELDE. Some of his early works were painted in collaboration with a specialist in wildfowl, and it is a nice point whether they are landscapes or animal pieces: otherwise, his charming views run to type and were much collected in the 18th and 19th centuries so that most galleries have one or more.

X

Y

YEATS, Jack B. (1871–1957), was the son of a painter and brother of the poet W. B. Yeats. He began his career as a watercolour painter and illustrator for the family press (later known as the Cuala Press). He exhibited at the ARMORY SHOW (1913), but did not begin to paint in oil until about 1915, evolving an intensely romantic, occasionally rather slapdash, landscape style which, in his last works, approaches ABSTRACT IMPRESSIONISM. It has been said that 'Irish romance is not easily exportable' but Yeats' works have been admired by painters like Kokoschka (who was a close friend). There are examples in Belfast, Cork, Dublin (Municipal Gall.), and London (Tate).

YSENBRANDT *see* ISENBRANDT.

Z

ZADKINE, Ossip (1890–1967), was born in Russia, came to London in 1907 and studied in Paris from 1911, where he met and was influenced by the Cubists. His works, in wood and stone, usually deal with figures from Greek mythology and are quasi-representational. Many of his wooden figures are very large, and have ingenious effects of silhouette obtained by cut-out shapes. Other works include a monument to van Gogh at Auvers-sur-Oise, and a memorial to the destruction of Rotterdam (*The Destroyed City*, 1952–3) which 'touched the imagination of the world'. There are examples in Antwerp, Edinburgh, Glasgow, Paris (Mus. d'Art Moderne), Philadelphia. He wrote an account of how he became a sculptor, and also published poems illustrated by himself.

ZAIS, Giuseppe (1709–84), was a Rococo landscape painter active in Venice. His early style was probably influenced by Marco RICCI, but his later landscapes have the brightness and prettiness of the style usually associated with ZUCCARELLI. There are characteristic examples in Venice and London (NG).

ZANDOMENEGHI, Federigo (1841–1917), was born in Venice, the son of a sculptor. He was in Sicily with Garibaldi in 1860, but from 1862–6 was in Florence in contact with the MACCHIAIOLI. From 1874 until his death he lived in Paris, often exhibiting with the Impressionists, although he was closest to DEGAS and the works of the two men have occasionally been confused. There are pictures by him in Florence, Milan, Piacenza, Philadelphia (Drexel Inst.), and Venice.

ZEVIO, Stefano da, *see* STEFANO.

ZICK, Januarius (1730–97), was one of the leading German Rococo painters. He was trained in Munich and then went to Paris, where he copied WATTEAU, after which (rather inappropriately) he went to Rome and worked in MENGS' studio (1757–8). In 1758 he returned to Germany and began his prolific career as a painter of altarpieces and decorative frescoes, the best of them being those at Mainz, Coblenz, and Wiblingen (1778–80), in the Klosterkirche. Many German museums have works and there is one in Kansas (University).

ZOFFANY, Johann (1725–1810), was a painter of portraits, conversation pieces, and theatrical scenes, who was born in Germany, studied in Italy, and worked mainly in England. He arrived about 1761 and was a Founder-Member of the RA (1768): in 1772, at the expense of George III, he went to Florence and spent some years there. One result of this was *The Tribuna of the Uffizi Gallery, Florence* (1772–80: Royal Coll.). He returned to England in 1779 but went to India and painted many portraits there 1783–9. He painted many theatrical scenes, usually representing an actual moment in a play, and many of them include portraits of Garrick – his first success was in 1762 with *Garrick in 'The Farmer's Return'* – and in this he was probably following HOGARTH, whose *Garrick as Richard III* was painted in 1746. There are works by him in Birmingham, Burnley, Edinburgh (NG), Glasgow, Liverpool, London (NG, NPG, Tate), Manchester, Newcastle, Ottawa, Springfield Mass., and elsewhere.

ZOPPO, Marco (*c.*1433–*c.*1478), was a Bolognese painter who was probably originally a pupil of TURA, but went, at the age of 21, to work for SQUARCIONE whose adopted son he became in 1455. In the same year he went to Venice and subsequently to Bologna. His style is a slightly softer version of the angular manner of both his masters and may reflect the influence of Giovanni Bellini. His main works are in Berlin and Bologna (San Clemente), but there are others in London and Oxford.

ZUCCARELLI, Francesco (1702–88), was a Florentine landscape painter who worked principally in Venice and England. He met Richard Wilson in Venice in 1751 and they exchanged paintings: in 1752 he went to London and remained until 1762. He returned to London in 1765 and stayed until 1771, being elected a Founder-Member of the Royal Academy in 1768. His light and facile style of landscape painting, with picturesque peasantry, was very popular in England and was preferred to the graver style of Wilson. There are several examples at Windsor Castle and others in Cambridge (Fitzwm), Glasgow, London (NG), Oxford (Ch. Ch.), Venice, and elsewhere.

ZUCCARO (Zuccari, Zuccheri), Taddeo (1529–66) and Federico (*c.*1540/3–1609), were brothers and represent the end of the MANNERIST tradition in Rome. Taddeo was the chief exponent of the style of the mid-16th century and his principal works were the fresco cycles in the Sala Regia of the Vatican and the *Farnese Deeds*, in the Villa Farnese at Caprarola, near Viterbo. Almost no oil paintings by him are known to survive, but there is a fine *Adoration* in Cambridge (Fitzwm). The two fresco cycles were completed by his younger brother, after which Federico went, in 1574, to France and Antwerp and, late in the year, to England. There he certainly made two drawings, one of Queen Elizabeth (both are in London, BM), but he was back in Italy by October 1575, so he cannot have painted all (or perhaps even any) of the portraits attributed to him in English houses. The *Queen Elizabeth* in Siena is certainly an Italian picture and the only one with a reasonable claim to be regarded as his, but the attribution is still controversial. Federico also worked in the Vatican, completed the frescoes of the dome of Florence Cathedral left incomplete by Vasari in 1574, and went to Spain in 1585, remaining until 1589 but finding little favour at the hands of Philip II, who was accustomed to the works of Titian. In 1593 he established the ACADEMY of S. Luke in his own Palazzo in Rome, becoming Principe of it in 1598, and devoting much thought in his last years to the theory of art and particularly of DISEGNO. Like the Cavaliere d'ARPINO, he was an eclectic Mannerist who lived on into a new era. Among the many pictures attributed to him are those in Florence (Uffizi, Pitti), Glasgow, Minneapolis, Milan (Brera), New York (Hist. Soc.), Rome (Borghese), and Vienna. His treatise 'L'Idea de' Scultori, Pittori e Architetti' was published in 1607, and his collected writings in 1961.

ZURBARÁN, Francisco de (1598–1664), was born near Bádajoz and was apprenticed in Seville in 1614 to a craftsman painter of devotional images. By 1617 he had settled in Llerena in southern Spain, but established himself in Seville at the invitation of the City Council in 1629. In 1634 he visited Madrid to paint a *Siege of Cadiz* for the King, to hang with Velazquez's *Surrender of Breda* and Maino's *Recovery of the Bay of S. Salvador*. He was back in Seville in 1635 to enter on his most productive and successful decade, during which he worked for monasteries and churches all over the south-west of Spain. He also painted pictures, some in long series, for religious houses in the Spanish colonies in the New World, and exported them as articles of trade, possibly through members of his second wife's family, established in Peru. Much of this production was shop work, but the argosies were not always successful, for there are many records of his difficulties in collecting the monies due to him. In 1658 he moved to Madrid in search of business, and renewed contact with Velazquez, for whom he was a witness in the proceedings that admitted him to the Order of Santiago. He died in Madrid.

The bleak, austere piety of his early pictures of saints, painted for the more severe religious orders, made him the ideal painter of simple doctrinal altarpieces, expressed in clear, sober colour, with figures of massive solidity and solemnity, and with a Tenebrism owing but little to Caravaggio or Ribera, but developed straight out of southern Spanish traditions of unidealized representation. He probably never saw a painting by Ribera until the mid 1630s, but he certainly knew his etchings. His ability to portray rather arid scenes from saintly lives, with a perfect union of the mystical and the realistic, accords well with Counter-Reformation theories of the purpose of paintings in churches and with the importance of subjects expressing the 'witness' aspect of a saint's life. The first journey to Madrid opened his eyes to other styles, and shows in something of a stronger feeling for Baroque magnificence. He still retained his hold on pure realism, but the splendour of his colour and the clarity and solidity of the masses in, for example, the *Adoration of the Shepherds* (1638: Grenoble) show how well he absorbed lessons learnt from Italian art. The rise of Murillo in the 1640s forced Zurbarán to compete with his softer, sweeter expression and more fused, smooth technique, and to abandon his own austerity of vision and colour, and impasted handling. His saints become more romantic in their devotion, his Madonnas ape the sentiment of Italian Mannerist painting, and in this competition with something entirely alien to him his own personality and individuality were lost.

Many of his works are in the churches and religious houses of Spain and Spanish America for which they were painted, but museums in Berlin, Boston (Mus., Gardner), Budapest, Cadiz, Chicago, Cincinnati, Cleveland Ohio, Dresden, Edinburgh (NG), Hartford Conn. (Wadsworth), Indianapolis, Lisbon, London (NG), Madrid (Prado and Acad.), Munich, New York (Hispanic Soc., Met. Mus.), Paris (Louvre), Philadelphia, St Louis, San Diego, São Paulo, Seville, Toledo Ohio, and Washington (NG) also have examples.

MORE ABOUT PENGUINS
AND PELICANS

Penguinews, which appears every month, contains details of all the new books issued by Penguins as they are published. From time to time it is supplemented by *Penguins in Print*, which is a complete list of all titles available. (There are some five thousand of these.)

A specimen copy of *Penguinews* will be sent to you free on request. For a year's issues (including the complete lists) please send 50p if you live in the British Isles, or 75p if you live elsewhere. Just write to Dept EP, Penguin Books Ltd, Harmondsworth, Middlesex, enclosing a cheque or postal order, and your name will be added to the mailing list.

In the U.S.A.: For a complete list of books available from Penguin in the United States write to Dept CS, Penguin Books Inc., 7110 Ambassador Road, Baltimore, Maryland 21207.

In Canada: For a complete list of books available from Penguin in Canada write to Penguin Books Canada Ltd, 41 Steelcase Road West, Markham, Ontario.

PENGUIN REFERENCE BOOKS

'Penguin Reference books are becoming indispensable; they are easy to travel with and, if they wear out, cheap to replace' – Cyril Connolly in the *Sunday Times*

A DICTIONARY OF GEOGRAPHY
W. G. Moore

Because geography is largely a synthetic subject the items in this Dictionary are derived from many sciences. The student will find in this revised and enlarged edition all the terms so frequently employed and seldom defined in geographical works.

A DICTIONARY OF MODERN HISTORY
1789–1945
A. W. Palmer

This book is intended as a reference-companion to personalities, events, and ideas. The prime emphasis is on British affairs and on political topics although the Dictionary aims to represent trends in the history of all the major regions of the world. There are entries on economic, social, religious and scientific developments, but not on the Arts.

AFRICA HANDBOOK*
Edited by Colin Legum

A modern and all-inclusive survey of the whole continent of Africa, in which experts have assembled a mass of reliable background information for the intelligent but non-expert reader. For each country the political development and economic situation are outlined and the basic geographical and racial facts given.

*NOT FOR SALE IN THE U.S.A.

PENGUIN REFERENCE BOOKS

THE PENGUIN DICTIONARY OF ARCHITECTURE
John Fleming, Hugh Honour and Nikolaus Pevsner

Every facet of architectural design and the art of building is covered. The entries are supplemented by more than a hundred clear and detailed architectural drawings set into the text they illustrate.

A NEW DICTIONARY OF MUSIC
Arthur Jacobs

A basic reference book for all who are interested in music, containing entries for composers (with biographies and details of compositions); musical works well known by their titles; orchestras, performers and conductors of importance today; musical instruments; and technical terms.

THE PENGUIN DICTIONARY OF THE THEATRE
John Russell Taylor

A world guide to past and present in the theatre, containing detailed information about both theoretical and practical aspects of everything to do with the theatre.

THE PENGUIN DICTIONARY OF SAINTS
Donald Attwater

An alphabetical reference book to the lives and legends of more than 750 saints, from Christ's apostles to the men and women who have been canonized in recent times, with full details of their work, feast-days and emblems.

Other subjects covered by Penguin Reference Books include: astronomy, biology, British natural history, building, civil engineering, commerce, computers, politics, psychology, quotations and modern quotations, science and surnames.